GOVERNMENT AND POLITICS IN INDIA
A Bibliographical Study of Contemporary Scenario Chronicling Rajiv Gandhi Era

CONCEPTS IN COMMUNICATION INFORMATICS & LIBRARIANSHIP (CICIL)

For a list of titles in this series, see pp. 366-68 at the end of the book.

About the Author

S.P. AGRAWAL (*b.* 1929) was Member Secretary Indian Assoication of Social Science Institution, and Director, National Social Science Documentation Centre, ICSSR. He was also the Vice-Chairman of the Asia and Pacific Information Network in Social Sciences (APINESS). In 1988 he was awarded the degree of Doctor of Philosophy in Education (Honoris Causa) by International University Foundation. Presently, he is Member, Round Table on Research in Reading, IFLA, and Member, International Committee for Social Science Information and Documentation. He is also Member of Board of Studies of National Archives of India and, Member Hindi Advisory Committee, Ministry of Coal, Government of India, New Delhi. Born and brought up in the cradle of our freedom movement which he joined at the tender age of twelve he gained an insight into problems political and developed a sense of responsibilities which bore fruits as an information scientist committed to Gandhiji's philosophy and action-plan in the field and its social concept. He has written extensively on various aspects of education, Indian polity and library and information science.

RAJEEV KUMAR SHARMA (*b.* 1966) Librarian in Directorate of Education, Delhi, has a Bachelor degree in Library and Information Science from Delhi University. He also earned Honours in Botany and Master's in Chemistry from Meerut University. He has a long experience of bibliographic documentation. His earlier publication jointly with S.P. AGRAWAL is *Weaker Section in Indian Society: Index to Writings in Indian Scholarly Journals (1886-1990)*. He is presently associated with a publication on Indian Writings on Science and Technology.

Concepts in Communication
Informatics & Librarianship-43

General Editor: **S.P. Agrawal**

Government and Politics in India

A Bibliographical Study of Contemporary Scenario Chronicling Rajiv Gandhi Era

S.P. AGRAWAL
Former Member Secretary
Indian Association of Social Science Institutions
New Delhi

RAJEEV KUMAR SHARMA
Librarian
Directorate of Education
Delhi

CONCEPT PUBLISHING COMPANY, NEW DELHI 110059

ISBN 81-7022-416-0

First Published 1993

Published and Printed by
Ashok Kumar Mittal
Concept Publishing Company
A/15-16, Commercial Block, Mohan Garden
NEW DELHI-110059 (India)

Lasertypeset by
Microtech Advance Printing Systems (Pvt.) Ltd.
H-13, Bali Nagar,
NEW DELHI-110015

GENERAL EDITOR'S INTRODUCTION

WHEN Rajiv Gandhi was at the pinnacle of his popularity and was expected to play a decisive role in the Indian politics in the second innings of his political career he was, as destiny would have it, snuffed out by the cruel hands of an assassin. It was generally believed that during the time he was not the Prime Minister and was free from strangle-hold of the coteric, his actions showed a changed man in him — matured and reflecting. Quite obviously, it was expected and not without some justification that he would thrive to provide a measure of stable relief to the nation in crisis that was unprecedented in the history of Independent India. His yearning to take the country into 21st century will be long remembered.

Rajiv Gandhi was born in Bombay on August 20, 1944 — three years before India got her Independence. His childhood was spent in Teen Murti, the then Prime Minister's official residence. In 1956 he was sent to Doon School where he pursued his studies and showed that he had a mechanical bent of mind. In 1958, when he was only 16, his father Feroze Gandhi who had differences with his wife Indira Gandhi died of heart attack. From the Doon School, Rajiv Gandhi moved to England and studied at Imperial College, London and Trinity College, Cambridge (for a course in mechanical engineering degree) from 1962 to 1965. There, he met Sonia Maino, an Italian lady and developed an intimacy with her which culminated into marriage in February 1968.

Unlike his younger brother Sanjay, Rajiv Gandhi did not show any outward signs of interest in politics, though he was born and bred in a political family which shaped the government and politics in India. He started his career as a pilot in Indian Airlines, thus preferring an aviator outfit to Jawahar waist-coat and lived a family life with his mother, Smt Indira Gandhi, in the Willingdon Crescent in New Delhi. He showed interest in his job as a pilot. Nonetheless as was destined, he entered political arena with a bang, despite disclaimers by Prime Minister Indira Gandhi, to fill the void created by the untimely death of his younger brother Sanjay Gandhi in an air crash in June 1980. Rajiv Gandhi resigned from the Indian Airlines in May 1981, fought by-election for Amethi's Parliamentary seat in August and won it. Later he was appointed as a General Secretary of Congress (I). After the assassination of his mother, Prime Minister Indira Gandhi, allegedly by her own bodyguards on October 31, 1984, Rajiv Gandhi, who had little experience about Government and politics in India, was hastened to succeed her mother, perhaps because faithfuls in Congress (I) as also Congress Party as such needed a member of Nehru family who could play charismatic role and attract sympathy wave to win the forthcoming 1984 elections for the Party. The assessment was correct and with Rajiv Gandhi at the helm of affairs and Indira sympathy wave blowing forcefully, Congress (I) won the elections by a land-side (415 of the 452 Lok Sabha Seats) .

It was clear from the thumping majority Rajiv Gandhi received that people had full faith and expectations that he would deliver the goods. In the beginning, his actions did show his sincerity of purpose and his seriousness in tackling the problems of the country. He appeared determined to change the face of the country politically, economically and socially. Like all young men, he was also in haste to bring about the rejuvenation of the country. Initially his efforts to rise to the expectation of the people were not without some success. His accords with Akali leaders on Punjab problem, with AASU in Assam and with Mizo leader Laldenga to end Mizo insurgency were cited as his initial achievements. He was also cited to have succeeded to a certain extent in improving India's relations with Sri Lanka. But it is also true that these accords failed to achieve their objectives and did not help to improve the situation in Punjab or in Assam. As was expected he permitted himself to be surrounded by unscrupulous and self-seeking politicians and advisers thus frustrating his attempts to do good to the people. Engulfed in intra-party intrigues and vested interests, he could not take any radical measures and reforms in regard to the Party as well as the Government. In the last two years of this tenure as Prime Minister it seemed as if he had completely surrendered himself to the coterie of his aides or may be that he was so overwhelmed by his initial success that he lost touch with the people. Ultimately in the 1989 general elections, the Congress Party came down from the commanding position and Rajiv Gandhi had to content himself with the position of a Leader of Opposition in the Parliament.

One of the failures of Rajiv Gandhi, it could be said, was that he could not bring about the democratisation of the Congress (I) Party by holding elections at all its levels which he promised at the Congress Centenary. He thundered at the Centenary in Bombay that he would rid the Party of the power brokers. But these power borkers proved so powerful that they did not allow the Party to hold the elections. Likewise, he failed to give direction to the bureaucracy which reacted sharply to the taming bid and stood road-blocks to any radical reform and change in the Government.

On the economic front, if the Government was not a great success, it was not a failure either. During his tenure of Prime Ministership over-all economic development was not so bad. Long-term Fiscal Policy did show signs of economic stability. Taxation laws were simplified. Certain industries under MRTP Act were delicensed and the asset limit for MRTP companies was raised from 20 to 100 crores. The other important measure was the liberalisation of the economy by relaxation of the imports for modernisation and for boosting exports. The relaxation of imports did increase the export earnings to some extent although in the long run, may be due to some unscrupulous businessmen's and bureaucratic machinations, it had adverse effect on the Balance of Payments resulting in the economic crisis.

On the international front, his Government was slightly better. Whichever country he visited he was warmly received because of his attractive personality. When Rajiv Gandhi assumed the Prime Ministership it was generally believed that an inexperienced youth unaware of the subtletics of the world politics would fumble before the seasoned world leaders. But it was surprising that, within a short time, he was able to establish a personal rapport with the world leaders like Gorbachev and Reagan. Even his adversaries would acknowledge that his Government raised the stature of India in the comity of nations. The measure of his Government's success in foreign affairs is the fact that the news of his assassination got considerable footage in international media. It was perhaps for the first time that UN Security Council paid homage to Rajiv Gandhi on May 25, 1991 by observing a minutes silence.

The main focus of the bibliographical references culled from various sources in the present CICIL publication is on Government and Politics in India bearing particular reference to the role, achievements and failures of Rajiv Gandhi during his five years as Prime Minister and the period when he was out of the office, tracing the contemporary scenario from his childhold as published/reported in Indian journals (53) and Newspaper (12). This documentation provides detailed information on most aspects of contemporary Government and Politics chronicling Rajiv Gandhi's era. Since his strength and weaknesses are linked with the Congress (I) Party and Government, Congress (I) activities and inroads have received a wide coverage. Every attempt has been made to include the material which represents the views of both his admirers and adversaries.

Since efforts have been made to make it as comprehensive as possible, it is hoped that this volume will prove an excellent guide for the researchers and the serious students of Indian history.

S.P. AGRAWAL

CONTENTS

LIST OF JOURNALS/NEWSPAPERS SCANNED

Journals

1 *African Quarterly* (Q)
Indian Council of Cultural Relations,
Azad Bhawan, Indraprastha Estate
New Delhi-110002

2. *Blitz* (W)
Blitz Publications (Pvt.) Ltd.,
17-17H, Cowasji Patel Street,
Fort,
Bombay-400 001

3. *Bulletin of the Association of Scienitic Workers of India* (M)
10, Rajendra Park,
New Delhi-110 060

4. *Business India* (F)
A.H. Advani,
Wadia Building,
17/19 Dalal Street,
Bombay-400 023

5. *Capital* (W)
1-2, Old Court House Corner,
Calcutta-700 001

6. *Caravan* (F)
Delhi Press Patra Prakashan (Pvt.) Ltd.,
Delhi Press Building,
E-3, Jhandewalan Estate,
New Delhi-110 055

7. *Commerce* (W)
NKM International House,
178, Backbay Reclamation,
Bombay-400 020

8. *Current* (W)
Current Publications (Pvt.) Ltd.,
Meher House, 15 Cowasji Patel Street, Post Box 1862,
Bombay-400 001

9. *Delhi Recorder* (M)
13 Deepak Building,
Room No. 44, 4th Floor,
Nehru Place,
New Delhi-110 010

10. *Democratic World* (W)
M. Gulab Singh and Sons (Pvt.) Ltd.,
6, Bahadur Shah Zafar Marg,
New Delhi-110 001

11. *Eastern Economist* (Q)
UCO Bank Building,
4th Floor, Parliament Street,
New Delhi-110 001

12. *Economic and Political Weekly* (W)
Sameksha Trust, Skylarke,
284, Shahid Bhagat Singh Road,
Bombay-400 038

13. *Foreign Affairs Report* (M)
Indian Council of World Affairs
Sapru House, Barakhamba Road,
New Delhi-110001

14. *Free Press Journal* (Irr)
Free Press House,
215 Nariman Point, 3rd Floor,
Bombay-400 021

15. *Frontline* (F)
Kasturi and Sons Ltd.,
Kasturi Buildings, Mount Road,
Madras-600 002

16. *Haryana Review* (M)
Public Relations Department,
S.C.O. No.189/191, Sector 17C,
Chandigarh-160 017

17. *IFTP Bulletin* (Q)
P 222, Block A, Lake Town,
Calcutta-700 089

18. *India Quarterly* (Q)
Indian Council of World Affairs,
Sapru House, Barakhamba Road,
New Delhi-110001

19. *India Today* (F)
Living Media India Ltd.,
F-14/15, Connaught Place,
New Delhi-110 001

20. *Indian and Foreign Review* (SA)
Ministry of Information and Broadcasting,
Government of India,
New Delhi-110001

21. *Indian Economic Review* (SA)
Delhi School of Economics,
University of Delhi,
Delhi-110 007

22. *Indian Horizons* (Q)
Indian Council of Cultural Relations
Azad Bhawan, Indraprastha State,
New Delhi-110 002

23. *Indian Journal of Public Administration* (Q)
Indian Institute of Public Administration,
Indraprastha Estate,
New Delhi-110002

24. *Indian Observer* (M)
26-F, Connaught Place,
New Delhi-110 011

25. *Indian Worker* (W)
Indian National Trade Union Congress,
17, Janpath,
New Delhi-110001

26. *Janata* (W)
National House,
6, Tulloch Road, Apollo Bundar,
Bombay-400 039

27. *Journal of Parliamentary Information* (Q)
Lok Sabha Secretariat,
Sansadiya Soudha,
New Delhi-110 001

28. *Kurukshetra* (M)
Publications Division,
Ministry of Information and Broadcasting,
Government of India
Patiala House,
New Delhi-110 001

29. *Link* (W)
Link House,
Bahadur Shah Zafar Marg,
New Delhi-110 002

30. *Mainstream* (W)
F-24, Bhagat Singh Market,
New Delhi-110 001

31. *Management in Government* (Q)
Department of Administrative Reforms,
Ministry of Home Affairs,
Government of India,
New Delhi-110001

32. *Monthly Commentary on Indian Economic Conditions* (M)
Indian Institute of Public Opinion (Pvt.) Ltd.,
2-A, National Insurance Building,
Parliament Street,
New Delhi-110001

33. *Muslim India* (M)
8, Ferozeshah Road,
New Delhi-110 001

34. *New Age* (W)
Ajoy Bhawan,
Kotla Road
New Delhi-110 002

35. *Onlooker* (F)
Publicity Society of India
20-G, Sleater Road,
Bombay-400 007

36. *Organiser* (W)
Bharat Prakashan (Delhi) Ltd.,
29, Rani Jhansi Marg,
New Delhi-110 055

37. *The Other Side*
26, Tughlaq Creseent,
New Delhi-110 011

38. *People's Democracy* (W)
4, Ashoka Road,
New Delhi-110 001

39. *Political Science Review* (Q)
Department of Political Science,
University of Ranchi,
Ranchi-834001

40. *Probe India* (M)
105, Rohit House,
3, Tolstoy Marg,
New Delhi-110 001

41. *Radical Humanist* (M)
B-17, Maharani Bagh,
New Delhi-110 065

42. *Rural India* (M)
Ishwardas Mansions,
Nana Chowk,
Bombay-400 007

43. *Secular Democracy* (M)
6B/8, Northern Extension Area,
Near Rajendra Nagar Market,
New Delhi-110 020

44. *Social Welfare* (M)
Central Social Welfare Board,
Jeewan Deep,
Parliament Street,
New Delhi-110001

45. *Southern Economist* (F)
106-108, Saleh Ahmed Building,
Infantry Road,
Bangalore-560 001

46. *Sunday* (W)
Ananda Bazar Patrika,
6, Prafulla Sarkar Street,
Calcutta-700 001

47. *Surya India* (M)
Youngman Printers and Publishers (Pvt.) Ltd.,
Kanchanjunga,
18, Barakhamba Road,
New Delhi-110 001

48. *Triveni* (Q)
Triveni Publishers,
Machilipatnam-521 001

49. *Vedanta Kesari* (M)
16, Sri Ramakrishna Math,
Mylapore,
Madras-600 004

50. *The Week* (W)
Malayala Manorama Company Ltd.,
Manorama Bldgs,
Post Box 2314,
Cochin-682 016

51. *Weekend Review* (W)
Hindustan Times House,
18/20 Kasturba Gandhi Marg,
New Delhi-110 001

52. *Yojana* (F)
Publications Division,
Ministry of Information and Broadcasting,
Government of India,
Patiala House,
New Delhi-110001

News-papers

1. *Amrita Bazar Patrika* (D)
Ulyan Kadma,
Jamshedpur-831 005

2. *Economic Times* (D)
7, Bahadur Shah Zafar Marg,
New Delhi-110 002

3. *Financial Express* (D)
Bahadur Shah Zafar Marg,
New Delhi-110 002

4. *Hindu* (D)
No. 5, IENS Building,
Rafi Marg,
New Delhi-110 001

5. *Hindustan Times* (D)
Hindustan Times House
18/20 Kasturba Gandhi Marg,
New Delhi-110 001

6. *Independent* (D)
Times of India
Suburban Press,
Bombay-400 101

7. *Indian Express* (D)
(including Sunday Standard)
Bahadur Shah Zafar Marg,
New Delhi-110 002

8. *National Herald* (D)
Herald House,
Bahadur Shah Zafar Marg,
New Delhi-110 002

9. *Patriot* (D)
Raisina Publications Ltd.,
United India Press,
Bahadur Shah Zafar Marg,
New Delhi-110 002

10. *Statesman* (D)
Statesman House,
Connaught Circus,
New Delhi-110001

11. *Telegraph* (D)
6, Prafulla Sarkar Street,
Calcutta-700 001

12. *Times of India* (D)
Bahadur Shah Zafar Marg,
New Delhi-110 002

13. *Tribune* (D)
(Chandigarh edition)
Chandigarh

Legend

D : Daily
F : Fortinghtly
Irr : Irregular
M : Monthly
Q : Quarterly
SA : Semi-Annual
W : Weekly

1

PRIMARY DOCUMENTATION

AICC (I)

=All-India Congress Committee(I)

AMU

=Aligarh Muslim University

ASEAN

=Association of South-East Asian Nations

Abbas, Khwaja Ahmad

Nizamuddin, D.E., 1982, Rajiv's friend Abbas, *Sunday* 8(9) September 7, p 66

Abdullah, Farooq

Anon, 1981, New dynasty: Abdullah Jr. is crowned, *Caravan* 12(704) September 16, p 11

Anon, 1982, Mrs Gandhi calls on Abdullah, *Hindustan Times*, June 25, p 16

Anon, 1982, Rajiv Gandhi's Aide meets Abdullah, *Hindustan Times*, May 19, p 8

Anon, 1982, Rajiv holds talks with Farooq, *Indian Express*, September 14, p 1

Dewan, Berindranath, 1981, Rajiv-Farooq talks for Congress (I)-N.C. coalition, *Hindu*, August 8, p 10

Nizamuddin, D.E., 1981, Farooq Abdullah's growing maturity, *Sunday* 9(22) Novermber 15, p 66

Abida Begum: Election to Lok Sabha

Anon, 1981, Rajiv and Begum Abida returned to Lok Sabha, *Hindu*, June 16, p 1

Academics : Political Use

Ghosh Chowdhury, Dilip, 1987, Academic platform used for Rajiv's political tirade, *New Age* 35(4), January 25, p 6

Access to Information

Times of India (Newspaper), 1985, The right to know, *Times of India*, June 20, p 6, col 1-2, editorial

Accords: Geographical Area: India: Assam

Anon, 1985, Accord to bring lasting peace to Assam: PM, *Times of India*, December 12, p 1, col 1-3, news-item

Anon, 1985, PM announces accord on Assam: Pakistan asked to abandon bomb: Sharper campaign against poverty: Call to combat extermism: Colourful Red Fort function, *Times of India*, August 16, p 1, col 1-4

Anon, 1985, Punjab and Assam solution: PM, *Times of India*, February 18, p 1, col 1-3, news-item

Accords: Geographical Area: India: Punjab

Anon, 1985, Punjab and Assam solution: PM, *Times of India*, February 18, p 1, col 1-3, news–item

Accords: Geographical Area: India-Afghanistan

Anon, 1988, India and the Afghan accords, *Link* 30(39) May 1, p 14-16

Accords: Geographical Area: India-Pakistan

Anon, 1989, India, Pak sign three accords: N-Plant not to be attacked, *Times of India*, January 1, p 1, col 1-3

Anon, 1989, Three Agreements signed, *National Herald*, January 1

Accords: Geographical Area: India-Sri Lanka

Anon, 1987, Indo-Sri Lanka Agreement, *Foreign Affairs Report* 36(7-10), July-October, p 93-237

Anon, 1987, Rajiv, JRJ sign accord as violence rocks Colombo, *Economic Times*, July 30, p 1, col 6-8+

Anon, 1989, Thoudaman calls for fresh accord, *Times of India*, July 10

Gangal, S.C., 1987, The India-Sri Lanka agreement, *Gandhi Marg* 9(5) August, p 259-263

Krishna Iyer, V.R., 1988, The Sri Lanka accord: An autopsy, *Illustrated Weekly of India* 109(14) April 3, p 32-35

Krishna Iyer, V.R., 1988, The Sri Lanka accord: A post mortem, *Illustrated Weekly of India* 109(15) April 10, p 38-41

Phadnis, Umashankar, 1989, Indo-Sri Lanka accord: Need for reassesing realities, *Mainstream* 27(40) July 1, p 5-6+

Times of India (Newspaper), 1989, A good agreement, *Times of India*, September 19, p 8, col 1-2, editorial

Acts and Bills, etc.: Geographical Area: India

See under name of the Acts and Bills, etc., e.g., Border Areas Bill.

Administrative Machinery: Geographical Area: India

Anon, 1984, Clean administration promise reiterated, *Financial Express*,

December 30, p 1, col 1-4

Anon, 1984, PM for result-oriented administration, *Times of India*, November 13, p 4, col 1-4

Anon, 1986, Need for better scientific administration, *Haryana Review* 20(11) November, p 3-5

Bhattacharya, Shubabrata, 1981, Government is much more pragmatic, *Sunday* 9(28) December 27, p 24-25

Mukarji, Nirmal, 1989, Decentratization below State level: Need for new system of governance, *Economic and Political Weekly* March 4

Administrative Machinery: Geographical Area: India: Punjab

Anon, 1981-1982, Darbara Singh Government blamed for Punjab unrest, *Delhi Recorder* 2(9) December 15-January 14, p 58-61

Anon, 1982, Rajiv rules out change in Punjab, *Hindustan Times*, July 4, p 8

Gandhi, Rajiv, 1981, Punjab Government not effective, *Hindustan Times*, November 21, p 1

Administrative Machinery: Geographical Area: India: Uttar Pradesh

Anon, 1981, Rajiv gives clean chit to U.P. Government, *Hindustan Times*, December 6, p 1

Administrative Machinery: Misuse

Times of India (Newspaper), 1981, Misuse of office, *Times of India*, November 12, p 8, col 1-2, editorial

Administrative Reforms

Anon, 1986, Need for better scientific administration, *Haryana Review* 20(11) November, p 3-5

Anon, 1986, PM for reforms in administration, *Indian Express*, February 7

Anon, 1989, Grassroot system to eleminate power brokers: PM, *Times of India*, May 11, p 1, col 1-3 +, news-item

Advani, L.K.: Impact as Leader of Opposition

Anon, 1991, Rajiv and V.P. Singh highly frustrated as Advani named Leader of the Opposition, *Organiser* 42(22) January 6, p 1, col 1-5+

Advani, L.K.: Views on Rajiv Gandhi's Working Style

Anon, 1986, Advani blames PM for crisis in the country, *Times of India*, December 26

Anon, 1986, The BJP leader L.K. Advani charged that ad hocism rather than a method governed Rajiv Gandhi's Cabinet changes, *Hindustan Times*, May 13; *Statesman*, May 13

Afghan Crisis

Anon, 1980, India has vital stake in resolution of Afghan crisis, says PM, *Hindustan Times*, March 3, news-item

Afghanistan

See also Geographical Area subdivision under main Decriptor

Afghanistan: Foreign Relations: Geographical Area: India

See under Indo-Afghanistan Relations

Africa

Chhabra, Hari Saran, 1991, Rajiv Gandhi and Africa, *Mainstream* 29 (32) June 1, p 6

See also Geographical Area subdivision under main Descriptors; Indo-African Relation.

Africa: South

See South Africa

Africa Fund

Anon, 1986, PM heads NAM Fund for Africa, *Telegraph*, September 7

Agra: Uttar Pradesh: India

Anon, 1991, Suspension over woman in Agra, *Hindustan Times*, June 7, col 8

See also Geographical Area subdivision under main Descriptors

Agreements

Anon, 1988, Six agreements signed, *National Herald*, November 21; *Times of India*, November 21

See also Accords

Agriculture: Geographical Area: India

Anon, 1981, Rajiv's top priority for Agriculture, *Times of India*, May 18
Anon, 1988, PM's talks with IFAD Chief, *Statesman*, March 31

Air Show: Geographical Area: United Kingdom

Anon, 1982, Rajiv in London as UK's biggest airshow begins, *Times of India*, September 6, p 9

Akalis

Anon, 1985, PM asks Akalis to publicity disown extremists, *Times of India*,

December 21, p 1 col 1-3 +, news-iem

Anon, 1985, Rajiv decries remarks by Akali leaders, *Times of India*, April 23, p 1, col 6-8, news-item

Anon, 1986, PM asks Akali to check terrorism, *Telegraph*, February 28, news-item

Anon, 1986, PM ready for talks with dissidents Akalis, *Telegraph*, July 13, news-item

Anon, 1986, Talks with Akali rebels if stand clarified: PM, *Times of India*, July 13, p 1, col 6-7+, news-item

Gandhi, Rajiv, 1981, Talks with Akalis have not broken down, *Hindustan Times*, November 21, p 16

Albania: Foreign Relations: Geographical: India

See under Indo-Albanian Relations

Algeria

See also Geographical Area subdivision under main Descriptor

Aligarh Muslim University

Anon, 1991, Rajiv wooing AMU students, *Organiser* 42(34) March 31, p 2, col 1-2

All India Congress Committee (I)

See also Congress (I)

All India Congress Committee (I): Homage to Gandhi, Sanjay

Anon, 1980, AICC-I tribute to Sanjay: Please to Rajiv, *Sunday-Standard*, December 7, p.7

All India Congress Committee (I): Plea to Gandhi, Rajiv

Anon, 1980, AICC-I tribute to Sanjay: Plea to Rajiv, *Sunday Standard*, December 7, p 7

Allahabad: Uttar Pradesh: India

See also Geographical Area Sub-division under main Descriptor

Ambedkar, B.R.

Anon, 1989, Ambedkar's portrait unveiled, *Indian Express*, August 10

America: Central

See Central America

Amethi: Uttar Pradesh: India

See also Geographical Area subdivision under main Descriptors, e.g, Elections:

Geographical Area: India: Uttar Pradesh, Amethi

Amethi: Uttar Pradesh: India: Poll

See Elections: Geographical Area: India: Uttar Pradesh: Amethi

Andaman and Nicobar Islands: India

Anon, 1986, PM in Andamans, *Hindu*, December 28

See also Geographical Area subdivision under main Descriptors

Andhra Pradesh: India

Anon, 1985, Rajiv made tactical error in Andhra, *Times of India*, January 1, p 12, col 1-2

Anon, 1992, Rajiv technology mission in AP, *National Herald*, May 23, p 10, col 1-2

Raghu, V., 1991, Andhra Pradesh vandalism after Rajiv's assassination, *Mainstream* 29(35) June 22, p 29-30

See also Geographical Area subdivision under main Descriptors

Angola

See also Geographical Area subdivision under main Descriptor

Angola: Foreign Relations: Geographical Area: India

See under Indo-Angolan Relations

Anjiah, T.

See also Chief Minister: Geographical Area: India: Andhra Pradesh: Anjiah, T.

Ankara: Turkey

See also Geographical Area subdivision under main Descriptor

Anti-Terrorism Day

Anon, 1992, BJP ridicules Cong on Anti-Terrorism Day, *Times of India*, May 23, p 5, col 1-4

Anon, 1992, Rajiv's death anniversary observed as Anti-Terrorism Day, *Economic Times*, May 22, p 13, col 1-6

Antonov Aircraft Plant

Anon, 1982, Rajiv visits Antonov Aircraft Plant, *Times of India*, September 26, p 9

Antulay, A.R.

Anon, 1980, Antulay requests Rajiv to join politics, *Times of India*, August 13

Anon, 1980, Rajiv blocks Antulay's nominees, *Blitz*, Septmber 6, p 7

Anon, 1980, Winning hand, *Current*, June 27, p 3

Anon, 1981, Antulay again: Misuse of political machinery, *Caravan* 1(709) December, p 17

Anon, 1981, Antulay meets PM, *Indian Express*, November 18, p 1

Anon, 1981, Antulay meets PM, Rajiv on border dispute, *Indian Express*, August 28, p 7

Anon, 1981, Antulay meets Rajiv on border issue, *Indian Express*, August 27, p 7

Anon, 1981, Antulay meets Rajiv Gandhi, *Hindustan Times*, August 27, p 5; *Times of India*, August 27, p 7

Anon, 1981, Antulay upset over Rajiv's remarks, *Hindustan Times*, Novermber 18, p 1

Anon, 1981, Dealing with Mr Antulay, *Indian Express*, November 14, p 6

Anon, 1981, Fruits of inaction, *Times of India*, November 24, p 8

Anon, 1981, Rajiv may visit Bombay soon, *Indian Express*, August 28, p 1

Anon, 1981, Rajiv on lawyer's crucial role, *Hindustan Times*, October, 31, p 3

Anon, 1981, Rajiv want PCC-I to decide Antulay fate, *Hindustan Times*, October 31, p 1

Anon, 1981, Rajiv's indictment of Antulay, *Indian Express*, November 11 p 1

Anon, 1982, Antulay and Solanki dropped from CWC, *Hindustan Times*, September 3, p 1

Anon, 1982, Antulay fall-out, *Link* 24(23) January 17, p 6

Anon, 1982, Antulay meets PM, Rajiv, *Times of India*, January 31, p 1

Anon, 1982, Rajiv to look into Antulay's new job, *Hindu*, February 6, p 9

Anon, 1982, Rebel leader snap links with Antulay, *Hindustan Times*, July 16, p 1

Anon, 1982, Why is Antulay still surviving: Reason he holds the Indira Pratisthan papers, *Sunday* 9(31) January 17, p 44

Antulay, A.R., 1981, I am disciplined soldier, *India Today* 6(16) August 16, p 40-41

Antulay, A.R., 1982, Political spiders weaving cobwebs, *Current*, April 17, p 3

Chander Uday Singh, 1981, Lawyer's conference utterly butterly, *India Today* 6(17) September 1, p 37

Chawla, Prabhu, 1982, One from the wings, *India Today* 7(3) February 15, p 19-20

Gandhi, Rajiv, 1981, Antulay misused political machinery, *Hindustan Times*, November 11, p 1

Gandhi, Rajiv, 1981, Antulay in state party affairs, *Indian Express*, October 13, p 1

Gandhi, Rajiv, 1981, Antulay stays, *Current*, October 17, p 1

Nayar, Kuldip, 1982, Mrs Gandhi likes sycophants, *Sunday* 9(37) March 6, p 9

Puri, Rajinder, 1981, Why Antulay will go? *Hindustan Times*, November 18, p 1

Shenoy, T.V.R., 1982, What the Congress (I) lost besides the election, *Onlooker* 44 (10) May 31, p 14-15

Talib, Rasheed, 1982, Not to perverse, *India Today* 7(5) March 15, p 27

Tellis, Olga, 1981, Maharashtra flats and barl licences to MLA's for support, *Sunday* 9(26) December 13, p 39-40

Tellis, Olga, 1982, Antulay verdict has not quelled dissension, *Sunday* 10(2) July

3, p 39-41

See also Chief Minister: Geographical Area: India: Maharashtra: Antulay, A.R.

Apartheid Problem

Anon, 1986, Apartheid must end, says PM, *Times of India*, June 17, news-item

Anon, 1986, India promises fresh initiative to end apartheid, *Times of India*, May 19

Anon, 1986, Rajiv Gandhi, Mikulic discuss aparthied, *Indian Express*, July 29

Aquino, Corazon

Anon, 1988, President Aquino's letter to Rajiv Gandhi, *Indian Express*, February 19

Arafat, Yasser: Homage paid to Gandhi, Rajiv

Anon, 1992, Arafat's homage to Rajiv, *Hindustan Times*, May 22, p 12, col 8

Anon, 1992, Yasser, Gayoom hail Rajiv, *National Herald*, May 22, p 10, col 3

Arafat, Yasser: Role

Sharma, P., 1991, Arafat had warned Rajiv, *Hindustan Times*, June 3, p 12, col 1-3.

Arjun Singh

Anon, 1982, V.C. Shukla and Arjun Singh meet, *Indian Express*, April 25, p 4

Anon, 1989, Arjun Singh was still seen as a potential threat to Rajiv Gandhi though his influence in M.P. evidently diminished sharply between 1985 and 1989, *Hindu*, March 22

Armacost, Michael Hayden

Anon, 1988, Armacost calls on Prime Minister, *Hindustan Times*, February 27; *Times of India*, February 27

Arms Proliferation

Anon, 1986, India has to match Pak arms build up, says PM, *Times of India*, October 16, p 1, col 1-4+, news-item

Anon, 1986, India will not allow arms imbalance, says PM, *Hindustan Times*, October 16, news-item

Gandhi, Rajiv, 1981, F-16s for Pak will spur arms race, *Hindustan Times*, July 10, p 4

Gandhi, Rajiv, 1981, US forcing arms on sub-continent, *Hindustan Times*, November 14, p 6

Gandhi, Rajiv, 1982, Pak reasoning for arms ridiculous, *Hindustan Times*, February 6, p 8

Army Commanders: Geographical Area: India

Anon, 1986, PM's address to Army Commanders, *Hindu*, April 25

Ashan, Altzaz

Anon, 1989, Ashan calls on Rajiv Gandhi, *National Herald*, April 12

Asia: South East

See South East Asia

Asiad: New Delhi: 1982

Anon, 1981, Edifice complex, *India Today* 6 (16) August 16, p 23
Anon, 1981, Games Minister's play, *India Today* 6(20) October 31, p 7
Anon, 1981, Politicians Games? *Onlooker* 43(21) November 30, p 7
Anon, 1982, Bhatnagar is NDMC Chief, *Hindustan Times*, September 2, p 3
Anon, 1982, Furniture for Asiad destroyed in fire, *Indian Express*, September 20, p 1
Anon, 1982, Images, *India Today* 7(1) January 15, p 66
Anon, 1982, Indian Officials at Asiad discriminated against, *Sunday* 9(45) May 1, p 9
Anon, 1982, PM happy with progress of Asiad complexes, *Hindustan Times*, May 1, p 1+
Anon, 1982, PM visit Asiad stadia, *National Herald*, May 4, p 1+
Anon, 1982, P.S. Bhatnagar replaces Behl as NDMC Chief, *Times of India*, September 2, p 3
Anon, 1982, Rajiv Gandhi goes round Aisad venues, *Times of India*, August 31, p 12
Anon, 1982, Rajiv shows his anger, *Times of India*, September 20, p 1
Anon, 1982, Rajiv tries food at Games Village, *Times of India*, September 18, p 4
Anon, 1982, Three furniture's factories gutted; Probe rodered, ACP, SI suspended, *Times of India*, September 20, p 1
Chawla, G.S., 1981, New Delhi and the Asiad, *Illustrated Weekly of India* 52(34) December 5, p 44-47
Chawla, Prabhu, 1982, Controversies: Asiad's other side, *India Today* 7(12) June 30, p 74-77
Dubashi, Jagannath, 1982 Asiad 82: Race against time, *India Today* 7(12) June 30, p 66-71
Grover, Satish, 1982, Building for the Asiad, *Illustrated Weekly of India* 103 (34) September 12, p 44-45
Kashyap, Krishan, 1982, Men behind ASIAD, *National Herald*, May 2, p 1, col 1-8+
Shastri, H. K., 1982, H.K. Shastu defends Rajiv Gandhi, *Times of India*, September 29 p 13.
Talyarkhan, A.F.S., 1981, Linkage of Asian Games with Delhi's development, *Blitz*, August 1, p 19

Tej Kumar, B., 1982, Preparations for Ninth Asiad, *Indian and Foreign Review* 19(14) May 1, p 19-20

Asian Games

See also Asiad: New Delhi: 1982

Assad, Hafiz-al

Anon, 1988, PM, Assad hold further talks, *National Herald*, June 6; *Statesman*, June 6

Assam: India

Anon, 1981, Rajiv arrives in Gauhati, *Hindustan Times*, October 12, p 7

Anon, 1981, Rajiv in Assam, *Indian Express*, October 12, p 5

Anon, 1985, Accord to bring lasting peace to Assam: PM, *Times of India*, December 12, p 1, col 1-3, news-item

Anon, 1985, Assam minorities safe, says PM, *Times of India*, December 14, p 1, col 1-3, news-item

Anon, 1985, Punjab and Assam solution: PM, *Times of India*, February 18, p 1, col 1-3, news-item

Anon, 1988, Mahanta refutes PM's charge, *Indian Express*, September 17

Anon, 1988, PM visits flood hit areas, *Times of India*, September 14

Anon, 1989, PM urged to visit Gohpur, *Times of India*, August 14

Mitra, Sumit and Chawla, P., 1982, Government: Sprucing up the band, *India Today* 7(3) February 15, p 62 -71

See also Bodoland Problem: Geographical Area subdivision under main Descriptors, e.g., Accords: Geographical Area: India: Assam

Assassination: Attempts and Probes: Gandhi, Rajiv

Anon, 1984, Assassination part of international conspiracy: Rajiv, *Times of India*, November 20, p 1, col 1-3, news-item

Anon, 1985, FBI uncovers plot of killing Rajiv during visit to US, *Times of India*, May 14, p 1, col 1-3

Anon, 1985, Terrorist wanted to kill Rajiv in France or Algeria, *Times of India*, May 17, p 1, col 1-3

Anon, 1986, Assassination attempt at Rajghat: PM, VIPs escape unhurt, *Economic Times*, October 3, p 1, col 1-4+

Anon, 1986, Bridge on PM's way blasted, *Statesman*, January 29, p 30

Anon, 1986, PM escapes attempt on life, *Indian Express*, October 3

Anon, 1986, PM, VIPs escape attempt on life, *Times of India*, October 3, p 1, col 1-4+

Anon, 1987, Attempt on Rajiv's life in Colombo, *Times of India*, July 31, p 1, col 3-6+

Anon, 1988, Pak hand seen in destabilisation bid: Concern at plot against PM, *Times of India*, August 3, p 1, col 1-3+

Anon, 1991, 2 refugees arrested, wireless set seized, *Hindustan Times*, July 10, p 1, col 5
Anon, 1991, 6 cops challenge their suspension, *Hindustan Times*, August 10, p 2, col 1-4
Anon, 1991, ASI among 6 suspended in Rajiv case, *Hindustan Times*, July 27, p 7, col 8
Anon, 1991, After Rajiv Gandhi, *Economic and Political Weekly*, 26(21) May 25, p 1307+
Anon, 1991, Allegation against Chandraswami, *Statesman*, August 10, p 4, col 3-4
Anon, 1991, Another judge soon to probe Rajiv murder, *Hindustan Times*, August 2, p 10, col 5
Anon, 1991, Assassin expelled from LTTE? *Hindustan Times*, May 31, p 9, col 7
Anon, 1991, Assassin identified, *Hindustan Times*, June 3, p 1, col 8+
Anon, 1991, The assassination: A confusing scenario, *Hindustan Times* (Sunday Magazine), June 2, p 1, col 1-8+
Anon, 1991, Assassination and after in North East, *Economic and Political Weekly*, 26(22-23) June 1-8, p 1383
Anon, 1991, Bail disallowed in Rajiv case, *Hindustan Times*, July 30, p 10, col 2-3.
Anon, 1991, BJP blames LTTE for killing, *Hindustan Times*, May 26, p 8, col 7
Anon, 1991, BJP seeks probe, *Hindustan Times*, May 30, p 10, col 1
Anon, 1991, BJP seeks wider probe, *Hindustan Times*, May 3, p 8, col 5-7
Anon, 1991, Bid to subvert Rajiv probe, *Hindustan Times*, August 10, p 9, col 1
Anon, 1991, Break through in Rajiv case: Woman, son held for sheltering assassin, *Hindustan Times*, June 13, p 1, col 6-8+
Anon, 1991, CBI raised reward to Rs 10 lakh, *Hindustan Times*, June 6, p 10, col 1
Anon, 1991, CBI team to visit Lanka today, *Hindustan Times*, May 30, p 16, col 1
Anon, 1999, CBI told to handover Rajiv's clothes, *Hindustan Times*, July 18, p 7, col 5
Anon, 1991, Capital is normal, *Hindustan Times*, May 26, p 5, col 4
Anon, 1991, Case against LTTE almost wrapped up, *Hindustan Times*, November 17, p 6, col 7-8.
Anon, 1991, Change in campaigning after assassination, *Hindustan Times*, June 3, p 10, col 2-4
Anon, 1991, Clinching evidence of LTTE hand: Aide of Sivarasan held, *Hindustan Times*, July 23, p 1, col 5-7.
Anon, 1991, Congress blames NF for killing, *Hindustan Times*, May 31, p 10, col 5-7
Anon, 1991, Conspiracy behind killing: Tiwari, *Hindustan Times*, June 6, p 7 col 2-7, news-item
Anon, 1991, Cowardly act, *Hindustan Times*, May 31, p 11, col 2-6, letters to the editor
Anon, 1991, Dead men tell tales? *Illustrated Weekly of India* July 6-July 12, p 10-11
Anon, 1991, Decision soon to widen Rajiv probe, *Hindustan Times*, July 18, p 9, col 1-4

Anon, 1991, The dry run: Sivarasan at V.P. Singh meeting, *Frontline* July 20-August 2, p 128 +
Anon, 1991, Era comes to an end, *Hindustan Times*, June 6, p 11, col 2-5, letter to the editor
Anon, 1991, Furore over remarks on Rajiv's killing, *Hindustan Times*, July 3, p 4, col 4-7
Anon, 1991,Getting away with murder, *India Today* June 15, p 53, col 1-2
Anon, 1991, Government flayed on assassination, *Hindustan Times*, May 30, p 3, col 1
Anon, 1991, Hunt for Kanthan in Bangalore, *Hindustan Times*, September 3
Anon, 1991, Information on Rajiv invited, *Hindustan Times*, June 24, p 7, col 8
Anon, 1991, Interrogation of DMK leaders demanded, *Hindustan Times*, June 4, p 4, col 3-4
Anon, 1991, Judges were against accepting probe offer, *Hindustan Times*, May, 28, p 5, col 5-6
Anon, 1991, Key suspect found hanging, *Hindustan Times*, July 21, p 1, col 4-7.
Anon, 1991, Killer was Sundari from Vauuniya in Sri Lanka? *Hindustan Times*, June 2, p 1, col 5-7
Anon, 1991, Killers used LTTE as cover: Kittu, *Hindustan Times*, June 2, p 15, col 8, new-item
Anon, 1991, Killers wanted to slip into Nepal, *Hindustan Times*, July 7, p 1, col 1-4
Anon, 1991, LTTE man detained, *Hindustan Times*, June 9, p 1, col 5
Anon, 1991, LTTE offer to help probe, *Hindustan Times*, June 7, p 1, col 8
Anon, 1991, LTTE owns 'onus' for Rajiv killing, *Hindustan Times*, July 15, p 1, col 1
Anon, 1991, LTTE planned mass killings in September, *Hindustan Times*, July 17, p 7, col 7-8
Anon, 1991, LTTE publication seized, *Hindustan Times*, July 23, p 6, col 1
Anon, 1991, LTTE refuses to own Rajiv's murder, *Organiser* 62(44) June 9, p 14, col 4-5 +
Anon, 1991, LTTE very much involved: Chavan, *Hindustan Times*, July 16, p 9, col 5-8, news-item
Anon, 1991, LTTE youth might spill the beams, says Lanka, *Hindustan Times*, June 10, p 13, col 2-4
Anon, 1991, Lanka rushes assassin's photo to SIT, *Hindustan Times*, July 10, p 12, col 6
Anon, 1991 Lankan says he knows 'accomplice', *Hindustan Times*, June 10, p 13, col 1-2
Anon, 1991, Lensman held in Rajiv case, *Hindustan Times*, July 3, p 1, col 1
Anon, 1991, Little headway in Rajiv murder case: Bhartiya Janta Party demand thorough judicial probe, *Organiser* 62(44) June 9, p 15, col 3-5
Anon, 1991, Major break in Rajiv murder case: 2 Lankans held in Delhi, *Hindustan Times*, July 6, p 1, col 5-7 +
Anon, 1991, Many Rajiv organs damaged, *Hindustan Times*, May 30, p 3, col 6-8
Anon, 1991, Maragatham meets Sonia, *Hindustan Times*, July 10, p 3, col 2

Anon, 1991, More suicides in some States, *Hindustan Times*, May 26, p 1, col 4-5 +

Anon, 1991, Murugan had affair with Nalini, *Hindustan Times*, July 6, p 10, col 5-8

Anon, 1991, Nalini, Murugan now in judicial custody, *Indian Express*, August 10, p 9, col 7-8

Anon, 1991, No change in SIT: Chavan, *Hindustan Times*, August 11, p 16, col 1-3, news-item

Anon, 1991, No hand in killing, insists LTTE, *Hindustan Time*, May 31, p 13, col 5-6

Anon, 1991, No headway in probe: Sahay, *Hindustan Times*, May 30, p 1, col 6-7, news-item

Anon, 1991, On the killer trail, *Frontline* June 22-July 5, p 21-28.

Anon, 1991, On leads, modes, linkages, *Frontline* June 22-July 5, p 37-38

Anon, 1991, One more held in assassination case, *Hindustan Times*, June 27, p 1, col 4-5

Anon, 1991, Other possibilities, *Hindustan Times* (Sunday Magazine), June 2, p 2, col 5-8

Anon, 1991, Panel probe on Rajiv urged, *Hindustan Times*, June 3, p 5, col 1

Anon, 1991, Petition in Rajiv case admitted, *Hindustan Times*, November 12, p 7, col 1.

Anon, 1991, Petition on Rajiv probe kept pending, *Hindustan Times*, July 9, p 4, col 5-6

Anon, 1991, Petitions for right to consult lawyers, *Hindustan Times*, July 9, p 4, col 2-3

Anon, 1991, Police had no metal detectors, *Hindustan Times*, May 28, p 16, col 4

Anon, 1991, Police questioning woman, *Hindustan Times*, May 28, p 1, col 1-3

Anon, 1991, Police wanted Rajiv poll meet venue changed, *Hindustan Times*, May 28, p 16, col 5-7

Anon, 1991 Policeman challenge suspension order, *Times of India*, August 10, p 3, col 4-5

Anon, 1991, Prabhakaran tried to reach Sivarasan, *Hindustan Times*, September 4

Anon, 1991, Prayer meet at Sriperumbudur, *Hindustan Times*, June 3, p 7, col 4

Anon, 1991, Rajiv bore most of blast impact, *Hindustan Times*, June 4, p 10, col 1

Anon, 1991, Rajiv case: Judicial custody for two, *Tribune*, August 10, p 5, col 1

Anon, 1991, Rajiv denies attack in Bihar town, *H idustan Times*, March 29, p 1, col 8+

Anon, 1991, Rajiv murder politicised, says BJP, *Hindustan Times*, May 30, p 7, col 3, news-item

Anon, 1991, Rajiv's last moments, *Frontline*, June 22-July 5, p 70+

Anon, 1991, Rajiv shoes handed over to Sonia, *Hindustan Times*, June 20, p 10, col 5

Anon, 1991, Rajya Sabha condemns Rajiv's assassination, *Hindustan Times*, June 4, p 1, col 2-4 +

Anon, 1991, Rangan keeps up disclosures, *Hindustan Times*, September 3

Anon, 1991, Reports on Rajiv case 'fiction', *Hindustan Times*, July 18, p 9, col 1

Anon, 1991, Revalue tumbles since Rajiv killing, *Hindustan Times*, July 10, p 15, col 1-2

Anon, 1991, SIT finds vital data on Padmanabha killing, *Hindustan Times*, July 27, p 1, col 1-3+

Anon, 1991, SIT hunting for youth, 2 women, *Hindustan Times*, June 12, p 1, col 1-2+

Anon, 1991, SIT seizes cache of explosives, *Hindustan Times*, July 20, p 20, col 1.

Anon, 1991, Sailor who hit Rajiv mourns death, *Hindustan Times*, May 30, p 11, col 1

Anon, 1991, Search for LTTE hide-outs, *Hindustan Times*, July 29, p 7, col 1-2

Anon, 1991, Search for Sivarasan accomplice, *Hindustan Times*, September 3

Anon, 1991, Search on for third accomplice, *Hindustan Times*, May 31, p 1, col 6-7 +

Anon, 1991, Secret link between NF, LTTE alleged, *Hindustan Times*, June 14, p 10, col 3

Anon, 1991, Shanmugam killed himself: Report, *Hindustan Times*, July 22, p 18, col 2-3.

Anon, 1991, Shanmugham's body is cremated, *Hindustan Times*, July 22, p 10, col 6.

Anon, 1991, Shanmugham's death: Judicial inquiry sought, *Hindustan Times*, July 30, p 1, col 5-7.

Anon, 1991, The shock wave, *Frontline* 8(12) June 8-June 21, p 28-29+

Anon, 1991, Shut up, *Hindustan Times*, July 18, p 9, col 4

Anon, 1991, Similar bomb had killed Wijeratne, *Hindustan Times*, May 20, p 20, col 1

Anon, 1991, Sivarasan made the bomb used by killer, *Hindustan Times*, June 17, p 4, col 1-2

Anon, 1991, Sivarasan may flee to Lanka, *Hindustan Times*, June 30, p 1, col 3

Anon, 1991, Sonia wants Rajiv's sneakers, *Hindustan Times*, June 13, p 8, col 1

Anon, 1991, Spectacles of assassin recovered, *Hindustan Times*, May 26, p 10, col 1-4

Anon, 1991, Sri Lankan officials see LTTE hand, *Hindustan Times*, May 26, p 12, col 2-3

Anon, 1991, Suspension for DIG in Rajiv case, *Hindustan Times*, July 14, p 1, col 8

Anon, 1991, Suspension over woman in Agra, *Hindustan Times*, June 7, col 8

Anon, 1991, Tamil Nadu witnessed maximum bomb shock and sympathy wave, *Democratic World* 20(25) June 3, p 8

Anon, 1991, Two LTTE men brought to capital, *Hindustan Times*, June 9, p 10, col 3

Anon, 1991, Verma to probe assassination, *Hindustan Times*, May 28, p 1, col 1-3

Anon, 1991, Viscious killing, *Hindustan Times*, May 28, p 9, col 2-5, letter to the editor

Anon, 1991, Vital links missing in Rajiv case, *Hindustan Times*, July 31, p 6, col 3-5

Anon, 1991, Who is to blame? *Hindustan Times* (Sunday Magazine), June 2, p 2,

col 5-8

Anon, 1991, Why LTTE high command ordered Rajiv's treacherous killing, *Link* 33(50) July 21, p 5-9

Anon, 1991, Why pick on the LTTE? *Sunday* June 23-June 29, p 64-65

Anon, 1991, Wife seeks property, *Hindustan Times*, September 3

Anon, 1991, Writ against CBI in Rajiv case, *Hindustan Times*, July 11, p 18, col 6

Anon, 1992, Affidavits by suspecıs discounted, *Hindustan Times*, February 20, p 9, col 5

Anon, 1992, Assassination case takes a new turn, *Sunday Statesman*, April 5, p 4, col 4-5

Anon, 1992, The case against the LTTE, *Independent*, May 22, p 4, col 1-2

Anon, 1992, Centre, organisers partly responsible, *Indian Express*, March 31, p 7, col 2-5

Anon, 1992, Chargesheet in Rajiv case filed: Killing plotted by Prabhakaran, *Hindustan Times*, May 21, p 1, col 1-3+

Anon, 1992, Chavan refutes charge in Rajiv killing case, *Hindustan Times*, March 13, p 15, col 5-6, news-item

Anon, 1992, Concern at erasure of Rajiv video film, *Times of India*, March 11, p 4, col 5-8

Anon, 1992, Cong leaders had idea of threat to Rajiv, *Times of India*, April 4, p 18, col 1-4

Anon, 1992, Cover up in Rajiv case, alleges Jaya, *Times of India*, p 14, col 4, news-items

Anon, 1992, DMK meeting was cancelled, *Hindustan Times*, February 10, p 8, col 6-8.

Anon, 1992, Evidence in Rajiv case being concealed: Jaya, *Indian Express*, March 31, p 1, col 8+, news-item

Anon, 1992, First hearing of Rajiv case on June 3, *Hindustan Times*, May 22, p 22, col 1

Anon, 1992, Gaps in crucial Rajiv Cassette, *The Independent*, April 3, p 6, col 5-6.

Anon, 1992, Garlander's list not correct, *Hindustan Times*, April 2, p 10, col 5-8.

Anon, 1992, Govt denies tampering video tape, *Hindustan Times*, March 12, p 12, col 5.

Anon, 1992, Jain panel yet to probe Rajiv assassination, *Indian Express*, March 27, p 7, col 5-6.

Anon, 1992, Justice J.S. Verma visits Sriperumbudur, *Hindustan Times*, March p 7, col 1-3.

Anon, 1992, LTTE blames Rajiv for massacre, *Hindustan Times*, March 4, p 22, col 3

Anon, 1992, LTTE planned for 9-months, *Tribune*, May 23, p 1, col 6-8

Anon, 1992, Lack of security, says Justice Verma, *National Herald*, April 4, p 1, col 5-6

Anon, 1992, Lanka Govt linked in Rajiv assassination case, *Hindustan Times*, April 10, p 12, col 2-4

Anon, 1992, Lanka willing to extradite Rajiv killers, *Hindustan Times*, May 22, p 1, col 1-3+

Anon, 1992, List of garlanders not genuine, says Counsel, *National Herald*, April 2, p 10, col 5-7

Anon, 1992, Move to find out assassin's route, *National Herald*, April 5, p 10, col 6-7

Anon, 1992, Music party arrival violated security, *Times of India*, March 16, p 3, col 4-5

Anon, 1992, No tampering with cassettes: Chavan, *Times of India*, March 12, p 4, col 7-8, news-item

Anon, 1992, Non-Congmen too garlanded Rajiv, *Hindustan Times*, January 25, p 17, col 2-6

Anon, 1992, Plea for testimony by suspended DIG, *Hindustan Times*, January 24, p 11, col 1-2

Anon, 1992, Police had provided 'full' security to Rajiv, panel told, *Hindustan Times*, March 30, p 12, col 5-7.

Anon, 1992, Probe must to clear Rajiv's name: Aiyar, *National Herald*, April 2, p 1, col 1-2+, news-item

Anon, 1992, Probe team holds LTTE responsible, *Hindustan Times*, March 2, p 22, col 6-7

Anon, 1992, Publication of Rajiv case trial banned, *Hindustan Times*, May 22, p 12, col 8

Anon, 1992, Rajiv case hearing in June 3, *Times of India*, May 22, p 11, col 6

Anon, 1992, Rajiv case proceedings to be kept secret, *Statesman*, May 22, p 9, col 5

Anon, 1992, Rajiv probe enters crucial phase, *Hindustan Times*, January 31, p 11, col 1-4

Anon, 1992, Rajiv was mobbed, Verma Panel told, *Times of India*, March 4, p 3, col 6-7

Anon, 1992, SIT: Dhanu was not gang-raped, *Hindustan Times*, May 23, p 7, col 6

Anon, 1992, SIT chargesheet: Assassination after 9-month planning, *Hindustan Times*, May 23, p 20, col 1-4

Anon, 1992, SIT Chief denies reports, *Times of India*, May 23, p 3, col 2, news-item

Anon, 1992, Security for Rajiv improper, panel told, *Hindustan Times*, April 28, p 10, col 6-7

Anon, 1992, Security lapses at Sriperumbudur: No escape for cops, leaders, *Hindustan Times*, April 4, p 4, col 4-6

Anon, 1992, Sivarasan had mole in AICC, *Statesman*, April 1, p 14, col 7-8

Anon, 1992, Sivarasan, Subha took shelter in TN, Kerala, *Sundary Tribune*, May 24, p 4, col 4-5

Anon, 1992, Six move held in Rajiv case, *Hindustan Times*, May 19, p 1, col 1+

Anon, 1992, Sonia's name not in SIT witnesses list, *Times of India*, May 23, p 3, col 1-2

Anon, 1992, Sonia to be examined in Rajiv case, *Hindustan Times*, May 20, p 12, col 5

Anon, 1992, TNCC Chief was not consulted about Rajiv's visit, *Indian Express*, April 1, p 3, col 2-6

Anon, 1992, TNCC(I), police responsible for security lapses: Justice Verma, *Economic Times*, April 4, p 16, col 1-6
Anon, 1992, Tamils abroad played an active role, *Hindustan Times*, January 28, p 12, col 3-4.
Anon, 1992, Testimony contradicts Organizer's claim, *Statesman*, April 2, p 6, col 6-7
Anon, 1992, Venue posed security risk, *Hindustan Times*, March 14, p 22, col 1-3
Anon, 1992, Verma Commission hearing: Cong leaders didn't agree to shift Rajiv meeting venue, *Hindustan Times*, March 8, p 12, col 2-4
Anon, 1992, Verma panel arguments commence in camera, *Hindustan Times* April 10, p 4, col 1-2
Anon, 1992, Verma panel flays AICC for delay, *Hindustan Times*, April 25, p 12, col 8
Anon, 1992, Verma panel gets extension, *Hindustan Times*, March 30, p 9, col 3-5
Anon, 1992, Verma panel hearing: AICC contributed to security lapses, *Indian Express*, April 4, p 11, col 1-4
Anon, 1992, Verma panel hearing: Cassettes screened again, *Indian Express*, April 3, p 11, col 6-8.
Anon, 1992, Verma panel hearing: Cop tried to stop 2 women, *Hindustan Times*, March 11, p 12, col 1-3
Anon, 1992, Verma penal hearing: Maragatham did not discuss security, *Hindustan Times*, March 6, p 10, col 4-7
Anon, 1992, Verma panel hearing: Police accused of lapses at meet, *Indian Express*, p 7, col 2-4
Anon, 1992, Verma panel hearing: Rajiv was not wearing bullet proof vest, *Hindustan Times*, January 4, p 5, col 1-4
Anon, 1992, Verma panel hearing re-scheduled, *Hindustan Times*, February 18, p 12, col 6.
Anon, 1992, Verma panel hearing: Security sketch plan not followed, *Hindustan Times*, January 30, p 10, col 7-8.
Anon, 1992, Verma panel hearing: Systematic erosion of security norms, *Hindustan Times*, March 13, p 12, col 7-8.
Anon, 1992, Verma panel hearing on SIT Chief, *Hindustan Times*, March 5, p 12, col 5
Anon, 1992, Verma panel probe: Intriguing aspect of garlanders, *Sunday Statesmen*, April 5, p 7, col 6-8.
Anon, 1992, Verma panel probe: Witness collapses while testifying, *Hindustan Times*, March 12, p 22, col 1-2
Anon, 1992, Verma panel report by May, *The Tribune*, March 30, p 12, col 5-7.
Anon, 1992, Verma panel starts video screening, *Hindustan Times*, Febraury 25, p 3, col 1-2.
Anon, 1992, Verma panel strictures on MP, *Hindustan Times*, February 26, p 24, col 8.
Anon, 1992, Verma panel to hand in report by May, *Indian Express*, March 30, p 7, col 7-8
Anon, 1992, Verma panel widens area of probe, *Times of India*, April 5, p 4, col

7-8

Anon, 1992, Verma panel's term extended, *Hindustan Times*, January 5, p 18, col 7.

Anon, 1992, Verma visits site of Rajiv's assassination, *Times of India*, March 23, p 3, col 1

Anon, 1992, Witness tells Verma panel: Lighting at meet was adequate, *Hindustan Times*, January 29, p 9, col 1-4

Anon, Sunita, 1991, BJP wants foreign connection probed, *Hindustan Times*, May 31, p 7, col 1-4

Badhwar, Inderjit, 1991, A water-shed of uncertainty, *India Today* June 15, p 6-7

Baird, Joel, 1986, This man tried to kill Rajiv Gandhi, *Illustrated Weekly of India* 107(19) May 4, p 26-29

Bandopadyay, Saumya, 1991, The last journey, *Sunday* June 9-June 15, p 30-31

Banerjee, Ruben, 1991, Presaging death, *India Today* June 15, p 16, col 1-2

Baruah, Amit, 1991, Security syndrome: The protection provided to Rajiv, *Forntline* 8(12) June 9-June 21, p 27

Baweja, Harinder, 1991, The Gandhi: Picking up the threads, *India Today* June 30, p 102-105

Baweja, Harinder and Vishwanthan, Anand, 1991, Darkness at mid-life, *India Today* June 15, p 10-19

Bhagwan Singh, R., 1991, Cracking the case, *Sunday* June 23-June 29, p 61-63

Bhagwan Singh, R., 1991, Eye witness: An on-the-spot report of Rajiv's assassinaion, *Sunday* June 2- June 8, p 12-13

Bidwai, Praful, 1991, Between despair and hope, *Illustrated Weekly of India* 112(23) June 1, p 12-13.

Buta Singh, 1988, MP's concern over plot to assassinate PM, *National Herald*, August 3

Chakravarti, Sudeep, 1991, The half-way house, *India Today* June 15, p 76-77

Chawla, Prabhu, 1991, Floundering for direction, *India Today* June 15, p 105-107

Crossette, Barbara, 1991, The last interview: Minutes before the blast, *Frontline* 8(12) June 8-June 21, p 19-20

D'Souza, Vincent, 1991, Ill-chosen venue, lax security, *The Week* June 9, p 36-37

D'Souza, Vincent, 1991, Elusive quarry, *The Week* June 30, p 10

D'Souza, Vincent, 1991, The hunt, *The Week* June 9, p 34-37

D'Souza, Vincent, 1991, Prized pictures, quick deals, *The Week* June 9, p 38-39

D'Souza, Vincent, 1991, Torturous trail, *The Week* June 30, p 9-10

D'Souza, Vincent, 1991, Will the snaps click as evidence? *The Week* June 9, p 42, col 1-3

Das, Sanjay K., 1991, The bomb that changed it all, *Onlooker* June 15, p 11-14

Das, Sanjay K., 1991, Murder night in Delhi, *Onlooker* June 15, p 16-18

Democratic World (Periodical), 1991, Rajiv's journey toward stability ends, *Democratic world* 20(21) May 26, p 3-4, col 2 +, editorial

Dharker, Anil, 1991, Who takes security seriously? *Sunday* June 23-June 29, p 16-17

Gupta, Shakhar, et al, 1991, An avoidable calamity, *India Today* June 15, p 38+

Gupta, Shakhar, et al, 1991, Assassination probe: Fitting the pieces, *India Today*

June 30, p 42-44

Gupta, Smita, 1992, Congress men no longer talk of chairsma, *Independent*, May 21, p 5, col 1-8

Hindustan Times (Newspaper), 1991, A thorough probe, *Hindustan Times*, June 6, p 11, col 1, editorial

Indian Express (Newspaper), 1992, Where is the evidence? *Indian Express*, April 2, p 8, col 1-2, editorial

Iyer, Mani Shankar, 1992, A loss of flair, *Independent*, May 21, p 5, col 1-4

Jayanth, V., et al, 1991, The gory end, *Frontline* 8(12) June 8-June 21, p 4-5 +

Jayaram, C.S., 1991, Blast device at forensic dept, *Hindustan Times*, May 30, p 1, col 5-7

Jayaram, C.S., 1991, A confusing scenario, *Hindustan Times* (Magazine), p 1, col 1-8+

Jayaram, C.S., 1991, Did killer's team visit Kanchi? *Hindustan Times*, June 6, p 18, col 3-6

Jayaram. C.S., 1991, Has the investigation been side tracked? *Hindustan Times* (Magazine), July 30, p 5, col 1-5.

Jeyaraj, D.B.S., 1991, Question of motive: Was it the LTTE? *Frontline* 8(12) June 8-June 21, p 25-26

Joshi, Chand, 1991, Last tipoff was from terrorists? *Hindustan Times*, June 3, p 1, col 1+

Joshi, Chand, 1991, Lax security at forensic lab, *Hindustan Times*, May 30, p 16, col 1-3

Jodhi, Chand, 1991, Rajiv assassination: More angles than facts, *Hindustan Times*, June 6, p 1, col 3-5

Joshi, Manoj, 1991, End of the road, *Frontline* 8(12) June 8-June 21, p 32-34+

Joshi, Manoj, 1991 A ruthless job: Who are the suspects? *Frontline* 8(12) June 8-June 21, p 21-22

Joshi, Manoj, 1991, Security puzzles, *Frontline* June 22-July 5, p 32-33

Kher, M.V., 1992, Naxal links with Rajiv assassins, *Times of India*, April 2, p 3, col 4-5

Kohli, M.S., 1991, An adventurous spirit, *Hindustan Times* (Magazine), July 20, p 3, col 1-8

Krishna Iyer, V.R., 1991, In search of truth, *Frontline* June 22-July 5, p 39-41

Krishnamurthy, R., 1991, Sleuths close in on Rajiv's killers, *Current*, July 6-July 12, p 9, col 1-5

Mahajan, Krishan, 1991, No SC judge to probe killing, *Hindustan Times*, May 26, p 1, col 1-4+

Malik, Suyash, 1991, Murder most foul, *Radical Humanist*, 55(3) June, p 4-6

Merchant, Minhaz, 1991, Rajiv and after, *Illustrated Weekly of India* 112(23) June 8, p 14-15

Mitra, Anirudhya, 1991, Rajiv assassination: The inside story, *India Today* July 15, p 22-29

Mitra, Anirudhya, 1991, Startling break through, *India Today* June 30, p 45, col 1-2

Mohan Ram, 1991, Who killed Rajiv? *Illustrated Weekly of India*, 112(23) June 8,

p 6-11

Mukarji, Apartim, 1991, Lanka TV fails to show assassin's photo, *Hindustan Times*, June 3, p 20, col 1-2

Mukarji, Apartim, 1992, LTTE extends olive branch to New Delhi, *Hindustan Times*, March 29, p 15, col 5-7

Mukarji, Apartim, 1992, Lanka assurance to India on Rajiv assassination, *Hindustan Times*, May 8, p 12, col 2-4

Mukarji, Apartim, 1992, Sri Lankan dilemma over Prabhakaran, *Hindustan Times*, January 6, p 15, col 7-8

Murthy, Sachidananda, 1991, Could SPG have saved Rajiv? *The Week* June 9, p 40-41

Nagi, Saroj, 1991, A tragic end, *Illustrated Weekly of India* 112(22) June 1, p 6-11.

New Age (Periodical), 1986, Grim warning, *New Age* 34(41) October 12, p 2, editorial

Nigam, R.L., 1991, Rajiv Gandhi assassination and assassins, *Radical Humanist* 55(3) June, p 1-3+

Noorani, A.G., 1991, A limited probe, *Frontline* June 22-July 5, p 42-44

Padmanabhan, Mukund, et al, 1991, How the arrests were made, *Sunday* June 23-June 29, p 62-63

Padmanabhan, Mukund, 1991, A question of identity, *Sunday* June 9-June 15, p 67-69

Padmanabhan, Mukund, et al, 1991, The hit: Who did it? And why? *Sunday* June 2-June 8, p 14-17

Pramar, Suresh K., 1991, Rajiv Gandhi's death orphans tribals, *Onlooker* June 15, p 46-47

Prasad, Srinivasa, 1992, Rajiv's assassins were ready to strike in 1990, *Independent*, May 23, p 1, col 2-6

Prasad, Srinivasa, 1992, SIT files chargesheet in Rajiv case: Prabhakaran, 40 others accused, *Independent*, May 21, p 1, col 5-7

Raghu, V., 1991, Andhra Pradesh vandalism after Rajiv's assassination, *Mainstream* 29(35) June 22, p 29-30

Raina, Askoh, 1991, Need he have died? *Hindustan Times* (Sunday Magazine), June 2, p 2, col 1-8

Sahay, Subodh Kant, 1991, Rajiv had been warned often, *India Today* June 15, p 46, col 1-2

Sahni, Ajai, 1991, The dynasty ends, *Surya India* June, p 6-14

Saksena, Rashmi, 1991, The pug mask, *The Week* June 9, p 38-39

Santosh Kumar, V.K., 1991, Last moment: A forensic view, *The Week* June 9, p 34-35

Shukla, Rajiv and Sarin, Ritu, 1991, After the dynasty, *Sunday* June 9-June 15, p 32-34

Shukla, Rajiv and Sarin, Ritu, 1991, A quiet sorrow, *Sunday* June 9-June 15, p 29

Sidhva, Shiraz, 1991, The Sonia enigma: The public loss of a private person, *Sunday* June 2-June 8, p 40

Subramanian, T.S., 1991, LTTE's overtures, *Frontline* 8(12) June 8-June 21, p 23

Sunil, K.P., 1991, The plot thickens, *Illustrated Weekly of India* 112(30) July 27,

p 20-12

Sunil, K.P., 1991, What is the LTTE up to? *Illustrated Weekly of India* 112(24) June 15, p 6-11

Talwar, Ashwini, 1991, Letter rogatory delivered to Lanka, *Times of India*, March 14, p 9, col 7-8

Thakur, Janardan, 1986, The intelligence network in a shambles, *Hindustan Times* (Magazine), October 12, p 1, col 1-6+

Theodore, Stanley, 1991, Madcap's blue noon, *The Week* June 9, p 42, col 1-3

Times of India (Newspaper), 1986, The shots at Rajghat, *Times of India*, October 3, p 8, col 1-2, editorial

Verekar, Raju, 1991, Rajiv death led to rout: Thackeray, *Hindustan Times*, June 22, p 7, col 1-4, news-item

Zehra, Nasim, 1991, Concern, disbelief in Pakistan, *Hindustan Times*, May 26, p 12, col 1-4

Assassination: Attempts and Probes: Gandhi, Rajiv: Bomb Scare

Anon, 1982, Bomb scare on Rajiv's flight, *Hindustan Times*, May 12, p 8

Assassination: Attempts and Probes: Gandhi, Rajiv: Dhanu Involvement

Anon, 1992, SIT: Dhanu was not gang-raped, *Hindustan Times*, May 23, p 7, col 6

Assassination: Attempts and Probes: Gandhi, Rajiv: Foreign Connection

Anon, 1991, 'Definite' foreign hand in blast, *Hindustan Times*, May 30, p 4, col 3

Aron, Sunita, 1991, BJP wants foreign connection probed, *Hindustan Times*, May 31, p 7, col 1-4

Assassination: Attempts and Probes: Gandhi, Rajiv: Influence on Elections

Anon, 1991, Rajiv wave caused BJP, Shiv Sena rout in Maharashtra, *Democratic World* 20(25) June 23, p 7

Assassination: Attempts and Probes: Gandhi, Rajiv: Murugan Involvement

Anon, 1991, Murugan had affair with Nalini, *Hindustan Times*, July 6, p 10, col 5-8

Anon, 1991, Nalini, Murugan now in judicial custody, *Indian Express*, August 10, p 9, col 7-8

Anon, 1991, Nalini, Murugan remanded, *Hindustan Times*, June 16, p 1, col 5+

Assassination: Attempts and Probes: Gandhi, Rajiv: Nalini Involvement

Anon, 1991, Murugan had affair with Nalini, *Hindustan Times*, July 6, col 5-8

Anon, 1991, Nalini, Murugan now in judicial custody, *Indian Express*, August, 10, p 9, col 7-8

Anon, 1991, Nalini, Murugan remanded, *Hindustan Times*, June 16, p 1, col 5+

Assassination: Attempts and Probes: Gandhi Rajiv: Padmanabha Involvement

Anon, 1991, SIT finds vital data on Padmanabha killing, *Hindustan Times*, July 27, p 1, col 1-3+

Assassination: Attempts and Probes: Gandhi Rajiv: Prabhakaran Involvement

Anon, 1992, Chargesheet in Rajiv case filed: Killing plotted by Prabhakaran, *Hindustan Times*, May 21, p 1, col 1-3+

Prasad, Srinivasa, 1992, SIT files chargesheet in Rajiv case: Prabhakaran, 40 others accused, *Independent*, May 21, p 1, col 5-7

Assassination: Attempts and Probes: Gandhi, Rajiv: Shanmugham Involvement

Anon, 1991, Shanmugham's body is cremated, *Hindsutan Times*, July 22, p 10, col 6.

Anon, 1991, Shanmugham's death: Judicial inquiry sought, *Hindustan Times*, July 30, p 1, col 5-7.

Anon, 1991, Shanmugham killed himself: Report, *Hindustan Times*, July 22, p 10, col 2-3

Assassination: Attempts and Probes: Gandhi, Rajiv: Sivarasan Involvement

Anon, 1991, Clinching evidence of LTTE hand: Aide of Sivarasan held, *Hindustan Times*, July 23, p 1, col 5-7

Anon, 1991, Pra'bhakaran tried to reach Sivarasan, *Hindustan Times*, September 4

Anon, 1991, Sivarasan made the bomb used by killer, *Hindustan Times*, June 17, p 4, col 1-2

Anon, 1991, Sivarasan may flee to Lanka, *Hindustan Times*, June 30, p 1, col 3+

Anon, 1992, Sivarasan had mole in AICC, *Statesman*, April 1, p 14, col 7-8

Anon, 1992, Sivarasan, Subha took shelter in TN, Kerala, *Sunday Tribune*, May 24, p 4, col 4-5

Assassination: Attempts and Probes: Gandhi, Rajiv: Special Investigation Team

Anon, 1991, Assassin an LTTE member: SIT, *Hindustan Times*, July 6, p 1, col 3, news-item

Anon, 1991, Assassins being given shelter: SIT, *Hindustan Times*, June 23, p 12, col 3, news-item

Anon, 1991, Hunt on for one-eyed jack: SIT, *Hindustan Times*, June 14, p 1, col 1+, news-item

Anon, 1991, Lanka rushes assassin's photo to SIT, *Hindustan Times*, July 10, p 12, col 6

Anon, 1991, Media probe irks SIT, *Hindustan Times*, May 28, p 7, col 6-8

Anon, 1991, No change in SIT: Chavan, *Hindustan Times*, June 12, p 1, col 1-2+,

news-item

Anon, 1991, SIT finds vital data on Padmanabha killing, *Hindustan Times*, July 27, p 1, col 1-3+

Anon, 1991, SIT hunting for youth, 2 women, *Hindustan Times*, June 12, p 1, col 1-2+

Anon, 1991, SIT seizes cache of explosives, *Hindustan Times*, July 20, p 20, col 1

Anon, 1992, SIT: Dhanu was not gang-raped, *Hindustan Times*, May 23, p 7, col 6, news-item

Anon, 1992, SIT chargesheet: Assassination after 9-month planning, *Hindustan Times*, May 23, p 20, col 1-4

Anon, 1992, SIT Chief denies reports, *Times of India*, May 23, p 3, col 2, news-item

Anon, 1992, Sonia's name not in SIT witnesses list, *Times of India*, May 23, p 3, col 1-2

Anon, 1992, Verma panel hearing on SIT Chief, *Hindustan Times*, March 5, p 12, col 5

Prasad, Srinivasa, 1992, SIT files chargesheet in Rajiv case: Prabhakaran, 40 others accused, *Independent*, May 21, p 1, col 5-7

Assassination: Attempts and Probes: Gandhi, Rajiv: Special Protection Group

Murthy, Sachidananda, 1991, Could SPG have saved Rajiv? *The Week* June 9, p 40-41

Assassination: Attempts and Probes: Gandhi, Rajiv: Subha Involvement

Anon, 1992, Sivarasan, Subha took shelter in TN, Kerala, *Sunday Tribune*, May 24, p 4, col 4-5

Assassination: Attempts and Probes: Gandhi, Rajiv: Sundari Involvement

Anon, 1991, Killer was Sundari from Vauuniya in Sri Lanka, *Hindustan Times*, June 2, p 1, col 5-7

Assassination: Attempts and Probes: Wijeratne, Ranjan Episode

Anon, 1991, Similar bomb had killed Wijeratne, *Hindustan Times*, May 20, p 20, col 1

Assembly

See Vidhan Sabha

Association of South East-Asian Nations

Anon, 1991, ASEAN watching India poll scene, *Hindustan Times*, May 31, p 12, col 1-4

Astrological Predictions: Gandhi, Rajiv

Tyagi, Sadanand, 1981, Rajiv is man of destiny but he won't be PM, *Current*, June 20, p 3

Atomic Bomb

See Nuclear Bomb

Australia

See also Geographical Area subdivision under main Descriptor

Australia: Foreign Relations: Geographical Area: India

See under Indo-Australian Relations

Awards and Honours: Geographical Area: India: Bharat Ratna: Gandhi, Rajiv

Anon, 1991, Bharat Ratna conferred on Rajiv, *Hindustan Times*, July 7, p 1, col 1

Anon, 1991, Bharat Ratna for Rajiv, Sardar Patel, *Hindustan Times*, June 18, p 1 col 5

Awards and Honours: Geographical Area: India: Bharat Ratna: Patel, Vallabhbhai

Anon, 1991, Bharat Ratna for Rajiv, Sardar Patel, *Hindustan Times*, June 18, p 1, col 5

Awards and Honours: Geographical Area: India: Indira Afforestation Award: Gandhi, Rajiv

Anon, 1986, Indira Afforestation Award presented, *Times of India*, November 20

Awards and Honours: Geographical Area: India: Indira Gandhi Peace Award: Gandhi, Rajiv

Anon, 1992, Indira Gandhi Peace Award for Rajiv, *Hindustan Times*, May 21, p 1, col 2-3

Anon, 1992, Rajiv Gandhi awarded Indira Peace Prize, *Independent*, May 21, p 6, col 3-8

Awards and Honours: Geographical Area: Nicaragua: Nicaraguan Award: Gandhi, Rajiv

Anon, 1986, Nicaraguan Award for the Prime Minister, *Statesman*, September 11

BHEL

=Bharat Heavy Electricals Limited

BJP

=Bhartiya Janata Party (Political Party)

Bachchan, Amitabh

Anon, 1982, Gandhi vote for Amitabh or Sivaji? *Indian Express*, February 5, p 5
Anon, 1982, Rajiv cuts short visit to see Amitabh, *Indian Express*, August 5, p 1
Anon, 1991, Amitabh as Party Chief demanded, *Hindustan Times*, May 28, p 7, col 1
Anon, 1991, No political role for me: Amitabh, *Hindustan Times*, June 2, p 1, col 3, news-item

Bachchan, Amitabh: Views on Gandhi, Rajiv

Anon, 1991, Rajiv was no quitter, says Amitabh, *Hindustan Times*, June 3, p 5, col 3-7, news-item

Bahuguna, H.N.,

Anon, 1989, Bahuguna cremated, *Times of India*, March 21
Chawla, Prabhu, 1982, Rahu, Ketu, Bahuguna, *India Today* 7(1) January 15, p 51

Bangalore: Karnataka: India

See also Geographical Area subdivision under main Descriptor

Bangla Desh

See also Geographical Area subdivision under main Descriptor

Bangla Desh: Foreign Relations: Geographical Area: India

See under Indo-Bangla Desh Relations

Bangrappa, S.

Anon, 1981, Bangrappa men meet Rajiv, *Indian Express*, December 31, p 7

Bansi Lal

Sharma, B.N., 1981, Bansi vs Bhajan: A battle for survival, *Caravan* 2(708) November 16, p 19

Barnala, Surjeet Singh

See also Chief Minister: Geographical Area: India: Punjab: Barnala, Surjeet Singh

Basu, Jyoti

See also Chief Minister: Geographical Area: India: West Bengal: Basu, Jyoti

Belgrade: Yugoslavia

See also Geographical Area subdivision under main Descriptor

Bengal Day

See West Bengal Day

Bhajan Lal

Anon, 1980, Darbara Singh and Bhajan Lal meet Rajiv Gandhi, *Statesman*, August 28

Anon, 1981, Bhajan Lal denies huge expences on Rajiv's visit, *Times of India*, November 23, p.5

Anon, 1982, Conductor Bhajan Lal, *Suday* 8(43) April 17, p 15

Mitra, Sumit, 1982, Bhajan Lal: The artful manipulator, *India Today* 7(12) June 30, p 78-82

Sharma, B.N.,1981, Bansi vs Bhajan: A battle for survival, *Caravan* 2(708) November 16, p 9

Sharma, Vichitra, 1982, Bhajan booed at Rajiv poll meeting, *Hindustan Times*, May 6, p 1+

Bhakti Movement

Ravindra Nath, 1981, New Bhakti movement, *Indian Express*, September 8, p 6

Bhandari, Nar Bahadur

See also Chief Minister: Geographical Area: India: Sikkim: Bhandari, Nar Bahadur

Bhanu Pratap Singh

See also Governer: Geographical Area: India: Goa: Bhanu Pratap Singh

Bharat Heavy Electricals Limited

Anon, 1982, Rajiv lays stone of BHEL plant, *Hindustan Times*, February 11, p 5

Bharat Krishak Samaj

Anon, 1989, PM's Address to Bharat Krishak Samaj, *National Herald* February 7, nesw-item

Bharat Ratna

See Awards and Honours: Geographical Area: India: Bharat Ratna

Bhartiya Janta Party (Political Party)

Anon, 1981, BJP charge on Rajiv rally, *Hindustan Times*, November 18, p 5

Anon, 1981, BJP, Congress (I) main rivals in MP poll, *Indian Express*, December 25, p 5

Anon, 1982, Rajiv blames BJP for Punjab incident, *Hindustan Times*, May 9, p 7

Anon, 1982, Rajiv lashes out at BJP-LD poll alliance, *Times of India*, May 7, p 7

Anon, 1986, The BJP leader, L.K. Advani charged that adhocism rather than a method governed Rajiv Gandhi's Cabinet changes, *Hindustan Times*, May 13, *Statesman*; May 13, nesw-item

Anon, 1986, BJP leader questions PM's stand on GNLF, *Times of India*, November 17

Anon, 1989, Rajiv questions BJP patriotism, *Times of India*, November 19, p 1

Anon, 1990, Rajiv for any non-BJP government, *Times of India*, October 21

Anon, 1991, Rajiv accuses NF, BJP of dividing country, *Hindustan Times*, April 19, p 1, col 1-3

Anon, 1991, Rajiv wave caused BJP, Shiv Sena rout in Maharashtra, *Democratic World* 20(25) June 23, p 7

Anon, 1992, BJP ridicules Cong on anti-terrorism day, *Times of India*, May 23, p 5, col 1-4

Chadha, Kumkum, 1991, BJP is my main enemy: Rajiv, *Hindustan Times*, March 28, p 1, col 1-4 +, news-item

Das, Rathin, 1991, No poll pact with BJP, says Rajiv, *Hindustan Times*, May 11, p 1, col 4-5 +, news-item

Gandhi, Rajiv, 1982, LD, BJP, alliance mere opportunism, fake, *Hindustan Times*, May 15, p 5

Janta (Periodical), 1985, Congress (I), RSS and BJP, *Janata* (Annual Number) 40(1), p 3-4, ediorial

Bharitya Janata Party: Election Cliches

Anon, 1991, Ram, Rajiv poll planks flayed, *Hindustan Times*, June 7, p 9, col 2

Bhartiya Janata Party: Views on Assassination of Gandhi, Rajiv

Anon, 1991, BJP blames LTTE for killing, *Hindustan Times*, May 26, p 8, col 7

Anon, 1991, BJP seeks probe, *Hindustan Times*, May 31, p 10, col 1

Anon, 1991, BJP seeks wider probe, *Hindustan Times* May 30, p 8, col 5-7

Anon, 1991, Rajiv murder politicised, says BJP, *Hindustan Times*, May 30, p 7, col 3

Aron, Sunita, 1991, BJP wants foreign connection probed, *Hindustan Times*, May 31, p 7, col 1-4

Bhatnagar, P.S.

Anon, 1982, Bhatnagar is NDMC Chief, *Hindustan Times*, September 2, p 3

Anon, 1982, P.S. Bhatnagar replaces behl as NDMC Chief, *Times of India*, September 2, p 3.

Bhave, Vinoba

Anon, 1982, Rajiv calls on Bhave, *Times of India*, September 16, p 5

Anon, 1982, Rajiv to call on Vinoba Bhave, *Hindustan Times*, September 10, p 12

Bhosle, Baba Saheb

Anon, 1982, Swamy meets Rajiv about Bhosle affairs, *Times of India*, March 27, p 9

Bhosle, Baba Saheb, 1982, I am Shivaji's descendent, *India Today* 7(3) February 15, p 20-21

Bhutan

See also Geographical Area subdivision under main Descriptor

Bhutan: Foreign Relations: Geographical Area: India

See under Indo-Bhutan Relations

Bhutto, Benazir

Anon, 1988, PM greets Benazir, *Indian Express*, December 3

Anon, 1988, Rajiv Gandhi holds discussions with Benazir, *National Herald*, December 31

Anon, 1989, Rajiv Gandhi holds talks with Banazir, *Indian Express*, July 17; *National Herald*, July 17

Bihar: India

Anon, 1982, Patna bridge hoax, *Sunday* March 27, p 22-23

Anon, 1982, World's longest river bridge opened in Bihar, *Hindu*, March 3, p 1

Anon, 1988, Government will not allow division of States, says PM, *National Herald*, May 26, news-item

Anon, 1988, PM turns down demand for Jharkhand State, *National Herald*, May 28

Anon, 1988, PM visits quake-affected areas, *Times of India*, August 23

Anon, 1991, Rajiv denies attack in Bihar town, *Hindustan Times*, March 29, p 1, col 8 +

Hemendra Narayan, 1982, No payment yet for Rajiv's air trip, *Indian Express*, April 10

See also Geographical Area subdivision under main Descriptors

Bihar Press Bill

Anon, 1982, PM denounces stir on Bihar Press Bill: Opposition obstructing Government work, *Hindustan Times*, September 2, p 1+

Bikaner: Rajasthan

See also Geographical Area subdivision under main Descriptor

Birendra, Bir Bikram Shah Dev

Anon, 1989, Rajiv, Birendra to meet on September 4, *Hindustan Times*, August 27

Blind

See Visually Handicapped

Bodoland Problem

Anon, 1989, The Bodoland imbroglio, *Indian Express*, March 28

Bofors Issue

Anon, 1987, Bofors audit report not contradictory: PM, *Times of India*, July 7, p 1, col 2-3+, news-item

Anon, 1987, Bofors Issues: Opposition asks PM to resign, *Times of India*, June 6, p 1, col 7-8+

Anon 1987, Opposition free to send team to Sweden: PM, *Times of India*, August 9, p 1, col 7-8+, news-item

Anon, 1987, Opposition meet with PM on Bofors Panel terms urged, *Economic Times*, August 12, p 1, col 1-4+

Anon, 1987, PM says he will move motion on Bofors Panel, *Times of India*, June 17, p 1, col 1-3+

Anon, 1988, Ardbo denies having met Rajiv Gandhi, *Hindu*, March 30

Anon, 1988, Genuine work for Bofors: Commission unquestionable: PM, *Economic Times*, November 12, p 1, col 2-5, news-item

Anon, 1988, PM showed extraordinary interest: Dissenting role, *Times of India*, April 27, p 1, col 6-8+

Anon, 1989, JD MPs write to PM on Bofors issue, *Times of India*, June 1

Anon, 1989, PM denies involvement in Bofors deal, *Sunday* November 1

Anon, 1991, Remember Bofors? *Sunday* May 12-May 18, p 88-93

Bombay: Maharashtra: India

See also Geographical Area subdivision under main Descriptor

Bonn: Germany

See also Geographical Area subdivision under main Descriptor

Border Areas Bill

Anon, 1986, PM's talks with opposition on Border Areas Bill, *Free Press Journal*, July 30; *Times of India*, July 30

Boundary Issues: Geographical Area: India

Anon, 1981, Antulay meets PM, Rajiv on border dispute, *Indian Express*, August 28, p 7

Anon, 1985, Border clashes may hit ties: PM, *Times of India*, December 7, p 1, col 1-3, news-item

Anon, 1986, No territorial concessions to China, says PM, *Times of India*, December 19, news-item

Anon, 1986, PM warns against bid to weaken border security, *Free Press Journal*,

September 12

Anon, 1988, Joint Panel set up to settle boundary issue, *Hindustan Times*, December 2

Anon, 1988, No territory to be ceded to China: PM, *Times of India*, September 28, p 1, col 1-3+, news-item

Anon, 1988, State borders not to be changed: PM, *Times of India*, May 22, p 1, col 5-8+, news-item

Breeder Reactor: Geographical Area: India

Anon, 1985, Rajiv invites Zia to inaguration of Breeder Reactor, *Times of India*, December 1, p 1, col 1-3+

Britain

See United Kingdom

Budget: Geographical Area: India

Ghosh, Arun, 1989, The Economy and the Budget, *Economic and Political Weekly*, March 11

Bureaucracy: Geographical Area: India

Anon, 1981, Rajiv asks bureaucrats to shed lethargy, *Hindustan Times*, December 20, p 7

Anon, 1982, Bureaucrats more powerful than politicians, *Sunday* 9(49) March 27, p 36-37

Nayar, Kuldip, 1981, No logic behind top bureaucrat's promotions, *Sunday* 9(8) August 9, p 37

Suresh Chandra, 1986, Rajiv Gandhi and the red-tape, *Economic Times*, March 11, p 5, col 7-8

Bush, George

See also President: Geographica Area: United States of America: Bush, George

Buta Singh

Anon, 1988, PM asks Buta to probe offer of funds to Zail, *Times of India*, March 3, p 1, col 1-3+

Anon, 1989, Sensitive parts of report not be tabled: Buta, *Times of India*, March 29, p 1, col 1-3, news-item

CAG

=Comptroller and Auditor General of India

CBI

=Central Bureau of Investigation, New Delhi

CHOGM

=Commonwealth Heads of Governments Meeting

CPB

=Congress Parliamentary Board

CPI

=Communist Party of India (Political Party)

CPM

=Communist Party of India (Marxist) (Political Party)

CPP

=Congress Party in Parliament

CWC

=Congress Working Committee

Cabinet: Geographical Area: India

Anon, 1986, The BJP leader, L.K. Advani charged that adhocism rather than a method governed Rajiv Gandhi's Cabinet changes, *Hindustant Times*, May 13; *Statesman*, May 13

Anon, 1986, Cabinet reshuffled, *Hindustan Times*, October 24

Anon, 1987, PM in no hurry to reshuffle Cabinet, *Times of India*, October 14, p 1, col 2-5+

Malhotra, Inder, 1985, Cabinet making and after, *Times of India*, January 3

Mitra, S. and Chawla, P., 1982, Cabinet-carousel, *India Today* 7(18) September 30, p 56-64

Calcutta: West Bengal: India

See also Geographical Area subdivision under main Descriptor

Cars

See under name of the car, e.g., Maruti Car

Caste: Geographical Area: India: Himachal Pradesh

Thukral, Gobind, 1982, Himachal Pradesh: Caste calculus, *India Today* 7(10) May 31, p 41-42

Casteism

Anon, 1988, PM warns against casteist front, *Times of India*, November 3

Castro, Fidel

Anon, 1985, Rajiv, Castro vow closer ties, *Times of India*, October 23, p 1, col 4-6+

Central America

Anon, 1986, PM decries outside intervention in Central America, *Telegraph*, August 9

Central Bureau of Investigation, New Delhi

Anon, 1991, CBI raises reward to Rs 10 lakh, *Hindustan Times*, June 6, p 10, col 1

Anon, 1991, CBI team to visit Lanka today, *Hindustan Times*, May 30, p 16, col 1

Anon, 1991, CBI told to hand over Rajiv's clothes, *Hindustan Times*, July 18, p 7, col 5

Anon, 1991, Writ against CBI in Rajiv case, *Hindustan Times*, July 11, p 18, col 6

Chandra Shekhar

Anon, 1991, Congress leaders 'rated' PM above Rajiv, *Hindustan Times*, April 26, p 8, col 2-3

Anon, 1991, Devi Lal seeking new equation with Rajiv as Chandra Shekhar's boat seems sinking, *Organiser* 42(25) January 27, p 64, col 1-3

Anon, 1991, PM briefs RV on law and order, *Hindustan Times*, May 28, p 1, col 5

Anon, 1991, PM hits back at Congress (I), *Organiser* 42(31) March 10, p 1, col 1-3+

Anon, 1991, PM, Rajiv meet President, *Times of India*, February 10

Anon, 1991, RV for Shekhar-Rajiv patch up, *Democratic World* 20(8) February 24, p 7, col 2-3

Anon, 1991, Rajiv apologised to Shekhar for a last minute patch-up, *Organiser* 42(33) March 24, p 5, col 1-5

Anon, 1991, Rajiv flays Shekhar's stand on Gulf War, *Link* 33(25) January 27, p 31-34

Anon, 1991, Rajiv Gandhi poised to take over as PM, *Organiser* 42(28) February 27, p 1, col 1-2+

Anon, 1991, Rajiv Gandhi's letter to PM, *Hindustan Times*, February 11, p 12, col 2

Anon, 1991, Rajiv hopes to present a populist budget after troppling Shekhar, *Organiser* 42(3) March 3, p 1, col 1-5

Anon, 1991, Rajivji's deepening displeasure with the defector PM, *Organier* 42(29) February 24, p 3, col 1-3+

Anon, 1991, Rajiv knew of refuelling: PM, *Hindustan Times*, April 13, col 1, p 1, news-item

Anon, 1991, Shekhar betrayed trust: Rajiv, *Hindustan Times*, April 10, p 9, col 1-3, news-item

Anon, 1991, The toppling of the turk: Rajiv Gandhi style, *Organiser* 42(33) March 24, p 3, col 2-4

Hafiz M. A., 1991, Rajiv, V.P., Shekhar on firm ground, *Hindustan Times*, April 2, p 10, col 5-8

Sanghvi, Vir, 1991, The odd couple: Rajiv Gandhi and Chandra Shekhar: What went wrong? *Sunday* March 17-March 23, p 35-42

Chandra Shekhar: Views on Diverse Issues

Chandra Shekhar, 1981, You cannot solve new problems with old minds, *Sunday* 9(28) December 27, p 17-18

Sanghvi, Vir, 1991, I cannot cling to office, *Sunday* March 17-March 23, p 66-69

Chandra Shekhar: Views on Gandhi, Rajiv

Anon, 1991, PM: Rajiv's statement not fair, *Hindustan Times*, May 9, p 7, col 1

Chandra Shekhar, 1980, Decries 'Draft Rajiv' campaign, *Statesman*, August 29, p 1

Chandraswami

Anon, 1991, Allegation against Chandraswami, *Statesman*, August 10, p 4, col 3-4

Jain, Girilal, 1988, Chandraswami as linchpin: Attempt to blackmail Rajiv Gandhi, *Times of India*, April 5, p 4, col 3-5

Charan Singh

Anon, 1981, Rajiv raps Charan for 'Lathi directive, *Hindustan Times*, June 1

Mehta, Dewang, 1981, Charan Singh: No visible sign of improvement, *Surya India* 5(4) January, p 24

Chavan, S.B.: Views on Assassination of Gandhi, Rajiv

Anon, 1991, Chavan: Foreign hand suspected in Rajiv killing, *Hindustan Times*, July 27, p 1, col 1-3+, news-items

Anon, 1991, LTTE very much involved: Chavan, *Hindustan Times*, July 16, p 9, col 5-8, news-item

Anon, 1991, No change in SIT: Chavan, *Hindustan Times*, August 11, p 16, col 1-3, news-item

Anon, 1991, Reports on Rajiv case 'fiction', *Hindustan Times*, July 18, p 9, col 1, news-item

Chief Minister: Geographical Area: India: Andhra Pradesh: Anjiah, T.,

Anjiah, T., 1982, Explians why Rajiv got angry, *Hindu*, February 4, p 9

Anon, 1982, Rajiv angry with Anjiah over arrangement, *Hindustan Times*, February 3, p 8

Anon, 1982, Rajiv Gandhi shouts at Anjiah for gaudy show, *Hindu*, February 3, p 1

Anon, 1982, Rajiv's anger: A part of the tamasha, *Caravan* 2(714) February, p 14

Hasan, Syed Majeedul, 1982, Rajiv Gandhi was displeased with Anjiah, *Sunday*

9(36) February 27, p 16-17

Nizamuddin, D.E., 1982, Anjiah's English was poor, *Sunday* 9(38) March 13, p 66

Chief Minister: Geographical Area: India: Assam: Mahanta, Praful Kumar

Anon, 1986, Mahanta meets PM, *Statesman*, June 11

Chief Minister: Geographical Area: India: Bihar: Yadav, Laloo Prasad

Anon, 1991, Laloo: Assassination won't influence voters, *Hindustan Times*, May 28, p 16, col 4+5

Chief Minister: Geographical Area: India: Haryana: Bansi Lal

See also Bansi Lal

Chief Minister: Geographical Area: India: Haryana: Bhajan Lal

See also Bhajan Lal

Chief Minister: Geographical Area: India: Haryana: Devi Lal

See also Devi Lal

Chief Minister: Geographical Area: India: Jammu and Kashmir: Abdullah, Farooq

See also Abdullah, Farooq

Chief Minister: Geographical Area: India: Maharashtra: Antulay, A.R.

Anon, 1982, Rajiv to have hand in Minister formation: CM, *Times of India*, January 22, p 9

See also Antuley, A.R.

Chief Minister: Geographical Area: India: Punjab: Barnala, Surjeet Singh

Anon, 1986, PM asks Barnala to curb violence, *Times of India*, June 24, p 1, col 1-3

Anon, 1986, PM assures all help to Barnala, *Telgraph*, December 9

Anon, 1986, PM expresses satisfaction over Barnala's performance, *Free Press Journal*, July 7

Chief Minister: Geographical Area: India: Punjab: Darbara Singh

Anon, 1980, Darbara Singh and Bhajan Lal meet Rajiv Gandhi, *Statesman*, August 28

Anon, 1981, Darbara Singh denies tension in Punjab, *Hindustan Times*, October 30, p 6

Anon, 1981-82, Darbara Singh Government blamed for Punjab unrest, *Delhi Recorder* 2(9) December 15-January 14, p 58-61

Chief Minister: Geographical Area: India: Sikkim : Bhandari, Nar Bahadur

Anon, 1986, PM's assurance to Bhandari, *Times of India*, August 28, news-item

Chief Minister: Geographical Area: India: Uttar Pradesh: Singh, V.P.

Saari Anil, 1981, Rajiv snubs UP CM, *Sunday* 9(25) December 6, p 37

Chief Minister: Geographical Area: India: Uttar Pradesh: Tiwari, Narain Dutt

Anon, 1986, PM invites Chief Minister, *Free Press Journal* December 18; *Times of India*, December 18

Chief Minister: Geographical Area: India: Uttar Pradesh: Yadav, Mulayam Singh

Anon, 1991, Mulayam Singh blackmils Rajiv with anti-Congress report on riots, *Organiser* 42(22) January 6, p 7, col 1-5+

Chadha, Kumkum: 1991, Rajiv all praise for Mulayam, *Hindustan Times*, April 2, p 1, col 5-7+

Chief Minister: Geographical Area: India: West Bengal: Basu, Jyoti

Anon, 1986, Prime Minister to hold talks on GNLF issue with CM, *Times of India*, December 19

Anon, 1986, Why Basu does'nt tax rich farmess? *Link* 29(8) September, p 10-12

Anon, 1988, Jyoti Basu calls on PM, *Hindustan Times*, June 29

Chief Minister: Geographical Area: India: West Bangal: Basu, Jyoti: Views on Gandhi, Rajiv

Anon, 1991, Basu flays Rajiv's remarks on polls, *Hindustan Times*, May 8, p 20, col 1-2

N. Ram, 1991, Rajiv had little time: Interview with Jyoti Basu, *Frontline* 8(12) June 8-June 21, p 113-115

Chief Ministers: Geographical Area: India

Anon, 1988, PM's Address to the Chief Ministers, *Hindustan Times*, March 19; *Times of India*, March 19

Anon, 1986, PM asks CMs to avert tension, *Times of India*, April 30

Children

Reddy, Sanjiva, 1981, Not enough done for children, *Indian Express*, November 15, p 4

China

See also Geographical Area subdivision under main Descriptor

China: Foreign Relations: Geographical Area: India

See under Indo-Chinese Relations

Chirac, Jacques Rene

Anon, 1986, Rajiv greets Chirac, *Statesman*, March 22

Clean, Mr

See Gandhi, Rajiv

Colombo: Sri Lanka

Abraham, Thomas, 1991, An enigma in Colombo, *Frontline* June 22-July 5, p 36
Anon, 1987, Attempt on Rajiv's life in Colombo, *Times of India*, July 31, p 1, col 3-6+
Anon, 1987, Rajiv, JRJ sign accord as violence rocks Colombo, *Economic Times*, July 30, p 6, col 6-8

See also Geographical Area subdivision under main Descriptors

Commerce Policy: Geographical Area: India

Anon, 1985, MNCs not being favoured, *Times of India*, May 5, p 1, col 5-7 +

Committee System: Geographical Area: India

Anon, 1986, PM's observations on Committee System, *Hindustan Times*, January 20; *Times of India*, January 20

Commonwealth Heads of Government Meet

Anon, 1989, PM not to attend CHOGM, *National Herald*, October 18

Commonwealth of Nations

Anon, 1986, No going back on South Africa, says PM, *Hindustan Times*, July 26, news-item
Anon, 1986, PM for C'Wealth aid to nations imposing sanction, *Times of India*, July 6, p 1, col 1-3+
Anon, 1986, PM for joint help to frontline States, *Indian Express*, August 15
Anon, 1986, UK isolated in Commonwealth, says PM, *Telegraph*, May 30, news-item

Commonwealth of Nations: Summit

Anon, 1986, Commonwealth mini-summit opens, *Free Press Journal*, August 4; *Times of India*, August 4
Anon, 1986, PM attacks British stand regarding sanctions against South Africa, *India Express*, August 3
Anon, 1989, Rajiv Gandhi's plan for planet protection fund to be considered,

Indian Express, November 21; *Times of India*, November 21

Communalism

Anon, 1982, Rajiv blames opposition for communal troubles, *Times of India*, May 9, p 9+

Anon, 1986, Arif's letter to PM: Communal divide in secular party, *Times of India*, September 25, p 1, col 2-5+

Anon, 1986, Prime Minister calls for new strategy to fight forces of communalism, *Indian Express*, September 13; *Times of India*, September 13

Anon, 1989, Opposition fanning communalism: Rajiv, *Times of India*, April 30, p 1, col 1-3, news-item

Anon, 1990, Congress-I convention against communalism, *Times of India*, May 20

Anon, 1991, Rajiv flays communal forces, *Hindustan Times*, April 3, p 7, col 1

Warier, K.U., 1989, Rajiv appeasing communalism: Daji, *New Age* 37(23) June 4, p 5, news-item

See also Fundamentalism

Communication Ministry: Geographical Area: India

Anon, 1989, PM takes charge of Communication Ministry, *Indian Express*, June 1

Communist Party of India (Marxist) (Political Party)

Anon, 1985, Surjeet hails Rajiv's lies, *People's Democracy* 8(51) December 16, p 9

Anon, 1988, CPM encouraging violence, says PM, *Times of India*, April 3, p 1, col 7-8, news-item

Surjeet, H.K., 1991, If Rajiv manages to maintain his present position, it will be a big achievement, *India Today* June 15, p 12, col 1-3

Comptroller and Auditor General of India

Mitra, Chandan, 1989, CAG-tag opposition: Neutralising Rajiv's populism, *Times of India*, July 26, p 6, col 3-5

Condolence Messages on Death of Gandhi, Rajiv

See also Gandhi, Rajiv: Homage paid to Him

Congress Centenary Celebration

Anon, 1985, Congress Centenary or Nehru family business? *Organiser* 36(52) May 12, p3

Gandhi, Rajiv, 1986, India towards 21st century: Speeches of Rajiv Gandhi at the Congress Centenary, *Secular Democracy* 19(1-2) January-February, p 20-28

Mathews, K.M., 1984, Bogus centenary of a bogus Congress, *Organiser* 35(34) January 8, p 7

Congress (I) (Political Party)

Abdi, S.H.M., 1986, At loggerheads, *Illustrated Weekly of India* 107(18) April 27, p 20-23

Abraham, A.S., 1983, Congress (I) bestirs itself: Mr Rajiv Gandhi builds his base, *Times of India*, October 7, p 8, col 3-5

Abraham, A.S., 1985, Revitalising the Congress: Challenges amidst the hurrahs, *Times of India*, May 24, p 8, col 3-5

Adhikari, Gautam, 1984, The Congress campaign: Crocodiles and wolves, *Times of India*, December 18, p 8, col 3-5

Advani, L.K., 1985, Congress (I) poll promises unredeemed, *Economic Times*, December 14, p 5, col 7-8

Ajay Kumar, 1989, PM: 'New fiza' in favour of Congress, *Times of India*, November 18, p 1, col 1-2, news-item

Ambegaokar, Nalini, 1985, The Congress (I) election manifesto: An economic analysis, *Commerce* 150(3842) January 12, p 56-58, tables

Anon, 1980, AICC-I tribute to Sanjay: Plea to Rajiv, *Sunday Standard*, December 7, p 7

Anon, 1981, BJP, Congress (I) main rivals in MP Poll, *Indian Express*, December 25, p 5

Anon, 1981, Decision on Rajiv on May 11, *National Herald*, May 9

Anon, 1981, Decision on Rajiv welcomed, *National Herald*, May 13

Anon, 1981, No decision yet on Rajiv, *Hindustan Times*, May 9, p 1

Anon, 1981, No quarter to dissidents, *Link* 24(11) October 25, p 6

Anon, 1981, Plea to make Rajiv Congress (I) Secretary, *Indian Express*, October 12, p 5

Anon, 1981, Pressure on Rajiv, *Current*, July 11, p 4

Anon, 1981, Rs 2 crores for Congress-I man, *Indian Express*, November 20, p 1

Anon, 1981, Rajiv calls for end to bickering, *Indian Express*, November 20, p 7

Anon, 1981, Rajiv is not expecting Party or Government post, *Times of India*, June 11, p 9, col 1-2

Anon, 1981, Rajiv may be made Party Secretary, *Hindustan Times*, p 1,

Anon, 1981, Rajiv's debut, *Blitz*, December 13, p 9

Anon, 1981, Rajiv to assume more responsibility, *Times of India*, December 31, p 1

Anon, 1981, Rajiv to be made AICC (I) Secretary, *Indian Express*, October 21, p 1

Anon, 1981, Rajiv to make Party change working style, *Times of India*, May 12, p 1, col 5+

Anon, 1982, AICC (I) General Secretaries, *Times of India*, September 18, p 7

Anon, 1982, Action against Orissa Congress (I) rebels urged, *Hindustan Times*, June 2, p 8

Anon, 1982 Antulay and Solanki dropped from CWC, *Hindustan Times*, September 3, p 1

Anon, 1982, Central surveillance tightens: Congress CMs on the mat, *Current*, March 13, p 3+

Anon, 1982, Congress (I) High command: Few options, *Link* 24(25) January 31,

p 60
Anon, 1982, Congress (I) offensive, *Link* 24(21) January 3, p 6
Anon, 1982, How A. F. Khan was side tracked? *Sunday* 9(31) January 17, p 37
Anon, 1982, Party system cracking up under pressure, *India Today* 7(1) January 15, p 78-79
Anon, 1982, Rajiv for better discipline among party workers, *Times of India*, January 7, p 7
Anon, 1982, Rajiv raps opposition, erring Cong-men, *Hindustan Times*, January 10, p 10
Anon, 1982, Year that wasn't! *India Today* 7(1) January 15, p 108-110
Anon, 1983, AICC (I) alaramed at nuclear threat, *Times of India*, December 29, p 11, col 4-7
Anon, 1983, Firm Congress (I) steps for peoples welfare: Rajiv, *Times of India*, October 19, p 6, col 3-4, news-item
Anon, 1983, From consensus to conflict, *Times of India*, January 7
Anon, 1983, Rajiv hits at factionalism, *Link* 26(13) Novermber 6, p 7-8
Anon, 1983, Rajiv blames Party for eclipse in South, *Times of India*, December 18, p 9, col 7-8
Anon, 1984, CPP endorses Rajiv's choice, *Times of India*, November 3, p 1, col 2-4+
Anon, 1984, Growing support for Rajiv as Party Chief, *Times of India*, November 6, p 1, col 4-5+
Anon, 1984, Rajiv elected Party Chief, *Times of India*, November 13, p 1, col 7-8+
Anon, 1984, Rajiv undecided on becoming Party President, *Times of India*, November 11, p 1, col 1-3
Anon, 1985, An arrangement of convenience, *Economic and Political Weekly* 20(5) February 2, p 174-175
Anon, 1985, A bulwark of world peace, *Patriot*, May 5, p 5, col 1-3
Anon, 1985, Cheer for Congress socialism, *Economic and Political Weekly*, 20(19) May 11, p 825-826
Anon, 1985, Congress Centenary or Nehru family business? *Organizer* 36(52) May 12, p 3
Anon, 1985, Congress (I) in the South: Down but by no means out, *Times of India*, May 15, p 8, col 3-5
Anon, 1985, Congress manifesto seeks suppot for accord, *Times of India*, September 11, p 1, col 4-5
Anon, 1985, CWC discusses Punjab, *Times of India*, May 4, p 1, col 4-6+
Anon, 1985, Indian National Congress (I): From Indira Gandhi to Rajiv Gandhi, *National Herald*, June 30
Anon, 1985, New face of loyalty, *Economic and Political Weekly* 20(6) February 9, p 214
Anon, 1985, No better guide for action than freedom struggle tenets, *Patriot*, May 5, p 5, col 1-8
Anon, 1985, PM has referred to army pull out at CPP meeting, *Times of India*, March 16, p 1, col 7-8+
Anon, 1985, Reverses dismay Congress leadership, *Times of India*, April 27, p 1,

col 5-6+

Anon, 1985, Splits have strengthened party: PM., *Times of India*, May 7, p 7, col 5-8, news-item

Anon, 1985, The state of the Congress I, *People's Democracy* 9(23) June 9, p 1-2+

Anon, 1985, Tytler among 12 AICC joint secretaries, *Times of India*, January 11, p 1, col 1-2

Anon, 1986, Another split? *Economic Times*, April 30, p 5, col 7-8

Anon, 1986, Arif's letter to PM: Communal divide in secular party, *Times of India*, September 25, col 2-5+

Anon, 1986, CWC drops move for action against Tripathi, *Times of India*, June 3, p 1, col 1-3

Anon, 1986, Communication gap between PM and his party, *Link* 29(19) December 14, p 6-8

Anon, 1986, Congress (I) fuelling regionalism, *Organiser* 37(36) January 19, p 1+

Anon, 1986, Dissent in Cong(I) due disillusionment, *New Age* 34(16) April 20, p 3

Anon, 1986, Fight new joint secretaries for Congress (I), *Indian Express*, January 23, p 24

Anon, 1986, Kamlapati slain with Aurangzeb-Shahjehan syndrome, *Organiser* 38(8) July 6, p 5

Anon, 1986, Major shake up in Congress (I), *Times of India*, January 20, p 1, col 1-5+

Anon, 1986, Mishra may be hauled up, *Times of India*, June 6, p 1, cpl 1-3

Anon, 1986, New turn to Sethi row, *Times of India*, October 16, p 1, col 1-3+

Anon, 1986, PM hails Congress (I), Congress (S) merger, *Times of India*, December 9

Anon, 1986, Pranab expelled from party for six years: Three others leaders suspended, *Times of India*, April 28, p 1, col 1-4

Anon, 1986, Rajiv drops three minister, major shake-up in Congress party, *Times of India*, January 20, p 1, col 2-4

Anon, 1986, Sethi suspended from Congress (I), *Times of India*, October 17, p 1, col 1-3+

Anon, 1986, Tripathi accepts CPB decision, *Times of India*, July 19, p 9, col 1-2

Anon, 1986, Tripathi criticises Rajiv's handling of affairs, *Times of India*, May 29, p 1, col 1-3

Anon, 1986, Tripathi may be eased out, *Times of India*, May 30, p 1, col 1-3+

Anon, 1986, Tripathi resigns as Working President of Congress (I), *Telegraph*, November 13

Anon, 1986, Tripathi should step down, says Anjiah, *Times of India*, July 11, p 1, col 4+, news-item

Anon, 1986, Tripathi supports Rajiv, *Hindustan Times*, June 1

Anon, 1986, Tripathi voices anguish, *Times of India*, April 25, p 1, col 4-6

Anon, 1986, Tripathi's letter to PM leaked, *Hindu*, May 29

Anon, 1986, Tirpathi's letter to Rajiv Gandhi, *Times of India*, May 29, p 8, col 7-8

Anon, 1986, Tripathi's tantalising tantrums, *Link* 28(39) May 4, p 19

Anon, 1986, Troubled Congress and its internal debate, *Link* 28(24) January 19, p 14-15

Anon, 1987, Rajiv expels V.P. Singh from Congress Party, *Times of India*, July 20, p 1, col 1-4+

Anon, 1988, AICC (I) session begins, *Statesman*, November 5; *Times of India*, November 5

Anon, 1988, AICC (I) session ends, *Times of India*, November 6

Anon, 1988, Gadgil appointed AICC (I) General Secretary, *National Herald*, September 2

Anon, 1988, Mature Rajiv best bet in next poll: Congressmen, *Times of India* Magazine (Section 1), May 5, p 1, col 2-8+

Anon, 1988, New AICC (I) General Secretary, *National Herald*, February 23

Anon, 1988, PM's address to CPP (I), *Hindu*, December 8

Anon, 1988, PM allows MP to vent views on party affairs, *Times of India*, July 21, p 1, col 2-4+

Anon, 1988, Party panel on policy persective set up, *Hindu*, March 11

Anon, 1988, Speech at the AICC session in New Delhi, *Times of India*, November 22

Anon, 1988, Tripathi's letter to Rajiv Gandhi, *Times of India*, July 7

Anon, 1988, Two AICC (I) General Secrataries replaced, *Free Press Jounral*, May 10

Anon, 1989, AICC (I) rewive dormant DCCs, *National Herald*, March 25

Anon, 1989, Congress leaders in mood of disaffection, *Link* 32(3) August 27, p 6-7

Anon, 1989, PM inagurates the National Convention of AICC (I) legal cell, *National Herald*, August 23; *Times of India*, August 23

Anon, 1990, AICC (I) meet continues, *National Herald*, July 24

Anon, 1990 AICC (I) session begins, *Statesman*, July 23; *Times of India*, July 23

Anon, 1990, AICC (I) session concludes, *Hindustan Times*, July 25

Anon, 1990, Enter Mr Gandhi, the Party Boss, *Economic Times*, July 28, p 1, col 2-5+

Anon, 1991, Congress (I) manifesto released, *Hindustan Times*, April 17,

Anon, 1991, The Congress concern over the current scenario, *Democratic World* 20(1) January 6, p 5, col 1-3

Anon, 1991, The Congress leaders 'rated' PM above Rajiv, *Hindustan Times*, April 26, p 18, col 2-3

Anon, 1991, Congress without Rajiv Gandhi, *Link*, 33(43) June 2, p 5-8.

Anon, 1991, Four new AICC (I) General Secretaries appointed, *Times of India*, February 15, p 16, col 2

Anon, 1991, PM hits back at Congress I, *Organiser* 42(31) March 10, p 1, col 1-3+

Anon, 1991, Security for Congress leaders beefed up, *Hindustan Times*, May 30, p 5, col 5-6

Anon, 1991, Succession struggle, *Frontline* 8(12) June 8-June 21, p 120-121

Anon, 1991, Why post-Rajiv Congress looks so empty? *Democratic World* 20(25) June 3, p 23

Anon, 1992, BJP ridicules Cong on anti-terrorism day, *Times of India*, May 23, p 5, col 1-4

Banyal, S.S., 1981, Rajiv disappoints CM's detractors, *Hindustan Times*, November 3, p 20-22

Barman, Ashis, 1986, Party bosses flox muscles, *Link* 28(33) March 23, p 11-12

Bharagava, G.S., 1986, Shadow boxing, Congress (I) style, *Indian Express* (Magazine), July 27, p 1, col 1-5+

Bhatt, S.C., 1986, Another acid test for Congress (I), *Economic Times*, October 21, p 5, col 7-8

Bhattacharya, Shubabrata, 1980, Homage to two brothers: AICC (I) 1980 was damp squib, *Sunday* 8(19) December 14, p 36-37

Chaddha, Kumkum, 1986, If I quit, it may damage the Congress (I): An interview with Kamlapati Tripathi, *Hindustan Times* (Magazine), September 14, p vii, col 1-6

Chakravartty, Nikhil, 1986, The goings on in Congress (I), *Times of India* (Sunday Review), May 11, p iv, col 1-4

Chandra Shekhar, 1984, AICC : Torrential rehatoric, *Janata* 38(39) January 8, p 3-4

Chawla, P. and Mitra, S., 1981, Congress (I): The enemy with in, *India Today* 6(4) February 28, p 64-73

Chawla, Prabhu, 1982, Congress (I): The Battle with in, *India Today* 7(19) October 15, p 18-19

Chawla, Prabhu, 1982, Uniting to divide, *India Today* 7(2) January 31, p 36-37

Chawla, Prabhu, 1982, Upper House scramble, *India Today* 7(6) March 31, p 26-27

Das, Sitanshu, 1986, Oxbridge and Ivy league screen between PM and Congress, *Link* 29(12) October 26, p 4-8

Das Gupta, Amalendu, 1989, Congress after Tamil Nadu: Gandhi faces danger of anarchy, *Times of India*, February 10, p 6, col 3-5

Dewan, Berindranath, 1981, Rajiv-Farooq talks for Congress (I)-N.C. coalition, *Hindu*, August 8, p 10

Dubey, Suman, et al, 1982, Zail Singh: The making of a President,*India Today* 7(13) July 15, p 50-55

Economic Times (Newspaper), 1986, Old wines, labels, *Economic Times*, January 21, p 5, col 1-2, editotial

Gadgil, V.N., 1990, No one attacked Rajiv Gandhi even indirectly, *Surya India* June, p 14, col 1-3

Gandhi, Rajiv, 1981, Congress (I) alone can provide stable Goverment, *Hindustan Times*, March 27, p 8

Gandhi, Rajiv, 1981, Opposed to re-entry of defectors, *Times of India*, November 23, p 5

Gandhi, Rajiv, 1981, Party office needs systemisation, *Blitz*, July 18, p 4

Gandhi, Rajiv, 1982, Congress (I) as strong as before, *National Herald*, April 25, p 3

Gandhi, Rajiv, 1982, Congress (I) enjoy people's support, *Times of India*, February 6, p 2

Gandhi, Rajiv, 1982, Opposition bid to tarnish Congress (I) image, *National Herald*, April 2, p 1

Gandhi, Rajiv, 1982, Party selections are all winners, *Hindustan Times*, April 25, p 1+

Gandhi, Rajiv, 1986, India towards 21st centary: Speeches of Rajiv Gandhi at the Congress Centenary, *Secular Democracy* 19(1-2) January-February, p 20-28

Gupta, O., 1980, Power equation after Kamalpati, *Onlooker* December 15, p 10-17

Inder Jit, 1985, More responsibility now on CPP (I), *Economic Times*, April 23, p 5, col 7-8

Jain, Girilal, 1985, A brush with Indian reality: Not by pragmatism and high tech, *Times of India*, May 7, p 6, col 3-5

Jain, Girilal, 1986, The challenge Rajiv faces: Continuing decay of Congress *Times of India*, August 27, p 8, col 3-5

Jain, Meenakshi, 1985, In search of a strategy, *Times of India* (Sunday Review), October 6, p 1, col 1-8

Janata (Periodical), 1985, Congress (I), RSS and BJP, *Janata* (Annual Number) 40 (1), p 3-4, editorial

Kamath, M.V., 1982, After Indira Gandhi, Who? *Indian Express*, March 7, p 2-6

Kamath. M.V., 1986, Bandying words with bandicoots, *Indian Express* (Magazine), June 22, p 2, col 6-8

Kamath, M.V., 1986, No bright ideas, *Indian Express* (Magazine), May 11, p 11, col 1-8

Khanna, Vinod, 1986, Vichar Vibhag : Miles to go, *National Herald*, March 23, p 10, col 2-5

Khare, Harish, 1986, Challenge to Rajiv Gandhi: Issue he can no longer skirt, *Times of India*, May 5, p 8, col 3-5

Khare, Harish, 1986, Congress and Rajiv Gandhi: Danger of Indian Marcoism, *Times of India*, September 6, p 8, col 3-5

Khare, Harish, 1986, Organisational elections: Coping with political vulnerabilities, *Times of India*, October 6, p 8, col 3-5

Khare, Harish, 1987, Dessidence in Congress: Rajiv Gandhi's strategy, *Times of India*, January 19, p 8, col 3-5

Khare, Harish, 1987, Reviving the Congress: Main challenge for Mr. Gandhi, *Times of India*, May 17, p 6, col 3-5

Khare, Harish, 1990 Congress dilemma: Alternative to Rajiv Gandhi, *Times of India*, March 26, p 6, col 3-5

Khursid, Salman, 1982, Inclement climate for Congress, *Delhi Recorder* 3(4) June, p 36-37

Koul, N. K., 1985, Congress (I) in an unenviable position in J and K, *Economic Times*, July 18, p 5, col 7-8

Kumar, D.P., 1991, Election scene: *Mainstream* 29(32) June 1, p 4-5

Lakshman, Nikhil, 1986, The Congress (I) cracking up, *Illustrated Weekly of India* 107(14) April 6, p 7-17

Mainstream (Periodical), 1986, The missing factor, *Mainstream* 24(21) January, p 3-4, ediorial

Malhotra, Vijay Kumar, 1981, Official funds used to project Congress (I), *Indian Express*, November 25, p 3

Mathews, K. M., 1984, Bogus Centrnary of a bogus Congress, *Organiser* 35(34) January 8, p 7

Mathur, Girish, 1981, Rajiv's rivals fight to save their deposits: Congress (I) battle to win Muslim minds, *Blitz*, June 13, p 11

Mathur, Girish, 1984, Will Congress (I) continue Indira's policies? *Link* 27(18) December 0, p 7-9

Mathur, Girish, 1986, How Prime Minister contains Congress unrest? *Link* 28(31) March 9, p 4-7

Mathur, Girish, 1986, Pranab: His business and Congress cultures, *Link* 28(44) June 8, p 14-16

Mathur, Girish, 1986, Whose Congress: Murli Deora's or Ram Kishan's? *Link* 28(40) May 11, p 4-7

Mathur, Girish, 1986, Why PM shouldn't let party drift to split? *Link* 28(37) April 20, p 10-12

Misra, Gopal, 1986, Revamping the ruling party, *Commerce* 152(3898) February 1, p 196 +

Misra, Panchanan, 1985, Indian National Congress: Towards technological revolution, *National Herald*, November 17, p 1, col 1-6 +

Mitra, Chandan, 1989, The odds get longer: Rajiv Gandhi after 'black Sunday', *Times of India*, January 24, p 6, col 3-5

Mitra, Chandan, 1989, The Pensive party: Rajiv's non-discovery of India, *Times of India*, March 22, p 6, col 3-5

Mitra, Chandan, 1989, Rajiv Gandhi moves up: Congress takes the offensive, *Times of India*, May 24, p 6, col 3-5

Moopnar, G.K., 1981, No meeting with Rajiv Gandhi, *Statesman*, February 10

Mukherjee, Sadhan, 1986, Congress (I) drama only starting, *New Age* 34(18) May 4, p 1+

Nandy, Pritish, 1986, Defiant: P.C. Sethi Ko Gussa Kyon Aata Hai, *Illustrated Weekly of India* 107(40) October 12, p 9-17

Nandy, Pritish, 1986, The man who knows too much, *Illustrated Weekly of India* 107(18) April 27, p 6-17

Nizamuddin, D.E., 1982, Congress (I) rally cancelled, *Sunday* 9(36) February 27, p 58

Organiser (Periodical), 1986, Ruling party crisis, *Organiser* 38(5) June 15, p 3, editorial

Parakal, Pauly V., 1987, Destabilisation cannot be fought Rajiv style, *New Age* 35(17) April 26, p 1-2

Parakal, Pauly V., 1990, Dubious role of Congress I, *New Age* 38(43), October 28, p 1.

Patil, Vasantdada, 1981, AICC (I) post for Rajiv soon, *Times of India*, October 22, p 5

Pawar, Sharad, 1989, Closing rank, *Illustratedd Weekly of India* 110(50) December 10, p 6-9

Pepole's Democracy (Periodical), 1989, The Congress (I) manifesto, *People's Democracy* 13(46) November 18, p 1, editorial

Raghavan, A., 1982, Bells toll for Congress (I), *Blitz*, May 29, p 1+

Raghavan, A., 1982, Congress (I) in 82... at sixes and sevens, *Blitz*, January 16, p 9

Rajeswara Rao, C., 1984, Congress has piled up problems, *Economic Times*, December 12, p 5, col 7-8

Rama Rao, G.J., 1985, Capitalism paraded as socialism at AICC, *New Age* 83(19) May 12, p 1+

Ranadive, B. T., 1985, On the AICC (I) session, *People's Democracy* 9(19) May 12, p 1+

Ranadive, B. T., 1986, Inner conflict inside the Congress (I), *People's Democracy* 10(19) May 11, p 1+

Ranga, N. G., 1985, Congress since 1971, *Rural India* 48(4-5) April-May, p 57-63

Rangarajan, R., 1983, Beyond the Bombay session, *Link* 26(12) October 30, p 12-13

Roy Choudhury, P.C., 1985, The Indian National Congress: Sowing the seeds of political consciousness, *Indian Express*, November 24, p 8, col 1-5

S.M., Pseud, 1982, What does all this add up to? *Indian Express*, January 9, p 6

Sham Lal, 1985, The national scene: Reading the fever chart, *Times of India*, January 12, p 8, col 3-5

Sharma, Narendra, 1983, AICC: The consensus call, *Mainstream* 22(9) October 29, p 4-5+

Shenoy, T.V.R., 1982, What the Congress (I) lost besides the election? *Onlooker* 44(10) May 31, p 14-15

Sheoery, W.G., 1985, Rajiv has wiped out the Congress (I) along with the opposition, *Organiser* 36(43) March 10, p 6

Shukla, Rajiv, 1990, Good bye? Can Rajiv Gandhi continue as Congress President? *Sunday* February 25-March 3, p 65-67+

Shukla, Satyendra R., 1981, Congress (I) still a divided house, *Hindustan Times*, November 17, p 24

Sinha, Bharati, 1984, No protection for weak under Congress (I) regime, *New Age* 32(48) November 25, p 8-9

Solanki, Madhavsinh, 1986, Congress decline in past year, *Times of India*, March 12, p 8, col 7-8

Srivastava, Manoj, 1985, Congress enters into a new dynamic phase, *National Herald*, July 7, p 1, col 1-6

Sundar Rajan, K.R., 1982, Is Congress (I) cracking up? *Illustrated Weekly of India* 103(13) April 17, p 8-12

Thakur, Janardan, 1986, Does his answer lie in the stars? *Hindustan Times* (Magazine), November 30, p 6, col 1-4

Thakur, Janardan, 1986, It is easy to quote Nehru, *Times of India* (Sunday Review), May 25, p 1, col 1-5

Thakur, Janardan, 1986, The stormy Arif, *Times of India* (Sunday Review), March 9, p 1, col 1-8

Thapar, Romesh, 1984, The Rajiv party and the Hindus, *Economic and Political Weekly* 19(50) December 15, p 2105

Times of India (Newspaper), 1985, Not just a party, *Times of India*, May 7, p 6, col 1-2, editorial

Times of India (Newspaper), 1985, Politics in war, *Times of India*, November 28, p 8, col 1-2, editorial

Times of India (Newspaper), 1986, Breaking conventions, *Times of India*, September 16, p 8, col 1-2. editorial

Times of India (Newspaper), 1986, Courageous Mr Khan, *Times of India*, September 27, p 8. col 1-2, editorial

Times of India (Newspaper), 1986, Death of illusion, *Times of India*, May 23, p 8, col 1-2, editorial

Times of India (Newspaper), 1986, Disciplinary action, *Times of India*, April 30, p 8, col 1-2, editorial

Times of India (Newspaper), 1986, Indira loyalists, *Times of India*, May 14, p 6, col 1-2, editorial

Times of India (Newspaper), 1986, Not to be written off, *Times of India*, November 14, p 8, col 1-2, editorial

Times of India, (Newspaper), 1986, Refusal to oblige, *Times of India* October 25, p 8, col 1-2, editorial

Times of India, (Newspaper), 1986, The Sethi episode, *Times of India*, October 18, p 8, col 1-2, editorial

Times of India, (Newspaper), 1986, Suppressing dissent, *Times of India*, March 14, p 8, col 1-2, editoiral

Times of India, (Newspaper), 1986, Test is not over, *Times of India*, June 4, p 8, col 1-3, editoiral

Times of India (Newspaper), 1986, Tripathi speaks out, *Times of India*, April 26, p 8, col 1-2, editorial

Tiwari, Narain Dutt, 1989, Waiting in the wings, *Illustrated Weekly of India* 110(51) December 17, p 6-7

Verma, Shrikant, 1985, An insider's view, *Illustrated Weekly of India* 106(31) December 8, p 38-41

Congress (I): Congress Party in Parliament

Anon, 1988, CPP-I general body meeting, *Hindustan Times*, May 14

Anon, 1988, PM's address to the CPP-I, *Hindu*, February 22, news-item

Anon, 1988, PM's address to CPP-I, *Hindu*, December 8, news-item

Anon, 1988, PM's address to CPP-I, *Hindustan Times*, July 28, news-item

Anon, 1988, PM's address to CPP-I, *Hindustan Times*, August 31, news-item

Anon, 1988, PM's address to CPP-I, *Hindustan Times*, February 21, news-item

Anon, 1988, PM's address to CPP-I, *National Herald*, May 13; *Times of India*, May 13, news-item

Congress (I): Congress Working Committee

Anon, 1988, CWC-I meet reviews bye-election reverses, *Times of India*, July 8

Anon, 1990. CWC-I meet begins *Hindu*, September 15; *Hindustan Times*, September 15; *Times of India*, September 15

Anon, 1990, CWC-I meeting, *Times of India*, June 19

Anon, 1990. CWC-I meets, *Hindustan Times*, April 7; *Times of India*, April 7

Anon, 1990, CWC-I re-constituted, *Times of India*, June 30

Anon, 1990, Dikshit resigns from CWC-I, *Times of India*, May 8

Congress (I): Dissidents

See also Dissidents

Congress (I): Dissidents: Geographical Area: India: Bihar

Janak Singh, 1986, Failure to curb Bihar dissidence, *Times of India*, May 20, p 8, col 7-8

Congress (I): Dissidents: Geographical Area: India: Rajasthan

Anon, 1982, Rajasthan dissidents stronger, *Sunday* 9(38) March 13, p 11

Nizamuddin, D.E., 1981, Rajiv tastes infighting, *Sunday* 9(15) September 21, p 66

Congress (I): Economic Resolution

Anon, 1983, Revive the Swadeshi spirit: Text of AICC(I) resolution on economic situation, *Mainstream* 22(9) October 29, p 31-33

Anon, 1984, Text of AICC(I) economic resolution, *Captial* 192(4772) January 23, p 43-46

Congress (I): Election Cliches

Anon, 1982, Rajiv asks people to vote for Congress (I), *Times of India*, May 15, p 13

Anon, 1983, From Garibi Hatao to Desh Bachao, *Organiser* 35(24) October 30, p 1+

Anon, 1989, Congress promises power to people: Vow to make DD Corporation, *Times of India*, November 7, p 1, col 1-3+

Congress (I): Election Nominees

Anon, 1981, Rajiv's silence delays decision on candidate, *Hindu*, May 6, p 9

Bhaumik, Kirti, 1982, Bad choice of nominees put Congress (I) in dump, *Times of India*, May 14, p 10

Gandhi, Rajiv, 1982, Part selections are all winners, *Hindustan Times*, April 25, p1+

Congress (I): Geographical Area: India: Andhra Pradesh

Anon, 1985, Congress Party's decline, *Economic and Political Weekly* 20(4) January 26, p 138-139

Chawla, Prabhu, 1982, Andhra Pradesh: Feeling unwanted, *India Today* 7(4) February 28, p 26

Pandit, Tooshar, 1982, Laughing stock of Andhra, *Sunday* 9(36) February 27, p 14+

Prasad Rao, V.G., 1986, Congress cross-voting in Andhra poll, *Times of India*, April 1, p 8, col 7-8

Congress (I): Geographical Area: India: Assam

Anon, 1985, List of Congress (I) candidates for Assam, *Times of India*, November 22, p 5, col 2-4

Misra, Prafulla, 1986, Factional squabble in Assam Congress (I), *New Age* 34(34) August 24, p 6

Congress (I): Geographical Area: India: Bihar

Anon, 1989, So much so that two AICC officials sent by Rajiv Gandhi to Patna to quieten the rebels had to "flee to Delhi" following skirmishes between two groups, *Statesman*, March 10

Sharan, Ranvhi, 1986, Dissidence on decline, *Link* 28(40) May 11, p 11

Congress (I): Geographical Area: India: Delhi

Anon, 1991, DPCC(I) for Sonia to be Party Chief, *Hindustan Times*, May 26, p 5, col 1

Congress (I): Geographical Area: India: Goa

Anon, 1984, Goa oriented politics, *Link* 27(16) November 25, p 15-17

Congress (I): Geographical Area: India: Gujarat

Pandya, Dinkar, 1986, No tears for the dissidents, *Link* 28(40) May 11, p 10

Congress (I): Geographical Area: India: Haryana

Anon, 1981, Haryana Congress (I) to be revamped, *Hindustan Times*, November 25, p 6

Inder Jit, 1987, Rajiv, Haryana Poll and new crisis, *Economic Times*, June 23, p 5, col 7-8+

Prem Kumar, 1982, Congress (I) stakes in Haryana, *Statesman*, May 18, p 4

Sud, S.K., 1986, Haryana Congress on its wane? *Link* 28(25) January 26, p 49

Congress (I): Geographical Area: India: Himachal Pradesh

Anon, 1986, New PCC(I) President appointed, *Indian Express*, February 7

Bharadwaj, A.K., 1986, No repercussions in Himachal, *Link* 28(40) May 11, p 14

Congress (I): Geographical Area: India: Jammu and Kashmir

Kaul, N.K., 1985, Congress(I) in an unenviable position in Jammu and Kashmir, *Economic Times*, July 18, p 5, col 7-8

Sayeed, Mohammad, 1986, State unit back High Command, *Link* 28(40) May 11, p 13

Congress (I): Geographical Area: India: Karnataka

Anon, 1982, Revolt imminent in Karnataka Congress I, *Indian Express*, June 30, p 4

Anon, 1991, Karnataka PCC offer to Rajiv, *Hindustan Times*, April 13, p 1, col 8

Chengappa, Raj, 1982, Gundu Rao grabs the show, *India Today* 7(2) January 31, p 53-54

Fernades, Louis, 1982, The son rose but did not shine, *Sunday* 9(31) January 17, p 34-35

Gadkari, J.P., 1986, Gundu on retreat as rival campaign grows, *Link* 28(40) May

11, p 9-10

Gadkari, J. P., 1986, KPCC(I) leadership reshuffled, *Link* 28(26) February 2, p 17

Congress (I): Geographical Area: India: Kerala

Anon, 1984, (Book Review), *Political Science Review* 23(3-4) July-December, p 309-312

Review of the Book: **Gopa Kumar, G.,** 1984, *The Congress Party and State politics: Emergence of new style politics*, Deep and Deep Publications, New Delhi

Congress (I): Geographical Area: India: Madhya Pradesh

Anon, 1982, V.C. Shukla and Arjun Singh meet, *Indian Express*, April 25, p 4

Anon, 1991, Free hand to Rajiv on MP candidates, *Hindustan Times*, March 30, p 12, col 4

Gupta, L.N., 1982, Tripude antics fail to amuse Rajiv, *Blitz*, May 22, p 4

Kher, M.V., 1982, Infighting cost Congress (I) Jabalpur seat, *Sunday* 9(51) July 12, p 31

Narayanan, K.P., 1982, Sagar poll: Storm signal for Congress (I), *Caravan* 1(713) February 1, p 35-36

Congress (I): Geographical Area: India: Maharashtra

Anon, 1981, Rajiv makes his 'debut' in Bombay, *Times of India*, January 14,

Anon, 1981, Rajiv's secret meeting, *Onlooker* 43(10) June 5, p 6

Anon, 1981, Shalinitai Patil meets Rajiv, *Indian Express*, September 6, p 7

Anon, 1985, Factional tussle for ticket in MPCC, *Times of India*, Janury 31, p 1, col 1-2+

Anon, 1985, I belong to the High Command and my leader? : An interview, *Indian Express* (Magazine), July 7, p 5, col 1-8

Anon, 1991, Party focus on Indira, Rajiv in Maharashtra, *Hindustan Times*, June 2, p 19, col 1-3

Mohite, Gopal, 1981, Politics of loyalty, *Sunday* 9(33) January 31, p 18-20

Times of India (Newspaper), 1985, Moves in Maharashtra, *Times of India*, November 9, p 8, col 1-2, editorial

Congress (I): Geographical Area: India: Maharashtra: Bombay Session

Mainstream (Periodical), 1983, Consensus and catcalls, *Mainstream* 22(9) October 29, p 1-2, editorial

Parakal, Pauly V., 1983, Bombay AICC (I) Session: Confrontation while talking consensus, *New Age* 31(44) October 30, p 1 +

Congress (I): Geographical Area: India: Orissa

Anon, 1982, Action against Orissa Congress (I) rebles urged, *Hindustan Times*, June 2, p 8

Anon, 1990, Will Rajiv save Orissa Congress? *Link* 32(37) April 22, p 12-14

Congress (I): Geographical Area: India: Punjab

Anon, 1982, Rajiv clips Zail's wings in Punjab PCC, *Current*, March 6, p 4

Times of India (Newspaper), 1985, The right to know, *Times of India*, June 20, p 6, col 1-2, editorial

Congress (I): Geographical Area: India: Rajasthan

Anon, 1982, No room for Pahadia, *Onlooker* 44(4) February 28, p 7

Anon, 1991, "Rajiv Jyoti" reveals changed picture in Rajasthan, *Hindustan Times*, June 10, p 10, col 6-8

Nizamuddin D.E., 1981, Rajiv tastes infighting, *Sunday* 9(15) September 21, p 66

Congress (I): Geographical Area: India: Tamil Nadu

Democratic World (Periodical), 1991, Rajiv gives Jaya bulk of seats, *Democratic World* 20(7) February 17, p 4, col 1-2, editorial

Congress (I): Geographical Area: India: Tripura

Chakravarty, S., 1986, No major contradiction, *Link* 28(40) May 11, p 12

Congress (I): Geographical Area: India: Uttar Pradesh

Anon, 1981, Rajiv critical of Garhwal strategy, *Sunday* 9(3) July 5, p 58

Anon, 1986, All is not well with UP Congress, *Link* 28(41) May 18, p 13

Anon, 1992, UP Youth Cong vows to follow Rajiv ideals, *National Herald*, May 23, p 10, col 1-3

Bahuguna, H.N., 1982, Garhwal will be a turning point, *Current*, May 1, p 5

Congress (I): Geographical Area: India: Uttar Pradesh: Convention

Anon, 1989, Rajiv Gandhi addresses UPCC(I) convention, *Times of India*, February 11

Congress (I): Geographical Area: India: West Bengal

Abdi, S.N.M., 1985, Back from the cold, *Illustrated Weekly of India* 106(9) July 7, p 32-33

Anon, 1982, Action against organisers of Congress (I) meeting, *Times of India*, May 13, p 1

Anon, 1982, Rajiv's call to return Congress (I) to power, *Amrit Bazar Patrika*, May 12, p 1+

Anon, 1982, Rajiv sure of Congress (I) Government in West Bengal, *Hindustan Times*, May 13, p 4

Anon, 1985, Revamping West Bengal Congress factions, *Link* 27(35) April 14, p 9-10

Anon, 1985, Unity bid by rival Bengal Congress factions, *Times of India*, January 8, p 1, col 2-5+

Anon, 1986, Another open show of Bengal Congress rift, *Times of India*, January

31, p 9, col 6-7

Bhattacharjee, Manindra, 1987, Rajiv's hysterical campaign style cost Congress I dear in West Bengal, *Organiser* 39(2) May 31, p 5+

Gandhi, Rajiv, 1982, 160 Bengal seats for Congress (I), *Hindustan Times*, May 12, p 8

Gandhi, Rajiv, 1982, Congress (I) sure to win in West Bengal, *Amrit Bazar Patrika*, May 13, p 7

Gandhi, Rajiv, 1982, No Congress (I) sponsored strikes, *Times of India*, January 1, p 9

Ghosh Chowdhury, Dilip, 1985, Bengal Congress (I) new line up, *New Age* 33(48) December 1, p 7

Ghosh Chowdhury, Dilip, 1985, Bombs parts of agitation for Bengal Congress (I), *New Age* 33(42) October 20, p 7

Ghosh Chowdhury, Dilip, 1985, West Bengal Congress (I) beset by trouble, *New Age* 33(40) October 6, p 15

Ghosh Chowdhury, Dilip, 1986, Feud in Bengal Cong (I) stepped up after poll, *New Age* 34(26), p 16

Sen, Sumanta, 1986, Factionalism in Bengal Congress, *Times of India*, April 21, p 8, col 7-8

Times of India (Newspaper), 1985, Another shake up, *Times of India* October 18, p 8, col 1-2, editorial

Congress (I): Leadership Issue

Anon, 1990, Congress rout in assembly polls: Rethinking on Rajiv's leadership, *Link* 32(30) March 4, p 5-7

Anon, 1991, All out effort to resolve Congress (I) leadership crisis, *Hindustan Times*, May 26, p 1, col 1-3 +

Anon, 1991, Amitabh as Party Chief demanded, *Hindustan Times*, May 28, p 7, col 1

Anon, 1991, No controversy, says Arjun Singh, *Hindustan Times*, May 31, p 7, col 2-3, news-item

Anon, 1991, Plea to dissolve Congress (I), *Hindustan Times*, May 31, p 10, col 1

Times of India (Newspaper), 1988, Leadership issue again, *Times of India*, July 27, p 4, col 1-2, editorial

Congress (I): Policies

Abraham, Abu, 1985, From Indira to Rajiv, *Mainstream* 24(9-10) November 2, p 9

Congress (I): Rajiv Brigade

Dev, Rahul, 1983, The Rajiv brigade, *Illustrated Weekly of India* 104(23) October 23, p 28-31

Congress (I): Role against Communalism

Anon, 1990, Congress (I) convention against communalism, *Times of India*,

May 20

Congress (I): Selection of Candidates for Election

See Congress (I): Election Nominees

Congress (I): Strategy

Anon, 1991, Congress plans new strategy, *Hindustan Times*, May 28, p 16, col 1-3

Anon, 1991, How Congress strategy failed? *Democratic World* 20(11) March 17, p 5, col 1-3 +

Congress (I): Views on National Front

Anon, 1991, Congress (I) blames NF for killing, *Hindustan Times*, May 31, p 10, col 5-7

Congress (I): Views on Refuelling Issue

Anon, 1991, Congress (I) asks for clarifications on refuelling issue, *Indian Express*, February 19

Anon, 1991, Congress (I) views on refuelling issue, *Hindustan Times*, February 17, p 18, col 2

Congress (I): Vote Bank

Kirpekar, Subhash, 1985, Congress vote bank that failed, *Times of India*, October 23, p 8, col 7-8

Congress (I) Parliamentary Board

Anon, 1991, CPB will urge Soina to contest, *Hindustan Times*, October 8, p 1, col 1

Congress Party (I) In Parliament

See Congress (I): Congress Party in Parliament

Congress (I) Working Committee

See Congress (I): Congress Working Committee

Congress (S): Merger with Congress (I)

Anon, 1986, PM hails Congress (I), Congress (S) merger, *Times of India*, December 9

Constituion: Geographical Area: India

Anon, 1987, A Prime Minister or a President? *Times of India* (Sunday Review), January 25, p iv, col 1-5

Inder Jit, 1987, Prime Minister and the Constitution, *Economic Times*, June 16, p

5, col 7-8+

Constitution: Geographical Area: India: Amendment

Anon, 1986, No Constitutional amendment to meet GNLF demand, *Free Press Journal*, October 9

Anon, 1986, Statute amendment hinted in National Anthem case, *Hindustan Times*, December 3

Constitution: Geographical Area: India: Eighth Schedule: Inclusion of Languages: Nepali

Anon, 1986, Clarification on PM's remarks on the inclusion of Nepali in the Eighth Schedule, *Free Press Journal* December 22

Constructive Co-operation

Anon, 1982, Rajiv asked people to co-operate with the government, *Hindustan Times*, January 9, p 7

Consumer Movement

Anon, 1981, Rajiv for strong consumer drive, *Hindustan Times*, November 20, p 3

Conventions

Times of India (Newspaper), 1986, Breaking conventions, *Times of India*, September 16, p 8, col 1-2, editorial

Corruption: Geographical Area: India

Anon, 1984, Rajiv pledges to fight corruption and inefficiency, *Times of India*, November 13, p 1, col 1-3 +

Anon, 1986, PM's call for probe into corruption roots, *Hindustan Times*, September 10

Anon, 1988, PM asks Buta to probe 'offer of funds' to Zail, *Times of India*, March 3, p 1, col 1-3 +

Anon, 1988, Probe into offer of money to favour President, *Hindu*, March 3; *Indian Express*, March 3

Sinha, B.M., 1981, Bonanza for tax-dodgers, *Probe India* 3(1) March p 25-27

Cuba

See also Geographical Area subdivision under main Descriptor

Cuba: Foreign Relations: Geographical Area: India

See under Indo-Cuban Relations

Cultural Affairs: Geographical Area: India

Anon, 1986, Pupul Jayekar Cultrural Adviser to PM, *Telegraph*, September 3

Cyprus

Anon, 1986, Cyprus to host Foreign Minister's Meet, *Statesman*, September 8

Czechoslovakia

See also Geographical Area Subdivision under main Descriptor

Czechoslovakia: Foreign Relations: Geographical Area: India

See under Indo-Czech Relations

DD

=Delhi Doordarshan

DDA

=Delhi Development Authority

DIG

=Deputy Inspector General

DMK

=Dravid Munnetkam Kajegam (Political Party)

Dacoits: Geographical Area: India: Madhya Pradesh

Anon, 1982, Malkhan, 19 of gang give up: Rajiv hails surrender, *Hindustan Times*, June 18, p 1 +

Dalits: Welfare

See Welfare Dalits: Geographical Area: India

Damascus: Syria

See also Geographical Area subdivision undermain Descriptor

Dandi March

Anon, 1988, The Dandi March, *Illustrated Weekly of India* 109(13) March 27, p 20-23

Dandi March: Replayed

Anon, 1988, Prime Minister flags off Dandi March, *Times of India*, March 13

Darbara Singh

See also Chief Minister: Geographical Area: India: Punjab: Darbara Singh

Darjiling: West Bengal: India

See also Geographical Area Subdivison under main Descriptor

Defamation Bill: Geographical Area: India

Anon, 1988, Defamation Bill withdrawn, *Hindustan Times*, September 23; *Indian Express*, September 23

Anon, 1988, PM for debate on all aspects of Defamation Bill, *National Herald*, September 7

Anon, 1988, PM's views on Defamation Bill, *Indian Express*, September 16; *National Herald*, September 16

Defence: Geographical Area: India

Anon, 1986, US offers help on arms, *Statesman*, October 12

Anon, 1988, India, Spain agree on defence tie up, *Hindustan Times*, July 17

Gandhi, Indira, 1982, Defence matters not on US talks agenda, *Hindustan Times*, July 28, p 3+

Karanjia, Russy, 1987, Case for the defence, *Illustrated Weekly of India* 108(28) July 19, p 32-35

Defence: Geographical Area: Spain

Anon, 1988, India, Spain agree on defence tie up, *Hindustan Times*, July 17

Defence Policy: Geographical Area: India

Anon, 1991, Rajiv wants review of defence policy, *Hindustan Times*, April 28, p 12, col 1-2

Delhi: India

Anon, 1981, Rajiv calls to fulfil mission, *Hindustan Times*, December 15, p 3

Anon, 1981, Unauthorised slums in Rajiv's name, *Onlooker* 43(21) November 30, p 17-18

Anon, 1981-1982, Remembering Sanjay Gandhi, *Delhi Recorder* 2(9) December 15-January 14, p 22-23

Anon, 1982, Noorjehan to give performance in Delhi, *Times of India*, March 11, p 2

Anon, 1982, Striking students seek Rajiv help, *Hindustan Times*, March 30, p 16

Anon, 1986, ASP suspended, *Hindustan Times*, October 3

Anon, 1988, PM visits flood-affected areas, *Hindustan Times*, September 28

Anon, 1988, Speech at the AICC Session in New Delhi, *Times of India*, November 22

Anon, 1989, So much so that two AICC Officials sent by Rajiv Gandhi to Patna to quiten the rebels had to flee to Delhi following skirmishes between two groups, *Statesman*, March 10

Anon, 1990, Congress (I) rally in Delhi, *Statesman*, May 6

Anon, 1991, Major break in Rajiv murder case: 2 Lankans held in Delhi, *Hindustan Times*, July 6, p 1, col 5-6+

Chawla, Prabhu, 1981, Cracks in the moonlith, *India Today* 6(21) November 15, p 26-29

Das, Sanjay K., 1991, Murder night in Delhi, *Onlooker* June 15, p 16-18

Kalbag, Chaitanya, 1981, Spate of senseless tragedies, *India Today* 6(24) December 31, p 48-51

Mukarji, Apartim, 1992, LTTE extends olive branch to New Delhi, *Hindustan Times*, March 19, p 15, col 7-8

Wig , A.R., 1991, Delhi will miss Rajiv Gandhi, *Hindustan Times*, May 26, p 5, col 1-4

See also Delhi Development Authority

Delhi: Killings

See Massacre: Geographical Area: India: Delhi

Delhi Development Authority

Anon, 1981, Delhi Development Authority to mark the launching of construction of 5,000 houses, *Hindustan Times*, November 19, p 3

Delhi Doordarshan

See Doordarshan

Democracy: Geographical Area: India

Anon, 1981, Dynastic rule has no place in democracy, *Indian Express*, December 19, p 4

Anon, 1991, India's democracy to respond 'sturdily', *Hindustan Times*, May 28, p 11, col 5-7

Gandhi, Rajiv, 1981, Democracy has strong base in India, *Hindustan Times*, July 29, p 16

Jain, Girilal, 1987, Prime Minister under siege: Compulsions of Indian democracy, *Times of India*, April 20, p 6, col 3-5

Sunder Rajan, K.R., 1982, Systematic strangling of democracy, *Caravan* August, p 15

Deng, Xiaoping

Anon, 1988, PM calls on Deng, Zhao, *Hindustan Times*, December 22; *Times of India*, December 22

Deora, Murli

Mathur, Girish, 1986, Whose Congress: Murli Deora's or Ram Krishan's? *Link* 28(40) May 11, p 4-7

Deportation: JKLF Chief from UK

Anon, 1986, UK explains causes for deportation of JKLF Chief, *Statesman*, October 27

Deputy Prime Minister: Geographical Area: India

See under Name of Deputy Prime Minister e.g. Devi Lal

Deshmukh, B.G.

Suroor, Hasan, 1991, At close quarters: B.G. Deshmukh recalls Rajiv days, *Frontline* 8(12) June-June 21, p 117

Devi Lal

Anon, 1991, Devi Lal seeking new equation with Rajiv as Chandra Sekhars's boat seems sinking, *Organiser* 42(25) January 27, p 64, col 1-3

Dibang, 1990, Rajiv plumped for Devi as PM, *Illustrated Weekly of India* December 1-2, p 1, col 1-5

Dhar, Vijay

Bhatt, B., 1982, Vijay Dhar still holding centre stage, *Caravan* 7(727) September, p 41

Dhawan, R.K.

Anon, 1980, Dhawan going down: Rajiv's entry certain, *Sunday Standard*, November 30, p 1

Diego Garcia Bases

Anon, 1986, PM for dismantling Diego Garcia bases, *Indian Express*, July 5

Dikshit, Umashankar: Resignation from CWC (I)

Anon, 1990, Dikshit resigns from CWC (I), *Times of India*, May 8

Disarmament

Anon, 1982, PM reiterates stand on peace, n-disarmament; Gulf between rich, poor dangerous, *Hindustan Times*, January 23, p 16

Anon, 1982, World youth to fight for disarmament, *Indian Express*, January 25, p 7

Anon, 1985, The Six Nation Summit on Nuclear Disarmament, New Delhi, January 28, *Monthly Commentary on Indian Economic Conditions* 26(6) January, p 7-8

Anon, 1986, Call for end to nuclear arms race, *Hindustan Times*, November 17

Anon, 1986, Disarmament move not against USA, says PM, *Telegraph*, August 7, news-item

Anon, 1986, MPs appeal for peace, *Telegraph*, August 3

Anon, 1986, N-Powers violating NPT, says PM, *Indian Express*, October 18, news-item

Anon, 1986, Nuclear arms main threat to peace, says Rajiv Gandhi, *Times of India*, March 6, news-item

Anon, 1986, PM calls for test ban treaty, *Times of India*, March 16, news-item

Anon, 1986, PM's address to the six nation summit, *Indian Express*, August 8; *Hindu*, August 8, news-item

Anon, 1986, Rajiv Gandhi, Palme hail Soviet move, *Times of India*, January 17

Anon, 1986, 'Star Wars' against world peace, says Rajiv, *National Herald*, February 17, news-item

Anon, 1988, Blueprint for comprehensive disarmament and security, *Mainstream* 26(36) June, 18, p 23-26+

Anon, 1988, PM for dismantling all nuclear weapons, *Hindustan Times*, November 15

Anon, 1988, PM's call for elemination of nuclear weapons, *National Herald*, November 25, news-item

Anon, 1988, PM urges NAM to help disarm efforts, *Times of India*, July 15, p 1, col 1-3+, news-item

Anon, 1988, Rajiv Gandhi's address to special session on disarmament, *Indian Express*, June 10, news-item

Disruptive Forces

See Divisive Forces

Dissanayake, Gamini

Anon, 1988, Dissanayake calls on PM, *Hindustan Times*, May 11

Dissidents

Anon, 1981, Congress (I) dissidence keeping leaders at logger heads, *Caravan* 2(702) August 16, p 15

Anon, 1981, Dissidents stay away from Rajiv meeting, *Indian Express*, November 20, p 8

Anon, 1981, No quarter to dissidents, *Link* 24(11) October 25, p 6

Anon, 1981, Rajiv calls for end to bickering, *Indian Express*, November 20, p 7

Anon, 1982, Action against Orissa Congress (I) rebels urged, *Hindustan Times*, June 2, p 8

Anon, 1982, Nation: 1981 in retrospect, *Probe India* 3(11) January, p 50-52

Anon, 1982, PM urged to punish Youth Congress rebels, *Times of India*, March 29, p 9

Anon, 1982, Rajasthan dissidents stronger, *Sunday* 9(38) March 13, p 11

Anon, 1982, Rajiv for better discipline among Party Workers, *Times of India*, January 7, p 7

Anon, 1982, Rebel leadership snap links with Antulay, *Hindustan Times*, July 16, p 1

Anon, 1982, Warning to YC (I) rebels against talking to Press, *Indian Express*,

August 21, p 9

Anon, 1986, The Arif Mohammad affair, *Times of India*, March 3, p 1, col 2-5+

Anon, 1986, Arif quits on Bill issue, *Times of India*, February 27, p 1, col 5-7

Anon, 1986, Dissent in Cong (I) due disillusionment, *New Age* 34(16) April 20, p 3

Anon, 1986, The dissenter, *Illustrated Weekly of India* 107(11) March 16, p 16-17

Anon, 1986, Pranab expelled from party for six years: Three other leaders suspended, *Times of India*, April 28, p 1, col 1-4+

Anon, 1986, Tripathi continues talks with rebels, *Times of India*, April 27, p 1, col 1-4

Anon, 1987, Dissidents hungry for power: PM, *Times of India*, August 30, p 1, col 1-3+, news-item

Anon, 1988, Seven of Rajiv's trusted men wanted Zail Singh to dismiss him, *Organiser* 39(42) April 3, p 8

Anon, 1989, An elderly Congress leader and Member of Rajya Sabha Chimmanbhai Mehta expelled from the Party, urged the Party to elect a new leader to replace Rajiv Gandhi: The first such voice to be raised, *Indian Express*, March 21

Barman, Ashish, 1986, Pranab's outer stems tide of revolt, *Link* 28(40) May 11, p 8-9

Bhatt, S.C., 1986, Dissidence in Congress (I): A new phase, *Economic Times*, June 17, p 5, col 7-8

Gandhi, Rajiv, 1981, Opposed to re-entry of defectors, *Times of India*, November 23, p 5

Gandhi, Rajiv, 1982, No dissent in public, *Indian Express*, January 10, p 5

Jain, Girilal, 1988, No anti-Rajiv conspiracy: Only convergence of interests, *Times of India*, December 16, p 6, col 3-5

Janak Singh, 1986, Failure to curb Bihar dissidence, *Times of India*, May 20, p 8, col 7-8

Karanjia, R.K., 1982, Congress for dissidents, *Blitz*, May 15, p 1

Kelkar, B.K., 1986, Dissidence in Congress (I): A new chewing gum, *Organiser* 38(1) May 18, p 7

Khare, Harish, 1987, Dissidence in Congress: Rajiv Gandhi's strategy, *Times of India*, January 19, p 8, col 3-5

Malik, Iqbal, 1981, Voices consonant and dissonant, *Indian Express*, November 23, p 6

Mathur, Girish, 1986, How Prime Minister contains Congress unrest, *Link* 38(31) March 9, p 4-7

Mishra, Sudhanshu, 1986, Mathur capable of stirring dissidence, *Link* 28(40) May 11, p 12

Misra, Prafulla, 1986, Factional squabble in Assam Congress (I), *New Age* 34(34) August 24, p 6

Pandya, Dinkar, 1986, No tears for the dissidents, *Link* 28(40) May 11, p 10

Quershy, Ahtesham, 1981, Rajiv's bid to stop infighting, *Indian Express*, November 24, p 20

Raghvan, A., 1982, Congress (I) in 82 ... at sixes and sevens, *Blitz*, January 16, p 9

Ranvhi, Sharan, 1986, Dissidence on decline, *Link* 28(40) May 11, p 11

Shukla, Satyendra R., 1981, Congress (I) still a divided house, *Hindustan Times*, November 17, p 24

Sud, S.K., 1986, No dissidents only opportunists in Haryana, *Link* 28(40) May 11, p 14

Thakur, Janardan, 1986, The stormy Arif, *Times of India* (Sunday Review), March 9, p 1, col 1-8

Times of India (Newspaper), 1986, Courageous Mr. Khan, *Times of India*, September 27, p 8, col 1-2, editorial

Times of India (Newspaper), 1986, Suppressing dissent, *Times of India*, March 14, p 8, col 1-2 editorial

Divisive Forces

Anon, 1981, Rajiv's call to crush divisive forces, *Indian Express*, November 15, p 4

Anon, 1985, Bid to weaken country not to be tolerated: PM, *Times of India*, May 7, p 1, col 1-4, news-item

Anon, 1985, No compromise on anti State elements: Rajiv, *Times of India* October 10, p 1, col 3-5, news-item

Anon, 1986, PM encouraging divisive forces, says Opposition, *Hindustan Times*, November 6

Anon, 1986, PM's call to fight disruptive forces, *Indian Express*, December 12

Anon, 1986, PM's call to fight divisive forces, *Times of India*, April 4

Anon, 1989, PM vows to fight seperatism, *Economic Times*, August 16, p 5, col 1-2

Anon, 1991, Plea to fight divisive forces, *Hindustan Times*, May 30, p 8, col 1-4

Anon, 1991, Rajiv accuses NF, BJP of dividing country, *Hindustan Times* April 19, p 1, col 1-3

Gandhi, Rajiv, 1981, Destroy divisive forces, *Hindustan Times*, November 15, p 15

Parakal, Pauly V., 1987, Destabilisation cannot be fought Rajiv style, *New Age* 35(17) April 26, p 1-2

Doordarhan

Anon, 1989, Congress promises power to people: Vow to make DD Corporation, *Times of India*, November 7, col 1-3+

Mitra, Sumit, 1982, Doordarshan : A slow fade-out, *India Today* 7(9) May 15, p 53

Dowry System: Geographical Area: India

Anon, 1982, Rajiv: Amend laws to combat dowry, *Indian Express*, July 21, p 3, news-item

Anon, 1982, Rajiv Gandhi call on dowry evil, *Hindustan Times*, July 21, p 3

Gandhi, Rajiv, 1982, Fight dowry evil, *National Herald*, September 4, p 3

Dravid Munetkam Kajegam (Political Party)

Anon, 1991, Interrogation of DMK leaders demanded, *Hindustan Times*, June 4, p 4, col 3-4

Anon, 1992, DMK meeting was cancelled, *Hindustan Times*, February 10, p 8, col 6-8

Dravidians

Fernades, George, 1989, The Dravidians and R. Gandhi, *The Other Side* March 26, p 6-13

Drought: Geographical Area: India

Anon, 1987, People asked to help fight drought, terrosism, *Times of India*, August 16, p 1, col 1-4

Dynastic Rule

Anon, 1981, Dynastic rule has no place in democracy, *Indian Express*, December 19. p 4

Anon, 1981, New dynasty: Abdullah Jr. is crowned, *Caravan* 12(704) September 16, p 11

Anon, 1981, Rajiv defends family succession, *Indian Express*, November 12, p 5

Anon, 1981, Rajiv denies being groomed as PM, *Indian Express*, June 20, p 5

Anon, 1981, Searching for successors, *India Today* 6(20) October 31, p 7

Anon, 1981, Times praise for Rajiv, *Hindustan Times*, August 1, p 16

Anon, 1982, Rajiv against family rule, *Indian Express*, January 9, p 5

Anon, 1982, Rajiv says he never justified family rule, *Times of India*, January 9, p 5

Anon, 1991, Family matters: Is this the end for the Gandhi dynasty, *Sunday* June 2-June 8, p 38-39

Dubey, Suman, 1982, Jammu and Kashmir son also rises, *India Today* 7(17) September 15, p 46-53

Gandhi, Indira, 1981, No build up of dynasty, *Hindustan Times*, November 14, p 6

Gandhi, Rajiv, 1981, Family succession not bad, *Hindustan Times*, November 12, p 4

Inder Jit, 1984, Indira, Rajiv and succession, *Economic Times*, November 6, p 5, col 7-8

Karanjia, R.K., 1982, Course of dynastic rule: Warning for Mrs. Gandhi, *Blitz*, April 10, p 1+

Karanjia, R.K., 1982, Dynastic crisis? *Blitz*, March 27, p 2

Karlekar, Hiranmay, 1981, Rajiv: The politics of dynastic succession, *Indian Express* (Magazine), June 21, p 1, col 1-8, p 8

Kripalani, J.B., 1981, Rajiv entitled to contest, *Hindustan Times*, June 2, p 13

Naik, J.A., 1980, India that Rajiv may inherit, *Janata* 35(41) December, June 2, p 13

Nihal Singh, S., 1981, Fall of the 'new' leader, *Indian Express*, September 9, p 6

Rath, Ramachandra, 1980, Let Indira choose the successor, *Current*, July 12, p 10-11

Sahni, Ajai, 1991, The dynasty ends, *Surya India* June, p 6-14

Saroj, Chiranjeev Joshi, 1982, Son will succeed Indira, *Current*, March 13, p 23

Sen Gupta, Barun, 1980, Astrology and succession, *Sunday* 8(11) September 21, p 37

Shukla, Rajiv and Sarin, Ritu, 1991, After the dynasty, *Sunday* June 9-June 15, p 23-34

Swamy, Subramaniam, 1982, Big game, *Current*, April 17, p1

Wariavwalla, Bharat, 1984, A dynastic democracy, *Illustrated Weekly of India* 105(33) December, p 34-35

Willey, Fay, 1977, Indira's sure thing, *News Week* 89(5) January 31, p 21-22

EEC

=European Economic Community

Eastern Europe

Kaushik, Devendra, 1985, India, USSR and East Europe: Emerging trends under Rajiv Gandhi, *India Quarterly* 41(1) January-March, p 6-16

Economic Conditions: Geographical Area: India

Banerjee, Subrata, 1989, Rajiv Gandhi government undermines Indian economy, *New Age* 37(42) October 15, p 8-9

Economic Development: Geographical Area: India

Anon, 1982, Rajiv stress on role of youths in economic order vital, *Hindustan Times*, January 25, p 1+

Anon, 1989, (Book Review), *Financial Express*, January 22, p 5, col 5-8

Review of the Book: *Venkateshwaran, R.J. and Mithani, D. M.*, 1989, *Rajiv Gandhi: Economic perspective towards 21st Century*, Himalaya Publishing House, Bombay, 239 p.

Chandra Shekhar, C.P., 1991, The economic record, *Frontline* 9(12) June 8-June 21, p 123-124

Dutt, Rudras, 1985, Rajiv Gandhi's economics, *Janata* 40(4) March 3, p 5-7

Economic Planning: Geographical Area: India

Anon, 1985, PM on planning, *Economic Times*, November 9, p 5, col 7-8

Banerjee, Subrata, 1985, Economic trust of Rajiv Gandhi, *New Age* 33(2) January 13, p 3

See also Planning: Geographical Area, India

Economic Policies: Geographical Area: India

Anon, 1987, Economic policies to stay: PM, *Economic Times*, January 21, p 1, col 1-5, news-item

Banerjee, Subrata, 1985, One year of Rajiv Gandhi minus on economic policy, *New Age* 33(45) November 10, p 5

Dutt, Rudras, 1985, Rajiv Gandhi's economics, *Janata* 40(4) March 3, p 5-7

Dwivedi, Devendra Nath, 1986, Rajiv pragmatic, not pragmatist, *Times of India*, December 25, p 8, col 8-9

Ghosh, Arun, 1989, The economy and the budget, *Economic and Political Weekly* March 11

Mishra, Chaturanan, 1989, Rajiv Gandhi policies on Perestroika, *New Age* 37(2) January 8, p 8

Paranjape, H.K., 1986, Mr Gandhi's economic policy, *Indian Economic Journal* 33(4) April-June, p 1-4

Paranjape, H.K., 1986, Mr Gandhi's economic policy: Throwing the baby with bath-water, *Times of India*, December 17, p 6, col 3-5

Roy, Subir, 1987, Economics of uncertainty: Policy options before Rajiv Gandhi, *Times of India*, April 10, p 6, col 3-5

Education: Geographical Area: India

Anon, 1986, New National Policy on Education, *Indian Journal of Public Administration* 32(3) July-September, p 435-460

Anon, 1986, Revamping the education system, *Haryana Review* 20(7) July, p 3-7

Anon, 1987, Education: The backbone of progress, *Haryana Review* 21(2) February, p 3-6

Egypt

See also Geographical Area Subdivision under main Descriptor

Egypt: Foreign Releations: Geographical Area: India

See under Indo-Egyptian Relations

Election Commission: Geographical Area: India: Seshan, Trunellai Narayabaiyer

See under Seshan, Trunellai Narayabaiyer

Election Mandates: Geographical Area: India

Anon, 1985, (Book Review), *National Herald*, May 26, p 7, col 1-4; *Times of India*, March 19, p 8, col 1-4

Review of the Book: **Mirchandani, G.S.**, and **Murthi, K.S.R.**, 1985, *Massive mandate for Rajiv Gandhi*, Sterling, New Delhi, xii, p 248

Anon, 1985, The mandate for Rajiv Gandhi, *Radical Humanist* 48(10) January, p 2-5

Anon, 1985, Mandate for unity strength and harmony, *Haryana Review* 19(1) Jaunary, p 3-5

Election Manifestoe: Congress (I)

Advani, L.K., 1985, Congress (I) poll promises unredeemed, *Economic Times*, December 14, p 5, col 7-8

Ambegaokar, Nalini, 1985, The Congress (I) election manifesto: An economic analysis, *Commerce* 150(3842) January 12, p 56-58, tables.

Anon, 1985, Congress manifesto seeks support for accord, *Times of India*, September 11, p 1, col 4-5

Anon, 1989, Congress promises power to people: Vow to make DD Corporation, *Times of India*, November 7, p 1, col 1-3+

Anon, 1991, Congress (I) manifesto released, *Hindustan Times*, April 17

Parakal, Pauly V., 1984, Cong (I) manifesto full of tall claims, *New Age* 32(51) December 16, p 1

People's Democracy (Periodical), 1989, The Congress (I) manifesto, *People's Democracy* 13(46) November 18, p 1, editorial

Elections: Analysis: Geographical Area: India

Ahmed, Bashiruddin, 1982, No foretelling the future: An analysis of the results of the 1982 mini general elections-2, *Indian Express*, June 13, p 4

Anon, 1988, CWC (I) meet reviews bye election reverses, *Times of India*, July 8

Elections: Assembly: Geographical Area: India

See Elections: Vidhan Sabha: Geographical Area: India

Elections: Cliches: Georgaphical Area: India

Anon, 1984, Rajiv's style of electioneering, *Times of India*, December 14, p 1, col 7-8

Mitra Chaudhury, Srerupa, 1991, Rajiv Gandhi: Vikas ki aandhi, *Democratic World* May 19, p 6, col 2

Elections: Geographical Area: India

Anita Pratap, 1982, Runaway kid goes to Rajya Sabha, *Sunday* 9(30) March 13, p 24-25

Anon, 1980, Rajiv for Amethi by election, *Blitz*, December 20, p 3

Anon, 1981, An expensive triumph, *India Today* 6(12) June 16, p 40-43

Anon, 1981, Is the government contesting the election? *Onlooker* June 30, p 34-35

Anon, 1981, No joint opposition candidate against Rajiv Gandhi, *Hindu*, May 13, p 1

Anon, 1981, Poll case against Rajiv dropped, *Indian Express*, October 13, p 17

Anon, 1981, Poll campaign for Rajiv begins, *Sunday Standard*, May 10, p 1

Anon, 1981, Rajiv and Begum Abida returned to Lok Sabha, *Hindu*, June 16, p 1

Anon, 1981, Rajiv denies misuse of official machinery, *Hindustan Times*, May 22, p 1

Anon, 1981, Rajiv for Lok Sabha? *Amrit Bazar Patrika*, May 9, p 1

Anon, 1981, Rajiv Gandhi: The triumph, *Surya India* 5(10) July, p 77

Anon, 1981, Rajiv Gandhi wins by record margin, *Hindustan Times*, June 16, p 1

Anon, 1981, Rajiv silence delays decision on candidates, *Hindu*, May 6, p 9

Anon, 1981, Rajiv's visit: Tailored versions, *Link* 24(2) August 22, p 20-21

Anon, 1981, Rajiv takes the plunge, *Surya India* 5(9) June, p 36-37

Anon, 1981, Rajiv wins his leadership spurs, *Blitz*, June 20, p 1

Anon, 1982, Asssembly elections: Mid-term warning, *India Today* 7(11) June 15, p 17-21

Anon, 1982, Charges on Rajiv visit, *Hindustan Times*, February 1, p 6

Anon, 1982, Election time: Gandhi time, *Onlooker* 44(10) May 31, p 37

Anon, 1982, Gandhi vote for Amitabh or Sivaji? *Indian Express*, February 5, p 5

Anon, 1982, Managing an election, *Onlooker* 14(10) May 31, p 7

Anon, 1982, Rajiv appeal to the people, *Times of India*, May 6, p 7

Anon, 1982, Rajiv asks people of vote for Congress (I), *Times of India*, May 15, p 13

Anon, 1982, Rajiv criticises LD-BJP alliance, *Times of India*, May 15, p 7

Anon, 1982, Rajiv hits out at LD-BJP alliance, *Amrit Bazar Patrika*, May 7, p 7

Anon, 1982, Rajiv lashes out at BJP-LD poll alliance, *Times of India*, May 7, p 7

Anon, 1982, Rajiv lashes out at self seekers, *Times of India*, April 25, p 9

Anon, 1982, Rajiv's hectic poll tour from May 11, *Amrit Bazar Patrika*, May 6, p 7

Anon, 1982, Rajiv starts poll tour in State today, *Amrit Bazar patrika*, May 11, p 7

Anon, 1982, Writing on the wall, *Surya India* 6(9-10) June-July, p 14-17

Anon, 1984, An election without focus, *Times of India*, December 15,

Anon, 1984, Rajiv as Campaigner, *Indian Express*, December 23; *Statesman*, December 15

Anon, 1984, Rajiv's style of electioneering, *Times of India*, December 14, p 1, col 7-8

Anon, 1985, Poll aims at urping out terrorism: Rajiv, *Times of India*, September 10, p 1, col 5-7, news-item

Anon, 1986, PM's election upheld, *Times of India*, April 26

Anon, 1987, PM will stick to Amethi, *Times fo India*, September 11, p 1, col 4-6

Anon, 1988, Mature Rajiv best bet in next poll: Congressmen, *Times of India* Magazine (Section II), May 5, p 1, col 2-8

Anon, 1989, (Book Review), *Tribune* (Sunday Review), August 6, p 2, col 1-6
Review of Book: **Rajput R.S.**, 1989, *Dynamics of democratic politics in India: A study of 1984 and 1985 Lok Sabha Election*, Deep and Deep Publishers, New Delhi, 185 p.

Anon, 1989, Rajiv Gandhi, V.P. Singh elected, *Hindustan Times*, November 30; *Times of India*, November 30

Anon, 1989, Rajiv in search of a poll strategy, *Link* 31(41) May 21, p 13-14

Anon, 1990, Writ against Rajiv Gandhi election dismissed, *Times of India*, April 11

Anon, 1991, ASEAN watching India poll scene, *Hindustan Times*, May 31, p 12, col 1-4

Anon, 1991, Free hand to Rajiv on MP candidates, *Hindustan Times*, March 30, p 12, col 4

Anon, 1991, Karnataka PCC offer to Rajiv, *Hindustan Times*, April 13, p 1, col 8

Anon, 1991, Rajiv calls for stable Government, *Hindustan Times* April 16, p 7, col 2-3

Anon, 1991, Rajiv denies reports on wooing Left, *Hindustan Times*, May 10, p 22, col 5

Anon, 1991, The Rajiv drive, *Frontline* May 25-Jnue 7, p 27

Anon, 1991, Rajiv files nomination, *Hindustan Times*, April 25, p 1, col 5-7

Anon, 1991, Rajiv Gandhi's election upheld, *Times of India*, February 8

Anon, 1991, Rajiv-Seshan flopshow, *Organiser* 62(38) April 28, p 16, col 4

Anon, 1991, Tamil Nadu witnessed maximum bomb-shock and sympathy wave, *Democratic World* 20(25) June 3, p 8

Bhattacharjee, Manindra, 1987, Rajiv's hysterical campaign style cost Congress (I) dear in West Bengal, *Organiser* 39(2) May 31, p 5

Bhaumik, Kirti, 1982, Bad choice of nominees put Cong (I) in dump, *Times of India*, May 14, p 10

Chadha, Kumkum, 1991, BJP is main enemy: Rajiv, *Hindustan Times*, March 28, p 1, col 1-4, news-item

Chakravarti, Prithvis, 1989, Elections: Rajiv's three pronged propaganda strategy, *Radical Humanist* 53(3) June, p 8-18

Chawla, P. and Thukral G., 1982, Himachal Pradesh: The photo finish, *India Today* 7(11) June 15, p 25

Das, Rahin, 1991, No poll pact with BJP, says Rajiv, *Hindustan Times*, May 11, p 1, col 4-5, news-item

Dhar M.K., 1991, Rajiv seeks decisive verdict, *Hindustan Times*, March 28, p 10, col 5-8

Gandhi, Rajiv, 1982, Congress (I) enjoys people's support, *Times of India*, February 6, p 2

Gandhi, Rajiv, 1982, Party selections are all winners, *Hindustan Times*, April 25, p 1+

Hafiz, M.A., 1991, V.P., Shekhar on firm ground, *Hindustan Times*, April 2, p 10, col 5-8

Jain, Girilal, 1987, Fight is for power: V.P. Singh's challenge to Rajiv Gandhi, *Times of India*, August 12, p 6, col 3-5

Jerath, Arati R., 1982, Collecting crowds for Rajiv, *Indian Express*, May 16, p 5

Kackar, Ranjana and Chaudhary, Shahid A., 1991, Will Rajiv be PM again? *Probe India* June 15, p 10-15

Kala, Arvind, 1989, Will a negative vote displace Mr Rajiv Gandhi? *Times of India*, October 17, p 11, col 1-6

Kumar D.P., 1991, Election scene: Congress prospects after Rajiv, *Mainstream* 29(32) June 1, p 4-5

Lamba, Asjeet, 1981, Rajiv campaign, *India Today* 6(24) December 31, p 4

Lamba, Asjeet, 1981, Rajiv Gandhi to fight Amethi seat, *Amrit Bazar Patrika* May 12, p 1

Mathur, Girish, 1981, Rajiv's rivals fight to save their deposits .. : Congress (I) battle to win Muslim minds, *Blitz*, June 13, p 11

Misra, Ravish, 1982, All set for 'mini' general poll, *National Herald* May 16, p 14

Mitra Chaudhury, Srerupa, 1991, Rajiv Gandhi: Vikas ki Aandhi, *Democratic World* 20(20) May 19, p 6, col 2

Mukerji, Debadhish, 1991, Power paralysis: Amethi yearns for the return of Rajiv as Prime Minister, *The Week*, April 28, p 38-39

Nihal Singh, S., 1982, Greatest show on earth, *Indian Express*, May 19, p 6

Nizamuddin, D.E., 1982, Missing the Rajya Sabha bus, *Sunday* 9(41) April 3, p 58

Padmanabhan, Mukund, 1991, The polls that weren't, *Sunday* June 2-8, p 18-19

Pandit, C.S., 1981, Mrs Indira Gandhi very sure of her ground, *Amrit Bazar Patrika*, May 14, p 6

Puri, Rajinder, 1981, Fighting Rajiv, *Hindustan Times*, June 3, p 9

Raghavan, Barun, 1982, Mrs Gandhi's troubles have only begun, *Sunday* 9(51) June 12, p 33

Sharma, Vichitra, 1982, Campaigning Rajiv style, *Weekened Review* 3(10) May 29, p 7

Subramaniam, Vidya, 1988, Will Rajiv Gandhi stand from Amethi? *Indian Express* (Magazine), November 6, p 1, col 1-8+

Surjeet, H.K., 1991, If Rajiv manages to maintain his present position, it will be a big achievement, *India Today* June 15, p 12, col 1-3

Times of India (Newspaper), 1987, Rajiv verses V.P. Singh, *Times of India*, March 27, p 6, col 1-2, editorial

Unnikrishan, K.P., 1991, I don't see Rajiv crossing 175-180 seats, *India Today* June 15, p 18, col 1-3

Elections: Geographical Area: India: Andhra Pradesh

Prased Rao, V.G., 1986, Congress cross voting in Andhra Poll, *Times of India*, April 1, p 8, col 7-8

Elections: Geographical Area: India: Assam

Anon, 1985, List of Congress candidates for Assam, *Times of India*, November 22, p 5, col 2-4

Elections: Geographical Area: India: Bihar

See Election: Sympathy Factor: Geographical Area: India: Bihar

Elections: Geographical Area: India: Gujarat

Anon, 1991, Patel, Rajiv talks on seat sharing, *Hindustan Times*, April 14, p 5 col 1

Elections: Geographical Area: India: Haryana

Anon, 1981, Rajiv rules out early poll in Haryana, *Hindustan Times*, August 13, p 13

Anon, 1982, Rajiv in Haryana, *Sunday* 9(48) March 22, p 13

Inder Jit, 1987, Rajiv Haryana Poll and new crises, *Economic Times*, June 23, p 5, col 7-8+

Elections: Geographical Area: India: Kerala

Anon, 1985, Kerala free to decide on poll: PM, *Times of India*, November 25, p 1, col 2-5, news-item

Elections: Geographical Area: India: Madhya Pradesh

Anon, 1981, BJP, Congress (I) main rivals in MP Poll, *Indian Express*, December 25, p 5

Anon, 1982, Health camp in V.C. Shukla's constituency, *Sunday* 9(41) April 3, p 13

Khandekar, Shreekant, 1982, Waves on the wane, *India Today* 7(12) January 31, p 48

Elections: Geographical Area: India: Madhya Pradesh: Jabalpur

Kher, M.V., 1982, Infighting cost Cong(I) Jabalpur seat, *Sunday* 9(51) June 12, p 31

Elections: Geographical Area: India: Madhya Pradesh: Sagar

Narayanan, K.P., 1982, Sagar Poll: Storm singal for Congress (I), *Caravan* 1(713) February 1, p 35-36

Elections: Geographical Area: India: Maharasthra

Anon, 1985, Factional tussle for ticket in MPCC, *Times of India*, January 31, p 1, col 1-2

Anon, 1991, Party focus on Indira, Rajiv in Maharashtra, *Hindustan Times*, June 2, p 19, col 1-3

Anon, 1991, Rajiv wave caused BJP-Shiv Sena rout in Maharasthra, *Democratic World* 20(25) June 23, p 7

Elections: Geographical Area: India: Orissa: Puri: Sympathy Factor

Anon, 1991, Sympathy wave may help Congress in Puri, *Hindustan Times*, May 30, p 7, col 4-5

Elections: Geographical Area: India: Punjab

Anon, 1990, Rajiv Gandhi's letter to PM on Punjab election, *Statesman*, September 22

Anon, 1991, Punjab not ready for polls: Rajiv, *Hindustan Times*, April 14, p 5, col 2-3, news–item

Kirpekar, Subash, 1985, Congress vote bank that failed, *Times of India*, October 23, p 8, col 7-8

Elections: Geographical Area: India: Rajasthan

Anon, 1991, Rajiv Jyoti reveals changed picture in Rajasthan, *Hindustan Times*, June 10, p 10, col 6-8

Elections: Geographical Area: India: Tamil Nadu

Anon, 1988, Rajiv's bid to woo Tamil Nadu voters, *Link* 31(18) December 11, p 12-13

Anon, 1991, Rajiv, Jayalalitha finalise poll pact, *Hindustan Times* March 31, p 1, col 1-3+

Democratic World (Periodical), 1991, Rajiv gives Jaya bulk of seats, *Democratic World* 20(7) February 17, p 4, col 1-2, editorial

Elections: Geographical Area: India: Uttar Pradesh: Amethi

Anon, 1980, Rajiv for Amethi by election, *Blitz*, December 20, p 3

Anon, 1980, Rajiv will add to party's strength, *Indian Express*, August 27

Anon, 1981, Big win for Rajiv, Begum Abida, *Amrit Bazar Patrika*, June 16, p 1

Anon, 1981, Feeling of gratitude for Mrs Gandhi in Amethi, *Hindustan Times*, June 9, p 11

Anon, 1981, Final decision on Rajiv tomorrow, *Sunday Standard*, May 3, p 7

Anon, 1981, Great debate: Has Amethi sanctioned hereditary democracy, *Probe India* 3(5) July, p 21

Anon, 1981, No decision yet on Rajiv's seat, *Amrit Bazar Patrika*, May 19, p 1

Anon, 1981, No wireless set in Rajiv jeep, *Hindustan Times*, June 4, p 8

Anon, 1981, Not yet Rajiv, *India Today* 6(5) March 15, p 5

Anon, 1981, Protest at Rajiv using Radio Ham, *Hindustan Times*, June 5, p 5

Anon, 1981, Rajiv disapproves of CM's frequent Delhi trips, *Hindustan Times*, July 22, p 13

Anon, 1981, Rajiv files poll papers for Amethi, *Hindustan Times*, May 12, p 1

Anon, 1981, Rajiv for Amethi, *Current*, July 12, p 9

Anon, 1981, Rajiv Gandhi makes his formal bow in politics, *National Herald*, May 12, p 1-4

Anon, 1981, Rajiv may consider party post, *Hindustan Times*, July 6

Anon, 1981, Rajiv not to join government, *Hindu*, June 17, p 1

Anon, 1981, Rajiv promises to pursue Sanjay goals, *Hindustan Times*, May 13, p 8

Anon, 1981, Rajiv's rival alleges use of government machinery, *Sunday Standard*, May 16, p 3

Anon, 1981, Rajiv wants to assist mother, *Amrit Bazar Patrika* June 17, p 1

Anon, 1982, MLA claims he brought Rajiv into lime light, *Hindustan Times*, May 31, p 12

Anon, 1982, Rajiv for watchdog panels in Amethi, *Hindustan Times*, August 31, p 5

Anon, 1982, Rajiv to use own car for Amethi tour, *Hindustan Times*, January 6, p 5

Anon, 1982, Sanjay Memorial Medical Institute for Amethi, *Hindustan Times*, September 1, p 7

Anon, 1987, PM will stick to Amethi, *Times of India*, September 11, p 1, col 1-6

Anon, 1988, Rajiv Gandhi to contest from Amethi, *Statesman*, November 23

Anon, 1989, Rajiv Gandhi files nomination from Amethi, *Times of India*, October 25

Anon, 1991, Rajiv firm on contesting from Amethi only, *Hindustan Times*, April 18, p 18, col 4

Chawla, P. and Mitra, S., 1981, Congress (I) the enemy within, *India Today* 6(4) February 28, p 64-73

Farid, Javeed, 1981, With Rajiv in Amethi, *Hindustan Times*, May 31, p 1+

Fishlock, Trever, 1981, Yet another Gandhi on the way to victory, *Times*, June 6

Gandhi, Indira, 1980, It's for Rajiv to decide, *Hindustan Times*, October 5, p 16

Gandhi, Indira, 1980, Rajiv not joining politics, *Sunday Standard*, October 12, p 1

Gandhi, Indira, 1981, Rajiv won't take Sanjay's place, *Hindu*, May 15, p 7

Gandhi, Rajiv, 1981, All Amethi villages to be electrified, *Hindustan Times*, May 30, p 16

Gandhi, Rajiv, 1981, Amethi my pilot project, *Blitz*, July 18, p 4

Gandhi, Rajiv, 1981, Amethi to be made model town, *Times of India*, July 4, p 5

Gandhi, Rajiv, 1981, Party comes first, *Hindustan Times*, December 30, p 8

Gandhi, Rajiv, 1981, Plan to make Amethi a model town, *Indian Express*, July 5, p 5

Kripalani, J.B., 1980, Rajiv Gandhi: The succession qestion, *Hindustan Times*, October 15

Lamba, Asjeet, 1981, Rajiv Gandhi to fight Amethi seat, *Amrit Bazar Patrika*, May 12, p 1

Louis, Arul B., 1981, India: The grandson also rises, *Far Eastern Economic Review* 112(27) June 26, p 22

Mukerji, Debashish, 1991, Power paralysis: Amethi yearns for the return of Rajiv as Prime Minister, *The Week*, April 28, p 38-39

Nehru, Arun, 1981, Charge baseless, *National Herald*, June 22

Nihal Singh, S., 1981, Art of muddling through, *Indian Express*, October 27, p 6

Nizamuddin, D.E., 1982, Even Amethi's animals are being nursed, *Sunday*, Febraury 27, p 38

Sadachari, 1981, Amethi wrong choice for Rajiv, *Blitz*, May 23, p 13

Singh, V.P., 1981, Rajiv's victory is sure, *Hindustan Times*, June 2, p 13

Subramaniam, Vidya, 1988, Will Rajiv Gandhi stand from Amethi? *Indian Express* (Magazine), November 6, p 1, col 1-8+

Tripathi, Srinivas, 1988, Prime Minister fighting shy of visit to Amethi, *New Age* 36(40) October 2, p 1

Verma, Kapil, 1981, PM's plea to Amethi as a mother, *Hindustan Times*, June 12, p 1, 16

Verma, Kapil, 1981, Rajiv rekindles Amethi hopes, *Hindustan Times*, June 12, p 1, 16

Verma, Kapil, 1981, Rajiv rekindles Amethi hopes, *Hindustan Times*, June 3, p 13

Vijay Dutt, 1981, Troubles of triunph: Can Indira-Rajiv work the Government that does not? *Probe India* 3(5) July, p 16-20

Elections: Geographical Area: India: West Bengal

Anon, 1982, Rajiv sure of Congress (I) Govt in West Bengal, *Hindustan Times*, May 13, p 4

Anon, 1982, Rajiv's call to return Congress (I) to power, *Amrit Bazar Patrika*,

May 12, p 1-7

Gandhi, Rajiv, 1982, 160 Bengal seats for Congress (I), *Hindustan Times*, May 12, p 8

Gandhi, Rajiv, 1982, Congress sure to win in West Bengal, *Amrit Bazar Patrika*, May 13, p 7

Elections: Mid Term: Geograph cal Area: India

Anon, 1987, PM rejects demand for Mid Term Poll, *Times of India*, July 5, p 1, col 1-4

Elections: Mid Term: Geographical Area: India: Karnataka

Raj Gopal, R., 1982, Karnataka: Little chance for Mid Term Poll, *Caravan* 2(714) February, 15-16

Elections: Poll Alliance: Geographical Area: India

Anon, 1991, Patel, Rajiv talks on seat sharing, *Hindustan Times*, April 14, p 5, col 1

Elections Rajya Sabha: Geographcal Area: India

Anon, 1986, Tripathi denied renomination to Rajya Sabha, *Times of India*, June 18, p 1, col 7-8

Elections: Sympathy Factor: Geographical Area: India

Anon, 1991, A clear Rajiv wave: Congress, *Hindustan Times*, March 28, p 5, col 1-3

Anon, 1991, More suicides in some States, *Hindustatn Times*, May 26, p 1, col 4-5+

Anon, 1991, Remember the wave? Rajiv Gandhi tries to recapture the spirit of 1984, *Sunday* May 5-May 11, p 28-31

Anon, 1991, Sympathy factor, *India Today* June 15, p 110-112

Anon, 1991, Sumpathy wave of no help in HP, *Hindustan Times*, May 26, p 9, col 7-8

Elections: Sympathy Factor: Geographical Area: India: Bihar

Anon, 1991, Laloo: Assassination won't influence voters, *Hindustan Times*, May 28, p 16, col 4-5, news-item

Elections: Vidhan Sabha: Geographical Area: India

Anon, 1990, Congress rout in assembly polls: Rethinking on Rajiv's leadership, *Link* 32(30) March 4, p 5-7.

Chawla, Prabhu, 1982, Assembly elections: The Acid test, *India Today*, 7(10) May 31, p 34-35

Chawla, Prabhu, 1982, State election confusion confounded, *India Today* 7(9) May 15, p 18-20

Electronics: Policy: Geographical Area: India

Anon, 1985, A new policy for electronics, *Commerce* (Supplement) 150(3850) March 9, p 1

Emergency: Geographical Area: India

Anon, 1985, Rajiv was not very much for emergency, *Times of India*, October 11, p 9, col 7-8

People's Democracy (Periodical), 1985, Rajiv threat of emergency, *People's Democracy* 9(28) July 14, p 1+2, editorial

Employment: Geographical Area: India

Anon, 1985, Job plans getting priority: PM, *Times of India*, November 24, p 1, col 1-3, news–item

Employment: Rural Sector: Geographical Area: India

Anon, 1981, YC (I) urges employment in rural sector, *Indian Express*, December 31, p 7

Anon, 1989, Government announces new rural job scheme, *National Herald*, April 29; *Telegraph*, April 29

Employment: Urban Job Plan: Geographical Aea: India

Anon, 1989, PM announces urban job plan, *Hindustan Times*, October 12

England

See United Kingdom

Environment

Anon, 1991, Rajiv's help to environment recalled, *Hindustan Times*, June 4, p 10, col 4

Ethnic Crisis: Geographical Area: Sri Lanka

Anon, 1986, Efforts continue for solution to ethnic crisis, *Free Press Journal* November 18

Anon, 1986, Prime Minister and Sri Lanka President discuss ethnic crisis, *Statesman*, November 16

Europe: East

See Eastern Europe

European Economic Community

Anon, 1986, PM criticises EEC for diluting sanctions, *Hindustan Times*, September 18

Extremists

Anon, 1982, Rajiv for eviction of extremists from Gurdwaras, *Indian Express*, October 6, p 7

Anon, 1985, PM asks Akalis to publicity disown extremists, *Times of India*, December 21, p 1, col 1-3+

Anon, 1986, PM asks MGR to ascertain militants views on Lanka offer, *Statesman*, October 11

Anon, 1986, Pak visit shelved: PM rules out talks with extremists, *Times of India*, July 19, p 1, col 1-3+

See also Terrorists

Extremists: Eviction from Gurdwaras

Anon, 1982, Rajiv for eviction of extremists from Gurdwaras, *Indian Express*, October 6, p 7

FBI

=Federal Bureau of Investigation

FP

=Family Planning

F-16

Anon, 1985, F-16s are for use against India: PM, *Times of India*, October 7, p 1, col 4-5, nwes-item

Gandhi, Indira, 1982, No plan for talks with US on F-16: Foreign fuel for Tarapur likely, *Indian Express*, July 20, p 1

Factionalism

Anon, 1983, PCC (I): Rajiv hits at factionalism, *Link* 26(13) November 6, p 7-8

Family Planning

Anon, 1989, Population control and grass-roots development, *Mainstream* 27(53) September 30, p 10-12+

Gandhi, Rajiv, 1982, Make FP a mass movement, *Hindustan Times*, March 10, p 3

Gandhi, Rajiv, 1982, FP needs people's support, *National Herald*, March 10, p 1

Farmers: Demands: Geographical Area: India

Anon, 1988, PM rejects farmer's demands, *Times of India*, February 21, p 1, col 4-6+

Anon, 1988, No concessions to farmers under pressure: PM, *Times of India*, October 28, p 1, col 1-3, news-item

Farmers: Taxation: Geographical Area: India: West Bengal

Anon, 1986, Why Basu does'nt tax rich farmers? *Link* 29(8) September, p 10-12

Farnborough Air Show

Anon, 1982, Rajiv sees Farnborough Air Show, *Hindustan Times*, September 6, p 11

Anon, 1982, Rajiv to attend air show, *Times of India*, September 5, p 11

Fashion Technology: Cardin's Design: Geographical Area: India

Anon, 1968, Cardin's new design in Indian silk catch the eye, *Hindu*, February 23, p 12

Fast

See Satyagrah

Federal Bureau of Investigation

Anon, 1985, FBI uncovers plot to kill Rajiv during visit to US, *Times of India*, May 14, p 1, col 1-3

Fernandes, George

Gandhi, Indira, 1982, Maneka had link with Fernandes, *Amrit Bazar Patrika*, April 5, p 1+

Fertiliser Subsidy: Geographical Area: India

Anon, 1991, Congress MPs warn against cut in fertiliser subsidy, *Hindustan Times*, August 12, p 1, col 2-4

Finland

See also Geographical Area subdivision under main Descriptor

Finland: Foreign Relations: Geographical Area: India

See under Indo-Finish Relations

Floods: Geographical Area: India

Anon, 1988, PM visits flood-affected areas, *Hindustan Times*, September 28

Foreign Debt: Geographical Area: India

See International Debt: Geographical Area: India

Foreign Minister's Meet

Anon, 1986, Cyprus to host Foreign Minister's Meet, *Statesman*, September 8

Foreign Policy: Geographical Area: India

Anon, 1985, India not to be a camp follower: PM, *Times of India*, October 24, p 9, col 7-8, news-item

Anon, 1985, India will not be a camp follower: PM told US Foreign Policy establishment, *Link* 28(3) November 3, p 9-10, news-item

Anon, 1985, Rajiv's foreign policy projections, *Mainstream* 23(20) January 12, p 3-4+

Anon, 1987, (Book Review), *Hindustan Times* (Magazine), June 28, col 4-6
Review of the Book: **Gupta, M.G.**, 1987, *Rajiv Gandhi's foregin policy : A study in continuity and change*, M.G. Publishers, Agra

Muni, S.D., 1986, Rajiv Gandhi's neighbourhood policy, *Mainstream* 24(25) February 22, p 4-6+

Prasanna Kumar, A., 1985, Form Nehru to Rajiv: Forty years of India's foreign policy, *Triveni* 54(1) April-June, p 39-46

Sen Gupta, Bhabani, 1988, The green leaves of December, *Hindustan Times*, October 10

Foreign Policy: Geographical Area: United States

See also Indo-U.S. Relation

Foreign Relations: Geographical Area: China-United States

Anon, 1986, Virk hoped for Chinese, Pak, US help, *Times of India*, March 12 p 1, col 2-5

Foreign Relations: Geographical Area: India-(Other Countries)

See under Indo- . . ., e.g., Indo-Afghanistan Relations

Foreign Relations: Geographical Area: Pakistan-United States

Anon, 1987, Pak exploiting links with US: PM, *Times of India*, July 8, p 1, col 1-6, news-item

Anon, 1986, Virk hoped for Chinese, Pak, US help, *Times of India*, March 12 p 1, col 2-5

Foreign Trade: Geographical Area: India

Anon, 1986, Steps to boost trade, *Times of India*, November 6

Anon, 1986, Steps to expand trade ties, *Hindustan Times*, October 8

Anon, 1986, Steps to explore new trade opportunities, *Statesman*, November 23

Anon, 1986, Trade Council set up, *Statesman*, October 7

Anon, 1988, Trade pact signed, *National Herald*, July 19

Forensic Lab: Geographical Area: India

Joshi, Chand, 1991, Lax security at forensic lab, *Hindustan Times*, May 30, p 16, col 1-3

Foundation Ceremonies: Geographical Area: India

Anon, 1981, Rajiv Gandhi to visit Haryana, *Indian Express*, November 3, p 4
Anon, 1982, PM opens world's longer river bridge today, *Hindustan Times*, March 2, p 5
Anon, 1982, Rajiv lays stone of BHEL plant, *Hindustan Times*, February 10, p 9
Anon, 1982, Rajiv lays stone of water project, *Hindustan Times*, January 8
Anon, 1982, Rajiv to lay foundation of ceramic unit, *Times of India*, February 1, p 5

France

See also Geographical Area subdivision under main Descriptors

France: Foreign Relations: Geographical Area: India

See under Indo-French Relations

Freedom Fighters: Geographical Area: India

Gupta, Ram Roop, 1985, Freedom fighters and Prime Minister: Intersting features of their horoscopes, *Organiser* 37(26) November 10, p 14-17

Freedom Struggle: Tenets: Geographical Area: India

Anon, 1985, No better guide for action than freedom struggle tenets, *Patriot*, May 5, p 5, col 1-8

Fundamentalism

Anon, 1986, PM's call to fight fundamentalism, *Times of India*, September 13, p 1, col 1-3+

See also Communalism

GNLF

=Gorkha National Liberation Front

Gadgil, V.N.

Anon, 1988, Gadgil appointed AICC (I) General Secratary, *National Herald*, September 2

Gandhi, Indira

Abraham, Abu, 1985, From Indira to Rajiv, *Manistream* 24(9-10) November 2, p 9
Anon, 1980, Mrs Gandhi leaves it to Rajiv, *Statesman*, August 8
Anon, 1981, Pahadia men appeal to PM and Rajiv, *Times of India*, July 9, p 9
Anon, 1981, PM will assess Gundu Government's performance, *Indian Express*, December 25, p 7
Anon, 1981-1982, Mrs Gandhi's Devoli visit heartens Harijan victins, *Delhi*

Recorder 2(9) December 15-June 14, p 26-28

Anon, 1982, Mrs Gandhi calls on Abdullah, *Hindustan Times*, June 25, p 16

Anon, 1982, Mrs Gandhi's report card, *India Today* 7(1) January 15, p 100-103

Anon, 1982, PM arrives in the US with good message: Mrs Gandhi in New York, *Indian Express*, July 29, p 1

Anon, 1982, PM opens world's longest river bridge today, *Hindustan Times*, March 2, p 5

Anon, 1982, PM may secure NC backing for Zail, *Hindustan Times*, June 26, p 16

Anon, 1982, PM reiterates stand on peace, n-disarmament: Gulf between rich, poor dangerous, *Hindustan Times*, January 23, p 16

Anon, 1982, PM rules out division of the State, *Telegraph*, September 19

Anon, 1982, PM seeking JK muslims backing for Rajiv, *Indian Express*, January 3, p 9

Anon, 1982, Rajiv's suceess depends on his ability: PM, *Times of India*, July 24, p 9, news-item

Anon, 1982, 'Star odyssey' of PM and Rajiv, *Times of India*, September 24, p 1

Anon, 1982, Zail's happiest days as Mrs Gandhi's Minister, *Hindustan Times*, July 1, p 5

Anon, 1982, Zail Singh reiterates loyalty to PM, *Indian Express*, June 30, p 7

Anon, 1984, Rajiv combines Nehru's liberalism, Indira's firmness, *Link* 27(21) December 30, p 4-7

Anon, 1990, (Book Review), *Hindustan Times* (Magazine), March 11, p 5, col 1-4
Review of the Book: **Hari Jai Singh**, 1990, *India after Indira: The turbulent years (1984-1989)*, Allied Publishers, New Delhi, 207 p

Anon, 1991, Party focus on Indira, Rajiv in Maharashtra, *Hindustan Times*, June 2, p 19, col 1-3

Balasubramanian, V., 1982, Not grooming Rajiv: PM, *Hindustan Times*, August 4, p 7

Bhattacharys, Shubhabrata, 1982, Gandhi vs Gandhi or why Surya was sold to the RSS, *Sunday* 9(37) March 6, p 12-15

Datta Ray, Sunanda K., 1981, Tremors in the Darbar: Will Mrs Gandhi declare herself? *Statesman*, April 8

Dhar, M.K., 1982, PM lauds joint Indo-Soviet space venture, *Hindustan Times*, September 24, p 1

Inder Jit, 1984, Indira, Rajiv and succession, *Economic Times*, November 6, p 5, col 7-8

Karanjia, R.K., 1976, The Nehrus: Father and daughter, *Illustrated Weakly of India* 97(46) November 14, p 6-19

Karanjia, R.K., 1981, Don't tampt fate, Mrs Gandhi, *Blitz*, May 30, p 1-2

Karanjia, R.K., 1982, Curse of dynastic rule: Warning for Mrs. Gandhi, *Blitz*, April 10, p 1+

Louis, Arul B., 1982, PM denies Sikhs being wronged: Injustice to Sikh denied, *Hindustan Times*, August 2, p 16

Niesewand, Peter, 1981, Indira without Sanjay: Rajiv no substitute, *Blitz*, September 20, p 20

Pandit, C.S., 1981, Indira Gandhi very sure of her ground, *Amrit Bazar Patrika*,

May 14, p 6

Rath, Ramachandra, 1980, Let Indira choose the successor, *Current*, July 12, p 10-11

Sen Gupta, Barun, 1980, Men who matter with the PM, *Sunday* 8(18) December 7, p 23

Sen Gupta, Barun, 1982, Mrs Gandhi's troubles have only begun, *Sunday* 9(51) June 12, p 33

Sen Gupta, Barun, 1982, Mrs Gandhi will make big changes in mid year, *Sunday* 9(51) June 12, p 33

Suri, Surinder, 1981, Mrs Gandhi's enigmatic charisma, *Illustrated Weekly of India* 102(33) November 15, p 30-31

Thakur, Janardan, 1981, Mrs Gandhi's thoughtless thinking tank: Will it now be different? *Probe India* 3(5) July, p 23-24+

Times of India (Newspaper), 1986, Indira loyalists, *Times of India*, May 14, p 6, col 1-2, editorial

Verma, Kewal, 1982, Where does Mrs Gandhi go from here? *Sunday* 9(51) June 12, p 25

Willey, Fay, 1977, Indira's sure thing, *News Week* 89(5) January 31, p 21-22

Gandhi, Indira: Homage Paid to Her

Anon, 1985, Unity of nation biggest tribute to Indira: PM, *Times of India*, November 1, p 1, col 1-3, news-item

Anon, 1986, Nation pays homage to Indira Gandhi, *Times of India*, November 1

Anon, 1986, Nation remembers Indira Gandhi, *Free Press Journal* November 20

Anon, 1988, Nation pays homage to Indira Gandhi, *Times of India*, November 20

Anon, 1990, Nation pays homage to Indira Gandhi, *Hindustan Times*, November 1

Gandhi, Indira: Policies

Anon, 1985, Plot to discard Indira policy defeated: PM tells where they got off, *Link* 27(46) June 23, p 4-6, news-item

Anon, 1985, Rajiv's style, priorities: Are they different from Indira's? *Link* 28(13) November 3, p 11-13

Jain, Girilal, 1984, Nehru, Indira and Rajiv: Different styles, one objective, *Times of India*, November 14, p 8, col 3-5

Mathur, Girish, 1984, Will Congress (I) continue Indira's policies? *Link* 27(18) December 9, p 7-9

Mitra, Ashok, 1989, Rajiv's reform agenda: Fulfilling the mother's dream, *Times of India*, July 3, p 6, col 3-5

Gandhi, Indira: Tributes Paid to Her

See Gandhi, Indira: Homage Paid to Her

Gandhi, Indira: Views on Antulay, A.R.

Nayar, Kuldip, 1982, Mrs Gandhi likes sycophants, *Sunday* 9(37) March 6, p 9

Gandhi, Indira: Views on Bihar Press Bill

Anon, 1982, PM denounces stir on Bihar Press Bill: Opposition obstructing Government work, *Hindustan Times*, September 2, p 1+

Gandhi, Indira: Views on Emergency

Anon, 1981, PM rules out emergency: No ambition for Rajiv, *Hindustan Times*, December 9, p 1+

Gandhi, Indira: Views on Gandhi, Rajiv in Politics

Anon, 1981, PM rules out emergency: No ambition for Rajiv, *Hindustan Times*, December 9, p 1+

Balasubramaniam, V., 1982, Not grooming Rajiv: PM, *Hindustan Times*, August 4, p 7

Gandhi, Indira, 1980, Rajiv not joining politics, *Sunday Standard*, October 12, p 1

Gandhi, Indira, 1980, Rajiv won't take Sanjay's place, *Hindu*, p 7

Gandhi, M.K.: Homage Paid to Him

Anon, 1981, Homage paid to Gandhi, *Hindustan Times*, October 3, p 1, 16

Anon, 1986, Nation pays tributes to Mathatma Gandhi, *Times of India*, October 3

Gandhi, M.K.: Relevance

Kripa Shankar, 1988, Relevance of Gandhi to India's rejuvenation, *Mainstream* 26(29) April 30, p 11-12

Gandhi, Maneka

Anon, 1980, Rajiv vs Maneka: Palace intrigues, *New Age*, 28(32) August 10, p 1+

Anon, 1982, Maneka gesture turn sour, *Hindustan Times*, June 24, p 8

Gandhi, Indira, 1982, Maneka had link with Fernades, *Amrit Bazar Patrika*, April 5, p 1+

Jain, Girilal, 1982, Political opponent or daughter-in-law, *Times of India*, April 11, p 2

Ramalingam, N.K., 1980, Rajiv, Maneka must play active role, *Current*, July 12, p 10-11

Gandhi, Priyanka

Mehta, Vinod, 1991, Enter Priyanka? *Sunday* June 9-15, p 10-11

Gandhi, Rahul

Anon, 1991, Rajiv denies grooming Rahul, *Hindustan Times*, March 31, p 18, col 17

Gandhi, Rajiv

Abdullah, Hasan, 1986, Politics of Rajiv Gandhi, *Mainstream* 24(30) March 29, p

23-25

Abraham, A.S., 1983, Congress (I) bestirs itself: Mr Rajiv Gandhi builds his base, *Times of India*, October 7, p 8, col 3-5

Abraham, A.S., 1987, PM at the half-way mark: Foreign and domestic perspectives, *Times of India*, July 11, p 6, col 3-5

Abraham, Abu, 1985, From Indira to Rajiv, *Mainstream* 24(9-10) November 2, p 9

Advani, L.K., 1988, Decline of Rajiv Government, *Mainstream* (Annual) October 8, p 31-32

Aiyar, Mani Shankar, 1991, The Rajiv I knew, *Sunday* June 2-June 8, p 42-44

Aiyar, Mani Shankar, 1992, The Satyagrahi who defied fear, *National Herald* (Supplement), p 10, col 1-6+

Aiyar, Mani Shankar, 1992, Why the Rajiv legacy will endure? *Independent*, May 23, p 8, col 2-5

Ajay Kumar, 1989, PM: 'New fiza' in favour of Congress, *Times of India*, November 18, p 1, col 1-2

Alexander, P.C., 1990, When Sonia urged Rajiv not to become PM, *Economic Times*, November 5, p 1, col 1-5+

Anjiah, T., 1982, Explains why Rajiv got angry, *Hindu*, February 4, p 9

Anon, 1980, Rajiv attends session, *Times of India*, December 7, p 1, col 1-2

Anon, 1980, Rajiv for Amethi by-election, *Blitz*, December 20, p 3

Anon, 1980, Rajiv likely to be Youth Congress leader, *Blitz*, July 26, p 3

Anon, 1980, Rajiv urged to lead YC (I) at Sanjay rally, *Indian Express*, December 15, p 17

Anon, 1980, Rajiv vs Maneka: Palace intrigues, *New Age* 28(32) August 10, p 1+

Anon, 1980, Strong appeal to Rajiv, *Hindustan Times*, December 7, p 7

Anon, 1980, Who needs Rajiv Gandhi? *Illustrated Weekly of India* 101(35) August 31, p 18-19

Anon, 1981, Bangrappa men meet Rajiv, *Indian Express*, December 31, p 7

Anon, 1981, BJP charge on Rajiv rally, *Hindustan Times*, November 18, p 5

Anon, 1981, I think I escaped, said Rajiv Gandhi, *Organiser* 33(28) November 29, p 15

Anon, 1981, New YC Chief, *Current*, November 22, p 2

Anon, 1981, Nirankaris meet Rajiv, *Indian Express*, November 21, p 7

Anon, 1981, No joint opposition candidate against Rajiv Gandhi, *Hindu*, May 13, p 1

Anon, 1981, Pahadia men appeal to PM and Rajiv, *Times of India*, July 9, p 9

Anon, 1981, Parliamentary system good, says Rajiv, *Times of India*, July 15, p 5, col 3-5, news-item

Anon, 1981, The pilot takes off, *Times of India* (Sunday Review), November 29, p 1, col 1-6

Anon, 1981, Politician with a difference, *Times of India*, June 9, p 1, col 2-4+

Anon, 1981, Poll case against Rajiv dropped, *Indian Express*, October 13, p 17

Anon, 1981, Rajiv a favourite among Pakistanis, *National Herald*, June 25

Anon, 1981, Rajiv agrees to lead IYC (I): Reslove to work for uplift of women, *Times of India*, December 30

Anon, 1981, Rajiv asked to lead Youth Congress (I), *Hindustan Times*, December

30, p 1+

Anon, 1981, Rajiv asks bureaucrats to shed lithargy, *Hindustan Times*, December 20, p 7

Anon, 1981, Rajiv asks youth to work for national uplift, *Times of India*, October 26, p 9, col 2-5

Anon, 1981, Rajiv assails concept of motley opposition, *Times of India*, December 30, p 7, col 3-6

Anon, 1981, Rajiv assails opposition on unity moves, *Hindustan Times*, December 14, p 1+

Anon, 1981, Rajiv assails on opposition unity move, *Times of India*, December 11

Anon, 1981, Rajiv axe to chop dead wood, *Current*, June 27, p 4

Anon, 1981, Rajiv critical of Garhwal strategy, *Sunday* 6(3) July 5, p 58

Anon, 1981, Rajiv Gandhi: The young inheritor, *India Today*, 6(10) May 16 p 56-62

Anon, 1981, Rajiv gives clean chit to UP government, *Hindustan Times*, December 6, p 1

Anon, 1981, Rajiv hints at new measures, *Hindustan Times*, November 19, p 8

Anon, 1981, Rajiv is not expecting Party or Government post, *Times of India*, June 11, p 9, col 1-2

Anon, 1981, Rajiv on YC (I) Council, *Hindustan Times*, June 25, p 1

Anon, 1981, Rajiv: Reluctant bridegroom, *Organiser* 33(2) May 31, p 6

Anon, 1981, Rajiv revitalises Youth Congress, *Blitz*, April 25, p 6

Anon, 1981, Rajiv new aim, *India Today* 6(18) October 1, p 8

Anon, 1981, Rajiv's secret meeting, *Onlooker* 43(10) June 15, p 36-37

Anon, 1981, Rajiv takes the plunge, *Surya India* 5(9) June, p 36-37

Anon, 1981, Rajiv to make Party change working style, *Times of India*, May 12, p 1, col 5+

Anon, 1981, Rajiv warns opposition, *Indian Express*, October 31, p 4

Anon, 1981, Rajiv will attend YC (I) Council meet, *Hindustan Times*, July 10, p 5

Anon, 1981, Rajiv wins his leadership spurs, *Blitz*, June 20, p 1

Anon, 1981. Will aim at new style of functioning, *Hindustan Times*, May 12, p 1

Anon, 1981, While Pranab and Zail quarreled over portocol, Rajiv officiated as PM, *Organiser* 33(29) December 6, p 5

Anon, 1982, (Book Review), *Hindustan Times*, May 2, P iv, col 4-7, *Link* 24(48) July 11, p 48; *National Herald*, May 9, p 11, col 4-6; *Tribune*, May 15, p 4, col 7-8

Review of the Book: **Mittal, Rajiv**, 1982, *Rajiv Gandhi: The theme of today*, Shakuntala Foundations, Chandigrah; Thomson Publication, New Delhi

Anon, 1982, Conspiracy to disturb Rajiv rally, *Hindustan Times*, September 20, p 5

Anon, 1982, Kidding with Rajiv's image, *Current*, March 20, p 4

Anon, 1982, Party post for Rajiv by February, *Hindustan Times*, September 18, p 11

Anon, 1982, Rajiv agrees to lead YC (I), pleads for unity, *Indian Express*, December 30, p 7

Anon, 1982, Rajiv and the fussy elephant, *Onlooker* 44(2) January 31, p 7

Anon, 1982, Rajiv angry with Anjiah over arrangements, *Hindustanm Times*, February 3, p 8

Anon, 1982, Rajiv asked people to cooperate with the governemnt, *Hindustan Times*, January 9, p 7

Anon, 1982, Rajiv blames BJP for Punjab incidents, *Hindustan Times*, May 9, p 7

Anon, 1982, Rajiv calls on Bhave, *Times of India*, September 16, p 5

Anon, 1982, Rajiv calls to rehabiltate the blind, *Hindustan Times*, August 23, p 16

Anon, 1982, Rajiv clips Zail's wings in Punjab PCC , *Current*, March 6, p 4

Anon, 1982, Rajiv exhorts people to work hard, *Hindustan Times*, February 14, p 7

Anon, 1982, Rajiv files papers for ICWA post, *Times of India*, August 7, p 3

Anon, 1982, Rajiv for better Public Sector performance, *Hindustan Times*, March 12, p 1, 10

Anon, 1982, Rajiv for eviction of extremists from Gurudawaras, *Indian Express*, October 6, p 7

Anon, 1982, Rajiv Gandhi not to take up YC post, *Indian Express*, January 1, p 7

Anon, 1982, Rajiv Gandhi's man, *Sunday* 10(5) July 24, p 57

Anon, 1982, Rajiv Gandhi shouts at Anjiah for 'gaudy-show', *Hindu*, February 3, p 1

Anon, 1982, Rajiv holds talks with Farooq, *Indian Express*, September 14, p 1

Anon, 1982, Rajiv lays stone of BHEL plant, *Hindustan Times*, February 11, p 5

Anon, 1982, Rajiv lays stone for water project, *Hindustan Times*, January 8

Anon, 1982, Rajiv not keen on YC (I) leadership, *Times of India*, April 2, p 7

Anon, 1982, Rajiv raps opposition, erring Congress-men, *Hindustan Times*, January 10, p 10

Anon, 1982, Rajiv ready to accept party post, *Hindustan Times*, September 16, p 8

Anon, 1982, Rajiv rules out change in Punjab, *Hindustan Times*, July 4, p 8

Anon, 1982, Rajiv's anger: A part of the tamasha, *Caravan* 2(714) February, p 14

Anon, 1982, Rajiv snubs Patnaik, *Blitz*, February 13, p 5

Anon, 1982, Rajiv's success depends on his ability: PM, *Times of India*, July 24, p 9, news-item

Anon, 1982, Rajiv to call on Vinoba Bhave, *Hindustan Times*, September 10, p 12

Anon, 1982, Rajiv to contest ICWA post, *Times of India*, September 7, p 3

Anon, 1982, Rajiv to have hand in Ministry formation: CM, *Times of India*, January 22, p 9, news-item

Anon, 1982, Rajiv to lay foundation of ceramic unit, *Times of India*, February 10, p 9

Anon, 1982, Rajiv willing to accept Party post, *Indian Express*, September 16, p 7

Anon, 1982, Rajiv willing to accept Party Secretaryship, *Times of India*, September 16, p 7

Anon, 1982, Sanjay-ignored YC men to back Rajiv Gandhi, *Hindustan Times*, May 4, p 6

Anon, 1982, Spotlight on Rajiv, *Times of India*, July 31, p 13

Anon, 1982, Spotlight on Rajiv about Bhosle affairs, *Times of India*, March 27, p 9

Anon, 1982, Will Rajiv Gandhi bow out of politics? *Organiser* 34(4) Jne 13, p 16

Anon, 1982, Will Sanjay cult overwhelm Rajiv? *Blitz*, March 13, p 6

Anon, 1983, (Book Review), *Hindustan Times* (Magazine), October 9, p 4, col 8

Review of the Book: **Sharma, Satinder and Sharma, Indira**, 1983, *Rajiv Gandhi: An annotated bibliography*, Sawan Publications, Delhi, 164p

Anon, 1983, Firm Congress (I) steps for people's welfare: Rajiv, *Times of India*, October 19, p 6, col 3-4, news-item

Anon, 1983, PCC (I): Rajiv hits at factionalism, *Link* 26(13) November 6, p 7-8

Anon, 1983, Rajiv blames party for eclipse in South, *Times of India*, December 18, p 9, col 7-8

Anon, 1983, Rajiv urges youth to build new India, *Times of India*, April 14, p 1, col 7-8 +

Anon, 1983, Rajiv: US interfering in Punjab affairs, *Times of India*, July 24, p 9, col 1-2

Anon, 1984, Assassination part of international conspiracy: Rajiv, *Times of India*, November 20, p 1, col 1-3 news-item

Anon, 1984, CPP endorses Rajiv's choice, *Times of India*, November 3, p 1, col 2-4+

Anon, 1984, (Book Review), *Journal of Parliamentary Information* 30(4) December, p 737-742

Review of the Book: **Pal, R.N., 1984, The office of the Prime Minister of India**, Ghanshyam Publication, New Delhi, 279p

Anon, 1984, Clean administration promise reiterated, *Financial Express*, December 30, p 1, col 1-4

Anon, 1984, Defeat selfish forces: PM, *Times of India*, December 26, p 9, col 6-8, news-item

Anon, 1984, Government committed to protect all: Rajiv, *Times of India*, December 20, p 1, col 7-8+, news-item

Anon, 1984, Growing support for Rajiv as Party Chief, *Times of India*, Novermber 6, p 1, col 4-5+

Anon, 1984, Hazards of novice as Prime Minister, *Organiser* 36(31) December 16, p 5+

Anon, 1984, He who rides a tiger, *Times of India* (Sunday Review), November 18, p 1, col 1-5

Anon, 1984, PM for result oriented administration, *Times of India*, November 13, p 4, col 1-4, news-items

Anon, 1984, Positive popular response to Rajiv, *Times of India*, December 16, p 1, col 2-5+

Anon, 1984, Priests resent Rajiv's remarks, *Times of India*, October 1, p 1, col 1-2+

Anon, 1984, Rajiv as campaigner, *Indian Express*, December 23; *Statesman*, December 15

Anon, 1984, Rajiv combines Nehru's liberalism, Indira's firmness, *Link* 27(21) December 30, p 4-7

Anon, 1984, Rajiv elected Party Chief, *Times of India*, November 13, p 1, col 7-8+

Anon, 1984, Rajiv Gandhi: An uncertain future, *Illustrated Weekly of India* 105(4) January 22, p 18-21

Anon, 1984, Rajiv Gandhi expounds Government policies, *Capital* 193(4794) November 26, p 49-51

Anon, 1984, Rajiv Gandhi firmly in the saddle, *Link* 27(15) November 18, p 26-28

Anon, 1984, Rajiv pledges to fight corruption and inefficiency, *Times of India*, November 13, p 1, col 1-3+

Anon, 1984, Rajiv's style of electioneering, *Times of India*, December 14, p 1, col 7-8

Anon, 1984, Rajiv sworn in new PM, *Times of India*, November 1, p 1, col 3-5+

Anon, 1984, Rajiv undecided on becoming Party President, *Times of India*, November 11, p 1, col 1-3

Anon, 1984, Timings of US study very significant, says Rajiv, *Times of India*, December 19, p 1, col 4-6+, news-item

Anon, 1984, Top priority to Punjab: PM, *Times of India*, December 30, p 1, col 4-5, news-item

Anon, 1984, Top priority to Punjab issue: Rajiv, *Times of India*, December 17, p 2, col 2-5+, news-item

Anon, 1984, Transfer of power to Rajiv, *Organiser* 35(46) April 1, p 1+

Anon, 1984, We live in India: They exist in Bharat, *Indian Express*, August 12

Anon, 1985, Accord to bring lasting peace to Assam: PM, *Times of India*, December 12, p 1, col 1-3

Anon, 1985, The Acid Test, *Mainstream* 23(42) June 15, p 1-2

Anon, 1985, Assam minorities safe, says PM, *Times of India*, December 14, p 1, col 1-3, news-item

Anon, 1985, Bid to weaken country not to be tolerated: PM, *Times of India*, May 7, p 1, col 1-4, news-item

Anon, 1985, (Book Review), *Hindustan Times* (Magazine), December 15, p 8, col 3-5
Review of the Book: **Mittal, Rajiv**, 1985, *Rajiv Gandhi: The theme of today*, Shakuntala Foundations, Chandigarh, 80p

Anon, 1985, (Book Review), *Hindustan Times* (Magazine), December 15, p 8, col 3-5
Review of the Book: **Murthi, V.K. and Sharma, Gautam**, 1985, *Rajiv Gandhi: Challenges and choices*, Radiant Publications, New Delhi, 141p

Anon, 1985, (Book Review), *Hindustan Times* (Magazine), December 15, p 8, col 3-5; *Link* 27(38) May 5, p 56; *National Herald*, April 14, p 7, col 1-4
Review of the Book: **Rai Singh**, 1985, *Resurgence of Rajiv Gandhi*, ABC Publishing House, New Delhi, 203p

Anon, 1985, (Book Review), *National Herald*, April 14, p 7, col 5-7
Review of the Book: **Desai, Dinesh N.**, 1985, *Rajiv's India*, Parijan Prakashan, Bombay, 73 p

Anon, 1985, (Book Review), *National Herald*, May 26, p 7, col 1-4, *Times of India*, March 19, p 8, col 1-4
Review of the Book: **Mirchandani, G.S.**, and **Murthi, K.S.R.**, 1985, *Massive mandate for Rajiv Gandhi*, Sterling, New Delhi, xii, 248p

Anon, 1985, Border clashes may hit ties: PM, *Times of India*, December 7, p 1, col 1-3, news-item

Anon, 1985, Can Rajiv overcome Nixon, Kissinger, Reagan? *Link* 27(44) June 9, p 13-16

Anon, 1985, Challenges before ILO: Rajiv Gandhi's Address, *Mainstream* 23(44) June 9, p 27-29

Anon, 1985, Conciliatory Rajiv can be tough, *Link* 27(49) July 14, p 13-15

Anon, 1985, Cross-roads before Rajiv, *Mainstream* 23(31) March 30, p 1-2

Anon, 1985, Efficiency, integrity, courtesy, *Link* 27(22) January 6, p 10-12

Anon, 1985, F-16s are for use against India: PM, *Times of India*, October 7, p 1, col 4-5, news-item

Anon, 1985, Govt not to yield to terrorists: PM, *Times of India*, May 18, p 1, col 1-3, news-item

Anon, 1985, India alive to threat for Pakistan: PM, *Times of India*, May 5, p 1, col 1-4, news-item

Anon, 1985, India has the resistance to absorb shocks, *Statesman*, August 11, p 1-2

Anon, 1985, India not to be a camp follower: PM, *Times of India*, October 14, p 9, col 7-8, news-item

Anon, 1985, India to take steps to meet Pak N-threat: Rajiv, *Times of India*, October 12, p 1, col 1-3, news-item

Anon, 1985, India will not sign NPT, says PM, *Times of India*, June 15, p 1, col 1-2, news-item

Anon, 1985, India willing to discuss all issues with Pak: PM, *Times of India*, November 12, p 1, col 1-3, news-item

Anon, 1985, Infiltrators from Pak behind terrorism: PM, *Times of India*, September 17, p 1, col 1-3, news-item

Anon, 1985, Job plans getting priority: PM, *Times of India*, November 24, p 1, col 1-3, news-item

Anon, 1985, Kerala free to decide on poll: PM, *Times of India*, November 25, p 1, col 2-5, news-item

Anon, 1985, Light and dark, *Mainstream* 23(39) May 25, p 1, col 1-3

Anon, 1985, The mandate for Rajiv Gandhi, *Radical Humanist* 48(10) January, p 2-5

Anon, 1985, Mandate for unity, strengh and harmony, *Haryana Review* 19(1) January, p 3-5

Anon, 1985, Measures sure to make impact: Rajiv, *Times of India*, October 22, p 1, col 2-3, news-item

Anon, 1985, The Minister doesn't have the answer, *Times of India* (Sunday Review), September 29, p 1, col 1-8

Anon, 1985, New direction to policies, programmes: Social justice within stipulated time frame, *Patriot*, January 6, p 1, col 3-7+

Anon, 1985, A new policy for electronics, *Commerce* (Supplement) 150(3850) March 9, p 1

Anon, 1985, No compromise on anti-State elements: Rajiv, *Times of India*, October 10, p 1, col 3-5, news-item

Anon, 1985, No progress in AP after Congress exit: PM, *Times of India*, December 25, p 6, col 1-4, news-item

Anon, 1985, No talks with Pak on N-issue: PM, *Times of India*, October 28, p 1, col 1-3, news-itme

Anon, 1985, On being buffeted about, *Mainstream* 23(33) April 13, p 5-6

Anon, 1985, Planning being geared to uplift poor: PM, *Economic Times*, August 16, p 1, col 1-4, news-item

Anon, 1985, Plot to discard Indira policy defeated: PM tells where they got off, *Link* 27(46) June 23, p 4-6

Anon, 1985, PM announces accord on Assam: Pakistan asked to abandon bomb: Sharper campaign against poverty: Call to combat extremism: Colourful Red Fort function, *Times of India*, August 16, p 1, col 1-4, news-items

Anon, 1985, PM asks Akalis to publicly disown extremists, *Times of India*, December 21, p 1, col 1-3+

Anon, 1985, PM for key role to public sector: Administrative accountability vital, *Economic Times*, January 6, p 1, col 1-6+

Anon, 1985, PM has refferred to army pull-out at CPP meeting, *Times of India*, March 16, p 1, col 7-8

Anon, 1985, PM: No problem in containing Pak, *Times of India*, October 14, p 16, col 1-5, news-item

Anon, 1985, PM on planning, *Economic Times*, November 9, p 5, col 7-8

Anon, 1985, PM, Opposition discuss Punjab, *Times of India*, January 12, p 1, col 7-8+

Anon, 1985, PM: Pull out depends on Sikh's response, *Times of India*, January 7, p 1, col 1-2+

Anon, 1985, PM's absense questioned, *Times of India*, November 19, p 1, col 4-6

Anon, 1985, PM's concern at build up in Ocean, *Times of India*, January 5, p 1, col 2-5+

Anon, 1985, PM's foreign tour plans unchanged, *Times of India*, May 16, p 1, col 1-3

Anon, 1985, Politics: PM's news style, *Economic and Political Weekly* 20(37) September 14, p 1536, col 1-2

Anon, 1985, Poll aims at wiping out terrorism: Rajiv, *Times of India*, September 10, p 1, col 5-7, news-item

Anon, 1985, Postings and policies, *Economic and political Weekly* 20(2) January 12, p 54-55

Anon, 1985, Prime Minister hits out at industry, *Economic Times*, October 12, p 1, col 1-5+

Anon, 1985, Prime Minister's broadcast to the Nation, *Commerce* 150(3843) January 19, p 18-119

Anon, 1985, Promises to State will be kept: PM, *Times of India*, March 24, p 1, col 1-3, news-item

Anon, 1985, Punjab and Assam solution: PM, *Times of India*, February 18, p 1, col 1-3, news-item

Anon, 1985, Rajiv decries remarks by Akali leaders, *Times of India*, April 13, p 1, col 6-8+

Anon, 1985, Rajiv for sanctions against Pretoria, *Times of India*, October 17, p 1, col 1-3

Anon, 1985, Rajiv Gandhi and the winds of change, January- September, *Monthly Commentary on Indian Economic Conditions* 27(1) August, p 17-18

Anon, 1985, Rajiv Gandhi speaks to the Nation, *Indian And Foreign Review* 22(6)

January 15, p 4-5

Anon, 1985, Rajiv Gandhi's first year: An exciting phase, *Link* 28(13) November 3, p 4-8

Anon, 1985, Rajiv Gandhi's policy projection, *Mainstream* 23(33) April 13, p 60-62

Anon, 1985, Rajiv invites Zia to inaguration of Breeder Reactor, *Times of India*, December 1, col 1-3+

Anon, 1985, Rajiv made tactical error in Andhra, *Times of India*, January 1, p 12, col 1-2

Anon, 1985, Rajiv's call to resist big-power politics, *Times of India*, October 1, p 1, col 5-7

Anon, 1985, Rajiv's foreign policy projection, *Mainstream* 23(20) January 12, p 3-4+

Anon, 1985, Rajiv's perspective on Indian development, *Economic Times*, October 16, p 5, col 7-8+

Anon, 1985, Rajiv's style, priorities: Are they different from Indira's? *Link* 28(13) November 3, p 11-13

Anon, 1985, Rajiv's unpublished interview, *Organiser* 37(38) Febraury 2, p 2

Anon, 1985, Rajiv urges UN to fight starvation, *Economic Times*, October 25, p 1, col 1-4+

Anon, 1985, Rajiv was not very much for emergency, *Times of India*, October 11, p 9, col 7-8

Anon, 1985, The Six Nation Summit on Nuclear Disarmament, New Delhi, January 28, *Monthly Commentary on Indian Economic Conditions* 26(6) January, p 7-8

Anon, 1985, Stern steps against hoarders: PM, *Times of India*, May 6, p 1, col 1-3, news-item

Anon, 1985, Surjeet hails Rajiv's lies, *Peoples's Demomcracy* 8(51) December 16, p 9, news-item

Anon, 1985, Top priority to Punjab: PM, *Indian Worker* 33(160 Jaunary 14, p 1+, news-item

Anon, 1985, Top priority to Punjab: PM, *Times of India*, January 6, p 1, col 1-3+, news-item

Anon, 1985, Two faces of American, *Link* 28(14) November 10, p 9-11

Anon, 1985, US treaty has retrospective effect: PM rejects terms for arms sale, *Times of India*, June 15, p 1, col 1-3, news-items

Anon, 1985, Unity of nation biggest tribute to Indira: PM, *Times of India*, November 1, p 1, col 1-3, news-item

Anon, 1985, Unquiet peace, unclear vista, *Mainstream* 23(41) June 8, p 1-3

Anon, 1985, Warning on 'Induced' sickness: PM's call to step up productivity, *Times of India*, September 20, p 1, col 1-3+

Anon, 1985, The Washington parade, *Organiser* 37(6) June 25, p 1+

Anon, 1985, We will build India of 21st century: PM, *Haryana Review* 18(11) November, p 38-40, news-item

Anon, 1985, What do people expect of Rajiv Gandhi? *Link* 27(24) January 20, p 30-31; *Patriot*, January 13, p 5, col 1-8

Anon, 1985, The year of Rajiv Gandhi, *Capital* 195(4819) December 23, p 17-28

Anon, 1986, Apartheid must end, says PM, *Times of India*, June 17, news-item

Anon, 1986, Arif's letter to PM: Communal divide in secular party, *Times of India*, September 25, p 1, col 2-5+

Anon, 1986, Asoke Sen defends PM's stand on GNLF, *Times of India*, October 3

Anon, 1986, BJP leader questions PM's stand on GNLF, *Times of India*, November 17

Anon, 1986, Big role for Navy in Ocean: PM, *Hindustan Times*, February 17, news-item

Anon, 1986, The BJP leader, L.K. Advani charged that adhocism rather than a method governed Rajiv Gandhi's Cabinet changes, *Hindustan Times*, May 13, *Statesman*, May 13

Anon, 1986, (Book Review), *India Quarterly* 42(1) January-March, p 93-95
Review of the Book: **Murthi, V.K. and Sharma Gautam**, 1986, *Rajiv Gandhi: Challenges and choices*, Radiant Publication, New Delhi 141p

Anon, 1986, Bridge on PM's way blasted, *Statesman*, January 29, p 30

Anon, 1986, Britain protests against PM's remarks on visa rule, *Hindu*, October 18; *Times of India*, October 18

Anon, 1986, Cabinet reshuffles, *Hindustan Times*, October 24

Anon, 1986, Call for national unity, *Hindustan Times*, November 7

Anon, 1986, Centre to announce anti-terrorist action, says PM, *Statesman*, December 2, news-item

Anon, 1986, Combat terrorism, says PM, *Hindustan Times*, April 8, news-item

Anon, 1986, Communication gap between PM and his party, *Link* 29(19) December 14, p 6-8

Anon, 1986, Crown Prince and Rajiv Gandhi discuss trade ties, *Hindustan Times*, February 5

Anon, 1986, Document presented to PM, *Hindu*, March 11

Anon, 1986, For the text of the speech, *Indian Express*, June 6; *Times of India*, January 30

Anon, 1986, Get to roots of grievances, says Rajiv, *Times of India*, October 16, p 1, col 7-8, news-item

Anon, 1986, Gorbachev's envoy meets PM, *Free Press Journal* July 18

Anon, 1986, Gorkhaland issue State's responsibility: PM, *Times of India*, September 20, news-item

Anon, 1986, Gorkha stir not anti-national, says PM, *Telegraph*, November 5, news-item

Anon, 1986, Implementation strategies, *Progressive Education Herald* 1(1) October, p 11-15

Anon, 1986, India fully prepared to repel attacks, says PM, *Indian Express*, December 13, news-item

Anon, 1986, India has to match Pak arms build up, says PM, *Times of India*, October 16, p 1, col 1-4+, news-item

Anon, 1986, India to go nuclear if challenged, says PM, *Times of India*, October 29, news-item

Anon, 1986, India will not allow arms imbalance, says PM, *Hindustan Times*,

October 16, news-item

Anon, 1986, India won't bow to pressures, says PM, *Times of India*, August 20, news-item

Anon, 1986, Indo-US ties better now, says PM, *Free Press Journal* March 6, news-item

Anon, 1986, Inflation under control: PM, *Economic Times*, March 6, p 1, col 2-4+, news-item

Anon, 1986, Intervention if GNLF stir truns secessionist, says PM, *Hindustan Times*, September 21, news-item

Anon, 1986, Irritating controls on small sector to go, says, PM, *Economic Times*, September 18, p 1, col 1-4, news-item

Anon, 1986, Kahmir issue to be solved bilaterally, says PM, *Hindustan Times*, January 21, news-item

Anon, 1986, Lyubomir, Rajiv agree on sanctions on South Africa, *Hindustan Times*, August 12

Anon, 1986, Madhu limaye's letter to PM, *Times of India*, June 1

Anon, 1986, Malviya criticises PM's stand on GNLF, *Indian Express*, October 4

Anon, 1986, Mandatory sanctions must for end of racism, says PM, *Hindustan Times*, July 6, news-item

Anon, 1986, MGR urges PM to withdraw circular, *Hindu*, September 21

Anon, 1986, Need for better scientific administration, *Haryana Review* 20(11) November, p 3-5, news-items

Anon, 1986, New National Policy on Education, *Indian Journal of Public Administration* 32(3) July-September, p 435-460, news-item

Anon, 1986, Nicaraguan award for the Prime Minister, *Statesman*, September 11

Anon, 1986, No compromise on unity, says PM, *Free Press Journal* December 15, news-item

Anon, 1986, No constitutional amendment to meet GNLF demands, *Free Press Journal* October 9, news-item

Anon, 1986, No going back on South Africa, says PM, *Hindustan Times*, June 26, news-item

Anon, 1986, No move to impose Hindi, says PM, *Statesman*, October 2, news-item

Anon, 1986, No territorial concessions to China, says PM, *Times of India*, December, news-item

Anon, 1986, Not much progress on terrorism, says PM, *Hindustan Times*, November 20, news-item

Anon, 1986, Nuclear option still open, says PM, *Indian Express*, April 9, news-item

Anon, 1986, No verbal understanding beyond accord, says Rajiv Gandhi, *Telegraph*, January 12, news-item

Anon, 1986, An open letter to Rajiv Gandhi, *Illustrated Weekly of India* 107(50) December 21, p 38-39

Anon, 1986, Opposition backs PM on Punjab, *Times of India*, April 1

Anon, 1986, Opposition made Bill religious issue: PM, *Times of India*, March 12, p 7, col 2-6, news-item

Anon, 1986, Opposition not to attend PM's meeting, *Statesman*, November 4

Anon, 1986, Ordinance on Article 249 only if necessary, says PM, *Telegraphy*, August 28, news-item

Anon, 1986, Our lifestyles must change, *Illustrated Weekly of India* 107(3) January 19, p 26-27, news-item

Anon, 1986, Pak aiding terrorists: PM, *Times of India*, October 13, p 1, col 1-3, news-item

Anon, 1986, Pak responsible for hijack tragedy, says PM, *Times of India*, September 7, p 1, col 1-3, news-item

Anon, 1986, Pak visit shelved: PM rules out talks with extremists, *Times of India*, July 19, p 1, col 1-3+

Anon, 1986, PM allays fears for migrants, *Hindustan Times*, June 27, news-item

Anon, 1986, PM asks Akali to check terrorism, *Telegraph*, February 28, news-item

Anon, 1986, PM asks Barnala to curb violence, *Times of India*, June 24, p 1, col 1-3, news-item

Anon, 1986, PM asks CMs to avert tension, *Times of India*, April 30, news-item

Anon, 1986, PM asks Jayewardne to find early solution, *Indian Express*, March 10, news-item

Anon, 1986, PM asks MGR to ascertain militants views on Lanka offer, *Statesman*, October 11, news-item

Anon, 1986, PM asks police to check infiltration, *Times of India*, March 20, news-item

Anon, 1986, PM asks Sri Lanka to clarify stand, *Indian Express*, February 10, news-item

Anon, 1986, PM assures all help to Barnala, *Telegraph*, December 9, news-item

Anon, 1986, PM assures support to Cuellar, *Telegraph*, October 12, news-item

Anon, 1986, PM briefed on Palestine meet, *National Heald*, April 27, news-item

Anon, 1986, PM clears pending State projects, *Hindustan Times*, September 19, news-item

Anon, 1986, PM concerned over Public Sector losses, *Indian Express*, August 24, news-item

Anon, 1986, PM concludes visit to Zambia, *Times of India*, May 16, news-item

Anon, 1986, PM condemns US action in Libya, *Hindu*, April 25, news-item

Anon, 1986, PM congratulates Shrestha, *Indian Express*, June 17, news-item

Anon, 1986, PM criticises EEC for diluting sanctions, *Hindustan Times*, September 18, news-item

Anon, 1986, PM decries obscurantism, *Times of India*, May 2, news-item

Anon, 1986, PM decries outside intervention in Central America, *Telegraph*, August 9, news-item

Anon, 1986, PM defends Law Minister's remarks, *Hindustan Times*, Sptember 30, news-item

Anon, 1986, PM defends price-hike, *Free Press Journal* Febraury 20; *Hindu*, February 20, news-item

Anon, 1986, PM defends Shankaranand, *Times of India*, August 1, news-item

Anon, 1986, PM encouraging divisive forces, says Opposition, *Hindustan Times*, November 6, news-item

Anon, 1986, PM expresses satisfaction over Barnala's performance, *Free Press*

Journal, July 7, news-item
Anon, 1986, PM for C'Wealth aid to nations imposing sanctions, *Times of India*, July 6, p 1, col 1-3+, news-item
Anon, 1986, PM for cautions approcach to terroirsm, *Tribune*, April 25, news-item
Anon, 1986, PM for dissmantling Diego Garcia bases, *Indian Express*, July 5, news-item
Anon, 1986, PM for dual war on terrorism, *Indian Express*, August 12, news-item
Anon, 1986, PM for immediate sanctions, *Hindustan Times*, August 30, news-item
Anon, 1986, PM for immediate sanctions by NAM, *Indian Express*, September 3, news-item
Anon, 1986, PM for joint efforts to fight terrorism, *Hindustan Times*, March 30, news-item
Anon, 1986, PM for joint help to frontline States, *Indian Express*, August 15, news-item
Anon, 1986, PM for non-violent movement in Punjab, *Times of India*, April 8, p 9, col 1-3, news-item
Anon, 1986, PM for reforms in administration, *Indian Express*, February 7, news-item
Anon, 1986, PM hails Congress (I), Congress (S) merger, *Times of India*, December 9, news-item
Anon, 1986, PM heads NAM fund for Africa, *Telegraphy*, September 7, news-item
Anon, 1986, PM justifies price-hike, *Times of India*, February 19, news-item
Anon, 1986, PM meets Opposition party leaders, *Times of India*, July 17, news-item
Anon, 1986, PM on new 20-point programme, *Telegraph*, August 23, news-item
Anon, 1986, PM opposed to linguistic States, *Statesman*, July 3, news-item
Anon, 1986, PM pleads for people's movement to curb terrorism, *Times of India*, October 9, news-item
Anon, 1986, PM ready for talks with dissident Akalis, *Telegraph*, July 13, news-item
Anon, 1986, PM reaffirms suppot to Namibian struggle, *Times of India*, May 9, news-item
Anon, 1986, PM reiterates Nehru's assurance on Hindi, *India Express*, November 7, news-item
Anon, 1986, PM reiterates stand on Gorkha stir, *Free Press Journal* Setember 30, news-item
Anon, 1986, PM rules out division of West Bengal, *Times of India*, September 19, p 1, col 1-3, news-item
Anon, 1986, PM rules out intervention in Punjab, *Hindustan Times*, March 23, news-item
Anon, 1986, PM's assurance to Bhandari, *Times of India*, August 28, news-item
Anon, 1986, PM's assurance to Punjab minorities, *Times of India*, May 30, news-item
Anon, 1986, PM call for probe into corruption roots, *Hindustan Times*, September 10, news-item
Anon, 1986, PM's call to fight divisive forces, *Times of India*, April 4, news-item

Anon, 1986, PM's call to fight fundamentalism, *Times of India*, September 13, p 1, col 1-3+, news-item

Anon, 1986, PM's call to safeguard NAM solidarity, *Free Press Jounral* August 27, news-item

Anon, 1986, PM's call to strengthen secularism, *Hindustan Times*, December 15, news-item

Anon, 1986, PM's call to uphold unity, *Times of India*, June 15, news-item

Anon, 1986, PM's charge against Pakistan, *Times of India*, November 5

Anon, 1986, PM's election upheld, *Times of India*, April 26

Anon, 1986, PM's message to NAM Ministers meet, *Indian Express*, January 10, news-item

Anon, 1986, PM's observations on Committee System, *Hindustan Times*, January 20l; *Times of India*, January 20, news-item

Anon, 1986, PM's remarks criticised, *Free Press Journal* September 23, news-item

Anon, 1986, PM stresses on need to streamline legal system, *Indian Express*, November 4

Anon, 1986, PM's talks with Opposition on Border Areas Bill, *Free Press Journal* July 30; *Times of India*, July 30

Anon, 1986, PM warns against bid to weaken border security, *Fress Press Journal* September 12, news-item

Anon, 1986, Pressure unity of India, says PM, *Free Press Journal* October 10, news-item

Anon, 1986, Primacy of public sector to stay, says PM, *Telegraph*, August 23, news-itme

Anon, 1986, Prime Minister and Sri Lankan President discuss ethnic crisis, *Statesman*, November 16

Anon, 1986, Prime Minister calls for new strategy to fight forces of communalism, *Indian Express*, September 13; *Times of India*, September 13, news-item

Anon, 1986, Prime Minister rejects demand for Gorkhaland, *Free Press Journal* December 20; *Times of India*, December 20, news-item

Anon, 1986, Prime Minister to hold talks on GNLF issue with CM, *Times of India*, December 19

Anon, 1986, Productivity improvement in Public Enterprises, *Management in Governemnt* 18(1) April-June, p 5-17

Anon, 1986, Pupul Jayekar cultural adviser to PM, *Telegraph*, September 3

Anon, 1986, Racism must end, says, PM, *Statesman*, June 16, news-itme

Anon, 1986, Rajiv detractors fossilised in the past, *Link* 29(7) September 21, p 14-16

Anon, 1986, Rajiv drops three Ministers: Major shake-up in Congress Party, *Times of India*, January 20, p 1, col 2-4

Anon, 1986, Rajiv Gandhi: On the razor's edge, *Illustrated Weekly of India* 107(17) April 20, p 26-35

Anon, 1986, Rajiv Gandhi: Where does he stand? *Hindustan Times* (Magazine), November 9, p 1, col 1-6+

Anon, 1986, Rajiv Gandhi abetting Gorkhaland agitation, *New Age* 34(35) August

31, p 3

Anon, 1986, Rajiv Gandhi lacks charisma, says Pranab, *Times of India*, June 1, news-item

Anon, 1986, Rajiv Gandhi, *Times of India*, March 6, p 8, col 6, *Times of India*, March 11, p 8, col 6; *Times of India*, March 17, p 8, col 6, letters to the editors

Anon, 1986, Rajiv Gandhi, MGR review situation, *Hindustan Times*, November 9

Anon, 1986, Rajiv Gandhi, Mikulic discuss apartheid, *Indian Express*, July 29

Anon, 1986, Rajiv Gandhi takes over as Chairman, *Hindustan Times*, November 17

Anon, 1986, Rajiv Gandhi warns rivalry in Indian Ocean, *Indian Express*, February 8

Anon, 1986, Rajiv, Jayewardne talks brighten peace-hope, *Statesman*, November 17; *Times of India*, November 17

Anon, 1986, Rajiv's India: Has the dream really faded? *Illustrated Weekly of India* 107(17) April 20, p 6-17

Anon, 1986, Revamping the education system, *Haryana Review* 20(7) July, p 3-7

Anon, 1986, Revitalize Panchayats, says PM, *Hindustan Times*, September 23, news-item

Anon, 1986, Security belt bill kept in abeyances, *Times of India*, August 21

Anon, 1986, Solanki issue is closed, says PM, *Times of India*, March 22, news-item

Anon, 1986, Soviet Minister meets PM, *Indian Express*, October 31

Anon, 1986, Soviets will stand by India, says PM, *Times of India*, December 3, news-item

Anon, 1986, Statute amendment hinted in National Anthem case, *Hindustan Times*, December 3

Anon, 1986, Strict minoriting of aid package for Bengal: PM, *Times of India*, September 21, p 1, col 1-3+, news-item

Anon, 1986, Stringent measures to meet terrorism, *Hindustan Times*, July 30, news-item

Anon, 1986, Talks with Akali rabels if stand clarified: PM, *Times of India*, July 13, p 1, col 6-7, news-item

Anon, 1986, Terrorism will be met at all costs, says PM, *Free Press Jouranl* July 29, news-item

Anon, 1986, To this course I plead myself, *Indian Worker* 34(17) January 27, p 9-15, news-item

Anon, 1986, Tripathi's letter to Rajiv Gandhi, *Times of India*, May 29, p 8, col 7-8

Anon, 1986, Tripathi criticises Rajiv's handling of affairs, *Times of India*, May 29, p 1, col 1-3

Anon, 1986, Tripathi supports Rajiv, *Hindustan Times*, June 1

Anon, 1986, UK isolated in Commonwealth, says PM, *Telegraph*, May 30, news-item

Anon, 1986, UN Namibia plan must prevail, says PM, *Hindustan Times*, July 8, news-item

Anon, 1986, What is Mr Gandhi's political base, *Illustrated Weekly of India* 107(23) June 1, p 16-17

Anon, 1986, Zia sends PM apology for attack on envoys, *Telegraph*, June 23

Anon, 1987, Bear hung for Rajiv, *Organiser* 39(1) May 24, p 1+

Anon, 1987, Bofors audit report not contradictory: PM, *Times of India*, July 7, p 1, col 2-3+, news-item

Anon, 1987, (Book Review), *Hindustan Times* (Magazine), January 18, p 8, col 1-4
Review of the Book: **Ponkshe, Satyawrat**, 1987, *Rajiv Gandhi: The Pragmatic Prime Minister of India*, Ponkshe Publications, Pune

Anon, 1987, (Book Review), *Hindustan Times* (Magazine), June 28, p 8, col 4-6
Review of the Book: **Gupta, M.G.**, 1987, *Rajiv Gandhi's foreign policy: A study in continuity and change*, M.G. Publishers, Agra

Anon, 1987, (Book Review), *Patriot*, July 5, p 4, col 2-5
Review of the Book: **Salvi, P.G.**, 1986, *Rajiv's new India*, Intellectual Publishers, New Delhi

Anon, 1987, Central rule till terrorism ends in Punjab: PM, *Times of India*, June 8, p 1, col 1-3, news-item

Anon, 1987, Destabilisation: Economic dimension, *Link* 29(41) May 17, p 11-12

Anon, 1987, Dissidents hungry for power: PM, *Times of India*, August 30, p 1, col 1-3+, news-item

Anon, 1987, Economic policies to stay: PM, *Economic Times*, January 21, p 1, col 1-5+, news-item

Anon, 1987, Education: The backbone of progress, *Haryana Review* 21(2) February, p 3-6, news-item

Anon, 1987, For a profile of the Gorkhaland agitation, *Illustrated Weekly of India* February 22, p 28, news-item

Anon, 1987, Government answerable only to people, Parliament: PM, *Times of India*, May 17, p 1, col 1-4+, news-itme

Anon, 1987, Harnessing Science and technology for development, *Yojana* 31(9) May 16, p 15-17, news-item

Anon, 1987, India to follow own path, *Times of India*, August 2, p 1, col 4-6+, news-item

Anon, 1987, Is Rajiv in trouble? *Illustrated Weekly of India* 108(15) April 12, p 9-11

Anon, 1987, Lives of landless to be insured: Iron hand for terrorists: PM, *Economic Times*, May 17, p 1, col 6-8, news-item

Anon, 1987, MGR, PM put all egges in LTTE basket, *Link* 30(17) November 29, p 4-7

Anon, 1987, The Mid Term blues Rajiv Gandhi, *Illustrated Weekly of India* 108(14) April 5, p 26-27

Anon, 1987, Opposition free to send team to Sweden: PM, *Times of India*, August 9, p 1, col 7-8+, news-item

Anon, 1987, Pak exploiting links with US: PM, *Times of India*, July 8, p 1, col 1-6, news-item

Anon, 1987, PM calls for world pressure on Lanka, *Times of India*, May 29, p 1, col 1-3, news-item

Anon, 1987, PM in no hurry to reshuffle Cabinet, *Times of India*, October 14, p 1, col 2-5+

Anon, 1987, PM lashes out at Pucblic Sector, *Times of India*, December 23, p 1, col 1-3, news-item

Anon, 1987, PM rejects demand for Mid Term Poll, *Times of India*, July 5, p 1, col 1-4

Anon, 1987, PM will stick to Amethi, *Times of India*, September 11, p 1, col 4-6

Anon, 1987, PM's behaviour, *Times of India*, March 24, p 6, col 6, letter to the editor

Anon, 1987, PM's prerogative, *Times of India*, March 25, p 6, col 6, letter to the editor

Anon, 1987, Political economy of Rajiv's regime, *Link* 29(25), p 12-15

Anon, 1987, President-PM differences being taken to absured length, *Organiser* 38(41) February 22, p 6

Anon, 1987, President rejects pleas for PM's prosecution, *Times of India*, July 23, p 1, col 1-3

Anon, 1987, A Prime Minister or a President? *Times of India*, (Sunday Review), January 25, p iv, col 1-5

Anon, 1987, Rai Bareli won't be neglected: PM, *Times of India*, September 13, p 9, col 4-5, news-item

Anon, 1987, Rajiv expels V.P. Singh from Congress Party, *Times of India*, July 20, p 1, col 1-4

Anon, 1987, Rajiv has damaged his image, V.P. Singh lacks courage, *Organiser* 39(10) August 2, p 5-6

Anon, 1987, Rajiv irresponsible leader: V.P. Singh, *Times of India*, August 20, p 1, col 1-4+, news-item

Anon, 1987, Rajiv's emergency plan to counter dismissal, *Organiser* 39(2) May 31, p 1-2

Anon, 1987, West confidence in Rajiv increasing, *Times of India*, October 15, p 1, col 2-5+

Anon, 1987, What would Gandhiji have done? *Indian Express* (Magazine), January 25, p 1, col 1-8+

Anon, 1987, When Rajivji gives his views, the others say "Okay", *Link* 30(21) December 27, p 6-8

Anon, 1987, Why pressures is mounting on Rajiv, *Link* 29(40) May 10, p 6-8

Anon, 1987, Will Zail dismiss Rajiv? *Organiser* 38(46) March 29, p 1+

Anon, 1988, All Party meet on Punjab soon: PM, *Times of India*, September 2, p 1, col 1-3, news-item

Anon, 1988, (Book Review), *Hindustan Times* (Magazine), May 29, p 4, col 1-8
Review of the Book: **Anon**, 1988, *From Raj to Rajiv*, BBC's Books, p 174

Anon, 1988, (Book Review), *Journal of Political Studies* 21(2) September, p 73-74
Review of the Book: **Pal, R.N.** and **Sudesh Rani**, 1988, *Information: Prime Minister's obligations*, Ghanshyam, New Delhi, p 249

Anon, 1988, Commentary: Thoughts on PM's foreign tour, *Mainstream* 26(41) July 23, p 3-4

Anon, 1988, Complications in dropping bill: PM, *Times of India*, September 16, p

1, col 1-3, news-item

Anon, 1988, CPM encoruaging violence, says PM, *Times of India*, April 3, p 1, col 7-8, news-itme

Anon, 1988, The Dandi March, *Illustrated Weekly of India*, 109(13) March 27, p 20-23

Anon, 1988, Defamation Bill withdrawn, *Hindustan Times*, September 23, *Indian Express*, September 23

Anon, 1988, Dissanayake calls on PM, *Hindustan Times*, May 11

Anon, 1988, The enemy within: Fears in PM's camp, *Link* 31(5) September 11, p 4-6

Anon, 1988, Genuine work for Bofors: Commission unquestionable: PM, *Economic Times*, November 12, p 1, col 2-5, news-item

Anon, 1988, Government firm on corridor plan, says PM, *Times of India*, June 10, news-item

Anon, 1988, Hindu report does not link politicians, says PM, *Tribune*, June 26, news-item

Anon, 1988, Independence day celebrated, *Hindu*, August 16; *Hindustan Times*, August 16

Anon, 1988, India has vital stake in resolution of Afghan crisis, says PM, *Hindustan Times*, March 3, news-item

Anon, 1988, India not to build N-arms, says PM, *National Herald*, June 6, news-item

Anon, 1988, Mature Rajiv best bet in next poll: Congressmen, *Times of India* Magazine (Section II), May 5, p 1, col 2-8+

Anon, 1988, NF rally calls for PM's resignation, *Times of India*, November 17, p 1, col 4-5+

Anon, 1988, Nations taxation policy and role of tax administration, *IFTP Bulletin* 8(2-3) September, p 5-8

Anon, 1988, No compromise on Siachen says PM, *Times of India*, February 10, p 1, col 1-3, news-item

Anon, 1988, No concession on farmers under pressure: PM, *Times of India*, October 28, p 1, col 1-3, nesw-item

Anon, 1988, No territory to be ceded to China: PM, *Times of India*, September 28, p 1, col 1-3, news-item

Anon, 1988, Opposition asks PM to quit, *Indian Express*, November 15

Anon, 1988, Opposition casteist, feudal: Rajiv, *Times of India*, November 6, p 1, col 7-8, news-item

Anon, 1988, Opposition nation's foe: PM, *Times of India*, November 1, p 1, col 5-7, news-item

Anon, 1988, Opposition rally asks PM to quit, *Hindu*, November 17

Anon, 1988, Opposition seeks PM's apology for remarks, *Hindustan Times*, July 28

Anon, 1988, Pak hand seen in destabilisation bid: Concern at plot against PM, *Times of India*, August 3, p 1, col 1-3

Anon, 1988, Party panel on policy perspective set up, *Hindu*, March 11

Anon, 1988, Pay off possibly for genuine work, says Rajiv, *Times of India*,

November 12, p 1, col 7-8, news-item

Anon, 1988, PM again warns Pakistan against aiding terrorists, *Times of India*, August 16, p 1, col 1-3

Anon, 1988, PM allows MP to vent views on party affairs, *Times of India*, June 6

Anon, 1988, PM asks Buta to probe 'offer of funds' to Zail, *Times of India*, March 3, p 1, col 1-3+

Anon, 1989, PM blames Pak for vitiating ties, *Times of India*, July 12, p 1, col 1-3+

Anon, 1988, PM calls on President, *Hindustan Times*, March 27

Anon, 1988, PM concludes visit to Bonn, *Hindu*, June 10; *Hindustan Times*, June 10

Anon, 1988, PM condemns Israeli atrocities, *Times of India*, February 7, news-item

Anon, 1988, PM condoles quake victims, *National Herald*, December 14; *Times of India* December 14, news-item

Anon, 1988, PM consistency lying: Opposition, *Times of India*, November 15, p 1, col 1-2

Anon, 1988, PM constitutes two committees, *National Herald*, July 2,

Anon, 1988, PM continues discussion, *Statesman*, June 12; *Times of India*, June 12

Anon, 1988, PM denies Swiss Bank accounts, *Hindustan Times*, November 11, news-item

Anon, 1988, PM for debate on all aspects of Defamation Bill, *National Herald*, September 7, news-item

Anon, 1988, PM for dismantling all nuclear weapons, *Hindustan Times*, November 15, news-item

Anon, 1988, PM for effective power devolution, *Hindustan Times*, August 24, news-item

Anon, 1988, PM, Governer review situation, *Free Press Journal* May 20; *National Herald*, May 20

Anon, 1988, PM hints at Bill to decentralise planning, *Hindustan Times*, November 26

Anon, 1988, PM, JRJ resolve to implement pact, *Times of India*, January 21, p 1, col 5-6+

Anon, 1988, PM not happy with relief, *Times of India*, October 14, p 1, col 2-3

Anon, 1988, PM offers dialogue on Bill, *Hindustan Times*, September 10; *Tribune*, September 10, news-item

Anon, 1988, PM: Press must be worthy of freedom, *Times of India*, September 10, p 1, col 5-6, news-item

Anon, 1988, PM rejects farmer's demands, *Times of India*, February 21, p 1, col 4-6

Anon, 1988, PM's apology demanded, *Times of India*, February 26

Anon, 1988, PM's call for elemination of nuclear weapons, *National Herald*, November 25, news-item

Anon, 1988, PM's call to fight reactionary forces, *Hindustan Times*, August 10 news-item

Anon, 1988, PM's conditions for talks, *Free Press Journal*, March 12

Anon, 1988, PM's confer, *Hindustan Times*, July 18

Anon, 1988, PM's interview to Sunday, *Times of India*, November 12

Anon, 1988, PM's secretariat toning up white paper on State Sector, *Economic Times*, July 30, p 1, col 1-4, news-item

Anon, 1988, PM views on Defamation Bill, *Indian Express*, September 16; *National Herald*, September 16

Anon, 1988, PM sees change in China's policy, *Times of India*, October 16, p 12, col 1-3

Anon, 1988, PM showed extraordinary interest: Dissenting role, *Times of India*, April 27, p 1, col 6-8+

Anon, 1988, PM's talks with IFAD Chief, *Statesman*, March 31

Anon, 1988, PM to head Seva Dal, *Telegraph*, May 11

Anon, 1988, PM turns down demand for Jharkhand State, *National Herald*, May 28, news-item

Anon, 1988, PM urges NAM to help disarm efforts, *Times of India*, July 15, p 1, col 1-3, news-item

Anon, 1988, PM urges to keep military out of politics, *Hindu*, November 13, news-item

Anon, 1988, PM warns against casteist front, *Times of India*, November 3, news-item

Anon, 1988, Prime Minister flags off Dandi March, *Times of India*, March 13

Anon, 1988, Prime Minister holds talks with Jordanian leaders, *Hindustan Times*, July 12; *Times of India*, July 12

Anon, 1988, Rajiv announces Rs. 175 crores relief, *Times of India*, October 15, p 1, col 1-3

Anon, 1988, Rajiv Gandhi briefed on Soviet troop withdrawal, *Hindu*, February 9

Anon, 1988, Rajiv Gandhi cannot solve Punjab problem: Who can? *Rual India* 51(3) March, p 31-33

Anon, 1988, Rajiv Gandhi criticises National Front, *Hindu*, November 28

Anon, 1988, Rajiv Gandhi's new honey-moon, *Commerce* 157(4041) November 23 p 12-13

Anon, 1988, Rajiv Gandhi's summer tour: Seeking roles for India, *Link* 30(46) June 19, p 8-9

Anon, 1988, Rajiv's bid to woo Tamil Nadu voters, *Link* 31(18) December 11, p 12-13

Anon, 1988, Rajiv has upbill task in Pakistan, *Link* 31(20) December, 25, p 4-5

Anon, 1988, Seven of Rajiv's trusted men wanted Zail Singh to dismiss him, *Orgniser* 39(42) April 3, p 8

Anon, 1988, State borders not to be changed: PM, *Times of India*, May 22, p 1, col 5-8, news-item

Anon, 1988, Sweeping electoral reforms soon: PM, *Times of India*, July 21, p 1, col 1-3, news-item

Anon, 1988, Talks on Punjab only if violence is given up: PM, *Times of India*, March 12, p 1, col 1-3, news-item

Anon, 1988, Tripathi's letter to Rajiv Gandhi, *Times of India* July 7

Anon, 1988, Uncertainty marks unity moves: Rajiv, *Times of India*, October 26, p

1, col 1-3, news-item

Anon, 1988, V.P. Singh exposes PM's Italian connection, *Organiser* 39(43) April 10, p 13

Anon, 1988, The vision of Jawaharlal Nehru, *Gandhi Marg* 10(8-9) Nvoember-December, p 456-460

Anon, 1988, Writ against PM dismissed, *National Herald*, March 4

Anon, 1989, 30 p.c. reservation for women in panchayats: Rajiv, *Times of India*, May 5, p 1, col 1-3, news-item

Anon, 1989, 'The Bodo land' imbroglio, *Indian Express*, March 28

Anon, 1989, (Book Review), *Financial Express*, January 22, p 5, col 5-8

Review of the Book: **Venkateswaran, R.J.** and **Mithani, D.M.**, 1989, *Rajiv Gandhi: Economic perspective towards 21st century*, Himalaya Publishing House, Bombay, 239p.

Anon, 1989, (Book Review), *Financial Express*, August 13, p 5, col 1-4; *Sunday Statesman*, December 31, p 11, *Tribune* (Mangazine), July 23, p 2, col 1-6

Reivew of the Book: **Sen Gupta, Bhabani**, 1989, *Rajiv Gandhi: A Political Study*, Konark Publishers, Delhi, 220 p.

Anon, 1989, (Book Review), *Gandhi Marg* 10(12) March, p 805-807

Review of the Book: **Pal, R.N.** and **Sudesh Rani**, 1988, *Information: Prime Minister's obligations*, Ghanshyam, New Delhi, 149 p.

Anon, 1989, (Book Review), *Patriot*, February 5, p 4, col 1-2

Review of the Book: **Pal, R.N.** and **Sudesh Rani**, 1988, *Information: Prime Minister's obligations*, Ghanshyam, New Delhi, 249p.

Anon, 1989, (Book Review), *Sunday Statesman*, August 13, p 11, col 1-4

Review of the Book: **Varma, Umeshwar Prasad**, 1989, *Rajiv Gandhi and morality in public affairs*, Mittal Publishers, Delhi

Anon, 1989, The compulsions of change, *Illustrated Weekly of India* 110(35) August 27, p 6-7

Anon, 1989, DMK MPs meet PM, *Indian Express*, April 6

Anon, 1989, Grassroot system to eliminate power brokers: PM, *Times of India*, May 11, p 1, col 1-3+, news-item

Anon, 1989, How much do we owe?, *Indian Express*, March 16

Anon, 1989, Independence Day celebrated, *Hindu*, August 16; *Hindustan Times*, August 16; *Times of India*, August 16

Anon, 1989, India ready for talks with Nepal, says Rajiv Gandhi, *National Herald*, April 17; *Statesman*, April 17, news-item

Anon, 1989, India will fulfil terms of treaty with Lanka: PM, *Times of India*, July 18, p 1, col 1-3+, news-item

Anon, 1989, Involve weaker section in PRIS, *Kurukshetra* 37(5) February, p 6-7, news-item

Anon, 1989, Lanka disputes Rajiv's stand on IPKF pull out, *Times of India*, June 16, p 1, col 1-3

Anon, 1989, Nagarpalika Bill introduced, *Indian Express*, August 8

Anon, 1989, Omansese leader calls on Rajiv Gandhi, *Hindustan Times*, March 9

Anon, 1989, On the comeback trail, *Illustrated Weekly of India*, 110(29) July 16, p 10-19

Anon, 1989, Opposition fanning communalism: Rajiv, *Times of India*, April 30, p 1, col 1-3+, news-item

Anon, 1989, Opposition walk out in LS over PM's remarks, *Hindustan Times*, April 6; *Telegraph*, April 6

Anon, 1989, PM addresses Panchayati Raj Sammelan, *Hindu*, April 4, news-item

Anon, 1989, PM affirms suppot for Panchayati Raj, *Statesman* April 30, news-item

Anon, 1989, PM announces probe into Thakkar report leak, *Telegraph*, April 11, news-item

Anon, 1989, PM announces urban job plan, *Hindustan Times*, October 12, news-item

Anon, 1989, PM dedicates Nhava Sheva port to the nation, *Hindustan Times*, May 27

Anon, 1989, PM expresses concern over Pak nuclear plan, *Free Press Journal* February 4; *Times of India*, Feburary 4, news-item

Anon, 1989, PM for unified plan for rural, urban areas, *National Herald*, June 9, news-item

Anon, 1989, PM inaugrates the National Convention of AICC (I) Legal Cell, *National Herald*, August 23, *Times of India*, August 23

Anon, 1989, PM not to attend CHOGM, *National Herald*, October 18

Anon, 1989, PM reaffirms support to PLO, *Times of India*, May 5

Anon, 1989, PM reviews Punjab package, *Hindustan Times*, April 22

Anon, 1989, PM reviews Punjab situation, *Hindustan Times*, March 30

Anon, 1989, Press conference, *Hindustan Times*, January 1; *Hindustan Times*, July 18

Anon, 1989, PM submits resignation, *Times of India*, November 30

Anon, 1989, PM submits resignation: Nominated CPP leader again, *Times of India*, November 30, p 1, col 1-4

Anon, 1989, PM takes charge of Communications Ministry, *Indian Express*, June 1

Anon, 1989, PM vows to fight seperatism, *Economic Times*, August 16, p 5, col 1-2, news-item

Anon, 1989, Population control and grassroots development, *Mainstream* 27(53) September 30, p 10-12

Anon, 1989, Premdasa's reply to Rajiv Gandhi's letter, *Hindustan Times*, July 14

Anon, 1989, Rajiv's Pak encounter, *Link* 31(50) July 23, p 5-7

Anon, 1989, Rajiv Leader of Opposition, *Telegraph*, December 21

Anon, 1989, Rajiv promises 'Ram Rajya', *Times of India*, November 4, p 1, col 2-3+

Anon, 1989, Rajiv questions BJP's patriotism, *Times of India*, November 19, p 1

Anon, 1989, Reaching the people, *Janata* 44(26) October 1, p 5-6+

Anon, 1989, So much so that two AICC officials sent by Rajiv Gandhi to Patna to quieten the rebles had to flee to Delhi following skirmishes between two groups, *Statesman*, March 10

Anon, 1990, (Book Review), *Financial Express*, December 2, p 9, col 1-4.
Review of the Book: **Rasgotra, Maharajakrishna**, ed., 1990, *Rajiv Gandhi's*

World View, New Delhi, Vikas Publishing House, 265p.,

Anon, 1990, (Book Review), *Indian Express* (Magazine), November 18, p 4, col 1-8.

Review of the Book: **Nungent, Nicholas**, 1990, *Rajiv Gandhi: Son of a dynasty*, BBC Books.

Anon, 1990, Congress rout in Assembly polls: Rethinking on Rajiv's leadership, *Link* 32(30) March 4, p 5-7

Anon, 1990, Enter Mr Gandhi, the Party boss, *Economic Times*, July 28, p 1, col 2-5

Anon, 1990, How long can Rajiv keep aflot? *Link* 32(37) April 22, p 10-11

Anon, 1990, National Front colluding with seperatists: Rajiv, *Economic Times*, July 24, p 1, col 6-8, news-item

Anon, 1990, Rajiv for any non-BJP government, *Times of India*, October 21, news-item

Anon, 1990, Rajiv Gandhi criticises NF government, *Times of India*, January 4

Anon, 1990, Rajiv Gandhi fails to make up lost ground, *Economic Times*, June 23, p 1, col 2-7+

Anon, 1990, Rajiv Gandhi leads fast, *Hindustan Times*, May 11

Anon, 1990, Rajiv Gandhi's letter to PM on Punjab election, *Statesman*, September 22

Anon, 1990, Rajiv under attack again, *Times of India*, April 18 p 1, col 2-8

Anon, 1990, Rajiv urged to correct style of functioning, *Times of India*, April 9, p 1, col 1-5

Anon, 1990, The loneliness of Rajiv Gandhi, *Illustrated Weekly of India* 111(9) March 4, p 11-19

Anon, 1990, Remembering Nana, *Times of India* (Sunday Review), May 27, p 2, col 1-6

Anon, 1990, Will Rajiv save Orissa Congress? *Link* 32(37) April 22, p 12-14

Anon, 1990, Writ against Rajiv Gandhi's election dismissed, *Times of India*, April 11

Anon, 1991, After Rajiv Gandhi, *Economic and Political Weekly* 26(21) May 25, p 1307, col 1-2

Anon, 1991, Ball is in Rajiv court, says Patil, *Hindustan Times*, March 28, p 10, col 4, news-item

Anon, 1991, Bengal poll may not be fair, *Hindustan Times*, May 7, p 9, col 6

Anon, 1991, Bharat Ratna conferred on Rajiv, *Hindustan Times*, July 7, p 1, col 1

Anon, 1991, Bharat Ratna for Rajiv, Sarder Patel, *Hindustan Times*, June 18, p 1, col 5

Anon, 1991, A clear Rajiv wave: Congress, *Hindustan Times*, March 28, p 5, col 1-3

Anon, 1991, The conspiracy that back-fired, *Organiser* 42(32) March 17, p 1+

Anon, 1991, Crisis in Kashmir Valley: Jagmohan's oppen letter to Rajiv, *Democratic World* 20(19) May 12, p 1, col 1-2

Anon, 1991, Era comes to an end, *Hindustan Times*, June 6, p 11, col 2-5, letters to editor

Anon, 1991, Family matters: Is this the end for the Gandhi dynasty, *Sunday* June

2-June 8, p 38-39

Anon, 1991, Free hand to Rajiv on MP candidates, *Hindustan Times*, March 30, p 12, col 4

Anon, 1991, Indian Leaders express shock, *Democratic World* 20(21) May 26, p 6, col 1-3

Anon, 1991, An insider's story, *Illustrated Weekly of India* (Supplement) 112(18), May 4, p 5

Anon, 1991, Jagmohan arraigns Rajiv for Kashmir crisis: Anyone trying to be fair is dubbed communal, *Organiser* 62(39) May 5, p 15+

Anon, 1991, Karnataka PCC offer to Rajiv, *Hindustan Times*, April 13, p 1, col 8

Anon, 1991, Kashmiri Pandits confront Rajiv, *Organiser* 42(25) January 27, p 65, col 1-2

Anon, 1991, Keeping an eye on Rajiv and making an extra buck, *Times of India*, March 10, p 1, col 2-7

Anon, 1991, Khashoggi Rajiv confabulation: Embarrasment for Cong? *Times of India*, February 1, p 1, col 6-8+

Anon, 1991, Moving ahead, *Illustrated Weekly of India*, 112(22) June 1, p 4.

Anon, 1991, Mulayam Singh blackmails Rajiv with anti-Congress reports on riots, *Organiser* 42(22) January 6, p 7, col 1-5

Anon, 1991, The New Rajiv: Five key questions about his style, *Sunday* May 11, p 32-35

Anon, 1991, No deviation from Rajiv path: PM, *Hindustan Times*, July 2, p 6, col 8, news-item

Anon, 1991, Party focus on Indira, Rajiv in Maharashtra, *Hindustan Times*, June 2 p 19, col 1-3

Anon, 1991, Patil, Rajiv talks on seat sharing, *Hindustan Times*, April 14, p 5, col 1q

Anon, 1991, PM, Rajiv meet President, *Times of India*, February 10

Anon, 1991, PM: Rajiv's statement not fair, *Hindustan Times*, May 9, p 7, col 1 news-item

Anon, 1991, Punjab not ready for polls: Rajiv, *Hindustan Times*, April 14, p 5, col 2-3, news-item

Anon, 1991, R.V. for Shekar-Rajiv patch-up, *Democratic World* 20(8) February 24, p 7, col 2-3

Anon, 1991, Rajiv accused of J and K mess, *Hindustan Times*, April 23, p 9, col 1-3

Anon, 1991, Rajiv accuses NF, BJP of dividing country, *Hindustan Times*, April 19, p 1, col 1-3

Anon, 1991, Rajiv and V.P. Singh highly frustrated as Advani named Leader of the Opposition, *Organiser* 42(22) January 6, p 1, col 1-5+

Anon, 1991, Rajiv apologised to Shekhar for a last minute patch-up, *Organiser* 42(3) March 24, p 5, col 1-5

Anon, 1991, Rajiv assails concept of motley Oppositaion, *Times of India* December 14, p 7

Anon, 1991, Rajiv bore most of blast impact, *Hindustan Times*, June 4, p 10, col 1

Anon, 1991, Rajiv calls for Dalit's uplift, *Hindustan Times*, April 15, p 1, col 1-2

news-item
Anon, 1991, Rajiv denies attack in Bihar town, *Hindustan Times*, March 29, p 1, col 8+, news-item
Anon, 1991, Rajiv denies reports on wooing Left, *Hindustan Times*, May 10, p 22, col 5, news-item
Anon, 1991, Rajiv drive, *Frontline* May 25-June 7, p 27
Anon, 1991, Rajiv files nomination, *Hindustan Times*, April 25, p 1, col 5-7
Anon, 1991, Rajiv flays non-Cong parties claim, *Hindustan Times*, March 27, p 20, col 5, news-item
Anon, 1991, Rajiv flays Patnik's remarks, *Hindustan Times*, March 31, p 17, col 1, news-item
Anon, 1991, Rajiv Gandhi calls for UNSC meeting on Gulf war, *Times of India*, February 8, news-item
Anon, 1991, Rajiv Gandhi calls on President, *Times of India*, February 14
Anon, 1991, Rajiv Gandhi on the come back trail? *Democratic World* 20(9) March 3, p 5, col 1-3+
Anon, 1991, Rajiv Gandhi poised to take over as PM, *Organiser* 42(28) February 27, p 1, col 1-2+
Anon, 1991, Rajiv Gandhi, Saddam and Bush, *Organiser* 42(33) March 24, p 16, col 4
Anon, 1991, Rajiv Gandhi's election upheld, *Times of India*, February 8
Anon, 1991, Rajiv going the Saddam way, *Organiser* 42(32) March 17, p 1, col 3-4+
Anon, 1991, Rajiv greetings on Bengal Day, *Hindustan Times*, April 15, p 10, col 3
Anon, 1991, Rajiv had faith in scientists, *Hindustan Times*, June 3, p 10, col 7-8
Anon, 1991, Rajiv hopes to present a populist budget after toppling Shekhar, *Organiser* 42(30) March 3, p 1, col 1-5
Anon, 1991, Rajiv, Jayalalitha finalise poll-pact, *Hindustan Times*, March 31, p 1, col 1-3+
Anon, 1991, Rajivji's deepening displeasure with the defector PM, *Organiser* 42(29) February 24, p 3, col 1-3+
Anon, 1991, Rajiv knew of refuelling: PM, *Hindustan Times*, April 13, p 1, col 1, news-item
Anon, 1991, Rajiv-Pawar tussle, *Organiser* 42(25) January 27, p 66, col 2
Anon, 1991, Rajiv's bid to play double role of the super PM and opposition leader, *Organiser* 42(23) January 13, p 3, col 2-4+
Anon, 1991, Rajiv's help to enviornment recalled, *Hindustan Times*, June 4, p 10, col 4
Anon, 1991, Rajiv's last moments, *Frontline* June 22-July 5, p 70+
Anon, 1991, Rajiv's optimism, *Democratic World* 20(11) March 17, p 7, col 2-3
Anon, 1991, Rajiv's personal contact, *Frontline* 8(12) June 8-June 21, p 24
Anon, 1991, Rajiv's zigzag, *India Today* April 30, p 38
Anon, 1991, Rajiv-Seshan flopshow, *Organiser* 62(380) April 28, p 16, col 4
Anon, 1991, Rajiv shoes handed over to Sonia, *Hindustan Times*, June 20, p 10, col 5

Anon, 1991, The Rajiv take-over plan? *Democratic World* 20(7) February 17, p 8, col 1-3

Anon, 1991, Rajiv trusted women folk, *Hindustan Times*, June 2, p 19, col 3

Anon, 1991, Rajiv wants review of defence policy, *Hindustan Times*, April 28, p 12, col 1-2, news-item

Anon, 1991, Rajiv was always smiling, says Sonia, *Hindustan Times*, June 16, p 15, co 1-2, news-item

Anon, 1991, Rajiv was leader of minorities, *Hindustan Times*, May 26, p 5, col 2-3

Anon, 1991, Rajiv wooing AMU students, *Organiser* 42(34) March 31, p 2 col 1-2

Anon, 1991, The reluctant politician, *Sunday* June 2-June 8, p 32-37

Anon, 1991, Remember the wave? Rajiv Gandhi tries to recapture the spirit of 1984, *Sunday* May 5-May 1, p 28-31

Anon, 1991, Reporters ire over Rajiv Gandhi, *Hindustan Times*, April 16, p 10, col 4

Anon, 1991, Sena leader for Rajiv's memorial, *Hindustan Times*, July 16, p 7, col 5

Anon, 1991, Shekhar betrayed trust: Rajiv, *Hindustan Times*, April 10, p 9, col 1-3, news-item

Anon, 1991, Somewhere we lost communication with the people, *India Today*, May 31, p 24-25, news-item

Anon, 1991, Speech dedicated to Rajiv, *Hindustan Times*, July 25, p 18, col 5-6.

Anon, 1991, Surveillance issue again rocks Parliament, *Hindustan Times*, March 6

Anon, 1991, Talking to Rajiv: Extracts from Sunday's interviews with the late leader, *Sunday* June 2-June 8, p 46-53

Anon, 1991, The toppling of the turk: Rajiv Gandhi style, *Organiser* 42(33) March 24, p 3, col 2-4

Anon, 1991, The twain met, *Sunday* January 13-January 19, p 36-37

Anon, 1991, Uproar in Parliament over surveillance of Rajiv Gandhi's house, *Times of India*, March 5

Anon, 1991, View point: Rajiv Gandhi, *Times of India* (Supplement), February 4, p 1, col 1-5+

Anon, 1991, Who switched off the Gulf War? Rajiv Gandhi, of course! *Organiser* 42(32) March 17, p 3, col 2-4

Anon, 1991, Why post-Rajiv Congress looks so empty, *Democratic World* 20(25) June 3, p 23

Anon, 1991, Will Rajiv Gandhi explain? Who is responsible for the begging bowl? *Organiser* 42(39) May 5, p 1, col 1-3+

Anon, 1991, Will Rajiv ultimately take over? *Democratic World* 20(5) February 3, p 5, col 1-3

Anon, 1992, Book on Rajiv released, *Indian Express*, May 22, p 4, col 2-3

Anon, 1992, Documentary on Rajiv, *Indian Express*, May 23, p 11, col 5, news-item

Anon, 1992, Emotional outbursts on Rajiv Gandhi, *Hindustan Times*, April 15, p 1, col 6-7

Anon, 1992, India without Rajiv, *National Herald*, May 22, p 6, col 1-2

Anon, 1992, Indira, Rajiv statues to be erected, *Hindustan Times*, May 20, p 7, col

1
Anon, 1992, No evidence on Rajiv's Swiss accounts, *Hindustan Times*, March 27, p 9, col 2-5

Anon, 1992, PM releases NH Supplement, *National Herald*, (Supplement), May 22, p 10, col 3

Anon, 1992, Rajiv alive in our programmes: PM, *National Herald*, May 22, p 1, col 5-7+, news-item

Anon, 1992, Rajiv Gandhi torch bearer of national interest, *National Herald*, May 22, p 3, col 1

Anon, 1992, Rajiv paved way for better ties with China, *National Herald*, May 23, p 16, col 6

Anon, 1992, Rajiv the human being: An excerpt from Mani Shankar Aiyar's biography 'Remembering Rajiv', *Hindustan Times* (Magazine), May 3, p 9, col 1-8+

Anon, 1992, Rajiv worked for modern India, *National Herald*, May 22, p 3, col 2-5

Arjun Singh, 1992, Campaigner for the new tech, *National Herald* (Supplement), p 5, col 1-3

Arunachalam, M., 1992, A believer in tradition and modernity, *National Herald* (Supplement), p 4, col 1-3

Azad, Ghulam Nabi, 1982, We want Rajiv, *Indian Today* 7(2) January 21

Badhwar, Inderjit, 1991, A water-shed of umcertainly, *India Today* June 15, p 6-7

Badhwar, Inderjit, and Chawla, Prabhu, 1991, Pulling apart, *India Today* February 28, p 32-41

Badhwar, Inderjit, and Chawla, Prabhu, 1991, Rising expectations, *India Today* April 30, p 28-31

Badola, V.M., 1989, PM fails to mollify Muslims, *Times of India*, November 22, p 4, col 1-3

Baird, Joel, 1986, This man tried to kill Rajiv Gandhi, *Illustrated Weekly of India* 107(19) May 4, p 26-29

Baja, Rajiv K., 1990, The fact, the farce and the fix, *Surya India* June, p 7-8

Balashankar, R., 1990, Do-or-die battle, *The Week* January, p 30-35

Banerjee, Ruben, 1991, Presaging death, *India Today* June 15, p 16, col 1-2

Banerjee, Subrata, 1985, Economic thrust of Rajiv Gandhi, *New Age* 33(2) January 13, p 3

Banerjee, Subrata, 1985, One year of Rajiv Gandhi minus on economic policy, *New Age* 33(45) November 10, p 5+

Banerjee, Subrata, 1988, Rajiv Gandhi brand socialism, *New Age* 36(19) May 8, p 5

Banerjee, Subrata, 1988, Rajiv Gandhi, Public-sector and socialism, *New Age* 36(2) January 10, p 3

Banyal, S. S., 1982, Rajiv steals show in Himachal Pradesh, *Hindustan Times*, May 17, p 5

Barman, Ashis, 1986, Party bosses flex muscles, *Link* 28(33) March 23, p 11-12

Barman, Ashis, 1986, Pranab's ouster stems tide of revolt, *Link* 28(40) May 11, p 8-9

Basavapunnaiah, M., 1985, Rajiv Gandhi's policy statements, *People's Democracy* 9(2) January 13, p 1+

Basavapunnaiah, M., 1986, Prime Minister and his brand of secularism, *People's Democracy* 10(43) October 26, p 1+

Basu, Soma, 1991, Living memories, *Frontline* 8(12) June 8-June 21, p 118-119

Baweja, Harinder, 1991, The Gandhis: Picking up the threads, *India Today* June 30, p 102-105

Baweja, Harinder and Viswanathan, Anand, 1991, Darkness at mid-life, *India Today* June 15, p 10-19

Baxi, Upendra, 1985, For Bunker Roy, a word of advice, *Mainstream* 23(32) April 6, p 28-31

Beant Singh, 1992, A valiant fighter of resurgent India, *National Herald* (Supplement), p 20, col 1-3

Bhajan Lal, 1992, Rajiv Gandhi and his vision, *National Herald* (Supplement), p 22, col 3-5

Bhambhri, C.P., From 1985 to 1986: Great challenges, *Patriot* (Magazine), December 29, p 1, col 1-5

Bhargava, G.S., 1982, Rajiv style of leadership, *Organiser* 33(41) February 28, p 6+

Bhargava, G.S., 1986, Rajiv's politicking style, *Janata* 41(23) November 9, p 3-4

Bhatnagar, R.K., 1992, Rajiv as I knew him, *Hindustan Times* (Magazine), May 17, p 4, col 1-8

Bhattachrya, M., 1981, YC (I) show to net regional support, boost Rajiv, *New Age* 29(43) October 25, p 11

Bhattachrya, Shubhabrata, 1981, Rajiv's team, *Sunday* 9(24) November 29, p 15

Bhattacharya, Shubhabrata, 1992, Rajiv Gandhi represented modern India, *National Herald* (Supplement), p 2, col 1-3

Bobb, Dilip, 1991, Ordeal of Prince charming, *India Today* June 15, p 62-68

Bokare, M.G., 1986, Politics of Rajiv Gandhi, *Mainstream* 24(32) April 12, p 27-28

Bokare, M.G., 1986, Sathe-Rajiv wave-length, *Mainstream* 25(8) November 8 p 27-29

Bose, Ajoy, 1988, At the court of Maha-Rajiv, *Indian Express* (Magazine), January 24, p 1, col 1-8+

Buta Singh, 1988, MP's concern over plot to assassinate PM, *National Herald*, August 3

Chacko, Arun, 1991, A fairy tale romance, *India Today* June 15, p 136-137+

Chadha, Kumkum, 1983, Suceess by devious means is not good, *Hindustan Times* (Magazine), December 25, p 1, col 1-8

Chadha, Kumkum, 1991, He had promised to return, *Hindustan Times*, August 20, p 19, col 1-4

Chadha, Kumkum, 1992, Perfect gentleman who spoke from his heart, *National Herald* (Supplement), p 11, col 1-6

Chakraborty, S.P., 1987, Rajiv has belied the Nation's hopes, *Organiser* 39(7) July 12, p 4+

Chakravarty, Nikhil, 1985, Whence the challenge to Rajiv Gandhi, *Economic*

Times, October 22, p 5, col 3-6

Chakravarty, Nikhil. 1986, A Balance sheet: The Rajiv government, *Times of India* (Sunday Review), August 17, p 1, col 1-8

Chakavarty, Nikhil, 1986, A new experiment, *Times of India* (Sunday Review), September 28, p 1, col 1-8+

Chakravarty, Nikhil, 1987, Our heroes and their fawning friends, *Times of India* (Sunday Review), July 12, p 1, col 1-6

Chakravaty, Sumit, 1988, At home and abroad, *Mainstream* 26(36) June 18, p 1-2

Chakravaty, Sumit, 1991, Rajiv Gandhi: A Balance-sheet, *Mainstream* 29(31) May 25, p 2-4

Chandramouli, I., 1991, Rajiv had no business: (Interview: Governer Bhanu Pratap Singh), *The Week* October 21, p 36-37

Chandra Shekhar, 1980, Chandra Shekhar Decries Draft Rajiv's campaign, *Statesman*, August 29, p 1

Chandrashekhar, C.P., 1991, The economic record, *Frontline* 8(12) June-June 21, p 123-124

Chandrashekhar Rao, C., 1985, A year of Rajiv Gandhi, *Indian Express*, April 22

Chatterji, Debasish, 1982, Youth Congress (I) happy days again: Will Rajiv Gandhi provide discipline to the hither to loose organisation? *Probe India* June, p 10-19

Chavan, S.B., 1992, Rajiv: The young inheritor, *National Herald* (Supplement), p 3, col 1-3

Chawla, Prabhu, 1991, Rajiv's revenge, *Indian Today* February 15, p 60, col 1-2

Chawla, Prabhu, 1991, Succession shenanigans, *India Today* June 15, p 90-91

Chhabra, Hari Saran, 1991, Rajiv Gandhi and Africa, *Mainstream* 29(32) June 1, p 6

Chidambaram, P., 1992, He wanted modern and confident India, *National Herald* (Supplement), p 8, col 5-6

Chopra, Pran, 1986, Rajiv Gandhi: Then and now: Shaky, but not about to fall, *Economic Times*, April 6, p 3, col 1-8; *Economic Times*, August 13, p 3, col 1-6+

Chopra, Pran, 1987, Rajiv Gandhi's coming bates, *Economic Times*, April 5, p 3, col 1-8

Chopra, Pran, 1987, Crucial year starts for Rajiv, *Times of India*, January 4, p 3, col 1-5+

Chopra, Pran, 1987, Universal vision: Rajiv Gandhi, *Haryana Review* 21(5) May, p 3-4+

Chopra, Pran, 1988, Benefit of doubt to Rajiv Gandhi, *Economic Times*, April 3, p 3, col 1-6

Chopra, Pran, 1989, Rajiv Gandhi in retrospect: Up like a rocker, down like a stick, *Economic Times*, November 2, p 5, col 1-5+

Chopra, Subhash, 1992, Man who kept us up in top space, *National Herald* (Supplement), p 18, col 3-4

Commerce (Periodical), 1985, Rajiv breaks the ice, *Commerce* 150(3865) June 22, p 11-81, editorial

Dandavate, Madhu, 1987, President, Prime Minister and Parliament, *Janata* (May

Day Number) 42(6), p 4-5

Das, Rathin, 1991, No poll pact with BJP, says Rajiv, *Hindustan Times*, may 11, p 1, col 4-5+, news-item

Das, Sitanshu, 1984, Rajiv wants reconciliation, *Link* 27(14) November 11, p 12-16

Das, Sitanshu, 1986, Oxbridge and Ivy league screen between PM and Congress, *Link* 29(12) October 26, p 4-8

Das Gupta, Amalendu, 1989, Congress after Tamil Nadu: Gandhi faces danger of anarchy, *Times of India*, February 10, col 3-5

Das Gupta, Amalendu and Datta-Ray, Sunanda K., 1985, Countering a Pakistani bomb, *Statesman*, August 18, p 1

Datta, Amlan, 1985, Start and way ahead: Challenge and opportunity for Mr Gandhi, *Statesman*, June 2, p 5, col 4-6

Datta-Ray, Sunanda K., 1989, Death of innocence: Rise and decline of Rajiv Gandhi, *Statesman*, March 12

Deming, Angus and Mazumdar, Sudip, 1990, Gandhi in the cheap seats, *News Week* July 23, p 34

Democratic World (Periodical), 1991, RV against Rajiv's take over? *Democratic World* 20(8) February 24, p 4, col 1-2, editorial

Democratic World (Periodical), 1991, Rajiv and after, *Democratic World* 20(21) May 26, p 4, col 2-3, editorial

Democratic World (Periodical), 1991, Rajiv calls for US forces in the Gulf, *Democratic World* 20(7) February 17, p 3, col 2, editorial

Democratic World (Periodical), 1991, Rajiv gives Jaya bulk of seats, *Democratic World* 20(7) February 17, p 4, col 1-2. editorial

Democratic World (Periodical), 1991, Rajiv's journey toward stability ends, *Democratic World* 20(21) May 26, p 3-4, col 2+, editorial

Democratic World (Periodical), 1991, Rajiv urges peace initiatives, *Democratic World* 20(6) February 10, p 3, col 2+, editorial

Desai, M.V., 1987, PM in North America: Yes, with a but, *Economic Times*, October 27, p 5, col 7-8

Desai, Mahesh, 1986, Assessing Rajiv Gandhi, *Janata* 41(24) November 16, p 14-15; *Janata* 41(25) November 30, p 13

Desai, Rajiv, 1989, The Mahalanobis mindset is Rajiv's real enemy, *Times of India*, March 17

Desai, Rajiv, 1990, Mr Rajiv Gandhi's second chance, *Times of India*, November 16, p 8, col 7-8

Dev, Rahul, 1983, The Rajiv brigade, *Illustrated Weekly of India* 104(23) October 23, p 28-31

Dev Dutt, 1981, The Rajiv factor, *Janata* 36(24) August 3, p 11-12

Dev Dutt, 1986, Images of Rajiv Gandhi, *Janata* 41(24) November 16, p 12-13

Devendra Mohan, 1982, Rajiv raises YC from the dead, *Blitz*, January 16, p 21

Dewan Berindranath, 1981, Rajiv-Farooq talks for Congress (I) NC coalition, *Hindu*, August 8, p 10

Dhar, M.K., 1991, Rajiv seeks decisive verdict, *Hindustan Times*, March 28, p 10, col 5-8

Dhar, P.N., 1989, The Prime Minister's office: Seeing through the mystique, *Times of India*, February 24, p 6, col 3-5

Dhar, Somnath, 1984, Rajiv: Dedication and humility, *National Herald*, August 26, p 3, col 1-4

Dibang, 1990, Rajiv plumped for Devi as PM, *Illustrated Weekly of India* December 1-2, p 1, col 1-5

Dikshit, Shiela, 1992, Rajiv Rattan, *Hindustan Times*, Mary 17, p 4, col 1-8

Dutt, Anuradha, 1990, Pilgrim's progress, *Illustrated Weekly of India* 111(29) July 22, p 34-37

Dutt, Rudras, 1985, Rajiv Gandhi's economics, *Janata* 40(4) March 3, p 5-7

Dwivedi, Devendra Nath, 1986, Assessing Rajiv Gandhi: Within Nehru Indira frame work, *Times of India*, December 24, p 8, col 3-5

Dwivedi, Devendra Nath, 1986, Rajiv pragmatic, not pragmatist, *Times of India*, December 25, p 8, col 7-8

Eastern Economist (Periodical), 1981, The new crown prince, *Eastern Economist* 76(21) May 22, p 1254, editorial

Economic and Political Weekly (Periodical), 1981, Painless induction, *Economic and Political Weekly* 16(20) May 16, p 877, editorial

Economic Times (News-Paper), 1984, Guidelines for action, *Economic Times*, November 14, p 5, col 1-2, editorial

Economic Times (Newspaper), 1985, PM at Press Club, *Economic Times*, October 14, p 5, col 1-2, editoral

Economic Times (Newspaper), 1985, Well begun, *Economic Times*. November 2, p 5, col 1-2, editorial

Economic Times (Newspaper), 1986, Doles and digs, *Economic Times*, September 22, p 5, col 1-2, editorial

Economic Times (Newspaper), 1989, From the frame parts, *Economic Times*, August 16, p 5, col 1-2, editorial

Economic Times (Newspaper) 1989, Prime Minister's plan, *Economic Times*, February 14, p 5, col 1-2, editorial

Economic Times (Newspaper), 1989, The Rajiv years, *Economic Times*, November 1, p 7, col 1-2, editorial

Fernades, George, 1989, The Dravidians and Rajiv Gandhi, *The Other Side* March 26, p 6-13

GPD, 1985, A day in the life of Rajiv Gandhi, *Economic and Political Weekly* 20(49) December 7, p 2141-2142

Gadgil, V.N., 1990, No one attacked Rajiv Gandhi even indirectly, *Surya India* June, p 14, col 1-3

Gajapathi, Gopi Nath, 1992, A leader par excellence, *National Herald* (Supplement), p 15, col 1-3

Gandhi, Rajiv, 1981, Involve people in development, *Hindustan Times*, May 18, p 1

Gandhi, Rajiv, 1981, People's role of watch dogs, *Blitz*, July 18, p 24

Gandhi, Rajiv, 1981, Punjab Government not effective, *Hindustan Times*, November 21, p 1

Gandhi, Rajiv, 1981, Talks with Akalis have not broken down, *Hindustan Times*,

November 21, p 16

Gandhi, Rajiv, 1981, US forcing arms on sub-continent, *Hindustan Times*, November 14, p 6

Gandhi, Rajiv, 1982, Congress (I) as strong as before, *National Herald*, April 25, p 3

Gandhi, Rajiv, 1982, LD, BJP alliance mere opportunism, fake, *Hindustan Times*, May 15, p 5

Gandhi, Rajiv, 1982, Sanjay plan not abandoned, *Indian Express*, March 31, p 1

Gandhi, Rajiv, 1982, YC (I) will do constructive work, *Hindustan Times*, January, p 4

Gandhi, Rajiv, 1984, 23rd INTUC plenary session: Message, *Indian Worker* 32(32-34) May 7-May 21

Gandhi, Rajiv, 1984, Prime Minister's broadcast to the Nation: Call to build India of 21st century, *Indian and Foreign Review* 22(3) November 30, p 12-13+

Gandhi, Rajiv, 1984, Rajiv's first message to the Nation, *Mainstream* 23(12), p 25-26

Gandhi, Rajiv, 1985, Funds plenty for engines of destruction and not for development, *Indian Worker* 33(39) June 24, p 3-5

Gandhi, Rajiv, 1985, It's time our scientists come out of their shell, *Yojana* 19(24) January 1, p 4-6

Gandhi, Rajiv, 1985, No giving up Nations thrust on socialism, *Indian Worker* 33(35) September 30, p 6-8

Gandhi, Rajiv, 1985, Text of PM's speech, *Times of India*, April 20, p 16, col 1-4

Gandhi, Rajiv, 1986, India towards 21st Century: Speeches of Rajiv Gandhi at the Congress Centenary, *Secular Democracy* 19(1-2) January-February, p 20-28

Gandhi, Rajiv, 1986, PM's Address to Army Commanders, *Hindu*, April 25

Gandhi, Rajiv, 1986, Thus spake Rajiv, *Illustrated Weekly of India* 107(20) May 11, p 40-41

Gandhi, Gandhi, 1987, Communalisation of politics, education, industry and commerce: Am imperialist strategy to impede national unity and freedom movement: Prime Minister Rajiv Gandhi's address to intellectuals, New Delhi, September 15, 1987, *Muslim India* 5(58) October, p 456-458

Gandhi Rajiv, 1987, We salute workers who do Gods work on earth: Prime Minister Rajiv Gandhi's address to the May day rally, 1987, *Indian Worker* 35(32-33) May 11-May 18, p 8-11

Gandhi, Rajiv, 1988, PM's Address at Silver Jubilee function of "Patriot", *Indian Express*, March 30

Gandhi, Rajiv, 1988, PM's Address to CPP (I), *Hindu*, December 8

Gandhi, Rajiv, 1988, PM's Address to the Chief Ministers, *Hindustan Times*, March 19; *Times of India*, March 19

Gandhi, Rajiv, 1988, PM's Address to Farmer's Rally, *Free Press Journal*, Febrary 21; *National Herald*, February 21

Gandhi, Rajiv, 1988, PM's Independence Day speech, *Economic Times*, August 16, p 4, col 5-8, news-item

Gandhi, Rajiv, 1988, PM's statement on Gorbachev's visit, *Hindu*, November 22

Gandhi, Rajiv, 1988, Speech at the AICC session in New Delhi, *Times of India*,

November 22

Gandhi, Rajiv, 1988, Speeches (Extract) Prime Minister Rajiv Gandhi, *Foreign Affairs Report* 37(9.10.11) September-November, p 101-124, figures

Gandhi, Rajiv, 1989, PM's Address to Bharat Krishak Samaj, *National Herald*, February 7

Gandhi, Rajiv, 1989, PM's Address to Municipal Officers, *Hindustan Times*, June 6; *National Herald*, June 6

Gandhi, Rajiv, 1989, PM's Address to Nagarpalika Sammelan, *Hindustan Times*, June 15

Gandhi, Rajiv, 1989, PM's Address to Panchayati Raj Conference, *Free Press Jouranl*, May 5

Gandhi, Rajiv, 1989, PM's statesmen tregarding terrorism, *Hindu*, March 1

Gandhi, Rajiv, 1989, Rajiv Gandhi's Address to Seva Dal Convention, *Times of India*, May 13

Gandhi, Rajiv, 1991, Rajiv Gandhi's letter to PM, *Hindustan Times*, Febrauary 11, p 12, col 2

Gangadhar, V., 1991, Rajiv-baiters, *Sunday* June 9-June 15, p 94-95

Gangal, S.C., 1987, President and the Prime Minister, *Gandhi Marg* 9(2) May, p 67-72

Ganguli, Amulya, 1989, Rajiv Gandhi in history, *Statesman* (Misc), November 26, p 1, col 1-5

Gani, H.A., 1989, Prime Minister's Panchayati Raj, *Janata* 44(19) Asgust 6, p 12+

Ghosh Chowdhury, Dilip, 1985, Bengal Congress (I) new line up, *New Age* 33(48) December 1, p 7

Ghosh Chowdhury, Dilip, 1996, Feud in Bengal Cong (I) stepped up after poll, *New Age* 34(20) June 29, p 16

Ghosh Chowdhury, Dilip, 1987, Academic platform used for Rajiv's political tirade, *New Age* 35(4) January 25, p 6

Gokhale, S.R., 1984, An adminocrat: New management concept, *Economic Times*, December 18, p 5, col 3-6

Guha, R., 1991, Rajiv Gandhi: Can he provide a stable alternative? *Sunday* March 24-March 30, p 4, letter to editor

Guha Thakurta, Paranjoy and Taneja, Shiv, 1991, Hard times get harder, *India Today* June 15, p 80-82

Gupta, Indrajit, 1988, Untenability of Rajiv Gandhi's rule, *Mainstream* (Annual) October 8, p 29-30+

Gupta, L.N., 1982, Tripude antics fail to amuse Rajiv, *Blitz*, May 22 p 4

Gupta, Ram Roop, 1985, Freedom fighters and Prime Minister: Interesting features of their horsocopes, *Organiser* 37(26) November 10, p 14-17+

Gupta, Ram Roop, 1987, Steep hildown trend in Rajiv Gandhi's life, *Organiser* 39(12) August 15, p 53-54

Gupta, Rajan, 1987, President-PM controvercy, *Mainstream* 25(28) March 28, p 6

Gupta, Shekhar, 1991, Friendly but lack lustre, *India Today* May 31, p 22-25

Gupta, Shakhar, et al, 1991, Planned Precise, Pulverising, *India Today* June 15, p 27-29

Hafiz, M.A., 1991, Rajiv, V.P., Shekhar on firm ground, *Hindustan Times*, April 2, p 10, col 5-8

Hanspal, H.S., 1992, An inspiring personality, *National Herald* (Supplement), p 11, col 4-6

Hari Kumar, K.N., 1988, Rajiv and the US: Trading Non-Alignment for Hi-tech? *Mainstream* 26(29) April 30, p 16-17

Hasan, Syed Majeedul, 1982, Why Rajiv Gandhi was displeased with Anjiah? *Sunday* 9(36) February 27, p 16-17

Hazarika, Sanjoy, 1991, For we shall never be young again, *Hindustan Times* (Sunday Magazine), June 2, p 4, col 1-8

Inder Jit, 1984, Indira, Rajiv and succession, *Economic Times*, Movember 6, p 5, col 7-8

Inder Jit, 1984, Rajiv and the talks ahead, *Economic Times*, November 13, p 5, col 7-8

Inder Jit, 1986, PM concedes basic Gorkha demand, *Economic Times*, December 23, p 5, col 7-8+

Inder Jit, 1987, Controversy ends, issue remains, *Economic Times*, May 26, p 5, col 7-8+

Inder Jit, 1987, Let Rajiv follow Nehru's example, *Economic Times*, June 9, p 5, col 7-8+

Inder Jit, 1987, PM's Darjelling visit and Gorkhas, *Economic Times*, February 17, p 5, col 7-8+

Inder Jit, 1987, Parliament must deabate gut issues, *Economic Times*, March 24, p 5, col 7-8+

Inder Jit, 1987, Prime Minister and the Constitution, *Economic Times*, June 16, p 5, col 7-8+

Inder Jit, 1987, Rajiv, Haryana Poll and new crises, *Economic Times*, June 23, p 5, col 7-8+

Inder Jit, 1987, Will Rajiv ride the rising crisis? *Economic Times*, July 28, p 5, col 7-8

Inder Jit, 1989, Singnificant gains of Rajiv's visit, *Economic Times*, July 25, p 5, col 7-8

Jaffer Shareef, C.K., 1992, Staunch votary of integration, *National Herald* (Supplement), p 9, col 3-6

Jain, Girilal, 1984, Grab for Rajiv Gandhi, *Times of India* (Sunday Review), December 2, p 1, col 1-8

Jain, Girilal, 1984, Nehru, Indira and Rajiv: Different styles, one objective, *Times of India*, November 14, p 8, col 3-5

Jain, Girilal, 1985, Promise and fufilment: Problems Rajiv Gandhi may face, *Times of India*, February 6, p 8, col 3-5

Jain, Girilal, 1985, The Rajiv phenomenon: India's search for a monarch, *Times of India*, March 19, p 8, col 3-5; *Times of India*, March 20, p 6, col 7-8; *Times of India*, Mach 22, p 6, col 7-8

Jain Girilal, 1985, Rajiv's India impatient to march ahead, *Times of India* (Sunday Review), January 27, p 1, col 1-8

Jain, Girilal, 1985, The year of Rajiv Gandhi : Pitfalls of accomodation, *Times of India*, December 31, p 8, col 3-5

Jain, Girilal, 1986, The challenge Rajiv faces: Continuing decay of Congress, *Times of India*, August 27, p 8, col 3-5

Jain, Girilal, 1986, Politics of Rajiv Gandhi, *Mainstream* 24(26) March 1, p 11-14

Jain, Girilal, 1986, Politics of Rajiv Gandhi: An outsider's view of India, *Times of India*, February 19, p 8, col 3-5, *Times of India*, February 20, p 8, col 3-5

Jain, Girilal, 1986, Rajiv Gandhi's personality: Impact on leadership style, *Times of India*, February 26, p 8, col 3-5; *Times of India*, Fecurary 27, p 8, col 3-5

Jain, Girilal, 1987, Challenge for Mr Gandhi: No room for compromise, *Times of India*, June 27, p 6, col 3-5

Jain, Girilal, 1987, Challenges to Rajiv Gandhi: President Zail Singh and V.P. Singh, *Times of India*, May 18, p 6, col 3-5

Jain, Girilal, 1987, A clash of interests: Rajiv Gandhi and V.P. Singh, *Times of India*, February 4, p 6, col 3-5

Jain, Girilal, 1987, Crisis of confidence: Challenge Rajiv Gandhi faces, *Times of India*, June 24, p 6, col 3-5

Jain, Girilal, 1987, Destabilisation in trouble: Rajiv Gandhi faces, *Times of India*, August 19, p 6, col 3-5

Jain, Girilal, 1987, Fight is for power: V.P. Singh's challenge to Rajiv Gandhi, *Times of India*, August 12, p 6, col 3-5

Jain, Girilal, 1987, Fight to the finish: Rajiv Gandhi versus V.P. Singh, *Times of India*, July 17, p 6, col 3-5

Jain, Girilal, 1987, Focus away from Rajiv: No natural allies for V.P. Singh, *Times of India*, September 9, p 6, col 3-5

Jain, Girilal, 1987, No anti-Rajiv conspiracy: Only convergence of interests, *Times of India*, December 16, p 6, col 3-5

Jain, Girilal, 1987, Political upheaval in India: Rajiv's blunder after blunder, *Times of India*, March 25, p 6, col 3-5

Jain, Girilal, 1987, President vs Prime Minster: New correlation of power, *Times of India*, July 29, p 6, col 3-5

Jain, Girilal, 1987, Prime Minister under siege: Compulsions of Indian democracy, *Times of India*, April 20, p 6, col 3-5

Jain. Girilal, 1987, Reagan has an agenda: Questions that Rajiv shold raise, *Times of India*, October 14, p 6, col 3-5

Jain, Girilal, 1988, Chandraswami as linchpin: Attempt to blackmail Rajiv Gandhi, *Times of India*, April 5, p 4, col 3-5

Jain, Girilal, 1988, No, anti-Rajiv conspiracy: Only convergence of interests, *Times of India*, December 16, p 6, col 3-5

Jain, Minu, 1991, What the stars don't fortell, *Sunday* June 9-June 15, p 60-61

Jakhar, Balram, 1992, The voice that stood for peace, *National Herald* (Supplement), p 9, col 1-2

Jalan, Bimal, 1991, Those were the days, *Sunday* June 23-June 29, p 54-56

Janardhana Reddy, 1992, Nothing stood between him and poeple, *National Herald* (Supplement), p 8, col 1-4

Janata (Periodical), 1981, Distinction without a difference, *Janata* 36(39) November 29, p 1-2, editorial

Jaura, Ramesh, 1986, Politics of Rajiv Gandhi, *Mainstream* 24(34) April 26,

p 26-27

Jayanth, V., et al, 1991, The gory end, *Frontline* 8(12) June 8-June 21, p 4-5+

Jha, Prem Shankar, 1985, New direction for politics: Rajiv Gaandhi's bold initiative, *Times of India*, January 8, p 8, col 3-5

Jha, Prem Shankar, 1986, Rajiv Gandhi's acid test: Revolt of the intermediate class, *Times of India*, February 24, p 8, col 3-4; *Times of India*, Feburary 25, p 8, col 7-8

Jhujhunwala, Bharat, 1986, Politics of Rajiv Gandhi, *Mainstream* 24(29) March 22, p 27-28

Joshi, Chand 1982, Rajiv to wield the 'big broom', *Hindustan Times*, March 13, p 1

Joshi, Murali Manohar, 1987, A diversionary exercise to defocus the moral failure of Rajiv Gandhi, *Organiser* 39(24) November 22, p 5+

Kackar, Ranjana and Chaudhary, Shahid A., 1991, Will Rajiv be PM again? *Probe India* October 17, p 11, col 1-6

Kalhan, Promila, 1991, A child who loved aeroplanes, *Hindustan Times* (Sunday Magazine), June 2, p 4, col 1-8

Kalkur, Ashok, 1991, The last post, *Frontline* 2(12) June 8-June 21, p 124-125

Kalra, Krishan, 1991, Fare well, my prince, *Hindustan Times*, June 4, p 11, col 2-5

Kamalanath, 1981, On Rajiv Gandhi: Nobody imposed him, *Probe India* 3(5) July, p 18-19

Kamalanath, 1981, Only the PM's son can fix the exploiters, *Onlooker* 43(12) July 15, p 38

Kamath, M.V., 1981, Why Rajiv Gandhi? *Illustrated Weekly of India* 102(19) May 31, p 6-11

Kamath, M.V., 1984, Rajiv Gandhi's Prime Ministership, *Organiser* 36(28) November 25, p 4

Kamath, M.V., 1984, Will Rajiv make good? *Indian Express* (Magazine), November 11, p 2, col 1-5

Kamath, M.V., 1986, Absence of malice? *Illustrated Weekly of India* 107(17) August 20, p 20-23

Kapoor, Coomi, 1990, A change of image: Rajiv tries to put his act together, *Illustrated Weekly of India* 111(27) July 8, p 10-19

Karanjia, Russy, 1987, Case for the defence, *Illustrated Weekly of India* 108(28) July 19, p 32-35

Karat, Prakash, 1987, Separating religion and politics: Rajiv style, *People's Democracy* 11(11) March 15, p 3

Karlekar, Hiranmay, 1981, Rajiv: The politics of dynastic succession, *Indian Express* (Magazine), June 21, p 1, col 1-8

Katyal, K.K., 1991, An aggregssive style, *Frontline* 8(12) June 8-June 21, p 122-123

Keshava Rao, K., 1992, Rajiv Gandhi Technology Mission for rural poor, *National Herald* (Supplement), p 19

Khanna, K.C., 1985, A young man in a hurry: Hopeful signs of dynamic change, *Times of India*, January 9, p 8, col 3-5

Khanna, K.C., 1986, Two-year of Rajiv Gandhi: A rudder jammed by drife wood,

Times of India, October 21, p 8, col 3-5
Khanna, Rajesh, 1992, Rajesh, we will make it, *National Herald* (Supplement), p 12, col 1-4
Khare, Harish, 1986, Challenge to Rajiv Gandhi: Issues he can no longer skirt, *Times of India*, May 5, p 8, col 3-5
Khare, Harish, 1986, Choice for Rajiv Gandhi: Away from charismatic leadership, *Times of India*, April 11, p 8, col 3-5
Khare, Harish, 1986, Congress and Rajiv Gandhi: Danger of Indian Marcoism, *Times of India*, September 6, p 8, col 3-5
Khare, Harish, 1986, Issues Tripathi has raised: Rajiv Gandhi should be grateful, *Times of India*, June 11, p 8, col 3-5
Khare, Harish, 1987, Dissidence in Congress: Rajiv Gandhi's strategy, *Times of India*, January 19, p 8, col 3-5
Khare, Harish, 1987, President, Prime Minister: No acquiescence, no confrontation, *Times of India*, March 2, p 6, col 3-5
Khare, Harish, 1987, Rajiv Gandhi on defensive: End of his brave new world, *Times of India*, March 24, p 6, col 3-5
Khare, Harish, 1987, Reviving the Congress: Main challenge for Rajiv Gandhi, *Times of India*, June 2, p 6, col 3-5
Khare, Harish, 1988, The repackaging of Rajiv Gandhi, *Times of India*, March 29, p 6, col 7-8
Khare, Harish, 1989, Preparing for the pool: Rajiv's overtures to party, *Times of India*, May 17, p 6, col 3-5
Khare, Harish, 1990, Anti-Congressism endures: Rajiv's failure to evolve, *Times of India*, October 10, p 8, col 3-5.
Khuswant Singh, 1991, Rajiv and the stars, *Sunday* June 23-June 29, p 20-21
Kirpekar, Subash, 1988, Rajiv warns Pak against medling in Punjab, *Times of India*, April 24, p 1, col 1-3+
Kothari, Rajini, 1985, Rajiv Gandhi's election: End or beginnning? *Economic Times*, January 6, p 3, col 1-5+
Kothari, Rajini, 1989, Rajiv's Panchayat: A bonapartist vision, *Mainstream* 27(34) May 20, p 2-3
Kottary, Sailesh, 1985, Target: Rajiv Gandhi, *Illustrated Weekly of India*, 106(4) June 2, p 6-11
Kripashankar, 1988, Relevance of Gandhi to India's rejuvenation, *Mainstream* 26(29) April 30, p 11-12
Lakshman, Nikhil, 1985, The men who will now rule India, *Illustrated Weekly of India*, 105, (37) January 20, p 6-13
Lakshman, Nikhil, 1985, Where are his men today? *Illustrated Weekly of India*, 105(52) May 5, p 6-13
Lal, Thanhawala, 1992, Man love for the poor, *National Herald* (Supplement), p 18, col 1
Mahavir Prasad, 1992, The end of an era, *National Herald* (Supplement), p 17, col 1-4
Mainstream (Periodical), 1985, Much ado about nothing, *Mainstream* 23(46) July 13, p 1-2, editorial

Mainstream (Periodical) 1991, Rajiv's stability, *Mainstream* 29(28) May 4, p 1-2, editorial

Malhotra, Inder, 1985, Cabinet making and after, *Times of India*, January 3

Malhotra, Inder, 1987, Political commentary: Britain's view of Rajiv, *Times of India*, July 2, p 6, col 3-5

Malhotra, Inder, 1987, Political commentary: Shades of the seventies, *Times of India*, March 20, p 6, col 3-5

Maniam, V.S., 1987, A dazzling meeting of minds, *Indian and Foreign Review* 24(10) March 15, p 10-12+

Manmohan, 1986, Danger in the air, *Hindustan Times* (Managzine), December 14, p 1, col 1-6+

Mansingh, Surjit, 1985, Rajiv Gandhi and Indo-American relations, *Mainstream* 24(9-10) November 2, p 49-53

Marakkar, V.P., 1989, Rajiv Gandhi and the working class, *Indian worker* 38(8) November 20, p 2-3

Mathur, Girish, 1985, The first 100 days in office, *Link* 27(27) Feburary 10, p 6-8

Mathur, Girish, 1986, How Prime Minister contains Congress unrest, *Link* 28(31) March 9, p 4-7

Mathur, Girish, 1986, Why PM shouldn't let party drift to split, *Link* 28(37) April 20, p 10-12

Mishra, Chaturanan, 1989, Rajiv Gandhi policies on Perestroika, *New Age* 37(2) January 8, p 8

Mishra, Chaturanan, 1989, Rajiv's promises and performance, *New Age* 37(40) October 1, p 1+

Mitra, Anirudhya, 1991, A formidable group, *India Today* June 30, p 46, col 1-2

Mitra, Ashok, 1989, Rajiv's reform agenda: Fulfilling the mother's dream, *Times of India*, July 3, p 6, col 3-5

Mitra, Chandam, 1989, A CAG-tag opposition: Neutralising Rajiv's populsim, *Times of India*, July 26, p 6, col 3-5

Mitra, Chandam, 1989, The odds get longer: Rajiv Gandhi after black Sunday, *Times of India*, January 24, p 6, col 3-5

Mitra, Chandam, 1989, Rajiv Gandhi moves up: Congress takes the offensive, *Times of India*, May 29, p 6, col 3-4

Mitra Chaudhury, Srerupa, 1991, Rajiv Gandhi: Vikas ki Aandhi, *Democratic World* 20(20) May 19, p 6, col 2

MItra, Sumit, 1992, Rajiv Gandhi: A dream made and unmade, *India Express* (Magazine), p 1, col 1-7

Mukarji, Nirmal, 1989, Decentralisation below State level: Need for new system of governance, *Economic and Political Weekly* March 4

Mukerji, Debashish, 1991, Power paralysis: Amethi yearns for the return of Rajiv as Prime Minister, *The Week* April 28, p 28-39

Mukherjee, Sadhan, 1986, Rajiv blues over Tripathi non-revolt, *New Age* 34(22), June 8, p 1

Mukherjee, Pranab, 1985, The Leader of the House and the whips in U.K. and India, *Journal of Parliamentary Information* December, p 598-604

Mukhopadhyay Ashim, 1986, Rajiv's gift to West Bengal, *India Express*

(Magazine), October 12, p 1, col 1-8+
Mumbal, Brihan, 1989, Maximum democracy and maximum devolution, *Mahanagarpalika Patrika* 36(6) August, p 2-6
Murthy, Sachidananda, 1991, Could SPG have saved Rajiv? *The Week* June 9, p 40-41
Murthy, Sachidananda, 1991, Power at hand, *The Week* Febuary, p 28-31
N.C., 1985 The chastening time, *Mainstream* 23(52) August 24, p 1-4
N.C., 1985, Chinks in the armour, *Mainstream* 23(49) August 3, p 1-2
Naik, J.A., 1980, India that Rajiv may inherit, *Janata* 35(41) December 7, p 6+
Naik, Subhakarrao, 1992, Rajiv: The innovator, *National Herald* (Supplement), p 20, col 1-3
Nalapai, M.D., 1992, The révolution unborn, *National Herald* (Supplement), p 14, col 1-6
Namboodripad, E.M.S., 1984, Will Rajiv Gandhi explain his stand: An open letter to Rajiv Gandhi, *People's Democracy* 8(52) December 23, p 7
Namboodripad, E.M.S., 1988, Rajiv Gandhi in his true colours, *People's Democracy* 12(15) August 10, p 1+
Nandy, Pritish, 1986, The men who tried to kill Rajiv Gandhi, *Illustrated Weekly of India* 107(27) July 6, p 8-17
Nandy, Pritish, 1986, Yesterday, tomorrow, *Illustrated Weekly of India* 107(2) January 12, p 8-17
Nandy, Pritish, 1989, The face-off at Amethi, *Illustrated Weekly of India*, 110(42) October 15, p 10-19
Nandy, Pritish, 1991, Stability and economic liberalism: Rajiv's new slogans, *Illustrated Weekly of India* (Supplement) 112(12) March 23, p 1
Narsimha Rao, P.V., 1992, A crusader for change, *National Herald* (Supplement), p 3, col 1-6
Nayar, Kuldip, 1981, Is Rajiv Gandhi really native? *Sunday* 9(25) December 6, p 13
Nayar, Kuldip, 1985, Rajiv Gandhi's 200 days, *Tribune*, July 25
New Age (Periodical), 1980, Rajiv vs Maneka: Palace intrigues, *New Age* 28(32) August 10, p 1+
New Age (Periodical), 1984, Pious platitudes, *New Age* 32(47) November 18, p 2, editorial
New Age (Periodical), 1984, Rajiv refrain, *New Age* 32(52) December 23, p 2, editoral
New Age (Periodical), 1985, Disturbing pronoucements, *New Age* 33(28) July 14, p 1, editorial
New Age (Periodical), 1985, Struggle for National unity, *New Age* 33(28) July 14, p 2, editorial
Nihal Singh, S., 1988, PM's propsoed China visit: Symbolism and substance, *Times of India*, May 28, p 6, col 3-5
Nihal Singh S., 1988, Rajiv and Govt battered: But oppostition fail to make gain, *Times of India*, May 10, p 6, col 3-5
Ninah, Sevanti, 1985, Rajiv's discovery of Bharat, *Indian Economics* (Magazine), October 20, p 1, col 1-8

Nizamuddin, D.E., 1980, Changing guard, *Sunday* 8(18) December 7, p 66

Nizamuddin, D.E., 1981, Rajiv looking after Punjab, *Sunday* 9(22) September 21, p 66

Nizamuddin, D.E., 1981, Rajiv tastes infighting, *Sunday* 9(15) September 21, p 66

Nizamuddin, D.E., 1982, Rajiv: A quarter person, *Sunday* 9(5) June 12, p 58

Noorani, A.G., 1988, Rajiv Gandhi: Immage and reality, *Indian Express* (Magazine), June 5, p 1, col 1-8

Noorani, A.G., 1988, Rajiv Gandhi's political invectives, *Indian Express* (Magazine), October 17

Nungent, Nicholas, 1990, Rajiv Gandhi: Son of a dynasty, *Tribune* (Magazine), November 25, p 1, col 1-7+

Oomen, T.K., 1987, Charisma and not king emperor, *Times of India*, January 22, p 8, col 7-8

Organiser (Periodical), 1985, PM's demagogy, *Organiser* 36(52) May 12, p 1+, editorial

Organiser (Periodical), 1985, Political pot-boiling, *Organiser* 36(43) March 10, p 3, editorial

Organiser (Periodical), 1988, PM's progress, *Organiser* 39(46) May 8, p 3, editorial

Padgaonkar, Dileep, 1990 The Congress will not deviate from secularism: An interview, *Times of India*, September 9, p 1, col 1-8.

Padmakumar, K., 1986, Politics of Rajiv Gandhi, *Mainstream* 24(33) April 19, p 31-33

Pandit, Tushar, 1991, A day with Rajiv, *Sunday* June 9-June 15, p 74

Panigrahi, Chintamani, 1992, Racing aganist time, *National Herald* (Supplement), p 8, col 4-6

Panja, Ajit Kumar, 1992, Facing challenges in Rajiv spirit, *National Herald* (Supplement), p 20, col 4-6

Parakal, Pauly V., 1987, Destabilisation cannot be fought Rajiv style, *New Age* 35(17) April 26, p 1-2

Parakal, Pauly V., 1987, Stark reality refutes Rajiv Gandhi's claims, *New Age* 35(5) Feburary 1, p 1

Parakal, Pauly V., 1988, Rajiv Gandhi's drive for one party rule, *New Age* 36(7) Feburary 14, p 1+

Parakal, Pauly V., 1988, Rajiv Gandhi in same old style, *New Age* 37(50) December 17, p 1+

Parakal, Pauly V., 1991, Rajiv Gandhi biggest destabiliser around, *New Age* 39(12), March 24, p 1, col 1-5

Parimoo, J.N., 1986, Virk's lawyers for dismissal of charge, *Times of India*, March 13, p 16, col 1-4

Parsai, K.B., 1981, What does the future hold for Rajiv? *Weekend Review* 2(14) January, p 2+

Parthasarthy, G., 1982, Rajiv to go to USSR with PM, *Indian Express*, September 5, p 9

People's Democracy (Periodical), 1985, Rajiv's threat of emergency, *People's Democracy* 9(28) July 14, p 1-2+, editorial

Pramar, Suresh K., 1991, Rajiv Gandhi's death orphans tribals, *Onlooker* June 15, p 46-47

Prasannan, R., 1991, Bond of blood, *The Week* April 28, p 36, col 1-3

Prasannan, R., 1991, The driving force, *The Week* April 28, p 31

Prasannan, R., 1991, Winning hand, *The Week* April 28, p 28-31+

Puri, Anjali, 1986, What's a nice kid like you donig in politics? *Indian Express* (Magazine), October 26, p 1, col 1-8+

Puri, Rajinder, 1981, Fighting Rajiv, *Hindustan Times*, June 3, p 9

Raghavan, C., 1991, A challenging role, *Frontline* June 22-July 5, p 29

Rahul Singh, 1986, Does Rajiv Gandhi still have anything to smile about? *Indian Express* (Magazine), November 2, p 1, col 1-8

Rai, Kalpanath, 1981, Rajiv has earned his place in politics, *Blitz*, June 13, p 4

Raina, Ashok, 1991, Need he have died? *Hindustan Times* (Sunday Magazine), June 2, p 2, col 1-8

Raina, Jay, 1991, Rajiv allays minorities apprehension, *Hindustan Times*, May 14, p 1, col 4+

Ram, N., 1991, Rajiv had little time: Interview with Jyoti Basu, *Frontline* 8(12) June 8-June 21, p 113-115

Rama Sarma, K.V.S., 1992, Man of destiny, *National Herald* (Supplement), p 5 vol 1-3

Raman, R., 1986, Rajiv in blunderland, *Indian Express* (Magazine), March 16, col 1-8+

Ramamurthy, Vazhapadi, K., 1992, An eminent Parliamentarian, *National Herald* (Supplement), p 18, col 1-4

Razdan, Deepak, 1991, Rajiv's oppoent for Govt of poor, *Hindustan Times*, May 7, p 9, col 1-2

Razi, Syed Sibtey, 1992, Rajiv Bhaiya: A man of the people, *National Herald* (Supplement), p 6, col 1-5

Reddy, G.K., 1987, PM retains image despite shortcomings, *Hindu*, January 1

Reddy, Pratap C., 1992, Rajiv's injection for high-tech medicare, *National Herald* (Supplement), p 12, col 5-6

Roy, Bhaskar, 1991, Ambiguous stand, *India Today* March 31, p 29-31

Roy Chowdhury, Nanda Dulal, 1991, Rajiv Gandhi: Can he provide a stable alternative? *Sunday* March 24-March 30, p 4, letter to editior

Roy, Bunker, 1985, For Prime Minister, a word of advice, *Mainstream* (Speical Number) 23(38) March 9, p 16-18

Rustamji, K.F., 1988, Good Morning India, *Illustrated Weekly of India* 109(30) July 24, p 20-21

S.V., 1985, Well-don, *Mainstream* 23(43) June 22, p 1-3

Saari, Anil, 1981, Rajiv snubs UP CM, *Sunday* 9(25) December 6, p 37

Sahay, Subodh Kant, 1991, Rajiv had been warned often, *India Today* June 15, p 46, col 1-2

Sahay, Vikant, 1986, Politics of Rajiv Gandhi: Measuring up to our expectations, *Mainstream* 24(29) March 22, p 28+

Sahni, Ajai and Dwivedi, S.K., 1991, The Bungler! *Surya India* April, p 22-23+

Sanghvi, Vir, 1991, Encounters with Rajiv Gandhi, *Sunday* June 9-June 15, p

18-28

Sanghvi, Vir, 1991, The odd couple: Rajiv Gandhi and Chandra Shekhar: What went wrong? *Sunday* March 17-March 23, p 35-42

Santosh Kumar, V.K., 1991, Last moment: A forensic view,*The Week* June 9, p 34-35

Satinder Singh, 1980, Rajiv to enter politics, *Tribune*, August 3

Satyanarayan Reddy, B., 1992, A messiah of down trodden, *National Herald* (Supplement), p 18, col 6

Scindia, Madhavrao, 1992, Progressive to the core, *National Herald* (Supplement), p 5, col 4-6+

Sengupta, Barun, 1980, And now, Rajiv, *Sunday* 8(3) July 27, p 35

Sengupta, Bhabhani, 1985, The year of living dangerously, *Indian Express* (Magaizne), November 3, p 1, col 1-8+

Sengupta, Bhabani, 1986, First year as Prime Minister, *Statesman* January 16

Sengupta, Bhabani, 1987, The fourth year, *Economic and Political Weekly* December 12

Sengupta, Bhabani, 1988, Rajiv Gandhi and his forty horses, *Economic and Political Weekly* May 7

Sengupta, Bhabani, 1988, Poised for peace, *India Today* Janary 15

Sengupta, Bhabani, 1989, The master and the novice, *Seminar* 363, November, p 31-34

Seth, N.K., 1988, Commentary: PM's office, *Mainstream* 26(25) April 2, p 3

Sethi, J.D., 1985, A year of Rajiv Gandhi, *Indian Express*, October 25

Sethi, J.D., 1988, All the PM's men, *Illustrated Weekly of India* 109(4) January 24, p 32-35

Sharan, R.H., 1986-1987, Prime Minister of India: The role of personality and social forces, *Calcutta Journal of Political Studies* 6(1-2), p 1-28, bibliography, footnotes

Sharma, Vasudev, 1981, Five star future for Rajiv: Golden era for Rajiv, *Current*, June 13, p 1+

Sheorey, W.G., 1985, Rajiv has wiped out the Congress (I) alones with the Opposition, *Organiser* 36(43) March 10, p 6

Shukla, Rajiv, 1990, Good bye? Can Rajiv Gandhi continue as Congress President? *Sunday* February 25-March 3, p 67+

Shukla, Rajiv, 1991, After Rajiv who? *Sunday* June 2-June 8, p 54-57

Shukla, Rajiv, 1991, Does Rajiv want out? *Sunday* January 13-January 19, p 30-35+

Shurygin, Veniamin, 1989, Rajiv Gandhi: A political profile, *Mainstream* 26(35) June 11, p 31-34

Sidhva, Shiraj, 1991, The letter bomb: Jagmohan accuses Rajiv Gandhi of misleading the nation over Kashmir, *Sunday* May 5-May 11, p 7

Sidhva, Shiraj, 1991, The Sonia enigma: The public loss of a private person, *Sunday* June 2-June 8, p 40

Silver, D.M., 1981, Indira's Rajiv gamble, *Onlooker* 43(10) June 15, p 20-22

Singhal, M.M., 1985, PM on test, *Mainstream* 23(38) May 18, p 11

Sood, Upendra, 1992, Rajiv gave his today for our tomorrow, *National Herald*

(Magazine) p 3, col 6

Southern Economist (Periodical), 1981, The Rajiv factor, *Southern Economist* 20(2) May 15, p 1-2, editiorial

Southern Economist (Periodical), 1984, The new dispensation, *Southern Economist* 23(14) November 15, p 1-2, editorial

Southern Economist (Periodical), 1985, Rajiv Gandhi at the helm, *Southern Economist* 23(19), Feburary 1, p 1-2, editorial

Sriman, R., 1992, Indian sports will always miss Rajiv, *National Herald* (Supplement), p 17, col 5-6

Srinivasan, S., 1984, Mr Prime Minister: Are you listening? *Indian Express* (Magazine), November 25, p 3, col 1-8

Subramaniam, Vidya, 1988, Will Rajiv Gandhi stand from Amethi? *Indian Express* (Magazine), November 6, p 1, col 1-8+

Surendra Mohan, 1985, Rajiv Gandhi on stump, *Janata*, 40(95) March 10, p 7-8

Surendra Mohan, 1987, The Prime Ministers outbrust, *Janata* 44(10) May 7, p 9-10

Suresh Chandra, 1986, Rajiv Gandhi and the red-tape, *Economic Times*, March 11, p 5, col 7-8

Surjeet, H.K., 1991, If Rajiv manages to maintain his present position, it will be a big achievement, *Indian Express*, June 15, p 12, col 1-3

Suroor, Hasan, 1991, At close quarters: B.G. Deshmukh recalls Rajiv days, *Frontline* 8(12) June 8-June 21, p 117

Suroor, Hasan, 1991, The man and the leader, *Frontline* 8(12) June 8-June 21, p 116

Suri, Surinder, 1985, Presidential Prime Minister: New trends in Indian politics, *Times of India*, November 30, p 8, col 3-5

Swarup, H., 1985, Rajiv Gandhi's triumphant visit to the dragon kingdom, *Indian and Foreign Review* 22(24) October 15, p 9-11+

Taban, Ghulam Rabbani, 1991, Post-Rajiv situation, *Mainstream* 29(34) June 15, p 19

Taksal, Vinod, 1985, Rajiv's timely initiatives, *Link* 27(36) April 21, p 28

Thakur, Janardan, 1986, Whoever spoke ill of Rajiv Gandhi? *Times of India* (Sunday Review), June 8, p 1, col 1-4

Thakur, Janardan, 1988, Rajiv Gandhi's discovery of rural India, *Hindustan Times* (Magazine), June 12, p 6, col 1-8+

Thakur, Rameshwar, 1992, Rajiv Gandhi: Visionary of New India, *National Herald* (Magazine), May 24, p 1, col 1-6

Thapar, Rajiv, 1985, Who is Rajiv protecting, *Economic and Political Weekly* 20(6) February 9, p 220-221

Thapar, Romesh, 1984, The Rajiv Party and the Hindus, *Economic and Political Weekly* 19(50) December 15, p 2105

Thapar, Romesh, 1985, Rajiv's Bharat Mata, *Economic and Political Weekly* 20(41) October 12, p 1723

Thapar, Romesh, 1986, A Damaged image, *Economic and Political Weekly* 21(49) December 6, p 2113

Times of India (Newspaper), 1980, Rajiv Gandhi, *Times of India*, August 16, col

1-2, editorial

Times of India (Newspaper), 1981, Misuse of office, *Times of India*, November 12, p 8, col 1-2, editorial

Times of India (Newspaper), 1982, Dangers of sycophancy, *Times of India*, February 5, p 8, col 1-2, editorial

Times of India (Newspaper), 1983, Rajiv's tasks, *Times of India*, May 20, p 8, col 1-2, editorial

Times of India (Newspaper), 1984, A clarion call, *Times of India* Novmber 14, p 8, col 1-2, editiorial

Times of India (Newspaper), 1984, Not by mollycoddling, *Times of India* May 1, p 8, col 1-2, editorial

Times of India (Newspaper), 1984, Mr Rajiv Gandhi, *Times of India*, November 3, p 6, col 1-2, editorial

Times of India (Newspaper), 1984, To the hustings, *Times of India*, November 15, p 8, col 1-2, editorial

Times of India (Neswpaper), 1985, After the mandate, *Times of India*, January 8, p 8, col 1-2, editorial

Times of India (Newspaper), 1985, A blunt instrument, *Times of India*, February 23, p 8, col 1-2, editorial

Times of India, (Newspaper), 1985, Mr Gandhi's odyssey, *Times of India*, October 30, p 8, col 1-2, editorial

Times of India (Newspaper), 1985, A new work ethic, *Times of India*, January 12, p 8, col 1-2, editorial

Times of India (Newspaper), 1985, PM darshan, *Times of India*, September 11, p 8, col 1-2, editorial

Times of India (Newspaper), 1985, Praise with purpose, *Times of India*, October 2, p 8, col 1-2, editorial

Times of India (Newspaper), 1985, War on India, *Times of India*, May 15, p 8, col 1-2, editorial

Times of India (Newspaper), 1985, On the wrong track, *Times of India*, November 25, p 8, col 1-2, editorial

Times of India (Newspaper), 1986, Issue is joined, *Times of India*, September 26, p 8, col 1-2, editorial

Times of India (Newspaper), 1986, An unresolved crisis, *Times of India*, April 14, p 8, col 1-2, editorial

Times of India (Newspaper), 1987, Anti Rajiv campaigns, *Times of India*, September 25, p 6, col 1-2, editorial

Times of India (Newspaper), 1987, Appeal to the President, *Times of India*, May 14, p 6, col 1-2, edtiorial

Times of India (Newspaper), 1987, Confrontation is on, *Times of India*, May 14, p 6, col 1-2, edtiorial

Times of India (Newspaper), 1987, No comfort for Giani, *Times of India*, January 28, p 7, col 1-2, editorial

Times of India (Newspaper), 1987, PM on growth, *Times of India*, January 28, p 7, col 1-2, editorial

Times of India (Newspaper), 1987, Rajiv versus V.P. Singh, *Times of India*, March

27, p 6, col 1-2, editorial

Times of India (Newspaper), 1987, Seeds of trouble, *Times of India*, May 5, p 6, col 1-2, editorial

Times of India (Newspaper), 1988, In a combative mood, *Times of India*, May 5, p 6, col 1-2, editorial

Times of India (Newspaper), 1988, The PM's trip, *Times of India*, April 19, p 6, col 1-2, editorial

Times of India (Newspaper), 1988, Rajiv Gandhi to blame, *Times of India*, February 25, p 6, col 1-2, editiorial

Times of India (Newspaper), 1988, State of the Nation, *Times of India*, August 16, p 4, col 1-2, editorial

Times of India (Newsparper), 1991, Best of both worlds, *Times of India*, Feburary 27, p 8, col 1-2, editorial.

Tripathi, Salil, 1986, Can the Prime Minister ever be safe? *Indian Express* (Magazine), October 18, p 1, col 1-8+

Tripahti, Srinivas, 1988, Prime Miniter fighting shy of visit to Amethi, *New Age* 36(40), October 2, p 1+

Tulasi Daas, Majji, 1992, The pride of the Nation, *National Herald* (Supplement), p 7, col 2-3

Tully, Mark and Masani, Zaheer, 1988, The Rajiv years, *Illustrated Weekly of India* 109(20) May 15, p 32-33

Unnikrishnan, K.P., 1991, I don't see Rajiv crossing 175-180 seats, *India Today* June 15, p 13, col 1-3

Vazeeruddin, Mohammad, 1985, Piloting the country, *Tribune*, August 18, p 1, col 1-8

Verghese, B.G., 1988, Getting more with less, *Indian Express*, March 10

Verma, Kewal, 1986, Rajiv Gandhi and secularism: Lessons from Muslim Women Bill debate, *Mainstream* 24(38) May 24, p 51-53+

Verma, Shrikant, 1985, An insider's view, *Illustrated Weekly of India* 106(31) December 8, p 38-39

Vidyadharan, Arvind, 1986, Rajiv's India, *Illustrated Weekly of India* 107(9) March 2, p 38-39

Vikramaditya, 1984, Will Mr Rajiv Gandhi be a better Prime Minister? *Commerce* 149(3834) November 24, p 814+

Viswam, S., 1984, Rajiv Gandhi faces history, *Mainstream* 23(14) December 1, p 7-10+

Wariavwalla, Bharat, 1984, A dynastic democracy, *Illustrated Weekly of India* 105(33) December 23, p 34-35

Warier, K.U., 1989, Rajiv Gandhi appeasing communalism: Daji, *New Age* 37(23) June 4, p 5

Zakaria, Rafiq, 1986, How strong is Rajiv? *Illustrated Weekly of India* 107(45) November 16, p 10-15

Gandhi, Rajiv: Activities

Anon, 1981, Rajiv calls to fulfil mission, *Hindustan Times*, December 15, p 3

Anon, 1991, Rajiv Gandhi's Bharat Darshan, *Democratic World* 20(21) May 26,

p 5

Gandhi, Rajiv: Address

See Prime Minister: Geographical Area: India: Gandhi, Rajiv Address

Gandhi, Rajiv: Apparels

Anon, 1991, CBI told to handover Rajiv's clothes, *Hindustan Times*, July 18, p 7, col 5

Anon, 1991, Sonia Counsel gets Rajiv's shoes, socks, *Hindustan Times*, June 18, p 9, col 5-6

Anon, 1991, Sonia wants Rajiv's sneakers, *Hindustan Times*, June 13, p 8, col 1

Gandhi, Rajiv: Assassination

See Assassination: Attempts and Probes: Gandhi, Rajiv

Gandhi, Rajiv: Biographical Sketch

Abbas, K.A., 1982, We will muddle thru, *Blitz*, January 9, p 24

Akbar, M.J., 1981, Better drawn, *Sunday* 9(2) Jnue 28, p 8

Anon, 1944, Grandson born to Pandit Nehru, *Hindustan Times*, August 21, p 1

Anon, 1981, Clean going places? *Sunday* 9(3) July 5, p 6

Anon, 1981, Eye-catchers, *India Today* 6(3) October 15, p 176

Anon, 1981, In Rajiv's raj, *Current*, July 4, p 4

Anon, 1981, No time yet for Rajiv to accept post: No more yet to nominate Rajiv, *Hindustan Times*, October 22, p 1-16

Anon, 1981, Rajiv and family dragged in, *Blitz*, January 3, p 3

Anon, 1981, Rajiv Gandhi: A calendar of events and stances, *Sunday* 9(24) November 29, p 18-19

Anon, 1981, Rajiv's man, *Indian Observer* 22(23) December 1, p 9

Anon, 1981, When the Rajiv wind blows, these heads will roll, 21, *Current*, May 23, p 1

Anon, 1982, Nehru dynasty: Rajiv Gandhi or Arun Nehru? *Blitz*, May 22, p 12-14

Anon, 1982, Stuff to choose from, *Delhi Recorder* 3(3) April 15-May 14, p 8

Azad, Ghulam Babi, 1980, Rajiv: An asset, *Current*, December 6, p 9

Devendrea Mohan, 1981, Rajiv the man to watch, *Biltz*, May 30, p 14

Gargi, Balwant, 1982, Rajiv Gandhi: A politician without hang-ups, *Illustrated Weekly of India* 103(2) January 30, p 12-13

Jain, Madhu, 1981, The family, *Sunday* 9(24) November 29, p 14

Jang, Bina, 1981, No babe in the woods, *Probe India* 3(5) July, p 20

Kalhan, Promila, 1980, A quite, young man in politics, *Hindustan Times*, October 27

Karanjia, R.K., 1976, The Nehrus: Father and dauguther, *Illustrated Weekly of India* 97(46) November 14, p 6-19

Karlekar, Hiranmay, 1981, Rajiv: The politics of dynastic succession, *Sunday Standard*, June 21, p 1

Khanna, K.C., 1982: Year of Rajiv Gandhi, *Illustrated Weekly of India* 103(2)

January 30, p 8-11

Nihal Singh, S., 1982, All of India is a stage, *Indian Express*, April 21, p 6

Silver, D.M., 1981, Mind of Rajiv Gandhi: Think Indian, think big, *Onlooker* 43(10) June 15, p 23-25

Singh, Khushwant, 1976, Man who gets the things done, *Illustrated Weekly of India* 97(33) August 15, p 6-15

Venkatraman, R., 1991, Rajiv excelled Nehru, *Hindustan Times*, July 3, p 1

Gandhi, Rajiv: Comparison with Hussain, Saddam

Anon, 1991, Rajiv going the Saddam way, *Orgainser* 42(32) March 17, p 1, col 3-4+

Gandhi, Rajiv: Denials regarding Misuse of Official Machinery

Anon, 1981, Rajiv denies misuse of offical machinery, *Hindustan Times*, May 22, p 1+

Gandhi, Rajiv: Election Appeal

Anon, 1982, Rajiv appeal to the people, *Times of India* May 6, p 7

Anon, 1982, Rajiv asks people of vote for Congress (I), *Times of India*, May 15, p 13

Gandhi, Rajiv: Election Campaign

Ajay Kumar, 1989, PM: New fiza in favour of Congress, *Times of India*, November 18, p 1, col 1-2, news-item

Anon, 1981, Poll campaign for Rajiv begins, *Sunday Standard*, May 10, p 1

Anon, 1982, Campaigning Rajiv style, *Weekend Review* 3(10) May 29, p 7

Anon, 1982, Rajiv in Harayana, *Sunday* 9(48) March 22, p 13

Anon, 1982, Rajiv's hectic poll tour from May 11, *Amrit Bazar Patrika*, May 6, p 7

Anon, 1982, Rajiv seeks votes for H.P. progress, *Hindustan Times* , May 8, p 16

Anon, 1982, Rajiv starts poll tour in State today, *Amrit Bazar Patrika*, May 11, p 7

Anon, 1982, Rajiv to launch mass contact drive in Nagpur, *Times of India*, September 8, p 9

Lamba, Asjeet, 1981, Rajiv campaign, *India Today* 6(24) December 31, p 4

Gandhi, Rajiv: Election: Campaigning Style

Bhattacharjee, Manindra, 1987, Rajiv's hysterical campaign style cost Congress (I) dear in West Bengal, *Organiser* 39(2) May 31, p 5+

Gandhi, Rajiv: Election Cliches

Anon, 1982, Rajiv hits out at LD-BJP alliance, *Amrit Bazar Patrika*, May 7, p 7

Anon, 1982, Rajiv criticises LD-BJP alliance, *Times of India*, May 15, p 7

Anon, 1982, Rajiv lashes out at BJP-LD poll alliance, *Times of India*, May 7, p 7

Anon, 1982, Rajiv sure of Congress (I) Government in West Bengal, *Hindustan*

Times, May 13, p 4, news-items

Anon, 1991, Prices, stability main issues: Rajiv, *Hindustan Times*, March 28, p 9, col 1-4, news-item

Anon, 1991, Rajiv accuses NF, BJP of dividing country, *Hindustan Times*, April 19, p 1, col 1-3

Anon, 1991, Rajiv calls for stable Govt, *Hindustan Times*, April 16, p 7, col 2-3; *Hindustan Times*, April 18, p 5, col 4

Anon, 1991, Rajiv pledges stable Govt, *Hindustan Times*, May 11, p 12, col 2-4

Chadha, Kumkum, 1991, BJP is main enemy: Rajiv, *Hindustan Times*, March 28, p 1, col 1-4+, news-item

Chakravarti, Prithvis, 1989, Elections: Rajiv's three pronged propaganda strategy, *Radical Humanist* 53(3) June, p 8-18

Gandhi, Rajiv, 1982, 160 Bengal seats for Congress (I), *Hindustan Times*, May 12, p 8

Gandhi, Rajiv, 1982, Congress (I) sure to win in West Bengal, *Amrit Bazar Patrika*, May 13, p 7

Mitra Chaudhury, Srerupa, 1991, Rajiv Gandhi: Vikas ki Aandhi, *Democratic World* 20(20) May 19, p 6, col 2

Prasannan, R., 1991, JD (S) will disappear: Rajiv Gandhi promises better contact with the masses, *The Week* April 28, p 32-33, news-item

Gandhi, Rajiv: Election to Lok Sabha

Anon, 1981, Rajiv and Begum Abida returned to Lok Sabha, *Hindu*, June 16, p 1

Anon, 1981, Rajiv for Lok Sabha? *Amrit Bazar Patrika*, May 9, p 1

Anon, 1981, Rajiv Gandhi: The triumph, *Surya India* 5(10) July, p 77

Anon, 1981, Rajiv Gandhi wins by record margin, *Hindustan Times*, June 16, p 1

Anon, 1989, Rajiv Gandhi, V.P. Singh elected, *Hindustan Times*, Novmebr 30; *Times of India*, November 30

Lamba, A., 1981, Rajiv Gandhi to fight Amethi seat, *Amrit Bazar Patrika*, May 12, p 1

Gandhi, Rajiv: Entry into Political Arena

Anon, 1980, AIFC asks Rajiv to join politics, *Times of India*, September 3

Anon, 1980, Antulay requests Rajiv to join politics, *Times of India*, August 13

Anon, 1980, Darbara Singh and Bhajan Lal meet Rajiv Gandhi, *Statesman*, August 28

Anon, 1980, Dhawan going down: Rajiv's entry certain, *Sunday Standard*, November 30, p 1

Anon, 1980, Mrs. Gandhi leaves it to Rajiv, *Statesman*, August 8

Anon, 1980, Goodbye to IAC, *Blitz*, July 26, p 3

Anon, 1980, More support for Rajiv Gandhi, *Statesman*, August 8

Anon, 1980, Pressure builds up on Rajiv Gandhi, *Statesman*, August 11

Anon, 1980, Rajiv Gandhi opposed to contesting by-election, *Statesman*, September 16

Anon, 1980, Rajiv makes his bow, *Indian Express*, August 2

Anon, 1980, Rajiv to quit IA, enter politics, *Times of India*, July 31

Anon, 1980, Rajiv urged to enter politics, *Sunday Standard*, June 29, p 5

Anon, 1980, Rajiv urged to enter public life, *National Herald*, July 31

Anon, 1980, Waiting for Rajiv, *Statesman*, October 30

Anon, 1981, Rajiv Gandhi to be projected in Kisan Rally, *Statesman*, February 12

Anon, 1981, Rajiv has arrived, *Blitz*, January 24, p 17

Anon, 1981, Rajiv's silence delays decision on candidates, *Hindu*, May 6, p 9

Anon, 1981, Rajiv to assume more responsibility, *Times of India*, December 31, p 1

Gupta, O., 1980, Power equation after Kamlapati, *Onlooker* December 15, p 10-17

Kumar, D.P., 1980, Rajiv Gandhi may join Party in October, *Statesman*, September 28

Satinder Singh, 1980, Rajiv to enter politics, *Tribune*, August 3

Gandhi, Rajiv: Foundation

See Rajiv Gandhi Foundation

Gandhi, Rajiv: Hobbies

Anon, 1982, Lords of the skies, *Sunday* 9(40) March 27, p 30-31

Kalhan, Promila, 1991, A child who loved aeroplanes, *Hindustan Times* (Magazine), June 2, p 4, col 1-8

Gandhi, Rajiv: Homage Paid by Him

See under the name of the person e.g. Jagjivan Ram: Homage Paid by Gandhi Rajiv

Gandhi, Rajiv: Homage Paid to Him

Anon, 1991, Bengal House pays tributes to Rajiv, *Hindustan Times*, July 20, p 10, col 5

Anon, 1991, Cherishing a Rajiv memento, *Hindustan Times*, May 30, p 8, col 4

Anon, 1991, Condolence messages continue to pour in, *Hindustan Times*, May 28, p 5, col 4-5

Anon, 1991, Farewell: India mourns a decent man, *Sunday* June 2-June 8, p 4-11

Anon, 1991, A Helmerian tribute to Rajiv Gandhi, *Bulletin of the Association of Scientific Workers of India* 21(7) July, p 97-100

Anon, 1991, Ideals of Rajiv called, *Hindustan Times*, June 16, p 7, col 4

Anon, 1991, Leaders recall fine qualities of Rajiv, *Hindustan Times*, June 2, p 7, col 4-7

Anon, 1991, Pledge to complete Rajiv tasks, *Hindustan Times*, May 31, p 6, col 6-8.

Anon, 1991, Rajiv: Voice of sanity lost, *Hindustan Times*, May 30, p 5, col 1-3

Anon, 1991, Rajya Sabha Session today: Elders to pay tributes to Rajiv, Dange, *Hindustan Times*, June 3, p 1, col 5-7, news-item

Anon, 1991, Rich tributes paid to Rajiv, *Hindustan Times*, May 28, p , col 6-8

Anon, 1991, Sad farewell from Delhi, *Hindustan Times*, May 28, p 1, col 5-7

Anon, 1991, A sombre affair at station, *Hindustan Times*, May 28, p 3, col 1-3

Anon, 1991, Tributes to Rajiv by MP House, *Hindustan Times*, June 27, p 5, col 6

Anon, 1991, UK House pays tributes to Rajiv, *Hindustan Times*, July 10, p 18, col 5

Anon, 1992, Briton's tribute to Rajiv, *Hindustan Times*, May 23, p 13, col 1

Anon, 1992, Capital remembers Rajiv, *Times of India*, May 22, p 11, col 3

Anon, 1992, China pays glowing tributes to Rajiv, *Patriot*, May 23, p 1, col 1

Anon, 1992, China pays homage to Rajiv, *Indian Express*, May 23, p 2, col 6-8

Anon, 1992, Devotional songs at Rajiv Samadhi, *National Herald*, May 22, p 10, col 1-2

Anon, 1992, Nation pays homage to Rajiv, *Indian Express*, May 22, p 1, col 5-7+; *Statesman*, May 22, p 1, col 2-3

Anon, 1992, PM pays homage, *Times of India*, May 22, p 3, col 1-2

Anon, 1992, Pledge to eradicate terrorism, *Indian Express*, May 22, p 4, col 2-5

Anon, 1992, Rajiv remembered with heavy heart, *National Herald*, May 22, p 1, col 4-5

Anon, 1992, Rooting out terrorism best tribute to Rajiv, *National Herald*, May 22, p 3, col 6-8

Anon, 1992, Tree plantation in memory of Rajiv Gandhi, *Tribune*, May 22, p 16, col 7

Anon, 1992, Tributes paid to Rajiv Gandhi in UK, *Times of India*, May 23, p 9, col 7-8

Anon, 1992, Vajpayee's tribute to Rajiv, *Hindustan Times*, May 20, p 24, col 1

Anon, 1992, Yasser, Gayoom hail Rajiv, *National Herald*, May 22, p 10, col 3

Bachchan, Amitabh, 1991, My friend, Rajiv, *Illustrated Weekly of India* July 6-July 12, p 19

Ghosh, Soumya K. and Parsai, Gargi, 1991, Asthi special let off steam of emotions, *Hindustan Times*, May 26, p 1, col 4.

Malhotra, Inder, 1991, Remembering Rajiv, *Sunday* June 9-June 15, p 83

Roy, Bhaskar, 1991, An emotional farewell, *India Today* June 15, p 108, col 1-2

Wig, A.R., 1991, Delhi will miss Rajiv Gandhi, *Hindustan Times*, May 26, p 5, col 1-4

See also Condolence Messages on Death of Gandhi, Rajiv

Gandhi, Rajiv: Homage Paid to Jagjivan Ram

Anon, 1986, Homage paid to Jagjivan Ram, *Times of India*, July 7

Gandhi, Rajiv: Homage Paid to Raj Narain

Anon, 1987, Homage to Raj Narain, *Hindu*, January 1.

Gandhi, Rajiv: Italian Connection

Anon, 1988, V.P. Singh exposes PM's Italian connection, *Organiser* 39(43) April 10, p 13

Gandhi, Rajiv: Jyoti

See Rajiv Jyoti

Gandhi, Rajiv: Last Interview

Crossette, Barbara, 1981, The last interview: Minutes before the blast, *Frontline* 8(12) June 8-June 21, p 19-20

Gandhi, Rajiv: Marriage

See Gandhi, Rajiv: Wedding

Gandhi, Rajiv: Memorial Lecture

See Rajiv Memorial Lecture

Gandhi, Rajiv: Name Exploitation

Anon, 1981, Unauthorised slums in Rajiv's name, *Onlooker* 43(21) November 30, p 17-18

Gandhi, Rajiv: Photographs

Anon, 1991, A rare Rajiv photo, *Hindustan Times*, June 3, p 8, col 6-8

Gandhi, Rajiv: Policies

Anon, 1989, PM for time frame for IPKF pull out, *Sunday* July 5, news-item

Anon, 1991, Sonia will launch Rajiv campaign, *Hindustan Times*, April 25, p 10, col 12

Gandhi, Rajiv: Role as Member of Parliament

Anon, 1980, Rajiv goes to Parliament House, *Current*, August 23, p 4

Anon, 1981, Rajiv favours joint decisions, *Hindustan Times*, August 19, p 12

Anon, 1982, Big brother is no better, *Caravan* 1(725) August, p 42

Anon, 1982, PM reiterates stand on peace, n-disarmament: Gulf between rich, poor, dangerous, *Hindustan Times*, January 23, p 16

Anon, 1982, Praise for Rajiv, *Hindustan Times*, July 31, p 5

Anon, 1982, Rajiv stress on role of youths in economic order vital, *Hindustan Times*, January 25, p 1+

Bali, Yogendra, 1981, Politician with a difference, *Times of India*, June 9, p 1, 4

Bobb, Dilip, 1982, Rajiv Gandhi flying higher, *India Today* 7(4) February 28, p 16-17

Datta-Ray, Sunanda K., 1981, High-flier in politics justifying Rajiv Gandhi's birth right, *Statesman*, May 13

Nizamuddin, D.E., 1982, Rajiv Gandhi's show: Who will pay this bill? *Sunday* 9(37) March 6, p 58

Sengupta, Barun, 1980, Men who matter with the PM, *Sunday* 8(18) December 7, p 23

Gandhi, Rajiv: Role as Pilot

Anon, 1980, Goodbye to IAC, *Blitz*, July 26, p 3
Anon, 1980, Rajiv to quit IA, enter politics, *Times of India*, July 31
Anon, 1981, Rajiv makes up his mind, *Current*, October 18, p 4
Anon, 1982, Precept and practices: An experiment with untruth, *Caravan* 1(175) March 1, p 12
Mehta, A.H., 1981, No complaint against Rajiv, *Hindustan Times*, January 21, p 8
Niesewand, Peter, 1981, Indira without Sanjay: Rajiv no substitute, *Blitz*, September 20, p 20
Sharma, A.P., 1982, No Rajiv hand in IA appointment, *Hindustan Times*, March 5, p 16
Sharma, Udayan, 1981, World of Rajiv Gandhi, *Sunday* 9(24) November 29, p 12-13
Tellis, Olgax, 1981, Why isn't Rajiv leaving Airlines? *Sunday* 8(24) January 18, p 36-37

Gandhi, Rajiv: Role in Diverse Issues

Anon, 1982, Election time: Gandhi time, *Onlooker* 44(10) May 31, p 37
Anon, 1988, PM showed extraordinary interest: Dissenting role, *Times of India*, April 27, p 1, vol 6-8+
Anon, 1989, Rajiv Gandhi's plan for Planet Protection Fund to be considered, *Indian Express*, November 21; *Times of India*, November 21
Anon, 1991, PM, Rajiv Gandhi meet President, *Times of India* February 10
Anon, 1991, Rajiv calls for Dalit's uplift, *Hindustan Times*, April 15, p 1, col 1-2
Anon, 1991, Rajiv Gandhi calls for UNSC meeting on Gulf war, *Times of India*, February 8
Quershy, Ahtesham, 1981, Rajiv's bid to stop infighting, *Indian Express*, November 24, p 20
Ramalingam, N.K., 1980, Rajiv, Maneka must play active role, *Current*, July 12, p 10-11
Saari, Anil, 1981, Can Rajiv save the Nirankaris? *Sunday* 9(25) December 6, p 43-45
Sanghvi, Vir, 1991, The odd couple: Rajiv Gandhi and Chandra Shekhar: What went wrong? *Sunday* March 17-March 23, p 34-42

Gandhi, Rajiv: Tours: Foreign

Anon, 1985, PM's foreign tour plans unchanged, *Times of India*, May 16, p 1, col 1-3
Anon, 1988, Commentary: Thoughts on PM's foreign tour, *Mainstream* 26(41) July 23, p 3-4
Anon, 1988, PM leaves on foreign tour, *National Herald*, June 5
Anon, 1988, Prime Minister returns home, *National Herald*, June 13
Anon, 1988, Rajiv Gandhi meets world leaders, *Hindustan Times*, June 11
Inder Jit, 1985, Rajiv and his fourth mission, abroad, *Economic Times*, October 15, p 5, col 7-8

Rahul Singh, 1985, Around the world with Rajiv Gandhi, *Indian Express*, June 30, p 6, col 1-8

Gandhi, Rajiv: Tours: Foreign: Africa

Anon, 1986, Rajiv's crusade in black Africa, *Link* 28(42) May 25, p 7-8

Gandhi, Rajiv: Tours: Foreign: Algeria

Anon, 1985, Terroirists wanted to kill Rajiv in France or Algeria, *Times of India*, May 17, p 1, col 1-3

Gandhi, Rajiv: Tours: Foreign: Australia

Anon, 1986, PM postpones visit, *Telegraph*, January 2

Gandhi, Rajiv: Tours: Foreign: Bhutan

Swarup, H., 1985, Rajiv Gandhi's triumphant visit to the dragon kingdom, *Indian and Foreign Review* 22(24) October 15, p 9-11+

Gandhi, Rajiv: Tours: Foreign: China

Anon, 1981, Rajiv Gandhi to visit China, *Hindustan Times*, September 28, p 6

Anon, 1981, Rajiv to visit China, *Indian Express*, September 28, p 1

Anon, 1982, China team invites Rajiv, *National Herald*, May 1, p 12

Anon, 1988, PM calls on Deng, Zhao, *Hindustan Times*, December 22; *Times of India*, December 22

Anon, 1988, PM's China visit concludes, *Indian Express*, December 24; *Times of India*, December 24

Anon, 1988, Rajiv Gandhi in Beijing, *Hindustan Times*, December 20; *Statesman*, December 20

Anon, 1988, Rajiv Gandhi meets Chinese President, *Hindustan Times*, December 12; *Tribune*, December 12

Nihal Singh, S., 1998, PM's proposed China visit: Symbolism and substance, *Times of India*, May 28, p 6, col 3-5

S.C., 1988, Focus: Rajiv's China visit: Balance sheet, *Mainstream* 27(14) December 31, p 3-4

Sinha Bhattcharya, Mira, 1988, Mission to Beijing, *Hindustn Times* (Magazine), December 18, p 1, col 1-8

Gandhi, Rajiv: Tours: Foreign: France

Anon, 1985, Rajiv to visit US, France in June, *Times of India*, January 4, p 1, col 1-2+

Anon, 1985, Terrorists wanted to kill Rajiv in France or Algeria *Times of India*, May 17, p 1, col 1-3

Gandhi, Rajiv: Tours: Foreign: France: Paris

Anon, 1989, Rajiv Gandhi arrives in Paris, *National Herald*, July 13

Gandhi, Rajiv: Tours: Foreign: Germany: Bonn

Anon, 1988, PM arrives in Bonn, *Hindu*, June 7; *National Herald*, June 7; *Times of India*, June 7

Anon, 1988, PM concludes visit to Bonn, *Hindu*, June 10; *Hindustan Times*, June 10

Anon, 1988, PM holds talk in Bonn, *Statesman*, June 7; *Times of India*, June 7

Gandhi, Rajiv: Tours: Foreign: Hungary

Anon, 1988, Rajiv Gandhi arrives in Hungary, *Telegraph*, June 11

Gandhi, Rajiv: Tours: Foreign: Hawaian Islands: Honolulu

Kalhan, Promila, 1982, PM visit to include Honolulu, *Hindustan Times*, July 11, p 8

Gandhi Rajiv: Tours: Foreign: Indonesia: Jakarta

Dhar, M.S., 1981, Warm Jakarta welcome to PM, *Hindustan Times*, September 24, p 1

Gandhi, Rajiv: Tours: Foreign: Japan

Times of India (Newspaper), 1985, A successful visit, *Times of India*, December 3, p 8, col 1-2, editorial

Gandhi, Rajiv: Tours: Foreign: North America

Desai, M.V., 1987, PM in North America: Yes, with a but, *Economic Times*, October 27, p 5, col 7-8

Gandhi, Rajiv: Tours: Foreign: Pakistan

Anon, 1986, Pak visit shelved: PM rules out talks with extremists, *Times of India*, July 19, p 1, col 1-3+

Anon, 1986, PM's visit to Pak cancelled, *Free Press Journal*, July 12

Anon, 1989, PM's visit concludes, *Telegraph*, July 18

Gandhi, Rajiv: Tours: Foreign: Pakistan: Islamabad

Anon, 1986, Rajiv Gandhi in Islamabad, *Indian Express*, December 30

Gandhi, Rajiv: Tours: Foreign: Russia

Anon, 1982, Rajiv meets Gilashvilli, *Patriot*, September 23, p 1

Anon, 1982, Rajiv to get VIP treatment in USSR, *Indian Express*, September 20, p 7

Anon, 1982, Rajiv visit Antonov Aircraft Plant, *Times of India*, September 26, p 9

Anon, 1982, Star Obyssey of PM and Rajiv, *Times of India*, September 24, p 1

Anon, 1982, VIP treatment awaits Rajiv, *Hindustan Times*, September 20, p 7

Anon, 1982, Wreath laid at Lenin's mausoleum, *Hindustan Times*, September 22,

p 8
Anon, 1985, Rajiv, Gorbachev exchange views on global issues, *Times of India*, March 14, p 1, col 1-3+
Anon, 1985, Soviet affront to Rajiv, *Organiser* 37(3) June 2, p 1+
Anon, 1987, Gorbachev, Rajiv discuss political situation in India, *Times of India*, July 3, p 1, col 1-3+
Dass, Ram, 1985, Rajiv Gandhi's Soviet visit, *People's Democracy* 9(22) June 2, p 2
Parthasarthy, G., 1982, Rajiv to go to USSR with PM, *Indian Express*, September 5, p 9

Gandhi, Rajiv: Tours: Foreign: Russia: Moscow

Anon, 1985, After Moscow, *Mainstream* 23(40) June 1, p 1-3
Jain, Girilal, 1985, Rajiv's mission to Moscow: No need to shirk issues, *Times of India*, May 18, p 8, col 3-5
Padgaonkar, Dilleep, 1987, Soviet backing for Rajiv: Significance of visit to Moscow, *Times of India*, July 7, p 6, col 3-5

Gandhi, Rajiv: Tours: Foreign: Saudi Arabia: Riyadh

Anon, 1982, Rajiv arrives in Riyadh, *National Herald*, April 19, p 1
Anon, 1982, Rajiv Gandhi in Riyadh, *Statesman*, April 19

Gandhi, Rajiv: Tours: Foreign: South East Asia Pacific

Gupta, Ranjan, 1986, Rajiv Gandhi's South East Asia Pacific tour, *Mainstream* 25(9) November 15, p 49-50

Gandhi, Rajiv: Tours: Foreign: Spain

Anon, 1988, Rajiv Gandhi in Spain, *Hindustan Times*, July 16

Gandhi, Rajiv: Tours: Foreign: Sri Lanka

Anon, 1987, Attempt on Rajiv's life in columbo, *Times of India*, July 31, p 1, col 3-6 +
Anon, 1987, PM to visit Sri Lanka despite rejection of plan by LTTE, *Times of India*, July 28, p 1, col 1-3

Gandhi, Rajiv: Tours: Foreign: Sweden: Stockholm

Anon, 1986, Rajiv meets Junejo in Stockholm, *Telegraph*, March 17

Gandhi, Rajiv: Tours: Foreign: Syria: Damascus

Anon, 1988, PM holds talks in Domascus, *Indian Express*, June 5; *Telegraph*, June 5; *Times of India*, June 5

Gandhi, Rajiv: Tours: Foreign: Turkey: Ankara

Anon, 1988, PM in Ankara, *Times of India*, July 18

Gandhi, Rajiv: Tours: Foreign: United Kingdom

Anon, 1980, British paper lauds Rajiv, *Indian Express*, August 22
Anon, 1981, All the Rajiv's men, *Indian Observer* 23(23) December 1, p 7-9
Anon, 1981, Rajiv still makes news in Britain, *Hindustan Times*, June 22, p 6
Anon, 1981, Who will be the Indian guest at Royal wedding? *Current*, June 27, p 4
Anon, 1982, Rajiv in London as UK's biggest airshow begins, *Times of India*, September 6, p 9
Anon, 1982, Rajiv sees Farnborough Air Show, *Hindustan Times*, September 6, p 11
Anon, 1982, Rajiv to attend air-show, *Times of India*, September 5, p 11

Gandhi, Rajiv: Tours: Foreign: United Kingdom: London

Anon, 1981, Rajiv calls on Mrs Thatcher, *Hindustan Times*, July 29, p 1
Anon, 1981, Rajiv featured in London paper, *National Herald*, June 23
Anon, 1981, Rajiv Gandhi in London, *Times of India*, July 24, p 1

Gandhi, Rajiv: Tours: Foreign: United States of America

Anon, 1985, FBI uncovers plot to kill Rajiv during visit to US, *Times of India*, May 14, p 1, col 1-3
Anon, 1985, Rajiv to visit US, France in June, *Times of India*, January 4, p 1, col 1-2+
Jain, Girilal, 1985, Rajiv Gandhi's visit to US: A possible turning point in policy, *Times of India*, June 4, p 8, col 3-5
New Age (Periodical), 1985, PM's US visit, *New Age* 33(25) June 23, p 2, editorial
Sengupta, Bhabani, 1985, A tale of two visits, *Illustrated Weekly of India* 106(8) June 30, p 22-23
Times of India (Newspaper), 1985, Significant gesture, *Times of India*, May 29, p 8, col 1-2, editorial

Gandhi, Rajiv: Tours: Foreign: United States of America: New York

Parimoo, J.N., 1982, Warm welcome to PM in New York, *Times of India*, July 29, p 1+

Gandhi, Rajiv: Tours: Foreign: United States of America: Washington

Gupta, Pranay, 1985, Mr Gandhi goes to Washington, *Illustrated Weekly of India* 106(8) June 30, p 20-21

Gandhi, Rajiv: Tours: Foreign: Yugoslavia: Belgrade

Anon, 1988, Prime Minister in Belgrade, *Hindustan Times*, July 14; *Times of India*, July 14

Gandhi, Rajiv: Tours: Foreign: Zambia

Anon, 1986, PM concludes visit to Zambia, *Times of India*, May 16

Gandhi, Rajiv: Tours: Foreign: Zimbabwe: Harare

Anon, 1986, Rajiv Zia meeting at Harare, *Hindustan Times*, September 6

Gandhi, Rajiv: Tours: Inland

Anon, 1981, Rajiv's visit: Tailored versions, *Link* 24(2) August 22, p 20-21

Anon, 1982, Charges on Rajiv visit, *Hindustan Times*, Febrauary 1, p 6

Anon, 1982, Rajiv starts poll tour in State today, *Amrit Bazar Patrika*, May 11, p 7

Anon, 1982, Rajiv's hectic poll tour from May 11, *Amrit Bazar Patrika*, May 6, p 7

Anon, 1991, Rajiv Gandhi's Bharat Darshan, *Democratic World* 20(21) May 26, p 5

Gandhi, Rajiv: Tours: Inland: Andhra Pradesh

Anon, 1981, Speculation over Rajiv's visit to AP, *Indian Express*, December 24, p 8

Economic Times (Newspaper), 1989, Yet another faux pas, *Economic Times*, August 23, p 5, col 1-2, editorial

Gandhi, Rajiv: Tours: Inland: Bihar

Anon, 1988, PM visits quake-affected areas, *Times of India*, August 23

Gandhi, Rajiv: Tours: Inland: Haryana

Anon, 1981, Bhjan Lal denies huge expense on Rajiv's visit, *Times of India*, November 23, p 5

Anon, 1981, Rajiv Gandhi to visit Haryana, *Indian Express*, November 3, p 4

Anon, 1982, Rajiv Haryana tour from May 5, *Hindustan Times*, May 4, p 1

Anon, 1982, Rajiv in Haryana, *Sunday* 9(48) March 22, p 13

Gandhi, Rajiv: Tours: Inland: Jammu and Kashmir

Anon, 1982, Rajiv family in Kashmir, *Hindustan Times*, January 2, p 13

Anon, 1981, Rajiv's Jammu and Kashmir visit cause confusion, *Times of India*, July 15, p 5

Gandhi, Rajiv: Tours: Inland: Jammu and Kashmir: Srinagar

Anon, 1981, Rajiv in Srinagar to attend YC(I) meet, *Times of India*, July 11, p 7

Anon, 1982, Rajiv in Srinagar, *Indian Express*, January 2, p 4

Gandhi, Rajiv: Tours: Inland: Karnataka

Anon, 1981, Gundu dreads Rajiv's visit, *Blitz*, August 8, p 3

Gandhi, Rajiv: Tours: Inland: Karnataka: Bangalore

Anon, 1981, Rajiv Gandhi in Bangalore, *Hindustan Times*, December 29, p 4

Gandhi, Rajiv: Tours: Inland: Madhya Pradesh

Anon, 1982, Rajiv Gandhi may visit Kestara, *Times of India*, February 11, p 5

Gandhi, Rajiv: Tours: Inland: Maharashtra

Anon, 1982, Rajiv to tour Maharashtra, *Hindustan Times*, September 8, p 8

Gandhi, Rajiv: Tours: Inland : Maharashtra; Bombay

Anon, 1981, Rajiv makes his 'debut' in Bombay, *Times of India*, January 14
Anon, 1982, Rajiv cuts short visit to see Amitabh, *Indian Express*, August 5, p 1
Anon, 1982, Rajiv in Bombay, *Times of India*, August 5, p 1

Gandhi, Rajiv: Tours: Inland: Maharashtra: Nagpur

Anon, 1982, Rajiv Nagpur visit significant, *Hindustan Times*, September 13, p 7

Gandhi, Rajiv: Tours: Inland: Orissa

Das, Ashok, 1982, Sober Orissa welcome for Rajiv planned, *Hindustan Times*, February 9, p 13

Gandhi, Rajiv: Tours: Inland: Punjab

Anon, 1988, PM's visit to Punjab, *Times of India*, September 22

Gandhi, Rajiv: Tours: Inland: Punjab: Ludhiana

Anon, 1982, Rajiv to open Ludhiana meet, *National Herald*, April 6, p 4

Gandhi, Rajiv: Tours: Inland: Rajasthan: Bikaner

Anon, 1982, Face-lift given to Bikaner to receive Rajiv, *Times of India*, January 30, p 6
Anon, 1982, Rajiv to open Bikaner meet, *Hindustan Times*, January 22, p 16

Gandhi, Rajiv: Tours: Inland: Tamil Nadu: Kanchi

Parakal, Pauly V., 1990, Rajiv trek back launch at Kanchi, *New Age* 88(24) June 17, p 1

Gandhi, Rajiv: Tours: Inland: Uttar Pradesh

Anon, 1989, Rajiv Gandhi addresses UPCC (I) Convention, *Times of India*, February 11

Gandhi, Rajiv: Tours: Inland: Uttar Pradesh: Allahabad

Mathur, Girish, 1988, PM on peace mission, as Allahabad hots up, *Link* 30(45) June 12, p 10-12

Gandhi, Rajiv: Tours: Inland: Uttar Pradesh: Amethi

Anon, 1982, Rajiv Gandhi will tour his constituency, *Hindustan Times*, July 3, p 12

Gandhi, Rajiv: Tours: Inland: Uttar Pradesh: Lucknow

Anon, 1981, Rajiv visiting Lucknow today, *Hindustan Times*, September 19, p 12

Gandhi, Rajiv: Tours: Inland: West Bengal: Calcutta

Anon, 1982, Rajiv to visit city in March, *Amrit Bazar Patrika*, February 20, p 5

Gandhi, Rajiv: Tours: Inland: West Bengal: Darjiling

Inderjeet, 1987, PM's Darjiling visit and Gorkhas, *Economic Times*, February 17, p 5,

Gandhi, Rajiv: Views on Border Dispute

Anon, 1981, Antulay meets PM, Rajiv on border dispute, *Indian Express*, August 28, p 7

Gandhi, Rajiv: Views on Budget

Anon, 1982, Budget dominates the debate, *Link*, 24(32) March 21, p 8

Anon, 1982, Lengthy budget speeches, but no fire works, *Hindustan Times*, March 15, p 8

Anon, 1982, Maiden over, *Hindustan Times*, March 15, p 9

Anon, 1982, Near-full house for maiden speech, *Times of India*, March 12, p 9

Anon, 1982, Rajiv's maiden speech superb, *National Herald*, March 14, p 5

Gandhi, Rajiv, 1982, Big cheer on maiden speech streamline vital sectors, *National Herald*, March 12, p 1

Gandhi, Rajiv: Views on Chandra Shekhar

Anon, 1991, Shekhar betrayed trust: Rajiv, *Hindustan Times*, April 10, p 9, col 1-3, news-item

Anon, 1991, Rajiv's deepening displeasure with the defector PM, *Organiser* 42(29) February 24, p 3, col 1-3+

Gandhi, Rajiv: Views on Communalism Forces

Anon, 1991, Rajiv flays communal forces, *Hindustan Times*, April 3, p 7, col 1

Gandhi, Rajiv: Views on Congress (I)

Gandhi, Rajiv, 1981, Congress (I) alone can provide stable government, *Hindustan Times*, March 27, p 8

Gandhi, Rajiv, 1982, Congress (I) enjoy people's support, *Times of India*, February 6, p 2

Gandhi, Rajiv: Views on Defectors

Gandhi, Rajiv, 1981, Opposed to reentry of defectors, *Times of India*, November 23, p 5

Gandhi, Rajiv: Views on Disarmament

Anon, 1986, Disarmament movement against USA, says PM, *Telegraph*, August 7, news-item

Anon, 1988, Blue print for comprehensive disarmanent and security, *Mainstream* 26(36) June 18, p 23-26+, news-item

Gandhi, Rajiv, 1988, Rajiv Gandhi's Address to Special Session on Disarmament, *Indian Express*, June 10

Gandhi, Rajiv: Views on Division of States

Anon, 1988, Government will not allow division of States, says PM, *National Herald*, May 26, news-item

Gandhi, Rajiv: Views on Divisive forces

Anon, 1981, Rajiv's call to crush divisive forces, *Indian Express*, November 15, p 4

Gandhi, Rajiv, 1981, Destroy divisive forces, *Hindustan Times*, November 15, p 15

Gandhi, Rajiv: Views on Dowry

Anon, 1982, Rajiv Gandhi call on dowry evil, *Hindustan Times*, July 21, p 3

Gandhi,Rajiv, 1982, Fight dowry evil, *National Herald*, September 4, p 3,

Gandhi, Rajiv: Views on Dynastic Rule

Anon, 1981, Rajiv defends family succession, *Indian Express*, November 12, p 5, news-item

Anon, 1982, Rajiv against family rule, *Indian Express*, January 9, p 5, news-item

Anon, 1982, Rajiv says he never justified family rule, *Times of India*, January 9, p 5, news-item

Gandhi, Rajiv, 1981, Family succession not bad, *Hindustan Times*, November 12, p 4

Gandhi, Rajiv: Views on Eviction of Extremists from Gurdwaras

Anon, 1982, Rajiv for eviction of extremists from Gurdwaras, *Indian Express*, October 6, p 7

Gandhi, Rajiv: Views on Family Planning

Gandhi, Rajiv, 1982, FP needs people's support, *National Herald*, March 10, p 1

Gandhi, Rajiv 1982, Make FP a mass movement, *Hindustan Times*, March 10, p 3

Gandhi, Rajiv: Views on Gandhi, Sanjay

Anon, 1981, Rajiv promises to pursue Sanjay Goals, *Hindustan Times*, May 13, p 8, news-item

Gandhi, Rajiv, 1982, Sanjay's plan being pursued with zest, *Times of India*, July 18, p 11

Gandhi, Rajiv, 1982, Sanjay's plan not abandoned, *Indian Express*, March 31, p 1

Gandhi, Rajiv: Views on Janata Government

Gandhi, Rajiv, 1981, Janata put country 20 years behind? *Indian Express*, December 31, p 7

Gandhi, Rajiv: Views on National Front (Political Party)

Anon, 1990, National Front colluding with separatists: Rajiv, *Economic Times*, July 24, p 1, col 6-8, news-item.

Gandhi, Rajiv: Views on Non-Congress Politicial Parties

Anon, 1981, Rajiv accuses NF, BJP of dividing country, *Hindustan Times*, April 19, p 1, col 1-3

Anon, 1982, Rajiv wants positive opposition, *Hindu*, January 1, p 9, news-item

Anon, 1990, CWC meet: Government vacillating: Rajiv, *Times of India*, April 7, p 1, col 1-3+, news-item

Chadha, Kumkum, 1991, BJP is my main enemy: Rajiv, *Hindustan Times*, March 28, p 1, col 1-4+, news-item

Das, Rathin, 1991, No poll pact with BJP, says Rajiv, *Hindustan Times*, May 11, p 1, col 4-5+, news-item

Khare, Harish, 1986, Rajiv Gandhi's world view: Anti-Congressism to anti-politics, *Times of India*, April 25, p 1, col 4-6+

Kirpekar, Subhash, 1988, Rajiv Gandhi attacks non-Congress govts, *Times of India*, April 25, p 1, col 4-6+

Gandhi, Rajiv: Views on Non Proliferation Treaty

Anon, 1986, N-Powers violating NPT, says PM, *Indian Express*, October 18, news-item

Gandhi, Rajiv: Views on Nuclear Arms

Anon, 1986, Nuclear arms main threat to peace, says Rajiv Gandhi, *Times of India*, March 6, news-item

Gandhi, Rajiv: Views on Nuclear Policy

Anon, 1991, Rajiv for Nuclear Policy review, *Times of India*, February 12, p 1, col 5-7+.

Gandhi, Rajiv: Views on Nuclear Powers

Anon, 1986, N-Powers violating NPT, says PM, *Indian Express*, October 18, news-item.

Gandhi, Rajiv: Views on Panchayats

Anon, 1982, Rajiv wants Panchayats made more effective, *Hindustan Times*, January 31, p 11.

Gandhi, Rajiv: Views on Parliamentary System

Anon, 1981, Find right men to do the job, *Blitz*, July 25, p 12-13, news-item

Anon, 1982, Party system cracking up under pressure, *India Today* 7(1) January 15, p 78-79, news-item

Anon, 1982, President pleasure Prime Minister's pain: Presidential system revisited, *Delhi Recorder* 3(2) March 15-April 14, p 10-13, news-item

Gandhi, Rajiv, 1981, Democracy has strong base in India, *Hindustan Times*, July 29, p 16

Gandhi, Rajiv, 1981, Parliamentary system good and sound, *Blitz*, July 18, p 24

Gandhi, Rajiv, 1981, Parliamentary system good, *Times of India*, July 15, p 5

Gandhi, Rajiv, 1981, Ram Rajya if we all do our duty, *Hindustan Times*, October 7, p 3

Gandhi, Rajiv 1982, Not for Presidential form of Government, *Amrit Bazar Patrika*, May 18, p 7

Kothari, Rajni, 1982, Stemming the rot, *Indian Express*, June 7, p 6

Gandhi, Rajiv: Views on Presidential System

Anon, 1982, President's pleasure Prime Minister's pain: Presidential System revisited, *Delhi Recorder* 3(2) March 15-April 14, p 10-13, news-item

Anon, 1982, Rajiv Gandhi not for Presidential system, *Hindu*, May 18, p 10, news-item

Gandhi, Rajiv, 1982, Not for Presidential form of Government, *Amrit Bazar Patrika*, May 18, p 7

Gandhi, Rajiv: Views on Press

Anon, 1982, Rajiv attacks press, calls for loyalty, *Indian Express*, April 25, p 4, news-item

Gandhi, Rajiv, 1982, Press writing irresponsible reports, *Indian Express*, October 6, p 1+

Gandhi, Rajiv: Views on Projects

Anon, 1982, Against projects at the cost of poor, *Hindustan Times*, February 13, p 5, news-item

Gandhi, Rajiv: Views on Racism

Anon, 1986, Mandatory sanctions must for end of racism, says PM, *Hindustan*

Times, July 6, news-item

Gandhi, Rajiv: Views on Separatism

Anon, 1989, PM vows to fight separatism, *Economic Times*, August 16, p 5, col 1-5, news-item

Gandhi, Rajiv: Views on Star War

Anon, 1986, 'Star Wars' against world peace, says Rajiv, *National Herald*, February 17, news-item

Gandhi, Rajiv: Views on Terrorism and Pakistan

Anon, 1988, Pakistan biggest supporter of terrorism, says Rajiv Gandhi, *Hindustan Times*, June 9, news-item

Gandhi, Rajiv: Views on West Bengal Day

Anon, 1991, Rajiv greetings on Bengal Day, *Hindustan Times*, April 15, p 10, col 3

Gandhi, Rajiv: Views on Youths

Anon, 1982, Rajiv urges youth to work for peace, *Hindustan Times*, September 23, p 8

Gandhi, Rajiv: Wedding

Anon, 1968, Cardin's new design in Indian silk catch the eye, *Hindu*, Feburary 23, p 12

Anon, 1968, Gandhi at Mehndi ceremony, *Hindustan Times*, February 25, p 1, col 2

Anon, 1968, India look for Sonia the bride, *Times of India*, February 25, p 1+

Anon, 1968, New reel, *Link* 10(30) March 3, p 7

Anon, 1968, Personalities, *Link* 10(26) February 4, p 33

Anon, 1968, Rajiv Gandhi weds, *Statesman*, February 26, p 1, 3

Anon, 1968, Rajiv weds Sonia in Indian style, *Hindu*, February 26, p 1

Anon, 1968, Sonia-Rajiv wedding marked by simplicity, *Times of India*, February 26, p 1+

Anon, 1968, Thousands felicitate Rajiv, Sonia, *Hindustan Times*, February 27, p 1+

Anon, 1968, Wedding scene: Turbans, tailors and fire works, *Hindustan Times*, February 26, p 7

Gandhi, Sanjay

Anon, 1981-1982, Remembering Sanjay Gandhi, *Delhi Recoder* 2(9) December 15, January 14, p 22-23

Anon, 1982, Sanjay ignored YC men to back Rajiv Gandhi, *Hindustan Times*, May 4, p 6

Anon, 1982, Will Sanjay cult overehelm Rajiv? *Blitz*, March 13, p 6

Gandhi, Rajiv, 1982, Sanjay's plan being pursued with zest, *Times of India*, July 18, p 11

Gandhi, Rajiv, 1982, Sanjay's plan not abondoned, *Indian Express*, March 31, p 1

Niewsewand, Peter, 1981, Indira without Sanjay: Rajiv no substitute, *Blitz*, September 20, p 20

Gandhi, Sanjay: Biography

Bhattacharya, Shubhabrata, 1980, Mystery: The delayed biography of Sanjay, *Sunday* 8(20) December 21, p 40-41

Gandhi, Sanjay: Homage Paid to Him

Anon, 1980, AICC (I) tribute to Sanjay, Plea to Rajiv, *Sunday Standard*, December 7, p 7

Anon, 1980, Ashes immersed, *Sunday Standard*, June 29, p 1

Anon, 1981, Blood in honour of Sanjay's memory, *National Herald*, April 10

Anon, 1981, Homage to Sanjay: A Great revolutionary? *Hindustan Times*, June, 24, p 1+

Anon, 1982, Sanjay Death Anniversary: Sanjay day, *Hindustan Times*, June 23, p 1+

Banerjee, Saumitra, 1980, Funeral: A last good bye, *Sunday* 8(1) June 19, P 27

Herle, Shashi, 1980, Trutu behind the demolition, *Onlooker* 42(19) October 31, p 9

Jain, Madhu, 1981, Nation remembers a leader but Subhash Saxena is forgotten, *Sunday* 9(3) July 5, p 32-33

Nihal Singh, S., 1983, The heart of the matter, *Indian Express*, May 5, p 6

Nizamuddin, D.E., 1982, Everybody is remembering Sanjay, *Sunday* 9(45) May 1, p 58

Saari, Anil 1982, Sanjay's death was a personal loss, *Sunday* 9(31) January 17, p 22-27

Sengupta, Barun, 1980, Politics after Sanjay, *Sunday* 8(1) June 29, p 14-15

Suri, Surinder, 1981, Mrs Gandhi's enigmatic charisma, *Illustrated Weekly of India*, 102(33) November 15, p 30-31

Swamy, Raman, 1981, Sanjay Gandhi: A controversial tribute, *India Today* 6(1) January 15, p 15

Gandhi, Sanjay: Homage Paid to Him by Family Members

Anon, 1982, Maneka gesture turn sour, *Hindustan Times*, June 24, p 8

Anon, 1982, Wreaths laid at Samadhi, *Hindustan Times*, June 24, p 1

Bhattcharya, Shubhabrata, 1981, Rajiv's team, *Sunday* 9(24) November 29, p 15

Joshi, Chand, 1980, Ashes imersed in many rivers, *Hindustan Times*, June 29, p 1+

Kaushik, Poonam I., 1982, Rajiv goes through his paces, *Weekend Review* 3(10) May 29, p 7

Gandhi, Sanjay: Plan

Anon, 1981, Rajiv promises to persue Sanjay goals, *Hindustan Times*, May 13, p

8, news-item

Gandhi, Rajiv, 1982, Sanjay's plan being pursued with zest, *Times of India*, July 18, p 11

Gandhi, Rajiv, 1982, Sanjay's plan not abandoned, *Indian Express*, March 31, p 1

Gandhi, Sanjay: Tributes Paid to Him

See Gandhi, Sanjay: Homage Paid to Him

Gandhi, Sanjay: Views of Gandhi, Rajiv

See Gandhi, Rajiv: Views on Gandhi, Sanjay

Gandhi, Sonia

Alexander, P.C., 1990, When Sonia urged Rajiv not to become PM, *Economic Times*, November 5, p 1, col 1-5+.

Anon, 1968, India look for Sonia the bride, *Times of India*, February 25, p 1+

Anon, 1982, Rajiv, Sonia trapped in lift, *Times of India*, August 1, p 1

Anon, 1991, CPB will urge Sonia to contest, *Hindustan Times*, October 8, p 1, col 1

Anon, 1991, DPCC-I for Sonia to be Party Chief, *Hindustan Times*, May 26, p 5, col 1.

Anon, 1991, Maragatham meets Sonia, *Hindustan Times*, July 10, p 3, col 2

Anon, 1991, Rajiv shoes handed over to Sonia, *Hindustan Times*, June 20, p 10, col 5

Anon, 1991, Rajiv was always smiling, says Sonia, *Hindustan Times*, June 16, p 15, col 1-2, news-item

Anon, 1991, Sonia Conusel gets Rajiv shoes, socks, *Hindustan Times*, June 18, p 9, col 5-6

Anon, 1991, Sonia detested politics, *Hindustan Times*, May 26, p 13, col 2-4.

Anon, 1991, Sonia no to grant for Trust, *Hindustan Times*, August 2, p 1, col 5

Anon, 1991, Sonia plea for consensus welcomed, *Hindustan Times*, May 28, p 6, col 8.

Anon, 1991, Sonia to chair Indira Trust, *Hindustan Times*, May 30, p 8, col 1.

Anon, 1991, Sonia to head Nehru Fund, *Hindustan Times*, May 31, p 10, col 4.

Anon, 1991, Sonia to retain Janpath bungalow, *Hindustan Times*, May 30, p 8, col 2-3.

Anon, 1991, Sonia wants Rajiv's sneakers, *Hindustan Times*, June 13, p 8, col 1

Anon, 1991, Sonia will launch Rajiv campaign, *Hindustan Times*, April 25, p 10, col 1

Anon, 1992, Mobile libraries flagged off, *National Herald*, May 23, p 10, col 6-7

Anon, 1992, Sonia handover keys of libraries, *Times of India*, May 23, p 4, col 5-6

Anon, 1992, Sonia not asked to depose: SIT, *National Herald*, May 23, p 10, col 8, *Hindustan Times*, May 23, p 20, col 1, news-item

Anon, 1992, Sonia present mobile libraries, *Hindustan Times*, May 23, p 1-2

Anon, 1992, Sonia's name not in SIT witnesses list, *Times of India*, May 23, p 3, col 1-2

Anon, 1992, Sonia's speech devoid of political hue, *Indian Express*, May 24, p 7, col 4

Anon, 1992, Sonia to be examined in Rajiv case, *Hindustan Times*, May 20, p 12,

Bhargava, G.S., 1991, Sonia Gandhi as a Hindu widow, *Mainstream* 29(35) June 22, p 9-10

KGK, 1991, Selection of Sonia Gandhi: Inside story, *Onlooker* June 15, p 47-50

Sehgal, Rashme, 1992, Trying to forget, *Independent*, May 21, p 5, col

Shiraz, 1991, The Sonia enigma: The public loss of a private person, *Sunday* June 2-June 8, p 40

Gandhi, Varun

Anon, 1981, Varun Star draw at Shantivana, *Hindustan Times*, June 24, p 3

Ganesan, Sivaji

Anon, 1982, Gandhi vote for Amitabh or Sivaji, *Indian Express*, February 5, p 5

Garhwal Issue

Anon, 1981, Rajiv critical of Garhwal strategy, *Sunday* 9(3) July 5, p 58

Bhauguna, H.N., 1982, Garhwal will be a turing point, *Current*, May 1, p 5

Raghavan, A., 1982, Garhwal: Threat to Congress (I) dynasty, *Blitz*, May 8, p 9

Gayoom, Maumoon Abdul

Anon, 1988, Gayoom, PM hold talks, *Indian Express*, December 8

Gayoom, Maumoon Abdul: Homage Paid to Gandhi, Rajiv

Anon, 1992, Yasser, Gayoom hail Rajiv, *National Herald*, May 22, p 10, col 3

Germany

See also Geographical Area subdivision under main Descriptor

Germany: FRG: Foreign Relations: Geographical Area: India

See Indo-German Relations

Gilashvilli

Anon, 1982, Rajiv meets Gilashvilli, *Patriot*, September 23, p 1

Global Issues

Anon, 1985, Rajiv, Gorbachev exchange views on global issues, *Times of India*, March 14, p 1, col 1-3+

Goa: India

Cabral-E-SA, Mario, 1981, Appealing for change, *Sunday* 9(28) December 27, p 50

See also Geographical Area subdivision under Descriptor

Gorbachev, Mikhail

Anon, 1985, Rajiv, Gorbachev exchange views on global issues, *Times of India*, March 14, p 1, col 1-3+

Anon, 1986, Tumultuous welcome to Gorbachev on arrival, *Indian Express*, November 26

Anon, 1987, Gorbachev, Rajiv discuss political situation in India, *Times of India*, July 3, p 1, col 1-3+

Anon, 1988, Gorbachev arrives in New Delhi, *Hindustan Times*, Novmber 19

Anon, 1988, PM's statesment on Gorbachev's visit, *Hindu*, November 22

Anon, 1989, PM holds talks with Gorbachev, *Hindustan Times*, July 16; *Times of India*, July 16

Gorkha National Libraration Front

Anon, 1986, Asoke Sen defends PM's stand on GNLF, *Times of India*, October 3

Anon, 1986, BJP leader questions PM's stand on GNLF, *Times of India*, November 17

Anon, 1986, Intervention if GNLF stir truns secessionist, says PM, *Hindustan Times*, September 21, news-item

Anon, 1986, Malviya criticises PM's stand on GNLF demands, *Free Press Journal*, October 9

Anon, 1986, No Constitutional amendment to meet GNLF demands, *Free Press Journal*, September 30

Anon, 1986, Prime Minister to hold talks on GNLF issue with CM, *Times of India*, December 19

See also Gorkhaland Problem

Gorkhaland Problem

Anon, 1986, Gorkhaland issue State's responsibility, says PM, *Times of India*, September 20, news-item

Anon, 1986, PM reiterates stand on Gorkha stir, *Free Press Journal*, Setember 30

Anon, 1986, Prime Minister rejects demand for Gorkhaland, *Free Press Journal*, December 20; *Times of India*, December 20

Anon, 1986, Rajiv Gandhi abetting Gorkhaland agitation, *New Age* 34(35) August 31, p 3

Anon, 1987, For a profile of the Gorkhaland agitation, *Illustrated Weekly of India*, February 22, p 28

Anon, 1989, PM, Ghising hold talks, *Indian Express*, May 19

Inder Jit, 1986, PM concedes basic Gorkha demand, *Economic Times*, December 23, p 5, col 7-8+

Inder Jit, 1987, PM's Darjiling visit and Gorkhas, *Economic Times*, February 17, p 5, col 7-8+

See also Gorkha National Libration Front

Governer: Geographical Area: India: Goa: Bhanu Pratap Singh

Chandramouli, I., 1991, Rajiv had no business (Interview: Governer Bhanu Pratap Singh), *The Week* October 21, p 36-37

Governer: Geographical Area: India: Punjab: Shankar Ray, S.

Anon, 1988, PM, Governer reviews situation, *Free Press Journal*, May 20; *National Herald*, May 20

Government and Politics: Geographical Area: India

Ahmad, S., 1991, Rajiv Gandhi: Can he provide a stable alternative? *Sunday* March 24-March 30, p 4, letter to editor

Anon, 1985, New direction to politics, programmes: Social justice within stipulated time frame, *Patriot*, January 6, p 1, col 3-7+

Anon, 1985, Politics: PM's new style, *Economic and Political Weekly* 20(37) September 14, p 1536, col 1-2

Anon, 1985, Postings and politics, *Economic and Political Weekly* 20(2) January 12, p 54-55

Anon, 1985, The Minister doesn't have the answer, *Times of India* (Sunday Review), September 29, p 1, col 1-8

Anon, 1986, Arif quits on Bill issue, *Times of India*, February 27, p 1, col 5-7

Anon, 1986, Rajiv drops three Ministers, major shake up in Congress Party, *Times of India*, January 20, p 1, col 2-4

Anon, 1986, Rajiv's India: Has the dream really faded? *Illustrated Weekly of India* 107(17) April 20, p 6-17

Anon, 1987, The mid-term blues: Rajiv Gandhi, *Illustrated Weekly of India* 108(14) April 5, p 26-27

Anon, 1987, Political economy of Rajiv's regime, *Link* 29(25) January 25, p 12-15

Anon, 1987, A Prime Minister or a President? *Times of India* (Sunday Review), January 25, p 4, col 1-5

Anon, 1987, Rajiv has damaged his image, V.P. Singh lacks courage, *Organiser* 39(10) August 2, p 5-6

Anon, 1987, Rajiv's emergency plan to counter dismissal, *Organiser* 39(2) May 31, p 1-2

Anon, 1987, What would Gandhiji have done? *Indian Express* (Magazine), January 25, p 1, col 1-8+

Anon, 1987, Will Zail dismiss Rajiv? *Organiser* 38(46) March 29, p 1+

Anon, 1988, PM urges to keep military out of politics, *Hindu*, November 13

Anon, 1988, V.P. Singh exposes PM's Italian connection, *Organiser* 39(43) April 10, p 13

Anon, 1989, Five Deputy ministers promoted, *Hindu*, July 5

Anon, 1989, On the come back trail, *Illustrated Weekly of India* 110(29) July 16, p 10-19

Anon, 1990, Rajiv for any non-BJP government, *Times of India*, October 21

Anon, 1991, After Rajiv Gandhi, *Economic and Political Weekly* 26(21) May 25, p 1307, col 1-2

Anon, 1991, Case for better equation between Shekhar and Rajiv, *Link* 33(23) January 18, p 12-15.

Anon, 1991, Congress leaders rated PM above Rajiv, *Hindustan Times*, April 26, p 18, col 2-3

Anon, 1991, Congress to support Shekhar from outside, *Times of India*, November 7, p 1, col 1-4.

Anon, 1991, Family matters: Is this the end for the Gandhi dynasty? *Sunday* June 2-June 8, p 38-39

Anon, 1991, Rajiv Gandhi on the come back trail? *Democratic World* 20(9) March 3, p 5, col 1-3

Anon, 1991, Rajiv Gandhi poised to take over as PM, *Organiser* 42(28) February 27, p 1, col 1-2+

Anon, 1991, Rajiv hopes to present a populist budget after toppling Shekhar, *Organiser* 42(30) March 3, p 1, col 1-5

Anon, 1991, The Rajiv take-over plan? *Democratic World* 20(7) February 17, p 8, col 1-3

Anon, 1991, The toppling of the Turk: Rajiv Gandhi style, *Organiser* 42(33) March 24, p 3, col 2-4

Anon, 1991, Will Rajiv ultimataly take over? *Democratic World* February 3, p 5, col 1-3

Advani, L.K., 1988, Decline of Rajiv Government, *Mainstream* (Annual) October 8, p 31-32

Chakravarti, Prithivis, 1989, Elections: Rajiv's three pronged propaganda strategy, *Radical Humanist* 53(3) June, p 8-18

Chowdhury, Dilip Ghosh, 1990, Shekhar at mercy of Cong (I) and Rajiv, *New Age* 38(49), December 9, p 7+.

Datta Ray, Sunanda K., 1989, Death of innocence: Rise and decline of Rajiv Gandhi, *Statesman*, March 12

Anon, 1990, (Book Review), *Hindustan Times* (Magazine), March 11, p 5, col 1-4 Review to the book: **Hari Jaisingh**, 1990, *India after Indira: The turbulent years (1984-1989)*, Allied Publishers, New Delhi, 207 p.

Democratic World (Periodical), 1991, Rajiv and after, *Democratic World* 20(21) May 26, p 4, col 2-3, editorial

Democratic World (Periodical), 1991, R.V. aginst Rajiv's take over? *Democratic World* 20(8) p 4, col 1-2, editorial

Dhar, P.N., 1987, Political economy of development in India, *Indian Economic Review* 22(1)

Dibang, 1990. Rajiv plumped for Devi as PM, *Illustrated Weekly of India* December 1-2, p 1, col 1-5

Guha, R., 1991, Rajiv Gandhi: Can he provide a stable alternative? *Sunday* March 24-March 30, p 4, letter to editor

Gupta, Ranjan, 1987, President, PM controversy, *Mainstream* 25(28) March 28, p 6

Jain, Girilal, 1987, Focus away from Rajiv: No natural allies for V.P. Singh, *Times of India*, September 9, p 6, col 3-5

Jain, Girilal, 1987, Political upheaval in India: Rajiv's blunder after blunder,

Times of India, March 25, p 6, col 3-5

Jain, Girilal, 1987, Prime Minister under siege: Compulsions of Indian democracy, *Times of India*, April 20, p 6, col 3-5

Jain, Girilal, 1988, No anti-Rajiv conspiracy: Only convergence of interests, *Times of India*, December 16, p 6, col 3-5

Joshi, Murali Manohar, 1987, A diversionary exercise to defocus the moral failure of Rajiv Gandhi, *Organiser* 39(24) November 22, p 5+

Khanna, K.C., 1986, Protecting precious lives: A "soft" State cannot endure, *Times of India*, October 7, p 8, col 3-5

Khare, Harish, 1980, Anti-Congressism endures: Rajiv's failure to evolve, *Times of India*, October 10, p 8, col 3-5.

Malhotra, Inder, 1987, Political commentary: Shades of the seventies, *Times of India*, March 20, p 6, col 3-5

Mitra, Chandan, 1989, A CAG-tag opposition: Neutralising Rajiv's populism, *Times of India*, July 26, p 6, col 3-5

Mukarji, Nirmal, 1989, Decentralization below State level: Need for new system of govrenance, *Economic and Political Weekly* March 4

Mumbal, Brihan, 1989, Maximum democracy and maximum devolution, *Mahanagarpalika Patrika* 36(6) August, p 2-6

Nihal Singh, S., 1988, Rajiv and government battered: But opposition fail to make gain, *Times of India*, May 10, p 6, col 3-5

Parakal, Pauly V., 1988, Rajiv Gandhi's drive for one-party rule, *New Age* 36(7) February 14, p 1+

Parakal, Pauly V., 1990, Dubious role of Congress I, *New Age* 38(430) October 28, p 1.

Razdan, Deepak, 1991, Rajiv's opponent for Government of poor, *Hindustan Times*, May 7, p 9, col 1-2

Roychowdhury, Nanda Dulal, 1991, Rajiv Gandhi: Can he provide a stable alternative? *Sunday* March 24-March 30, p 4, letter to editor

Sanghvi, Vir, 1991, The odd couple Rajiv Gandhi and Chandra Shekhar: What went wrong? *Sunday* March 17-March 23, p 35-42

Shukla, Rajiv, 1991, After Rajiv? *Sunday* June 2-June 8, p 54-57

Sinha, S.K., 1984, A soldier looks at political scene, *Statesman*, July 8

Suri, Surinder, 1985, Presidential Prime Minister: New trends in politics, *Times of India*, November 30, p 8, col 3-5

Taban, Ghulam, Rabbani, 1991, Post-Rajiv situation, *Mainstream* 29(34) June 15, p 19

Times of India (Newspaper), 1987, Anti-Rajiv campaigns, *Times of India*, September 25, p 6, col 1-2, editorial

Times of India (Newspaper), 1988, Rajiv Gandhi to blame, *Times of India*, February 25, p 6, col 1-2, editorial

Times of India (Newspaper), 1988, State of the Nation, *Times of India*, August 16, p 4, col 1-2, editorial

See also National Affairs: Geographical Area: India

Government and Politics: Geographical Area: India: Andhra Pradesh

Anon, 1985, No progress in AP after Congress exit: PM, *Times of India*, December 25, p 6, col 1-4, news-tem

Government and Politics: Geographical Area: India: Janata Government

Anon, 1984, Janata lifted ban on Chauhan: PM, *Times of India*, December 16, p 1, col 1-2+, news-item

Government Policy: Geographical Area: India

Anon, 1984, Goverment committed to protect all: Rajiv, *Times of India*, December 20, p 1, col 7-8+, news-item

Great Britian

See United Kingdom

Grievances

Anon, 1986, Get to roots of grievances, says Rajiv, *Times of India*, October 16, p 1, col 7-8, news-item

Gulf Crisis

See Gulf War

Gulf Policy

Sarojangi, 1991, Congress wants its way on Gulf policy, *Illustrated Weekly of India* January 26-January 27, p 1, col 1-5

Gulf War

Anon, 1988, PM's call to ease tension in the Gulf, *Hindustan Times*, July 15; *National Herald*, July 15; *Statesman*, July 15

Anon, 1991, Rajiv Gandhi calls for UNSC meeting on Gulf War, *Times of India*, February 8

Anon, 1991, Who switched off the Gulf War? Rajiv Gandhi of course! *Organiser* 42(32) March 17, p 3, col 2-4

Democratic World (Periodical), 1991, Rajiv calls for US Forces in the Gulf, *Democratic World* 20(7) February 17, p 3, col 2, editorial

Gundu Rao

Anon, 1981, Gundu dreads Rajiv's visit, *Blitz*, August 8, p 3

Anon, 1981, PM will assess Gundu Goverment's performance, *Indian Express*, December 25, p 7

Chenappa, Raj, 1982, Gundu Rao grabs the show, *India Today* 7(2) January 31, p 53-54

Gurdwaras: Eviction of Extremists

Anon, 1982, Rajiv for eviction of extremists from Gurdwaras, *Indian Express*, October 6, p 7

Haq, Zia-ul

See Zia-ul Haq

Harare: Zimbaabwe

See also: Geographical Area subdivision under main Descriptor

Harijan Welfare

See Welfare: Harijan

Haryana: India

Anon, 1981, Bhajan Lal denies huge expenses on Rajiv's visit, *Times of India*, November 23, p 5

Anon, 1981, Haryana Congress (I) to be revamped, *Hindustan Times*, November 25, p 6

Anon, 1982, Rajiv Haryana tour from May 5, *Hindustan Times*, May 4, p 1

Anon, 1986, Prime Minister announces Rs. 400 crore package for Haryana, *Indian Express*, December 19

Mitra, Sumit, 1982, Bhajan Lal: The artful manipulator, *India Today* 7(12) June 30, p 78-82

Premkumar, 1982, Congress (I) stakes in Haryana, *Statesman*, May 18, p 4

See also Geographical Area subdivision under main Descriptors

Haryana: India: Political Scenario

See Political Scenario: Geographical Area: India: Haryana

Haryana Problem

Inder Jit, 1987, Rajiv, Haryana Poll and new crises, *Economic Times*, June 23, p 5, col 7-8

Hawaian Islands

See also Geographical Area subdivision under main Descriptor

Hawke, Bob

Anon, 1989, Bob Hawke's talks in New Delhi, *Times of India*, February 10

Hegde, Ram Krishan: Views on Congress Unity

Anon, 1991, Hegde call for Cong men's unity, *Hindustan Times*, May 28, p 7, col 1-2

High Command: Congress (I)

See Congress (I)

High Technology

Hari Kumar, K.N., 1988, Rajiv and the US trading Non-Alignment for Hi-tech? *Mainstream* 26(29) April 30, p 17-26

Hijack Incident

Anon, 1986, Pak responsibility for hijak tragedy, says PM, *Times of India*, September 7, p 1, col 1-3+. news-item

Himachal Pradesh: India

Anon, 1982, Rajiv seeks votes for HP progress, *Hindustan Times*, May 8, p 16

Anon, 1986, New PCC (I) President appointed, *Indian Express*, February 7

Banyal, S.S., 1982, Rajiv steals the show in Himachal Pradesh, *Hindustan Times*, May 17. p 5

Bharadwaj, A.K., 1986, No repercussions in Himachal, *Link* 28(40) May 11, p 14

Chawla, P. and Thukral, G., 1982, Himachal Pradesh: The photo finish, *India Today* 7(11) June 15, p 25

Malhotra, Inder, 1982, Warming up for 1985, *Times of India*, May 16, p 1

Thukral, Gobind, 1982, Himachal Pradesh: Caste calculus, *India Today* 7(10) May 31, p 41-42

See also Geographical Area subdivision under main Descriptors

Hindi Language

See Language: Hindi

Hindu (Newspaper): Report on Bofors

Anon, 1988, Hindu report does not link politicians, says PM, *Tribune*, June 26, news-item

Hinduja, S.P.: Homage Paid to Gandhi, Rajiv

Anon, 1991, Sad loss, says S.P. Hinduja, *Hindustan Times*, May 26, p 12, col 3

Hindus

Thapar, Romesh, 1984, The Rajiv party and the Hindus, *Economic and Political Weekly* 16(50) December 15, p 2105

Hoarders: Geographical Area: India

Anon, 1985, Stern steps against hoarders: PM, *Times of India*, May 6, p 1, col 1-3+, news-item

Home Minister: Geographical Area: India

See under name of the Home Minister, e.g., Buta Singh, Chavan, S.V.

Hun Sen

See Prime Minister: Geographical Area: Kampuchea

Hungary

See also Geographical Area subdivison under main Descriptor

Hungary: Foreign Relations: Geographical Area: India

See under Indo-Hungarian Relations

Hunger

See Starvation

Hussain, Saddam

Anon, 1991, Rajiv going the Saddam way, *Organiser* 42(32) March 17, p 1, col 3-4+

Anon, 1991, Rajiv Gandhi, Saddam and Bush, *Organiser* 42(33) March 24, p 16, col 4

IA

=Indian Airlines

IAC

=Indian Airlines Corporation

IAF

=Indian Air Force

ICWA

=Indian Council of World Affairs

IFAD

=International Fund for Agricultural Development

IFC

=International Finance Corporation

ILO

=International Labour Organisation

INTUC

=Indian National Trade Union Congress

IPKF

=Indian Peace Keeping Force

India: North-East

See North East India

India: Political Parties

See under name of the Political Party, e.g., Bhartiya Janata Party

Indian Air Fore

Bob, Dilip, 1982, Indian Air Force: Spectacle in the sky, *India Today* 7(6) March 31, p 36-39

Indian Air Force: Copter: Use by Gandhi, Rajiv

Moopnar, G.K., 1982, No IAF copter for Rajiv, *Hindustan Times*, May 15, p 5

Inidan Airlines: Appointments

Sharma, A.P., 1982, No Rajiv hand in IA appointment, *Hindustan Times*, March 5, p 16

Indian Council of World Affairs

Anon, 1982, Hectic scenes at ICWA elections, *Hindustan Times*, September 7, p 3
Anon, 1982, ICWA: Indian Council of World Affairs, *Caravan* 12(727) September p 27-29
Anon, 1982, Rajiv files papers for ICWA post, *Times of India*, August 7, p 3
Anon, 1982, Rajiv to contest ICWA post, *Times of India*, September 7, p 3

Indian National Congress

See also All India Congress Committee; Congress (I)

Indian National Trade Union Congress

Gandhi, Rajiv, 1984, 23rd INTUC Plenary session: Message, *Indian Worker* 32(32-34) May 7-May 21, p 29-30

Indian Ocean

Anon, 1986, Call for global meet on Indian Ocean, *Hindustan Times*, October 14
Anon, 1986, Rajiv Gandhi warns rivalry in Indian Ocean, *Indian Express*, Febraury 14

Indian Peace Keeping Force

Anon, 1988, Phased withdrawl of IPKF agreed upon, *Statesman*, May 14
Anon, 1989, Lanka disputes Rajiv's stand on IPKF pull out, *Times of India*, June 16, p 1, col 1-3
Anon, 1989, PM for time frame for IPKF pull out, *Sunday* July 5

Indian Silk

Anon, 1968, Cardin's new design in Indian Silk catch the eye, *Hindu*, February 23, p 12

Indira Gandhi Trust

Anon, 1991, Sonia to chair Indira Trust, *Hindustan Times*, May 30, p 8, col 1

Indira Pratisthan

Anon, 1982, Why is Antulay still surviving: Reason he holds the Indira Pratisthan papers, *Sunday* 9(31) January 17, p 44

Indo-Afghan Relations

Anon, 1988, Abdul Vakil calls on PM, *Hindustan Times*, September 4
Anon, 1988, India and the Afghan accords, *Link* 30(39) May 1, p 14-16
Anon, 1988, Najib holds further discussion with PM, *Hindustan Times*, May 6; *Times of India* May 6
Anon, 1988, Najibullah holds talks in New Delhi, *National Herald*, May 5, *Times of India*, May 5
Anon, 1988, PM, Najib call for Geneva pact success, *Times of India*, May 5, p 1, col 6-8+
Anon, 1989, Wakil holds talks with Rajiv Gandhi, *Hindustan Times*, March 4

See also Afghan Crisis

Indo-African Relations

Chabra, Hari Saran, 1991, Rajiv Gandhi and Africa, *Mainstream* 29(32) June 1, p 6

See also Africa, Fund; Gandhi, Rajiv: Tours: Foreign: Africa; Indo-South African Relations

Indo-Albanian Relations

Anon, 1988, Bandh passes off peacefully, *Hindustan Times*, September 15

Indo-Algerian Relations

See also Gandhi, Rajiv: Tours: Foreign: Algeria

Indo-American Relations

See Indo-US Relations

Indo-Angola Relations

Anon, 1986, India, Angola assail West on sanctions, *Times of India*, May 17

Indo-Australian Relations

Anon, 1986, India will not allow arms imbalance, says PM, *Hindustan Times*, October 16, news-item

Anon, 1986, PM postpones visit, *Telegraph*, January 2

Anon, 1986, Trade Council set up, *Statesman*, October 17

Anon, 1988, Australian Minister in New Delhi, *Times of India*, December 2

Anon, 1989, Bob Hawk's talks in New Delhi, *Times of India*, February 10

Indo-Bangladesh Relations

Anon, 1988, President Ershad in New Delhi, *Free Press Journal*, September 30; *Hindustan Times*, September 30

Indo-Bhutanese Relations

Anon, 1985, Rajiv's call to resist big power politics, *Times of India*, October 1, p 1, col 5-7

Anon, 1988, PM, Bhutan King hold more talks, *Hindustan Times*, September 25

Anon, 1988, PM holds discussions with Bhutan King, *Hindustan Times*, July 11

Anon, 1988, PM holds talks with Bhutan King, *Hindustan Times*, September 24

Sen, Sumanta, 1985, PM's visit boisters Bhutan's confidence, *Times of India*, October 4, p 7, col 1-4

See also Gandhi, Rajiv: Tours: Foreign: Bhutan

Indo-Chinese Relations

Anon, 1981, Hindi-Chini once again Bhai-Bhai, *Current*, July 4, p 4

Anon, 1981, Rajiv Gandhi to visit China, *Hindustan Times*, September 28, p 6

Anon, 1982, China team inivites Rajiv, *National Herald*, May 1, p 12

Anon, 1985, Stiffer line at border talks: China spurns Rajiv's peace overtures, *Organiser* 37(33) December 29, p 1+

Anon, 1986, No territorial conessions to China, says PM, *Times of India*, December 19, news-item

Anon, 1988, China keen on PM's visit, *Times of India*, November 30, p 1, col 2-4+

Anon, 1988, Joint Panel set up to settle boundary issue, *Hindustan Times*, December 23; *Times of India*, December 23

Anon, 1988, No territory to be ceded to China: PM, *Times of India*, September 28, p 1, col 1-3, news-item

Anon, 1988, PM brings border issue with China to the fore, *Economic Times*, December 2, p 1, col 2-5

Anon, 1988, PM calls on Deng, Zhao, *Hindustan Times*, December 22; *Times of India*, December 22

Anon, 1988, PM sees change in China's policy, *Times of India*, October 16, p 1, col 1-3

Anon, 1988, PM's China visit concludes, *Indian Express*, December 24; *Times of India*, December 24

Anon, 1988, Rajiv Gandhi in Beijing, *Hindustan Times*, December 20; *Statesman*, December 20

Anon, 1988, Rajiv Gandhi meets Chinese President, *Hindustan Times*, December 12; *Tribune*, December 12

Anon, 1988, Rajiv, Li Peng hopeful of border accord, *Times of India*, December 20, p 1, col 1-4+

Anon, 1988, Why is the PM going to China? *Economic and Political Weekly* 23(4) October 8, p 2087

Anon, 1989, Liang calls on Rajiv Gandhi, *National Herald*, March 2; *Statesman*, March 2

Anon, 1989, PM, Wu optimistic on border, *Times of India*, October 14, p 1, col 2-4+

Anon, 1989, Wu meets Rajiv Gandhi, *Hindustan Times*, October 14

Anon, 1992, China pays glowing tributes to Rajiv, *Patriot*, May 23, p 1, col 1

Bhattacharya, Mira Sinha, 1988, Mission to Beijing, *Hindustan Times* (Magazine), December 18, p 1, col 1-8

Inder Jit, 1988, Rajiv's China visit and Nehru, *Economic Times*, December 20, p 5, col 7-8

Nihal Singh, S., 1988, PM's proposed China visit: Symbolism and substance, *Times of India*, May 28, p 6, col 3-5

Nihal Singh, S., 1989, Rajiv's China visit: Much work lies ahead, *Times of India*, January 3, p 6, col 3-5

S.C., 1988, Focus: Rajiv's China visit: Balance sheet, *Mainstream* 27(14) December 331, p 3-4

Times of India (Newspaper), 1988, A significant visit, *Times of India*, December 24, p 6, col 1-2, editorial

Venkatcharya, R., 1988, PM must prepare groundwork, *Economic Times*, December 18, p 3, col 1-8

See also Gandhi, Rajiv: Tours: Foreign: China

Indo-Cuban Relations

Anon, 1985, Rajiv, Castro vow closer ties, *Times of India*, October 23, p 1, col 4-6+

Indo-Czech Relations

Anon, 1986, Lyubomir, Rajiv agree on sanctions on South Africa, *Hindustan Times*, August 12

Indo-Dutch Relations

Anon, 1985, Rajiv, Dutch PM hold talks on trade, technology, *Times of India*, October 26, p 1, col 1-3

Indo-Egyptian Relations

Anon, 1989, Ghali calls on PM, *Hindustan Times*, Apri 29

Indo-Finnish Relations

Anon, 1986, Finnish leaders felicitated, *Hindustan Times*, December 6

Indo-French Relations

Anon, 1985, Rajiv, Mitterand hold talks, *Times of India*, June 7, p 1, col 1-3
Anon, 1985, Rajiv to visit US, France in June, *Times of India*, Jaunary, p 1, col 1-2+
Anon, 1986, Rajiv greets Chirac, *Statesman*, March 22
Anon, 1988, French Defence Minister calls on PM, *Statesman*, December 18
Anon, 1988, PMs confer, *Hindustan Times*, July 18
Anon, 1989, PM, Mitterand hold talks with Rajiv Gandhi, *Hindu*, February 2; *Hindustan Times*, February 2
Anon, 1989, Rajiv Gandhi arrives in Paris, *National Herald*, July 13
Anon, 1989, Rajiv Gandhi, Mitterand hold talks, *National Herald*, July 14; *Times of India*, July 14

See also Gandhi, Rajv: Tours: Foreign: France

Indo-German Relations

Anon, 1988, PM arrives in Bonn, *Hindu*, June 7; *National Herald*, June 7; *Times of India*, June 7
Anon, 1988, PM concludes visit to Bonn, *Hindu*, June 10; *Hindustan Times*, June 10
Anon, 1988, PM holds talks in Bonn, *Statesman*, June 7; *Times of India*, June 7

Indo-Hawaian Islands Relations

See also Gandhi, Rajiv: Tours: Foreign: Hawain Islands

Indo-Hungarian Relations

Anon, 1988, Hungarian Foreign Minister calls on Rajiv Gandhi, *Times of India*, March 2
Anon, 1988, PM continues discussions, *Statesman*, June 12; *Times of India*, June 12
Anon, 1988, Rajiv Gandhi arrives in Hungary, *Telegraph*, June 11
Anon, 1986, Call for global meet on Indian Ocean, *Hindustan Times*, October 14

Indo-Indonesian Relations

See also Gandhi, Rajiv: Tours: Foreign: Indonesia

Indo-Iranian Relations

Anon, 1989, Iranian leader calls on Rajiv Gandhi, *National Herald*, April 27

Anon, 1989, President, PM express grief over Khomeini's death, *Times of India*, June 5

Anon, 1989, Velayati, PM hold talks, *Hindustan Times*, August 30

Indo-Israeli Relations

Anon, 1988, India not to play Israel, *Hindustan Times*, March 24

Anon, 1988, PM condemns Israeli atrocities, *Times of India*, February 7

Indo-Italian Relations

Anon, 1986, Steps to boost trade, *Times of India*, November 6

Anon, 1988, V.P. Singh exposes PM's Italian connection, *Organiser* 39(43) April 10, p 3

Indo-Jambian Relations

Anon, 1986, PM concludes visit to Zambia, *Times of India*, May 16

Indo-Japanese Relations

See also Gandhi, Rajiv: Tours: Foreign: Japan

Indo-Jordanian Relations

Anon, 1986, Steps to expand trade ties, *Hindustan Times*, October 8

Anon, 1988, PM holds further discussions, *Statesman*, July 13

Anon, 1988, Prime Minister holds talks with Jordanian leaders, *Hindustan Times* July 12, *Times of India*, July 12

Indo-Kampuchean Relations

Anon, 1986, Political solution to Kampuchean issue urged, *Statesman*, October 20

Anon, 1988, Hun Sen holds talks with Rajiv Gandhi, *Times of India*, November 17

Indo-Korean Relations

See also Indo-North Korean Relations

Indo-Kuwait Relations

Anon, 1991, Rajiv flays Shekhar's stand on Gulf war, *Link* 33(25) January 27, p 31-34

Indo-Libyan Relations

Anon, 1986, PM condemns US action in Libya, *Hindu*, April 25

Anon, 1986, PM voice NAM support to Libya, *Times of India*, April 17, p 1, col 1-3

Indo-Maldives Relations

Anon, 1986, PM warns against rivalry in Indian Ocean, *Times of India*, February 3, p 1, col 1-3

Anon, 1986, Rajiv Gandhi for North South dialogue, *Indian Express*, February 9

Anon, 1986, Rajiv Gandhi warns rivalary in Indian Ocean, *Indian Express*, February 8

Anon, 1988, Gayoom, PM hold talks, *Indian Express*, December 8

Anon, 1988, Indian troops crush coup bid, *Times of India*, November 5

Anon, 1992, Yasser, Gayoom hail Rajiv, *Naitonal Herald*, May 22, p 10, col 3

Indo-Mauritius Relations

Anon, 1986, Mandatory sanctions must for end to racism, says PM, *Hindustan Times*, July 6, news-item

Anon, 1988, Ringadoo meets PM, *Statesman*, November 17

Indo-Mexican Relations

Anon, 1986, PM decries outside intervention in Central America, *Telegraph*, August 9

Indo-Mozambique Relations

Anon, 1988, India to assist Mozambique, *Indian Express*, December 3

Anon, 1986, PM expresses grief, *Hindu*, October 21

Anon, 1988, Mozambique President holds talks in New Delhi, *Hindustan Times*, May 15; *National Herald*, May 15

Indo-Namibian Relations

Anon, 1986, Call for Namibian independence, *Indian Express*, May 18

Anon, 1986, PM reaffirms support to Namibian struggle, *Times of India*, May 29

Anon, 1986, UN Namibia plan must prevail, says PM, *Hindustan Times*, July 6 news-item

Indo-Nepalese Relations

Anon, 1986, PM congratulates Shrestha, *Indian Express*, June 17

Anon, 1989, India ready for talks with Nepal: China not behind trouble, PM, *Times of India*, April 17, p 1, col 1-3+

Anon, 1989, India ready for talks with Nepal, says Rajiv Gandhi, *National Herald*, April 17; *Statesman*, April 17, news-item

Anon, 1989, Nepal welcomes offer to hold talks, *Times of India*, April 19

Anon, 1991, Killers wanted to slip into Nepal, *Hindustan Times*, July 7, p 1,

col 1-4

Anon, 1991, Rich tributes paid to Rajiv in Nepal, *Hindustan Times*, May 28, p 10, col 8

See also Birendra, Bir Bikram Shah Dev

Indo-Nicaraguan Relations

Anon, 1986, Nicaraguan Award for the Prime Minister, *Statesman* September 11

Anon, 1986, Nicaraguan leader's talks in New Delhi, *Hindustan Times*, August 24

Indo-North American Relations

Desai, M.V., 1987, PM in North America: Yes, with a but, *Economic Times*, October 27, p 5, col 7-8

Indo-North Korean Relations

Anon, 1988, North Korean PM in New Delhi, *National Herald*, Febraury 19

Indo-Norway Relations

Anon, 1986, Crown Prince and Rajiv Gandhi discuss trade ties, *Hindustan Times*, February 5

Indo-Omanese Relations

Anon, 1989, Omanese leader calls on Rajiv Gandhi, *Hindustan Times*, March 9

Indo-Pacific Relations

See also Gandhi, Rajiv: Tours: Foreign: South East Asia Pacific

Indo-Pak Relations

Anon, 1981, Failure to communicate, *India Today* 6(24) December 31, p 25

Anon, 1981, Rajiv: Favourite among Pakistanis, *National Herald*, June 25

Anon, 1985, Border clashes may hit ties: PM, *Times of India*, December 7, col 1-3, news-item

Anon, 1985, F-16s are for use against India: PM, *Times of India*, October 7, p 1, col 4-5, news-item

Anon, 1985, India alive to threat for Paksitan: PM, *Times of India*, May 5, p 1, col 1-4, news-item

Anon, 1985, India to take steps to meet Pak N-therat: Rajiv, *Times of India*, October 12, p 1, col 1-3, news-item

Anon, 1985, India willing to discuss all issues with Pak: PM, *Times of India*, November 12, p 1, col 1-3+, news-item

Anon, 1985, Infiltrators from Pak behind terrorism: PM, *Times of India*, September 17, p 1, col 1-3, news-item

Anon, 1985, No talks with Pak on N-issue: PM, *Times of India*, October 28, p 1, col 1-3, news-item

Anon, 1985, PM announces accord on Assam: Pakistan asked to abandon bomb: Sharper campaign against poverty: Call to combat extremism: Colourful Red Fort function, *Times of India*, Agust 16, p 1, col 1-4

Anon, 1985, PM: No Problem in containing Pak, *Times of India*, October 14, p 16, col 1-5, news-item

Anon, 1985, Rajiv invites Zia to inaguration of Breeder Reactor, *Times of India*, December 1, p 1, col 1-3+

Anon, 1986, India fully prepared to repel attacks, says PM, *Indian Express*, December 13, news-item

Anon, 1986, India to go nuclear if challenged, says PM, *Times of India* October 29, news-item

Anon, 1986, Junejo hails Rajiv Gandhi's role in bettering ties, *Telegraph* July 29

Anon, 1986, Nuclear option still open, says PM, *Indian Express*, April 9, news-item

Anon, 1986, Pak aiding terrorists: PM, *Times of India*, October 13, p 1, col 1-3, news-item

Anon, 1986, Pak responsiblity for hijack tragedy, says PM, *Times of India*, September 7, p 1, col 1-3, news-item

Anon, 1986, Pak visit shelved: PM rules out talks with extremists, *Times of India*, July 19, p 1, col 1-3+, news-item

Anon, 1986, PM holds Pakistan responsible, *Statesman*, September 7, news-item

Anon, 1986, PM's charge against Pakistan, *Times of India*, November 5, news-item

Anon, 1986, PM's visit to Pak cancelled, *Free Press Journal*, July 12

Anon, 1986, Rajiv meets Junejo in Stockholm, *Telegraph*, March 17

Anon, 1986, Rajiv-Zia meeting at Harare, *Hindustan Times*, September 6

Anon, 1986, Yaqub meets PM, *Times of India*, April 18

Anon, 1986, Zia expresses concern, *Telegraph*, October 3

Anon, 1986, Zia sends PM apology for attack on envoys, *Telegraph*, June 23

Anon, 1987, Pak exploting links with US: PM, *Times of India*, July 8, p 1, col 1-6, news-item

Anon, 1988, Foreign Secretaries meet ends, *Hindu*, June 3

Anon, 1988, No compromise on Siachen, says Rajiv Gandhi, *Hindu*, February 10, news-item

Anon, 1988, Paksitan biggest supporter of terrosim, says Rajiv Gandhi, *Hindustan Times*, June 9, news-item

Anon, 1988, PM again warns Pakistan against aiding terrorists, *Times of India*, August 16, p 1, col 1-3+, news-item

Anon, 1988, PM blames Pak for vitiating ties, *Times of India*, July 12, p 1, col 1-3+, news-item

Anon, 1988, PM greets Benazir, *Indian Express*, December 3

Anon, 1988, PM invites Zia for talks, *Hindu*, February 26; *Tribune*, Febraury 26

Anon, 1988, Rajiv Gandhi holds discussions with Benazir, *National Herald*, December 31

Anon, 1988, Rajiv Gandhi in Islamabad, *Indian Express*, December 30

Anon, 1989, Ashan calls on Rajiv Gandhi, *National Herald*, April 12

Anon, 1989, Indiaa, Pak sign these Records: N-Plant not to be attacked, *Times of India*, January 1, p 1, col 1-3.

Anon, 1989, PM's visit concludes, *Telegraph* July 18

Anon, 1989, Rajiv Gandhi holds talks with Benazir, *Indian Express*, July 7; *National Herald*, July 7

Anon, 1989, Three agreements signed, *National Herald*, January 1

Anon, 1989, Yaqub Khan calls on PM, *Hindustan Times*, July 26

Das Gupta, Amalendu and Datta-Ray, Sunanda, K., 1985, Countering a Pakistani bomb, *Statesman*, August 18, p 1

Gandhi, Rajiv, 1981, F-16s for Pak will spur arms race, *Hindustan Times*, July 10, p 4

Gandhi, Rajiv, 1982, Pak reasoning for arms ridiculous, *Hindustan Times*, Febraury 6, p 8

Kirpekar, Subash, 1988, Rajiv warns Pak against meddling in Punjab, *Times of India*, April 24, p 1, col 1-3+

Louis, Arul B., 1982, Arms for Pak will be discussed: PM, *Hindustan Times*, July 29, p 1, news-item

Organiser (Periodical), 1986, Rajiv-Zia see-saw, *Organiser* 37(44) March 16, p 3, editorial

Zehra, Nasim, 1991, Concern, disbelief in Pakistan, *Hindustan Times*, May 26, p 12, col 1-4

See also Gandhi, Rajiv: Tour: Foreign: Pakistan

Indo-Phillipines Relations

Anon, 1988, President Aquino's letter to Rajiv Gandhi, *Indian Express*, February 19

Indo-Polish Relations

Anon, 1985, Polish assurance to PM on spying probe, *Times of India*, February 13, p 1, col 1-2+

Anon, 1989, PM holds talks with Polish Vice-President, *National Herald*, April 13

Indo-Russian Relations

Anon, 1981, Rajiv lauds friendship with Soviet Union, *Hindustan Times*, October 26, p 1+

Anon, 1982, PM's Russia visit from September 20, *Times of India*, September 5, p 1

Anon, 1985, After Moscow, *Mainstream* 23(40) June 1, p 1-3

Anon, 1985, Gorbachyov pledges support for 'united, strong India': Rajiv in USSR, *Link* 27(42) May 26, p 4-10

Anon, 1985, PM confers with Gorbachev, *Times of India*, October 27, p 1, col 1-3

Anon, 1986, Call for ban on nuclear arms, *Times of India*, November 28

Anon, 1986, Gorbachev's envoy meets PM, *Free Press Journal*, July 18

Anon, 1986, Rajiv, Gorbachev hold talks on bilateral, global matters, *Economic*

Times, November 26, p 1, col 1-5+

Anon, 1986, Soviet Minister meets PM, *Indian Express*, October 31

Anon, 1986, Soviet will stand by India, says PM, *Times of India*, December 3, news-item

Anon, 1986, Tumultuous welcome to Gorbachev on arrival, *Indian Express*, November 26

Anon, 1987, Gorbachev, Rajiv discuss political situation in India, *Times of India*, July 3, p 1, col 1-3+

Anon, 1987, Gorbachev arrives in New Delhi, *Hindustan Times*, November 19

Anon, 1988, High level talks contiune, *Indian Express*, November 20

Anon, 1988, PM condoles quake victims, *National Herald*, December 14; *Times of India*, December 14

Anon, 1988, President, Prime Minister condole Armenian quake deaths, *Times of India*, December 9

Anon, 1988, Rajiv Gandhi briefed on Soviet troop withdrawl, *Hindu*, February 9

Anon, 1988, Six agreements signed, *National Herald*, November 21; *Times of India*, November 21

Anon, 1988, Speeches (Extracts): Prime Minister Rajiv Gandhi, *Foreign Affairs Report* 37(9-10-11) September-November, p 101-124, figures

Anon, 1989, Kamentsev meets Rajiv Gandhi, *Hindu*, March 10

Anon, 1989, PM holds talks with Gorbachev, *Hindustan Times*, July 16, *Times of India*, July 16

Anon, 1989, Soviet Minister calls on PM, *National Herald*, May 25

Anon, 1989, Vorontsov holds talks with Rajiv Gandhi, *Hindustan Times*, February 17

Chakravartty, Nikhil, 1989, Mr Gandhi's weekend visit to Moscow, *Times of India*, July 14, p 6, col 7-8

Dass, Ram, 1985, Rajiv Gandhi's Soviet visit, *People's Democracy* June 2, p 2

Dhar, M.K., 1982, PM lauds joint Indo-Soviet space venture, *Hindustan Times*, September 24, p 1

Jain, Girilal, 1985, Rajiv's mission to Moscow: No need to shirk issues, *Times of India*, May 18, p 8, col 3-5

Kausnik, Devendra, 1985, India, USSR and East Europe: Emerging trends under Rajiv Gandhi, *India Quaterly* 41(1) January-March, p 6-16

Khan, Masood Ali, 1985, Immensely successful Rajiv to USSR, *New Age* 33(22) June 2, p 8-9+

Khan, Masood Ali, 1985, Rajiv in Moscow, *New Age* 33(21) May 26, p 1+

Mishra, Chaturanan, 1989, Rajiv Gandhi policies on Perestroika, *New Age* 37(2) January 8, p 8

Murarka Dev, 1984, The assassination and after, *Mainstream* 23(15) December 8, p 5-6+

Padgaonkar, Dileep, 1987, Soviet backing for Rajiv: Significance of visit to Moscow, *Times of India*, July 7, p 6, col 3-5

Roy Chodhury, P., 1984, Soviet support for Rajiv Gandhi, *Link* 27(19) December 16, p 30-31

Sardesai, 1989, Gandhi, Gorbachev and India today, *Mainstream* 27(35) May 27,

p 53-55

Segon, Harish, 1987, Rajiv Gandhi's sueecssful visit, *Indian and Foreign Review* 24(21) August 31, p 6-9

See also Gandhi, Rajiv: Tours: Foreign: Russia

Indo-Saudi Arabian Relations

Reddy, G.K., 1982, India-Saudi Arabia joint Commission likley, *Hindu*, April 13, p 1

See also Gandhi, Rajiv: Tours: Foreign: Saudi-Arabia

Indo-Singapore Relations

Anon, 1988, Singapore PM's talks in New Delhi, *Times of India*, March 17

Indo-South African Relations

Anon, 1985, Rajiv for sanctions against Pretoria, *Times of India*, October 17, p 10, col 4, news item

Anon, 1986, Apartheid must end, says PM, *Times of India*, June 17, news-item

Anon, 1986, India promises fresh initiative to end apartheid, *Times of India*, May 19

Anon, 1986, India, Zambia call for world action against pretoria Government *Times of India*, Mat 15

Anon, 1986, Lyubomir, Rajiv agree on sanctions on South Africa, *Hindustan Times*, August 12

Anon, 1986, Mandatory sanctions against South Africa stressed, *Hindustan Times*, May 23

Anon, 1986, No going back on South Africa, says PM, *Hindustan Times*, July 26, news-item

Anon, 1986, PM attacks British stand regarding sanctions against South Africa, *Indian Express*, August 3, news-item

Anon, 1986, PM criticises EEC for diluting sanctions, *Hindustan Times*, September 18, news-item

Anon, 1986, PM for immediate sanctions, *Hindustan Times*, August 30, news-item

Anon, 1986, PM for immediate sanctions by NAM, *Indian Express*, September 3, news-item

Anon, 1986, PM for joint help to frontline States, *Indian Express*, Agust 15, news-item

Anon, 1986, Racism must end, says PM, *Statesman*, June 16, news-item

Anon, 1986, Rajiv's crusade in black Africa, *Link* 28(42) May 25, p 7-8

Anon, 1986, Sanctions against South Africa, *Times of India*, May 26

Anon, 1988, India wants Mandela's release, *Indian Express*, July 19

Indo-South-East Asian Relations

See also Gandhi, Rajiv: Tours: Foreign: South East Asian Pacific

Indo-Soviet Relations

See Indo-Russian Relations

Indo-Spanish Relations

Anon, 1988, India, Spain agree on defence tie up, *Hindustan Times*, July 13
Anon, 1988, PMs confer, *Hindustan Times*, July 18
Anon, 1988, Rajiv Gandhi in Spain, *Hindustan Times*, July 16

Indo-Sri Lankan Relations

Abraham, Thomas, 1991, An enigma in Colombo, *Front-line* June 22-July 5, p.2
Anon, 1986, Efforts continue for solution to ethnic crisis, *Free Press Journal*, November 18
Anon, 1986, JRJ hits out at Rajiv Gandhi, *Free Press Journal* May 19
Anon, 1986, Lanka Minister meets PM, *Indian Express*, April 18
Anon, 1986, PM asks Jayewardne to find early solution, *Indian Express*, March 10, news-item
Anon, 1986, PM asks MGR to ascertain militants views on Lanka offer, *Statesman*, October 11, news-item
Anon, 1986, PM asks Sri Lanka to clarify stand, *Indian Express*, February 10, news-item
Anon, 1986, Prime Minister and Sri Lanka President discuss ethnic crisis, *Statesman*, November 16
Anon, 1986, Rajiv Gandhi, MGR review situation, *Hindustan Times*, November 17; *Times of India*, November 17
Anon, 1986, Rajiv -Jayewardne talks brighten peace-hope, *Statesman*, November 17; *Times of India*, November 17
Anon, 1986, Rajiv voices concern to Sri Lankan envoy, *Hindu*, February 19, news-item
Anon, 1986, Talks fail over Tamil homeland, *Hindustan Times*, November 26
Anon, 1987, Attempt on Rajiv's life in Colombo, *Times of India*, July 31, p 1, col 3-6+
Anon, 1987, Indo-Sri Lanka agreement, *Foreign Affairs Report* 36(7-10) July-October, p 93-237
Anon, 1987, MGR, PM put all egges in LTTE basket, *Link* 30(17) November 29, p 4-7
Anon, 1987, PM calls for world pressure on Lanka, *Times of India*, May 29, p 1, col 1-3, news-item
Anon, 1987, PM to visit Lanka despite rejection of plan by LTTE, *Times of India*, July 28, p 1, col 1-3+
Anon, 1987, Rajiv, JRJ sign accord as violence rocks Colombo, *Economic Times*, July 30, p 1, col 6-8+
Anon, 1988, Dissanaayake calls on PM, *Hindustan Times*, May 11
Anon, 1988, PM, JRJ resolve to implement pact, *Times of India*, January 1, p 1, col 5-6+
Anon, 1988, Phased withdraw of IPKF agreed upon, *Statesman*, May 14

Anon, 1989, India to decide on pull out if no talks held, *National Herald*, July 13

Anon, 1989, India will fulfil terms of treaty with Lanka: PM, *Times of India*, July 18, p 1, col 1-3+

Anon, 1989, Lanka disputes Rajiv's stand on IPKF pull out, *Times of India*, June 16, p 1, col 1-3

Anon, 1989, Perumal calls for decisive move, *Times of India*, July 20

Anon, 1989, Perumal holds further talks, *National Herald*, March 22; *Statesman*, March 22

Anon, 1989, PM for time frame for IPKF pull out, *Sunday* July 5, news-item

Anon, 1989, PM's reply to Premdasa, *Hindustan Times*, July 1, news-item

Anon, 1989, PM writes to Premdasa, *Times of India*, June 21, news-item

Anon, 1989, Premdasa's reply to Rajiv Gandhi's letter, *Hindustan Times*, July 14

Anon, 1989, Premdasa writes to Rajiv Gandhi, *Hindustan Times*, July 23

Anon, 1989, Rajiv Gandhi, Perumal hold discussion, *Hindustan Times*, August 13

Anon, 1989, Thondaman calls for fresh accord, *Times of India*, July 10

Anon, 1989, Thondaman calls on Rajiv Gandhi, *Times of India*, July 9

Anon, 1989, Wijeratne calls on Rajiv Gandhi, *National Herald*, August 1

Anon, 1991, CBI team to visit Lanka today, *Hindustan Times*, May 30, p 16, col 1

Anon, 1991, Lanka rushes assassin's photo to SIT, *Hindustan Times*, July 10, p 12, col 6

Anon, 1991, Lankan says he knows accomplice, *Hindustan Times*, June 10, p 13, col 1-3

Anon, 1991, Sivarasan may flee to Lanka, *Hindustan Times*, June 30, p 1, col 3+

Anon, 1991, Sri Lanka officials see LTTE hand, *Hindustan Times*, May 26, p 12, col 2-3

Anon, 1992, Lanka willing to extradite Rajiv killers, *Hindustan Times*, May 22, p 1, col 1-3+

Gangal, S.C., 1987, The India-Sri Lanka agreement, *Gandhi Marg* 9(5) August, p 259-265

Krishna Iyer, V.R., 1988, The Sri Lanka accord: An autopsy, *Illustrated Weekly of India* 109(14) April 3, p 32-35

Krishna Iyer, V.R., 1988, The Sri Lanka accord: A post mortem, *Illustrated Weekly of India* 109(15) April 10, p 38-41

Mukarji, Apartim, 1991, Lanka TV fails to show assassin's photo, *Hindsutan Times*, June 3, p 20, col 1-2

Mukarji, Apartim, 1992, Lanka assurance to India on Rajiv assassination, *Hindustan Times*, May 8, p 12, col 2-4

Mukarji, Apartim, 1992, Sri Lanka dilemma over Prabhakaran, *Hindustan Times*, January 6, p 15, col 7-8

Phadnis, Umashankar, 1989, Indo-Sri Lanka accord: Need for reassesing realitics, *Mainstream* 27(40) July 1, p 5-6+

Talwar, Ashwini, 1991, Letter rogatory delivered to Lanka, *Times of India*, March 14, p 9, col 7-8

Times of India (Newspaper), 1989, A good agreement, *Times of India*, September 19, p 8, col 1-2, editorial

Indo-Sweden Relations

Anon, 1987, Opposition free to send team to Sweden: PM, *Times of India*, August 9, p 1, col 7-8+, news-item

See also Gandhi, Rajiv: Tours: Foreign: Sweden

Indo-Syrian Relations

Anon, 1988, PM, Assad hold further talks, *National Herald*, June 6; *Statesman*, June 6

Anon, 1988, PM hold talks in Damascus, *Indian Express*, June 5; *Telegraph*, June 5; *Time of India*, June 5

Anon, 1989, Syrian Minister calls on Rajiv Gandhi, *Hindustan Times*, April 26

Indo-Thai Relations

Anon, 1989, Joint panel to be set up, *Hindustan Times*, March 30

Anon, 1989, Thailand PM holds further talks with Rajiv Gandhi, *Telegraph*, March 31

Indo-Turkish Relations

Anon, 1986, Steps to explore new trade opportunities, *Statesman*, November 23

Anon, 1988, PM holds talks, *Indian Express*, July 20

Anon, 1988, PM in Ankara, *Times of India*, July 18

Anon, 1988, Trade pact signed, *National Herald*, July 19

Anon, 1988, Turkey ban export of components, *Telegraph*, July 19

Anon, 1988, Turkish President in New Delhi, *Statesman*, February 23

Indo-UK Relations

Anon, 1982, Rajiv sees Farnborough Air Show, *Hindustan Times*, September 6, p 11

Anon, 1986, Britain protests against PM's remarks on visa rule, *Hindu*, October 18; *Times of India*, October 18

Anon,1986, UK explains causes for deportation of JKLF Chief, *Statesman* October 27

Anon, 1986, United Kingdom isolated in Commonwealth, says PM, *Telegraph*, May 30, news-item

Anon, 1988, Lord Machay calls on Rajiv Gandhi, *Hindustan Times*, August 17

Anon, 1989, Rajiv Gandhi holds talks with Thatcher, *Indian Express*, July 15

Anon, 1991, UK House pays tributes to Rajiv, *Hindustan Times*, July 10, p 18, col 5

Anon, 1992, Tribes paid to Rajiv Gandhi in UK, *Times of India*, May 23, p 9, col 7-8.

See also Gandhi, Rajiv: Tours: Foreign: United Kingdom

Indo-US Relations

Aggarwal, A.K., 1986, Rajiv's u-turn toward USA, *Organiser* 37(43) March 9, p 1+

Anon, 1982, Indo-US retations breaking the ice, *India Today* 7(16) August 31, p 66-72

Anon, 1982, Side tracking, *India Today* 7(16) August 31, p 74-75

Anon, 1982, Spotlight on Rajiv, *Times of India*, July 31, p 13

Anon, 1983, Rajiv: US interfering in Punjab affairs, *Times of India*, July 24, p 9, col 1-2, news-item

Anon, 1984, Timings of US study very significant, says Rajiv, *Times of India*, December 19, p 1, col 4-6+, news-item

Anon, 1985, Image building and exploration in Rajiv's US visit, *Radical Humanist* 49(4) July, p 1-3

Anon, 1985, India will not be a camp follower: PM told US Foreign Policy Establishment, *Link* 28(3) November 3, p 9-10, news-item

Anon, 1985, Two faces of American pique with Rajiv Gandhi, *Link* 28(14) November 10, p 9-11

Anon, 1986, US treaty has retrospective effect: PM rejects terms for arms sale, *Times of India*, June 15, p 1, col 1-3

Anon, 1986, Disarmament movement against USA, says PM, *Telegraph*, August 7, news-item

Anon, 1986, Indo-US ties better now, says PM, *Free Press Journal* March 6, news-item

Anon, 1986, PM condemns US action in Libya, *Hindu*, April 25, news-item

Anon, 1986, PM-Solarz talks on arms threat, *Times of India*, December 16

Anon, 1986, President, Prime Minister greet Reagan, *Times of India*, July 4

Anon, 1986, US offers help on arms, *Statesman* October, 12

Anon, 1988, Armacost calls on Prime Minister, *Hindustan Times*, May 26, p 12, col 5-7

Anon, 1991, US wanted Rajiv back, *Hindustan Times*, May 26, p 12, col 5-7

Gandhi, Indira, 1982, Defence matters not on US talks, *Hindustan Times*, July 28, p 3+

Gandhi, Indira, 1982, No plan for talks with US on F-16 foregin fuel for Tarapur likely, *Indian Express*, July 28, p 1

Gandhi. Indira, 1982, US policies not in India's interest, *Hindustan Times*, July 12, p 1

Jain, Girilal, 1985, Rajiv Gandhi's visit to US: A possible turning point in policy, *Times of India*, June 4, p 8, col 3-5

Jain, Girilal, 1987, Reagan has an agenda: Questions that Rajiv should raise, *Times of India*, October 14, p 6, col 3-5

Hari Kumar, K.N., 1988, Rajiv and the US: Trading Non-Alignemnt for Hi-tech? *Mainstream* 26(29) April 30, p 17-26

Hari Kumar, K.N., 1988, Trading Non-Alignment for High Tech: Rajiv's record US visit, *Economic and Politied Weekly* 23(17) April 23, p 840-853

Louis, Arul B., 1982, Arms for Pak will be discussed: PM, *Hindustan Times*

July 29, p 1, news-item

Man Singh, Surjit, 1985, Rajiv Gandhi and Indo-American relations, *Mainstream* 24(9-10) November 2, p 49-53

Mathur, Girish, 1985, Rajiv's US visit may be as futile as Indira's was in 1982, *Link* 27(45) June 16, p 15-16

Parimoo, J.N., 1985, Rajiv charms American: But US policy is another matter, *Times of India*, June 22, p 8, col 3-5

Sethi, Patricia J., 1985, Rajiv impact lasts in United States, *Times of India*, July 3, p 8, col 7-8

Shankhdher, M.M., 1987, Rajiv-Reagan talks can open new chapter in Indo-US relations, *Organiser* 39(24) November 22, p 6

Subrahamanyam, K., 1987, Rajiv must resist US plea on NPT, *Times of India*, October 10, p 6, col 7-8

Thakur, Janardan, 1986, No big toy for Rajiv, *Times of India* (Sunday Review), July 6, p 1, col 1-5

See also Gandhi, Rajiv: Tours: Foreign: United States of America

Indo-Yugoslav Relations

Anon, 1986, Rajiv Gandhi, Mikulic discuss apartheid, *Indian Express*, July 29

Anon, 1988, Prime Minister in Belgrade, *Hindustan Times*, July 14; *Times of India*, July 14

Anon, 1989, Budhimir Loncar calls on PM, *National Herald*, May 4

Indo-Zambian Relations

Anon, 1986, Indo-Zambia call for world action against Pretoria Governmnet, *Times of India*, May 15

Anon, 1986, PM concludes visit to Zambia, *Times of India*, May 16

Indo-Zimbabwe Relations

Anon, 1986, India, Zimbabwe to set up joint commission, *Statesman*, May 17

Anon, 1986, PM visit Zimbabwe, *Times of India*, May 16

See also Gandhi, Rajiv: Tours: Foreign: Zimbabwe

Indonesia

See also Geographical Area subdivision under main Descriptor

Indoor Stadium: Geographical Area: India: Karnataka

Anon, 1992, Stadium named after Rajiv, *National Herald*, May 22, p 8 col 7-8

Industrial Growth: Geographical Area: India

Gandhi, Rajiv, 1982, Industrial growth vital for country, *Times of India*, February 11, p 5

Industry: Geographical Area: India

Anon, 1985, Prime Minister hits out at industry, *Economic Times*, October 12, p 1, col 1-5+

Anon, 1985, Warning on Induced sickness: PM's call to step up productivity, *Times of India*, September 20, p 1, col 1-3+, news item

Anon, 1988, What govenment expects from industry, *Business India* (Special Number), April 30, p 14-15

Infiltration: Geographical Area: India

Anon, 1985, Infiltrators from Pak behind terrorism: PM, *Times of India*, September 17, p 1, col 1-3, news-item

Anon, 1986, PM asks police to check infiltration, *Times of India*, March 20

Inflation: Geographical Area: India

Anon, 1986, Inflation under control: PM, *Economic Times*, March 6, p 1, col 2-4+, news-item

Infiltrators from Pakistan

Anon, 1985, Infiltrators from Pak behind terrorism: PM, *Times of India*, September 17, p 1, col 1-3, news-item

Inquiries

Anon, 1991, Politicising inquiries, *India Today*, June 30, p 11, col 1-2

International Debt: Geographical Area: India

Anon, 1991, Will Rajiv Gandhi explain? Who is responsible for the begging bowl? *Organiser* 62(39) May 5, p 1, col 1-3+

Internatioanl Fund for Agricultural Development

Anon, 1988, PM's talks with IFAD Chief, *Statesman*, March 31

International Labour Organisation

Anon, 1985, Challenges before ILO: Rajiv Gandhi's Address, *Mainstream* 23(44) June 9, p 27-29

International Relations

See Foreign Relations
See also Indo-. . . Relations, e.g. Indo-African Relations

International Youth Conference

Anon, 1982, World youth to fight for disarmament, *Indian Express*, January 25, p 7

Gandhi, Rajiv, 1982, Internatinal Youth Conference work for peace, *Current*,

January 30, p 6

Iran

See also Geographical Area Subdivision under main Descriptor

Iran: Foreign Relations: Geographical Area: India

See under Indo-Iranian Relations

Islamabad: Pakistan

See also Geographical Area subdivision under main Descriptor

Israel

See also Geographical Area subdivision under main Descriptor

Israel: Atroctities

Anon, 1988, PM condemn Israeli atrocitics, *Times of India*, February 7,

Israel: Foreign Relations: Geographical Area: India

See under Indo-Israel Relations

Italy

See also Geographical Area subdivision under main Descriptor

Italy: Foreign Relations: Geographical Area: India

See under Indo-Italian Relations

IVY League

Das, Sitanshu, 1986, Oxbridge and IVY league screen between PM and Congress, *Link* 29(12) October, p 4-8

JKLF

=Jammu Kashmir Liberation Front

Jagjivan Ram: Homage Paid by Gandhi, Rajiv

Anon, 1986, Homage paid to Jagjivan Ram, *Times of India*, July 7

Jagjivan Ram: Views on Gandhi, Rajiv

Anon, 1981, J.Ram's jibe at Rajiv Gandhi, *Indian Express*, August 24, p 10

Jagmohan

Anon, 1986, Jagmohan calls on PM, *Telegrph*, July 27

Anon, 1991, Crisis in Kashmir valley: Jagmohan's open letter to Rajiv,

Democratic World 20(19) May 12, p 1, col 1-2

Anon, 1991, Jagmohan arraigns Rajiv for Kashmir crisis: Anyone trying to be fair is dubbed communal, *Organiser* 40(39) May 5, p 15+

Sidhva, Shirj, 1991, The letter bomb: Jagmohan accuses Rajiv Gandhi of misleading the Nation over Kashmir, *Sunday* May 5-May 11, p 17

Jag Pravesh Chandra: Views on Assassination of Gandhi, Rajiv

Anon, 1991, Nation will emerge stronger: Chandra, *Hindustan Times*, May 31, p 3, col 2-3

Jakarta: Indonesia

See also Geographical Area subdivision under main Descriptor

Jambia

See also Geographical Area subdivision under main Descriptor

Jambia: Foreign Relations: Geographical Area: India

See also Indo-Jambian Relations

Jammu and Kashmir: India

N.C., 1986, Sunshine in Kashmir, *Mainstream* 25(9) November 15, p 6-7

Anon, 1982, PM seeking J.K. Muslims backing for Rajiv, *Indian Express*, January 3, p 9

See also Geographical Area Subdivision under main Descriptor

Jammu and Kashmir Liberation Front

Anon, 1986, UK explains causes for deportation of JKLF Cheif, *Statesman*, October 27

See also Kashmiri Pandits

Jammu and Kashmir Problem

Anon, 1986, Kashmir issue to be solved bilaterally, says PM, *Hindustan Times*, January 21, news-item

Anon, 1991, Crisis in Kashmir valley: Jagmohan's open letter to Rajiv, *Democratic World* 20(19) May 12, p 1, col 1-2

Anon, 1991, Jagmohaan arraigns Rajiv for Kashmir crisis: Anyone trying to be fair is dubbed communal, *Organiser* 62(39) May 5, p 15+

Anon, 1991, Kashmiri Pandits confront Rajiv, *Organiser* 42(25) January 27, p 65, col 1-2

Anon, 1991, Rajiv accused of J and K mess, *Hindustan Times*, April 23, p 9, col 1-3

Sidhva, Shiraj, 1991, The letter bomb: Jagmohan accuses Rajiv Gandhi of misleading the Nation over Kashmir, *Sunday* May 5-May 11, p 17

Janata Dal (Political Party)

Anon, 1984, Janata lifted ban on Chauhan: PM, *Times of India*, December 16, p 1, col 1-2+, news-item

Gandhi, Rajiv, 1982, Raps Janata, LD Leadership, *Hindustan Times*, May 28, p 6, col 6-7

Janata Dal (Samajvadi) (Political Party)

Prasannan, R., 1991, JD(S) will disappear: Rajiv Gandhi promises better contact with the masses, *The week* April 28, p 32-33

Janata Government

See Non-Congress Governments

Japan

See also Geographical Area subdivision under main Descriptor

Japan: Foreign Relations: Geographical Area: India

See under Indo-Japanese Relations

Jawaharlal Nehru Memorial Fund

Anon, 1991, Sonia to head Nehru Fund, *Hindustan Times*, May 31, p 10, col 4

Jawaharlal Nehru Rojgar Yojana

Anon, 1989, Government announces new rural job scheme, *National Herald*, April 29; *Telegraph*, April 29

Jayalalitha, J.

Anon, 1991, Rajiv, Jayalalitha finalise poll pact, *Hindustan Times*, March 31, p 1, col 1-3+

Democratic World (Periodical), 1991, Rajiv gives Jaya bulk of seats, *Democratic World*, 20(7) February 17, p 4, col 1-2, editorial

Jayalalitha, J.: Views on Assassination of Gandhi, Rajiv

Anon, 1992, Cover-up in Rajiv case, alleges Jaya, *Times of India*, p 14, col 4, news-item

Anon, 1992, Evidence in Rajiv case being concealed: Jaya, *Indian Express*, March 31, p 1, col 8+, news-item

Jayekar, Pupul

Anon, 1986, Pupul Jayekar cultural adviser to PM, *Telegraph*, September 3

Jayewardne, Junius Ranjan

Anon, 1986, JRJ hits out at Rajiv Gandhi, *Free Press Journal*, May 19

Anon, 1986, PM asks Jayewardne to find early solution, *Indian Express*, March 10

Anon, 1986, Rajiv, Jayewardne talks brighten peace-hope, *Statesman*, November 17; *Times of India*, November 17

Anon, 1987, Rajiv, JRJ sign accord as violence rocks Colombo, *Economic Times*, July 30, p 1, col 6-8+

Anon, 1988, PM, JRJ resolve to implement pact, *Times of India*, Jaunary 21, p 1, col 5-6+

Jharkhand Problem

Anon, 1988, PM turns down demand for Jharkhand State, *National Herald*, May 28

Jordan

See also Geographical Area subdivision under main Descriptor

Jordan: Foreign Relations: Geographical Area: India

See under Indo-Jordan Relations

Junejo, Muhammad Khan

Anon, 1986, Junejo hails Rajiv Gandhi's role in bettering ties, *Telegraph*, July 29

Anon, 1986, Rajiv meets Junejo in Stockholm, *Telegraph*, March 17

Kamentesv, Veladimir Mikhailovich

Anon, 1989, Kamentsev meets Rajiv Gandhi, *Hindu*, March 10

Kampuchea

See also Geographical Area Subdivision under main Descriptor

Kampuchea: Foreign Relations: Geographical Area: India

See under Indo-Kampuchean Relations

Kanchi: Tamil Nadu: India

Jayaram, C.S., 1991, Did killer's team visit Kanchi? *Hindustan Times*, June 6, p 18, col 3-6

See also Geographical Area Subdivision under main Descriptor

Kapoor, Yashpal

Nizamuddin D.E., 1982, Who is Yashpal Kapoor fooling? *Sunday* 9(37) March 6, p 58

Saari, Anil 1982, Yashpal Kapoor: The end is near, *Sunday* 9(33) January 31, p 42

Karanjia, R.K.: Views on Congress (I)

Karanjia, R.K., 1982, Congress for dissidents, *Blitz*, May 15, p 1

Karnataka: India

Anon, 1981, Bangappa men meet Rajiv, *Indian Express*, December 31, p 7

Anon, 1981, Gundu dreads Rajiv's visit, *Blitz*, August 8, p 3

Anon, 1981, PM will assess Gundu Govt's performance, *Indian Express*, December 25, p 7

Anon, 1982, A.M. Khan was side tracked? *Sunday* 9(31) January 17, p 37

Anon, 1982, Raja Rajiv snubs Khan, *Blitz*, January 9, p 5

Anon, 1982, Revolt imminent in Karnataka Congress (I), *Indian Express*, June 30, p 4

Anon, 1991, Karnataka House mourns Rajiv, *Hindustan Times*, July 6, p 9, col 1

Chawla, Prabhu, 1982, Uniting to divide, *India Today* 7(2) January 31, p 36-37

Kamath, M.V., 1982, Importance of being a sycophant, *Indian Express*, February 7, p 2

Raj Gopal, R., 1982, Karnataka: Little chance for mid-term poll, *Caravan* 2(714) February, p 15-16

See also Geographical Area subdivision under main Descriptors

Karthikeyan, R.,

Anon, 1992, SIT Chief denies reports, *Times of India*, May 23, p 3, col 2, news-item

Anon, 1992, Verma Panel hearing on SIT Chief, *Hindustan Times*, March 5, p 12, col 5

Karunanidhi, Muthuvel

Anon, 1991, Karunanidhi blames Central rule, *Hindustan Times*, June 2, p 12, col 5-8

Kashmir

See Jammu and Kashmir

Kashmiri Pandits

Anon, 1991, Kashmiri Pandits confront Rajiv, *Organiser* 42(25) January 27, p 65, col 1-2

Kerala: India

Anon, 1992, Sivarasan, Subha took shelter in TN, Kerala, *Sunday Tribune*, May 24, p 4, col 4-5

See also Geographical Area subdivision under main Descriptors

Khan, Abdul Ghaffar

Anon, 1981, Ghaffar Khan arrives for treatment, *Times of India*, November 7, p 1
Anon, 1981, Ghaffar Khan in India, *Indian Express*, Novmber 7, p 1

Khan, Arif Mohammad

Anon, 1982, How A.M. Khan was side tracked? *Sunday* 9(31) January 17, p 37
Anon, 1982, Raja Rajiv snubs Khan, *Blitz*, January 9, p 5
Anon, 1986, Arif quit on Bill issue, *Times of India*, February 27, p 1, col 5-7
Anon, 1986, Arif's letter to PM: Communal divide in secular party, *Times of India*, September 25, p 1, col 2-5+
Anon, 1986, The Arif Mohammad affair, *Times of India*, March 3, p 1, col 2-5+
Thakur, Janardan, 1986, The stormy Arif, *Times of India* (Sunday Review), March 9, p 1, col 1-8
Times of India (Newspaper), 1986, Courageous Mr. Khan, *Times of India*, September 27, p 8, col 1-2, editorial
Times of India (Newspaper), 1986, Unanswered questions, *Times of India*, March 6, p 8, col 1-2, editorial

Khan, Syed Murtuga Ali

See Rampur Nawab of

Khashoggi, Adnan M.

Anon, 1991, Khashoggi-Rajiv confabulation: Embarrassment for Cong? *Times of India*, February 1, p 1, col 6-8+.

Khomeini, Ayatollah Ruhollah: Homage Paid by Gandhi, Rajiv

Anon, 1989, President, PM express grief over Khomeini's death, *Times of India*, June 5

Khomeini, Ayatollah Ruhollah: Homage Paid by Venkataranam

Anon, 1989, President, PM express grief over Khomeini's death, *Times of India*, June 5

Khushwant Singh: Views on Gandhi, Rajiv

Khushwant Singh, 1981, Rajiv: Reluctant bridegroom, *Hidustan Times*, May 13, p 9

Kisan Rally

Anon, 1981, Rajiv Gandhi to be projected in Kisan Rally, *Statesman*, February 12
Mitra, Sumit, 1981, Kisan Rally: Operation Ego message, *India Today*, 6(5) March 15, p 16-21

Kissinger, Henry Alferd

Anon, 1985, Can Rajiv overcome Nixon, Kissinger and Reagan? *Link* 27(44) June 9, p 13-16

Kittu

Anon, 1991, Killers used LTTE as cover: Kittu, *Hindustan Times*, June 2, p 15, col 8

Kohl, Helmut

Anon, 1986, Helmut Kohl writes to Rajiv Gandhi, *Statesman*, May 23

Korea: North

See North Korea

Kuwait

See also Geographical Area subdivision under main Descriptor

Kuwait: Foreign Relations: Geographical Area: India

See under Indo-Kuwait Relations

LD

=Lok Dal (Political Party)

LF

=Left Front

LS

=Lok Sabha

LTTE

=Liberation Tigers of Tamil Elam

Language: Hindi

Anon, 1986, No move to impose Hindi, says PM, *Statesman*, October 2, news-item

Anon,1986, PM reiterates Nehru's assurance on Hindi, *Indian Express*, November 7

Language: Nepali

Anon, 1986, Clarification on PM's remarks on the inclusion of Nepali in the Eighth schedule, *Free Press Journal*, December 22

Lanka

See Sri Lanka

Law and Order: Geographical Area: India

Anon, 1991, PM briefs RV on law and order, *Hindustan Times*, May 28, p 1, col 5

Law Minister: Geographical Area: India

Anon, 1986, PM defends Law Minister's remarks, *Hindustan Times*, September 30

Leader of Opposition in Parliament: Geographical Area: India: Advani, L.K.

Anon, 1991, Rajiv and V.P. Singh highly frustrated as Advani named Leader of the Opposition, *Organiser* 42(22) January 6, p 1, col 1-5+

Leader of Opposition in Parliament: Geographical Area: India: Gandhi, Rajiv

Anon, 1989, Rajiv: Leader of Opposition, *Telegraph*, December 21

Anon, 1991, Rajiv's bid to play the double role of the super PM and Opposition Leader, *Organiser* 42(23) January 13, p 3, col 2-4+

Left Front: Boycott of Meet on Gandhi, Rajiv

Anon, 1991, LF to boycott meet on Rajiv, *Hindustan Times*, May 26, p 9, col 1-2

Legal System: Geographical Area: India

Anon, 1986, PM stresses on need to streamline legal system, *Indian Express*, November 4

Lenin: Homage Paid to Him

Anon, 1982, Wreath laid at Lenin's mausoleum, *Hindustan Times*, September 22, p 8

Li Peng

Anon, 1988, Rajiv, Li Peng hopeful of border accord, *Times of India*, December 20, p 1, col 1-4+

Liang-Kim Bang

Anon, 1989, Liang calls on Rajiv Gandhi, *National Herald*, March 2; *Statesman*, March 2

Liberation Tigers of Tamil Elam

Anon, 1986, PM asks MGR to ascertain militants views on Lanka offer, *Statesman*, October 11

Anon, 1987, LTTE chief to meet Rajiv today, *Times of India*, July 25, p 1, col

1-3+

Anon, 1987, MGR, PM put all eggs in LTTE basket, *Link* 30(17) November 29, p 4-7

Anon, 1987, PM to visit Lanka despite rejection of plan by LTTE, *Times of India*, July 28, p 1, col 1-3+

Anon, 1991, Prime Minister rules out truce with LTTE, *Hindu*, August 6, news-item

Anon, 1991, Assassin an LTTE member: SIT, *Hindustan Times*, July 6, p 1, col 3, news-item

Anon, 1991, Assassin expelled fron LTTE? *Hindustan Times*, May 31, p 9, col 7

Anon, 1991, BJP blame LTTE for killing, *Hindustan Times*, May 26, p 8, col 7

Anon, 1991, Case against LTTE almost wrapped up, *Hindustan Times*, November 17, p 6, col 7-8

Anon, 1991, Killers used LTTE as cover: Kittu, *Hindustan Times*, June 2, p 15, col 8, news-item

Anon, 1991, LTTE cadres panic in UK, *Hindustan Times*, June 16, p 15, col 3

Anon, 1991, LTTE man detained, *Hindustan Times*, June 9, p 12, col 5

Anon, 1991, LTTE offer to help probe, *Hindustan Times*, June 7, p 1, col 8

Anon, 1991, LTTE owns 'onus' for Rajiv killing, *Hindustan Times*, July 15, p 1, col 1

Anon, 1991, LTTE planned mass killings in Sept, *Hindustan Times*, July 17, p 7, col 7-8

Anon, 1991, LTTE publication seized, *Hindustan Times*, July 23, p 6, col 1

Anon, 1991, LTTE refuses to own Rajiv's murder, *Organiser* 62(44) June 9, p 14, col 4-5+

Anon, 1991, LTTE very much involved: Chavan, *Hindustan Times*, May 31', p 13, col 5-6, news-item

Anon, 1991, LTTE youth might spill the beams, says Lanka, *Hindustan Times*, June 10, p 13, col 2-4

Anon, 1991, No hand in killing, insists LTTE, *Hindustan Times*, May 31, p 13, col 5-6

Anon, 1991, Search for LTTE hide outs, *Hindustan Times*, July 29, p 7, col 1-2.

Anon, 1991, Secret link between NF, LTTE alleged, *Hindustan Times*, June 14, p 10, col 3

Anon, 1991, Sri Lankan officials see LTTE hand, *Hindustan Times*, May 26, p 12, col 2-3

Anon, 1991, Two LTTE men brought to Capital, *Hindustan Times*, June 9, p 10, col 3

Anon, 1991, Why LTTE High Command ordered Rajiv's treacherous killing? *Link* 33(50) July 21, p 5-9

Anon, 1991, Why pick on the LTTE? *Sunday* June 23-june 29, p 64-65

Anon, 1992, The case against the LTTE, *Independent*, May 24, p 4, col 1-3

Anon, 1992, Evidence of LTTE hand in Rajiv murder, *Hindustan Times*, April 17, p 10, col 4

Anon, 1992, LTTE blames Rajiv for massacre, *Hindustan Times*, March 4, p 22, col 5

Anon, 1992, LTTE planned for 9 months, *Tribune*, May 23, p 1, col 6-8

Anon, 1992, Probe team holds LTTE responsible, *Hindustan Times*, March 2, p 22, col 6-7.

Jeyaraj, D.B.S., 1991, Question of motive: Was it the LTTE? *Frontline* 8(12) June 8-June 21, p 25-26

Mukarji, Apartim, 1992, LTTE extends olive branch to New Delhi, *Hindustan Times*, March 29, p 15, col 5-7

Subramanian, T.S., 1991, LTTE's overtures, *Frontline* 8(12) June 8-June 21, p 23

Sunil, K.P., 1991, What is the LTTE up to? *Illustrated Weekly of India* 112(24) June 15, p 6-11

Liberation Tigers of Tamil Elam: Geographical Area: United Kingdom

Anon, 1991, LTTE cadres panic in UK, *Hindustan Times*, June 16, p 15, col 13

Libya

See also Geographical Area subdivision under main Descriptor

Libya: Foreign Relations: Geographical Area: India

See under Indo-Libyan Relations

Limaye, Madhu

Anon, 1986, Madhu Limaye's letter to PM, *Times of India*, June 1

Linguistic States: Geographical Area: India

Anon, 1986, PM opposed to linguistic States, *Statesman*, July 3

Parakal, Pauly V., 1986, Rajiv Gandhi should know some facts on linguistic States, *New Age* 34(42) December 28, p 3

Lok Dal (Political Party)

Anon, 1982, Rajiv lashes out at BJP-LD Poll alliance, *Times of India*, May 7, p 7

Gandhi, Rajiv, 1982, LD-BJP alliance mere opportunism, fake, *Hindustan Times*, May 15, p 5

Gandhi, Rajiv, 1982, Raps Janata, LD Leadership, *Hindustan Times*, May 14

Lok Sabha: Proceedings: Geographical Area: India

Anon, 1988, Opposition seeks PM's apology for remarks, *Hindustan Times*, July 28

Anon, 1989, Opposition walkout in LS over PM's remarks, *Hindustan Times*, April 6, *Telegraph*, April 6

Anon, 1991, Surveillance issue again rocks Parliament, *Hindustan Times*, March 6

Loncar, Budimir

Anon, 1989, Budimir Loncar calls on PM, *National Herald*, May 4

Lucknow: Uttar Pradesh: India

See also Geographical Area Subdivision under main Descriptor

Ludhiana: Punjab: India

See also Geographical Area subdivision under main Descriptor

MNC

=Multi National Corporation/Company

Mr Clean

See Gandhi, Rajiv

M'Bow, A.M.

Anon, 1986, M'Bow meets PM, *Times of India*, August 22

Mackay, Lord

Anon, 1988, Lord Mackay calls on Rajiv Gandhi, *Hindustan Times*, August 17

Madhya Pradesh: India

See also Geographical Area subdivision under main Descriptor

Mahanta, Prafulla Kumar

See Chief Minister: Geographical Area: India: Assam: Mahanta, Prafulla Kumar

Maharashtra: India

See also Geographical Area subdivision under main Descriptors

Mahatab, H.

Anon, 1989, Mahatab's portrait unveiled, *National Herald*, August 8

Makwana, Yogendra

Anon, 1988, Yogendra Makwana forwards resignation letter, *Indian Express*, September 18

Maldives

See also Geographical Area subdivision under main Descriptors

Maldives: Foreign Relations: Geographical Area: India

See under Indo-Maldives Relations

Malkhan Singh

Anon, 1982, Malkhan, 19 of gang give up: Rajiv hails surrender, *Hindustan Times*,

June 18, p 1+

Malviya, Satya Prakash: Views on Gandhi, Rajiv

Anon, 1986, Malviya criticises PM's stand on GNLF, *Indian Express*, October 4

Mandela, Nelson

Anon, 1988, India wants Mandala's release, *Indian Express*, July 19

Maragatham, Chandra Shekhar

Anon, 1991, Maragatham meets Sonia, *Hindustan Times*, July 10, p 3, col 2

Anon, 1992, Maragatham didn't discuss security, *Hindustan Times*, March 6, p 10, col 4-7.

Marcoism

Khare, Harish, 1986, Congress and Rajiv Gandhi: Danger of Indian Marcoism, *Times of India*, September 6, p 8, col 3-5

Maruti Cars

Anon, 1982, Goodbye, Maruti, *Onlooker* 44(2) June 31, p 7

Mass Killings

See Massacre

Massacre

Anon, 1991, LTTE planned mass killings in September, *Hindustan Times*, July 17, p 7, col 7-8

Massacre: Geographical Area: India: Devoli

Anon, 1981-1982, Mrs Gandhi's Devoli visit heartens Harijan victims, *Delhi Recorder* 2(9) December 15-June 14, p 26-28

Mauritius

See also Geographical Area subdivision under main Descriptors

Mauritius: Foreign Relations: Geographical Area: India

See under Indo-Mauritius Relations

May Day

Gandhi, Rajiv, 1987, We salute workers who do Gods work on earth: Prime Minsiter Rajiv Gandhi's Address to the May day rally, 1987, *Indian Worker* 35(32-33) May 11-May 18, p 8-11

Mehta, Chiman Bhai

Anon, 1989, An elderly Congress leader and Member of the Rajya Sabha, B. Chiman Bhai Mehta expelled from the Party, urged the Party to elect a new leader to replace Rajiv Gandhi: The first such vocie to be raised, *Indian Express*, March 21

Member of Parliament: Geographical Area: India: Congress (I): Views on Fertiliser Subsidy

Anon, 1991, Congress MPs warn against cut in fertiliser subsidy, *Hindustan Times*, August 2, p 1, col 2-4

Member of Parliament: Geographical Area: India: DMK

Anon, 1989, DMK MPs meet PM, *Indian Express*, April 6

Member of Parliament: Geographical Area: India: Lok Sabha: Gandhi, Rajiv

1981, June, elected
1981, August 17, sworn

Member of Parliament: Geographical Area: India: Mehta, Chiman Bhai

Anon, 1989, An elderly Congress leader and Member of the Rajya Sabha, Chimman Bhai Mehta expelled fron the Party, urged the Pary to elect a new leader to replace Rajiv Gandhi: The first such voice to be raised, *Indian Express*, March 21

Mexico

See also Geographical Area subdivision under main Descriptors

Mexico: Foreign Relations: Geographical Area: India

See also Indo-Mexican Relations

Mid Term Poll

See Elections: Mid Term: Geographical Area: India

Migrants: Geographical Area: India

Anon, 1986, PM allays fears of migrants, *Hindustan Times*, June 27

Mikulic, Branko

Anon, 1986, Rajiv Gandhi, Mikulic discuss apartheid, *Indian Express*, July 29

Militants

Anon, 1986, PM asks MGR to ascestain Militant's views on Lanka offer, *Statesman*, October 11

See also Extremists: Terrorists

Military: Geographical Area: India

Anon, 1988, PM urges to keep military out of politics, *Hindu*, November 13

Ministry: Geographical Area: India

Sen Gupta, Barun, 1981, Cabinet shake up has merely been post- pond, *Sunday* 9(10) August 23, p 23

Minorities: Geographical Area: India

Anon, 1991, Rajiv was leader of minorites, *Hindustan Times*, May 26, p 5, col 2-3

Raina, Jay, 1991, Rajiv allays minorities apprehension, *Hindustan Times*, May 14, p 1, col 4+

Minorities: Geographical Area: India: Assam

Anon, 1985, Assam minorities safe, says PM, *Times of India*, December 14, p 1, col 1-3, news-item

Minorities: Geographical Area: India: Punjab

Anon, 1986, PM's assurance to Punjab minorities, *Times of India*, May 30

Mitterand, Francois

Anon, 1989, PM, Mitterand hold talks with Rajiv Gandhi, *Hindu*, February 2; *Hindustan Times*, Febraury 2

Anon, 1989, Rajiv Gandhi, Mitterand hold talks, *National Herald*, July 14; *Times of India*, July 14

Mobile Libraries: Geographical Area: India

Anon, 1992, Mobile libraries flagged off, *National Herald*, May 23, p 10, col 6-7

Anon, 1992, Sonia handover keys of libraries, *Times of India*, May 23, p 4, col 5-6

Anon, 1992, Sonia presents mobile libraries, *Hindustan Times*, May 23

Morals and Morality

Anon, 1989, (Book Review), *Sunday Statesman*, August 13, p 11, col 1-4

Review of the Book: **Varma, Umeshwar Prasad**, 1989, *Rajiv Gandhi and morality in public affairs*, Mittal Publishers, Delhi

Moscow: Russia

See also Geographical Area subdivision under main Descriptors

Mountaineering

Anon, 1981, Mountaineer's bid to scale Nanda Devi, *Hindustan Times*, August 7, p 8

Anon, 1981, Three women climb Nanda Devi peak, *Hindustan Times*, September 23, p 1-16

Mozambique

See also Geographical Area subdivision under main Descriptors

Mozambique: Foreign Relations: Geographical Area: India

See under Indo-Mozambique Relations

Mozambique: President

See under President: Geographical Area: Mozambique

Mukherjee, Pranab

Anon, 1981, While Pranab and Zail quarreled over protocol Rajiv officiated as PM, *Organiser* 33(29) December 6, p 5

Anon, 1986, Pranab expelled from Party for six years: Three other leaders suspended, *Times of India*, April 28, p 1, col 1-4

Anon, 1986, Rajiv Gandhi lacks charisma, says Pranab, *Times of India*, June 1, news-item

Barman, Ashish, 1986, Pranab's ouster stems tide of revolt, *Link* 28(40) May 11, p 8-9

Mathur, Girish, 1986, Pranab: His business and culture, *Link* 28(44) July 8, p 14-16

Mukherjee, Pranab, 1982, New blood in politics, *Illustrated Weekly of India*, 103(3) January 31, p 30-33

Multinational Corporation/Company: Geographical Area: India

Anon, 1985, MNCs not being favoured, *Times of India*, May 5, p 1, col 5-7+

Municipal Officers: Geographical Area: India

Gandhi, Rajiv, 1989, PM's address to Municipal Officers, *Hindustan Times*, June 6; *National Herald*, June 6

Murtuza Ali Khan, Syed

See Rampur, Nawab of

Murugan

See Assassination: Attempts and Probes: Gandhi, Rajiv: Murugan Involvement

Muslim Women Bill

Verma, Kewal, 1986, Rajiv Gandhi and secularism: Lessons from Muslim Women Bill debate, *Mainstream* 24(38) May 24, p 51-53+

Muslims: Vote Bank

Anon, 1982, PM seeking JK Muslims backing for Rajiv, *Indian Express*, January 3, p 9

Badola, V.M., 1989, PM fails to mollify Muslims, *Times of India*, November 22, p 4, col 1-3

Mathur, Girish, 1981, Rajiv's rivals fight to save their deposits . . . Congress (I) battle to win Muslim minds, *Blitz*, June 13, p 4

NAM

=Non-Aligned Movement

NC

=National Conference (Political Party)

NDMC

=New Delhi Municipal Committee

NF

=National Front (Political Party

NPT

=Non Proliferation Treaty

NSUI

=National Students Union of India

Nagarpalika Bill

Anon, 1989, Nagarpalika Bill introduced, *Indian Express*, August 8

Nagarpalika Sammelan

Gandhi, Rajiv, 1989, PM's Address to Nagarpalika Sammelan, *Hindustan Times*, June 15

Nagpur: Maharashtra: India

Anon, 1982, Rajiv to launch mass contact drive in Nagpur, *Times of India*, September 8, p 9

See also Geographical Area subdivision under main Descriptors

Najibullah

Anon, 1988, Najib holds further discussion with PM, *Hindustan Times*, May 6; *Times of India*, May 6

Anon, 1988, Najibullah holds talks in New Delhi, *National Herald*, May 5; *Times of India*, May 5

Nalini

See Assassination: Attempts and Probes: Gandhi, Rajiv: Nalini Involvement

Namibia

See also Geographical Area subdivision under main Descriptors

Namibia: Foreign Relations: Geographical Area: India

See under Indo-Namibian Relations

Nanda Devi Peak

Anon, 1981, Mountaineer's bid to scale Nanda Devi, *Hindustan Times*, August 7, p 8

Anon, 1981, Three women climb Nanda Devi peak, *Hindustan Times*, September 23, p 1-16

Narsimha Rao, P.V.

See also Prime Minister: Geographical Area: India: Narsimha Rao, P.V.

National Affairs: Geographical Area: India

Anon, 1982, Uniform policy, *India Today* 7(7) April 15, p 8

Anon, 1989, Five Deputy ministers promoted, *Hindu*, July 5

Ghosh, Arun, 1989, The economy and the Budget, *Economic and Political Weekly* March 11

Grant, Bruce, 1982, Of diplomats and politicians, *Indian Express*, April 25, p 1

Joshi, Manoj, 1991, The changing political scene, *Frontline* 8(12) June 8-June 21, p 18

Kothari, Rajni, 1987, Decline of institutions, *Hindustan Times*, August 10

Sahni, Ajai, et al, 1991, The age of the pygmy, *Surya India* March, p 23-30

Silvera. D.M., 1980, Meet the Government that works, *Onlooker* 42(19) October 31, p 10-13

See also Government and Politics: Geographicala Area: India

National Affairs: Geographical Area: India: Tamil Nadu

Viswanth, 1991, Tamil Nadu under the Tiger's away, *Indian Today* June 15, p 50+

National Affairs: Geographical Area: India: Uttar Pradesh

Jaffer, S.M., 1981, Uttar Pradesh: The political cauldron, *Probe India*, 3(10) December, p 18-19+

Sharma, Rajat, 1982, Uttar Pradesh batting caste, dissent and crime, *Onlooker* 44(3) February 15, p 17-19

National Anthem: Geographical Area: India

Anon, 1986, Statute amendment hinted in National Anthem case, *Hindustan Times*, December 3

National Conference (Political Party)

Anon, 1982, PM may secure NC backing for Zail, *Hindustan Times*, June 26, p 16
Dewan, Berindranath, 1981, Rajiv-Farooq talks for Congress (I)-N.C. coatlition, *Hindu*, August 8, p 10

National Conference: Views on Panchayati Raj and Scheduled Tribes

Anon, 1989, National Conference on Panchayati Raj and Scheduled Tribes, *Statesman*, March 5

National Development: Geographical Area: India

Abraham, A.S., 1987, PM at the half way mark: Foreign and domestic perspectives, *Times of India*, July 11, p 6, col 3-5
Anon, 1981, Rajiv asks youth to work for national uplift, *Times of India*, October 26, p 9, col 2-5
Anon, 1981, Will aim at new style of functioning, *Hindustan Times*, May 12, p 1
Anon, 1982, Rajiv for better Public Sector performance, *Hindustan Times*, March 12, p 1+
Anon, 1982, Rajiv exhorts people to work hard, *Hindustan Times*, February 14, p 7
Anon, 1985, Rajiv perspective on Indian development, *Economic Times*, October 16, p 5, col 7-8+
Anon, 1987, Harnessing Science and Technology for development, *Yojana* 31(9) May 16, p 15-17
Anon, 1987, PM for unified plan for rural, urban area, *National Herald*, June 9
Anon, 1989, Population control and grass roots development, *Mainstream* 27(53) September 30, p 10-12+
Gandhi, Rajiv, 1981, Involve people in development, *Hindustan Times*, May 18, p 1
Gandhi, Rajiv, 1981, People's role of watch dogs, *Blitz*, July 18, p 24
Gandhi, Rajiv, 1982, Industrial growth vital for country, *Times of India*, Febraury 11, p 5
Gandhi, Rajiv, 1985, Funds plenty for engines of destruction and not for development, *Indian Worker* 33(39) June 24, p 3-5
Gandhi, Rajiv, 1989, Population control and grass-roots development: Document, *Mainstream* 27(53) September 30, p 10-12
Kripa Shankar, 1988, Relevance of Gandhi to India's rejuvenation, *Mainstream* 26(29) April 30, p 11-12
Mitra, Ashok, 1989, Rajiv's reform agenda: Fulfilling the mother's dream, *Times of India*, July 3, p 6, col 3-5

National Development: Geographical Area: India: Andhra Pradesh

Anon, 1985, No progress in Andhra Pradesh after Congress exit: PM, *Times of India*, December 25, p 6, col 1-4, news-item

National Front (Political Party)

Anon, 1988, NF rally calls for PM's resignation, *Times of India*, November 17, p 1, col 4-5+

Anon, 1988, Rajiv Gandhi criticises National Front, *Hindu*, November 28

Anon, 1990, National Front colluding with seperatisits: Rajiv, *Economic Times*, July 24, p 1, col 6-8, news-item

Anon, 1990, Rajiv Gandhi criticies NF government, *Times of India*, January 4

Anon, 1991, Rajiv accuses NF, BJP of dividing country, *Hindustan Times*, April 19, p 1, col 1-3

Anon, 1991, Secret link between NF, LTTE alleged, *Hindustan Times*, June 14, p 10, col 3

National Planning

Anon, 1988, PM hints at Bill to decentralise planning, *Hindustan Times*, November 26

National Policy on Education

Anon, 1986, New Educational Policy on Education, *Indian Journal of Public Administration* 32(3) July-September, p 435-460

National Reconsturction: Geographical Area: India

See National Development: Geographical Area: India

National Students Union of India: Convention

Gandhi, Rajiv, 1989, Rajiv Gandhi's Address to NSUI Convention, *Hindustan Times*, April 5

National Students Union of India: Suggestion on Name of University of Delhi

Anon, 1991, Name DU after Rajiv: NSUI, *Hindustan Times*, May 30, p 3, col 4

National Unity: Geographical Area: India

Anon, 1985, Mandate for unity, strength and harmony, *Haryana Review* 19(1) January p 3-5

Anon, 1985, No compromise on anti-State elements: Rajiv, *Times of India*, October 10, p 1, col 3-5, news-item

Anon, 1986, Call for national unity, *Hindustan Times*, November 7

Anon, 1986, India won't bow to pressure, says PM, *Times of India*, August 20, news-item

Anon, 1986, PM's call to uphold unity, *Times of India*, June 15, news-item

Anon, 1991, Unity of India will be safeguarded, says Rao, *Hindustan Times*, July 2, p 1, col 1-3+, news-item

Gandhi, Rajiv, 1984, Prime Minister's broadcast to the Nation: Call to build India of 21st centry, *Indian and Foreign Review* 23(3) November 30, p 12-13

New Age (Periodical), 1985, Struggle for national unity, *New Age* 33(2) January 13, p 2, editorial

Navy: Geographical Area: India

Anon, 1986, Big role for Navy in Ocean: PM, *Hindustan Times*, February 17, news-item

Nehru, Arun

Anon, 1982, Arun Nehru could have done better, *India Today* 7(11) June 15, p 18-19

Nehru, Jawaharlal

Anon, 1984, Rajiv combines Nehru's liberalism, Indira's firmness, *Link* 27(21) December 30, p 4-7

Anon, 1989, Government announces new rural job scheme, *National Herald*, April 29, *Telegraph*, April 29

Anon, 1990, Remembering 'Nana', *Times of India* (Sunday Review), May 27, p 2, col 1-6

Anon, 1991, Nehru too came to Sriperumbudur, *Hindustan Times*, June 3, p 7, col 1-4

Jain, Girilal, 1984, Nehru, Indira and Rajiv: Different styles, one objective, *Times of India*, November 14, p 8, col 3-5

Karanjia, R.K., 1976, The Nehrus: Father and daughter, *Illustrated Weekly of India* 97(46) November 14, p 6-19

Thakur, Janardan, 1986, It is lazy to quote Nehru..., *Times of India* (Sunday Review), May 25, p 1, col 1-5

Venkatraman, R., 1991, Rajiv excelled Nehru, *Hindustan Times*, July 3, p 1

Nehru, Jawaharlal: Homage Paid to Him

Anon, 1981, Delhi homage to Nehru: Children pay homage to Jawaharlal Nehru, *Hindustan Times*, November 15, p 1+

Anon, 1981, Nation pays homage to Nehru, *Indian Express*, November 15, p 1

Anon, 1988, Nation pays homage to Nehru, *Times of India*, November 15

Nehru, Jawaharlal: Policies

Anon, 1984, Rajiv combines Nehru's liberalism, Indira's firmness, *Link* 27(21) December 30, p 4-7

Anon, 1988, The vision of Jawaharlal Nehru, *Gandhi Marg* 10(8-9) November-December, p 456-460

Dwivedi, Devendranath, 1986, Assessing Rajiv Gandhi: Within Nehru-Indira frame-work, *Times of India*, December 24, p 8, col 3-5

Inder Jit, 1987, Let Rajiv follow Nehru's example, *Economic Times*, June 9, p 5, col 7-8+

Nehru, R.K: Homage Paid to Him

Anon, 1981, R.K. Nehru cremated, *Hindustan Times*, April 4, p 7

Nepal

See also Geographical Area subdivision under main Descriptor

Nepal: Foreign Relations: Geographical Area: India

See under Indo-Nepal Relations

Nepali Language

See Language: Nepali

Netherlands: Foreign Relations: Geographical Area: India

See under Indo-Dutch Relations

New Delhi Municipal Committee

Anon, 1982, Bhatnagar is NDMC Cheif, *Hindustan Times*, September 2 p 3

Anon, 1982, P.S. Bhatnagar replaces Behl as NDMC Chief, *Times of India*, September 2, p 3

New York: United States of America

See also Geographical Area Subdivision under main Descriptor

New York Times (Periodical): Views on Legacy

Anon, 1991, Legacy flayed: NYT, *Hindustan Times*, May 28, p 10, col 4

Nhava Sheva Port

Anon, 1989, PM dedicates Nhava Sheva Port to the Nation, *Hindustan Times*, May 27

Nicaragua: Foreign Relations: India

See under Indo-Nicaraguan Relations

Nirankaris

Anon, 1981, Nirankaris meet Rajiv, *Indian Express*, Novmber 21, p 7

Anon, 1981, Nirankaris turn violent, *Indian Express*, November 19, p 7

Saari, Anil 1981, Can Rajiv save the Nirankaris? *Sunday* 9(25) December 6, p 43-45

Nixon, Richard Mithous

Anon, 1985, Can Rajiv overcome Nixon, Kissinger and Reagan? *Link* 27(44) June 9, p 13-16

Non-Aligned Minister's Conference, Harare, 1986

Anon, 1986, Pak responisble for hijack tragedy, says PM, *Times of India*, September 7, p 1, col 1-3+, news-item

Non-Aligned Movement

Anon, 1984, The movenment of non-aligned countries, *Africa Quarterly* 23(3-4), p 1-9

Anon, 1985, PM flays Pretoria move for suppert to Government in Namibia, *Times of India*, April 20, p 1, col 1-3

Anon, 1986, PM for immediate sanctions by NAM, *Indian Express*, September 3

Anon, 1986, PM for immediate sanctions, *Hindustan Times*, August 30

Anon, 1986, PM heads NAM Fund for Africa, *Telegraph*, September 7

Anon, 1986, PM voice NAM support to Libya, *Times of India*, April 17, p 1, col 1-3

Anon, 1986, PM's call to safeguard NAM solidarity, *Free Press Jouranal* August 27

Anon, 1986, PM's message to NAM minister's meet, *Indian Express*, January 10

Anon, 1988, PM urge NAM to help disarm efforts, *Times of India*, July 15, p 1, col 1-3, news-item

Gandhi, Rajiv, 1985, Text of PM's speech, *Times of India*, April 20, p 16, col 1-4

Gandhi, Rajiv 1986, The substance of non-alignment, *Monthly Commentary on Indian Economic Conditions* 28(1) August, p 23

Hari Kumar, K.N., 1988, Rajiv and the US: Trading Non-Alignment for Hi-Tech? *Mainstream* 26(29) April 30, p 17-26

Taksal, Vinod, 1985, Rajiv's timely initiatives, *Link* 17(36) April 21, p 28

Non-Aligned Movement: Fund for Africa

See Africa Fund

Non-Congress Governments: Geographical Area: India

Gandhi, Rajiv, 1981, Janata put country 20 years behing? *Indian Express*, December 31, p 7

Kirpekar, Subash, 1988, Rajiv Gandhi attaks Non-Congress Governments, *Times of India*, April 25, p 1, col 4-6+

Non-Congress Parties: Geographical Area

Anon, 1981, Rajiv assails concept of motley opposition, *Times of India*, December 14, p 7, col 3-6

Anon, 1984, Opposition: Stooping to hair splitting, *Hindustan Times*, November 4, p 9, col 1-6, news-item

Anon, 1988, Opposition casteist, feudal: Rajiv, *Times of India*, Nvoember 6, p 1, col 7-8, news-item

Anon, 1988, Opposition Nation's foe: PM, *Times of India*, November 1, p 1, col 5-7+, news-item

Anon, 1991, Rajiv flays non-Congress Parties claim, *Hindustan Times* March 27, p 20, col 5

Nihal Singh, S., 1988, Rajiv and Government battered: But Opposition fail to make gain, *Times of India*, May 10, p 6, col 3-5

Sheorey, W.G., 1986, Rajiv has wiped out the Congress (I) along with the Opposition, *Organiser* 36(43) March 10, p 6

See also under name of non-Congress Political Parties, e.g., Bharatiya Party

Non-Proliferation Treaty

Anon, 1985, India will not sign NPT say PM, *Times of India*, June 15, p 1, col 1-2, news-item

Anon, 1986, N-Powers violating NPT, says PM, *Indian Express*, October 18, news-item

Subramanyam, K., 1987, Rajiv must resist US plea on NPT, *Times of India*, October 10, p 6, col 7-8

North America

See also Geographical Area subdivision under main Descriptor

North-East India

Kamaruppe, 1991, Assassination and after in North-East, *Economic and Political Weekly* 26(22-23) June 1-June 8, p 1383, col 1-3

North Korea

See also Geographical Area subdivision under main Descriptor

North Korea: Foreign Relations: Geographical Area: India

See under Indo-North Korean Relations

North-South Dialogue

Anon, 1986, Rajiv Gandhi for North South dialogue, *Indian Express*, February 9

Norway

See also Geographical Area subdivision under main Descriptor

Norway: Foreign Relations: Geographical Area: India

See under Indo-Norway Relations

Nuclear Fuel

Gandhi, Indira, 1982, No plan for talks with US on F-16s foreign fuel for Tarapur likely, *Indian Express*, July 28, p 1

Nuclear Policy: Geographical Area: India

Anon, 1985, No talks with Pak on N-issue: PM, *Times of India*, October 28, p 1, col 1-3, news-item

Anon, 1985, India's option to make bomb still open: PM, *Times of India*, Novmber 2, p 1, col 1-3, news-item

Anon, 1986, India to go nuclear if challenged, says PM, *Times of India*, October 29, news-item

Anon, 1986, Nuclear option still open, says PM, *Indian Express*, April 9, news-item

Anon, 1988, India not to build N-arms, says PM, *National Herald*, June 6, news-item

Gandhi, Indira, 1982, No plan for talks with US on F-16s foreign fuel for Tarapur likely, *Indian Express*, July 28, p 1

Nuclear Threat

Anon, 1983, AICC (I) alarmed at nuclear threat, *Times of India*, December 29, p 11, col 4-7

Nuclear Weapons

Anon, 1982, PM reiterates stand on peace, N-disarmament: Gulf between rich, poor dangerous, *Hindustan Times*, January, 23, p 16

Anon, 1985, The Six Nation Summit on Nuclear Disarmament, New Delhi, January 28, *Monthly Commentary on Indian Economic Conditions* 26(6) January, p 7-8

Anon, 1986, Call for ban on nuclear arms, *Times of India*, November 28

Anon, 1986, Call for end to nuclear arms race, *Hindustan Times*, Novmber 17

Anon, 1986, Nuclear arms main threat to peace, says Rajiv Gandhi, *Times of India*, March 6, news-item

Anon, 1988, PM for dismantling all nuclear weapons, *Hindustan Times*, November 15, news-item

Anon, 1988, PM's call for elemination of nuclear weapons, *National Herald*, November 25, news-item

Nuclear Weapons: Geographical Area: India

Anon, 1988, India not to build N-arms, says PM, *National Herald*, June 6, news-item

Nuclear Weapons: Geographical Area: Pakistan

Anon, 1985, India to take steps to meet Pak N threat: Rajiv, *Times of India*, October 12, p 1, col 1-3, news-item

Anon, 1989, PM expresses concern over Pak, *Free Press Journal*,Febraury 4; *Times of India*, February 4, news-item

Obscurantism

Anon, 1986, PM decries obscurantism, *Times of India*, May 2, news-item

Official Language: Geographical Area: India

Anon, 1986, MGR urges PM to withdraw circular, *Hindu*, September 21

Anon, 1986, PM reiterates Nehru's assurance on Hindi, *Indian Express*, November 7

Oman

See also Geographical Area subdivision under main Descriptor

Oman: Foreign Relations: Geographical Area: India

See under Indo-Omanese Relations

One Party Rule

Giri, V.V., 1980, Poll for one party rule ... Prelude to Presidential form of Government, *Illustrated Weekly of India* 101(21) May 31, p 6-9

Opposition Parties in Parliament: Geographical Area: India

Anon, 1981, Quiet debut amid sound and fury, *Hindustan Times*, August 18, p 8

Anon, 1981, Rajiv assails concept of motley Opposition, *Times of India*, December 14, p 7

Anon, 1981, Rajiv assails Opposition on unity moves, *Hindustan Times*, December 14, p 1+

Anon, 1981, Rajiv raps Charan for 'Lathi directive', *Hindustan Times*, June 1

Anon, 1981, Rajiv warns Opposition, *Indian Express*, October 21, p 4

Anon, 1981, Vehicle minus battery, *Hindustan Times*, December 30, p 8

Anon, 1982, Rajiv blames Opposition for communal troubles, *Times of India*, May 9, p 9+

Anon, 1982, Rajiv raps Opposition, erring Cong mem, *Hindustan Times*, January 10, p 10

Anon, 1982, Rajiv wants positive Opposition, *Hindu*, January 1, p 9

Anon, 1984, Opposition: Stooping to hair splitting, *Hindustan Times*, November 4, p 9, col 1-6, news-item

Anon, 1985, PM, Opposition discuss Punjab, *Times of India*, January 12, p 1, col 7-8+

Anon, 1985, Talks with Opposition promised: PM hopes Punjab situation will cease, *Times of India*, July 8, p 1, col 1-3

Anon, 1986, BJP leader question PM's stand on GNLF, *Times of India*, November 17

Anon, 1986, Opposition backs PM on Punjab, *Times of India*, April 7

Anon, 1986, Opposition not to attend PM's meeting, *Statestman*, Novmber 4

Anon, 1986, Opposition made Bill, religious issue: PM, *Times of India*, March 12, p 7, col 2-6, news-item

Anon, 1986, PM encouraging divisive forces, says Opposition, *Hindustan Times*, November 6, news-item

Anon, 1986, PM meets Oppostion Party leaders, *Times of India*, July 17

Anon, 1986, PM's talks with Opposition on Border Areas Bill, *Free Press Journal* July 30; *Times of India*, July 30

Anon, 1987, Opposition free to send team to Sweden: PM, *Times of India*, August 1-9, p 1, col 7-8+, news-item

Anon, 1988, Opposition asks PM to quit, *Indian Express*, November 15

Anon, 1988, Opposition casteist, feudal: Rajiv, *Times of India*, November 6, p 1, col 7-8, news-item

Anon, 1988, Opposition Nation's foe: PM, *Times of India*, November 1, p 1, col 5-7+, news-item

Anon, 1988, Opposition rally asks PM to quit, *Hindu*, November 17

Anon, 1988, Opposition seeks PM's apology for remarks, *Hindustan Times*, July 28

Anon, 1988, PM conistently lying: Opposition, *Times of India*, Novmber 15, p 1, vol 1-2

Anon, 1989, Oppostion fanning communalism: Rajiv, *Times of India*, April 30, p 1, col 1-3+, news-item

Anon, 1989, Opposition walkout in LS over PM's remarks, *Hindustan Times*, April 6; *Telegraph*, April 6

Gandhi, Rajiv, 1982, Opposition bid to tarnish Congress (I) image, *National Herald*, April 2, p 1

Kal Bag, Chaitanyanya, 1982, The Opposition: The games old men play, *India Today* 7(4) February 28, p 14-15

Mitra, Chandan, 1989, A CAG-tag Opposition: Neutralising Rajiv's populism, *Times of India* July 26, p 6, col 3-5

Nihal Singh, S., 1982, Making a leader to order, *Indian Express*, January 6, p 6

Nihal Singh, S., 1988, Rajiv and Govt battered: But Opposition fail to make again, *Times of India*, May 10, p 6, col 3-5

Sagar, Anand, 1982, In and out, *India Today* 7(5) March 16, p 35

Sharma, Rajat, 1982, Opposition unity: Putting the piece together, *Onlooker* 44(2) January 31, p 17-19

Optimism: Geographical Area: India: Gandhi, Rajiv

Anon, 1991, Rajiv's optimism, *Democratic World*, 20(11) March 17, p 7, col 2-3

Orissa: India

Anon, 1982, Action against Orissa Congress (I) rebels urged, *Hindustan Times*, June 2, p 8

See also Geographical Area subdivision under main Descriptors

Osibisa

Mitra, Sumit, 1981, Osibisa costly razze-dazze, *India Today* 6(21) November 15, p 129-131

Overbridge

See Flyover

Oxbridge League

Das, Sitanshu, 1986, Oxbridge and IVY League sereen between PM and Congress, *Link* 29(12) October 26, p 4-8

PLO

=Palestine Liberation Organisation

PM

=Prime Minister

Pahadia, Jagannath

Anon, 1981, Pahadia men appeal to PM and Rajiv, *Times of India*, July 9, p 9
Anon, 1982, No room for Pahadia, *Onlooker* 44(4) February 28, p 7

Pakistan

See also Geographical Area Subdivision under main Descriptor

Pakistan: Foreign Relations: Geographical Area: India

See under Indo-Pak Relations

Palestine Liberation Organisation

Anon, 1986, PLO seeks India's help, *Free Press Journal* December 6
Anon, 1986, PM briefed on Palestine meet, *National Herald*, April 27
Anon, 1989, PM reaffirms support to PLO, *Times of India*, May 5

Palme, Olaf

Anon, 1986, Rajiv, Palme hail Soviet move, *Times of India*, January 17

Panchayati Raj

Anon, 1989, National Conference on Panchayati Raj and Seheduled Tribes, *Statesman*, March 5

Anon, 1989, PM affirms support for Panchayati Raj, *Statesman*, April 30, news-Item

Gani, H.A., 1989, Prime Minister's Panchayati Raj, *Janata* 44(19) August 6, p 12+

Kothari, Rajni, 1989, Rajiv's Panchayati: A bonapartist vision, *Mainstream* 27(34)

May 20, p 2-3

Panchyati Raj Conference

Gandhi, Rajiv, 1989, PM's Address to Panchayati Raj Conference, *Free Press Journal* May 5

See also Panchayati Raj Sammelan

Panchayati Raj Sammelan

Anon, 1989, PM addresses Panchayati Raj Sammelan, *Hindu*, April 4, news-Item
Gandhi, Rajiv, 1989, PM's Address to the Panchayati Raj Sammelan, *Hindustan Times*, April 8; *Telegraph*, April 8

See also Panchayati Raj Conference

Panchyats

Anon, 1982, Rajiv wants Panchayats made more effective, *Hindustan Times*, January 31, p 11

Anon, 1986, Revitalize Panchayats, says PM, *Hindustan Times*, September 23, news-item

Anon, 1989, 30 p.c. reservation for women in panchayats: Rajiv, *Times of India*, May 5, p 1, col 1-3+, news-item

Paris: France

See also Geographical Area subdivision under main Descriptor

Parliament: Geographical Area: India

Anon, 1987, Govt answerable only to people, Parliament: PM, *Times of India*, May 17, p 1, col 1-4+, news-item

Anon, 1991, Rajiv's bid to play the double role of the super PM and Opposition leader, *Organiser* 42(23) January 13, p 3, col 2-4+

non, 1991, Surveillance issue again rocks Parliament, *Hindustan Times*, March 6
Dandavate, Madhu, 1987, President, Prime Minister and Parliament, *Janata* (May Day Number), 42(6), p 4-5

Inder Jit, 1987, Parliament must debate gun issue, *Economic Times*, March 24, p 5, col 7-8+

Parliament: Leader of the House: Geographical Area: India

Mukherjee, Pranab, 1984, The Leader of the House and the whips in United Kingdom and India, *Journal of Parliamentary Information* December, p 598-604

Parliament: Leader of the House: Geographical Area: United Kingdom

Mukherjee, Pranab, 1984, The Leader of the House and the whips in UK and India, *Journal of Parliamentary Information* December, p 598-604

Parliament: Rajya Sabha: Geographical Area: India

Anon, 1991, Rajya Sabha condemns Rajiv assassination, *Hindustan Times*, June 4, p 1, col 2-4+

Parliament: Rajya Sabha: Geographical Area: India: Rajya Sabha: Homage Paid to Gandhi, Rajiv

Anon, 1991, Rajya Sabha session today: Elders to pay tributes to Rajiv, Dange, *Hindustan Times*, June 3, p 1, col 5-7

Parliamentary System

Anon, 1981, Parliamentary system good, says Rajiv, *Times of India*, July 15, p 5, col 3-5, news-item

Gandhi, Rajiv, 1981, Parliamentary system good and sound, *Blitz*, July 18, p 24

Patel, Chiman Bhai

Anon, 1991, Chiman, Rajiv to resume talks, *Hindustan Times*, April 15, p 9, col 5

Anon, 1991, Patel, Rajiv talks on seat-sharing, *Hindustan Times*, April 14, p 5, col 1

Patel, Vallabhbhai

Anon, 1991, Bharat Ratna for Rajiv, Sardar Patel, *Hindustan Times*, June 18, p 1, col 5

Patil, Shalini Tai

Anon, 1981, Shalinitai Patil meets Rajiv, *Indian Express*, September 6, p 7

Patna: Bihar: India

Anon, 1989, So much so that two AICC officials sent by Rajiv Gandhi to Patna to quieten the rebels had to flee to Delhi following skirmishes between two groups, *Statesman* March 10

See also Geographical Area subdivision under main Descriptors

Patnaik, Biju

Anon, 1982, Rajiv snubs Patnaik, *Blitz*, February 13, p 5

Anon, 1986, Patnaik meet PM, *Telegraph*, May 30

Anon, 1991, Biju flays Rajiv, BJP, *Hindustan Times*, April 3, p 7, col 2-4

Anon, 1991, Rajiv flays Patnaik's remarks, *Hindustan Times*, March 31, p 17, col 1

Patriot (Newspaper): Silver Jubilee

Anon, 1988, PM's Address at Silver Jubilee function of "Patriot", *Indian Express*, March 30, news-item

Pawar, Sharad

Anon, 1991, The Pawar game, *Organiser* 42(27) February 10, p 2, col 1-5
Anon, 1991, Rajiv-Pawar tussle, *Organiser* 42(25) January 27, p 66, col 1-2
Pawar, Sharad, 1989, Closing rank, *Illustrated Weekly of India*, 110(50) December 10, p 6-9

Peace

Anon, 1982, PM reiterates stand on peace, N-disarmament: Gulf between rich, poor dangerous, *Hindustan Times*, January 23, p 16
Anon, 1984, The imperative of peace, *Indian Horizons* 33(3-4), p 5-8
Anon, 1986, Nuclear arms main threat to peace, says Rajiv Gandhi, *Times of India*, March 6, news-item
Anon, 1986, 'Star Wars' against world peace, says Rajiv, *National Herald*, February 17, news-item
Democratic World (Periodical), 1991, Rajiv urges peace inititives, *Democratic World* 20(6) February 10, p 3, col 2+, editorial
Gandhi, Rajiv, 1982, International Youth Conference work for peace, *Current*, January 30, p 6

Perestroika

Mishra, Charuranan, 1989, Rajiv Gandhi policies on Perestroika, *New Age* 37(2) January 8, p 8

Perumal

Anon, 1989, Perumal calls for decisive move, *Times of India*, July 20
Anon, 1989, Perumal holds further talks, *National Herald*, March 22; *Statesman*, March 22
Anon, 1989, Rajiv Gandhi, Perumal hold discussion, *Hindustan Times*, August 13

Philippines

See also Geographical Area subdivision under main Descriptor

Philippines: Foreign Relations: Geographical Area: India

See under Indo-Philippines Relations

Planet Protections Fund

Anon, 1989, Rajiv Gandhi's plan for Planet Protection Fund to be considered, *Indian Express*, November 21; *Times of India*, November 21

Planning: Geographical Area: India

Anon, 1985, Planning being geared to uplift poor: PM, *Economic Times*, August 16, p 1, col 1-4, news-item

See also Economic Planning: Geographical Area: India, National Development:

Geographical Area: India

Poland

See also Geographical Area subdivision under main Descriptor

Poland: Foreign Relations: Geographical Area: India

See under Indo-Polish Relations

Policemen: Geographical Area: India

Anon, 1991, 6 cops challenge their suspension, *Hindustan Times*, August 10, p 20, col 1-4

Anon, 1991, Policemen challenge suspension order, *Times of India* August 10, p 3, col 4-5

Political Alliances: Geographical Area: India

Anon, 1981, New-found alliance, *India Today* 6(16) August 16, p 7

Anon, 1982, Mrs Gandhi calls on Abdullah, *Hindustan Times*, June 25, p 16

Anon, 1982,. PM seeking JK Muslims backing for Rajiv, *Indian Express*, January 3, p 9

Anon, 1982, Rajiv Gandhi's Aide meets Abdullah, *Hindustan Times*, May 19, p 8

Anon, 1991, RV for Shekhar-Rajiv patch up, *Democratic World* 20(8) February 24, p 7, col 2-3

Dewan, Berindranath, 1981, Rajiv-Farooq talks for Congress (I)-NC coalition, *Hindu*, August 8, p 10

Karunakaran, K., 1982, Last laugh, *India Today* 7(2) January 31, p 51

Khayal, Ghulam Nabi, 1981, All in the family, *India Today* 6(17) September 1, p 45-46

Tellis, Olga, 1982, I was not surprised, *Sunday* 9(33) January 31, p 21-22

Political Alliances: Geographical Area: India: BJP-LD

Anon, 1982, Rajiv criticises LD-BJP alliance, *Times of India*, May 15, p 7

Anon, 1982, Rajiv hits out at LD-BJP Poll alliance, *Amrit Bazar Patrika*, May 7, p 7

Anon, 1982, Rajiv lashes out at BJP-LD Poll alliance, *Times of India*, May 7, p 7

Gandhi, Rajiv, 1982, LD-BJP alliance more opprtunism fake, *Hindustan Times*, May 15, p 5

Political Parties: Geographical Area: India

See under Name of the Politcical Party, e.g., Bhartiya Janata Party

Political Parties: Non-Congress Parties: Geographical Area: India:

See Non-Congress Parties: Geographical Area: India

Political Problems: Geographical Area: Indian States

See under name of the State, e.g., Assam Problem

Political Scenario: Geographical Area: India

Anon, 1991, End of cold war 'disoriented' India, *Hindustan Times*, May 31, p 13, col 2-3

See also Government and Politics: Geographical Area: India

Political Scenario: Geographical Area: India: 1981

Kanju, N., 1982, 1981: A year of turbulence for India, *Caravan* 2(712) January, p 16-18

Political Scenario: Geographical Area: India: 1982

Bhasin, Prem, 1982, Politics of 1982: Can '1984' be far behind, *Indian Express*, Marchd 7, p 1+

Political Scenario: Geographical Area: India: 1984-1985

Anon, 1989, (Book Review), *Tribune* (Sunday Review), August 6, p 2, col 1-6
Review of the Book: **Rajput R.S.**, 1989, *Dynamics of democratic politics in India: A study of 1984 and 1985 Lok Sabha Election*, Deep and Deep Publishers, New Delhi, 185p.

Political Scenario: Geographical Area: India: 1987

Ghosh Chowdhury, Dilip, 1987, Academic platform used for Rajiv's poitical tirade, *New Age* 35(4) January 25, p 6

Karat, Prakash, 1987, Seperating religion and politics: Rajiv style, *People's Democracy* 11(11) March 15, p 3

Political Scenario: Geographical Area: India: 1988

Times of India (Newspaper), 1988, State of the Nation, *Times of India*, August 16, p 4, col 1-2, editorial

Political Scenario: Geographical Area: India: 1991 –

Anon, 1991, The Congress concern over the current scenario, *Democratic World* 20(1) January 6, p 5, col 1-3

Anon, 1991, Nation will emerge stronger: Chandra, *Hindustan Times*, May 31, p 3, col 2-3, news-item

Anon, 1991, Political scenario changes due to Gulf War, *Democratic World* 20(4) January 27, p 5, col 1-3+

Jha, Ajay N., 1991, Post-Rajiv scene murky, *Hindustan Times*, May 31, p 7, col 1-3

Kumar, D.P., 1991, Election scene: Congress prospects after Rajiv, *Mainstream* 29(32) June 1, p 4-5

Shukla, Rajiv and Sarin, Ritu, 1991, After the dynasty, *Sunday* June 9-June 15, p 32-34

Stewart, William, 1991, The next generation: Can India's republican dynasty produce more leaders? *Times International*, June 3, p 13

Political Scenario: Geographical Area: India: Haryana

Anon, 1982, Art of eleminating rivals, *Sunday* 9(51) June 12, p 17

Anon, 1982, "Conductor" Bhajan Lal, *Sunday* 9(43) April 17, p 15

Sharma, B,N., 1981, Bansi vs Bhajan: A battle for survival, *Caravan* 2(708) November 16, p 19

Sharma, Vichitra, 1982, Bhajan booed at Rajiv poll meeting, *Hindustan Times*, May 6, p 1+

Sud, S.K., 1986, No dissidents only opportunists in Haryana, *Link* 28(40) May 11, p 14

Political Scenario: Geographical Area: India: Jammu and Kashmir

Anon, 1981, New dynasty: Abdullah Jr is crowned, *Caravan* 12(704) September 16, p 11

Dubey, Suman, 1982, Jammu and Kashmir son also rises, *India Today* 7(17) September 15, p 46-53

Political Scenario: Geographical Area: India: West Bengal

Chalapathi Rau, M., 1982, Democracy at work, *Link* 24(42) May 30, p 12

Poll

See Elections

Population Control

Gandhi, Rajiv, 1989, Population control and grass-roots development: Document, *Mainstream* 27(53) September 30, p 10-12+

Post-Rajiv Scene

See Political Scenario: Geographical Area: India 1991–

Poverty Alleviation

Anon, 1985, PM announces accord on Assam: Pakistan asked to abandon bomb: Sharper campaign against poverty: Call to combat extremism: Colourful Red Fort Function, *Times of India*, August 16, p 1, col 1-4, news-item

Anon, 1985, Rajiv Gandhi urges UN to fight starvation, *Economic Times*, October 25, p 1, col 1-4+

Anon, 1988, Reorder global priorities for poverty uplift: PM, *Economic Times*, March 26, p 1, col 60-8, news-item

Power Brokers: Geographical Area: India

Anon, 1989, Grass-root system to eleminate power broker: PM, *Times of India*, May, p 1, col 1-3, news-item

Power Devolution

Anon, 1988, PM for effective power devolution, *Hindustan Times*, August 24

Prabhakaran, Velupillai

Anon, 1991, Prabhakaran tried to reach Sivarasan, *Hindustan Times*, September 4

Mukarji, Apartim, 1992, Sri Lankan dilemma over Prabhakaran, *Hindustan Times*, January 6, p 15, col 7-8.

Premdasa, Ranasinghe

Anon, 1989, PM's reply to Premdasa, *Hindustan Times*, July 1, news-item

Anon, 1989, PM writes to Premdasa, *Times of India*, June 21, news-item

Anon, 1989, Premádasa writes to Rajiv Gandhi, *Hindustan Times*, July 23

Anon, 1989, Premdasa's reply to Rajiv Gandhi's letter, *Hindustan Times* July 14

President: Geographical Area: Bangladesh: Ershad, Hossain Mohammed

Anon, 1988, President Ershad in New Delhi, *Free Press Journal* September 30; *Hindustan Times*, September 30

President: Geographical Area: China

Anon, 1988, Rajiv Gandhi meets Chinese President, *Hindustan Times*, December 12; *Tribune*, December 12

President: Geographical Area: India: Venkataraman, R. (July 25, 1987 – July 24, 1992)

Anon, 1988, PM calls on President, *Hindustan Times*, March 27

Anon, 1991, PM briefs RV on law and order, *Hindustan Times*, May 28, p 1, col 5

Anon, 1991, PM, Rajiv meet President, *Times of India*, February 10

Anon, 1991, Rajiv Gandhi calls on President, *Times of India*, February 14

Anon, 1991, R.V. for Shekhar-Rajiv patch up, *Democratic World* 20(8) February 24, p 7, col 2-3

Dandavate, Madhu, 1987, President, Prime Minister and Parliament, *Janata* (May Day Mumber) 42(6), p 4-5

Democratic World (Periodical), 1991, RV against Rajiv's take over? *Democratic World* 20(8) February 24, p 4, col 1-2, editorial

Gangal, S.S., 1987, President and the Prime Minister, *Gandhi Marg* 9(2) May, p 67-72

Gupta, Ranjan, 1987, President, PM controversy, *Mainstream* 25(28) March 28, p 6

Jain, Girilal, 1987, President versus Prime Minister: New correlation of power, *Times of India*, July 29, p 6, col 3-5

Khare, Harish, 1987, President Prime Minister: No acquiescence on confrontation, *Times of India*, March 2, p 6, col 3-5

Masani, Minoo, 1987, Roots of President PM clash, *Times of India*, (Sunday Review), March 29, p 1, col 7-8

Sen Gupta, Barun, 1981, Could the next President be Mr Venkatraman? *Sunday* 9(25) December 6, p 30

Suri, Surinder, 1985, Presidential Prime Minister: New trends in Indian politics, *Times of India*, November 30, p 8, col 3-5

Times of India (Newspaper), 1987, Appeal to the President, *Times of India*, April 24, p 6, col 1-2, editorial

President: Geographical Area: India: Venkataraman, R.: Condolences by Him

Anon, 1988, President, Prime Minister condole Armenian quake deaths, *Time of India*, December 9

See also President: Geographical Area: India: Venkataraman, R. Homage Paid to Khomeinie, Ayatollah Ruhollah

President: Geographical Area: India: Venkataraman, R.: Homage Paid to Gandhi, Rajiv

Anon, 1992, President pays tribute to Rajiv, *Hindustan Times*, January 6, p 18, col 8

Anon, 1992, RV recalls Rajiv's vision, *Hindustan Times*, May 22, p 12, col 8

Anon, 1992, RV's call to live up to Rajiv ideals, *Hindustan Times*, May 21, p 12, col 1-4

President: Geographical Area: India: Venkataraman, R.: Homage Paid to Khomeinie: Ayatollah Ruhollah

Anon, 1989, President, PM express grief over Khomeinie's death, *Times of India*, June 5.

President: Geographical Area: India: Zail Singh (July 1982-July 1987)

See also Zail Singh

President: Geographical Area: Mozambique: Chissano, Joaquim Mohammad

Anon, 1988, Mozambique's President holds talk in New Delhi, *Hindustan Times*, May 15; *National Herald*, May 15

President: Geographical Area: Philippines: Aquino, Corazon

Anon, 1988, President Aquino's letter to Rajiv Gandhi, *Indian Express*, February 19

President: Geographical Area: Sri Lanka: Jayawardne, Junius Ranjan

Anon, 1986, Prime Minister and Sri Lankan President discuss ethnic crisis, *Statesman*, November 16

President: Geographical Area: Turkey: Evren, Kenan

Anon, 1989, Turkish President in New Delhi, *Stetesman*, February 23

President: Geographical Area: United States of America: Bush, George

Anon, 1991, Rajiv Gandhi, Saddam and Bush, *Organiser* 42(33) March 24, p 16, col 4

President: Geographical Area: United States of America: Reagan, Ronald

Anon, 1985, Can Rajiv overcome Nixon, Kessinger, Reagan? *Link* 27(44) June 9, p 13-16

Anon, 1986, President, Prime Minister greet Reagan, *Times of India*, July 4

Jain, Girilal, 1987, Reagan has an agenda: Questions that Rajiv should raise, *Times of India*, October 14, p 6, col 3-5

Shankhdher, M.M., 1987, Rajiv-Reagan talks can open new chapter in Indo-US relations, *Organiser* 39(24) November 22, p 6

Presidential Form of Government

See Presidential System: Geographical Area: India

Presidential System: Geographical Area: India

Anon, 1982, President's pleasure Prime Minister's pain: Presidential system revisited, *Delhi Recorder* 3(2) March 15-April 14, p 10-13

Anon, 1982, Rajiv Gandhi not for Presidential system, *Hindu*, May 18, p 10

Giri, V.V., 1980, Poll for one party rule ... Prelude to Presidential form of Government, *Illustrated Weekly of India*, 101(21) May 31, p 6-9

President's Rule: Geographical Area: India: Punjab

Anon, 1987, Central rule till terrorism ends in Punjab: PM, *Times of India*, June, p 1, col 1-3, news-item

President's Rule: Geographical Area: India: Tamil Nadu

Anon, 1991, Karunanidhi blames Central rule, *Hindustan Times*, June 2, p 12, col 5-8

Press: Geographical Area: India

Anon, 1982, IYC (I) keeps out Press from meet, *Indian Express*, January 24, p 3

Anon, 1982, Rajiv attacks Press, call for loyalty, *Indian Express*, April 25, p 4

Anon, 1988, PM: Press must be worthy of freedom, *Times of India*, September 10, p 1, col 5-6+, news-item

Gandhi, Rajiv, 1982, Press writing irresponsible reports, *Indian Express*, October 6, p 1+

See also Press Reporters of Gandhi, Rajiv

Press Conference

Sahay, S., 1985, Mr Gandhi's Press Conference, *Statesman*, July 11

Press Reporters

Anon, 1991, Reporters ire over Rajiv Gandhi, *Hindustan Times*, April 16, p 10, col 4

Pretoria Governmnet

See under Indo-South Africa Relations

Prices and Pricing: Geographical Area: India

Anon, 1986, PM defends price-hike, *Free Press Journal* February 20; *Hindu*, February 20

Anon, 1986, PM justifies price hike, *Times of India*, February 19

Anon, 1991, Prices, Stability main issues: Rajiv, *Hindustan Times*, March 28, p 9, col 1-4, news-item

Priests: Geographical Area: India

Anon, 1984, Priests resent Rajiv's remarks, *Times of India*, October 1, p 1, col 1-2+

Prime Minister: Geographical Area: France

Anon, 1988, PMs confer, *Hindustan Times*, July 18

Prime Minister: Geographical Area: India: Chandra Shekhar (November 10, 1990–21st June 1991)

See also Chandra Shekhar

Prime Minister: Geographical Area: India: Charan Singh (July 28, 1979–January 14, 1980)

See also Charan Singh

Prime Minister: Geographical Area: India: Gandhi Indira (January 24, 1966–March 24, 1977; January 14, 1980–October 31, 1984)

See also Gandhi, Indira

Prime Minister: Geographical Area: India: Gandhi, Rajiv (October 31, 1984–November 30, 1989)

See also Gandhi, Rajiv

Prime Minister: Geographical Area: India: Gandhi, Rajiv: Address on Independence Day

See Prime Minister: Geographical Area: India: Gandhi, Rajiv: Independence Day Address

Prime Minister: Geographical Area: India: Gandhi, Rajiv: Address to Army Commanders

Gandhi, Rajiv, 1986, PM's Address to Army Commanders, *Hindu*, April 25

Prime Minister: Geographical Area: India: Gandhi, Rajiv: Address to Bharat Krishak Samaj

Gandhi, Rajiv, 1989, PM's Address to Bharat Krishak Samaj, *National Herald*, February 7, news-item

Prime Minister: Geographical Area: India: Gandhi, Rajiv: Address to Chief Ministers

Gandhi, Rajiv, 1988, PM's Address to the Chief Minister, *Hindustan Times*, March 19

Prime Minister: Geographical Area: India: Gandhi, Rajiv: Address to Congress Party in Parliament

Gandhi, Rajiv, 1988, PM's Address to CPP (I) *Hindu*, February 22; *Hindu*, December 8; *Hindustan Times*, February 21; *Hindustan Times*, July 28; *Hindustan Times*, August 31; *National Herald*, May 13; *Times of India*, May 13

Prime Minister: Geographical Area: India: Gandhi, Rajiv: Address to Farmer's Rally

Gandhi, Rajiv, 1988, PM's Address to Farmer's Rally, *Free Press Journal*, February 21; *National Herald*, February 21

Prime Minister: Geographical Area: India: Gandhi, Rajiv: Address to Intellectuals

Gandhi, Rajiv, 1987, Communalisation of politics, education, industry and commerce: An imperialist strategy to impede national unity and freedom movement: Prime Minister Rajiv Gandhi's Address to intellectuals, New Delhi, September 15, 1987, *Muslim India* 5(58) October, p 457-458

Prime Minister: Geographical Area: India: Gandhi, Rajiv: Address to May Day Rally

Gandhi, Rajiv, 1987, We salute workers who do Gods work on earth, Prime Minister Rajiv Gandhi's Address to the May Day rally, *Indian Worker*

35(32-33) May 11-May 18, p 8-11

Prime Minister: Geographical Area: India: Gandhi, Rajiv: Address to Municipal Officers

Gandhi, Rajiv, 1989, PM's Address to Municipal Officers, *Hindustan Times*, June 6; *National Herald*, June 6

Prime Minister: Geographical Area: India: Gandhi, Rajiv: Address to NSUI Convention

Gandhi, Rajiv, 1989, Rajiv Gandhi's Address to NSUI convention, *Hindustan Times*, April 5

Prime Minister: Geographical Area: India: Gandhi, Rajiv: Address to Nagarpalika Sammelan

Gandhi, Rajiv, 1989, PM's Address to Nagarpalika Sammelan, *Hindustan Times*, June 15

Prime Minister: Geographical Area: India: Gandhi, Rajiv: Address to Panchayati Raj Conference

Gandhi, Rajiv, 1989, PM's Address to Panchayati Raj Conference, *Free Press Journal*, May 5

Prime Minister: Geographical Area: India: Gandhi, Rajiv: Address to Panchayati Raj Sammelan

Gandhi, Rajiv, 1989, PM Addresses Panchayati Raj Sammelan, *Hindu*, April 4, news-item

Prime Minister: Geographical Area: India: Gandhi, Rajiv: Address to Seva Dal Convention

Gandhi, Rajiv, 1989, Rajiv Gandhi's Address to Seva Dal convention, *Times of India*, May 13

Prime Minister: Geographical Area: India: Gandhi, Rajiv: Address to Six Nations Summit

Gandhi, Rajiv, 1986, PM's Address to the Six Nations Summit, *Indian Express*, August 3; *Hindu*, August 8

Prime Minister: Geographical Area: India: Gandhi, Rajiv: Address to Special Session on Disarmament

Gandhi, Rajiv, 1988, Rajiv Gandhi's Address to Special Session on Disarmament, *Indian Express*, June 10

Prime Minister: Geographical Area: India: Gandhi, Rajiv: Address to UPCC (I) Convention

Gandhi, Rajiv, 1989, Rajiv Gandhi addresses UPCC (I) Convention, *Times of India*, February 11, news-item

Prime Minister: Geographical Area: India: Gandhi, Rajiv: Administrative Machinery

Dhar, R.N., 1989, The Prime Minister's Office: Seeing through the mystique, *Times of India*, February 24, p 6, col 3-5

Prime Minister: Geographical Area: India: Gandhi, Rajiv: Condolences by Him

Anon, 1988, PM condoles quake victims, *National Herald*, December 14; *Time of India*, December 14

Anon, 1988, President, Prime Minister condole Armenian quake deaths, *Times of India*, December 9

See also Gandhi, Rajiv, Homage paid

Prime Minister: Geographical Area: India: Gandhi, Rajiv: Independence Day Address

Anon, 1985, PM announces accord on Assam: Pakistan asked to abandon bomb: Sharper campaing against poverty: Colourful Red Fort function, *Times of India*, August 16, p 1, col 1-4, news-item

Anon, 1986, Updated 20-Point plan soon: PM, *Economic Times*, August 16, p 1, col 1-4, news-item

Anon, 1987, People asked to help fight drought, terrorism, *Times of India*, August 16, p 1, col 1-4, news-item

Economic Times (Newspaper), 1989, From the framparts, *Economic Times*, August 16, p 5, col 1-2, editorial

Gandhi, Rajiv, 1988, PM's Independence Day speech, *Economic Times*, August 16, p 4, col 5-8

Prime Minister: Geographical Area: India: Gandhi, Rajiv: Interview to Sunday (Magazine)

Anon, 1988, PM's interview to "Sunday", *Times of India*, November 12, news-item

Prime Minister: Geographical Area: India: Gandhi, Rajiv: Italian Connection

Anon, 1988, V.P. Singh exposes PM's Italian connection, *Organiser* 39(43) April 10, p 13

Prime Minister: Geographical Area: India: Gandhi, Rajiv: Statement on Gorbachev's Visit

Gandhi, Rajiv, 1988, PM's statement on Gorbachev's visit, *Hindu*, November 22

Prime Minister: Geographical Area: India: Gandhi, Rajiv: Support to PLO

Anon, 1989, PM reaffirms support to PLO, *Time of India*, May 5

Prime Minister: Geographical Area: India: Gandhi, Rajiv: Tours

See Gandhi, Rajiv: Tours

Prime Minister: Geographical Area: India: Gandhi, Rajiv: Views on Defamation Bill

Anon, 1988, PM's views on Defamation Bill, *Indian Express*, September 16; *National Herald*, September 16

Prime Minister: Geographical Area: India: Narsimha Rao, P.V. (June 21, 1991—)

Anon, 1991, No deviation from Rajiv path: PM, *Hindustan Times*, July 2, p 6, col 8, news-item

Anon, 1991, PM trustee of Rajiv Foundation, *Hindustan Times*, July 14, p 12, col 1

Anon, 1991, Unity of India will be safeguarded, says Rao, *Hindustan Times*, June 2, p 1, col 1-3+, news-item

See also Narsimha Rao, P.V.

Prime Minister: Geographical Area: India: Narsimha Rao, P.V.: Homage Paid to Gandhi, Rajiv

Anon, 1992, Fight terrorism, says PM, *Hindustan Times*, May 22, p 1, col 5-7+, news-item

Prime Minister: Geographical Area: India: Singh, V.P.

See also Singh, V.P.

Prime Minister: Geographical Area: Kampuchea: Hun Sen

Anon, 1989, Hun Sen holds talks with Rajiv Gandhi, *Times of India*, November 17

Prime Minister: Geographical Area; North Korea

Anon, 1988, North Korean PM in New Delhi, *National Herald*, February 19

Prime Minister: Geographical Area: Pakistan: Bhutto, Benazir

See Bhutto, Benazir

Prime Minister: Geographical Area: Singapore

Anon, 1988, Singapore PM's talks in New Delhi, *Time of India*, March 17

Prime Minister: Geographical Area: Spain

Anon, 1988, PMs confer, *Hindustan Times*, July 18

Prime Minister: Geographpical Area: Thailand

Anon, 1989, Thailand PM hold further talks with Rajiv Gandhi, *Telegraph*, March 31

Prime Minister's Office: Geographical Area: India: Gandhi, Rajiv

See Prime Minister: Geographical Area: India: Gandhi, Rajiv: Administrative Mechinary

Productivity: Geographical Area: India

Anon, 1985, Warning on induced sickness: PM's call to step up productivity, *Times of India*, September 20, p 1, col 1-3+, news-item

Anon, 1986, Productivity improvement in Public Interprises, *Management in Government* 18(1) April-June, p 5-17, news-item

Projects: Geographical Area: India: West Bengal

Anon, 1986, PM clears State projects, *Hindustan Times*, September 19

Projects: Implementation Strategies: Geographical Area: India

Anon, 1986, Implementation Strategies, *Progressive Education Herald* 1(1) October, p 11-15

Public Enterprises

See Public Sector Undertakings

Public Grievances

See Grievances

Public Sector Undertakings: Geographical Area: India

Anon, 1982, Rajiv for better public sector performance, *Hindustan Times*, March 12, p 1+

Anon, 1982, Rajiv to lay foundation of ceramic unit, *Times of India*, February 10, p 9

Anon, 1985, PM for key role to Public Sector: Aministrative accountability vital, *Economic Times*, January 6, p 1, col 1-6+

Anon, 1986, Primacy of Public Sector to stay, says PM, *Telegraph*, August 23, news-item

Anon, 1986, Productivity improvement in Public Interprises, *Management in*

Government 18(1) April-Jnue, p 5+

Anon, 1987, PM lashes out at Public Sector, *Times of India*, December 23, p 1, col 1-3

Banerjee, Subrata, 1988, Rajiv Gandhi, Public Sector and socialism, *New Age* 36(2) January 10, p 3

Punjab: India

See also Geographical subdivision under main Descriptor, e.g., Accords: Geographical Area: India: Punjab

Punjab Problem

Anon, 1981, Darbara Singh denies tension in Punjab, *Hindustan Times*, October 30, p 6

Anon, 1981, Nirankaries meet Rajiv, *Indian Express*, November 21, p 7

Anon, 1981, Rajiv hints at new measures, *Hindustan Times*, November 19, p 8

Anon, 1981-1982, Darbara Singh Government blamed for Punjab unrest, *Delhi Recorder* 2(9) December 15-January 14, p 58-61

Anon, 1982, Rajiv blames BJP for Punjab incidents, *Hindustan Times*, May 9, p 7

Anon, 1982, Rajiv clips Zail's wings in Punjab PCC, *Current*, March 6, p 4

Anon, 1982, Rajiv rules out change in Punjab, *Hindustan Times*, July 4, p 8

Anon, 1982, Rajiv to open Ludhiana meet, *National Herald*, April 6, p 4

Anon, 1983, Rajiv: US interfering in Punjab affairs, *Times of India*, July 24, p 9, col 1-2, news-item

Anon, 1984, Janata lifted ban on Chauhan: PM, *Times of India*, December 16, p 1, col 1-2+, news-item

Anon, 1984, Top priority to Punjab issue: Rajiv, *Times of India*, December 17, p 2, col 2-5+, news-item

Anon, 1984, Top priority to Punjab: PM, *Times of India*, December 30, p 1, col 4-5, news-item

Anon, 1985, CWC discusses Punjab, *Times of India*, May 4, p 1, col 4-6+

Anon, 1985, PM asks Akalis to publicity disown extremists, *Times of India*, December 21, p 1, col 1-3+

Anon, 1985, PM, Opposition discuss Punjab, *Times of India*, January 12, p 1, col 7-8+

Anon, 1985, PM: Pull out depends on Sikh's response, *Times of India*, January 7, p 1, col 1-2+, news-item

Anon, 1985, Punjab and Assam solution: PM, *Times of India*, March 24, p 1, col 1-3, news-item

Anon, 1985, Rajiv decries remarks by Akali leaders, *Times of India*, April 23, p 1, col 6-8+, news-item

Anon, 1985, Talks with opposition promised: PM hopes Punjab situation will cease, *Times of India*, July 8, p 1, col 1-3, news-item

Anon, 1985, Top priority to Punjab: PM, *Indian Worker* 33(16) January 14, p 1, news-item

Anon, 1985, Top priority to Punjab: PM, *Times of India*, January 6 p 1, col 1-3,

news-item
Anon, 1986, Opposition backs PM on Punjab, *Times of India*, April 1,
Anon, 1986, PM asks Akali to check terrorism, *Telegraph*, February 28
Anon, 1986, PM asks Barnala to curb violence, *Times of India*, June 24, p 1, col 1-3
Anon, 1986, PM assures all help to Barnala, *Telegraph*, December 9
Anon, 1986, PM expresses satisfaction over Barnala's performance, *Free Press Jounral* July 7
Anon, 1986, PM for non-violent movement in Punjab, *Times of India*, April 8, p 9, col 1-3
Anon, 1986, PM ready for talks with dissidents Akalies, *Telegraph*, July 13
Anon, 1986, PM rules out intervention in Punjab, *Hindustan Times*, March 23
Anon, 1986, PM's assurance to Punjab minorities, *Times of India*, May 30
Anon, 1986, Talks with Akali rebels if stand clarified: PM, *Times of India*, July 13, col 6-7+, news-item
Anon, 1987, Central rule till terrosism ends in Punjab: PM, *Times of India*, June 8, p 1, col 1-3, news-item
Anon, 1988, All Party meet on Punjab soon: PM, *Times of India*, Sepptember 2, p 1, col 1-3, news-item
Anon, 1988, PM's condition for talks, *Free Press Journal* March 12
Anon, 1988, PM's visit to Punjab, *Times of India*, September 22
Anon, 1988, Rajiv Gandhi cannot solve Punjab problem: Who can? *Rural India* 51(3) March, p 31-33
Anon, 1988, Talks on Punjab only if violence is given up: PM, *Time of India* March 12, p 1, col 1-3, news-item
Anon, 1989, PM reviews Punjab package, *Hindustan Times*, April 22
Anon, 1989, PM reviews Punjab situation, *Hindustan Times*, March 30
Anon, 1989, PM's package for Punjab, *Hindu*, March 4; *National Herald*, March 4
Anon, 1991, Punjab not ready for polls: Rajiv, *Hindustan Times*, April 14, p 5, co 2-3, news-item
Chawla, Prabhu, 1981, Beating the dead line, *India Today* 6(24) December 31, p 23
Chawla, Prabhu, 1981, Punjab talks and terror, *India Today* 6(21) November 15, p 31-33
Gandhi, Rajiv, 1981, Aliens backing secessionist move, *Indian Express*, Octobe 13, p 7
Gandhi, Rajiv, 1981, Punjab Government not effective, *Hindustan Times* November 21, p 1
Gandhi, Rajiv, 1981, Talks with Akalis have not broken down, *Hindustan Times* November 21, p 16
Gandhi, Rajiv, 1990, Rajiv Gandhi's letter to PM on Punjab election, *Statesman* September 22
Kirpekar, Subash, 1988, Rajiv warns Pak against medding in Punjab, *Times of India*, April 24, p 1, col 1-3+
Nizamuddin, D.E., 1981, Rajiv looking after Punjab, *Sunday* 9(22) Novmeber 15 p 66

Tukral, Gobind, 1982, Punjab seeking peace, *India Today* 7(5) March 15, p 38-39

See also Akalis, Sikhs

Puri: Orissa: India

Anon, 1991, Sympathy wave may help Congress in Puri, *Hindustan Times*, May 30, p 7, col 4-5

See also Geographical Area subdivision under main Descriptors

Quakes: Geographical Area: India: Bihar

Anon, 1988, PM visits quake-affected areas, *Times of India*, August 23

Quakes: Geographical Area: USSR

Anon, 1988, PM condoles quake victims, *National Herald*, December 14; *Times of India*, December 14

Quakes: Geographical Area: USSR: Armenia

Anon, 1988, President, Prime Minister condole Armenian quake deaths, *Times of India*, December 9

RSS

=Rashtriya Swam-sevak Sangh

Rachpal Singh Jatthedar: Views on Assassination of Gandhi, Rajiv

Anon, 1991, Govt flayed on assassination, *Hindustan Times*, May 30, p 3, col 1

Racism

Anon, 1986, Mandatory sanctions must for end to racism, says PM, *Hindustan Times*, July 6, news-item

Anon, 1986, Racism must end, says PM, *Statesman*, June 16, news-item

Rai Bareli: Uttar Pradesh: India

Anon, 1987, Rai Bareli won't be neglected: PM, *Times of India*, September 13, p 9, col 4-5, news-item

See also Geographical Area subdivision under main Descriptors

Raj Naraian: Homage Paid by Gandhi, Rajiv

Anon, 1987, Homage to Raj Narain, *Hindu*, January 1

Rajasthan: India

Anon, 1981, Pahadia men appeal to PM and Rajiv, *Times of India*, July 9, p 9

Anon, 1982, Rajiv wants Panchayats made more effective, *Hindustan Times*,

January 31, p 11

See also Geographical Area subdivision under main Descriptors

Rajiv Assassination

See Assassination: Attemps and Probes: Gandhi, Rajiv

Rajiv Brigade

See Congress (I): Rajiv Brigade

Rajiv Death Anniversary

Anon, 1992, Rajiv's death anniversary observed as Anti-Terrorism Day, *Economic Times*, May 22, p 13, col 1-6

See also Anti-Terrorism Day

Rajiv Gandhi Foundation

Anon, 1991, 100 cr for Rajiv Foundation, *Hindustan Times*, July 25, p 3, col 6

Anon, 1991, PM trustee of Rajiv Foundation, *Hindustan Times*, July 14, p 12, col 1

Anon, 1991, Rajiv Gandhi Foundation set up, *Hindustan Times*, June 22, p 3, col 3

Habibullah, Wajahat, 1992, The Rajiv Gandhi Foundation, *National Herald* (Supplement), p 13, col 1-4

Rajiv Jyoti and Sandesh Yatra

Anon, 1991, Plan to take "Rajiv Jyoti" across country, *Hindustan Times*, July 30, p 5, col 2-3.

Anon, 1991, 'Rajiv Jyoti' reveals changed picture in Rajastan, *Hindustan Times*, June 10, p 10, col 6-8

Anon, 1992, Offer on Rajiv Jyoti: Antony group in tight spot, *Hindustan Times*, April 30, p 7, col 5-7

Anon, 1992, Rajiv Jyoti arrives in Bangalore, *Hindustan Times*, May 21, p 12, col 4

Anon, 1992, Rajiv Jyoti Yatra from May 10, *Hindustan Times*, May 9, p 3, col 1-3

Anon, 1992, Rajiv Sandesh Yatra begins, *Hindustan Times*, May 11, p 1, col 4-5+

Anon, 1992, Shadow of infighting dim Rajiv Jyoti, *Times of India*, May 22, p 3, col 2-5

Rajiv Memorial Lecture

Anon, 1991, Rajiv Memorial Lecture, *Hindustan Times*, July 10, p 4, col 6

Rajiv Trust

Anon, 1991, Sharp exchanges over Rajiv Trust, *Hindustan Times*, July 31, p 9, col 4-5

Anon, 1991, Sonia no to grant for Trust, *Hindustan Times*, August 2, p 1, col 5

Rallies: Geographical Area: India: Congress (I)

Anon, 1990, Congress (I) rally in Delhi, *Statesman*, May 6

Rallies: Geographical Area: India: Farmers

Anon, 1981, Rajiv Gandhi to be projectrd in Kisan rally, *Statesman*, February 12

Gandhi, Rajiv, 1988 PM's Address to Farmer's Rally, *Free Press Journal*, February 21; *National Herald*, February 21

Mitra, Sumit 1981, Kisan Rally: Operation Ego message, *India Today* 6(5) March 15, p 16-21

Rallies: Geographical Area: India: May Day

Gandhi, Rajiv, 1987, We salute workers who do Gods work on earth, Prime Minister Rajiv Gandhi's Address to the May Day rally, 1987, *Indian Worker* 35(32-33) May 11, May 18, p 8-11

Rallies: Geographical Area: India: National Front

Anon, 1988, NF calls for PM's resignation, *Times of India*, November 17, p 1, col 4-5+

Rallies: Geographical Area: India: Opposition Parties

Anon, 1988, Opposition rally asks PM to quit, *Hindu*, November 17

Rallies: Geographical Area: India: Rajiv Rally

Anon, 1981, BJP charge on Rajiv rally, *Hindustan Times*, November 18, p 5

Anon, 1982, Conspiracy to disturb Rajiv rally, *Hindustan Times*, September 20, p 5

Ram Rajya

Gandhi, Rajiv, 1981, Ram Rajya if we all do our duty, *Hindustan Times*, October 7, p 3

Ramchandran, M.G.

Anon, 1986, MGR urges PM to withdraw circular, *Hindu*, September 21

Anon, 1986, PM asks MGR to ascertain militants views on Lanka offer, *Statesman*, October 11

Anon, 1986, Rajiv Gandhi, MGR review situation, *Hindustan Times*, November 9

Anon, 1987, MGR, PM put all eggs in LTTE basket, *Link* 30(17) November 29, p 4-7

Ramakrishna Paramhans

Anon, 1987, Sri Ramkrishna and the Ramkrishna order, *Vedanta Kesari* April 14, p 151-152

Rampur, Nawab of Homage Paid by Gandhi, Rajiv

Anon, 1982, Nawab Rampur mourned, *National Herald*, March 29, p 5

Rashtriya Swam-sevak Sangh

Bhattacharya, Shubhabrata, 1982, Gandhi vs Gandhi or why Surya was sold to the RSS, *Sunday* 9(37) March 6, p 12-15

Janata (Periodical), 1985, Congress (I), RSS and BJP, *Janata* (Annual Number) 40(1), p 3-4, editorial

Ray, Siddharth Shankar

Abdi, S.N.M., 1985, Back from the cold, *Illustrated Weekly of India* 106(9) July 7, p 32-33

Ghosh Chowdhry, Dilip, 1985, West Bengal Congress (I) beset by new trouble, *New Age* 33(40) October 6, p 15

Ray, Siddharth Shankar: Views on Assassination of Gandhi, Rajiv

Anon, 1991, Ray denies statemant on Rajiv death, *Hindustan Times*, May 28, p 8, col 8

Reactionary Forces

Anon, 1988, PM's call to fight reactionary forces, *Hindustan Times*, August 10

Reagan, Ronald

See also President: Geographical Area: United States of America: Reagan, Ronald

Refuelling Issue

Anon, 1991, Congress (I) asks for clarifications on refuelling issue, *Indian Express*, February 19

Anon, 1991, Congress (I) views on refuelling issue, *Hindustan Times*, February 17, p 18, col 2

Anon, 1991, Rajiv knew of refuelling: PM, *Hindustan Times*, April 13, p 1, col 1, news-item

Reservation for Women

Anon, 1989, 30 p.c. reservation for woman in panchayats: Rajiv, *Times of India*, May 5, p 1, col 1-3+, news-item

Ringadoo, Veerasamy

Anon, 1988, Ringadoo meets PM, *Statesman*, November 16

Riots: Geographical Area: India: Uttar Pradesh

Anon, 1991, Mulayam Singh blackmails Rajiv with anti-Congress reports on riots,

Organiser 42(22) January, p 7, col 1-5+

Rituals/Rites: Funeral: Gandhi, Rajiv

Anon, 1991, Ashes immersed as sun set over Yamuna, *Hindustan Times*, May 31, p 5, col 1-2

Anon, 1991, Ashes immersion at 'Sangam', *Hindustan Times*, May 26, p 7, col 1-2

Anon, 1991, Ashes scattered over Himalayas, *Hindustan Times*, May 30, p 5, col 1-4

Anon, 1991, Ashes to be immersed in Yamuna, *Hindustan Times*, May 30, p 5, col 4

Anon, 1991, 'Havan' for Rajiv's soul, *Hindustan Times*, May 31, p 5, col 1-3

Anon, 1991, JD warning on urn with ashes, *Hindustan Times*, May 28, p 6, col 6-7

Anon, 1991, Kalash train leaves behind journalists, *Hindustan Times*, May 30, p 5, col 5

Anon, 1991, Multi-faith prayer meet, *Hindustan Times*, May 26, p 12, col 1

Anon, 1991, Shaktisthal lost in silence again, *Hindustan Times*, May 26, p 7, col 4-5

Ghosh, Soumya K. and Parsai, Gargi, 1991, Asthi special let off steam of emotions, *Hindustan Times*, May 28, p 1, col 4

River Bridge: Geographical Area: India: Bihar

Anon, 1982, PM opens world's longest river bridge today, *Hindustan Times*, March 2, p 5

Anon, 1982, World's longest river bridge opened in Bihar, *Hindu*, March 3, p 1

Riyadh: Saudi Arabia

See also Geographical Area subdivision under main Descriptor

Rojgar Yojana

See Jawaharlal Nehru Rojgar Yojana

Roy, Bunker

Baxi, Upendra, 1985, For Bunker Roy, a word of advice, *Mainstream* 23(32) April 6, p 28-31

Rural Sector: Geographical Area: India

Anon, 1981, YC (I) urges employment in rural sector, *Indian Express*, December 31, p 7

Russia

See also Geographical Area Subdivision under main Descriptor

Russia: Foreign Relations: Geographical Area: India

See under Indo-Russian Relation

SAARC

=South Asian Association for Regional Co-operation

SIT

=Special Investigation Team

SPG

=Special Protection Group

Sahay, Subodh Kant: Views on Assassination of Gandhi, Rajiv

Anon, 1991, No headway in probe: Sahay, *Hindustan Times*, May 30, p 1, col 6-7, news-item

Sanjay Memorial Medical Institute

Anon, 1982, Sanjay Memorial Medical Institute for Amethi, *Hindustan Times*, September 1, p 7

Santokh Singh

See Assassination: Attempts and Probes: Santokh Singh

Sathe, Vasant

Bokare, M.G., 1986, Sathe-Rajiv wavelength, *Mainstream* 25(8) Novmeber 8, p 27-29

Satyagrah: Gandhi, Rajiv

Anon, 1990, Rajiv Gandhi leads fast, *Hindustan Times*, May 11

Saudi Arabia

See also Geographical Area subdivision under main Descriptor

Saudi Arabia: Foreign Relations: Geographical Area: India

See under Indo-Saudi Arabian Relations

Saxena, Subhash

Jain, Madhu, 1981, Nation remembers a leader but Subhash Saxena is forgotten, *Sunday* 9(3) July 5, p 32-33

Scheduled Tribes: Geographical Area: India

Anon, 1989, National Conference on Panchayati Raj and Scheduled Tribes, *Statesman*, March 5

Pramar, Suresh K., 1991, Rajiv Gandhi's death orphans tribals, *Onlooker* June 15, p 46-47

Science and Technology: Geographical Area: India

Anon, 1986, Need for better scientific administration, *Haryana Review* 20(11) November, p 3-5

Anon, 1987, Harnessing Science and Technology for development, *Yojana* 31(9) May 16, p 15-17

Scientists

Anon, 1991, Rajiv had faith in scientists, *Hindustan Times*, June 3, p 10, col 7-8

Scientists: Geographical Area: India

Anon, 1985, It's time our scientists came out of their shell, *Yojana* 29(24) January 1, p 4-6

Scindia, Madhav Rao

Anon, 1991, Scindia's call to combat violence, *Hindustan Times*, June 3, p 5, col 2-3

Scindia, Madhav Rao: Views on Assassination of Gandhi, Rajiv

Anon, 1991, Rajiv's death a national tragedy, says Scindia, *Hindustan Times*, May 31, p 3, col 1-3, news-item

Scindia, Madhav Rao: Views on Plans of Gandhi, Rajiv

Anon, 1992, Rajiv's dream will come true: Scindia, *Hindustan Times*, May 22, p 12, col 5-8

Seat Sharing in Elections

Anon, 1991, Patel, Rajiv talks on seat sharing, *Hindustan Times*, April 14, p 5, col 1

Secularism

Anon, 1991, Arif's letter to PM: Communal divide in secular party, *Times of India*, September 25, p 1, col 2-5+

Anon, 1986, PM's call to strengthen secularism, *Hindustan Times*, December 15

Basavapunalah, M., 1986, Prime Minister and his brand of secularism, *People's Democracy* 10(43) October 26, p 1+

Karat, Prakash, 1987, Separating religion and politics: Rajiv style, *People's Decmocracy* 11(11) March 15, p 3

Verma, Kewal, 1986, Rajiv Gandhi and secularism: Lessons from Muslim Woman Bill debate, *Mainstream* 24(38) May 24, p 51-53+

Security Belt Bill

Anon, 1986, Security Belt Bill kept in abeyances, *Times of India*, August 21

Security Matters: Geographical Area: India

Anon, 1986, Probe into security lapses, *Hindu*, October 5
Anon, 1987, No compromise on security: PM, *Times of India*, February 1, p 1, col 1-3, news-item
Anon, 1991, No change in PM security, *Hindustan Times*, June 6, p 10, col 1
Anon, 1991, Security for Congress leaders beefed up, *Hindustan Times*, May 30, p 5, col 5-6
Baruah, Amit, 1991, Secruity syndrome: The protection provided to Rajiv, *Frontline* 8(12) June 8-June 21, p 27
Dharker, Anil, 1991, Who takes security seriously? *Sunday* June 23-June 29, p 16-17
Joshi, Chand, 1991, Lax secuirty at Forensic Lab, *Hindustan Times*, May 30, p 16, col 1-3
Murty, Sachidananda, 1991, Could SPG have saved Rajiv? *The Week* June 9, p 40-41
Shukla, Rajiv, 1990, Security isn't cheap, *Sunday* February 25-March 3, p 7

Sen, Ashok

Anon, 1986, Askoh Sen defends PM's stand on GNLF, *Times of India*, October 3

Separatism

See Divisive Forces

Secessionist

Anon, 1986, Intervention if GNLF stir turns secessionist, says PM, *Hindustan Times*, September 21, news-item
Anon, 1990, National Front colluding with separatists: Rajiv, *Economic Times*, July 24, p 1, col 6-8, news-item
Gandhi, Rajiv 1981, Aliens backing secessionist move, *Indian Express*, October 13, p 7

See also Divisive Forces

Seshan, Trunellai Narayabaiyer

Anon, 1991, Rajiv-Seshan flop show, *Organiser* 42(38) April 28, p 16, col 4

Sethi, P.C.

Anon, 1986, New turn to Sethi row, *Times of India*, October 16, p 1, col 1-3+
Anon, 1986, Sethi suspended from Congress, *Times of India*, October 17, p 1, col 1-3+
Bhatt, S.C., 1986, Another acid test for Congress (I), *Economic Times*, October 21, p 5, col 7-8
Nandy, Pritish, 1986, Defiant! P.C Sethi Ko Gussa Kyon Aata Hai? *Illustrated Weekly of India* 107(40) October 12, p 9-12

Times of India (Newspaper), 1986, The Sethi episode, *Times of India*, October 18, p 8, col 1-2, editorial

Seva Dal

Anon, 1988, PM to head Seva Dal, *Telegraph*, May 11

Seva Dal Convention

Anon, 1989, Rajiv Gandhi's Address to Seva Dal Convention, *Times of India*, May 14

Shaktisthal

Anon, 1991, Shaktisthal lost in silence again, *Hindustan Times*, May 26, p 7, col 4-5

Shankaranand, B.

Anon, 1986, PM defends Shankaranand, *Times of India*, August 1

Shanmugham

See Assassination: Attempts and Probes: Gandhi, Rajiv: Shanmu- gham Involvement

Shantivana

Anon, 1981, Varun star draw at Shantivana, *Hindustan Times*, June 24, p 3

Sharma, Satish

Ghose, Arabinda, 1991, Captain basking in Rajiv glory, *Hindustan Times*, November 10, p 16, col 5-8

Sharma, Shankar Dayal: Homage Paid to Gandhi, Rajiv

Anon, 1991, Rajiv was a crusader for peace, justice: Dr Sharma, *Hindustan Times*, May 26, p 7, col 5-7, news-item

Shastri, H.K.: Views on Gandhi, Rajiv

Shastri, H.K., 1982, Defends Rajiv Gandhi, *Times of India*, September 29, p 13

Shipping: Geographical Area: India

Anon, 1989, PM dedicates Nhava Sheva Port to the Nation, *Hindustan Times*, May 29

Shiva Sena (Political Party)

Anon, 1991, Sena leader for Rajiv's memorial, *Hindustan Times*, July 16, p 7, col 5

Shrestha, Maricham Singh

Anon, 1986, PM congratulates Shrestha, *Indian Express*, June 17

Shukla, V.C.

Anon, 1982, VC Shukla and Arjun Singh meet, *Indian Express*, April 25, p 4

Shukla, V.C.: Election Cliches

Anon, 1982, Health camp in V.C. Shukla's constituency, *Sunday* 9(41) April 3, p 13

Siachen: India

Anon, 1988, No compromise on Siachen, says PM, *Times of India*, February 10, p 1, col 1-3+, news-item

Anon, 1988, No compromise on Siachen, says Rajiv Gandhi, *Hindu*, February 10, news-item

See also Geographical Area subdivision under main Descriptors

Sikhs

Anon, 1985, PM: Pull out depends on Sikh's response, *Times of India*, January 7, p 1, col 1-2+

Louis, Arul, B., 1982, PM denies Sikhs being wronged: Injustice to Sikhs denied, *Hindustan Times*, August 2, p 1+

Sikkim: India

Anon, 1989, CM calls on PM, *Times of India*, April 27

See also Geographical Area subdivision under main Descriptors

Singapore

See also Geographical Area subdivision under main Descriptor

Singapore: Foreign Relations: Geographical Area: India

See under Indo-Singapore Relations

Singh, Vishwantah Pratap

Anon, 1987, No confrontation with Rajiv, says V.P. Singh, *Times of India*, August 20, p 1, col 1-4+, news-item

Anon, 1988, V.P. Singh exposes PM's Italian connection, *Orgainser* 39(43) April 10, p 13

Anon, 1991, Rajiv and V.P. Singh highly frustrated as Advani named Leader of the Opposition, *Organiser* 42(22) January 6, p 1, col 1-5+

Hafiz, M.A., 1991, Rajiv, V.P., Shekhar on firm ground, *Hindustan Times*, April 2, p 10, col 5-8

Jain, Girilal, 1987, A clash of interests: Rajiv Gandhi and V.P. Singh, *Times of India*, May 18, p 6, col 3-5

Jain Girilal, 1987, Fight is for power: V.P. Singh's challenge to Rajiv Gandhi, *Times of India*, August 12, p 6, col 3-5

Jain, Girilal, 1987, Fight to the finish: Rajiv Gandhi versus V.P. Singh, *Times of India*, July 17, p 6, col 3-5

Jain, Girilal, 1987, Focus away from Rajiv: No "Natural allies" for V.P. Singh, *Times of India*, September 9, p 6, col 3-5

Times of India (Newspaper), 1987, Rajiv versus V.P. Singh, *Times of India*, March 27, p 6, col 1-2, editorial

See also Chief Minister: Geographical Area: India: Uttar Pradesh: Singh, V.P. ; Prime Minister: Geographical Area: India: Singh, V.P. (December 2, 1989-10 November 1990)

Singh, Vishwanath Pratap: Election to Parliament

Anon, 1989, Rajiv Gandhi, V.P. Singh elected, *Hindustan Times*, November 30; *Times of India*, November 30

Singh, Vishwanath Pratap: Views on Italian Connection of Gandhi, Rajiv

Anon, 1988, V.P. Singh exposes PM's Italian connection, *Organiser* 39(43) April 10, p 13

Sivarasan

See Assassination: Attempts and Probes: Gandhi, Rajiv: Sivarasan Involvement

Six Nation Summit

Anon, 1985, The Six Nation Summit on Nuclear Disarmament, New Delhi, January 28, *Monthly Commentary on Indian Economic Conditions* 26(6) January, p 7-8

Slums: Geographical Area: India

Anon, 1981, Unauthorised slums in Rajiv's name, *Onlooker* 43(21) November 30, p 17-18

Small Scales Industries: Geographical Area: India

Anon, 1986, Irritating controls on small sector to go, says PM, *Economic Times*, September 18, p 1, col 1-4, news-item

Social Justice

Anon, 1985, New direction to policies, programmes: Social justice within stipulated time frame, *Patriot*, January 6, p 1, col 3-7+

Socialism

Anon, 1985, No giving up of Nations thrust on socialism, *Indian Worker* 33(53) September 30, p 6-8

Banerjee, Subrata, 1988, Rajiv Gandhi, Public sector and socialism, *New Age* 36(2) January 10, p 3

Solanki, Madhavsinh

Anon, 1982, Antulay and Solanki dropped from CWC, *Hindustan Times*, September 3, p 1

Anon, 1986, Solanki issue is closed, says PM, *Times of India*, March 22, news-item

South Africa

See also Geographical Area subdivision under main Descriptor

South Africa: Foreign Relations: Geographical Area: India

See under Indo-South African Relations

South Asian Association for Regionsal Co-operation

Anon, 1986, Broad concensus on terrorism, *Indian Express*, November 16

Anon, 1986, Call for end to nuclear arms race, *Hindustan Times*, November 17

Anon, 1986, Not much progress on terrorism, says PM, *Hindustan Times*, November 20, news-item

Anon, 1986, Rajiv Gandhi takes over as Chairman, *Hindustan Times*, November 17

Anon, 1986, SAARC initiates action in new areas, *Times of India*, Novmeber 18

Anon, 1986, SAARC meet on women, *Indian Express*, May 7

Anon, 1988, SAARC summit begins, *Hindustan Times*, December 30

South East Asia Pacific

See also Geographical Area subdivision under main Descriptor

Soviet Festival

Anon, 1988, Soviet Festival concludes, *Hindu*, November 20

Space: Indo-Russian Alliance

Dhar, M.K., 1982, PM lauds joint Indo-Soviet space venture, *Hindustan Times*, September 24, p 1

See also Geographical Area Subdivison under main Descriptor

Spain: Foreigen Relations: Geographical Area: India

See under Indo-Spanish Relations

Special Investigation Team

See Assassination: Attempts and Probes: Gandhi, Rajiv: Special Investigation Team

Special Protection Group

Murty, Sachidananda, 1991, Could SPG have saved Rajiv? *The Week* June 9, p 40-41

See also Security Matters

Sri Lanka

See also: Colombo: Sri Lanka; Geographical Area subdivision under main Descriptor

Sri Lanka: Foreign Relations: Geographical Area: India

See under Indo-Sri Lankan Relations

Sri Nagar: Jammu and Kashmir: India

See also Geographical Area subdivision under main Descriptor

Sriperumbudur: Tamil Nadu: India

Anon, 1991, Nehru too came to Sriperumbudur, *Hindustan Times*, June 3, p 7, col 1-4

Anon, 1991, Prayer meet at Sriperumbudur, *Hindustan Times*, June, p 7, col 4

Anon, 1992, Justice J.S. Verma visits Sriperumbudur, *Hindustan Times*, March 23, p 7, col 1-3

Anon, 1992, Security lapses at Sriperumbudur: No escape for cops, leaders, *Hindustan Times*, April 4, p 4, col 4-6

See also Geographical Area subdivision under main Descriptors

Stability

Anon, 1991, Prices, stability main issues: Rajiv, *Hindustan Times*, March 28, p 9, col 1-4, news-item

Democratic World (Periodical), 1991, Rajiv's journey towards stability ends, *Democratic World* 20(21) May 26, p 3-4, col 2+, editorial

See also Stable Government

Stable Government

Anon, 1991, Rajiv calls for stable Government, *Hindustan Times*, April 10, p 5, col 4, news Item

Anon, 1991, Rajiv pledges stable Government, *Hindustan Times*, May 11, p 12, col 2-4, news-item

Starvation

Anon, 1985, Rajiv Gandhi urges UN to fight starvation, *Economic Times*, October 25, p 1, col 1-4+

Starwars

Anon, 1986, 'Starwars' against world peace, says Rajiv, *National Herald*, February 17, news-item

State Grant in Aid

Anon, 1991, Sonia no to grant for Trust, *Hindustan Times*, August 2, p 1, col 5

State Assembly

See Vidhan Sabha

State Borders

See under Boundary: Geographical Area: India: States

State Election

See Elections: Vidhan Sabha

State Enterprises

See Public Sector Undertakings

State Funds

Anon, 1985, Funds plenty for engines of destruction and not for development, *Indian Worker* 33(39) June 24, p 3-5

State Projects: Geographical Area: India: West Bengal

See Projects: Geographical Area: India: West Bengal

State Sector

See Public Sector Undertakings

Stockholm

See also Geographical Area Subdivision under main Descriptor

Strikes: Geographical Area: India: West Bengal

Gandhi, Rajiv, 1982, No Congress (I) sponsored strikes, *Times of India*, January 1, p 9

Strougal, Lyubomir

Anon, 1986, Lyubomir, Rajiv agree on sanctions on South Africa, *Hindustan*

Times, August 12

Students: Help Sought from Gandhi, Rajiv

Anon, 1982, Striking students seek Rajiv help, *Hindustan Times*, March 30, p 16

Subramanian Swamy

See Swamy, Subramanian

Succession Struggle: Geographical Area: India

Anon, 1991, Succession struggle, *Frontline*, 8(12) Jnue 8-June 21, p 120-121

Suicide Killers

Jayaraj, D.B.S., 1991, The suicide killers, *Frontline* June 22-July 5, p 30-31

Sundari

See Assassination: Attempts and Probes: Gandhi, Rajiv: Sundari Involvement

Suresh Ram

Anon, 1981, Suresh Ram greater than Rajiv, *Blitz*, July 11, p 8

Surveillance Issue

Anon, 1991, Surveillance issue again rocks Parliament, *Hindustan Times*, March 6

Anon, 1991, Uproar in Parliament over Surveillance of Rajiv Gandhi's house, *Times of India*, March 5

Surya (Periodical)

Bhattacharya, Shubharata, 1982, Gandhi vs Gandhi or why Surya was sold to the RSS, *Sunday* 9(37) March 6, p 12-15

Swamy, Subramanian

Anon, 1991, Move to destabilise India: Swamy, *Hindustan Times*, June 2, p 19, col 1-4, news-item

Sweden: Foreign Relations: Geographical Area: India

See under Indo-Sweden Relations

Swiss Bank Accounts

Anon, 1986, PM denies Swiss Bank accounts, *Hindustan Times*, November 11

Sycophants

Anon, 1987, When Rajivji gives his views, the others say 'okay', *Link* 30(21 December 27, p 6-8

Sympathy Wave in Elections

See Elections: Sympathy Factor

Syria

See also Geographical Area subdivision under main Descriptor

Syria: Foreign Relations: Geographical Area: India

See under Indo-Syrian Relations

T V

=Television

T V: Geographical Area: India

See Doordarshan

Tamil Nadu: India

Anon, 1986, MRG urges PM to withdraw circular, *Hindu*, September 21
Anon, 1989, DMK MPs meet PM, *Indian Express*, April 6
Anon, 1991, Karunanidhi blames Central rule, *Hindustan Times*, June 2, p 12, col 5-8
Anon, 1991, Rajiv, Jayalalitha finalise poll pact, *Hindustan Times*, March 31, p 1, col 1-3+
Anon, 1991, TN witnessed maximum bomb shock and sympathy wave, *Democratic World* 20(15) June 3, p 8
Anon, 1992, Sivarasan, Subha took shelter in TN, Kerala, *Sunday Tribure*, May 24, p 4, col 45
Viswanatha, 1991, Tamil Nadu under the Tiger's sway, *India Today* June 15, p 50+

See also Geographical Area subdivision under main Descriptors

Tamilians: Geographical Area: Sri Lanka

Anon, 1986, Talks fail over "Tamil homeland", *Hindustan Times*, November 26

Tarapur: India

Gandhi, Indira, 1982, No plan for talks with US on F-16 foreign fuel for Tarapur likely, *Indian Express*, July 28, p 1

See also Geographical Area subdivision under main Descriptors

Taxation: Geographical Area: India

Anon, 1988, Nation's taxation policy and role of tax administration, *IFTP Bulletin* 8(2-3) September, p 5-8
Anon, 1986, Why Basu does't tax rich farmers? *Link* 29(8) Setember, p 10-12

Tax Evasion: Geographical Area: India

Sinha, B.M., 1981, Bonanza for tax dodgers, *Probe India* 3(1) March, p 25-27

Terrorism: Geographical Area: India

Anon, 1985, Govt not to yield to terrorists: PM, *Times of India*, May 18, p 1, col 1-3, news-item

Anon, 1985, Infitrators from Pak behind terrorism: PM, *Times of India*, September 17, p 1, col 1-3, news-item

Anon, 1985, Poll aims at wiping out terrorism: Rajiv, *Times of India*, September 10, p 1, col 5-7, news-item

Anon, 1986, Broad concensus on terrorism, *Indian Express*, November 16

Anon, 1986, Centre to announce anti-terrorist action, says PM, *Statesman*, December 2, news-item

Anon, 1986, Combat terrorism, says PM, *Hindustan Times*, April 8, news-item

Anon, 1986, Not much progress on terrorism, says PM, *Hindustan Times*, November 20, news-item

Anon, 1986, PM asks Akali to check terrorism, *Telegraph*, February 28, news-item

Anon, 1986, PM for cautious approach to terrorism, *Times of India*, April 25

Anon, 1986, PM for dual war on terrorism, *Indian Express*, August 12

Anon, 1986, PM for joint efforts to fight terrorism, *Hindustan Times*, March 30

Anon, 1986, PM pleads for people's movement to curb terrorism, *Times of India*, October 9, news-item

Anon, 1986, Stringent measures to meet terrorism, *Hindustan Times*, July 30

Anon, 1986, Terrorism will be met at all costs, says PM, *Free Press Journal* July 29, news-item

Anon, 1987, Cenral rule till terrorism ends in Punjab: PM, *Times of India*, June 8, p 1, col 1-3

Anon, 1987, People asked to help fight drought, terrorism, *Times of India*, August 16, p 1, col 1-4

Anon, 1988, Pakistan biggest supporter of terrorism, says Rajiv Gandhi, *Hindustan Times*, June 9, news-item

Gandhi, Rajiv, 1989, PM's statement regarding terrorism, *Hindu*, March 1

Mitra Chauddhury, Sreerupa, 1991, Is terrorism, the way to all solutions? *Democratic World* 20(21) May 26, p 5, col 1-3

See also Terrorists: Geographical Area: India

Terrorism: Geographical Area: India: Punjab

Chawla, Prabhu, 1981, Punjab talks and terror, *India Today*, 6(21)

Terrorists: Geographical Area: Algeria

Anon, 1985, Terrorist wanted to kill Rajiv in France or Algeria, *Times of India*, May 17, p 1, col 1-3

Terrorists: Geograhical Area: France

Anon, 1985, Terrorist wanted to kill Rajiv in France or Algeria, *Times of India*, May 17, p 1, col 1-3

Terrorists: Geographical Area: India

Anon, 1986, Pak aiding terrorists: PM, *Times of India*, October 13, p 1, col 1-3, news-item

Anon, 1987, Lives of landless to be insured: Iron hand for terrorists: PM, *Economic Times*, May 17, p 1, col 6-8, news-item

Anon, 1988, PM again warns Paksistan against aiding terrorists, *Times of India*, August 16, p 1, col 1-3+

See also Terrorism: Geographical Area: India

Thackeray, Bal: Views on Assassination of Gandhi, Rajiv

Vernekar, Raju, 1991, Rajiv death led to rout: Thackeray, *Hindustan Times*, June 22, p 7, col 1-4

Thailand

See also Geographical Area subdivision under main Descriptor

Thailand: Foreign Relations: Geographical Area: India

See under Indo-Thai Relations

Thakkar Report

Anon, 1989, PM announces probe into Thakkar report leak, *Telegraph*, April 11

Thatcher, Margaret

Anon, 1981, Rajiv Gandhi calls on Mrs Thatcher, *Hindustan Times*, July 29, p.

Anon, 1989, Rajiv Gandhi holds talks with Thatcher, *Indian Express*, July 15

Thondaman, S.

Anon, 1989, Thondaman calls on Rajiv Gandhi, *Times of India*, July 9

Anon, 1989, Thondaman calls for fresh accord, *Times of India*, July 10 -

Tina Factor

Anon, 1988, Rajiv's 'Tina' factor, *India Today*, February 29

Tiwari, Narain Dutta

Anon, 1982, Rajiv keen on Tiwari becoming UP CM, *Indian Express*, July 1, p 1

See also Chief Minister: Geographical Area: India: Uttar Pradesh: Tiwari, Narain Dutta

Tiwari, Narain Dutta: Views on Assassination of Gandhi, Rajiv

Anon, 1991, Conspiracy behind killing: Tiwari, *Hindustan Times*, June 6, p 7, col 2-7, news-item

Tributes

See under Name of the person, e,g., Gandhi, Indira: Homage Paid to Her

Tripathi, Kamlapati

Anon, 1986, CWC drops move for action against Tripathi, *Times of India*, June 3, p 1, col 1-3

Anon, 1986, Kamlapati slain with Aurangeb-Shahjehan syndrome, *Orgainser* 38(8) July 6, p 5

Anon, 1986, Tripathi accepts CPB decision, *Times of India*, June 19, p 9, col 1-2

Anon, 1986, Tripathi continues talk with rebels, *Times of India*, April 27, p 1, col 1-4

Anon, 1986, Tripathi criticises Rajiv's handling of affairs, *Times of India*, May 29, p 1, col 1-3

Anon, 1986, Tripathi denied renomination to Rajya Sabha, *Times of India*, June 18, p 1, col 7-8

Anon, 1986, Tripathi may be eased out, *Times of India*, May 30, p 1, col 1-3+

Anon, 1986, Tripathi resigns as Working President of Congress (I), *Telegraph*, November 13

Anon, 1986, Tripathi resings on PM's demand, *Times of India*, November 13, p 1, col 1-3

Anon, 1986, Tripathi's letter to PM leaked, *Hindu*, May 29

Anon, 1986, Tripathi's letter to Rajiv Gandhi, *Times of India*, May 29, p 8, col 7-8

Anon, 1986, Tripathi should quit, says Anjiah, *Times of India*, May 31, p 1, col 4+, news-item

Anon, 1986, Tripathi supports Rajiv, *Hindustan Times*, June 1

Anon, 1986, Tripathi's tantalising tantrums, *Link* 28(39) May 4, p 19

Anon, 1986, Tripathi voices anguish, *Times of India*, April 25, p 1, col 4-6

Anon, 1986, Tripathi won't take any more insults, *Times of India*, September 4, p 1, col 1-4

Anon, 1988, Tripathi's letter to Rajiv Gandhi, *Times of India*, July 7

Chadha, Kumkum, 1986, If I quit, it may damage the Congress (I): An interview with Kamlapati Tripathi, *Hindustan Times* (Magazine), September 14, p 7, col 1-6

Gupta, O., 1980, Power equation after Kamlapati, *Onlooker* December 15, p 10-17

Kamath, M.V., 1986, Bandying words with bandicoots, *Indian Express* (Magazine), June 22, p 2, col 6-8

Khare, Harish, 1986, Issues Tripathi has raised: Rajiv Gandhi should be grateful, *Times of India*, June 11, p 8, col 3-5

Mukherjee, Sadhan, 1986, Rajiv blues over Tripathi non-revolt, *New Age* 34(22) June 8, p 1

Thakur, Janardan, 1986, Does his answer lie in the stars? *Hindustan Times*

(Magazine), November 30, p 6, col 1-4

Times of India (Newspaper), 1986, Not to be written off, *Times of India*, Nvoember 14, p 8, col 1-2, editorial

Times of India (Newspaper) 1986, Refusal to oblige, *Times of India*, October 25, p 8, col 1-2, editorial

Times of India (Newspaper), 1986, Test is not over, *Times of India*, June 4, p 8, col 1-2, editorial

Times of India (Newspaper), 1986, Tripathi speaks out, *Times of India*, April 26, p 8, col 1-2, editorial

Times of India (Newspaper), 1986, Tripathi strikes again, *Times of India*, July 10, p 8, col 1-2, editorial

Tripura: Geographical Area: India

Chakravarty, S., 1986, No major contradiction, *Link* 28(40) May 11, p 12

See also Geographical Area subdivision under main Descriptors

Turkey

See also Geographical Area subdivision under main Descriptor

Turkey: Foreign Relations: Geographical Area: India

See under Indo-Turkish Relations

Twenty Point Programme: Geographical Area: India

Anon, 1986, PM on new 20 Point Programme, *Telegrph*, August 23

Tytler, Jagdish

Anon, 1985, Tytler among 12 AICC joint secretaries, *Times of India*, January 11, p 1, col 1-2

UK

=United Kingdom

UN

=United Nation

UNESCO

=United Nations Educational, Scientific and Cultural Organization

USA

=United States of America

USSR

=Union of Soviet Socialist Republics (Erstwhile)

USSR: Foreign Relations: Geographical Area: India

See under Indo-Russian Relations

United Kingdom

See also Geographical Area subdivision under main Descriptor

United Kingdom: Foreign Relations: Geographical Area: India

See under Indo-UK Relations

United Nations

Anon, 1986, Aparthied must ends, says PM, *Times of India*, June 17, news-item
Anon, 1986, PM assures support to Cuellar, *Telegraph*, October 12
Anon, 1988, Rajiv Gandhi meets world leaders, *Hindustan Times*, June 11
Anon, 1989, PM, Cuellar meet, *Indian Express*, February 28

United Nations: Homage Paid to Gandhi, Rajiv

Anon, 1991, UN Council homage to Rajiv, *Hindustan Times*, May 26, p 12, col 4

United Nations: Namibia Plan

Anon, 1986, UN Namibia Plan must prevail, says PM, *Hindustan Times*, July 8, news-item

United Nations Educational, Scientific and Cultural Organization

Anon, 1986, M'Bow meets PM, *Times of India*, August 22

United Nations Organisation

See United Nation

United Nations Security Council

Anon, 1991, Rajiv Gandhi calls for UNSC meeting on Gulf war, *Times of India*, February 18

Unity: National

See National Unity

United States of America

See also Geographical Area Subdivision under main Descriptor

United States of America: Arms Supply

Gandhi, Rajiv, 1981, US forcing arms on sub-continent, *Hindustan Times*, November 14, p 6

United States of America: Arms Supply to Pakistan

Louis, Arul B., 1982, Arms for Pak will be discussed: PM, *Hindustan Times*, July 29, p 1, news-item

United States of America: Foreign Relations: Geographical Area: India

See under Indo-US Relations

Unnikrishan, K.P.: Election Cliches

Unnikrishan, K.P., 1991, I don't see Rajiv crossing 175-180 seats, *India Today* June 15, p 13, col 1-3

Uttar Pradesh: India

Anon, 1981, December 24 will not come, *Hindustan Times*, December 8, p 2
Chawla, Prabhu, 1982, Rahu, Ketu, Bahuguna, *India Today* 7(1) January 15, p 51
Gandhi, Rajiv, 1988, PM's Address to Farmer's Rally, *Free Press Journal* February 21; *National Herald*, February 21
Singh, Vishwanath Pratap, 1982, My failure is total, *Onlooker* 44(3) February 15, p 20+

See also Geographical Area subdivision under main Descriptors

Uttar Pradesh Government

See Administrative Machinery: Geographical Area: India: Uttar Pradesh

Vajpayee, Atal Behari: Homage Paid to Gandhi, Rajiv

Anon, 1992, Vajpayee's tribute to Rajiv, *Hindustan Times*, May 20, p 24, col 1

Vakil, Abdul

Anon, 1988, Abdul Vakil calls on PM, *Hindustan Times*, September 4

Vauuniya: Sri Lanka

Anon, 1991, Killer was Sundari from Vauuniya in Sri Lanka? *Hindustan Times*, June 2, p 1, col 5-7

Velayati, Ali Akbar

Anon, 1989, Velayati, PM hold talks, *Hindustan Times*, August 30

Venkataraman, R.

See President: Geographical Area: India: Venkataraman, R. (25th July 25, 1987

– July 24, 1992)

Verma, J.S.

Anon, 1992, Justice J.S. Verma visits Sriperumbudur, *Hindustan Times*, March 4, p 7, col 1-3

Vice-President: Geographical Area: India: Sharma, Shankar Dayal (1987 – 1992)

See also Sharma, Shankar Dayal

Vice-President:Geographical Area: Poland

Anon, 1989, PM holds talks with Polish Vice-President, *National Herald*, April 13

Vidhan Sabha: Geographical Area: India: Karnataka: Homage Paid to Gandhi, Rajiv

Anon, 1991, Karnatka House mourns Rajiv, *Hindustan Times*, July 6, p 9, col 1

Vidhan Sabha: Geographical Area: India: Madhya Pradesh: Homage Paid to Gandhi, Rajiv

Anon, 1991, Tributes to Rajiv by MP House, *Hindustan Times*, June 27, p 5, col 6

Voilence: Geographical Area: India

Anon, 1988, CPM encouraging violence, says PM, *Times of India*, April 3, p 1, col 7-8, news-item

Anon, 1991, Politics of violence, *Hindustan Times*, June 4, p 11, col 2-5, letter to the editor

Anon, 1991, Scindia's call to combat violence, *Hindustan Times*, June 3, p 5, col 21-3

Violence: Geographical Area: India: Punjab

Anon, 1986, PM asks Barnala to curb violence, *Times of India*, June 24, p 1, col 1-3

Anon, 1988, Talks on Punjab only if violence is given up: PM, *Times of India*, March 12, p 1, col 1-3, news-item

Visa Policy: Geograhical Area: United Kingdom

Anon, 1986, Britain protests against PM's remarks on Visa rule, *Hindu*, October 18; *Times of India*, October 18

Visually Handicapped

Anon, 1982, Rajiv calls to rehabilitate the blind, *Hindustan Times*, August 23, p 16

Vorontsov, Yuliy Mikhailovich

Anon, 1989, Vorontsov holds talks with Rajiv Gandhi, *Hindustan Times*, February 17

Wakil, Abdul

Anon, 1989, Wakil holds talks with Rajiv Gandhi, *Hindustan Times*, March 4

Washington: United States of America

See also Geographical Area subdivision under main Descriptor

Water Project: Geographical Area: India

Anon, 1982, Rajiv lays stone for water project, *Hindustan Times*, January 8

Welfare: Dalits: Geographical Area: India

Anon, 1991, Rajiv calls for Dalit's uplift, *Hindustan Times*, April 15, p 1, col 1-2

Welfare: Geographical Area: India

Anon, 1983, Firm Congress (I) steps for people's welfare: Rajiv, *Times of India*, October 19, p 6, col 3-4, news-item

Anon, 1985, New direction to policies, programmes: Social Justice within stipulated time frame, *Patriot*, January 6, p 1, col 3-7+

Welfare: Geographical Area: India

Anon, 1981, Delhi Development Authority to mark the launching of construction of 5,000 houses, *Hindustan Times*, November 19, p 3

Anon, 1985, Planning being geared to uplift poor: PM, *Economic Times*, August 16, p 1, col 1-4, news-item

Anon, 1988, Reorder global priorities for poverty uplift: PM, *Economic Times*, March 26, p 1, col 6-8+, news-item

Gandhi, Indira, 1982, Welfare schemes not known to poor, *Indian Express*, September 1, p 3

Razdan, Deepak, 1991, Rajiv's opponent for Govt of poor, *Hindustan Times*, May 7, p 9, col 1-2

Sinha, Bharati, 1984, No protection for weak under Congress (I) regime, *New Age* 32(42) November 25, p 8-9

Welfare: Harijans: Geographical Area: India

Anon, 1981, Houses handed over to Harijans, *Hindustan Times*, August 10, p 8

Anon, 1981, Of house, buffaloes and bank aid, *Times of India*, August 10, p 9

Anon, 1981-1982, Mrs Gandhi's Devoli visit heartens Harijan victims, *Delhi Recorder* 2(9) December 15-June14, p 26-28

Welfare: Landless: Geographical Area: India:

Anon, 1987, Lives of landless to be insured: Iron hand for terrorists, PM: *Economic Times*, May 17, p 1, col 6-8, news-item

Welfare: Visually Handicapped Geographical Area: India

Anon, 1982, Rajiv calls to rehabilitate the blind, *Hindustan Times*, August 23, p 16

Welfare: Women: Geographical Area: India

Gandhi, Rajiv, 1982, Fight dowry evil, *National Herald*, September 4, p 3

West Bengal: India

Anon, 1982, Bomb scare on Rajiv's flight, *Hindustan Times*, May 12, p 8

Anon, 1986, PM rules out division of the State, *Telegraph*, September 19, news-item

Anon, 1986, Prime Mininster rejects demand for Gorkhaland, *Free Press Journal* December 20, *Times of India*, December 20, news-item

Anon, 1986, PM, Ghising hold talks, *Indian Express*, May 19

Mukhopadhyay, Ashim, 1986, Rajiv's gift to West Bengal, *Indian Express* (Magazine), October 12, p 1, col 1-8+

See also Geographical Area subdivision under main Descriptors

West Bengal Day

Anon, 1991, Rajiv greeting on Bengal Day, *Hindustan Times*, April 15, p 10, col 3

Wijeratne, Ranjan

Anon, 1989, Wijeratne calls on Rajiv Gandhi, *National Herald*, August 1

Anon, 1991, Similar Bomb had killed Wijeratne, *Hindustan Times*, May 20, p 20, col 1

Wives: Political Role

Anon, 1991, How wives make politicians, *Probe India* June, p 55-58

Women

Anon, 1981, Three women climb Nanda Devi peak, *Hindustan Times*, September 23, p 1-16

Anon, 1985, Woman: The social conscience of the country, *Social Welfare* 32(2) May, p 4-5

Anon, 1986, SAARC meet on women, *Indian Express*, May 7

Anon, 1989, 30 p.c reservation for women in panchayats: Rajiv, *Times of India*, May 5, col 1-3, news-item

Anon, 1991, Rajiv trusted women folk, *Hindustan Times*, June 2, p 19, col 3

See also Welfare: Geographical Area: India: Women; Women: Respective Plan

Women: Perspective Plan

Anon, 1988, Perspective plan for women presented, *Hindu*, November 13

Working Class: Geographical Area: India

Marakkar, V.P., 1989, Rajiv Gandhi and the working class, *Indian Worker* 38(8) November 20, p 2-3

YC (I)

= Youth Congress (I)

Yadav, Laloo Prasad

See also Chief Minister: Geographical Area: India: Bihar: Yadav, Laloo Prasad

Yadav, Mulayam Singh

See also Chief Minister: Geographical Area: India: Uttar Pradesh: Yadav, Mulayam Singh

Yaqub Khan

Anon, 1989, Yaqub Khan calls on PM, *Hindustan Times*, July 26

Anon, 1989, Yaqub meets PM, *Times of India*, April 18

Youth

Anon, 1981, Rajiv asks youth to work for national uplift, *Times of India*, October 26, p 9, col 2-5

Anon, 1982, Experiment with the young, *Link*, 25(5) September 12, p 6

Anon, 1982, Rajiv urges youth to work for peace, *Hindustan Times*, September 23, p 8

Youth: Role in National Development

Anon, 1982, Rajiv stress on role of youth's in economic order vital, *Hindustan Times*, January 25, p 1+

Youth: Rural

Anon, 1982, Rajiv's call to rural youth to stay in villages, *Times of India*, January 31, p 9

Youth Congress (I)

Akbar, M.J., 1980, What is happening in the Youth Congress, *Sunday* 8(5) August 10, p 24-25

Anon, 1980, Rajiv likely to be Youth Congress leader, *Blitz*, July 26, p 3

Anon, 1980, Rajiv urged to lead YC (I) at Sanjay Rally, *Indian Express*, December 15, p 1+

Anon, 1980, Strong appeal to Rajiv, *Hindustan Times*, December 7, p 7

Anon, 1981, Fight bid to create chaos YC (I) told: Youth Congress (I) to implement 25-point plan, *Hindustan Times*, December 31, p 1+, nes-items

Anon, 1981, New YC Chief, *Current*, November 22, p 2

Anon, 1981, Rajiv agrees to lead IYC (I): Resolve to work for uplift of women, *Times of India*, December 30

Anon, 1981, Rajiv asked to lead Youth Congress (I), *Hindustan Times*, December 30, p 1+

Anon, 1981, Rajiv Gandhi: The young inheritor, *India Today* 6(10) May 16, p 56-62

Anon, 1981, Rajiv in Srinagar to attend YC (I) meet, *Times of India*, July 11, p 7

Anon, 1981, Rajiv jets into politics without power, *Current*, November 29, p 1-2

Anon, 1981, Rajiv on YC (I) Council, *Hindustan Times*, June 25, p 1

Anon, 1981, Rajiv revitalises Youth Congress, *Blitz*, April 25, p 6

Anon, 1981, Rajiv will attend YC (I) Council meet, *Hindustan Times*, July 10, p 5

Anon, 1981, Rath regains Rajiv's confidence, *Sunday* 9(14) September 20, p 65

Anon, 1981, Weathering the storm, *India Today* 6(5) March 15, p 5

Anon, 1981, YC (I) assured 'due share' of Poll tickets, *Indian Express*, November 15, p 2

Anon, 1981, YC (I) to have job-oriented programme, *Hindustan Times*, December 29, p 4

Anon, 1981, YC (I) urges employment in rural sector, *Indian Express*, December 31, p 7

Anon, 1982, IYC (I) keeps out Press from Meet, *Indian Express*, January 24, p 3

Anon, 1982, PM urged to punish Youth Congress rebles, *Times of India*, March 29, p 9

Anon, 1982, Rajiv and the fussy elephant, *Onlooker* 44(2) January 31, p 7

Anon, 1982, Rajiv Gandhi not ot take up YC post, *Indian Express*, January 1, p 7

Anon, 1982, Rajiv not keen on YC (I) leadership, *Times of India*, April 2, p 7

Anon, 1982, Rajiv's call to rural youth to stay in villages, *Times of India*, January 31, p 9

Anon, 1982, Sanjay-ignored YC men to back Rajiv Gandhi, *Hindustan Times*, May 4, p 6

Anon, 1982, State YC (I) team sees Rajiv, *Amrit Bazar Patrika*, April 7, p 8

Anon, 1982, Warning to YC (I) rebels against talking to Press, *Indian Express*, August 21, p 9

Anon, 1982, Will Sanjay cult overwhelm Rajiv? *Blitz*, March 13, p 6

Anon, 1983, Rajiv urges youth to build 'new India', *Times of India*, April 14, p 1, col 7-8+

Anon, 1984, YC charge against Opposition, *Times of India*, May 8, p 1, col 5-6+

Azad, Ghulm Nabi, 1982, 'We want Rajiv', *India Today* 7(2) January 21, p 27

Bhattacharya, M., 1981, YC (I) show to net regional support, boost Rajiv, *New Age* 29(43) October 25, p 11

Chatterji, Debasish, 1982, YC (I) happy days again: Will Rajiv Gandhi provide discipline to the hitherto loose organisation? *Probe India* 3(12) February, p 57-58

Chawla, P. and Mitra, S., 1982, Sycophancy unleashed, *India Today* 7(2)

January 31, p 68-83

Chengappa, Raj, 1982, Logistics: A costly coronation, *India Today* 7(2) January 31, p 80-81

Datta-Ray, Sundnda K., 1981, Tremors in the Darbar: Will Mrs Gandhi declare herself? *Statesman*, April 8

Davendra, Mohan, 1982, Rajiv raises YC from the dead, *Blitz*, January 16, p 21

Gandhi, Rajiv, 1982, YC (I) will do constructive work, *Hindustan Times*, January, p 4

Khushwant Singh, 1980, Destiny's cruelty, *Sunday* 8(1) June 29, p 8

Nihal Singh, S., 1981, Few signs of hope, *Indian Express*, December 30, p 6

Nizamuddin, D.E., 1980, Changing guard, *Sunday* 8(18) December 7, p 66

Nizamuddin, D.E., 1980, Tears of many colours, *Sunday*, 8(2) July 20, p 58

Nizamuddin, D.E., 1982, Rewarded for misconduct, *Sunday* 9(47) May 15, p 66

Puri, Anjali, 1986, What's nice kid like you doing in politics? *Indian Express* (Magazine), October 26, p 1, col 1-8+

Rai, Kalpnath, 1981, Rajiv carrying the Nehru flag, *Current*, July 11, p 5

Ramalingam, N.K., 1980, Rajiv, Maneka must play active role, *Current*, July 12, p 10-11

Sulekh, 1982, Youth power no answer to gangster politics, *Blitz*, February 13, p 9

Thakur, Janardan, 1986, Who ever spoke ill of Rajiv Gandhi? *Times of India*, (Sunday Review), June 8, p 1, col 1-4

Times of India (Newspaper), 1983, Rajiv's tasks, *Times of India*, May 20, p 8, col 1-2. editorial

Times of India (Newspaper), 1984, Thugs at large, *Times of India*, September 15, p 6, col 1-2, editroial

Youth Congress (I): Geographical Area: India: West Bengal

Ghosh Chowdhury, Dilip 1984, Faction flight in Youth Congress come to fore in Bengal, *New Age*, 32(36) September 2, p 14

Youth Congress (I): Rebels

Sharma, Padam Singh, 1982, PM urged to punish Youth Congress rebels, *Times of India*, March 29, p 9

Yugoslavia

See also Geographical Area subdivision under main Descriptor

Yugoslavia: Foreign Relations: Geographical Area: India

See under Indo-Yugoslav Relations

Zail Singh

Anon, 1981, While Pranab and Zail quarreled over protocol, Rajiv officiated as PM, *Organier* 33(29) December 6, p 5

Anon, 1982, PM may secure NC backing for Zail, *Hindustan Times*, June 26, p 16

Anon, 1982, Rajiv clips Zail's wings in Punjab PCC, *Current*, March 6, p 4

Anon, 1982, Zail's happiest days as Mrs Gandhi's Minister, *Hindustan Times*, July 1, p 5

Anon, 1982, Zail Singh reiterates loyalty to PM, *Indian Express*, June 30, p 7

Anon, 1986, President, Prime Minister greet Reagan, *Times of India*, July 4

Anon, 1987, A Prime Minister or a President? *Times of India* (Sunday Review), January 25, p iv, col 1-5

Anon, 1987, President-PM differences being taken to absured length, *Organiser* 38(41) February 22, p 6

Anon, 1987, President rejects pleas for PM's prosecution, *Times of India*, July 23, p 1, col 1-3

Anon, 1987, Will Zail dismiss Rajiv? *Orgainser* 38(46) March 29, p 1+

Anon, 1988, PM asks to probe 'offer of funds' to Zail, *Times of India*, March 3, p 1, col 1-3+

Anon, 1988, Probe into offer of money to former President, *Hindu*, March 3; *Indian Express*, March 3

Anon, 1988, Seven of Rajiv's trusted men wanted Zail Singh to dismiss him, *Orgainser* 39(42) April 3, p 8

Dubey, Sumam, et al, 1982, Zail Singh: The making of a President, *India Today* 7(13) July 15, p 50-55

Gandhi, Rajiv, 1982, Men with conscience will back Zail Singh, *Hindustan Times*, June 30, p 7

Jain, Girilal, 1987, Challenges to Rajiv Gandhi: President Zail Singh and V.P. Singh, *Times of India*, May 18, p 6, col 3-5

Times of India (Newspapper), 1987, No comfort for Giani, *Times of India*, May 2, p 6, col 1-2, editorial

See also President: Geographical Area: India: Zail Singh

Zail Singh: Public Relations

Anon, 1982, Ladoos, cold drinks for asking at Zail house, *Hindustan Times*, July 16, p 3

Zambia

See also Geographical Area subdivision under main Descriptor

Zambia: Foreign Relations: India

See under Indo-Zambian Relations

Zhao, Ziyang

Anon, 1988, PM calls on Deny, Zhao, *Hindustan Times*, December 22; *Times of India*, December 22

Zia-ul-Haq

Anon, 1985, Rajiv invites Zia to inaguration of Breeder Reactor, *Times of India*,

December 1, p 1, col 1-3

Anon, 1986, Rajiv Gandhi's criticism not based on facts, says Zia, *Times of India*, September 9, news-item

Anon, 1986, Rajiv-Zia meeting at Harare, *Hindustans Times*, September 6

Anon, 1986, Zia sends PM apology for attack on envoys, *Telegraph*, June 23

Anon, 1987, PM, Zia review bilateral ties, *Times of India*, February 22, p 1, col 1-3+

Anon, 1988, PM invites Zia for talks, *Hindu*, February 26; *Tribune*, February 26

Zia-ul-Haq: Condolence to Him

Anon, 1988, President Zia's death condoled, *National Herald*, August 19; *Telegraph*, August 19

Zimbabwe

See also Geographical Area Subdivision under main Descriptor

Zueqian, Wu

Anon, 1989, Wu meets Rajiv Gandhi, *Hindustan Times*, October 14

2

SELECT RELEVENT MONOGRAPHS

(not included in the Printary Documentation)

BOOKS

Aggarwal, J.C. and Agrawal, S.P., 1992, *Modern History of Punjab: A look back into ancient peaceful Punjab focusing confrontation and failures leading to present Punjab problem and a peep ahead*, Concept Publishing Company, New Delhi

Agrawal, S.P. 1985, *India since Independence*, rev edn., Ministry of Information and Broadcasting, Publication Division, Government of India, New Delhi, 137p

Agrawal, S.P. and Aggarwal, J.C., 1988, *Nehru on Social Issues*, Concept Publishing Company, New Delhi

Agrawal, S.P. and Aggarwal, J.C., 1989, *Information India: Global View: 1988*, Concept Publishing Company, New Delhi

Agrawal, S.P. and Aggarwal, J.C., 1989-1990, *Information India: Global View: 1990*, Concept Publishing Company, New Delhi

Agrawal, S.P. and Aggarwal, J.C., 1990, Lok Sabha and Vidhan Sabha Elections in India 1989-1990: Process and Results with Comparative Study of Manifestoes, Concept Publishing Company, New Delhi

Agrawal, S.P. and Aggarwal, J.C., 1990-1991, *Information India: Global View: 1991*, Concept Publishing Company, New Delhi

Agrawal, S.P. and Aggarwal, J.C., 1991, *Educational and Social Uplift of Backward Classes: At What Cost and How? Mandal Commission and After*, Concept Publishing Company, New Delhi

Agrawal, S.P. and Aggarwal, J.C., 1991, *Nation in Crisis: Achievement, Failures and Non-function of the Government*, Concept Publishing Company, New Delhi

Agrawal, S.P. and Aggarwal, J.C., 1991, *Rise and Fall of Non-Congress Government of India*, Shipra Publications, New Delhi, viii, 292p.

Agrawal, S.P. and Aggarwal, J.C., 1991-1992, *Information India: Global View: 1992*, Concept Publishing Company, New Delhi

Ahluwalia, B.K. and Ahluwalia, S., 1985, *Rajiv Gandhi: Breaking New Grounds*, Cosmo, New Delhi, xiv, 202p., illustrations

Ahluwalia, B.K. and Ahluwalia, Shashi, 1985, *Rajiv Gandhi: A Profile in Courage*, Intellectual Publishing House, New Delhi, xii, 152p

Ali, Tariq, 1985, *An Indian Dynasty: The Story of the Nehru Gandhi Family*, Putnam, New York, 318p, plates

Anu, 1986, *Rajiv Gandhi: New Era in Economic Development*, Institute of

Economic Studies, New Delhi

Bedi, P.S. and Sharma, Raj, 1985, *Rajiv Gandhi: Our National Hero*, Ranubdera Publications, Jalandhar, 188p

Bhambhari, Chandra Prakash, 1987, *Politics in India: 1947-1987*, Vikas, New Delhi

Bhasin, Prem, 1971, *Politics: National and International*, Associated Publications, New Delhi, 231p

Boble, Dilip, 1990, *Rajiv Years: Decline of a Dynasty*, Vikas, New Delhi,

Das, B.C., 1979, *Indian Government and Politics: A Critical Commentary*, Pragati Prakashan, Meerut, xii, 598p

Fadia, B.L., 1992, *Indian Government and Politics*, Sahitya Bhawan, Agra, 644p, appendices, select bibliography

Gandhi, Rajiv, 1987, *Responsive Administration: Speeches by Rajiv Gandhi at the Workshop of District Magistrates and Collectors (at) Bhopal, December 10, 1987*, p 1-6

Gandhi, Rajiv, 1987, *Selected Speeches and Writings*, Ministry of Information and Broadcasting, Publications Division, Government of India, New Delhi, 4 vols.; V1, xvi, 541p, includes index; V2, xii, 416p; V3, xvi, 499p; V4, xv, 537p, includes index

Gandhi, Rajiv, 1988, *Responsive Administration: Speeches by Rajiv Gandhi at the Workshop of District Magistrates and Collectors (at) Hyderabad, Febraury 13, 1988*, p 7-16

Gandhi, Rajiv, 1988, *Responsive Administration: Speeches by Rajiv Gandhi at the Workshop of District Magistrates and Collectors (at) Imphal, April 2, 1988*, p 17-24

Gandhi, Rajiv, 1988, *Responsive Administration: Speeches by Rajiv Gandhi at the Workshop of District Magistrates and Collectors (at) Jaipur, April 30, 1988*, p 25+

Gonsalves, Fric, 1990, *Rajiv Gandhi's World View*, Vikas, New Delhi, 400p

Goyal, Om Prakash, 1979, *India: Government and Politics*, Light and Life, New Delhi, rev edn 2, viii, 345p

Grover, V., 1987, *Gandhi and Politics in India*, Deep and Deep, New Delhi, 240p

Gupta, D.C., 1983, *Indian Government and Politics (1947-1981)*, 6th edn., Vikas, New Delhi, vi, 672p

Gupta, M.G., 1989, *The Prime Ministers of India*, M.G. Publishers, Agra, 608p

Gupta. M.G., *Rajiv Gandhi's Foreign Policy: A Study in Continuity and Change*, M.G. Publishers, Agra

Hardgrave, Robert L. Jr., 1984, *India under Pressure: Prospects for Political Stability*, Westview Press, Boulder, Colorado, 92p

Hardgrave, Robert L., 1979, *India: Government and Politics in a Developing Nation*, 2nd edn., Freeman Book Company, Delhi, vi, 250p

Haskins, James, 1989, *India under Indira and Rajiv Gandhi*, Enslow Publications, New Jersey, 104p

Healy, Kathlean, 1989, *Rajiv Gandhi: The Years of Power*, Vikas Publishing House, New Delhi, 307p.

Innaiah, N., 1986, *State Government and Politics*, Scientific Service, Hyderabad,

271p,

Kamal, K.L., 1987, *Contemporary Indian Politics: Tradition, Structures and Progress*, RBSA, Jaipur

Miradchandani, G.G., 1985, *Massive Mandate for Rajiv Gandhi*, Asia Book Corporation, New York

Mittal, Rajiv, 1985, *Rajiv Gandhi: The Theme of Today*, Shakuntala Foundations, Chandigarh, 80p

Morris Jones, W.H., 1989, *Government and Politics of India,* UBS, New Delhi, 296p

Murthi, V.K. and Sharma, G., 1986, *Rajiv Gandhi: Challenges and Choices*, Radiant, New Delhi, viii, 141p

Narang, A.S., 1985, *Indian Government and Politics*, Gitanjali, New Delhi, 381p

Nurul, Huda, 1989, *The New Choices: Thoughts and Ideas of Rajiv Gandhi*, Commonwealth Publishers, New Delhi, 180p

Ponkshe, Satyawrat, 1986, *Rajiv Gandhi: The Pragmatic Prime Minister of India*, Bhate and Ponkshe Publications, Pune, 345p

Rai Singh, 1985, *Resurgence of Rajiv Gandhi: Assassination of Indira Gandhi and After*, ABC Publishing House, New Delhi, 203p, appendix

Rasgotra, Maharajakrishna, ed, 1991, *Rajiv Gandhi's World View*, Vikas, New Delhi, 256p

Salvi, P.G., 1986, *Rajiv's New India*, Intellectual, New Delhi, 140p

Sen Gupta, Bhabani, 1989, *Rajiv Gandhi: A Political Study*, Konark Publishers, Delhi, ix, 120p

Sharan, P., 1986, *Government and Politics of India: Recent Developemnts*, Metropolitan, New Delhi, 103p

Sharma, Satinder and Sharma, Indira, 1983, *Rajiv Gandhi: An Annotated Bibliography (1944-1982)*, Sawan Publications, Delhi, 164p

Sood, P., 1986, *Rajiv Gandhi: The Brave New Leader*, Marwah Publications, New Delhi, xxviii, 227p

Tokas, Jagdish Chander, 1987, *Rajiv Gandhi: Future of India*, Pustakayan, New Delhi, 134p

Vakil, F.D. and Shivaji Rao, K.H., 1990, *Indian Government and Politics*, 5th edn., Sterling, New Delhi, viii, 371p

Varma, Umeshwar Prasad, 1988, *Rajiv Gandhi and Morality in Public Affairs*, Mittal Publications, New Delhi, ix, 163p

Venkateswaran, R.J. and Mithani, D.M., 1989, *Rajiv Gandhi: Economic Perspective towards 21st Century*, Himalaya, Bomaby, xii, 543p

Verma, Shrikant, 1985, *A Protrait of Rajiv Gandhi*, Arnold Heinemann Publishers, New Delhi, 99p, illustrations

GRAY LITERATURE: DISSERTATIONS

Azam, Kousar J., 1974, *National Integration in India: Some Major Political Aspects: The First Two Decades of Indepenence 1947-1967*, Osmania University, Osmania.

Hans Raj, 1975, *Privileges of the Members of Parliament in India*, Aligarh Muslim University, Aligarh.

Kulsum, C., 1970, *The Role of the Congress High Command in the Working of State Governments: 1950-1962*, Aligarh Muslim University, Aligarh.

Mishra, Krishna Kant, 1988, *USSR's Role in India's Security*, Department of Military Science, Univeristy of Gorakhpur, Gorakhpur

Pandey, Dinesh Chandra, 1969, *Principles and Practices of Non-alignment with Special Reference to India from 1947 to 1962*, Agra University, Agra.

Patil, S.H., 1976, *The Congress Policy towards Princely India*, Karnataka University

Prasad, Ghan Shyam, 1988, *Pakistan as a Factor in India's Security*, Department of Military Science, University of Gorakhpur, Gorakhpur

Ram Sunder Singh, 1988, *India's Nuclear Policy: An Analytical Study*, Department of Militiary Science, University of Gorakhpur, Gorakhpur

Rathore, Babu Ram, 1987, *Kendra-Rajyon ke Sambandh mein Pradhanmantri kee Bhumika (1967-1984)*, Rohilkhand University (in Hindi)

Shukla, Anil Kumar, 1988, *Comparative Studies of Sixth and Seventh Lok Sabha*, R. R. College, Amethi, Sultanpur, (Avadh, Department of Political Science)

Siwach, J.R., 1969, *The Indian Presidency*, Kurukshetra University, Kurukshetra.

Thakur, J.S., 1988, *India's Role in the Non-aligned Movement*, Kumaun University,

Tiwari, Rashmi, 1988, *Bharat Soviet Sambandh San 1971 ke uprant 1987 tak*, School of Studies in Political Science, Vikaram University, Ujjain (in Hindi)

Tiwari, Suman, 1988, *Bharatiya Rashtrapati kee Apatkaleen Shaktiyan*, School of Studies in Political Science, Vikram University, Ujjain (in Hindi)

Usmani, Abul Fazl, 1970, *The Role of Opposition Parties in Indian Parliament (Lok Sabha) 1962-1967*, Aligarh Muslim University, Aligarh

Vaish, Shiv Om, 1987, *President's Rule in India: A Study of its Range and Scope*, NMSN Dass College, Budaun, (Rohilkhand University, Department of Political Science)

Virender Singh, 1987, *Pakistan ka Shastra Sanchay evam Bhartiya Suraksha*, Department of Military Science, University of Gorakhpur, Gorakhpur

3

AUTHOR APPROACH

Abbas, K.A., 1982, We will muddle thru, *Blitz*, January 9, p 24

Abdi, S.H.M., 1986, At loggerheads, *Illustrated Weekly of India* 107(18) April 27, p 20-23

Abdi, S.N.M., 1985, Back from the cold, *Illustrated Weekly of India* 106(9) July 7, p 32-33

Abdullah, Hasan, 1986, Politics of Rajiv Gandhi, *Mainstream* 24(30) March 29, p 23-25

Abraham, A.S., 1983, Congress (I) bestirs itself: Mr Rajiv Gandhi builds his base, *Times of India*, October 7, p 8, col 3-5

Abraham, A.S., 1985, Revitalising the Congress: Challenges amidst the hurrahs, *Times of India*, May 24, p 8, col 3-5

Abraham, A.S., 1987, PM at the half way mark: Foreign and domestic perspectives, *Times of India*, July 11, p 6, col 3-5

Abraham, Abu, 1985, From Indira to Rajiv, *Mainstream* 24(9-10) November 2, p 9

Abraham, Thomas, 1991, An enigma in Colombo, *Frontline* June 22-July 5, p 36

Adhikari, Gautam, 1984, The Congress campaign: Crocodiles and wolves, *Times of India*, December 18, p 8, col 3-5

Advani, L.K., 1985, Congress (I) poll promises unredeemed, *Economic Times*, December 14, p 5, col 7-8

Advani, L.K., 1988, Decline of Rajiv Government, *Mainstream* (Annual) October 8, p 31-32

Aggarwal, A.K., 1986, Rajiv's u-turn toward USA, *Organiser* 37(43) March 9, p 1+

Ahmad, S., 1991, Rajiv Gandhi: Can he provide a stable alternative? *Sunday* March 24-March 30, p 4, letter to editor

Ahmed, Bashiruddin, 1982, No foretelling the future: An analysis of the results of the 1982 mini general elections-2, *Indian Express*, June 13, p 4

Aiyar, Mani Shankar, 1991, The Rajiv I knew, *Sunday* June 2-June 8, p 42-44

Aiyar, Mani Shankar, 1992, The Satyagrahi who defied fear, *National Herald* (Supplement), p 10, col 1-6+

Aiyar, Mani Shankar, 1992, Why the Rajiv legacy will endure? *Independent*, May 23, p 8, col 2-5

Ajay Kumar, 1989, PM: 'New fiza' in favour of Congress, *Times of India*, November 18, p 1, col 1-2, news-item

Akbar, M.J., 1980, What is happening in the Youth Congress, *Sunday* 8(5) August 10, p 24-25

Akbar, M.J., 1981, Better drawn, *Sunday* 9(2) June 28, p 8

Alexander, P.C., 1990, When Sonia urged Rajiv not to become PM, *Economic

Times, November 5, p 1, col 1-5+.

Ambegaokar, Nalini, 1985, The Congress (I) election manifesto: An economic analysis, *Commerce* 150(3842) January 12, p 56-58, tables

Anita Pratap, 1982, Runaway kid goes to Rajya Sabha, *Sunday* 9(30) March 13, p 24-25

Anjiah, T., 1982, Explains why Rajiv got angry, *Hindu*, February 4, p 9

Anon, 1944, Grandson born to Pandit Nehru, *Hindustan Times*, August 21, p 1

Anon, 1968, Cardin's new design in Indian Silk catch the eye, *Hindu*, February 23, p 12

Anon, 1968, Gandhi at Mehndi ceremony, *Hindustan Times*, February 25, p 1, col 2

Anon, 1968, India look for Sonia the bride, *Times of India*, February 25, p 1+

Anon, 1968, New reel, *Link* 10(30) March 3, p 7

Anon, 1968, Personalities, *Link* 10(26) February 4, p 33

Anon, 1968, Rajiv Gandhi weds, *Statesman*, February 26, p 1, 3

Anon, 1968, Rajiv weds Sonia in Indian style, *Hindu*, February 26, p 1

Anon, 1968, Sonia-Rajiv wedding marked by simplicity, *Times of India*, February 26, p 1+

Anon, 1968, Thousands felicitate Rajiv, Sonia, *Hindustan Times*, February 27, p 1+

Anon, 1968, Wedding scene: Turbans, tailors and fire works, *Hindustan Times*, February 26, p 7

Anon, 1980, AICC (I) tribute to Sanjay, Plea to Rajiv, *Sunday Standard*, December 7, p 7

Anon, 1980, AIFC asks Rajiv to join politics, *Times of India*, September 3

Anon, 1980, Antulay requests Rajiv to join politics, *Times of India*, August 13

Anon, 1980, Ashes immersed, *Sunday Standard*, June 29, p 1

Anon, 1980, British paper lauds Rajiv, *Indian Express*, August 22

Anon, 1980, Darbara Singh and Bhajan Lal meet Rajiv Gandhi, *Statesman*, August 28

Anon, 1980, Dhawan going down: Rajiv's entry certain, *Sunday Standard*, November 30, p 1

Anon, 1980, Goodbye to IAC, *Blitz*, July 26, p 3

Anon, 1980, India has vital stake in resolution of Afghan crisis, says PM, *Hindustan Times*, March 3, news-item

Anon, 1980, Mrs Gandhi leaves it to Rajiv, *Statesman*, August 8

Anon, 1980, More support for Rajiv Gandhi, *Statesman*, August 8

Anon, 1980, Pressure builds up on Rajiv Gandhi, *Statesman*, August 11

Anon, 1980, Rajiv attends session, *Times of India*, December 7, p 1, col 1-2

Anon, 1980, Rajiv blocks Antulay's nominees, *Blitz*, Septmber 6, p 7

Anon, 1980, Rajiv for Amethi by-election, *Blitz*, December 20, p 3

Anon, 1980, Rajiv Gandhi opposed to contesting by-election, *Statesman*, September 16

Anon, 1980, Rajiv goes to Parliament House, *Current*, August 23, p 4

Anon, 1980, Rajiv likely to be Youth Congress leader, *Blitz*, July 26, p 3

Anon, 1980, Rajiv makes his bow, *Indian Express*, August 2

Anon, 1980, Rajiv to quit IA, enter politics, *Times of India*, July 31

Anon, 1980, Rajiv urged to enter politics, *Sunday Standard*, June 29, p 5

Anon, 1980, Rajiv urged to enter public life, *National Herald*, July 31

Anon, 1980, Rajiv urged to lead YC (I) at Sanjay Rally, *Indian Express*, December 15, p 1+

Anon, 1980, Rajiv vs Maneka: Palace intrigues, *New Age* 28(32) August 10, p 1+

Anon, 1980, Rajiv will add to party's strength, *Indian Express*, August 27

Anon, 1980, Strong appeal to Rajiv, *Hindustan Times*, December 7, p 7

Anon, 1980, Waiting for Rajiv, *Statesman*, October 30

Anon, 1980, Who needs Rajiv Gandhi? *Illustrated Weekly of India* 101(35) August 31, p 18-19

Anon, 1980, Winning hand, *Current*, June 27, p 3

Anon, 1981, All the Rajiv's men, *Indian Observer* 23(23) December 1, p 7-9

Anon, 1981, Antulay again: Misuse of political machinery, *Caravan* 1(709) December, p 17

Anon, 1981, Antulay meets PM, *Indian Express*, November 18, p 1

Anon, 1981, Antulay meets PM, Rajiv on border dispute, *Indian Express*, August 28, p 7

Anon, 1981, Antulay meets Rajiv Gandhi, *Hindustan Times*, August 27, p 5; *Times of India*, August 27, p 7

Anon, 1981, Antulay meets Rajiv on border issue, *Indian Express*, August 27, p 7

Anon, 1981, Antulay upset over Rajiv's remarks, *Hindustan Times*, November 18, p 1

Anon, 1981, BJP charge on Rajiv rally, *Hindustan Times*, November 18, p 5

Anon, 1981, BJP, Congress (I) main rivals in MP poll, *Indian Express*, December 25, p 5

Anon, 1981, Bangarappa men meet Rajiv, *Indian Express*, December 31, p 7

Anon, 1981, Bhajan Lal denies huge expenses on Rajiv's visit, *Times of India*, November 23, p 5

Anon, 1981, Big win for Rajiv, Begum Abida, *Amrit Bazar Patrika*, June 16, p 1

Anon, 1981, Blood in honour of Sanjay's memory, *National Herald*, April 10

Anon, 1981, Clean going places? *Sunday* 9(3) July 5, p 6

Anon, 1981, Congress (I) dissidence keeping leaders at logger heads, *Caravan* 2(702) August 16, p 15

Anon, 1981, Darbara Singh denies tension in Punjab, *Hindustan Times*, October 30, p 6

Anon, 1981, Dealing with Mr Antulay, *Indian Express*, November 14, p 6

Anon, 1981, December 24 will not come, *Hindustan Times*, December 8, p 2

Anon, 1981, Decision on Rajiv on May 11, *National Herald*, May 9

Anon, 1981, Decision on Rajiv welcomed, *National Herald*, May 13

Anon, 1981, Delhi Development Authority to mark the launching of construction of 5,000 houses, *Hindustan Times*, November 19, p 3

Anon, 1981, Delhi homage to Nehru: Children pay homage to Jawaharlal Nehru, *Hindustan Times*, November 15, p 1+

Anon, 1981, Dissidents stay away from Rajiv meeting, *Indian Express*, November 20, p 8

Anon, 1981, Dynastic rule has no place in democracy, *Indian Express*, December 19, p 4
Anon, 1981, Edifice complex, *India Today* 6 (16) August 16, p 23
Anon, 1981, An expensive triumph, *India Today* 6(12) June 16, p 40-43
Anon, 1981, Eye-catchers, *India Today* 6(3) October 15, p 176
Anon, 1981, Failure to communicate, *India Today* 6(24) December 31, p 25
Anon, 1981, Feeling of gratitude for Mrs Gandhi in Amethi, *Hindustan Times*, June 9, p 11
Anon, 1981, Fight bid to create chaos YC (I) told: Youth Congress (I) to implement 25-point plan, *Hindustan Times*, December 31, p 1+, news-items
Anon, 1981, Final decision on Rajiv tomorrow, *Sunday Standard*, May 3, p 7
Anon, 1981, Find right men to do the job, *Blitz*, July 25, p 12-13, news-item
Anon, 1981, Fruits of inaction, *Times of India*, November 24, p 8
Anon, 1981, Games Minister's play, *India Today* 6(20) October 31, p 7
Anon, 1981, Ghaffar Khan arrives for treatment, *Times of India*, November 7, p 1
Anon, 1981, Ghaffar Khan in India, *Indian Express*, Novmber 7, p 1
Anon, 1981, Great debate: Has Amethi sanctioned hereditary democracy, *Probe India* 3(5) July, p 21
Anon, 1981, Gundu dreads Rajiv's visit, *Blitz*, August 8, p 3
Anon, 1981, Haryana Congress (I) to be revamped, *Hindustan Times*, November 25, p 6
Anon, 1981, Hindi-Chini once again Bhai-Bhai, *Current*, July 4, p 4
Anon, 1981, Homage paid to Gandhi, *Hindustan Times*, October 3, p 1, 16
Anon, 1981, Homage to Sanjay: A Great revolutionary? *Hindustan Times*, June, 24, p 1+
Anon, 1981, Houses handed over to Harijans, *Hindustan Times*, August 10, p 8
Anon, 1981, I think I escaped, said Rajiv Gandhi, *Organiser* 33(28) November 29, p 15
Anon, 1981, In Rajiv's raj, *Current*, July 4, p 4
Anon, 1981, Is the government contesting the election? *Onlooker* June 30, p 34-35
Anon, 1981, J.Ram's jibe at Rajiv Gandhi, *Indian Express*, August 24, p 10
Anon, 1981, Mountaineer's bid to scale Nanda Devi, *Hindustan Times*, August 7, p 8
Anon, 1981, Nation pays homage to Nehru, *Indian Express*, November 15, p 1
Anon, 1981, New dynasty: Abdullah Jr is crowned, *Caravan* 12(704) September 16, p 11
Anon, 1981, New YC Chief, *Current*, November 22, p 2
Anon, 1981, New-found alliance, *India Today* 6(16) August 16, p 7
Anon, 1981, Nirankaries meet Rajiv, *Indian Express*, November 21, p 7
Anon, 1981, Nirankaries turn violent, *Indian Express*, November 19, p 7
Anon, 1981, No decision yet on Rajiv's seat, *Amrit Bazar Patrika*, May 19, p 1
Anon, 1981, No joint opposition candidate against Rajiv Gandhi, *Hindu*, May 13, p 1
Anon, 1981, No quarter to dissidents, *Link* 24(11) October 25, p 6
Anon, 1981, No time yet for Rajiv to accept post: No more yet to nominate Rajiv, *Hindustan Times*, October 22, p 1-16

Anon, 1981, No wireless set in Rajiv jeep, *Hindustan Times*, June 4, p 8
Anon, 1981, Not yet Rajiv, *India Today* 6(5) March 15, p 5
Anon, 1981, Of house, buffaloes and bank aid, *Times of India*, August 10, p 9
Anon, 1981, PM rules out emergency: No ambition for Rajiv, *Hindustan Times*, December 9, p 1+
Anon, 1981, PM will assess Gundu Goverment's performance, *Indian Express*, December 25, p 7
Anon, 1981, Pahadia men appeal to PM and Rajiv, *Times of India*, July 9, p 9
Anon, 1981, Parliamentary system good, says Rajiv, *Times of India*, July 15, p 5, col 3-5, news-item
Anon, 1981, The pilot takes off, *Times of India* (Sunday Review), November 29, p 1, col 1-6
Anon, 1981, Plea to make Rajiv Congress (I) Secretary, *Indian Express*, October 12, p 5
Anon, 1981, Politician with a difference, *Times of India*, June 9, p 1, col 2-4+
Anon, 1981, Politicians games? *Onlooker* 43(21) November 30, p 7
Anon, 1981, Poll campaign for Rajiv begins, *Sunday Standard*, May 10, p 1
Anon, 1981, Poll case against Rajiv dropped, *Indian Express*, October 13, p 17
Anon, 1981, Pressure on Rajiv, *Current*, July 11, p 4
Anon, 1981, Protest at Rajiv using Radio Ham, *Hindustan Times*, June 5, p 5
Anon, 1981, Quiet debut amid sound and fury, *Hindustan Times*, August 18, p 8
Anon, 1981, R.K. Nehru cremated, *Hindustan Times*, April 4, p 7
Anon, 1981, Rs 2 crores for Congress-I man, *Indian Express*, November 20, p 1
Anon, 1981, Rajiv: Favourite among Pakistanis, *National Herald*, June 25
Anon, 1981, Rajiv: Reluctant bridegroom, *Organiser* 33(2) May 31, p 6
Anon, 1981, Rajiv a favourite among Pakistanis, *National Herald*, June 25
Anon, 1981, Rajiv agrees to lead IYC (I): Resolve to work for uplift of women, *Times of India*, December 30
Anon, 1981, Rajiv and Begum Abida returned to Lok Sabha, *Hindu*, June 16, p 1
Anon, 1981, Rajiv and family dragged in, *Blitz*, January 3, p 3
Anon, 1981, Rajiv arrives in Gauhati, *Hindustan Times*, October 12, p 7
Anon, 1981, Rajiv asked to lead Youth Congress (I), *Hindustan Times*, December 30, p 1+
Anon, 1981, Rajiv asks bureaucrats to shed lethargy, *Hindustan Times*, December 20, p 7
Anon, 1981, Rajiv asks youth to work for national uplift, *Times of India*, October 26, p 9, col 2-5
Anon, 1981, Rajiv assails concept of motley Opposition, *Times of India*, December 14, p 7, col 3-6
Anon, 1981, Rajiv assails Opposition on unity moves, *Hindustan Times*, December 14, p 1+
Anon, 1981, Rajiv axe to chop dead wood, *Current*, June 27, p 4
Anon, 1981, Rajiv calls for end to bickering, *Indian Express*, November 20, p 7
Anon, 1981, Rajiv calls on Mrs Thatcher, *Hindustan Times*, July 29, p 1
Anon, 1981, Rajiv critical of Garhwal strategy, *Sunday* 9(3) July 5, p 58
Anon, 1981, Rajiv defends family succession, *Indian Express*, November 12, p 5,

news-item

Anon, 1981, Rajiv denies being groomed as PM, *Indian Express*, June 20, p 5

Anon, 1981, Rajiv denies misuse of official machinery, *Hindustan Times*, May 22, p 1

Anon, 1981, Rajiv disapproves of CM's frequent Delhi trips, *Hindustan Times*, July 22, p 13

Anon, 1981, Rajiv favours joint decisions, *Hindustan Times*, August 19, p 12

Anon, 1981, Rajiv featured in London paper, *National Herald*, June 23

Anon, 1981, Rajiv files poll papers for Amethi, *Hindustan Times*, May 12, p 1

Anon, 1981, Rajiv for Amethi, *Current*, July 12, p 9

Anon, 1981, Rajiv for Lok Sabha? *Amrit Bazar Patrika*, May 9, p 1

Anon, 1981, Rajiv for strong consumer drive, *Hindustan Times*, November 20, p 3

Anon, 1981, Rajiv Gandhi: A calendar of events and stances, *Sunday* 9(24) November 29, p 18-19

Anon, 1981, Rajiv Gandhi: The young inheritor, *India Today* 6(10) May 16, p 56-62

Anon, 1981, Rajiv Gandhi: The triumph, *Surya India* 5(10) July, p 77

Anon, 1981, Rajiv Gandhi in Bangalore, *Hindustan Times*, December 29, p 4

Anon, 1981, Rajiv Gandhi in London, *Times of India*, July 24, p 1

Anon, 1981, Rajiv Gandhi makes his formal bow in politics, *National Herald*, May 12, p 1-4

Anon, 1981, Rajiv Gandhi to be projected in Kisan Rally, *Statesman*, February 12

Anon, 1981, Rajiv Gandhi to visit China, *Hindustan Times*, September 28, p 6

Anon, 1981, Rajiv Gandhi to visit Haryana, *Indian Express*, November 3, p 4

Anon, 1981, Rajiv Gandhi wins by record margin, *Hindustan Times*, June 16, p 1

Anon, 1981, Rajiv gives clean chit to U.P. Government, *Hindustan Times*, December 6, p 1

Anon, 1981, Rajiv has arrived, *Blitz*, January 24, p 17

Anon, 1981, Rajiv hints at new measures, *Hindustan Times*, November 19, p 8

Anon, 1981, Rajiv in Assam, *Indian Express*, October 12, p 5

Anon, 1981, Rajiv in Srinagar to attend YC(I) meet, *Times of India*, July 11, p 7

Anon, 1981, Rajiv is not expecting Party or Government post, *Times of India*, June 11, p 9, col 1-2

Anon, 1981, Rajiv jets into politics without power, *Current*, November 29, p 1-2

Anon, 1981, Rajiv lauds friendship with Soviet Union, *Hindustan Times*, October 26, p 1+

Anon, 1981, Rajiv makes his 'debut' in Bombay, *Times of India*, January 14

Anon, 1981, Rajiv makes up his mind, *Current*, October 18, p 4

Anon, 1981, Rajiv may be made Party Secretary, *Hindustan Times*, p 1,

Anon, 1981, Rajiv may consider party post, *Hindustan Times*, July 6

Anon, 1981, Rajiv may visit Bombay soon, *Indian Express*, August 28, p 1

Anon, 1981, Rajiv new aim, *India Today* 6(18) October 1, p 8

Anon, 1981, Rajiv not to join government, *Hindu*, June 17, p 1

Anon, 1981, Rajiv on lawyer's crucial role, *Hindustan Times*, October, 31, p 3

Anon, 1981, Rajiv on YC (I) Council, *Hindustan Times*, June 25, p 1

Anon, 1981, Rajiv promises to pursue Sanjay goals, *Hindustan Times*, May 13, p

8, news-item
Anon, 1981, Rajiv raps Charan for 'Lathi directive', *Hindustan Times*, June 1
Anon, 1981, Rajiv revitalises Youth Congress, *Blitz*, April 25, p 6
Anon, 1981, Rajiv rules out early poll in Haryana, *Hindustan Times*, August 13, p 13
Anon, 1981, Rajiv silence delays decision on candidates, *Hindu*, May 6, p 9
Anon, 1981, Rajiv still makes news in Britain, *Hindustan Times*, June 22, p 6
Anon, 1981, Rajiv takes the plunge, *Surya India* 5(9) June, p 36-37
Anon, 1981, Rajiv to assume more responsibility, *Times of India*, December 31, p 1
Anon, 1981, Rajiv to be made AICC (I) Secretary, *Indian Express*, October 21, p 1
Anon, 1981, Rajiv to make Party change working style, *Times of India*, May 12, p 1, col 5+
Anon, 1981, Rajiv to visit China, *Indian Express*, September 28, p 1
Anon, 1981, Rajiv visiting Lucknow today, *Hindustan Times*, September 19, p 12
Anon, 1981, Rajiv wants PCC-I to decide Antulay fate, *Hindustan Times*, October 31, p 1
Anon, 1981, Rajiv wants to assist mother, *Amrit Bazar Patrika* June 17, p 1
Anon, 1981, Rajiv warns Opposition, *Indian Express*, October 21, p 4
Anon, 1981, Rajiv will attend YC (I) Council meet, *Hindustan Times*, July 10, p 5
Anon, 1981, Rajiv wins his leadership spurs, *Blitz*, June 20, p 1
Anon, 1981, Rajiv's call to crush divisive forces, *Indian Express*, November 15, p 4
Anon, 1981, Rajiv's debut, *Blitz*, December 13, p 9
Anon, 1981, Rajiv's indictment of Antulay, *Indian Express*, November 11 p 1
Anon, 1981, Rajiv's Jammu and Kashmir visit cause confusion, *Times of India*, July 15, p 5
Anon, 1981, Rajiv's man, *Indian Observer* 22(23) December 1, p 9
Anon, 1981, Rajiv's rival alleges use of government machinery, *Sunday Standard*, May 16, p 3
Anon, 1981, Rajiv's secret meeting, *Onlooker* 43(10) June 5, p 6
Anon, 1981, Rajiv's silence delays decision on candidates, *Hindu*, May 6, p 9
Anon, 1981, Rajiv's top priority for Agriculture, *Times of India*, May 18
Anon, 1981, Rajiv's visit: Tailored versions, *Link* 24(2) August 22, p 20-21
Anon, 1981, Rath regains Rajiv's confidence, *Sunday* 9(14) September 20, p 65
Anon, 1981, Searching for successors, *India Today* 6(20) October 31, p 7
Anon, 1981, Shalinitai Patil meets Rajiv, *Indian Express*, September 6, p 7
Anon, 1981, Speculation over Rajiv's visit to AP, *Indian Express*, December 24, p 8
Anon, 1981, Suresh Ram greater than Rajiv, *Blitz*, July 11, p 8
Anon, 1981, Three women climb Nanda Devi peak, *Hindustan Times*, September 23, p 1-16
Anon, 1981, Times praise for Rajiv, *Hindustan Times*, August 1, p 16
Anon, 1981, Unauthorised slums in Rajiv's name, *Onlooker* 43(21) November 30, p 17-18
Anon, 1981, Varun star draw at Shantivana, *Hindustan Times*, June 24, p 3

Anon, 1981, Vehicle minus battery, *Hindustan Times*, December 30, p 8

Anon, 1981, Weathering the storm, *India Today* 6(5) March 15, p 5

Anon, 1981, When the Rajiv wind blows, these heads will roll, 21, *Current*, May 23, p 1

Anon, 1981, While Pranab and Zail quarreled over protocol, Rajiv officiated as PM, *Organiser* 33(29) December 6, p 5

Anon, 1981, Who will be the Indian guest at Royal wedding? *Current*, June 27, p 4

Anon, 1981, Will aim at new style of functioning, *Hindustan Times*, May 12, p 1

Anon, 1981, YC (I) assured 'due share' of Poll tickets, *Indian Express*, November 15, p 2

Anon, 1981, YC (I) to have job-oriented programme, *Hindustan Times*, December 29, p 4

Anon, 1981, YC (I) urges employment in rural sector, *Indian Express*, December 31, p 7

Anon, 1981-1982, Darbara Singh Government blamed for Punjab unrest, *Delhi Recorder* 2(9) December 15-January 14, p 58-61

Anon, 1981-1982, Mrs Gandhi's Devoli visit heartens Harijan victims, *Delhi Recorder* 2(9) December 15-June 14, p 26-28

Anon, 1981-1982, Remembering Sanjay Gandhi, *Delhi Recoder* 2(9) December 15, January 14, p 22-23

Anon, 1982, AICC (I) General Secretaries, *Times of India*, September 18, p 7

Anon, 1982, A.M. Khan was side tracked? *Sunday* 9(31) January 17, p 37

Anon, 1982, Action against organisers of Congress (I) meeting, *Times of India*, May 13, p 1

Anon, 1982, Action against Orissa Congress (I) rebels urged, *Hindustan Times*, June 2, p 8

Anon, 1982, Against projects at the cost of poor, *Hindustan Times*, February 13, p 5, news-item

Anon, 1982, Antulay and Solanki dropped from CWC, *Hindustan Times*, September 3, p 1

Anon, 1982, Antulay fall-out, *Link* 24(23) January 17, p 6

Anon, 1982, Antulay meets PM, Rajiv, *Times of India*, January 31, p 1

Anon, 1982, Art of eleminating rivals, *Sunday* 9(51) June 12, p 17

Anon, 1982, Arun Nehru could have done better, *India Today* 7(11) June 15, p 18-19

Anon, 1982, Asssembly elections: Mid-term warning, *India Today* 7(11) June 15, p 17-21

Anon, 1982, Bhatnagar is NDMC Cheif, *Hindustan Times*, September 2 p 3

Anon, 1982, Big brother is no better, *Caravan* 1(725) August, p 42

Anon, 1982, Bomb scare on Rajiv's flight, *Hindustan Times*, May 12, p 8

Anon, 1982, (Book Review), *Hindustan Times*, May 2, P iv, col 4-7, *Link* 24(48) July 11, p 48; *National Herald*, May 9, p 11, col 4-6; *Tribune*, May 15, p 4, col 7-8

Review of the Book: **Mittal, Rajiv**, 1982, *Rajiv Gandhi: The theme of today*, Shakuntala Foundations, Chandigrah; Thomson Publication, New Delhi

Anon, 1982, Budget dominates the debate, *Link*, 24(32) March 21, p 8

Anon, 1982, Bureaucrats more powerful than politicians, *Sunday* 9(49) March 27, p 36-37

Anon, 1982, Campaigning Rajiv style, *Weekend Review* 3(10) May 29, p 7

Anon, 1982, Central surveillance tightens: Congress CMs on the mat, *Current*, March 13, p 3+

Anon, 1982, Charges on Rajiv visit, *Hindustan Times*, February 1, p 6

Anon, 1982, China team inivites Rajiv, *National Herald*, May 1, p 12

Anon, 1982, Conductor Bhajan Lal, *Suday* 8(43) April 17, p 15

Anon, 1982, Congress (I) High Command: Few options, *Link* 24(25) January 31, p 60

Anon, 1982, Congress (I) offensive, *Link* 24(21) January 3, p 6

Anon, 1982, Conspiracy to disturb Rajiv rally, *Hindustan Times*, September 20, p 5

Anon, 1982, E!ection time: Gandhi time, *Onlooker* 44(10) May 31, p 37

Anon, 1982, Experiment with the young, *Link*, 25(5) September 12, p 6

Anon, 1982, Face-lift given to Bikaner to receive Rajiv, *Times of India*, January 30, p 6

Anon, 1982, Furniture for Asiad destroyed in fire, *Indian Express*, September 20, p 1

Anon, 1982, Gandhi vote for Amitabh or Sivaji, *Indian Express*, February 5, p 5

Anon, 1982, Goodbye, Maruti, *Onlooker* 44(2) June 31, p 7

Anon, 1982, Health camp in V.C. Shukla's constituency, *Sunday* 9(41) April 3, p 13

Anon, 1982, Hectic scenes at ICWA elections, *Hindustan Times*, September 7, p 3

Anon, 1982, How A.M. Khan was side tracked? *Sunday* 9(31) January 17, p 37

Anon, 1982, ICWA: Indian Council of World Affairs, *Caravan* 12(727) September p 27-29

Anon, 1982, IYC (I) keeps out Press from meet, *Indian Express*, January 24, p 3

Anon, 1982, Images, *India Today* 7(1) January 15, p 66

Anon, 1982, Indian Officials at Asiad discriminated against, *Sunday* 9(45) May 1, p 9

Anon, 1982, Indo-US retations breaking the ice, *India Today* 7(16) August 31, p 66-72

Anon, 1982, Kidding with Rajiv's image, *Current*, March 20, p 4

Anon, 1982, Ladoos, cold drinks for asking at Zail house, *Hindustan Times*, July 16, p 3

Anon, 1982, Lengthy budget speeches, but no fire works, *Hindustan Times*, March 15, p 8

Anon, 1982, Lords of the skies, *Sunday* 9(40) March 27, p 30-31

Anon, 1982, MLA claims he brought Rajiv into lime light, *Hindustan Times*, May 31, p 12

Anon, 1982, Mrs Gandhi calls on Abdullah, *Hindustan Times*, June 25, p 16

Anon, 1982, Mrs Gandhi's report card, *India Today* 7(1) January 15, p 100-103

Anon, 1982, Maiden over, *Hindustan Times*, March 15, p 9

Anon, 1982, Malkhan, 19 of gang give up: Rajiv hails surrender, *Hindustan Times*, June 18, p 1+

Anon, 1982, Managing an election, *Onlooker* 14(10) May 31, p 7
Anon, 1982, Maneka gesture turn sour, *Hindustan Times*, June 24, p 8
Anon, 1982, Nation: 1981 in retrospect, *Probe India* 3(11) January, p 50-52
Anon, 1982, Nawab Rampur mourned, *National Herald*, March 29, p 5
Anon, 1982, Near-full house for maiden speech, *Times of India*, March 12, p 9
Anon, 1982, Nehru dynasty: Rajiv Gandhi or Arun Nehru? *Blitz*, May 22, p 12-14
Anon, 1982, No room for Pahadia, *Onlooker* 44(4) February 28, p 7
Anon, 1982, Noorjehan to give performance in Delhi, *Times of India*, March 11, p 2
Anon, 1982, PM arrives in the US with good message: Mrs Gandhi in New York, *Indian Express*, July 29, p 1
Anon, 1982, PM denounces stir on Bihar Press Bill: Opposition obstructing Government work, *Hindustan Times*, September 2, p 1+
Anon, 1982, PM happy with progress of Asiad complexes, *Hindustan Times*, May 1, p 1+
Anon, 1982, PM may secure NC backing for Zail, *Hindustan Times*, June 26, p 16
Anon, 1982, PM opens world's longest river bridge today, *Hindustan Times*, March 2, p 5
Anon, 1982, PM reiterates stand on peace, N-disarmament: Gulf between rich, poor, dangerous, *Hindustan Times*, January 23, p 16
Anon, 1982, PM rules out division of the State, *Telegraph*, September 19
Anon, 1982, PM seeking JK Muslims backing for Rajiv, *Indian Express*, January 3, p 9
Anon, 1982, PM urged to punish Youth Congress rebles, *Times of India*, March 29, p 9
Anon, 1982, PM visit Asiad stadia, *National Herald*, May 4, p 1+
Anon, 1982, PM's Russia visit from September 20, *Times of India*, September 5, p 1
Anon, 1982, P.S. Bhatnagar replaces Behl as NDMC Chief, *Times of India*, September 2, p 3
Anon, 1982, Party post for Rajiv by February, *Hindustan Times*, September 18, p 11
Anon, 1982, Party system cracking up under pressure, *India Today* 7(1) January 15, p 78-79, news-item
Anon, 1982, Patna bridge hoax, *Sunday* March 27, p 22-23
Anon, 1982, Praise for Rajiv, *Hindustan Times*, July 31, p 5
Anon, 1982, Precept and practices: An experiment with untruth, *Caravan* 1(175) March 1, p 12
Anon, 1982, President pleasure Prime Minister's pain: Presidential system revisited, *Delhi Recorder* 3(2) March 15-April 14, p 10-13, news-item
Anon, 1982, Raja Rajiv snubs Khan, *Blitz*, January 9, p 5
Anon, 1982, Rajasthan dissidents stronger, *Sunday* 9(38) March 13, p 11
Anon, 1982, Rajiv: Amend laws to combat dowry, *Indian Express*, July 21, p 3, news-item
Anon, 1982, Rajiv, Sonia trapped in lift, *Times of India*, August 1, p 1
Anon, 1982, Rajiv against family rule, *Indian Express*, January 9, p 5, news-item

Anon, 1982, Rajiv agrees to lead YC (I), pleads for unity, *Indian Express*, December 30, p 7

Anon, 1982, Rajiv and the fussy elephant, *Onlooker* 44(2) January 31, p 7

Anon, 1982, Rajiv angry with Anjiah over arrangement, *Hindustan Times*, February 3, p 8

Anon, 1982, Rajiv appeal to the people, *Times of India* May 6, p 7

Anon, 1982, Rajiv arrives in Riyadh, *National Herald*, April 19, p 1

Anon, 1982, Rajiv asked people to co-operate with the government, *Hindustan Times*, January 9, p 7

Anon, 1982, Rajiv asks people of vote for Congress (I), *Times of India*, May 15, p 13

Anon, 1982, Rajiv attacks press, calls for loyalty, *Indian Express*, April 25, p 4, news-item

Anon, 1982, Rajiv blames BJP for Punjab incidents, *Hindustan Times*, May 9, p 7

Anon, 1982, Rajiv blames Opposition for communal troubles, *Times of India*, May 9, p 9+

Anon, 1982, Rajiv calls on Bhave, *Times of India*, September 16, p 5

Anon, 1982, Rajiv calls to rehabilitate the blind, *Hindustan Times*, August 23, p 16

Anon, 1982, Rajiv clips Zail's wings in Punjab PCC, *Current*, March 6, p 4

Anon, 1982, Rajiv criticises LD-BJP alliance, *Times of India*, May 15, p 7

Anon, 1982, Rajiv cuts short visit to see Amitabh, *Indian Express*, August 5, p 1

Anon, 1982, Rajiv exhorts people to work hard, *Hindustan Times*, February 14, p 7

Anon, 1982, Rajiv family in Kashmir, *Hindustan Times*, January 2, p 13

Anon, 1982, Rajiv files papers for ICWA post, *Times of India*, August 7, p 3

Anon, 1982, Rajiv for better discipline among party workers, *Times of India*, January 7, p 7

Anon, 1982, Rajiv for better Public Sector performance, *Hindustan Times*, March 12, p 1+

Anon, 1982, Rajiv for watchdog panels in Amethi, *Hindustan Times*, August 31, p 5

Anon, 1982, Rajiv Gandhi call on dowry evil, *Hindustan Times*, July 21, p 3

Anon, 1982, Rajiv Gandhi goes round Aisad venues, *Times of India*, August 31, p 12

Anon, 1982, Rajiv Gandhi in Riyadh, *Statesman*, April 19

Anon, 1982, Rajiv Gandhi may visit Kestara, *Times of India*, February 11, p 5

Anon, 1982, Rajiv Gandhi not for Presidential system, *Hindu*, May 18, p 10, news-item

Anon, 1982, Rajiv Gandhi not to take up YC post, *Indian Express*, January 1, p 7

Anon, 1982, Rajiv Gandhi shouts at Anjiah for gaudy show, *Hindu*, February 3, p 1

Anon, 1982, Rajiv Gandhi will tour his constituency, *Hindustan Times*, July 3, p 12

Anon, 1982, Rajiv Gandhi's Aide meets Abdullah, *Hindustan Times*, May 19, p 8

Anon, 1982, Rajiv Gandhi's man, *Sunday* 10(5) July 24, p 57

Anon, 1982, Rajiv Haryana tour from May 5, *Hindustan Times*, May 4, p 1

Anon, 1982, Rajiv hits out at LD-BJP alliance, *Amrit Bazar Patrika*, May 7, p 7

Anon, 1982, Rajiv holds talks with Farooq, *Indian Express*, September 14, p 1
Anon, 1982, Rajiv in Bombay, *Times of India*, August 5, p 1
Anon, 1982, Rajiv in Harayana, *Sunday* 9(48) March 22, p 13
Anon, 1982, Rajiv in London as UK's biggest airshow begins, *Times of India*, September 6, p 9
Anon, 1982, Rajiv in Srinagar, *Indian Express*, January 2, p 4
Anon, 1982, Rajiv keen on Tiwari becoming UP CM, *Indian Express*, July 1, p 1
Anon, 1982, Rajiv lashes out at BJP-LD poll alliance, *Times of India*, May 7, p 7
Anon, 1982, Rajiv lays stone for water project, *Hindustan Times*, January 8
Anon, 1982, Rajiv lays stone of BHEL plant, *Hindustan Times*, February 11, p 5
Anon, 1982, Rajiv meets Gilashvilli, *Patriot*, September 23, p 1
Anon, 1982, Rajiv Nagpur visit significant, *Hindustan Times*, September 13, p 7
Anon, 1982, Rajiv not keen on YC (I) leadership, *Times of India*, April 2, p 7
Anon, 1982, Rajiv raps Opposition, erring Cong mem, *Hindustan Times*, January 10, p 10
Anon, 1982, Rajiv ready to accept party post, *Hindustan Times*, September 16, p 8
Anon, 1982, Rajiv rules out change in Punjab, *Hindustan Times*, July 4, p 8
Anon, 1982, Rajiv says he never justified family rule, *Times of India*, January 9, p 5, news-item
Anon, 1982, Rajiv seeks votes for H.P. progress, *Hindustan Times* , May 8, p 16
Anon, 1982, Rajiv sees Farnborough Air Show, *Hindustan Times*, September 6, p 11
Anon, 1982, Rajiv shows his anger, *Times of India*, September 20, p 1
Anon, 1982, Rajiv snubs Patnaik, *Blitz*, February 13, p 5
Anon, 1982, Rajiv starts poll tour in State today, *Amrit Bazar Patrika*, May 11, p 7
Anon, 1982, Rajiv stress on role of youths in economic order vital, *Hindustan Times*, January 25, p 1+
Anon, 1982, Rajiv sure of Congress (I) Government in West Bengal, *Hindustan Times*, May 13, p 4
Anon, 1982, Rajiv to attend air show, *Times of India*, September 5, p 11
Anon, 1982, Rajiv to call on Vinoba Bhave, *Hindustan Times*, September 10, p 12
Anon, 1982, Rajiv to contest ICWA post, *Times of India*, September 7, p 3
Anon, 1982, Rajiv to get VIP treatment in USSR, *Indian Express*, September 20, p 7
Anon, 1982, Rajiv to have hand in Ministry formation: CM, *Times of India*, January 22, p 9, news-item
Anon, 1982, Rajiv to launch mass contact drive in Nagpur, *Times of India*, September 8, p 9
Anon, 1982, Rajiv to lay foundation of ceramic unit, *Times of India*, February 10, p 9
Anon, 1982, Rajiv to look into Antulay's new job, *Hindu*, February 6, p 9
Anon, 1982, Rajiv to open Bikaner meet, *Hindustan Times*, January 22, p 16
Anon, 1982, Rajiv to open Ludhiana meet, *National Herald*, April 6, p 4
Anon, 1982, Rajiv to tour Maharashtra, *Hindustan Times*, September 8, p 8
Anon, 1982, Rajiv to use own car for Amethi tour, *Hindustan Times*, January 6, p 5

Anon, 1982, Rajiv to visit city in March, *Amrit Bazar Patrika*, February 20, p 5
Anon, 1982, Rajiv tries food at Games Village, *Times of India*, September 18, p 4
Anon, 1982, Rajiv urges youth to work for peace, *Hindustan Times*, September 23, p 8
Anon, 1982, Rajiv visit Antonov Aircraft Plant, *Times of India*, September 26, p 9
Anon, 1982, Rajiv wants Panchayats made more effective, *Hindustan Times*, January 31, p 11.
Anon, 1982, Rajiv wants positive opposition, *Hindu*, January 1, p 9, news-item
Anon, 1982, Rajiv willing to accept Party post, *Indian Express*, September 16, p 7
Anon, 1982, Rajiv willing to accept Party Secretaryship, *Times of India*, September 16, p 7
Anon, 1982, Rajiv's anger: A part of the tamasha, *Caravan* 2(714) February, p 14
Anon, 1982, Rajiv's call to return Congress (I) to power, *Amrit Bazar Patrika*, May 12, p 1+
Anon, 1982, Rajiv's call to rural youth to stay in villages, *Times of India*, January 31, p 9
Anon, 1982, Rajiv's hectic poll tour from May 11, *Amrit Bazar Patrika*, May 6, p 7
Anon, 1982, Rajiv's maiden speech superb, *National Herald*, March 14, p 5
Anon, 1982, Rajiv's success depends on his ability: PM, *Times of India*, July 24, p 9, news-item
Anon, 1982, Rebel leader snap links with Antulay, *Hindustan Times*, July 16, p 1
Anon, 1982, Revolt imminent in Karnataka Congress (I), *Indian Express*, June 30, p 4
Anon, 1982, Sanjay Death Anniversary: Sanjay day, *Hindustan Times*, June 23, p 1+
Anon, 1982, Sanjay ignored YC men to back Rajiv Gandhi, *Hindustan Times*, May 4, p 6
Anon, 1982, Sanjay Memorial Medical Institute for Amethi, *Hindustan Times*, September 1, p 7
Anon, 1982, Side tracking, *India Today* 7(16) August 31, p 74-75
Anon, 1982, Spotlight on Rajiv, *Times of India*, July 31, p 13
Anon, 1982, Spotlight on Rajiv about Bhosle affairs, *Times of India*, March 27, p 9
Anon, 1982, Star Obyssey of PM and Rajiv, *Times of India*, September 24, p 1
Anon, 1982, State YC (I) team sees Rajiv, *Amrit Bazar Paktrika*, April 7, p 8
Anon, 1982, Striking students seek Rajiv help, *Hindustan Times*, March 30, p 16
Anon, 1982, Stuff to choose from, *Delhi Recorder* 3(3) April 15-May 14, p 8
Anon, 1982, Swamy meets Rajiv about Bhosle affairs, *Times of India*,
Anon, 1982, Three furniture's factories gutted; Probe rodered, ACP, SI suspended, *Times of India*, September 20, p 1
Anon, 1982, Uniform policy, *India Today* 7(7) April 15, p 8
Anon, 1982, V.C. Shukla and Arjun Singh meet, *Indian Express*, April 25, p 4
Anon, 1982, VIP treatment awaits Rajiv, *Hindustan Times*, September 20, p 7
Anon, 1982, Warning to YC (I) rebels against talking to Press, *Indian Express*, August 21, p 9
Anon, 1982, Why is Antulay still surviving: Reason he holds the Indira Pratisthan

papers, *Sunday* 9(31) January 17, p 44
Anon, 1982, Will Rajiv Gandhi bow out of politics? *Organiser* 34(4) Jne 13, p 16
Anon, 1982, Will Sanjay cult overehelm Rajiv? *Blitz*, March 13, p 6
Anon, 1982, World youth to fight for disarmament, *Indian Express*, January 25, p 7
Anon, 1982, World's longest river bridge opened in Bihar, *Hindu*, March 3, p 1
Anon, 1982, Wreath laid at Lenin's mausoleum, *Hindustan Times*, September 22, p 8
Anon, 1982, Wreaths laid at Samadhi, *Hindustan Times*, June 24, p 1
Anon, 1982, Writing on the wall, *Surya India* 6(9-10) June-July, p 14-17
Anon, 1982, Year that wasn't! *India Today* 7(1) January 15, p 108-110
Anon, 1982, Zail Singh reiterates loyalty to PM, *Indian Express*, June 30, p 7
Anon, 1982, Zail's happiest days as Mrs Gandhi's Minister, *Hindustan Times*, July 1, p 5
Anon, 1983, AICC (I) alaramed at nuclear threat, *Times of India*, December 29, p 11, col 4-7
Anon, 1983, (Book Review), *Hindustan Times* (Magazine), October 9, p 4, col 8
Review of the Book: **Sharma, Satinder** and **Sharma, Indira,** 1983, *Rajiv Gandhi: An annotated bibliography,* Sawan Publications, Delhi, 164p
Anon, 1983, Firm Congress (I) steps for people's welfare: Rajiv, *Times of India*, October 19, p 6, col 3-4, news-item
Anon, 1983, From consensus to conflict, *Times of India*, January 7
Anon, 1983, PCC (I): Rajiv hits at factionalism, *Link* 26(13) November 6, p 7-8
Anon, 1983, Rajiv: US interfering in Punjab affairs, *Times of India*, July 24, p 9, col 1-2
Anon, 1983, Rajiv blames Party for eclipse in South, *Times of India*, December 18, p 9, col 7-8
Anon, 1983, Rajiv hits at factionalism, *Link* 26(13) Novermber 6, p 7-8
Anon, 1983, Rajiv urges youth to build 'new India', *Times of India*, April 14, p 1, col 7-8+
Anon, 1983, Revive the Swadeshi spirit: Text of AICC(I) resolution on economic situation, *Mainstream* 22(9) October 29, p 31-33
Anon, 1984, Assassination part of international conspiracy: Rajiv, *Times of India*, November 20, p 1, col 1-3, news-item
Anon, 1984, (Book Review), *Journal of Parliamentary Information* 30(4) December, p 737-742
Review of the Book: **Pal, R.N.**, 1984, *The office of the Prime Minister of India*, Ghanshyam Publication, New Delhi, 279p
Anon, 1984, (Book Review), *Political Science Review* 23(3-4) July-December, p 309-312
Review of the Book: **Gopa Kumar, G.**, 1984, *The Congress Party and State politics: Emergence of new style politics*, Deep and Deep Publications, New Delhi
Anon, 1984, CPP endorses Rajiv's choice, *Times of India*, November 3, p 1, col 2-4+
Anon, 1984, Clean administration promise reiterated, *Financial Express*, Decem-

ber 30, p 1, col 1-4

Anon, 1984, Defeat selfish forces: PM, *Times of India*, December 26, p 9, col 6-8, news-item

Anon, 1984, An election without focus, *Times of India*, December 15,

Anon, 1984, Goa oriented politics, *Link* 27(16) November 25, p 15-17

Anon, 1984, Goverment committed to protect all: Rajiv, *Times of India*, December 20, p 1, col 7-8+, news-item

Anon, 1984, Growing support for Rajiv as Party Chief, *Times of India*, November 6, p 1, col 4-5+

Anon, 1984, Hazards of novice as Prime Minister, *Organiser* 36(31) December 16, p 5+

Anon, 1984, He who rides a tiger, *Times of India* (Sunday Review), November 18, p 1, col 1-5

Anon, 1984, The imperative of peace, *Indian Horizons* 33(3-4), p 5-8

Anon, 1984, Janata lifted ban on Chauhan: PM, *Times of India*, December 16, p 1, col 1-2+, news-item

Anon, 1984, The movement of non-aligned countries, *Africa Quarterly* 23(3-4), p 1-9

Anon, 1984, Opposition: Stooping to hair splitting, *Hindustan Times*, November 4, p 9, col 1-6, news-item

Anon, 1984, PM for result oriented administration, *Times of India*, November 13, p 4, col 1-4, news-items

Anon, 1984, Positive popular response to Rajiv, *Times of India*, December 16, p 1, col 2-5+

Anon, 1984, Priests resent Rajiv's remarks, *Times of India*, October 1, p 1, col 1-2+

Anon, 1984, Rajiv as campaigner, *Indian Express*, December 23; *Statesman*, December 15

Anon, 1984, Rajiv combines Nehru's liberalism, Indira's firmness, *Link* 27(21) December 30, p 4-7

Anon, 1984, Rajiv elected Party Chief, *Times of India*, November 13, p 1, col 7-8+

Anon, 1984, Rajiv Gandhi: An uncertain future, *Illustrated Weekly of India* 105(4) January 22, p 18-21

Anon, 1984, Rajiv Gandhi expounds Government policies, *Capital* 193(4794) November 26, p 49-51

Anon, 1984, Rajiv Gandhi firmly in the saddle, *Link* 27(15) November 18, p 26-28

Anon, 1984, Rajiv pledges to fight corruption and inefficiency, *Times of India*, November 13, p 1, col 1-3 +

Anon, 1984, Rajiv sworn in new PM, *Times of India*, November 1, p 1, col 3-5+

Anon, 1984, Rajiv undecided on becoming Party President, *Times of India*, November 11, p 1, col 1-3

Anon, 1984, Rajiv's style of electioneering, *Times of India*, December 14, p 1, col 7-8

Anon, 1984, Text of AICC(I) economic resolution, *Captial* 192(4772) January 23, p 43-46

Anon, 1984, Timings of US study very significant, says Rajiv, *Times of India*,

December 19, p 1, col 4-6+, news-item

Anon, 1984, Top priority to Punjab: PM, *Times of India*, December 30, p 1, col 4-5, news-item

Anon, 1984, Top priority to Punjab issue: Rajiv, *Times of India*, December 17, p 2, col 2-5+, news-item

Anon, 1984, Transfer of power to Rajiv, *Organiser* 35(46) April 1, p 1+

Anon, 1984, We live in India: They exist in Bharat, *Indian Express*, August 12

Anon, 1984, YC charge against Opposition, *Times of India*, May 8, p 1, col 5-6+

Anon, 1985, The Acid Test, *Mainstream* 23(42) June 15, p 1-2

Anon, 1985, Accord to bring lasting peace to Assam: PM, *Times of India*, December 12, p 1, col 1-3, news-item

Anon, 1985, After Moscow, *Mainstream* 23(40) June 1, p 1-3

Anon, 1985, An arrangement of convenience, *Economic and Political Weekly* 20(5) February 2, p 174-175

Anon, 1985, Assam minorities safe, says PM, *Times of India*, December 14, p 1, col 1-3, news-item

Anon, 1985, Bid to weaken country not to be tolerated: PM, *Times of India*, May 7, p 1, col 1-4, news-item

Anon, 1985, Border clashes may hit ties: PM, *Times of India*, December 7, col 1-3, news-item

Anon, 1985, (Book Review), *Hindustan Times* (Magazine), December 15, p 8, col 3-5; *Link* 27(38) May 5, p 56; *National Herald*, April 14, p 7, col 1-4
Review of the Book: **Rai Singh**, 1985, *Resurgence of Rajiv Gandhi*, ABC Publishing House, New Delhi, 203p

Anon, 1985, (Book Review), *Hindustan Times* (Magazine), December 15, p 8, col 3-5
Review of the Book: **Mittal, Rajiv**, 1985, *Rajiv Gandhi: The theme of today*, Shakuntala Foundations, Chandigarh, 80p

Anon, 1985, (Book Review), *Hindustan Times* (Magazine), December 15, p 8, col 3-5
Review of the Book: **Murthi, V.K.** and **Sharma, Gautam**, 1985, *Rajiv Gandhi: Challenges and choices*, Radiant Publications, New Delhi, 141p

Anon, 1985, (Book Review), *National Herald*, April 14, p 7, col 5-7
Review of the Book: **Desai, Dinesh N.**, 1985, *Rajiv's India*, Parijan Prakashan, Bombay, 73 p

Anon, 1985, (Book Review), *National Herald*, May 26, p 7, col 1-4; *Times of India*, March 19, p 8, col 1-4
Review of the Book: **Mirchandani, G.S.**, and **Murthi, K.S.R.**, 1985, *Massive mandate for Rajiv Gandhi*, Sterling, New Delhi, xii, p 248

Anon, 1985, A bulwark of world peace, *Patriot*, May 5, p 5, col 1-3

Anon, 1985, Border clashes may hit ties: PM, *Times of India*, December 7, p 1, col 1-3, news-item

Anon, 1985, CWC discusses Punjab, *Times of India*, May 4, p 1, col 4-6+

Anon, 1985, Can Rajiv overcome Nixon, Kissinger and Reagan? *Link* 27(44) June 9, p 13-16

Anon, 1985, Challenges before ILO: Rajiv Gandhi's Address, *Mainstream* 23(44)

June 9, p 27-29
Anon, 1985, Cheer for Congress socialism, *Economic and Political Weekly*, 20(19) May 11, p 825-826
Anon, 1985, Conciliatory Rajiv can be tough, *Link* 27(49) July 14, p 13-15
Anon, 1985, Congress (I) in the South: Down but by no means out, *Times of India*, May 15, p 8, col 3-5
Anon, 1985, Congress Centenary or Nehru family business? *Organiser* 36(52) May 12, p3
Anon, 1985, Congress manifesto seeks suppot for accord, *Times of India*, September 11, p 1, col 4-5
Anon, 1985, Congress Party's decline, *Economic and Political Weekly* 20(4) January 26, p 138-139
Anon, 1985, Cross-roads before Rajiv, *Mainstream* 23(31) March 30, p 1-2
Anon, 1985, Efficiency, integrity, courtesy, *Link* 27(22) January 6, p 10-12
Anon, 1985, F-16s are for use against India: PM, *Times of India*, October 7, p 1, col 4-5, news-item
Anon, 1985, FBI uncovers plot to kill Rajiv during visit to US, *Times of India*, May 14, p 1, col 1-3
Anon, 1985, Factional tussle for ticket in MPCC, *Times of India*, Janury 31, p 1, col 1-2+
Anon, 1985, Funds plenty for engines of destruction and not for development, *Indian Worker* 33(39) June 24, p 3-5
Anon, 1985, Gorbachev pledges support for 'united, strong India': Rajiv in USSR, *Link* 27(42) May 26, p 4-10
Anon, 1985, Govt. not to yield to terrorists: PM, *Times of India*, May 18, p 1, col 1-3, news-item
Anon, 1985, I belong to the High Command and my leader? : An interview, *Indian Express* (Magazine), July 7, p 5, col 1-8
Anon, 1985, Image building and exploration in Rajiv's US visit, *Radical Humanist* 49(4) July, p 1-3
Anon, 1985, India alive to threat for Paksitan: PM, *Times of India*, May 5, p 1, col 1-4, news-item
Anon, 1985, India has the resistance to absorb shocks, *Statesman*, August 11, p 1-2
Anon, 1985, India not to be a camp follower: PM, *Times of India*, October 24, p 9, col 7-8, news-item
Anon, 1985, India to take steps to meet Pak N-therat: Rajiv, *Times of India*, October 12, p 1, col 1-3, news-item
Anon, 1985, India will not be a camp follower: PM told US Foreign Policy Establishment, *Link* 28(3) November 3, p 9-10, news-item
Anon, 1985, India will not sign NPT says PM, *Times of India*, June 15, p 1, col 1-2, news-item
Anon, 1985, India willing to discuss all issues with Pak: PM, *Times of India*, November 12, p 1, col 1-3+, news-item
Anon, 1985, India's option to make bomb still open: PM, *Times of India*, Novmber 2, p 1, col 1-3, news-item
Anon, 1985, Indian National Congress (I): From Indira Gandhi to Rajiv Gandhi.

National Herald, June 30

Anon, 1985, Infiltrators from Pak behind terrorism: PM, *Times of India*, September 17, p 1, col 1-3, news-item

Anon, 1985, It's time our scientists came out of their shell, *Yojana* 29(24) January 1, p 4-6

Anon, 1985, Job plans getting priority: PM, *Times of India*, November 24, p 1, col 1-3, news-item

Anon, 1985, Kerala free to decide on poll: PM, *Times of India*, November 25, p 1, col 2-5, news-item

Anon, 1985, Light and dark, *Mainstream* 23(39) May 25, p 1, col 1-3

Anon, 1985, List of Congress (I) candidates for Assam, *Times of India*, November 22, p 5, col 2-4

Anon, 1985, MNCs not being favoured, *Times of India*, May 5, p 1, col 5-7+

Anon, 1985, The mandate for Rajiv Gandhi, *Radical Humanist* 48(10) January, p 2-5

Anon, 1985, Mandate for unity, strength and harmony, *Haryana Review* 19(1) January p 3-5

Anon, 1985, Measures sure to make impact: Rajiv, *Times of India*, October 22, p 1, col 2-3, news-item

Anon, 1985, The Minister doesn't have the answer, *Times of India* (Sunday Review), September 29, p 1, col 1-8

Anon, 1985, New direction to policies, programmes: Social justice within stipulated time frame, *Patriot*, January 6, p 1, col 3-7+

Anon, 1985, New face of loyalty, *Economic and Political Weekly* 20(6) February 9, p 214

Anon, 1985, A new policy for electronics, *Commerce* (Supplement) 150(3850) March 9, p 1

Anon, 1985, No better guide for action than freedom struggle tenets, *Patriot*, May 5, p 5, col 1-8

Anon, 1985, No compromise on anti-State elements: Rajiv, *Times of India*, October 10, p 1, col 3-5, news-item

Anon, 1985, No giving up of Nations thrust on socialism, *Indian Worker* 33(53) September 30, p 6-8

Anon, 1985, No progress in AP after Congress exit: PM, *Times of India*, December 25, p 6, col 1-4, news-item

Anon, 1985, No talks with Pak on N-issue: PM, *Times of India*, October 28, p 1, col 1-3, news-item

Anon, 1985, On being buffeted about, *Mainstream* 23(33) April 13, p 5-6

Anon, 1985, PM: No Problem in containing Pak, *Times of India*, October 14, p 16, col 1-5, news-item

Anon, 1985, PM: Pull out depends on Sikh's response, *Times of India*, January 7, p 1, col 1-2+, news-item

Anon, 1985, PM, Opposition discuss Punjab, *Times of India*, January 12, p 1, col 7-8+

Anon, 1985, PM announces accord on Assam: Pakistan asked to abandon bomb: Sharper campaign against poverty: Call to combat extremism: Colourful Red

Fort function, *Times of India*, Agust 16, p 1, col 1-4

Anon, 1985, PM asks Akalis to publicity disown extremists, *Times of India*, December 21, p 1, col 1-3+

Anon, 1985, PM confers with Gorbachev, *Times of India*, October 27, p 1, col 1-3

Anon, 1985, PM flays Pretoria move for support to Government in Namibia, *Times of India*, April 20, p 1, col 1-3

Anon, 1985, PM for key role to Public Sector: Aministrative accountability vital, *Economic Times*, January 6, p 1, col 1-6+

Anon, 1985, PM has referred to army pull out at CPP meeting, *Times of India*, March 16, p 1, col 7-8+

Anon, 1985, PM on planning, *Economic Times*, November 9, p 5, col 7-8

Anon, 1985, PM's absensc questioned, *Times of India*, November 19, p 1, col 4-6

Anon, 1985, PM's concern at build up in Ocean, *Times of India*, January 5, p 1, col 2-5+

Anon, 1985, PM's foreign tour plans unchanged, *Times of India*, May 16, p 1, col 1-3

Anon, 1985, Planning being geared to uplift poor: PM, *Economic Times*, August 16, p 1, col 1-4, news-item

Anon, 1985, Plot to discard Indira policy defeated: PM tells where they got off, *Link* 27(46) June 23, p 4-6, news-item

Anon, 1985, Polish assurance to PM on spying probe, *Times of India*, February 13, p 1, col 1-2+

Anon, 1985, Politics: PM's new style, *Economic and Political Weekly* 20(37) September 14, p 1536, col 1-2

Anon, 1985, Poll aims at wiping out terrorism: Rajiv, *Times of India*, September 10, p 1, col 5-7, news-item

Anon, 1985, Postings and politics, *Economic and Political Weekly* 20(2) January 12, p 54-55

Anon, 1985, Prime Minister hits out at industry, *Economic Times*, October 12, p 1, col 1-5+

Anon, 1985, Prime Minister's broadcast to the Nation, *Commerce* 150(3843) January 19, p 18-119

Anon, 1985, Promises to State will be kept: PM, *Times of India*, March 24, p 1, col 1-3, news-item

Anon, 1985, Punjab and Assam solution: PM, *Times of India*, March 24, p 1, col 1-3, news-item

Anon, 1985, Rajiv decries remarks by Akali leaders, *Times of India*, April 23, p 1, col 6-8+, news-item

Anon, 1985, Rajiv for sanctions against Pretoria, *Times of India*, October 17, p 10, col 4, news item

Anon, 1985, Rajiv Gandhi and the winds of change, January-September, *Monthly Commentary on Indian Economic Conditions* 27(1) August, p 17-18

Anon, 1985, Rajiv Gandhi speaks to the Nation, *Indian And Foreign Review* 22(6) January 15, p 4-5

Anon, 1985, Rajiv Gandhi urges UN to fight starvation, *Economic Times*, October 25, p 1, col 1-4+

Anon, 1985, Rajiv Gandhi's first year: An exciting phase, *Link* 28(13) November 3, p 4-8

Anon, 1985, Rajiv Gandhi's policy projection, *Mainstream* 23(33) April 13, p 60-62

Anon, 1985, Rajiv invites Zia to inaguration of Breeder Reactor, *Times of India*, December 1, p 1, col 1-3+

Anon, 1985, Rajiv made tactical error in Andhra, *Times of India*, January 1, p 12, col 1-2

Anon, 1985, Rajiv perspective on Indian development, *Economic Times*, October 16, p 5, col 7-8+

Anon, 1985, Rajiv to visit US, France in June, *Times of India*, January 4, p 1, col 1-2+

Anon, 1985, Rajiv urges UN to fight starvation, *Economic Times*, October 25, p 1, col 1-4+

Anon, 1985, Rajiv was not very much for emergency, *Times of India*, October 11, p 9, col 7-8

Anon, 1985, Rajiv, Castro vow closer ties, *Times of India*, October 23, p 1, col 4-6+

Anon, 1985, Rajiv, Dutch PM hold talks on trade, technology, *Times of India*, October 26, p 1, col 1-3

Anon, 1985, Rajiv, Gorbachev exchange views on global issues, *Times of India*, March 14, p 1, col 1-3+

Anon, 1985, Rajiv, Mitterand hold talks, *Times of India*, June 7, p 1, col 1-3

Anon, 1985, Rajiv's call to resist big power politics, *Times of India*, October 1, p 1, col 5-7

Anon, 1985, Rajiv's perspective on Indian development, *Economic Times*, October 16, p 5, col 7-8+

Anon, 1985, Rajiv's style, priorities: Are they different from Indiras? *Link* 28(13) November 3, p 11-13

Anon, 1985, Rajiv's unpublished interview, *Organiser* 37(38) Febraury 2, p 2

Anon, 1985, Revamping West Bengal Congress factions, *Link* 27(35) April 14, p 9-10

Anon, 1985, Reverses dismay Congress leadership, *Times of India*, April 27, p 1, col 5-6+

Anon, 1985, The Six Nation Summit on Nuclear Disarmament, New Delhi, January 28, *Monthly Commentary on Indian Economic Conditions* 26(6) January, p 7-8

Anon, 1985, Soviet affront to Rajiv, *Organiser* 37(3) June 2, p 1+

Anon, 1985, Splits have strengthened party: PM., *Times of India*, May 7, p 7, col 5-8, news-item

Anon, 1985, The state of the Congress I, *People's Democracy* 9(23) June 9, p 1-2+

Anon, 1985, Stern steps against hoarders: PM, *Times of India*, May 6, p 1, col 1-3+, news-item

Anon, 1985, Stiffer line at border talks: China spurns Rajiv's peace overtures, *Organiser* 37(33) December 29, p 1+

Anon, 1985, Surjeet hails Rajiv's lies, *People's Democracy* 8(51) December 16, p

9

Anon, 1985, Talks with Opposition promised: PM hopes Punjab situation will cease, *Times of India*, July 8, p 1, col 1-3

Anon, 1985, Terrorists wanted to kill Rajiv in France or Algeria, *Times of India*, May 17, p 1, col 1-3

Anon, 1985, Top priority to Punjab: PM, *Indian Worker* 33(16) January 14, p 1, news-item

Anon, 1985, Two faces of American pique with Rajiv Gandhi, *Link* 28(14) November 10, p 9-11

Anon, 1985, Tytler among 12 AICC joint secretaries, *Times of India*, January 11, p 1, col 1-2

Anon, 1985, US treaty has retrospective effect: PM rejects terms for arms sale, *Times of India*, June 15, p 1, col 1-3, news-items

Anon, 1985, Unity bid by rival Bengal Congress factions, *Times of India*, January 8, p 1, col 2-5+

Anon, 1985, Unity of nation biggest tribute to Indira: PM, *Times of India*, November 1, p 1, col 1-3, news-item

Anon, 1985, Unquiet peace, unclear vista, *Mainstream* 23(41) June 8, p 1-3

Anon, 1985, Warning on Induced sickness: PM's call to step up productivity, *Times of India*, September 20, p 1, col 1-3+, news item

Anon, 1985, The Washington parade, *Organiser* 37(6) June 25, p 1+

Anon, 1985, We will build India of 21st century: PM, *Haryana Review* 18(11) November, p 38-40, news-item

Anon, 1985, What do people expect of Rajiv Gandhi? *Link* 27(24) January 20, p 30-31; *Patriot*, January 13, p 5, col 1-8

Anon, 1985, Woman: The social conscience of the country, *Social Welfare* 32(2) May, p 4-5

Anon, 1985, The year of Rajiv Gandhi, *Capital* 195(4819) December 23, p 17-28

Anon, 1986, ASP suspended, *Hindustan Times*, October 3

Anon, 1986, Advani blames PM for crisis in the country, *Times of India*, December 26

Anon, 1986, All is not well with UP Congress, *Link* 28(41) May 18, p 13

Anon, 1986, Another open show of Bengal Congress rift, *Times of India*, January 31, p 9, col 6-7

Anon, 1986, Another split? *Economic Times*, April 30, p 5, col 7-8

Anon, 1986, Apartheid must end, says PM, *Times of India*, June 17, news-item

Anon, 1986, The Arif Mohammad affair, *Times of India*, March 3, p 1, col 2-5+

Anon, 1986, Arif quits on Bill issue, *Times of India*, February 27, p 1, col 5-7

Anon, 1986, Arif's letter to PM: Communal divide in secular party, *Times of India*, September 25, p 1, col 2-5+

Anon, 1986, Ashok Sen defends PM's stand on GNLF, *Times of India*, October 3

Anon, 1986, Assassination attempt at Rajghat: PM, VIPs escape unhurt, *Economic Times*, October 3, p 1, col 1-4+

Anon, 1986, The BJP leader, L.K. Advani charged that adhocism rather than a method governed Rajiv Gandhi's Cabinet changes, *Hindustan Times*, May 13, *Statesman*; May 13, news-item

Anon, 1986, BJP leader questions PM's stand on GNLF, *Times of India*, November 17

Anon, 1986, Big role for Navy in Ocean: PM, *Hindustan Times*, February 17, news-item

Anon, 1986, (Book Review), *India Quarterly* 42(1) January-March, p 93-95
Review of the Book: **Murthi, V.K.** and **Sharma Gautam**, 1986, *Rajiv Gandhi: Challenges and Choices*, Radiant Publication, New Delhi, 141p

Anon, 1986, Bridge on PM's way blasted, *Statesman*, January 29, p 30

Anon, 1986, Britain protests against PM's remarks on visa rule, *Hindu*, October 18; *Times of India*, October 18

Anon, 1986, Broad concensus on terrorism, *Indian Express*, November 16

Anon, 1986, CWC drops move for action against Tripathi, *Times of India*, June 3, p 1, col 1-3

Anon, 1986, Cabinet reshuffled, *Hindustan Times*, October 24

Anon, 1986, Call for ban on nuclear arms, *Times of India*, November 28

Anon, 1986, Call for end to nuclear arms race, *Hindustan Times*, November 17

Anon, 1986, Call for global meet on Indian Ocean, *Hindustan Times*, October 14

Anon, 1986, Call for Namibian independence, *Indian Express*, May 18

Anon, 1986, Call for national unity, *Hindustan Times*, November 7

Anon, 1986, Centre to announce anti-terrorist action, says PM, *Statesman*, December 2, news-item

Anon, 1986, Clarification on PM's remarks on the inclusion of Nepali in the Eighth Schedule, *Free Press Journal* December 22

Anon, 1986, Combat terrorism, says PM, *Hindustan Times*, April 8, news-item

Anon, 1986, Commonwealth mini-summit opens, *Free Press Journal*, August 4; *Times of India*, August 4

Anon, 1986, Communication gap between PM and his party, *Link* 29(19) December 14, p 6-8

Anon, 1986, Congress (I) fuelling regionalism, *Organiser* 37(36) January 19, p 1+

Anon, 1986, Crown Prince and Rajiv Gandhi discuss trade ties, *Hindustan Times*, February 5

Anon, 1986, Cyprus to host Foreign Minister's Meet, *Statesman*, September 8

Anon, 1986, Disarmament move not against USA, says PM, *Telegraph*, August 7, news-item

Anon, 1986, Dissent in Cong(I) due disillusionment, *New Age* 34(16) April 20, p 3

Anon, 1986, The dissenter, *Illustrated Weekly of India* 107(11) March 16, p 16-17

Anon, 1986, Document presented to PM, *Hindu*, March 11

Anon, 1986, Efforts continue for solution to ethnic crisis, *Free Press Journal* November 18

Anon, 1986, Fight new joint secretaries for Congress (I), *Indian Express*, January 23, p 24

Anon, 1986, Finnish leaders felicitated, *Hindustan Times*, December 6

Anon, 1986, For the text of the speech, *Indian Express*, June 6; *Times of India*, January 30

Anon, 1986, Get to roots of grievances, says Rajiv, *Times of India*, October 16, p 1, col 7-8, news-item

Anon, 1986, Gorbachev's envoy meets PM, *Free Press Journal* July 18

Anon, 1986, Gorkha stir not anti-national, says PM, *Telegraph*, November 5, news-item

Anon, 1986, Gorkhaland issue State's responsibility: PM, *Times of India*, September 20, news-item

Anon, 1986, Helmut Kohl writes to Rajiv Gandhi, *Statesman*, May 23

Anon, 1986, Homage paid to Jagjivan Ram, *Times of India*, July 7

Anon, 1986, Implementation strategies, *Progressive Education Herald* 1(1) October, p 11-15

Anon, 1986, India fully prepared to repel attacks, says PM, *Indian Express*, December 13, news-item

Anon, 1986, India has to match Pak arms build up, says PM, *Times of India*, October 16, p 1, col 1-4+, news-item

Anon, 1986, India promises fresh initiative to end apartheid, *Times of India*, May 19

Anon, 1986, India to go nuclear if challenged, says PM, *Times of India*, October 29, news-item

Anon, 1986, India will not allow arms imbalance, says PM, *Hindustan Times*, October 16, news-item

Anon, 1986, India won't bow to pressures, says PM, *Times of India*, August 20, news-item

Anon, 1986, India, Angola assail West on sanctions, *Times of India*, May 17

Anon, 1986, India, Zambia call for world action against pretoria Government *Times of India*, Mat 15

Anon, 1986, India, Zimbabwe to set up joint commission, *Statesman*, May 17

Anon, 1986, Indira Afforestation Award presented, *Times of India*, November 20

Anon, 1986, Indo-US ties better now, says PM, *Free Press Journal* March 6, news-item

Anon, 1986, Indo-Zambia call for world action against Pretoria Governmnet, *Times of India*, May 15

Anon, 1986, Inflation under control: PM, *Economic Times*, March 6, p 1, col 2-4+, news-item

Anon, 1986, Intervention if GNLF stir truns secessionist, says PM, *Hindustan Times*, September 21, news-item

Anon, 1986, Irritating controls on small sector to go, says, PM, *Economic Times*, September 18, p 1, col 1-4, news-item

Anon, 1986, JRJ hits out at Rajiv Gandhi, *Free Press Journal*, May 19

Anon, 1986, Jagmohan calls on PM, *Telegraph*, July 27

Anon, 1986, Junejo hails Rajiv Gandhi's role in bettering ties, *Telegraph*, July 29

Anon, 1986, Kahmir issue to be solved bilaterally, says PM, *Hindustan Times*, January 21, news-item

Anon, 1986, Kamlapati slain with Aurangzeb-Shahjehan syndrome, *Organiser* 38(8) July 6, p 5

Anon, 1986, Kashmir issue to be solved bilaterally, says PM, *Hindustan Times*, January 21, news-item

Anon, 1986, Lanka Minister meets PM, *Indian Express*, April 18

Anon, 1986, Lyubomir, Rajiv agree on sanctions on South Africa, *Hindustan Times*, August 12

Anon, 1986, MGR urges PM to withdraw circular, *Hindu*, September 21

Anon, 1986, MPs appeal for peace, *Telegraph*, August 3

Anon, 1986, M'Bow meets PM, *Times of India*, August 22

Anon, 1986, Madhu Limaye's letter to PM, *Times of India*, June 1

Anon, 1986, Mahanta meets PM, *Statesman*, June 11

Anon, 1986, Major shake up in Congress (I), *Times of India*, January 20, p 1, col 1-5+

Anon, 1986, Malviya criticises PM's stand on GNLF, *Indian Express*, October 4

Anon, 1986, Mandatory sanctions against South Africa stressed, *Hindustan Times*, May 23

Anon, 1986, Mandatory sanctions must for end to racism, says PM, *Hindustan Times*, July 6, news-item

Anon, 1986, Mishra may be hauled up, *Times of India*, June 6, p 1, cpl 1-3

Anon, 1986, N-Powers violating NPT, says PM, *Indian Express*, October 18, news-item

Anon, 1986, Nation pays homage to Indira Gandhi, *Times of India*, November 1

Anon, 1986, Nation pays tributes to Mathatma Gandhi, *Times of India*, October 3

Anon, 1986, Nation remembers Indira Gandhi, *Free Press Journal*, November 20

Anon, 1986, Need for better scientific administration, *Haryana Review* 20(11) November, p 3-5

Anon, 1986, New Educational Policy on Education, *Indian Journal of Public Administration* 32(3) July-September, p 435-460

Anon, 1986, New PCC (I) President appointed, *Indian Express*, February 7

Anon, 1986, New turn to Sethi row, *Times of India*, October 16, p 1, col 1-3+

Anon, 1986, Nicaraguan Award for the Prime Minister, *Statesman*, September 11

Anon, 1986, Nicaraguan leader's talks in New Delhi, *Hindustan Times*, August 24

Anon, 1986, No compromise on unity, says PM, *Free Press Journal*, December 15, news-item

Anon, 1986, No going back on South Africa, says PM, *Hindustan Times*, July 26, news-item

Anon, 1986, No move to impose Hindi, says PM, *Statesman*, October 2, news-item

Anon, 1986, No territorial concessions to China, says PM, *Times of India*, December 19, news-item

Anon, 1986, No verbal understanding beyond accord, says Rajiv Gandhi, *Telegraph*, January 12, news-item

Anon, 1986, Not much progress on terrorism, says PM, *Hindustan Times*, November 20, news-item

Anon, 1986, Nuclear arms main threat to peace, says Rajiv Gandhi, *Times of India*, March 6, news-item

Anon, 1986, Nuclear option still open, says PM, *Indian Express*, April 9, news-item

Anon, 1986, An open letter to Rajiv Gandhi, *Illustrated Weekly of India* 107(50) December 21, p 38-39

Anon, 1986, Opposition backs PM on Punjab, *Times of India*, April 1

Anon, 1986, Opposition made Bill, religious issue: PM, *Times of India*, March 12, p 7, col 2-6, news-item

Anon, 1986, Opposition not to attend PM's meeting, *Statesman*, November 4

Anon, 1986, Ordinance on Article 249 only if necessary, says PM, *Telegraphy*, August 28, news-item

Anon, 1986, Our lifestyles must change, *Illustrated Weekly of India* 107(3) January 19, p 26-27, news-item

Anon, 1986, PLO seeks India's help, *Free Press Journal* December 6

Anon, 1986, PM, Ghising hold talks, *Indian Express*, May 19

Anon, 1986, PM, VIPs escape attempt on life, *Times of India*, October 3, p 1, col 1-4+

Anon, 1986, PM-Solarz talks on arms threat, *Times of India*, December 16

Anon, 1986, PM allays fears for migrants, *Hindustan Times*, June 27, news-item

Anon, 1986, PM asks Akali to check terrorism, *Telegraph*, February 28, news-item

Anon, 1986, PM asks Barnala to curb violence, *Times of India*, June 24, p 1, col 1-3

Anon, 1986, PM asks CMs to avert tension, *Times of India*, April 30

Anon, 1986, PM asks Jayewardne to find early solution, *Indian Express*, March 10, news-item

Anon, 1986, PM asks MGR to ascertain militants views on Sri Lanka offer, *Statesman*, October 11

Anon, 1986, PM asks police to check infiltration, *Times of India*, March 20, news-item

Anon, 1986, PM asks Sri Lanka to clarify stand, *Indian Express*, February 10, news-item

Anon, 1986, PM assures all help to Barnala, *Telegraph*, December 9

Anon, 1986, PM assures support to Cuellar, *Telegraph*, October 12, news-item

Anon, 1986, PM attacks British stand regarding sanctions against South Africa, *Indian Express*, August 3

Anon, 1986, PM briefed on Palestine meet, *National Herald*, April 27, news-item

Anon, 1986, PM call for probe into corruption roots, *Hindustan Times*, September 10, news-item

Anon, 1986, PM calls for test ban treaty, *Times of India*, March 16, news-item

Anon, 1986, PM clears pending State projects, *Hindustan Times*, September 19

Anon, 1986, PM concerned over Public Sector losses, *Indian Express*, August 24, news-item

Anon, 1986, PM concludes visit to Zambia, *Times of India*, May 16, news-item

Anon, 1986, PM condemns US action in Libya, *Hindu*, April 25, news-item

Anon, 1986, PM congratulates Shrestha, *Indian Express*, June 17, news-item

Anon, 1986, PM criticises EEC for diluting sanctions, *Hindustan Times*, September 18

Anon, 1986, PM decries obscurantism, *Times of India*, May 2, news-item

Anon, 1986, PM decries outside intervention in Central America, *Telegraph*, August 9, news-item

Anon, 1986, PM defends Law Minister's remarks, *Hindustan Times*, Sptember 30, news-item

Anon, 1986, PM defends price-hike, *Free Press Journal*, Febraury 20; *Hindu*, February 20, news-item

Anon, 1986, PM defends Shankaranand, *Times of India*, August 1, news-item

Anon, 1986, PM denies Swiss Bank accounts, *Hindustan Times*, November 11

Anon, 1986, PM encouraging divisive forces, says Opposition, *Hindustan Times*, November 6, news-item

Anon, 1986, PM escapes attempt on life, *Indian Express*, October 3

Anon, 1986, PM expresses grief, *Hindu*, October 21

Anon, 1986, PM expresses satisfaction over Barnala's performance, *Free Press Journal*, July 7

Anon, 1986, PM for C'Wealth aid to nations imposing sanction, *Times of India*, July 6, p 1, col 1-3+

Anon, 1986, PM for cautious approach to terrorism, *Times of India*, April 25

Anon, 1986, PM for dismantling Diego Garcia bases, *Indian Express*, July 5

Anon, 1986, PM for dual war on terrorism, *Indian Express*, August 12, news-item

Anon, 1986, PM for immediate sanctions, *Hindustan Times*, August 30, news-item

Anon, 1986, PM for immediate sanctions by NAM, *Indian Express*, September 3, news-item

Anon, 1986, PM for joint efforts to fight terrorism, *Hindustan Times*, March 30, news-item

Anon, 1986, PM for joint help to frontline States, *Indian Express*, August 15

Anon, 1986, PM for non-violent movement in Punjab, *Times of India*, April 8, p 9, col 1-3, news-item

Anon, 1986, PM for reforms in administration, *Indian Express*, February 7

Anon, 1986, PM hails Congress (I), Congress (S) merger, *Times of India*, December 9

Anon, 1986, PM heads NAM Fund for Africa, *Telegraph*, September 7

Anon, 1986, PM holds Pakistan responsible, *Statesman*, September 7, news-item

Anon, 1986, PM in Andamans, *Hindu*, December 28

Anon, 1986, PM invites Chief Minister, *Free Press Journal*, December 18; *Times of India*, December 18

Anon, 1986, PM justifies price-hike, *Times of India*, February 19, news-item

Anon, 1986, PM meets Opposition party leaders, *Times of India*, July 17, news-item

Anon, 1986, PM on new 20-Point Programme, *Telegraph*, August 23

Anon, 1986, PM opposed to linguistic States, *Statesman*, July 3, news-item

Anon, 1986, PM pleads for people's movement to curb terrorism, *Times of India*, October 9, news-item

Anon, 1986, PM postpones visit, *Telegraph*, January 2

Anon, 1986, PM ready for talks with dissidents Akalis, *Telegraph*, July 13, news-item

Anon, 1986, PM reaffirms suppot to Namibian struggle, *Times of India*, May 9, news-item

Anon, 1986, PM reiterates Nehru's assurance on Hindi, *India Express*, November 7, news-item

Anon, 1986, PM rules out division of the State, *Telegraph*, September 19, news-item

Anon, 1986, PM rules out division of West Bengal, *Times of India*, September 19, p 1, col 1-3, news-item

Anon, 1986, PM rules out intervention in Punjab, *Hindustan Times*, March 23, news-item

Anon, 1986, PM stresses on need to streamline legal system, *Indian Express*, November 4

Anon, 1986, PM visit Zimbabwe, *Times of India*, May 16

Anon, 1986, PM voice NAM support to Libya, *Times of India*, April 17, p 1, col 1-3

Anon, 1986, PM warns against bid to weaken border security, *Fress Press Journal*, September 12, news-item

Anon, 1986, PM warns against rivalry in Indian Ocean, *Times of India*, February 3, p 1, col 1-3

Anon, 1986, PM's address to Army Commanders, *Hindu*, April 25

Anon, 1986, PM's address to the six nation summit, *Indian Express*, August 8; *Hindu*, August 8, news-item

Anon, 1986, PM's assurance to Bhandari, *Times of India*, August 28, news-item

Anon, 1986, PM's assurance to Punjab minorities, *Times of India*, May 30, news-item

Anon, 1986, PM's call for probe into corruption roots, *Hindustan Times*, September 10, news-item

Anon, 1986, PM's call to fight disruptive forces, *Indian Express*, December 12, news-item

Anon, 1986, PM's call to fight fundamentalism, *Times of India*, September 13, p 1, col 1-3+, news-item

Anon, 1986, PM's call to safeguard NAM solidarity, *Free Press Journal*, August 27, news-item

Anon, 1986, PM's call to strengthen secularism, *Hindustan Times*, December 15, news-item

Anon, 1986, PM's call to uphold unity, *Times of India*, June 15, news-item

Anon, 1986, PM's charge against Pakistan, *Times of India*, November 5

Anon, 1986, PM's election upheld, *Times of India*, April 26

Anon, 1986, PM's message to NAM Ministers meet, *Indian Express*, January 10, news-item

Anon, 1986, PM's observations on Committee System, *Hindustan Times*, January 20; *Times of India*, January 20

Anon, 1986, PM's remarks criticised, *Free Press Journal*, September 23, news-item

Anon, 1986, PM's talks with Opposition on Border Areas Bill, *Free Press Journal*, July 30; *Times of India*, July 30

Anon, 1986, PM's visit to Pak cancelled, *Free Press Journal*, July 12

Anon, 1986, Pak aiding terrorists: PM, *Times of India*, October 13, p 1, col 1-3, news-item

Anon, 1986, Pak responisble for hijack tragedy, says PM, *Times of India*, September 7, p 1, col 1-3+, news-item

Anon, 1986, Pak visit shelved: PM rules out talks with extremists, *Times of India* July 19, p 1, col 1-3+

Anon, 1986, Patnaik meet PM, *Telegraph*, May 30

Anon, 1986, Political solution to Kampuchean issue urged, *Statesman*, October 20

Anon, 1986, Pranab expelled from party for six years: Three others leaders suspended, *Times of India*, April 28, p 1, col 1-4

Anon, 1986, President, Prime Minister greet Reagan, *Times of India*, July 4

Anon, 1986, Pressure unity of India, says PM, *Free Press Journal* October 10 news-item

Anon, 1986, Primacy of public sector to stay, says PM, *Telegraph*, August 23 news-itme

Anon, 1986, Prime Minister and Sri Lanka President discuss ethnic crisis, *Statesman*, November 16

Anon, 1986, Prime Minister announces Rs. 400 crore package for Haryana, *Indian Express*, December 19

Anon, 1986, Prime Minister calls for new strategy to fight forces of communalism *Indian Express*, September 13; *Times of India*, September 13

Anon, 1986, Prime Minister rejects demand for Gorkhaland, *Free Press Journal* December 20; *Times of India*, December 20, news-item

Anon, 1986, Prime Minister to hold talks on GNLF issue with CM, *Times of India* December 19

Anon, 1986, Probe into security lapses, *Hindu*, October 5

Anon, 1986, Productivity improvement in Public Enterprises, *Management in Government* 18(1) April-June, p 5-17

Anon, 1986, Pupul Jayekar Cultural Adviser to PM, *Telegraph*, September 3

Anon, 1986, Racism must end, says, PM, *Statesman*, June 16, news-itme

Anon, 1986, Rajiv, Gorbachev hold talks on bilateral, global matters, *Economic Times*, November 26, p 1, col 1-5+

Anon, 1986, Rajiv, Jayewardne talks brighten peace-hope, *Statesman*, November 17; *Times of India*, November 17

Anon, 1986, Rajiv detractors fossilised in the past, *Link* 29(7) September 21, p 14-16

Anon, 1986, Rajiv drops three Ministers, major shake up in Congress Party, *Times of India*, January 20, p 1, col 2-4

Anon, 1986, Rajiv Gandhi, *Times of India*, March 6, p 8, col 6; *Times of India* March 11, p 8, col 6; *Times of India*, March 17, p 8, col 6, letters to the editor

Anon, 1986, Rajiv Gandhi: On the razor's edge, *Illustrated Weekly of India* 107(17) April 20, p 26-35

Anon, 1986, Rajiv Gandhi: Where does he stand? *Hindustan Times* (Magazine) November 9, p 1, col 1-6+

Anon, 1986, Rajiv Gandhi, MGR review situation, *Hindustan Times*, November 9

Anon, 1986, Rajiv Gandhi, Mikulic discuss apartheid, *Indian Express*, July 29

Anon, 1986, Rajiv Gandhi, Palme hail Soviet move, *Times of India*, January 17

Anon, 1986, Rajiv Gandhi abetting Gorkhaland agitation, *New Age* 34(35) August 31, p 3

Anon, 1986, Rajiv Gandhi for North South dialogue, *Indian Express*, February 9

Anon, 1986, Rajiv Gandhi in Islamabad, *Indian Express*, December 30

Anon, 1986, Rajiv Gandhi lacks charisma, says Pranab, *Times of India*, June 1, news-item

Anon, 1986, Rajiv Gandhi takes over as Chairman, *Hindustan Times*, November 17

Anon, 1986, Rajiv Gandhi warns rivalry in Indian Ocean, *Indian Express*, February 8

Anon, 1986, Rajiv Gandhi's criticism not based on facts, says Zia, *Times of India*, September 9, news-item

Anon, 1986, Rajiv greets Chirac, *Statesman*, March 22

Anon, 1986, Rajiv meets Junejo in Stockholm, *Telegraph*, March 17

Anon, 1986, Rajiv voices concern to Sri Lankan envoy, *Hindu*, February 19, news-item

Anon, 1986, Rajiv Zia meeting at Harare, *Hindustan Times*, September 6

Anon, 1986, Rajiv's crusade in black Africa, *Link* 28(42) May 25, p 7-8

Anon, 1986, Rajiv's India: Has the dream really faded? *Illustrated Weekly of India* 107(17) April 20, p 6-17

Anon, 1986, Revamping the education system, *Haryana Review* 20(7) July, p 3-7

Anon, 1986, Revitalize Panchayats, says PM, *Hindustan Times*, September 23, news-item

Anon, 1986, SAARC initiates action in new areas, *Times of India*, November 18

Anon, 1986, SAARC meet on women, *Indian Express*, May 7

Anon, 1986, Sanctions against South Africa, *Times of India*, May 26

Anon, 1986, Security Belt Bill kept in abeyances, *Times of India*, August 21

Anon, 1986, Sethi suspended from Congress (I), *Times of India*, October 17, p 1, col 1-3+

Anon, 1986, Solanki issue is closed, says PM, *Times of India*, March 22, news-item

Anon, 1986, Soviet Minister meets PM, *Indian Express*, October 31

Anon, 1986, Soviet will stand by India, says PM, *Times of India*, December 3, news-item

Anon, 1986, 'Star Wars' against world peace, says Rajiv, *National Herald*, February 17, news-item

Anon, 1986, Statute amendment hinted in National Anthem case, *Hindustan Times*, December 3

Anon, 1986, Steps to boost trade, *Times of India*, November 6

Anon, 1986, Steps to expand trade ties, *Hindustan Times*, October 8

Anon, 1986, Steps to explore new trade opportunities, *Statesman*, November 23

Anon, 1986, Strict minoriting of aid package for Bengal: PM, *Times of India*, September 21, p 1, col 1-3+, news-item

Anon, 1986, Stringent measures to meet terrorism, *Hindustan Times*, July 30, news-item

Anon, 1986, Talks fail over Tamil homeland, *Hindustan Times*, November 26

Anon, 1986, Talks with Akali rebels if stand clarified: PM, *Times of India*, July 13, col 6-7+, news-item

Anon, 1986, Terrorism will be met at all costs, says PM, *Free Press Journal*, July

29, news-item
Anon, 1986, Tirpathi's letter to Rajiv Gandhi, *Times of India*, May 29, p 8, col 7-8
Anon, 1986, To this course I plead myself, *Indian Worker* 34(17) January 27, p 9-15, news-item
Anon, 1986, Trade Council set up, *Statesman*, October 7
Anon, 1986, Tripathi accepts CPB decision, *Times of India*, July 19, p 9, col 1-2
Anon, 1986, Tripathi continues talks with rebels, *Times of India*, April 27, p 1, col 1-4
Anon, 1986, Tripathi criticises Rajiv's handling of affairs, *Times of India*, May 29, p 1, col 1-3
Anon, 1986, Tripathi denied renomination to Rajya Sabha, *Times of India*, June 18, p 1, col 7-8
Anon, 1986, Tripathi may be eased out, *Times of India*, May 30, p 1, col 1-3+
Anon, 1986, Tripathi resigns as Working President of Congress (I), *Telegraph*, November 13
Anon, 1986, Tripathi resings on PM's demand, *Times of India*, November 13, p 1, col 1-3
Anon, 1986, Tripathi should quit, says Anjiah, *Times of India*, May 31, p 1, col 4+, news-item
Anon, 1986, Tripathi should step down, says Anjiah, *Times of India*, July 11, p 1, col 4+, news-item
Anon, 1986, Tripathi supports Rajiv, *Hindustan Times*, June 1
Anon, 1986, Tripathi voices anguish, *Times of India*, April 25, p 1, col 4-6
Anon, 1986, Tripathi won't take any more insults, *Times of India*, September 4, p 1, col 1-4
Anon, 1986, Tripathi's letter to PM leaked, *Hindu*, May 29
Anon, 1986, Tripathi's letter to Rajiv Gandhi, *Times of India*, May 29, p 8, col 7-8
Anon, 1986, Tripathi's tantalising tantrums, *Link* 28(39) May 4, p 19
Anon, 1986, Troubled Congress and its internal debate, *Link* 28(24) January 19, p 14-15
Anon, 1986, Tumultuous welcome to Gorbachev on arrival, *Indian Express*, November 26
Anon, 1986, UK explains causes for deportation of JKLF Chief, *Statesman*, October 27
Anon, 1986, UK isolated in Commonwealth, says PM, *Telegraph*, May 30, news-item
Anon, 1986, UN Namibia plan must prevail, says PM, *Hindustan Times*, July 8, news-item
Anon, 1986, US offers help on arms, *Statesman*, October 12
Anon, 1986, US treaty has retrospective effect: PM rejects terms for arms sale, *Times of India*, June 15, p 1, col 1-3
Anon, 1986, United Kingdom isolated in Commonwealth, says PM, *Telegraph*, May 30, news-item
Anon, 1986, Updated 20-Point plan soon: PM, *Economic Times*, August 16, p 1, col 1-4, news-item
Anon, 1986, Virk hoped for Chinese, Pak, US help, *Times of India*, March 12 p 1,

col 2-5

Anon, 1986, What is Mr Gandhi's political base, *Illustrated Weekly of India* 107(23) June 1, p 16-17

Anon, 1986, Why Basu doesn't tax rich farmers? *Link* 29(8) September, p 10-12

Anon, 1986, Yaqub meets PM, *Times of India*, April 18

Anon, 1986, Zia expresses concern, *Telegraph*, October 3

Anon, 1986, Zia sends PM apology for attack on envoys, *Telegraph*, June 23

Anon, 1987, Attempt on Rajiv's life in columbo, *Times of India*, July 31, p 1, col 3-6 +

Anon, 1987, Bear hung for Rajiv, *Organiser* 39(1) May 24, p 1+

Anon, 1987, Bofors audit report not contradictory: PM, *Times of India*, July 7, p 1, col 2-3+, news-item

Anon, 1987, Bofors Issues: Opposition asks PM to resign, *Times of India*, June 6, p 1, col 7-8+

Anon, 1987, (Book Review), *Hindustan Times* (Magazine), January 18, p 8, col 1-4

Review of the Book: **Ponkshe, Satyawrat**, 1987, *Rajiv Gandhi: The Pragmatic Prime Minister of India*, Ponkshe Publications, Pune

Anon, 1987, (Book Review), *Hindustan Times* (Magazine), June 28, p 8, col 4-6

Review of the Book: **Gupta, M.G.**, 1987, *Rajiv Gandhi's foreign policy: A study in continuity and change*, M.G. Publishers, Agra

Anon, 1987, (Book Review), *Patriot*, July 5, p 4, col 2-5

Review of the Book: **Salvi, P.G.**, 1986, *Rajiv's new India*, Intellectual Publishers, New Delhi

Anon, 1987, Cenral rule till terrorism ends in Punjab: PM, *Times of India*, June 8, p 1, col 1-3

Anon, 1987, Destabilisation: Economic dimension, *Link* 29(41) May 17, p 11-12

Anon, 1987, Dissidents hungry for power: PM, *Times of India*, August 30, p 1, col 1-3+, news-item

Anon, 1987, Economic policies to stay: PM, *Economic Times*, January 21, p 1, col 1-5, news-item

Anon, 1987, Education: The backbone of progress, *Haryana Review* 21(2) February, p 3-6

Anon, 1987, For a profile of the Gorkhaland agitation, *Illustrated Weekly of India*, February 22, p 28

Anon, 1987, Gorbachev, Rajiv discuss political situation in India, *Times of India*, July 3, p 1, col 1-3+

Anon, 1987, Gorbachev arrives in New Delhi, *Hindustan Times*, November 19

Anon, 1987, Government answerable only to people, Parliament: PM, *Times of India*, May 17, p 1, col 1-4+, news-item

Anon, 1987, Harnessing Science and Technology for development, *Yojana* 31(9) May 16, p 15-17

Anon, 1987, Homage to Raj Narain, *Hindu*, January 1

Anon, 1987, India to follow own path, *Times of India*, August 2, p 1, col 4-6+, news-item

Anon, 1987, Indo-Sri Lanka Agreement, *Foreign Affairs Report* 36(7-10) July-

October, p 93-237
Anon, 1987, Is Rajiv in trouble? *Illustrated Weekly of India* 108(15) April 12, p 9-11
Anon, 1987, LTTE chief to meet Rajiv today, *Times of India*, July 25, p 1, col 1-3+
Anon, 1987, Lives of landless to be insured: Iron hand for terrorists: PM, *Economic Times*, May 17, p 1, col 6-8, news-item
Anon, 1987, MGR, PM put all egges in LTTE basket, *Link* 30(17) November 29, p 4-7
Anon, 1987, The Mid Term blues Rajiv Gandhi, *Illustrated Weekly of India* 108(14) April 5, p 26-27
Anon, 1987, No compromise on security: PM, *Times of India*, February 1, p 1, col 1-3, news-item
Anon, 1987, No confrontation with Rajiv, says V.P. Singh, *Times of India*, August 20, p 1, col 1-4+, news-item
Anon, 1987, Opposition free to send team to Sweden: PM, *Times of India*, August 1-9, p 1, col 7-8+, news-item
Anon, 1987, Opposition meet with PM on Bofors Panel terms urged, *Economic Times*, August 12, p 1, col 1-4+
Anon, 1987, PM, Zia review bilateral ties, *Times of India*, February 22, p 1, col 1-3+
Anon, 1987, PM calls for world pressure on Lanka, *Times of India*, May 29, p 1, col 1-3, news-item
Anon, 1987, PM for unified plan for rural, urban area, *National Herald*, June 9
Anon, 1987, PM in no hurry to reshuffle Cabinet, *Times of India*, October 14, p 1, col 2-5+
Anon, 1987, PM lashes out at Public Sector, *Times of India*, December 23, p 1, col 1-3
Anon, 1987, PM rejects demand for Mid Term Poll, *Times of India*, July 5, p 1, col 1-4
Anon, 1987, PM says he will move motion on Bofors Panel, *Times of India*, June 17, p 1, col 1-3+
Anon, 1987, PM will stick to Amethi, *Times fo India*, September 11, p 1, col 4-6
Anon, 1987, PM's beháviour, *Times of India*, March 24, p 6, col 6, letter to the editor
Anon, 1987, PM's prerogative, *Times of India*, March 25, p 6, col 6, letter to the editor
Anon, 1987, Pak exploiting links with US: PM, *Times of India*, July 8, p 1, col 1-6, news-item
Anon, 1987, People asked to help fight drought, terrorism, *Times of India*, August 16, p 1, col 1-4, news-item
Anon, 1987, Political economy of Rajiv's regime, *Link* 29(25) January 25, p 12-15
Anon, 1987, President-PM differences being taken to absured length, *Organiser* 38(41) February 22, p 6
Anon, 1987, President rejects pleas for PM's prosecution, *Times of India*, July 23, p 1, col 1-3

Anon, 1987, A Prime Minister or a President? *Times of India* (Sunday Review), January 25, p 4, col 1-5

Anon, 1987, Rai Bareli won't be neglected: PM, *Times of India*, September 13, p 9, col 4-5, news-item

Anon, 1987, Rajiv, JRJ sign accord as violence rocks Colombo, *Economic Times*, July 30, p 1, col 6-8+

Anon, 1987, Rajiv expels V.P. Singh from Congress Party, *Times of India*, July 20, p 1, col 1-4+

Anon, 1987, Rajiv has damaged his image, V.P. Singh lacks courage, *Organiser* 39(10) August 2, p 5-6

Anon, 1987, Rajiv irresponsible leader: V.P. Singh, *Times of India*, August 20, p 1, col 1-4+, news-item

Anon, 1987, Rajiv's emergency plan to counter dismissal, *Organiser* 39(2) May 31, p 1-2

Anon, 1987, Sri Ramkrishna and the Ramkrishna order, *Vedanta Kesari*, April 14, p 151-152

Anon, 1987, West confidence in Rajiv increasing, *Times of India*, October 15, p 1, col 2-5+

Anon, 1987, What would Gandhiji have done? *Indian Express* (Magazine), January 25, p 1, col 1-8+

Anon, 1987, When Rajivji gives his views, the others say 'okay', *Link* 30(21) December 27, p 6-8

Anon, 1987, Why pressures is mounting on Rajiv, *Link* 29(40) May 10, p 6-8

Anon, 1987, Will Zail dismiss Rajiv? *Organiser* 38(46) March 29, p 1+

Anon, 1988, AICC (I) session begins, *Statesman*, November 5; *Times of India*, November 5

Anon, 1988, Abdul Vakil calls on PM, *Hindustan Times*, September 4

Anon, 1988, All Party meet on Punjab soon: PM, *Times of India*, September 2, p 1, col 1-3, news-item

Anon, 1988, Ardbo denies having met Rajiv Gandhi, *Hindu*, March 30

Anon, 1988, Armacost calls on Prime Minister, *Hindustan Times*, May 26, p 12, col 5-7

Anon, 1988, Australian Minister in New Delhi, *Times of India*, December 2

Anon, 1988, Bandh passes off peacefully, *Hindustan Times*, September 15

Anon, 1988, Blue print for comprehensive disarmament and security, *Mainstream* 26(36) June 18, p 23-26+, news-item

Anon, 1988, (Book Review), *Hindustan Times* (Magazine), May 29, p 4, col 1-8
Review of the Book: **Anon**, 1988, *From Raj to Rajiv*, BBC's Books, p 174

Anon, 1988, (Book Review), *Journal of Political Studies* 21(2) September, p 73-74
Review of the Book: **Pal, R.N.** and **Sudesh Rani**, 1988, *Information: Prime Minister's obligations*, Ghanshyam, New Delhi, p 249

Anon, 1988, CPM encouraging violence, says PM, *Times of India*, April 3, p 1, col 7-8, news-itme

Anon, 1988, CPP-I general body meeting, *Hindustan Times*, May 14

Anon, 1988, CWC (I) meet reviews bye election reverses, *Times of India*, July 8

Anon, 1988, China keen on PM's visit, *Times of India*, November 30, p 1, col 2-4+

Anon, 1988, Commentary: Thoughts on PM's foreign tour, *Mainstream* 26(41) July 23, p 3-4

Anon, 1988, Complications in dropping bill: PM, *Times of India*, September 16, p 1, col 1-3, news-item

Anon, 1988, The Dandi March, *Illustrated Weekly of India* 109(13) March 27, p 20-23

Anon, 1988, Defamation Bill withdrawn, *Hindustan Times*, September 23; *Indian Express*, September 23

Anon, 1988, Dissanaayake calls on PM, *Hindustan Times*, May 11

Anon, 1988, The enemy within: Fears in PM's camp, *Link* 31(5) September 11, p 4-6

Anon, 1988, Foreign Secretaries meet ends, *Hindu*, June 3

Anon, 1988, French Defence Minister calls on PM, *Statesman*, December 18

Anon, 1988, Gadgil appointed AICC (I) General Secretary, *National Herald*, September 2

Anon, 1988, Gayoom, PM hold talks, *Indian Express*, December 8

Anon, 1988, Genuine work for Bofors: Commission unquestionable: PM, *Economic Times*, November 12, p 1, col 2-5, news-item

Anon, 1988, Gorbachev arrives in New Delhi, *Hindustan Times*, Novmber 19

Anon, 1988, Government firm on corridor plan, says PM, *Times of India*, June 10, news-item

Anon, 1988, Government will not allow division of States, says PM, *National Herald*, May 26, news-item

Anon, 1988, High level talks contiune, *Indian Express*, November 20

Anon, 1988, Hindu report does not link politicians, says PM, *Tribune*, June 26, news-item

Anon, 1988, Hun Sen holds talks with Rajiv Gandhi, *Times of India*, November 17

Anon, 1988, Hungarian Foreign Minister calls on Rajiv Gandhi, *Times of India*, March 2

Anon, 1988, Independence day celebrated, *Hindu*, August 16; *Hindustan Times*, August 16

Anon, 1988, India, Spain agree on defence tie up, *Hindustan Times*, July 17

Anon, 1988, India and the Afghan accords, *Link* 30(39) May 1, p 14-16

Anon, 1988, India has vital stake in resolution of Afghan crisis, says PM, *Hindustan Times*, March 3, news-item

Anon, 1988, India not to build N-arms, says PM, *National Herald*, June 6, news-item

Anon, 1988, India not to play Israel, *Hindustan Times*, March 24

Anon, 1988, India to assist Mozambique, *Indian Express*, December 3

Anon, 1988, India wants Mandela's release, *Indian Express*, July 19

Anon, 1988, Indian troops crush coup bid, *Times of India*, November 5

Anon, 1988, Joint Panel set up to settle boundary issue, *Hindustan Times*, December 23; *Times of India*, December 23

Anon, 1988, Jyoti Basu calls on PM, *Hindustan Times*, June 29

Anon, 1988, Lord Mackay calls on Rajiv Gandhi, *Hindustan Times*, August 17

Anon, 1988, Mahanta refutes PM's charge, *Indian Express*, September 17

Anon, 1988, Mature Rajiv best bet in next poll: Congressmen, *Times of India* (Magazine Section 1), May 5, p 1, col 2-8+

Anon, 1988, Mozambique President holds talks in New Delhi, *Hindustan Times*, May 15; *National Herald*, May 15

Anon, 1988, NF rally calls for PM's resignation, *Times of India*, November 17, p 1, col 4-5+

Anon, 1988, Najib holds further discussion with PM, *Hindustan Times*, May 6; *Times of India* May 6

Anon, 1988, Najibullah holds talks in New Delhi, *National Herald*, May 5; *Times of India*, May 5

Anon, 1988, Nation pays homage to Indira Gandhi, *Times of India*, November 20

Anon, 1988, Nation pays homage to Nehru, *Times of India*, November 15

Anon, 1988, Nation's taxation policy and role of tax administration, *IFTP Bulletin* 8(2-3) September, p 5-8

Anon, 1988, New AICC (I) General Secretary, *National Herald*, February 23

Anon, 1988, No compromise on Siachen says PM, *Times of India*, February 10, p 1, col 1-3, news-item

Anon, 1988, No compromise on Siachen, says Rajiv Gandhi, *Hindu*, February 10, news-item

Anon, 1988, No concession on farmers under pressure: PM, *Times of India*, October 28, p 1, col 1-3, nesw-item

Anon, 1988, No territory to be ceded to China: PM, *Times of India*, September 28, p 1, col 1-3, news-item

Anon, 1988, North Korean PM in New Delhi, *National Herald*, Febraury 19

Anon, 1988, Opposition asks PM to quit, *Indian Express*, November 15

Anon, 1988, Opposition casteist, feudal: Rajiv, *Times of India*, November 6, p 1, col 7-8, news-item

Anon, 1988, Opposition Nation's foe: PM, *Times of India*, November 1, p 1, col 5-7+, news-item

Anon, 1988, Opposition rally asks PM to quit, *Hindu*, November 17

Anon, 1988, Opposition seeks PM's apology for remarks, *Hindustan Times*, July 28

Anon, 1988, PM: Press must be worthy of freedom, *Times of India*, September 10, p 1, col 5-6+, news-item

Anon, 1988, PM, Assad hold further talks, *National Herald*, June 6; *Statesman*, June 6

Anon, 1988, PM, Bhutan King hold more talks, *Hindustan Times*, September 25

Anon, 1988, PM, Governer reviews situation, *Free Press Journal*, May 20; *National Herald*, May 20

Anon, 1988, PM, JRJ resolve to implement pact, *Times of India*, January 1, p 1, col 5-6+

Anon, 1988, PM, Najib call for Geneva pact success, *Times of India*, May 5, p 1, col 6-8+

Anon, 1988, PM again warns Pakistan against aiding terrorists, *Times of India*, August 16, p 1, col 1-3+, news-item

Anon, 1988, PM allows MP to vent views on party affairs, *Times of India*, July 21, p 1, col 2-4+
Anon, 1988, PM arrives in Bonn, *Hindu*, June 7; *National Herald*, June 7; *Times of India*, June 7
Anon, 1988, PM asks Buta to probe offer of funds to Zail, *Times of India*, March 3, p 1, col 1-3+
Anon, 1988, PM blames Pak for vitiating ties, *Times of India*, July 12, p 1, col 1-3+, news-item
Anon, 1988, PM brings border issue with China to the fore, *Economic Times*, December 2, p 1, col 2-5
Anon, 1988, PM calls on Deng, Zhao, *Hindustan Times*, December 22; *Times of India*, December 22
Anon, 1988, PM calls on President, *Hindustan Times*, March 27
Anon, 1988, PM concludes visit to Bonn, *Hindu*, June 10; *Hindustan Times*, June 10
Anon, 1988, PM condemn Israeli atrocities, *Times of India*, February 7,
Anon, 1988, PM condoles quake victims, *National Herald*, December 14; *Times of India*, December 14
Anon, 1988, PM conistently lying: Opposition, *Times of India*, November 15, p 1, vol 1-2
Anon, 1988, PM constitutes two committees, *National Herald*, July 2,
Anon, 1988, PM continues discussions, *Statesman*, June 12; *Times of India*, June 12
Anon, 1988, PM denies Swiss Bank accounts, *Hindustan Times*, November 11, news-item
Anon, 1988, PM for debate on all aspects of Defamation Bill, *National Herald*, September 7
Anon, 1988, PM for dismantling all nuclear weapons, *Hindustan Times*, November 15, news-item
Anon, 1988, PM for effective power devolution, *Hindustan Times*, August 24
Anon, 1988, PM greets Benazir, *Indian Express*, December 3
Anon, 1988, PM hints at Bill to decentralise planning, *Hindustan Times*, November 26
Anon, 1988, PM hold talks in Damascus, *Indian Express*, June 5; *Telegraph*, June 5; *Time of India*, June 5
Anon, 1988, PM holds discussions with Bhutan King, *Hindustan Times*, July 11
Anon, 1988, PM holds further discussions, *Statesman*, July 13
Anon, 1988, PM holds talk in Bonn, *Statesman*, June 7; *Times of India*, June 7
Anon, 1988, PM holds talks, *Indian Express*, July 20
Anon, 1988, PM holds talks with Bhutan King, *Hindustan Times*, September 24
Anon, 1988, PM in Ankara, *Times of India*, July 18
Anon, 1988, PM invites Zia for talks, *Hindu*, February 26; *Tribune*, Febraury 26
Anon, 1988, PM leaves on foreign tour, *National Herald*, June 5
Anon, 1988, PM not happy with relief, *Times of India*, October 14, p 1, col 2-3
Anon, 1988, PM offers dialogue on Bill, *Hindustan Times*, September 10; *Tribune*, September 10, news-item

Anon, 1988, PM rejects farmer's demands, *Times of India*, February 21, p 1, col 4-6+

Anon, 1988, PM sees change in China's policy, *Times of India*, October 16, p 1, col 1-3

Anon, 1988, PM showed extraordinary interest: Dissenting role, *Times of India*, April 27, p 1, vol 6-8+

Anon, 1988, PM to head Seva Dal, *Telegraph*, May 11

Anon, 1988, PM turns down demand for Jharkhand State, *National Herald*, May 28

Anon, 1988, PM urges NAM to help disarm efforts, *Times of India*, July 15, p 1, col 1-3, news-item

Anon, 1988, PM urges to keep military out of politics, *Hindu*, November 13

Anon, 1988, PM views on Defamation Bill, *Indian Express*, September 16; *National Herald*, September 16

Anon, 1988, PM visits flood-affected areas, *Hindustan Times*, September 28

Anon, 1988, PM visits quake-affected areas, *Times of India*, August 23

Anon, 1988, PM warns against casteist front, *Times of India*, November 3

Anon, 1988, PM's Address at Silver Jubilee function of "Patriot", *Indian Express*, March 30, news-item

Anon, 1988, PM's Address to CPP (I), *Hindu*, February 22; *Hindu*, December 8; *Hindustan Times*, February 21; *Hindustan Times*, July 28; *Hindustan Times*, August 31; *National Herald*, May 13; *Times of India*, May 13, news-item

Anon, 1988, PM's Address to the Chief Ministers, *Hindustan Times*, March 19; *Times of India*, March 19

Anon, 1988, PM's apology demanded, *Times of India*, February 26

Anon, 1988, PM's call for elemination of nuclear weapons, *National Herald*, November 25, news-item

Anon, 1988, PM's call to ease tension in the Gulf, *Hindustan Times*, July 15; *National Herald*, July 15; *Statesman*, July 15

Anon, 1988, PM's call to fight reactionary forces, *Hindustan Times*, August 10

Anon, 1988, PM's China visit concludes, *Indian Express*, December 24; *Times of India*, December 24

Anon, 1988, PM's condition for talks, *Free Press Journal*, March 12

Anon, 1988, PM's confer, *Hindustan Times*, July 18

Anon, 1988, PM's interview to "Sunday", *Times of India*, November 12, news-item

Anon, 1988, PM's secretariat toning up white paper on State Sector, *Economic Times*, July 30, p 1, col 1-4, news-item

Anon, 1988, PM's statement on Gorbachev's visit, *Hindu*, November 22

Anon, 1988, PM's talks with IFAD Chief, *Statesman*, March 31

Anon, 1988, PM's views on Defamation Bill, *Indian Express*, September 16; *National Herald*, September 16

Anon, 1988, PM's visit to Punjab, *Times of India*, September 22

Anon, 1988, Pak hand seen in destabilisation bid: Concern at plot against PM, *Times of India*, August 3, p 1, col 1-3+

Anon, 1988, Pakistan biggest supporter of terrorism, says Rajiv Gandhi, *Hindustan*

Times, June 9, news-item

Anon, 1988, Party panel on policy persective set up, *Hindu*, March 11

Anon, 1988, Pay off possibly for genuine work, says Rajiv, *Times of India*, November 12, p 1, col 7-8, news-item

Anon, 1988, Perspective plan for women presented, *Hindu*, November 13

Anon, 1988, Phased withdrawl of IPKF agreed upon, *Statesman*, May 14

Anon, 1988, President, Prime Minister condole Armenian quake deaths, *Times of India*, December 9

Anon, 1988, President Aquino's letter to Rajiv Gandhi, *Indian Express*, February 19

Anon, 1988, President Ershad in New Delhi, *Free Press Journal*, September 30; *Hindustan Times*, September 30

Anon, 1988, President Zia's death condoled, *National Herald*, August 19; *Telegraph*, August 19

Anon, 1988, Prime Minister flags off Dandi March, *Times of India*, March 13

Anon, 1988, Prime Minister holds talks with Jordanian leaders, *Hindustan Times*, July 12; *Times of India*, July 12

Anon, 1988, Prime Minister in Belgrade, *Hindustan Times*, July 14; *Times of India*, July 14

Anon, 1988, Prime Minister returns home, *National Herald*, June 13

Anon, 1988, Probe into offer of money to former President, *Hindu*, March 3; *Indian Express*, March 3

Anon, 1988, Rajiv, Li Peng hopeful of border accord, *Times of India*, December 20, p 1, col 1-4

Anon, 1988, Rajiv announces Rs. 175 crores relief, *Times of India*, October 15, p 1, col 1-3

Anon, 1988, Rajiv Gandhi arrives in Hungary, *Telegraph*, June 11

Anon, 1988, Rajiv Gandhi briefed on Soviet troop withdrawal, *Hindu*, February 9

Anon, 1988, Rajiv Gandhi cannot solve Punjab problem: Who can? *Rual India* 51(3) March, p 31-33

Anon, 1988, Rajiv Gandhi criticises National Front, *Hindu*, November 28

Anon, 1988, Rajiv Gandhi holds discussions with Benazir, *National Herald*, December 31

Anon, 1988, Rajiv Gandhi in Beijing, *Hindustan Times*, December 20; *Statesman*, December 20

Anon, 1988, Rajiv Gandhi in Islamabad, *Indian Express*, December 30

Anon, 1988, Rajiv Gandhi in Spain, *Hindustan Times*, July 16

Anon, 1988, Rajiv Gandhi meets Chinese President, *Hindustan Times*, December 12; *Tribune*, December 12

Anon, 1988, Rajiv Gandhi meets world leaders, *Hindustan Times*, June 11

Anon, 1988, Rajiv Gandhi to contest from Amethi, *Statesman*, November 23

Anon, 1988, Rajiv Gandhi's address to special session on disarmament, *Indian Express*, June 10, news-item

Anon, 1988, Rajiv Gandhi's new honey-moon, *Commerce* 157(4041) November 23 p 12-13

Anon, 1988, Rajiv Gandhi's summer tour: Seeking roles for India, *Link* 30(46)

June 19, p 8-9

Anon, 1988, Rajiv has uphill task in Pakistan, *Link* 31(20) December, 25, p 4-5

Anon, 1988, Rajiv's bid to woo Tamil Nadu voters, *Link* 31(18) December 11, p 12-13

Anon, 1988, Rajiv's 'Tina' factor, *India Today*, February 29

Anon, 1988, Reorder global priorities for poverty uplift: PM, *Economic Times*, March 26, p 1, col 60-8, news-item

Anon, 1988, Ringadoo meets PM, *Statesman*, November 17

Anon, 1988, SAARC summit begins, *Hindustan Times*, December 30

Anon, 1988, Seven of Rajiv's trusted men wanted Zail Singh to dismiss him, *Organiser* 39(42) April 3, p 8

Anon, 1988, Singapore PM's talks in New Delhi, *Times of India*, March 17

Anon, 1988, Six agreements signed, *National Herald*, November 21; *Times of India*, November 21

Anon, 1988, Soviet Festival concludes, *Hindu*, November 20

Anon, 1988, Speech at the AICC session in New Delhi, *Times of India*, November 22

Anon, 1988, Speeches (Extracts): Prime Minister Rajiv Gandhi, *Foreign Affairs Report* 37(9-10-11) September- November, p 101-124, figures

Anon, 1988, State borders not to be changed: PM, *Times of India*, May 22, p 1, col 5-8, news-item

Anon, 1988, Sweeping electoral reforms soon: PM, *Times of India*, July 21, p 1, col 1-3, news-item

Anon, 1988, Talks on Punjab only if violence is given up: PM, *Times of India*, March 12, p 1, col 1-3, news-item

Anon, 1988, Trade pact signed, *National Herald*, July 19

Anon, 1988, Tripathi's letter to Rajiv Gandhi, *Times of India*, July 7

Anon, 1988, Turkey ban export of components, *Telegraph*, July 19

Anon, 1988, Turkish President in New Delhi, *Statesman*, February 23

Anon, 1988, Two AICC (I) General Secrataries replaced, *Free Press Jounral*, May 10

Anon, 1988, Uncertainty marks unity moves: Rajiv, *Times of India*, October 26, p 1, col 1-3, news-item

Anon, 1988, V.P. Singh exposes PM's Italian connection, *Organiser* 39(43) April 10, p 13

Anon, 1988, The vision of Jawaharlal Nehru, *Gandhi Marg* 10(8-9) November-December, p 456-460

Anon, 1988, What government expects from industry, *Business India* (Special Number), April 30, p 14-15

Anon, 1988, Why is the PM going to China? *Economic and Political Weekly* 23(4) October 8, p 2087

Anon, 1988, Writ against PM dismissed, *National Herald*, March 4

Anon, 1988, Yogendra Makwana forwards resignation letter, *Indian Express*, September 18

Anon, 1989, 30 p.c. reservation for women in panchayats: Rajiv, *Times of India*, May 5, col 1-3, news-item

Anon, 1989, AICC (I) revives dormant DCCs, *National Herald*, March 25

Anon, 1989, Ambedkar's portrait unveiled, *Indian Express*, August 10

Anon, 1989, Arjun Singh was still seen as a potential threat to Rajiv Gandhi though his influence in M.P. evidently diminished sharply between 1985 and 1989, *Hindu*, March 22

Anon, 1989, Ashan calls on Rajiv Gandhi, *National Herald*, April 12

Anon, 1989, Bahuguna cremated, *Times of India*, March 21

Anon, 1989, Bob Hawk's talks in New Delhi, *Times of India*, February 10

Anon, 1989, The Bodoland imbroglio, *Indian Express*, March 28

Anon, 1989, (Book Review), *Financial Express*, January 22, p 5, col 5-8
Review of the Book: **Venkateswaran, R.J.** and **Mithani, D.M.**, 1989, *Rajiv Gandhi: Economic perspective towards 21st century*, Himalaya Publishing House, Bombay, 239p.

Anon, 1989, (Book Review), *Financial Express*, August 13, p 5, col 1-4; *Sunday Statesman*, December 31, p 11, *Tribune* (Mangazine), July 23, p 2, col 1-6
Reivew of the Book: **Sen Gupta, Bhabani**, 1989, *Rajiv Gandhi: A Political Study*, Konark Publishers, Delhi, 220 p.

Anon, 1989, (Book Review), *Gandhi Marg* 10(12) March, p 805-807

Anon, 1989, (Book Review), *Patriot*, February 5, p 4, col 1-2
Review of the Book: **Pal, R.N.** and **Sudesh Rani**, 1988, *Information: Prime Minister's obligations*, Ghanshyam, New Delhi, 149 p.

Anon, 1989, (Book Review), *Sunday Statesman*, August 13, p 11, col 1-4
Review of the Book: **Varma, Umeshwar Prasad**, 1989, *Rajiv Gandhi and morality in public affairs*, Mittal Publishers, Delhi

Anon, 1989, (Book Review), *Tribune* (Sunday Review), August 6, p 2, col 1-6
Review of the Book: **Rajput, R.S.**, 1989, *Dynamics of democratic politics in India: A study of 1984 and 1985 Lok Sabha Election*, Deep and Deep Publishers, New Delhi, 185p.

Anon, 1989, Budhimir Loncar calls on PM, *National Herald*, May 4

Anon, 1989, CM calls on PM, *Times of India*, April 27

Anon, 1989, The compulsions of change, *Illustrated Weekly of India* 110(35) August 27, p 6-7

Anon, 1989, Congress leaders in mood of disaffection, *Link* 32(3) August 27, p 6-7

Anon, 1989, Congress promises power to people: Vow to make DD Corporation, *Times of India*, November 7, col 1-3+

Anon, 1989, DMK MPs meet PM, *Indian Express*, April 6

Anon, 1989, An elderly Congress leader and Member of the Rajya Sabha, B. Chiman Bhai Mehta expelled from the Party, urged the Party to elect a new leader to replace Rajiv Gandhi: The first such vocie to be raised, *Indian Express*, March 21

Anon, 1989, Five Deputy ministers promoted, *Hindu*, July 5

Anon, 1989, Ghali calls on PM, *Hindustan Times*, Apri 29

Anon, 1989, Government announces new rural job scheme, *National Herald*, April 29; *Telegraph*, April 29

Anon, 1989, Grass-root system to eleminate power broker: PM, *Times of India*, May, p 1, col 1-3, news-item

Anon, 1989, How much do we owe?, *Indian Express*, March 16

Anon, 1989, Hun Sen holds talks with Rajiv Gandhi, *Times of India*, November 17

Anon, 1989, Independence Day celebrated, *Hindu*, August 16; *Hindustan Times*, August 16; *Times of India*, August 16

Anon, 1989, India ready for talks with Nepal, says Rajiv Gandhi, *National Herald*, April 17; *Statesman*, April 17, news-item

Anon, 1989, India ready for talks with Nepal: China not behind trouble, PM, *Times of India*, April 17, p 1, col 1-3+

Anon, 1989, India to decide on pull out if no talks held, *National Herald*, July 13

Anon, 1989, India will fulfil terms of treaty with Lanka: PM, *Times of India*, July 18, p 1, col 1-3+

Anon, 1989, India, Pak sign three accords: N-Plant not to be attacked, *Times of India*, January 1, p 1, col 1-3

Anon, 1989, Involve weaker section in PRIS, *Kurukshetra* 37(5) February, p 6-7, news-item

Anon, 1989, Iranian leader calls on Rajiv Gandhi, *National Herald*, April 27

Anon, 1989, JD MPs write to PM on Bofors issue, *Times of India*, June 1

Anon, 1989, Joint panel to be set up, *Hindustan Times*, March 30

Anon, 1989, Kamentsev meets Rajiv Gandhi, *Hindu*, March 10

Anon, 1989, Lanka disputes Rajiv's stand on IPKF pull out, *Times of India*, June 16, p 1, col 1-3

Anon, 1989, Liang calls on Rajiv Gandhi, *National Herald*, March 2; *Statesman*, March 2

Anon, 1989, Mahatab's portrait unveiled, *National Herald*, August 8

Anon, 1989, Nagarpalika Bill introduced, *Indian Express*, August 8

Anon, 1989, National Conference on Panchayati Raj and Seheduled Tribes, *Statesman*, March 5

Anon, 1989, Nepal welcomes offer to hold talks, *Times of India*, April 19

Anon, 1989, Omanese leader calls on Rajiv Gandhi, *Hindustan Times*, March 9

Anon, 1989, On the come back trail, *Illustrated Weekly of India* 110(29) July 16, p 10-19

Anon, 1989, Opposition fanning communalism: Rajiv, *Times of India*, April 30, p 1, col 1-3+, news-item

Anon, 1989, Opposition walkout in LS over PM's remarks, *Hindustan Times*, April 6, *Telegraph*, April 6

Anon, 1989, PM, Cuellar meet, *Indian Express*, February 28

Anon, 1989, PM, Ghising hold talks, *Indian Express*, May 19

Anon, 1989, PM, Mitterand hold talks with Rajiv Gandhi, *Hindu*, February 2; *Hindustan Times*, February 2

Anon, 1989, PM, Wu optimistic on border, *Times of India*, October 14, p 1, col 2-4+

Anon, 1989, PM addresses Panchayati Raj Sammelan, *Hindu*, April 4, news-item

Anon, 1989, PM affirms support for Panchayati Raj, *Statesman* April 30, news-item

Anon, 1989, PM announces probe into Thakkar report leak, *Telegraph*, April 11, news-item

Anon, 1989, PM announces urban job plan, *Hindustan Times*, October 12, news-item

Anon, 1989, PM blames Pak for vitiating ties, *Times of India*, July 12, p 1, col 1-3+

Anon, 1989, PM dedicates Nhava Sheva port to the nation, *Hindustan Times*, May 27

Anon, 1989, PM denies involvement in Bofors deal, *Sunday* November 1

Anon, 1989, PM expresses concern over Pak nuclear plan, *Free Press Journal* February 4; *Times of India*, Feburary 4, news-item

Anon, 1989, PM for time frame for IPKF pull out, *Sunday* July 5, news-item

Anon, 1989, PM for unified plan for rural, urban areas, *National Herald*, June 9, news-item

Anon, 1989, PM holds talks with Gorbachev, *Hindustan Times*, July 16; *Times of India*, July 16

Anon, 1989, PM holds talks with Polish Vice-President, *National Herald*, April 13

Anon, 1989, PM inagurates the National Convention of AICC (I) legal cell, *National Herald*, August 23; *Times of India*, August 23

Anon, 1989, PM not to attend CHOGM, *National Herald*, October 18

Anon, 1989, PM reaffirms support to PLO, *Times of India*, May 5

Anon, 1989, PM reviews Punjab package, *Hindustan Times*, April 22

Anon, 1989, PM reviews Punjab situation, *Hindustan Times*, March 30

Anon, 1989, PM submits resignation: Nominated CPP leader again, *Times of India*, November 30, p 1, col 1-4

Anon, 1989, PM takes charge of Communications Ministry, *Indian Express*, June 1

Anon, 1989, PM urged to visit Gohpur, *Times of India*, August 14

Anon, 1989, PM vows to fight seperatism, *Economic Times*, August 16, p 5, col 1-2, news-item

Anon, 1989, PM writes to Premdasa, *Times of India*, June 21, news-item

Anon, 1989, PM's Address to Bharat Krishak Samaj, *National Herald* February 7, news-item

Anon, 1989, PM's package for Punjab, *Hindu*, March 4; *National Herald*, March 4

Anon, 1989, PM's reply to Premdasa, *Hindustan Times*, July 1, news-item

Anon, 1989, PM's visit concludes, *Telegraph*, July 18

Anon, 1989, Perumal calls for decisive move, *Times of India*, July 20

Anon, 1989, Perumal holds further talks, *National Herald*, March 22; *Statesman*, March 22

Anon, 1989, Population control and grassroots development, *Mainstream* 27(53) September 30, p 10-12

Anon, 1989, Premadasa writes to Rajiv Gandhi, *Hindustan Times*, July 23

Anon, 1989, Premdasa's reply to Rajiv Gandhi's letter, *Hindustan Times*, July 14

Anon, 1989, President, PM express grief over Khomeini's death, *Times of India*, June 5

Anon, 1989, Press conference, *Hindustan Times*, January 1; *Hindustan Times*, July 18

Anon, 1989, Rajiv, Birendra to meet on September 4, *Hindustan*

Anon, 1989, Rajiv: Leader of Opposition, *Telegraph*, December 21

Anon, 1989, Rajiv Gandhi addresses UPCC (I) Convention, *Times of India*, February 11

Anon, 1989, Rajiv Gandhi, Mitterand hold talks, *National Herald*, July 14; *Times of India*, July 14

Anon, 1989, Rajiv Gandhi, Perumal hold discussion, *Hindustan Times*, August 13

Anon, 1989, Rajiv Gandhi, V.P. Singh elected, *Hindustan Times*, November 30; *Times of India*, November 30

Anon, 1989, Rajiv Gandhi arrives in Paris, *National Herald*, July 13

Anon, 1989, Rajiv Gandhi files nomination from Amethi, *Times of India*, October 25

Anon, 1989, Rajiv Gandhi holds talks with Benazir, *Indian Express*, July 7; *National Herald*, July 7

Anon, 1989, Rajiv Gandhi holds talks with Thatcher, *Indian Express*, July 15

Anon, 1989, Rajiv Gandhi's Address to Seva Dal Convention, *Times of India*, May 14

Anon, 1989, Rajiv Gandhi's plan for Planet Protection Fund to be considered, *Indian Express*, November 21; *Times of India*, November 21

Anon, 1989, Rajiv in search of a poll strategy, *Link* 31(41) May 21, p 13-14

Anon, 1989, Rajiv Leader of Opposition, *Telegraph*, December 21

Anon, 1989, Rajiv promises 'Ram Rajya', *Times of India*, November 4, p 1, col 2-3+

Anon, 1989, Rajiv questions BJP's patriotism, *Times of India*, November 19, p 1

Anon, 1989, Rajiv's Pak encounter, *Link* 31(50) July 23, p 5-7

Anon, 1989, Reaching the people, *Janata* 44(26) October 1, p 5-6+

Anon, 1989, Sensitive parts of report not be tabled: Buta, *Times of India*, March 29, p 1, col 1-3, news-item

Anon, 1989, So much so that two AICC officials sent by Rajiv Gandhi to Patna to quieten the rebels had to flee to Delhi following skirmishes between two groups, *Statesman*, March 10

Anon, 1989, Soviet Minister calls on PM, *National Herald*, May 25

Anon, 1989, Syrian Minister calls on Rajiv Gandhi, *Hindustan Times*, April 26

Anon, 1989, Thailand PM holds further talks with Rajiv Gandhi, *Telegraph*, March 31

Anon, 1989, Thondaman calls for fresh accord, *Times of India*, July 10

Anon, 1989, Thondaman calls on Rajiv Gandhi, *Times of India*, July 9

Anon, 1989, Three agreements signed, *National Herald*, January 1

Anon, 1989, Turkish President in New Delhi, *Stetesman*, February 23

Anon, 1989, Velayati, PM hold talks, *Hindustan Times*, August 30

Anon, 1989, Vorontsov holds talks with Rajiv Gandhi, *Hindustan Times*, February 17

Anon, 1989, Wakil holds talks with Rajiv Gandhi, *Hindustan Times*, March 4

Anon, 1989, Wijeratne calls on Rajiv Gandhi, *National Herald*, August 1

Anon, 1989, Wu meets Rajiv Gandhi, *Hindustan Times*, October 14

Anon, 1989, Yaqub Khan calls on PM, *Hindustan Times*, July 26

Anon, 1989, Yaqub meets PM, *Times of India*, April 18

Anon, 1990, AICC (I) meet continues, *National Herald*, July 24

Anon, 1990 AICC (I) session begins, *Statesman*, July 23; *Times of India*, July 23

Anon, 1990, AICC (I) session concludes, *Hindustan Times*, July 25

Anon, 1990, (Book Review), *Financial Express*, December 2, p 9, col 1-4.
Review of the Book: **Rasgotra, Maharajakrishna**, ed., 1990, *Rajiv Gandhi's World View*, New Delhi, Vikas Publishing House, 265p.,

Anon, 1990, (Book Review), *Hindustan Times* (Magazine), March 11, p 5, col 1-4
Review of the book: **Hari Jaisingh**, 1990, *India after Indira: The turbulent years (1984-1989)*, Allied Publishers, New Delhi, 207 p.

Anon, 1990, (Book Review), *Indian Express* (Magazine), November 18, p 4, col 1-8.
Review of the Book: **Nungent, Nicholas**, 1990, *Rajiv Gandhi: Son of a dynasty*, BBC Books.

Anon, 1990, CWC meet: Government vacillating: Rajiv, *Times of India*, April 7, p 1, col 1-3+, news-item

Anon, 1990. CWC-I meet begins *Hindu*, September 15; *Hindustan Times*, September 15; *Times of India*, September 15

Anon, 1990, CWC-I meeting, *Times of India*, June 19

Anon, 1990. CWC-I meets, *Hindustan Times*, April 7; *Times of India*, April 7

Anon, 1990, CWC-I re-constituted, *Times of India*, June 30

Anon, 1990, Congress (I) convention against communalism, *Times of India*, May 20

Anon, 1990, Congress (I) rally in Delhi, *Statesman*, May 6

Anon, 1990, Congress rout in Assembly polls: Rethinking on Rajiv's leadership, *Link* 32(30) March 4, p 5-7

Anon, 1990, Dikshit resigns from CWC-I, *Times of India*, May 8

Anon, 1990, Enter Mr Gandhi, the Party boss, *Economic Times*, July 28, p 1, col 2-5

Anon, 1990, How long can Rajiv keep aflot? *Link* 32(37) April 22, p 10-11

Anon, 1990, The loneliness of Rajiv Gandhi, *Illustrated Weekly of India* 111(9) March 4, p 11-19

Anon, 1990, Nation pays homage to Indira Gandhi, *Hindustan Times*, November 1

Anon, 1990, National Front colluding with seperatists: Rajiv, *Economic Times*, July 24, p 1, col 6-8, news-item

Anon, 1990, Rajiv for any non-BJP government, *Times of India*, October 21, news-item

Anon, 1990, Rajiv Gandhi criticises NF government, *Times of India*, January 4

Anon, 1990, Rajiv Gandhi fails to make up lost ground, *Economic Times*, June 23, p 1, col 2-7+

Anon, 1990, Rajiv Gandhi leads fast, *Hindustan Times*, May 11

Anon, 1990, Rajiv Gandhi's letter to PM on Punjab election, *Statesman*, September 22

Anon, 1990, Rajiv under attack again, *Times of India*, April 18 p 1, col 2-8

Anon, 1990, Rajiv urged to correct style of functioning, *Times of India*, April 9, p 1, col 1-5

Anon, 1990, Remembering Nana, *Times of India* (Sunday Review), May 27, p 2,

col 1-6

Anon, 1990, Will Rajiv save Orissa Congress? *Link* 32(37) April 22, p 12-14

Anon, 1990, Writ against Rajiv Gandhi election dismissed, *Times of India*, April 11

Anon, 1991, 2 refugees arrested, wireless set seized, *Hindustan Times*, July 10, p 1, col 5

Anon, 1991, 6 cops challenge their suspension, *Hindustan Times*, August 10, p 20, col 1-4

Anon, 1991, 100 cr for Rajiv Foundation, *Hindustan Times*, July 25, p 3, col 6

Anon, 1991, ASEAN watching India poll scene, *Hindustan Times*, May 31, p 12, col 1-4

Anon, 1991, ASI among 6 suspended in Rajiv case, *Hindustan Times*, July 27, p 7, col 8

Anon, 1991, After Rajiv Gandhi, *Economic and Political Weekly* 26(21) May 25, p 1307, col 1-2

Anon, 1991, All out effort to resolve Congress (I) leadership crisis, *Hindustan Times*, May 26, p 1, col 1-3 +

Anon, 1991, Allegation against Chandraswami, *Statesman*, August 10, p 4, col 3-4

Anon, 1991, Amitabh as Party Chief demanded, *Hindustan Times*, May 28, p 7, col 1

Anon, 1991, Another judge soon to probe Rajiv murder, *Hindustan Times*, August 2, p 10, col 5

Anon, 1991, Arif's letter to PM: Communal divide in secular party, *Times of India*, September 25, p 1, col 2-5+

Anon, 1991, Ashes immersed as sun set over Yamuna, *Hindustan Times*, May 31, p 5, col 1-2

Anon, 1991, Ashes immersion at 'Sangam', *Hindustan Times*, May 26, p 7, col 1-2

Anon, 1991, Ashes scattered over Himalayas, *Hindustan Times*, May 30, p 5, col 1-4

Anon, 1991, Ashes to be immersed in Yamuna, *Hindustan Times*, May 30, p 5, col 4

Anon, 1991, Assassin an LTTE member: SIT, *Hindustan Times*, July 6, p 1, col 3, news-item

Anon, 1991, Assassin expelled from LTTE? *Hindustan Times*, May 31, p 9, col 7

Anon, 1991, Assassin identified, *Hindustan Times*, June 3, p 1, col 8+

Anon, 1991, Assassination and after in North East, *Economic and Political Weekly*, 26(22-23) June 1-8, p 1383

Anon, 1991, The assassination: A confusing scenario, *Hindustan Times* (Sunday Magazine), June 2, p 1, col 1-8+

Anon, 1991, Assassins being given shelter: SIT, *Hindustan Times*, June 23, p 12, col 3, news-item

Anon, 1991, BJP blame LTTE for killing, *Hindustan Times*, May 26, p 8, col 7

Anon, 1991, BJP seeks probe, *Hindustan Times*, May 30, p 10, col 1

Anon, 1991, BJP seeks wider probe, *Hindustan Times* May 30, p 8, col 5-7

Anon, 1991, Bail disallowed in Rajiv case, *Hindustan Times*, July 30, p 10, col 2-3.

Anon, 1991, Ball is in Rajiv court, says Patil, *Hindustan Times*, March 28, p 10, col 4, news-item

Anon, 1991, Basu flays Rajiv's remarks on polls, *Hindustan Times*, May 8, p 20, col 1-2

Anon, 1991, Bengal House pays tributes to Rajiv, *Hindustan Times*, July 20, p 10, col 5

Anon, 1991, Bengal poll may not be fair, *Hindustan Times*, May 7, p 9, col 6

Anon, 1991, Bharat Ratna conferred on Rajiv, *Hindustan Times*, July 7, p 1, col 1

Anon, 1991, Bharat Ratna for Rajiv, Sarder Patel, *Hindustan Times*, June 18, p 1, col 5

Anon, 1991, Bid to subvert Rajiv probe, *Hindustan Times*, August 10, p 9, col 1

Anon, 1991, Biju flays Rajiv, BJP, *Hindustan Times*, April 3, p 7, col 2-4

Anon, 1991, Break through in Rajiv case: Woman, son held for sheltering assassin, *Hindustan Times*, June 13, p 1, col 6-8+

Anon, 1991, CBI raises reward to Rs 10 lakh, *Hindustan Times*, June 6, p 10, col 1

Anon, 1991, CBI team to visit Lanka today, *Hindustan Times*, May 30, p 16, col 1

Anon, 1991, CBI told to handover Rajiv's clothes, *Hindustan Times*, July 18, p 7, col 5

Anon, 1991, CPB will urge Sonia to contest, *Hindustan Times*, October 8, p 1, col 1

Anon, 1991, Capital is normal, *Hindustan Times*, May 26, p 5, col 4

Anon, 1991, Case against LTTE almost wrapped up, *Hindustan Times*, November 17, p 6, col 7-8

Anon, 1991, Case for better equation between Shekhar and Rajiv, *Link* 33(23) January 18, p 12-15.

Anon, 1991, Change in campaigning after assassination, *Hindustan Times*, June 3, p 10, col 2-4

Anon, 1991, Chavan: Foreign hand suspected in Rajiv killing, *Hindustan Times*, July 27, p 1, col 1-3+, news-items

Anon, 1991, Cherishing a Rajiv memento, *Hindustan Times*, May 30, p 8, col 4

Anon, 1991, Chiman, Rajiv to resume talks, *Hindustan Times*, April 15, p 9, col 5

Anon, 1991, A clear Rajiv wave: Congress, *Hindustan Times*, March 28, p 5, col 1-3

Anon, 1991, Clinching evidence of LTTE hand: Aide of Sivarasan held, *Hindustan Times*, July 23, p 1, col 5-7.

Anon, 1991, Condolence messages continue to pour in, *Hindustan Times*, May 28, p 5, col 4-5

Anon, 1991, The Congress concern over the current scenario, *Democratic World* 20(1) January 6, p 5, col 1-3

Anon, 1991, Congress (I) asks for clarifications on refuelling issue, *Indian Express*, February 19

Anon, 1991, Congress (I) blames NF for killing, *Hindustan Times*, May 31, p 10, col 5-7

Anon, 1991, Congress (I) manifesto released, *Hindustan Times*, April 17,

Anon, 1991, Congress (I) views on refuelling issue, *Hindustan Times*, February 17, p 18, col 2

Anon, 1991, Congress leaders rated PM above Rajiv, *Hindustan Times*, April 26, p 18, col 2-3

Anon, 1991, Congress MPs warn against cut in fertiliser subsidy, *Hindustan Times*, August 2, p 1, col 2-4

Anon, 1991, Congress plans new strategy, *Hindustan Times*, May 28, p 16, col 1-3

Anon, 1991, Congress to support Shekhar from outside, *Times of India*, November 7, p 1, col 1-4.

Anon, 1991, Congress without Rajiv Gandhi, *Link*, 33(43) June 2, p 5-8.

Anon, 1991, Conspiracy behind killing: Tiwari, *Hindustan Times*, June 6, p 7 col 2-7, news-item

Anon, 1991, The conspiracy that back-fired, *Organiser* 42(32) March 17, p 1+

Anon, 1991, Cowardly act, *Hindustan Times*, May 31, p 11, col 2-6, letters to the editor

Anon, 1991, Crisis in Kashmir Valley: Jagmohan's open letter to Rajiv, *Democratic World* 20(19) May 12, p 1, col 1-2

Anon, 1991, DPCC(I) for Sonia to be Party Chief, *Hindustan Times*, May 26, p 5, col 1

Anon, 1991, Dead men tell tales? *Illustrated Weekly of India* July 6-July 12, p 10-11

Anon, 1991, Decision soon to widen Rajiv probe, *Hindustan Times*, July 18, p 9, col 1-4

Anon, 1991, 'Definite' foreign hand in blast, *Hindustan Times*, May 30, p 4, col 3

Anon, 1991, Devi Lal seeking new equation with Rajiv as Chandra Shekhar's boat seems sinking, *Organiser* 42(25) January 27, p 64, col 1-3

Anon, 1991, The dry run: Sivarasan at V.P. Singh meeting, *Frontline* July 20-August 2, p 128 +

Anon, 1991, End of cold war 'disoriented' India, *Hindustan Times*, May 31, p 13, col 2-3

Anon, 1991, Era comes to an end, *Hindustan Times*, June 6, p 11, col 2-5, letters to editor

Anon, 1991, Family matters: Is this the end for the Gandhi dynasty, *Sunday* June 2-June 8, p 38-39

Anon, 1991, Farewell: India mourns a decent man, *Sunday* June 2-June 8, p 4-11

Anon, 1991, Four new AICC (I) General Secretaries appointed, *Times of India*, February 15, p 16, col 2

Anon, 1991, Free hand to Rajiv on MP candidates, *Hindustan Times*, March 30, p 12, col 4

Anon, 1991, Furore over remarks on Rajiv's killing, *Hindustan Times*, July 3, p 4, col 4-7

Anon, 1991, Getting away with murder, *India Today* June 15, p 53, col 1-2

Anon, 1991, Government flayed on assassination, *Hindustan Times*, May 30, p 3, col 1

Anon, 1991, 'Havan' for Rajiv's soul, *Hindustan Times*, May 31, p 5, col 1-3

Anon, 1991, Hegde call for Cong men's unity, *Hindustan Times*, May 28, p 7, col 1-2

Anon, 1991, A Helmerian tribute to Rajiv Gandhi, *Bulletin of the Association of*

Scientific Workers of India 21(7) July, p 97-100

Anon, 1991, How Congress strategy failed? *Democratic World* 20(11) March 17, p 5, col 1-3 +

Anon, 1991, How wives make politicians, *Probe India* June, p 55-58

Anon, 1991, Hunt for Kanthan in Bangalore, *Hindustan Times*, September 3

Anon, 1991, Hunt on for one-eyed jack: SIT, *Hindustan Times*, June 14, p 1, col 1+, news-item

Anon, 1991, Ideals of Rajiv called, *Hindustan Times*, June 16, p 7, col 4

Anon, 1991, India's democracy to respond 'sturdily', *Hindustan Times*, May 28, p 11, col 5-7

Anon, 1991, Indian Leaders express shock, *Democratic World* 20(21) May 26, p 6, col 1-3

Anon, 1991, Information on Rajiv invited, *Hindustan Times*, June 24, p 7, col 8

Anon, 1991, An insider's story, *Illustrated Weekly of India* (Supplement) 112(18), May 4, p 5

Anon, 1991, Interrogation of DMK leaders demanded, *Hindustan Times*, June 4, p 4, col 3-4

Anon, 1991, JD warning on urn with ashes, *Hindustan Times*, May 28, p 6, col 6-7

Anon, 1991, Jagmohan arraigns Rajiv for Kashmir crisis: Anyone trying to be fair is dubbed communal, *Organiser* 62(39) May 5, p 15+

Anon, 1991, Judges were against accepting probe offer, *Hindustan Times*, May, 28, p 5, col 5-6

Anon, 1991, Kalash train leaves behind journalists, *Hindustan Times*, May 30, p 5, col 5

Anon, 1991, Karnataka House mourns Rajiv, *Hindustan Times*, July 6, p 9, col 1

Anon, 1991, Karnataka PCC offer to Rajiv, *Hindustan Times*, April 13, p 1, col 8

Anon, 1991, Karunanidhi blames Central rule, *Hindustan Times*, June 2, p 12, col 5-8

Anon, 1991, Kashmiri Pandits confront Rajiv, *Organiser* 42(25) January 27, p 65, col 1-2

Anon, 1991, Keeping an eye on Rajiv and making an extra buck, *Times of India*, March 10, p 1, col 2-7

Anon, 1991, Key suspect found hanging, *Hindustan Times*, July 21, p 1, col 4-7.

Anon, 1991, Khashoggi Rajiv confabulation: Embarrassment for Cong? *Times of India*, February 1, p 1, col 6-8+

Anon, 1991, Killer was Sundari from Vauuniya in Sri Lanka? *Hindustan Times*, June 2, p 1, col 5-7

Anon, 1991, Killers used LTTE as cover: Kittu, *Hindustan Times*, June 2, p 15, col 8

Anon, 1991, Killers wanted to slip into Nepal, *Hindustan Times*, July 7, p 1, col 1-4

Anon, 1991, LF to boycott meet on Rajiv, *Hindustan Times*, May 26, p 9, col 1-2

Anon, 1991, LTTE cadres panic in UK, *Hindustan Times*, June 16, p 15, col 3

Anon, 1991, LTTE man detained, *Hindustan Times*, June 9, p 12, col 5

Anon, 1991, LTTE offer to help probe, *Hindustan Times*, June 7, p 1, col 8

Anon, 1991, LTTE owns 'onus' for Rajiv killing, *Hindustan Times*, July 15, p 1, col 1

Anon, 1991, LTTE planned mass killings in Sept, *Hindustan Times*, July 17, p 7, col 7-8

Anon, 1991, LTTE publication seized, *Hindustan Times*, July 23, p 6, col 1

Anon, 1991, LTTE refuses to own Rajiv's murder, *Organiser* 62(44) June 9, p 14, col 4-5+

Anon, 1991, LTTE very much involved: Chavan, *Hindustan Times*, May 31', p 13, col 5-6, news-item

Anon, 1991, LTTE youth might spill the beams, says Lanka, *Hindustan Times*, June 10, p 13, col 2-4

Anon, 1991, Laloo: Assassination won't influence voters, *Hindustan Times*, May 28, p 16, col 4+5

Anon, 1991, Lanka rushes assassin's photo to SIT, *Hindustan Times*, July 10, p 12, col 6

Anon, 1991, Lankan says he knows accomplice, *Hindustan Times*, June 10, p 13, col 1-3

Anon, 1991, Leaders recall fine qualities of Rajiv, *Hindustan Times*, June 2, p 7, col 4-7

Anon, 1991, Legacy flayed: NYT, *Hindustan Times*, May 28, p 10, col 4

Anon, 1991, Lensman held in Rajiv case, *Hindustan Times*, July 3, p 1, col 1

Anon, 1991, Little headway in Rajiv murder case: Bhartiya Janta Party demand thorough judicial probe, *Organiser* 62(44) June 9, p 15, col 3-5

Anon, 1991, Major break in Rajiv murder case: 2 Lankans held in Delhi, *Hindustan Times*, July 6, p 1, col 5-7 +

Anon, 1991, Many Rajiv organs damaged, *Hindustan Times*, May 30, p 3, col 6-8

Anon, 1991, Maragatham meets Sonia, *Hindustan Times*, July 10, p 3, col 2

Anon, 1991, Media probe irks SIT, *Hindustan Times*, May 28, p 7, col 6-8

Anon, 1991, More suicides in some States, *Hindustan Times*, May 26, p 1, col 4-5 +

Anon, 1991, Move to desabilise India: Swamy, *Hindustan Times*, June 2, p 19, col 1-4, news-item

Anon, 1991, Moving ahead, *Illustrated Weekly of India*, 112(22) June 1, p 4.

Anon, 1991, Mulayam Singh blackmails Rajiv with anti-Congress reports on riots, *Organiser* 42(22) January 6, p 7, col 1-5

Anon, 1991, Multi-faith prayer meet, *Hindustan Times*, May 26, p 12, col 1

Anon, 1991, Murugan had affair with Nalini, *Hindustan Times*, July 6, p 10, col 5-8

Anon, 1991, Nalini, Murugan now in judicial custody, *Indian Express*, August, 10, p 9, col 7-8

Anon, 1991, Nalini, Murugan remanded, *Hindustan Times*, June 16, p 1, col 5+

Anon, 1991, Name DU after Rajiv: NSUI, *Hindustan Times*, May 30, p 3, col 4

Anon, 1991, Nation will emerge stronger: Chandra, *Hindustan Times*, May 31, p 3, col 2-3

Anon, 1991, Nehru too came to Sriperumbudur, *Hindustan Times*, June 3, p 7, col 1-4

Anon, 1991, The New Rajiv: Five key questions about his style, *Sunday* May 11, p

32-35
Anon, 1991, No change in PM security, *Hindustan Times*, June 6, p 10, col 1
Anon, 1991, No change in SIT: Chavan, *Hindustan Times*, August 11, p 16, col 1-3, news-item
Anon, 1991, No controversy, says Arjun Singh, *Hindustan Times*, May 31, p 7, col 2-3, news-item
Anon, 1991, No deviation from Rajiv path: PM, *Hindustan Times*, July 2, p 6, col 8, news-item
Anon, 1991, No hand in killing, insists LTTE, *Hindustan Times*, May 31, p 13, col 5-6
Anon, 1991, No headway in probe: Sahay, *Hindustan Times*, May 30, p 1, col 6-7, news-item
Anon, 1991, No political role for me: Amitabh, *Hindustan Times*, June 2, p 1, col 3, news-item
Anon, 1991, On leads, modes, linkages, *Frontline* June 22-July 5, p 37-38
Anon, 1991, On the killer trail, *Frontline* June 22-July 5, p 21-28.
Anon, 1991, One more held in assassination case, *Hindustan Times*, June 27, p 1, col 4-5
Anon, 1991, Other possibilities, *Hindustan Times* (Sunday Magazine), June 2, p 2, col 5-8
Anon, 1991, PM: Rajiv's statement not fair, *Hindustan Times*, May 9, p 7, col 1, news-item
Anon, 1991, PM, Rajiv Gandhi meet President, *Times of India*, February 10
Anon, 1991, PM briefs RV on law and order, *Hindustan Times*, May 28, p 1, col 5
Anon, 1991, PM hits back at Congress (I), *Organiser* 42(31) March 10, p 1, col 1-3+
Anon, 1991, PM trustee of Rajiv Foundation, *Hindustan Times*, July 14, p 12, col 1
Anon, 1991, Panel probe on Rajiv urged, *Hindustan Times*, June 3, p 5, col 1
Anon, 1991, Party focus on Indira, Rajiv in Maharashtra, *Hindustan Times*, June 2, p 19, col 1-3
Anon, 1991, Patel, Rajiv talks on seat-sharing, *Hindustan Times*, April 14, p 5, col 1
Anon, 1991, The Pawar game, *Organiser* 42(27) February 10, p 2, col 1-5
Anon, 1991, Petition in Rajiv case admitted, *Hindustan Times*, November 12, p 7, col 1.
Anon, 1991, Petition on Rajiv probe kept pending, *Hindustan Times*, July 9, p 4, col 5-6
Anon, 1991, Petitions for right to consult lawyers, *Hindustan Times*, July 9, p 4, col 2-3
Anon, 1991, Plan to take "Rajiv Jyoti" across country, *Hindustan Times*, July 30, p 5, col 2-3.
Anon, 1991, Plea to dissolve Congress (I), *Hindustan Times*, May 31, p 10, col 1
Anon, 1991, Plea to fight divisive forces, *Hindustan Times*, May 30, p 8, col 1-4
Anon, 1991, Pledge to complete Rajiv tasks, *Hindustan Times*, May 31, p 6, col 6-8.

Anon, 1991, Police had no metal detectors, *Hindustan Times*, May 28, p 16, col 4

Anon, 1991, Police questioning woman, *Hindustan Times*, May 28, p 1, col 1-3

Anon, 1991, Police wanted Rajiv poll meet venue changed, *Hindustan Times*, May 28, p 16, col 5-7

Anon, 1991, Political scenario changes due to Gulf War, *Democratic World* 20(4) January 27, p 5, col 1-3+

Anon, 1991, Politicising inquiries, *India Today*, June 30, p 11, col 1-2

Anon, 1991, Politics of violence, *Hindustan Times*, June 4, p 11, col 2-5, letter to the editor

Anon, 1991, Prabhakaran tried to reach Sivarasan, *Hindustan Times*, September 4

Anon, 1991, Prayer meet at Sriperumbudur, *Hindustan Times*, June, p 7, col 4

Anon, 1991, Prices, stability main issues: Rajiv, *Hindustan Times*, March 28, p 9, col 1-4, news-item

Anon, 1991, Prime Minister rules out truce with LTTE, *Hindu*, August 6, news-item

Anon, 1991, Punjab not ready for polls: Rajiv, *Hindustan Times*, April 14, p 5, col 2-3, news-item

Anon, 1991, R.V. for Shekar-Rajiv patch-up, *Democratic World* 20(8) February 24, p 7, col 2-3

Anon, 1991, Rajiv: Voice of sanity lost, *Hindustan Times*, May 30, p 5, col 1-3

Anon, 1991, Rajiv, Jayalalitha finalise poll-pact, *Hindustan Times*, March 31, p 1, col 1-3+

Anon, 1991, Rajiv-Pawar tussle, *Organiser* 42(25) January 27, p 66, col 2

Anon, 1991, Rajiv-Seshan flop show, *Organiser* 42(38) April 28, p 16, col 4

Anon, 1991, Rajiv accused of J and K mess, *Hindustan Times*, April 23, p 9, col 1-3

Anon, 1991, Rajiv accuses NF, BJP of dividing country, *Hindustan Times*, April 19, p 1, col 1-3

Anon, 1991, Rajiv and V.P. Singh highly frustrated as Advani named Leader of the Opposition, *Organiser* 42(22) January 6, p 1, col 1-5+

Anon, 1991, Rajiv apologised to Shekhar for a last minute patch-up, *Organiser* 42(3) March 24, p 5, col 1-5

Anon, 1991, Rajiv assails concept of motley Oppositaion, *Times of India*, December 14, p 7

Anon, 1991, Rajiv bore most of blast impact, *Hindustan Times*, June 4, p 10, col 1

Anon, 1991, Rajiv calls for Dalit's uplift, *Hindustan Times*, April 15, p 1, col 1-2

Anon, 1991, Rajiv calls for stable Government, *Hindustan Times* April 16, p 7, col 2-3

Anon, 1991, Rajiv case: Judicial custody for two, *Tribune*, August 10, p 5, col 1

Anon, 1991, Rajiv denies attack in Bihar town, *Hindustan Times*, March 29, p 1, col 8+, news-item

Anon, 1991, Rajiv denies grooming Rahul, *Hindustan Times*, March 31, p 18, col 17

Anon, 1991, Rajiv denies reports on wooing Left, *Hindustan Times*, May 10, p 22, col 5, news-item

Anon, 1991, Rajiv drive, *Frontline*, May 25-June 7, p 27

Anon, 1991, Rajiv files nomination, *Hindustan Times*, April 25, p 1, col 5-7
Anon, 1991, Rajiv firm on contesting from Amethi only, *Hindustan Times*, April 18, p 18, col 4
Anon, 1991, Rajiv flays communal forces, *Hindustan Times*, April 3, p 7, col 1
Anon, 1991, Rajiv flays non-Congress Parties claim, *Hindustan Times*, March 27, p 20, col 5
Anon, 1991, Rajiv flays Patnik's remarks, *Hindustan Times*, March 31, p 17, col 1, news-item
Anon, 1991, Rajiv flays Shekhar's stand on Gulf war, *Link* 33(25) January 27, p 31-34
Anon, 1991, Rajiv for Nuclear Policy review, *Times of India*, February 12, p 1, col 5-7+.
Anon, 1991, Rajiv Gandhi, Saddam and Bush, *Organiser* 42(33) March 24, p 16, col 4
Anon, 1991, Rajiv Gandhi calls for UNSC meeting on Gulf war, *Times of India*, February 8
Anon, 1991, Rajiv Gandhi calls on President, *Times of India*, February 14
Anon, 1991, Rajiv Gandhi calls for UNSC meeting on Gulf war, *Times of India*, February 18
Anon, 1991, Rajiv Gandhi Foundation set up, *Hindustan Times*, June 22, p 3, col 3
Anon, 1991, Rajiv Gandhi on the come back trail? *Democratic World* 20(9) March 3, p 5, col 1-3+
Anon, 1991, Rajiv Gandhi poised to take over as PM, *Organiser* 42(28) February 27, p 1, col 1-2+
Anon, 1991, Rajiv Gandhi's Bharat Darshan, *Democratic World* 20(21) May 26, p 5
Anon, 1991, Rajiv Gandhi's election upheld, *Times of India*, February 8
Anon, 1991, Rajiv Gandhi's letter to PM, *Hindustan Times*, February 11, p 12, col 2
Anon, 1991, Rajiv going the Saddam way, *Organiser* 42(32) March 17, p 1, col 3-4+
Anon, 1991, Rajiv greetings on Bengal Day, *Hindustan Times*, April 15, p 10, col 3
Anon, 1991, Rajiv had faith in scientists, *Hindustan Times*, June 3, p 10, col 7-8
Anon, 1991, Rajiv hopes to present a populist budget after toppling Shekhar, *Organiser* 42(30) March 3, p 1, col 1-5
Anon, 1991, Rajiv Jyoti reveals changed picture in Rajasthan, *Hindustan Times*, June 10, p 10, col 6-8
Anon, 1991, Rajiv knew of refuelling: PM, *Hindustan Times*, April 13, p 1, col 1, news-item
Anon, 1991, Rajiv Memorial Lecture, *Hindustan Times*, July 10, p 4, col 6
Anon, 1991, Rajiv murder politicised, says BJP, *Hindustan Times*, May 30, p 7, col 3, news-item
Anon, 1991, Rajiv pledges stable Govt, *Hindustan Times*, May 11, p 12, col 2-4
Anon, 1991, Rajiv shoes handed over to Sonia, *Hindustan Times*, June 20, p 10, col 5

Anon, 1991, The Rajiv take-over plan? *Democratic World* 20(7) February 17, p 8, col 1-3
Anon, 1991, Rajiv trusted women folk, *Hindustan Times*, June 2, p 19, col 3
Anon, 1991, Rajiv wants review of defence policy, *Hindustan Times*, April 28, p 12, col 1-2, news-item
Anon, 1991, Rajiv was a crusader for peace, justice: Dr Sharma, *Hindustan Times*, May 26, p 7, col 5-7, news-item
Anon, 1991, Rajiv was always smiling, says Sonia, *Hindustan Times*, June 16, p 15, co 1-2, news-item
Anon, 1991, Rajiv was leader of minorities, *Hindustan Times*, May 26, p 5, col 2-3
Anon, 1991, Rajiv was no quitter, says Amitabh, *Hindustan Times*, June 3, p 5, col 3-7, news-item
Anon, 1991, Rajiv wave caused BJP, Shiv Sena rout in Maharashtra, *Democratic World* 20(25) June 23, p 7
Anon, 1991, Rajiv wooing AMU students, *Organiser* 42(34) March 31, p 2 col 1-2
Anon, 1991, Rajiv's bid to play double role of the super PM and opposition leader, *Organiser* 42(23) January 13, p 3, col 2-4+
Anon, 1991, Rajiv's death a national tragedy, says Scindia, *Hindustan Times*, May 31, p 3, col 1-3, news-item
Anon, 1991, Rajiv's deepening displeasure with the defector PM, *Organiser* 42(29) February 24, p 3, col 1-3+
Anon, 1991, Rajiv's help to enviornment recalled, *Hindustan Times*, June 4, p 10, col 4
Anon, 1991, Rajiv's last moments, *Frontline* June 22-July 5, p 70+
Anon, 1991, Rajiv's optimism, *Democratic World* 20(11) March 17, p 7, col 2-3
Anon, 1991, Rajiv's personal contact, *Frontline* 8(12) June 8-June 21, p 24
Anon, 1991, Rajiv's zigzag, *India Today* April 30, p 38
Anon, 1991, Rajivji's deepening displeasure with the defector PM, *Organiser* 42(29) February 24, p 3, col 1-3+
Anon, 1991, Rajya Sabha condemns Rajiv assassination, *Hindustan Times*, June 4, p 1, col 2-4+
Anon, 1991, Rajya Sabha Session today: Elders to pay tributes to Rajiv, Dange, *Hindustan Times*, June 3, p 1, col 5-7, news-item
Anon, 1991, Ram, Rajiv poll planks flayed, *Hindustan Times*, June 7, p 9, col 2
Anon, 1991, Rangan keeps up disclosures, *Hindustan Times*, September 3
Anon, 1991, A rare Rajiv photo, *Hindustan Times*, June 3, p 8, col 6-8
Anon, 1991, Ray denies statemant on Rajiv death, *Hindustan Times*, May 28, p 8, col 8
Anon, 1991, The reluctant politician, *Sunday* June 2-June 8, p 32-37
Anon, 1991, Remember Bofors? *Sunday* May 12-May 18, p 88-93
Anon, 1991, Remember the wave? Rajiv Gandhi trics to recapture the spirit of 1984, *Sunday* April 25-May 1, p 28-31
Anon, 1991, Reporters irc over Rajiv Gandhi, *Hindustan Times*, April 16, p 10, col 4
Anon, 1991, Reports on Rajiv case 'fiction', *Hindustan Times*, July 18, p 9, col 1
Anon, 1991, Revalue tumbles since Rajiv killing, *Hindustan Times*, July 10, p 15,

col 1-2

Anon, 1991, Rich tributes paid to Rajiv, *Hindustan Times*, May 28, p , col 6-8

Anon, 1991, SIT finds vital data on Padmanablia killing, *Hindustan Times*, July 27, p 1, col 1-3+

Anon, 1991, SIT hunting for youth, 2 women, *Hindustan Times*, June 12, p 1, col 1-2+

Anon, 1991, SIT seizes cache of explosives, *Hindustan Times*, July 20, p 20, col 1.

Anon, 1991, Sad farewell from Delhi, *Hindustan Times*, May 28, p 1, col 5-7

Anon, 1991, Sad loss, says S.P. Hinduja, *Hindustan Times*, May 26, p 12, col 3

Anon, 1991, Sailor who hit Rajiv mourns death, *Hindustan Times*, May 30, p 11, col 1

Anon, 1991, Scindia's call to combat violence, *Hindustan Times*, June 3, p 5, col 2-3

Anon, 1991, Search for LTTE hide outs, *Hindustan Times*, July 29, p 7, col 1-2.

Anon, 1991, Search for Sivarasan accomplice, *Hindustan Times*, September 3

Anon, 1991, Search on for third accomplice, *Hindustan Times*, May 31, p 1, col 6-7 +

Anon, 1991, Secret link between NF, LTTE alleged, *Hindustan Times*, June 14, p 10, col 3

Anon, 1991, Security for Congress leaders beefed up, *Hindustan Times*, May 30, p 5, col 5-6

Anon, 1991, Sena leader for Rajiv's memorial, *Hindustan Times*, July 16, p 7, col 5

Anon, 1991, Shaktisthal lost in silence again, *Hindustan Times*, May 26, p 7, col 4-5

Anon, 1991, Shanmugam killed himself: Report, *Hindustan Times*, July 22, p 18, col 2-3.

Anon, 1991, Shanmugham's body is cremated, *Hindustan Times*, July 22, p 10, col 6.

Anon, 1991, Shanmugham's death: Judicial inquiry sought, *Hindustan Times*, July 30, p 1, col 5-7.

Anon, 1991, Sharp exchanges over Rajiv Trust, *Hindustan Times*, July 31, p 9, col 4-5

Anon, 1991, Shekhar betrayed trust: Rajiv, *Hindustan Times*, April 10, p 9, col 1-3, news-item

Anon, 1991, The shock wave, *Frontline* 8(12) June 8-June 21, p 28-29+

Anon, 1991, Shut up, *Hindustan Times*, July 18, p 9, col 4

Anon, 1991, Similar Bomb had killed Wijeratne, *Hindustan Times*, May 20, p 20, col 1

Anon, 1991, Sivarasan made the bomb used by killer, *Hindustan Times*, June 17, p 4, col 1-2

Anon, 1991, Sivarasan may flee to Lanka, *Hindustan Times*, June 30, p 1, col 3+

Anon, 1991, A sombre affair at station, *Hindustan Times*, May 28, p 3, col 1-3

Anon, 1991, Somewhere we lost communication with the people, *India Today*, May 31, p 24-25, news-item

Anon, 1991, Sonia Conusel gets Rajiv shoes, socks, *Hindustan Times*, June 18, p

9, col 5-6

Anon, 1991, Sonia detested politics, *Hindustan Times*, May 26, p 13, col 2-4.

Anon, 1991, Sonia no to grant for Trust, *Hindustan Times*, August 2, p 1, col 5

Anon, 1991, Sonia plea for consensus welcomed, *Hindustan Times*, May 28, p 6, col 8.

Anon, 1991, Sonia to chair Indira Trust, *Hindustan Times*, May 30, p 8, col 1.

Anon, 1991, Sonia to head Nehru Fund, *Hindustan Times*, May 31, p 10, col 4.

Anon, 1991, Sonia to retain Janpath bungalow, *Hindustan Times*, May 30, p 8, col 2-3.

Anon, 1991, Sonia wants Rajiv's sneakers, *Hindustan Times*, June 13, p 8, col 1

Anon, 1991, Sonia will launch Rajiv campaign, *Hindustan Times*, April 25, p 10, col 12

Anon, 1991, Spectacles of assassin recovered, *Hindustan Times*, May 26, p 10, col 1-4

Anon, 1991, Speech dedicated to Rajiv, *Hindustan Times*, July 25, p 18, col 5-6.

Anon, 1991, Sri Lankan officials see LTTE hand, *Hindustan Times*, May 26, p 12, col 2-3

Anon, 1991, Succession struggle, *Frontline*, 8(12) Jnue 8-June 21, p 120-121

Anon, 1991, Surveillance issue again rocks Parliament, *Hindustan Times*, March 6

Anon, 1991, Suspension for DIG in Rajiv case, *Hindustan Times*, July 14, p 1, col 8

Anon, 1991, Suspension over woman in Agra, *Hindustan Times*, June 7, col 8

Anon, 1991, Sympathy factor, *India Today* June 15, p 110-112

Anon, 1991, Sympathy wave of no help in HP, *Hindustan Times*, May 26, p 9, col 7-8

Anon, 1991, Sympathy wave may help Congress in Puri, *Hindustan Times*, May 30, p 7, col 4-5

Anon, 1991, Talking to Rajiv: Extracts from Sunday's interviews with the late leader, *Sunday* June 2-June 8, p 46-53

Anon, 1991, Tamil Nadu witnessed maximum bomb-shock and sympathy wave, *Democratic World* 20(25) June 3, p 8

Anon, 1991, The toppling of the turk: Rajiv Gandhi style, *Organiser* 42(33) March 24, p 3, col 2-4

Anon, 1991, Tributes to Rajiv by MP House, *Hindustan Times*, June 27, p 5, col 6

Anon, 1991, The twain met, *Sunday* January 13-January 19, p 36-37

Anon, 1991, Two LTTE men brought to Capital, *Hindustan Times*, June 9, p 10, col 3

Anon, 1991, UK House pays tributes to Rajiv, *Hindustan Times*, July 10, p 18, col 5

Anon, 1991, UN Council homage to Rajiv, *Hindustan Times*, May 26, p 12, col 4

Anon, 1991, US wanted Rajiv back, *Hindustan Times*, May 26, p 12, col 5-7

Anon, 1991, Unity of India will be safeguarded, says Rao, *Hindustan Times*, July 2, p 1, col 1-3+, news-item

Anon, 1991, Uproar in Parliament over surveillance of Rajiv Gandhi's house, *Times of India*, March 5

Anon, 1991, Verma to probe assassination, *Hindustan Times*, May 28, p 1, col 1-3

Anon, 1991, View point: Rajiv Gandhi, *Times of India* (Supplement), February 4, p 1, col 1-5+

Anon, 1991, Viscious killing, *Hindustan Times*, May 28, p 9, col 2-5, letter to the editor

Anon, 1991, Vital links missing in Rajiv case, *Hindustan Times*, July 31, p 6, col 3-5

Anon, 1991, Who is to blame? *Hindustan Times* (Sunday Magazine), June 2, p 2, col 5-8

Anon, 1991, Who switched off the Gulf War? Rajiv Gandhi, of course! *Organiser* 42(32) March 17, p 3, col 2-4

Anon, 1991, Why LTTE High Command ordered Rajiv's treacherous killing? *Link* 33(50) July 21, p 5-9

Anon, 1991, Why pick on the LTTE? *Sunday* June 23-june 29, p 64-65

Anon, 1991, Why post-Rajiv Congress looks so empty, *Democratic World* 20(25) June 3, p 23

Anon, 1991, Wife seeks property, *Hindustan Times*, September 3

Anon, 1991, Will Rajiv Gandhi explain? Who is responsible for the begging bowl? *Organiser* 42(39) May 5, p 1, col 1-3+

Anon, 1991, Will Rajiv ultimately take over? *Democratic World* 20(5) February 3, p 5, col 1-3

Anon, 1991, Writ against CBI in Rajiv case, *Hindustan Times*, July 11, p 18, col 6

Anon, 1992, Affidavits by suspects discounted, *Hindustan Times*, February 20, p 9, col 5

Anon, 1992, Arafat's homage to Rajiv, *Hindustan Times*, May 22, p 12, col 8

Anon, 1992, Assassination case takes a new turn, *Sunday Statesman*, April 5, p 4, col 4-5

Anon, 1992, BJP ridicules Cong on Anti-Terrorism Day, *Times of India*, May 23, p 5, col 1-4

Anon, 1992, Book on Rajiv released, *Indian Express*, May 22, p 4, col 2-3

Anon, 1992, Briton's tribute to Rajiv, *Hindustan Times*, May 23, p 13, col 1

Anon, 1992, CBI told to handover Rajiv's clothes, *Hindustan Times*, July 18, p 7, col 5

Anon, 1992, Capital remembers Rajiv, *Times of India*, May 22, p 11, col 3

Anon, 1992, Centre, organisers partly responsible, *Indian Express*, March 31, p 7, col 2-5

Anon, 1992, Chargesheet in Rajiv case filed: Killing plotted by Prabhakaran, *Hindustan Times*, May 21, p 1, col 1-3+

Anon, 1992, Chavan refutes charge in Rajiv killing case, *Hindustan Times*, March 13, p 15, col 5-6, news-item

Anon, 1992, China pays glowing tributes to Rajiv, *Patriot*, May 23, p 1, col 1

Anon, 1992, China pays homage to Rajiv, *Indian Express*, May 23, p 2, col 6-8

Anon, 1992, Concern at erasure of Rajiv video film, *Times of India*, March 11, p 4, col 5-8

Anon, 1992, Cong leaders had idea of threat to Rajiv, *Times of India*, April 4, p 18, col 1-4

Anon, 1992, Cover up in Rajiv case, alleges Jaya, *Times of India*, p 14, col 4, news-items

Anon, 1992, DMK meeting was cancelled, *Hindustan Times*, February 10, p 8, col 6-8.

Anon, 1992, Devotional songs at Rajiv Samadhi, *National Herald*, May 22, p 10, col 1-2

Anon, 1992, Documentary on Rajiv, *Indian Express*, May 23, p 11, col 5, news-item

Anon, 1992, Emotional outbursts on Rajiv Gandhi, *Hindustan Times*, April 15, p 1, col 6-7

Anon, 1992, Evidence in Rajiv case being concealed: Jaya, *Indian Express*, March 31, p 1, col 8+, news-item

Anon, 1992, Evidence of LTTE hand in Rajiv murder, *Hindustan Times*, April 17, p 10, col 4

Anon, 1992, Fight terrorism, says PM, *Hindustan Times*, May 22, p 1, col 5-7+, news-item

Anon, 1992, First hearing of Rajiv case on June 3, *Hindustan Times*, May 22, p 22, col 1

Anon, 1992, Gaps in crucial Rajiv Cassette, *The Independent*, April 3, p 6, col 5-6.

Anon, 1992, Garlander's list not correct, *Hindustan Times*, April 2, p 10, col 5-8.

Anon, 1992, Govt. denies tampering video tape, *Hindustan Times*, March 12, p 12, col 5.

Anon, 1992, India without Rajiv, *National Herald*, May 22, p 6, col 1-2

Anon, 1992, Indira Gandhi Peace Award for Rajiv, *Hindustan Times*, May 21, p 1, col 2-3

Anon, 1992, Indira, Rajiv statues to be erected, *Hindustan Times*, May 20, p 7, col 1

Anon, 1992, Jain panel yet to probe Rajiv assassination, *Indian Express*, March 27, p 7, col 5-6.

Anon, 1992, Justice J.S. Verma visits Sriperumbudur, *Hindustan Times*, March 23, p 7, col 1-3

Anon, 1992, LTTE blames Rajiv for massacre, *Hindustan Times*, March 4, p 22, col 5

Anon, 1992, LTTE planned for 9 months, *Tribune*, May 23, p 1, col 6-8

Anon, 1992, Lack of security, says Justice Verma, *National Herald*, April 4, p 1, col 5-6

Anon, 1992, Lanka Govt. linked in Rajiv assassination case, *Hindustan Times*, April 10, p 12, col 2-4

Anon, 1992, Lanka willing to extradite Rajiv killers, *Hindustan Times*, May 22, p 1, col 1-3+

Anon, 1992, List of garlanders not genuine, says Counsel, *National Herald*, April 2, p 10, col 5-7

Anon, 1992, Maragatham didn't discuss security, *Hindustan Times*, March 6, p 10, col 4-7.

Anon, 1992, Mobile libraries flagged off, *National Herald*, May 23, p 10, col 6-7

Anon, 1992, Move to find out assassin's route, *National Herald*, April 5, p 10, col 6-7

Anon, 1992, Music party arrival violated security, *Times of India*, March 16, p 3, col 4-5

Anon, 1992, Nation pays homage to Rajiv, *Indian Express*, May 22, p 1, col 5-7+; *Statesman*, May 22, p 1, col 2-3

Anon, 1992, No evidence on Rajiv's Swiss accounts, *Hindustan Times*, March 27, p 9, col 2-5

Anon, 1992, No tampering with cassettes: Chavan, *Times of India*, March 12, p 4, col 7-8, news-item

Anon, 1992, Non-Congmen too garlanded Rajiv, *Hindustan Times*, January 25, p 17, col 2-6

Anon, 1992, Offer on Rajiv Jyoti: Antony group in tight spot, *Hindustan Times*, April 30, p 7, col 5-7

Anon, 1992, PM pays homage, *Times of India*, May 22, p 3, col 1-2

Anon, 1992, PM releases NH Supplement, *National Herald*, (Supplement), May 22, p 10, col 3

Anon, 1992, Plea for testimony by suspended DIG, *Hindustan Times*, January 24, p 11, col 1-2

Anon, 1992, Pledge to eradicate terrorism, *Indian Express*, May 22, p 4, col 2-5

Anon, 1992, Police had provided 'full' security to Rajiv, panel told, *Hindustan Times*, March 30, p 12, col 5-7.

Anon, 1992, President pays tribute to Rajiv, *Hindustan Times*, January 6, p 18, col 8

Anon, 1992, Probe must to clear Rajiv's name: Aiyar, *National Herald*, April 2, p 1, col 1-2+, news-item

Anon, 1992, Probe team holds LTTE responsible, *Hindustan Times*, March 2, p 22, col 6-7.

Anon, 1992, Publication of Rajiv case trial banned, *Hindustan Times*, May 22, p 12, col 8

Anon, 1992, RV recalls Rajiv's vision, *Hindustan Times*, May 22, p 12, col 8

Anon, 1992, RV's call to live up to Rajiv ideals, *Hindustan Times*, May 21, p 12, col 1-4

Anon, 1992, Rajiv alive in our programmes: PM, *National Herald*, May 22, p 1, col 5-7+, news-item

Anon, 1992, Rajiv case hearing in June 3, *Times of India*, May 22, p 11, col 6

Anon, 1992, Rajiv case proceedings to be kept secret, *Statesman*, May 22, p 9, col 5

Anon, 1992, Rajiv Gandhi awarded Indira Peace Prize, *Independent*, May 21, p 6, col 3-8

Anon, 1992, Rajiv Gandhi torch bearer of national interest, *National Herald*, May 22, p 3, col 1

Anon, 1992, Rajiv the human being: An excerpt from Mani Shankar Aiyar's biography 'Remembering Rajiv', *Hindustan Times* (Magazine), May 3, p 9, col 1-8+

Anon, 1992, Rajiv Jyoti arrives in Bangalore, *Hindustan Times*, May 21, p 12, col 4

Anon, 1992, Rajiv Jyoti Yatra from May 10, *Hindustan Times*, May 9, p 3, col 1-3

Anon, 1992, Rajiv paved way for better ties with China, *National Herald*, May 23, p 16, col 6

Anon, 1992, Rajiv probe enters crucial phase, *Hindustan Times*, January 31, p 11, col 1-4

Anon, 1992, Rajiv remembered with heavy heart, *National Herald*, May 22, p 1, col 4-5

Anon, 1992, Rajiv Sandesh Yatra begins, *Hindustan Times*, May 11, p 1, col 4-5+

Anon, 1992, Rajiv technology mission in AP, *National Herald*, May 23, p 10, col 1-2

Anon, 1992, Rajiv was mobbed, Verma Panel told, *Times of India*, March 4, p 3, col 6-7

Anon, 1992, Rajiv worked for modern India, *National Herald*, May 22, p 3, col 2-5

Anon, 1992, Rajiv's death anniversary observed as Anti-Terrorism Day, *Economic Times*, May 22, p 13, col 1-6

Anon, 1992, Rajiv's dream will come true: Scindia, *Hindustan Times*, May 22, p 12, col 5-8

Anon, 1992, Rooting out terrorism best tribute to Rajiv, *National Herald*, May 22, p 3, col 6-8

Anon, 1992, SIT: Dhanu was not gang-raped, *Hindustan Times*, May 23, p 7, col 6

Anon, 1992, SIT chargesheet: Assassination after 9-month planning, *Hindustan Times*, May 23, p 20, col 1-4

Anon, 1992, SIT Chief denies reports, *Times of India*, May 23, p 3, col 2, news-item

Anon, 1992, Security for Rajiv improper, panel told, *Hindustan Times*, April 28, p 10, col 6-7

Anon, 1992, Security lapses at Sriperumbudur: No escape for cops, leaders, *Hindustan Times*, April 4, p 4, col 4-6

Anon, 1992, Shadow of infighting dim Rajiv Jyoti, *Times of India*, May 22, p 3, col 2-5

Anon, 1992, Sivarasan had mole in AICC, *Statesman*, April 1, p 14, col 7-8

Anon, 1992, Sivarasan, Subha took shelter in TN, Kerala, *Sunday Tribure*, May 24, p 4, col 45

Anon, 1992, Six move held in Rajiv case, *Hindustan Times*, May 19, p 1, col 1+

Anon, 1992, Sonia handover keys of libraries, *Times of India*, May 23, p 4, col 5-6

Anon, 1992, Sonia not asked to depose: SIT, *National Herald*, May 23, p 10, col 8, *Hindustan Times*, May 23, p 20, col 1, news-item

Anon, 1992, Sonia present mobile libraries, *Hindustan Times*, May 23, p 1-2

Anon, 1992, Sonia to be examined in Rajiv case, *Hindustan Times*, May 20, p 12,

Anon, 1992, Sonia's name not in SIT witnesses list, *Times of India*, May 23, p 3, col 1-2

Anon, 1992, Sonia's speech devoid of political hue, *Indian Express*, May 24, p 7, col 4

Anon, 1992, Stadium named after Rajiv, *National Herald*, May 22, p 8 col 7-8

Anon, 1992, TNCC Chief was not consulted about Rajiv's visit, *Indian Express*, April 1, p 3, col 2-6

Anon, 1992, TNCC(I), police responsible for security lapses: Justice Verma,

Economic Times, April 4, p 16, col 1-6

Anon, 1992, Tamils abroad played an active role, *Hindustan Times*, January 28, p 12, col 3-4.

Anon, 1992, Testimony contradicts Organizer's claim, *Statesman*, April 2, p 6, col 6-7

Anon, 1992, The case against the LTTE, *Independent*, May 24, p 4, col 1-3

Anon, 1992, Tree plantation in memory of Rajiv Gandhi, *Tribune*, May 22, p 16, col 7

Anon, 1992, Tributes paid to Rajiv Gandhi in UK, *Times of India*, May 23, p 9, col 7-8.

Anon, 1992, UP Youth Cong vows to follow Rajiv ideals, *National Herald*, May 23, p 10, col 1-3

Anon, 1992, Vajpayee's tribute to Rajiv, *Hindustan Times*, May 20, p 21, col 1

Anon, 1992, Venue posed security risk, *Hindustan Times*, March 14, p 22, col 1-3

Anon, 1992, Verma Commission hearing: Cong. leaders didn't agree to shift Rajiv meeting venue, *Hindustan Times*, March 8, p 12, col 2-4

Anon, 1992, Verma panel arguments commence in camera, *Hindustan Times* April 10, p 4, col 1-2

Anon, 1992, Verma panel flays AICC for delay, *Hindustan Times*, April 25, p 12, col 8

Anon, 1992, Verma panel gets extension, *Hindustan Times*, March 30, p 9, col 3-5

Anon, 1992, Verma panel hearing: AICC contributed to security lapses, *Indian Express*, April 4, p 11, col 1-4

Anon, 1992, Verma panel hearing: Cassettes screened again, *Indian Express*, April 3, p 11, col 6-8.

Anon, 1992, Verma panel hearing: Cop tried to stop 2 women, *Hindustan Times*, March 11, p 12, col 1-3

Anon, 1992, Verma penal hearing: Maragatham did not discuss security, *Hindustan Times*, March 6, p 10, col 4-7

Anon, 1992, Verma panel hearing: Police accused of lapses at meet, *Indian Express*, p 7, col 2-4

Anon, 1992, Verma panel hearing: Rajiv was not wearing bullet proof vest, *Hindustan Times*, January 4, p 5, col 1-4

Anon, 1992, Verma panel hearing: Security sketch plan not followed, *Hindustan Times*, January 30, p 10, col 7-8.

Anon, 1992, Verma panel hearing: Systematic erosion of security norms, *Hindustan Times*, March 13, p 12, col 7-8.

Anon, 1992, Verma panel hearing on SIT Chief, *Hindustan Times*, March 5, p 12, col 5

Anon, 1992, Verma panel hearing re-scheduled, *Hindustan Times*, February 18, p 12, col 6.

Anon, 1992, Verma panel probe: Intriguing aspect of garlanders, *Sunday Statesmen*, April 5, p 7, col 6-8.

Anon, 1992, Verma panel probe: Witness collapses while testifying, *Hindustan Times*, March 12, p 22, col 1-2

Anon, 1992, Verma panel report by May, *The Tribune*, March 30, p 12, col 5-7.

Anon, 1992, Verma panel starts video screening, *Hindustan Times*, Febraury 25, p 3, col 1-2.

Anon, 1992, Verma panel strictures on MP, *Hindustan Times*, February 26, p 24, col 8.

Anon, 1992, Verma panel to hand in report by May, *Indian Express*, March 30, p 7, col 7-8

Anon, 1992, Verma panel widens area of probe, *Times of India*, April 5, p 4, col 7-8

Anon, 1992, Verma panel's term extended, *Hindustan Times*, January 5, p 18, col 7.

Anon, 1992, Verma visits site of Rajiv's assassination, *Times of India*, March 23, p 3, col 1

Anon, 1992, Witness tells Verma panel: Lighting at meet was adequate, *Hindustan Times*, January 29, p 9, col 1-4

Anon, 1992, Yasser, Gayoom hail Rajiv, *National Herald*, May 22, p 10, col 3

Antulay, A.R., 1981, I am disciplined soldier, *India Today* 6(16) August 16, p 40-41

Antulay, A.R., 1982, Political spiders weaving cobwebs, *Current*, April 17, p 3

Anuradha, Dutt

See Dutt, Anuradha

Arjun Singh, 1992, Campaigner for the new tech, *National Herald* (Supplement), p 5, col 1-3

Aron, Sunita, 1991, BJP wants foreign connection probed, *Hindustan Times*, May 31, p 7, col 1-4

Arunachalam, M., 1992, A believer in tradition and modernity, *National Herald* (Supplement), p 4, col 1-3

Azad, Ghulam Nabi, 1980, Rajiv: An asset, *Current*, December 6, p 9

Azad, Ghulam Nabi, 1982, We want Rajiv, *Indian Today* 7(2) January 21

Bachchan, Amitabh, 1991, My friend, Rajiv, *Illustrated Weekly of India* July 6-July 12, p 19

Badhwar, Inderjit, 1991, A water-shed of uncertainty, *India Today* June 15, p 6-7

Badhwar, Inderjit, and Chawla, Prabhu, 1991, Pulling apart, *India Today* February 28, p 32-41

Badhwar, Inderjit, and Chawla, Prabhu, 1991, Rising expectations, *India Today* April 30, p 28-31

Badola, V.M., 1989, PM fails to mollify Muslims, *Times of India*, November 22, p 4, col 1-3

Bahuguna, H.N., 1982, Garhwal will be a turning point, *Current*, May 1, p 5

Baird, Joel, 1986, This man tried to kill Rajiv Gandhi, *Illustrated Weekly of India* 107(19) May 4, p 26-29

Baja, Rajiv K., 1990, The fact, the farce and the fix, *Surya India* June, p 7-8

Balashankar, R., 1990, Do-or-die battle, *The Week* January, p 30-35

Balasubramaniam, V., 1982, Not grooming Rajiv: PM, *Hindustan Times*, August 4, p 7

Bali, Yogendra, 1981, Politician with a difference, *Times of India*, June 9, p 1, 4

Bandopadyay, Saumya, 1991, The last journey, *Sunday* June 9-June 15, p 30-31

Banerjee, Ruben, 1991, Presaging death, *India Today* June 15, p 16, col 1-2

Banerjee, Saumitra, 1980, Funeral: A last good bye, *Sunday* 8(1) June 19, P 27

Banerjee, Subrata, 1985, Economic trust of Rajiv Gandhi, *New Age* 33(2) January 13, p 3

Banerjee, Subrata, 1988, Rajiv Gandhi, Public-sector and socialism, *New Age* 36(2) January 10, p 3

Banerjee, Subrata, 1988, Rajiv Gandhi brand socialism, *New Age* 36(19) May 8, p 5

Banerjee, Subrata, 1989, Rajiv Gandhi government undermines Indian economy, *New Age* 37(42) October 15, p 8-9

Banyal, S.S., 1981, Rajiv disappoints CM's detractors, *Hindustan Times*, November 3, p 20-22

Banyal, S.S., 1982, Rajiv steals the show in Himachal Pradesh, *Hindustan Times*, May 17. p 5

Barman, Ashis, 1986, Party bosses flex muscles, *Link* 28(33) March 23, p 11-12

Barman, Ashis, 1986, Pranab's ouster stems tide of revolt, *Link* 28(40) May 11, p 8-9

Baruah, Amit, 1991, Secruity syndrome: The protection provided to Rajiv, *Frontline* 8(12) June 8-June 21, p 27

Basavapunnaiah, M., 1985, Rajiv Gandhi's policy statements, *People's Democracy* 9(2) January 13, p 1+

Basavapunnaiah, M., 1986, Prime Minister and his brand of secularism, *People's Democracy* 10(43) October 26, p 1+

Basu, Soma, 1991, Living memories, *Frontline* 8(12) June 8-June 21, p 118-119

Baweja, Harinder, 1991, The Gandhis: Picking up the threads, *India Today* June 30, p 102-105

Baweja, Harinder and Vishwanthan, Anand, 1991, Darkness at mid- life, *India Today* June 15, p 10-19

Baxi, Upendra, 1985, For Bunker Roy, a word of advice, *Mainstream* 23(32) April 6, p 28-31

Beant Singh, 1992, A valiant fighter of resurgent India, *National Herald* (Supplement), p 20, col 1-3

Bhagwan Singh, R., 1991, Cracking the case, *Sunday* June 23-June 29, p 61-63

Bhagwan Singh, R., 1991, Eye witness: An on-the-spot report of Rajiv's assassinaion, *Sunday* June 2- June 8, p 12-13

Bhajan Lal, 1992, Rajiv Gandhi and his vision, *National Herald* (Supplement), p 22, col 3-5

Bhambhri, C.P., From 1985 to 1986: Great challenges, *Patriot* (Magazine), December 29, p 1, col 1-5

Bharadwaj, A.K., 1986, No repercussions in Himachal, *Link* 28(40) May 11, p 14

Bhargava, G.S., 1982, Rajiv style of leadership, *Organiser* 33(41) February 28, p 6+

Bhargava, G.S., 1986, Rajiv's politicking style, *Janata* 41(23) November 9, p 3-4

Bharagava, G.S., 1986, Shadow boxing, Congress (I) style, *Indian Express* (Magazine), July 27, p 1, col 1-5+

Bhargava, G.S., 1991, Sonia Gandhi as a Hindu widow, *Mainstream* 29(35) June

22, p 9-10

Bhasin, Prem, 1982, Politics of 1982: Can '1984' be far behind, *Indian Express*, Marchd 7, p 1+

Bhatnagar, R.K., 1992, Rajiv as I knew him, *Hindustan Times* (Magazine), May 17, p 4, col 1-8

Bhatt, B., 1982, Vijay Dhar still holding centre stage, *Caravan* 7(727) September, p 41

Bhatt, S.C., 1986, Another acid test for Congress (I), *Economic Times*, October 21, p 5, col 7-8

Bhatt, S.C., 1986, Dissidence in Congress (I): A new phase, *Economic Times*, June 17, p 5, col 7-8

Bhattacharjee, Manindra, 1987, Rajiv's hysterical campaign style cost Congress (I) dear in West Bengal, *Organiser* 39(2) May 31, p 5+

Bhattacharya, M., 1981, YC (I) show to net regional support, boost Rajiv, *New Age* 29(43) October 25, p 11

Bhattacharya, Mira Sinha
See Sinha-Bhattacharya Mira

Bhattacharya, Shubabrata, 1980, Homage to two brothers: AICC (I) 1980 was damp squib, *Sunday* 8(19) December 14, p 36-37

Bhattacharya, Shubabrata, 1980, Mystery: The delayed biography of Sanjay, *Sunday* 8(20) December 21, p 40-41

Bhattacharya, Shubabrata, 1981, Government is much more pragmatic, *Sunday* 9(28) December 27, p 24-25

Bhattacharya, Shubabrata, 1981, Rajiv's team, *Sunday* 9(24) November 29, p 15

Bhattacharya, Shubabrata, 1982, Gandhi vs Gandhi or why Surya was sold to the RSS, *Sunday* 9(37) March 6, p 12-15

Bhattacharya, Shubhabrata, 1992, Rajiv Gandhi represented modern India, *National Herald* (Supplement), p 2, col 1-3

Bhauguna, H.N., 1982, Garhwal will be a turing point, *Current*, May 1, p 5

Bhaumik, Kirti, 1982, Bad choice of nominees put Cong (I) in dump, *Times of India*, May 14, p 10

Bhosle, Baba Saheb, 1982, I am Shivaji's descendent, *India Today* 7(3) February 15, p 20-21

Bidwai, Praful, 1991, Between despair and hope, *Illustrated Weekly of India* 112(23) June 1, p 12-13.

Bina, Jang,
See Jang, Bina

Bob, Dilip, 1982, Indian Air Force: Spectacle in the sky, *India Today* 7(6) March 31, p 36-39

Bobb, Dilip, 1982, Rajiv Gandhi flying higher, *India Today* 7(4) February 28, p 16-17

Bobb, Dilip, 1991, Ordeal of Prince charming, *India Today* June 15, p 62-68

Bokare, M.G., 1986, Politics of Rajiv Gandhi, *Mainstream* 24(32) April 12, p 27-28

Bokare, M.G., 1986, Sathe-Rajiv wavelength, *Mainstream* 25(8) Novmeber 8, p 27-29

Bose, Ajoy, 1988, At the court of Maha-Rajiv, *Indian Express* (Magazine), January 24, p 1, col 1-8+

Buta Singh, 1988, MP's concern over plot to assassinate PM, *National Herald*, August 3

C.N.
See N.C.

Cabral-E-SA, Mario, 1981, Appealing for change, *Sunday* 9(28) December 27, p 50

Chacko, Arun, 1991, A fairy tale romance, *India Today* June 15, p 136-137+

Chaddha, Kumkum, 1983, Succeess by devious means is not good, *Hindustan Times* (Magazine), December 25, p 1, col 1-8

Chadha, Kumkum, 1986, If I quit, it may damage the Congress (I): An interview with Kamlapati Tripathi, *Hindustan Times* (Magazine), September 14, p 7, col 1-6

Chadha, Kumkum, 1991, BJP is main enemy: Rajiv, *Hindustan Times*, March 28, p 1, col 1-4, news-item

Chadha, Kumkum, 1991, He had promised to return, *Hindustan Times*, August 20, p 19, col 1-4

Chadha, Kumkum, 1992, Perfect gentleman who spoke from his heart, *National Herald* (Supplement), p 11, col 1-6

Chakraborty, S.P., 1987, Rajiv has belied the Nation's hopes, *Organiser* 39(7) July 12, p 4+

Chakravarti, Prithivis, 1989, Elections: Rajiv's three pronged propaganda strategy, *Radical Humanist* 53(3) June, p 8-18

Chakravarti, Sudeep, 1991, The half-way house, *India Today* June 15, p 76-77

Chakravarty, Nikhil, 1985, Whence the challenge to Rajiv Gandhi, *Economic Times*, October 22, p 5, col 3-6

Chakravarty, Nikhil. 1986, A Balance sheet: The Rajiv government, *Times of India* (Sunday Review), August 17, p 1, col 1-8

Chakravarty, Nikhil, 1986, The goings on in Congress (I), *Times of India* (Sunday Review), May 11, p iv, col 1-4

Chakravarty, Nikhil, 1986, A new experiment, *Times of India* (Sunday Review), September 28, p 1, col 1-8+

Chakravarty, Nikhil, 1987, Our heroes and their fawning friends, *Times of India* (Sunday Review), July 12, p 1, col 1-6

Chakravarty, Nikhil, 1989, Mr Gandhi's weekend visit to Moscow, *Times of India*, July 14, p 6, col 7-8

Chakravarty, S., 1986, No major contradiction, *Link* 28(40) May 11, p 12

Chakravarty, Sumit, 1988, At home and abroad, *Mainstream* 26(36) June 18, p 1-2

Chakravarty, Sumit, 1991, Rajiv Gandhi: A Balance-sheet, *Mainstream* 29(31) May 25, p 2-4

Chalapathi Rau, M., 1982, Democracy at work, *Link* 24(42) May 30, p 12

Chander Uday Singh, 1981, Lawyer's conference utterly butterly, *India Today* 6(17) September 1, p 37

Chandra
See also full name e.g., Suresh Chandra

Chandra Shekhar, 1980, Decries 'Draft Rajiv' campaign, *Statesman*, August 29, p 1

Chandra Shekhar, 1981, You cannot solve new problems with old minds, *Sunday* 9(28) December 27, p 17-18

Chandra Shekhar, 1984, AICC : Torrential rehatoric, *Janata* 38(39) January 8, p 3-4

Chandramouli, I., 1991, Rajiv had no business: (Interview: Governer Bhanu Pratap Singh), *The Week* October 21, p 36-37

Chandrashekhar, C.P., 1991, The economic record, *Frontline* 8(12) June-June 21, p 123-124

Chandrashekhar Rao, C., 1985, A year of Rajiv Gandhi, *Indian Express*, April 22

Chatterji, Debasish, 1982, YC (I) happy days again: Will Rajiv Gandhi provide discipline to the hitherto loose organisation? *Probe India* 3(12) February, p 57-58

Chauddhury, Sreerupa Mitra,
See Mitra Chauddhury, Sreerupa

Chaudhary, Shahid 17, jt. author
See Kackar, Ranjana and Chaudhary, Shahid A.

Chavan, S.B., 1992, Rajiv: The young inheritor, *National Herald* (Supplement), p 3, col 1-3

Chawla, G.S., 1981, New Delhi and the Asiad, *Illustrated Weekly of India* 52(34) December 5, p 44-47

Chawla, P., jt. author,
See Mitra, S. and Chawla

Chawla, P. and Mitra, S., 1981, Congress (I): The enemy with in, *India Today* 6(4) February 28, p 64-73

Chawla, P. and Mitra, S., 1982, Sycophancy unleashed, *India Today* 7(2) January 31, p 68-83

Chawla, P. and Thukral, G., 1982, Himachal Pradesh: The photo finish, *India Today* 7(11) June 15, p 25

Chawla, Prabhu, 1981, Beating the dead line, *India Today* 6(24) December 31, p 23

Chawla, Prabhu, 1981, Cracks in the moonlith, *India Today* 6(21) November 15, p 26-29

Chawla, Prabhu, 1981, Punjab talks and terror, *India Today* 6(21) November 15, p 31-33

Chawla, Prabhu, 1982, Andhra Pradesh: Feeling unwanted, *India Today* 7(4) February 28, p 26

Chawla, Prabhu, 1982, Assembly elections: The Acid test, *India Today*, 7(10) May 31, p 34-35

Chawla, Prabhu, 1982, Congress (I): The Battle with in, *India Today* 7(19) October 15, p 18-19

Chawla, Prabhu, 1982, Controversies: Asiad's other side, *India Today* 7(12) June 30, p 74-77

Chawla, Prabhu, 1982, One from the wings, *India Today* 7(3) February 15, p 19-20

Chawla, Prabhu, 1982, Rahu, Ketu, Bahuguna, *India Today* 7(1) January 15, p 51

Chawla, Prabhu, 1982, State election confusion confounded, *India Today* 7(9) May 15, p 18-20

Chawla, Prabhu, 1982, Uniting to divide, *India Today* 7(2) January 31, p 36-37

Chawla, Prabhu, 1982, Upper House scramble, *India Today* 7(6) March 31, p 26-27

Chawla, Prabhu, 1991, Floundering for direction, *India Today* June 15, p 105-107

Chawla, Prabhu, 1991, Rajiv's revenge, *India Today* February 15, p 60, col 1-2

Chawla, Prabhu, 1991, Succession shenanigans, *India Today* June 15, p 90-91

Chenappa, Raj, 1982, Gundu Rao grabs the show, *India Today* 7(2) January 31, p 53-54

Chengappa, Raj, 1982, Logistics: A costly coronation, *India Today* 7(2) January 31, p 80-81

Chhabra, Hari Saran, 1991, Rajiv Gandhi and Africa, *Mainstream* 29(32) June 1, p 6

Chidambaram, P., 1992, He wanted modern and confident India, *National Herald* (Supplement), p 8, col 5-6

Chopra, Pran, 1986, Rajiv Gandhi: Then and now: Shaky, but not about to fall, *Economic Times*, April 6, p 3, col 1-8; *Economic Times*, August 13, p 3, col 1-6+

Chopra, Pran, 1987, Crucial year starts for Rajiv, *Times of India*, January 4, p 3, col 1-5+

Chopra, Pran, 1987, Rajiv Gandhi's coming bates, *Economic Times*, April 5, p 3, col 1-8

Chopra, Pran, 1987, Universal vision: Rajiv Gandhi, *Haryana Review* 21(5) May, p 3-4+

Chopra, Pran, 1988, Benefit of doubt to Rajiv Gandhi, *Economic Times*, April 3, p 3, col 1-6

Chopra, Pran, 1989, Rajiv Gandhi in retrospect: Up like a rocker, down like a stick, *Economic Times*, November 2, p 5, col 1-5+

Chopra, Subhash, 1992, Man who kept us up in top space, *National Herald* (Supplement), p 18, col 3-4

Commerce (Periodical), 1985, Rajiv breaks the ice, *Commerce* 150(3865) June 22, p 11-81, editorial

Crossette, Barbara, 1981, The last interview: Minutes before the blast, *Frontline* 8(12) June 8-June 21, p 19-20

D'Souza, Vincent, 1991, Elusive quarry, *The Week* June 30, p 10

D'Souza, Vincent, 1991, The hunt, *The Week* June 9, p 34-37

D'Souza, Vincent, 1991, Ill-chosen venue, lax security, *The Week* June 9, p 36-37

D'Souza, Vincent, 1991, Prized pictures, quick deals, *The Week* June 9, p 38-39

D'Souza, Vincent, 1991, Torturous trail, *The Week* June 30, p 9-10

D'Souza, Vincent, 1991, Will the snaps click as evidence? *The Week* June 9, p 42, col 1-3

Dandavate, Madhu, 1987, President, Prime Minister and Parliament, *Janata* (May Day Number), 42(6), p 4-5

Das, Ashok, 1982, Sober Orissa welcome for Rajiv planned, *Hindustan Times*, February 9, p 13

Das, Rahin, 1991, No poll pact with BJP, says Rajiv, *Hindustan Times*, May 11, p

1, col 4-5, news-item

Das, Sanjay K., 1991, The bomb that changed it all, *Onlooker* June 15, p 11-14

Das, Sanjay K., 1991, Murder night in Delhi, *Onlooker* June 15, p 16-18

Das, Sitanshu, 1984, Rajiv wants reconciliation, *Link* 27(14) November 11, p 12-16

Das, Sitanshu, 1986, Oxbridge and IVY League sereen between PM and Congress, *Link* 29(12) October 26, p 4-8

Das Gupta, Amalendu, 1989, Congress after Tamil Nadu: Gandhi faces danger of anarchy, *Times of India*, February 10, col 3-5

Das Gupta, Amalendu and Datta-Ray, Sunanda K., 1985, Countering a Pakistani bomb, *Statesman*, August 18, p 1

Dass, Ram, 1985, Rajiv Gandhi's Soviet visit, *People's Democracy* 9(22) June 2, p 2

Datta, Amlan, 1985, Start and way ahead: Challenge and opportunity for Mr Gandhi, *Statesman*, June 2, p 5, col 4-6

Datta-Ray, Sunanda K., 1981, High-flier in politics justifying Rajiv Gandhi's birth right, *Statesman*, May 13

Datta-Ray, Sunanda K., 1981, Tremors in the Darbar: Will Mrs Gandhi declare herself? *Statesman*, April 8

Datta-Ray, Sunanda K., 1989, Death of innocence: Rise and decline of Rajiv Gandhi, *Statesman*, March 12

Deming, Angus and Mazumdar, Sudip, 1990, Gandhi in the cheap seats, *News Week* July 23, p 34

Democratic World (Periodical), 1991, Rajiv's journey towards stability ends, *Democratic World* 20(21) May 26, p 3-4, col 2+, editorial

Democratic World (Periodical), 1991, R.V. aginst Rajiv's take over? *Democratic World* 20(8) p 4, col 1-2, editorial

Democratic World (Periodical), 1991, Rajiv and after, *Democratic World* 20(21) May 26, p 4, col 2-3, editorial

Democratic World (Periodical), 1991, Rajiv calls for US Forces in the Gulf, *Democratic World* 20(7) February 17, p 3, col 2, editorial

Democratic World (Periodical), 1991, Rajiv gives Jaya bulk of seats, *Democratic World*, 20(7) February 17, p 4, col 1-2, editorial

Democratic World (Periodical), 1991, Rajiv urges peace initiatives, *Democratic World* 20(6) February 10, p 3, col 2+, editorial

Democratic World (Periodical), 1991, Rajiv's journey toward stability ends, *Democratic world* 20(21) May 26, p 3-4, col 2 +, editorial

Desai, Dinesh, 1985,
See Anon, 1985, (Book Review)

Desai, M.V., 1987, PM in North America: Yes, with a but, *Economic Times*, October 27, p 5, col 7-8

Desai, Mahesh, 1986, Assessing Rajiv Gandhi, *Janata* 41(24) November 16, p 14-15; *Janata* 41(25) November 30, p 13

Desai, Rajiv, 1989, The Mahalanobis mindset is Rajiv's real enemy, *Times of India*, March 17

Desai, Rajiv, 1990, Mr Rajiv Gandhi's second chance, *Times of India*, November

16, p 8, col 7-8

D'Souza,

See after Crossette, Barbara

Dev Dutt, 1981, The Rajiv factor, *Janata* 36(24) August 3, p 11-12

Dev Dutt, 1986, Images of Rajiv Gandhi, *Janata* 41(24) November 16, p 12-13

Dev, Murarka

See Murarka Dev

Dev, Rahul, 1983, The Rajiv brigade, *Illustrated Weekly of India* 104(23) October 23, p 28-31

Devendra Mohan, 1981, Rajiv the man to watch, *Biltz*, May 30, p 14

Devendra Mohan, 1982, Rajiv raises YC from the dead, *Blitz*, January 16, p 21

Dewan, Berindranath, 1981, Rajiv-Farooq talks for Congress (I) NC coalition, *Hindu*, August 8, p 10

Dhar, M.K., 1982, PM lauds joint Indo-Soviet space venture, *Hindustan Times*, September 24, p 1

Dhar, M.K., 1991, Rajiv seeks decisive verdict, *Hindustan Times*, March 28, p 10, col 5-8

Dhar, M.S., 1981, Warm Jakarta welcome to PM, *Hindustan Times*, September 24, p 1

Dhar, P.N., 1987, Political economy of development in India, *Indian Economic Review* 22(1)

Dhar, P.N., 1989, The Prime Minister's office: Seeing through the mystique, *Times of India*, February 24, p 6, col 3-5

Dhar, Somnath, 1984, Rajiv: Dedication and humility, *National Herald*, August 26, p 3, col 1-4

Dharker, Anil, 1991, Who takes security seriously? *Sunday* June 23-June 29, p 16-17

Dibang, 1990, Rajiv plumped for Devi as PM, *Illustrated Weekly of India* December 1-2, p 1, col 1-5

Dikshit, Shiela, 1992, Rajiv Rattan, *Hindustan Times*, Mary 17, p 4, col 1-8

D'Souza

See after Crossette Barbara

Dubashi, Jagannath, 1982, Asiad 82: Race against time, *India Today* 7(12) June 30, p 66-71

Dubey, Suman, 1982, Jammu and Kashmir son also rises, *India Today* 7(17) September 15, p 46-53

Dubey, Suman, et al, 1982, Zail Singh: The making of a President,*India Today* 7(13) July 15, p 50-55

Dutt

See also under full name, e.g., Dev Dutt; Vijay Dutt

Dutt, Anuradha, 1990, Pilgrim's progress, *Illustrated Weekly of India* 111(29) July 22, p 34-37

Dutt, Rudras, 1985, Rajiv Gandhi's economics, *Janata* 40(4) March 3, p 5-7

Dwivedi, Devendranath, 1986, Assessing Rajiv Gandhi: Within Nehru-Indira frame-work, *Times of India*, December 24, p 8, col 3-5

ESA, Mario Cabral

See Cabral-ESA, Mario

Eastern Economist (Periodical), 1981, The new crown prince, *Eastern Economist* 76(21) May 22, p 1254, editorial

Economic and Political Weekly (Periodical), 1981, Painless induction, *Economic and Political Weekly* 16(20) May 16, p 877, editorial

Economic Times (News-Paper), 1984, Guidelines for action, *Economic Times*, November 14, p 5, col 1-2, editorial

Economic Times (Newspaper), 1985, PM at Press Club, *Economic Times*, October 14, p 5, col 1-2, editoral

Economic Times (Newspaper), 1985, Well begun, *Economic Times*, November 2, p 5, col 1-2, editorial

Economic Times (Newspaper), 1986, Doles and digs, *Economic Times*, September 22, p 5, col 1-2, editorial

Economic Times (Newspaper), 1986, Old wines, labels, *Economic Times*, January 21, p 5, col 1-2, editotial

Economic Times (Newspaper), 1989, From the framparts, *Economic Times*, August 16, p 5, col 1-2, editorial

Economic Times (Newspaper) 1989, Prime Minister's plan, *Economic Times*, February 14, p 5, col 1-2, editorial

Economic Times (Newspaper), 1989, The Rajiv years, *Economic Times*, November 1, p 7, col 1-2, editorial

Economic Times (Newspaper), 1989, Yet another faux pas, *Economic Times*, August 23, p 5, col 1-2, editorial

Farid, Javeed, 1981, With Rajiv in Amethi, *Hindustan Times*, May 31, p 1+

Fernades, George, 1989, The Dravidians and Rajiv Gandhi, *The Other Side* March 26, p 6-13

Fernades, Louis, 1982, The son rose but did not shine, *Sunday* 9(31) January 17, p 34-35

Fishlock, Trever, 1981, Yet another Gandhi on the way to victory, *Times*, June 6

GPD, 1985, A day in the life of Rajiv Gandhi, *Economic and Political Weekly* 20(49) December 7, p 2141-2142

Gadgil, V.N., 1990, No one attacked Rajiv Gandhi even indirectly, *Surya India* June, p 14, col 1-3

Gadkari, J.P., 1986, Gundu on retreat as rival campaign grows, *Link* 28(40) May 11, p 9-10

Gadkari, J.P., 1986, KPCC(I) leadership reshuffled, *Link* 28(26) February 2, p 17

Gajapathi, Gopi Nath, 1992, A leader par excellence, *National Herald* (Supplement), p 15, col 1-3

Gandhi, Indira, 1980, It's for Rajiv to decide, *Hindustan Times*, October 5, p 16

Gandhi, Indira, 1980, Rajiv not joining politics, *Sunday Standard*, October 12, p 1

Gandhi, Indira, 1981, No build up of dynasty, *Hindustan Times*, November 14, p 6

Gandhi, Indira, 1981, Rajiv won't take Sanjay's place, *Hindu*, May 15, p 7

Gandhi, Indira, 1982, Defence matters not on US talks, *Hindustan Times*, July 28, p 3+

Gandhi, Indira, 1982, Maneka had link with Fernandes, *Amrit Bazar Patrika*, April 5, p 1+

Gandhi, Indira, 1982, No plan for talks with US on F-16s foreign fuel for Tarapur likely, *Indian Express*, July 28, p 1
Gandhi, Indira, 1982, Welfare schemes not known to poor, *Indian Express*, September 1, p 3
Gandhi, Rajiv 1981, Aliens backing secessionist move, *Indian Express*, October 13, p 7
Gandhi, Rajiv, 1981, All Amethi villages to be electrified, *Hindustan Times*, May 30, p 16
Gandhi, Rajiv, 1981, Amethi my pilot project, *Blitz*, July 18, p 4
Gandhi, Rajiv, 1981, Amethi to be made model town, *Times of India*, July 4, p 5
Gandhi, Rajiv, 1981, Antulay misused political machinery, *Hindustan Times*, November 11, p 1
Gandhi, Rajiv, 1981, Antulay in State party affairs, *Indian Express*, October 13, p 1
Gandhi, Rajiv, 1981, Antulay stays, *Current*, October 17, p 1
Gandhi, Rajiv, 1981, Congress (I) alone can provide stable government, *Hindustan Times*, March 27, p 8
Gandhi, Rajiv, 1981, Democracy has strong base in India, *Hindustan Times*, July 29, p 16
Gandhi, Rajiv, 1981, Destroy divisive forces, *Hindustan Times*, November 15, p 15
Gandhi, Rajiv, 1981, F-16s for Pak will spur arms race, *Hindustan Times*, July 10, p 4
Gandhi, Rajiv, 1981, Family succession not bad, *Hindustan Times*, November 12, p 4
Gandhi, Rajiv, 1981, Involve people in development, *Hindustan Times*, May 18, p 1
Gandhi, Rajiv, 1981, Janata put country 20 years behing? *Indian Express*, December 31, p 7
Gandhi, Rajiv, 1981, Opposed to reentry of defectors, *Times of India*, November 23, p 5
Gandhi, Rajiv, 1981, Parliamentary system good and sound, *Blitz*, July 18, p 24
Gandhi, Rajiv, 1981, Party comes first, *Hindustan Times*, December 30, p 8
Gandhi, Rajiv, 1981, Party office needs systemisation, *Blitz*, July 18, p 4
Gandhi, Rajiv, 1981, People's role of watch dogs, *Blitz*, July 18, p 24
Gandhi, Rajiv, 1981, Plan to make Amethi a model town, *Indian Express*, July 5, p 5
Gandhi, Rajiv, 1981, Punjab Government not effective, *Hindustan Times*, November 21, p 1
Gandhi, Rajiv, 1981, Ram Rajya if we all do our duty, *Hindustan Times*, October 7, p 3
Gandhi, Rajiv, 1981, Talks with Akalis have not broken down, *Hindustan Times*, November 21, p 16
Gandhi, Rajiv, 1981, US forcing arms on sub-continent, *Hindustan Times*, November 14, p 6
Gandhi, Rajiv, 1982, 160 Bengal seats for Congress (I), *Hindustan Times*, May 12,

p 8

Gandhi, Rajiv, 1982, Big cheer on maiden speech streamline vital sectors, *National Herald*, March 12, p 1

Gandhi, Rajiv, 1982, Congress (I) as strong as before, *National Herald*, April 25, p 3

Gandhi, Rajiv, 1982, Congress (I) enjoys people's support, *Times of India*, February 6, p 2

Gandhi, Rajiv, 1982, Congress (I) sure to win in West Bengal, *Amrit Bazar Patrika*, May 13, p 7

Gandhi, Rajiv, 1982, FP needs people's support, *National Herald*, March 10, p 1

Gandhi, Rajiv, 1982, Fight dowry evil, *National Herald*, September 4, p 3

Gandhi, Rajiv, 1982, Industrial growth vital for country, *Times of India*, February 11, p 5

Gandhi, Rajiv, 1982, International Youth Conference work for peace, *Current*, January 30, p 6

Gandhi, Rajiv, 1982, LD, BJP alliance mere opportunism, fake, *Hindustan Times*, May 15, p 5

Gandhi, Rajiv, 1982, Make FP a mass movement, *Hindustan Times*, March 10, p 3

Gandhi, Rajiv, 1982, Men with conscience will back Zail Singh, *Hindustan Times*, June 30, p 7

Gandhi, Rajiv, 1982, No Congress (I) sponsored strikes, *Times of India*, January 1, p 9

Gandhi, Rajiv, 1982, No dissent in public, *Indian Express*, January 10, p 5

Gandhi, Rajiv, 1982, Not for Presidential form of Government, *Amrit Bazar Patrika*, May 18, p 7

Gandhi, Rajiv, 1982, Opposition bid to tarnish Congress (I) image, *National Herald*, April 2, p 1

Gandhi, Rajiv, 1982, Pak reasoning for arms ridiculous, *Hindustan Times*, Febraury 6, p 8

Gandhi, Rajiv, 1982, Party selections are all winners, *Hindustan Times*, April 25, p 1+

Gandhi, Rajiv, 1982, Press writing irresponsible reports, *Indian Express*, October 6, p 1+

Gandhi, Rajiv, 1982, Raps Janata, LD leadership, *Hindustan Times*, May 28, p 6, col 6-7

Gandhi, Rajiv, 1982, Sanjay's plan not abandoned, *Indian Express*, March 31, p 1

Gandhi, Rajiv, 1982, Sanjay's plan being pursued with zest, *Times of India*, July 18, p 11

Gandhi, Rajiv, 1982, YC (I) will do constructive work, *Hindustan Times*, January, p 4

Gandhi, Rajiv, 1984, 23rd INTUC plenary session: Message, *Indian Worker* 32(32-34) May 7-May 21

Gandhi, Rajiv, 1984, Prime Minister's broadcast to the Nation: Call to build India of 21st century, *Indian and Foreign Review* 22(3) November 30, p 12-13+

Gandhi, Rajiv, 1984, Rajiv's first message to the Nation, *Mainstream* 23(12), p 25-26

Gandhi, Rajiv, 1985, Funds plenty for engines of destruction and not for development, *Indian Worker* 33(39) June 24, p 3-5

Gandhi, Rajiv, 1985, It's time our scientists come out of their shell, *Yojana* 19(24) January 1, p 4-6

Gandhi, Rajiv, 1985, No giving up Nations thrust on socialism, *Indian Worker* 33(35) September 30, p 6-8

Gandhi, Rajiv, 1985, Text of PM's speech, *Times of India*, April 20, p 16, col 1-4

Gandhi, Rajiv, 1986, India towards 21st Century: Speeches of Rajiv Gandhi at the Congress Centenary, *Secular Democracy* 19(1-2) January-February, p 20-28

Gandhi, Rajiv, 1986, PM's Address to Army Commanders, *Hindu*, April 25

Gandhi, Rajiv, 1986, PM's Address to the Six Nations Summit, *Indian Express*, August 3; *Hindu*, August 8

Gandhi, Rajiv 1986, The substance of non-alignment, *Monthly Commentary on Indian Economic Conditions* 28(1) August, p 23

Gandhi, Rajiv, 1986, Thus spake Rajiv, *Illustrated Weekly of India* 107(20) May 11, p 40-41

Gandhi, Rajiv, 1987, Communalisation of politics, education, industry and commerce: An imperialist strategy to impede national unity and freedom movement: Prime Minister Rajiv Gandhi's Address to intellectuals, New Delhi, Sep. 15, 1987, *Muslim India* 5(58) Oct., p 457-458

Gandhi, Rajiv, 1987 We salute workers who do Gods work on earth, Prime Minister Rajiv Gandhi's Address to the May Day rally, *Indian Worker* 35(32-33) May 11-May 18, p 8-11

Gandhi, Rajiv, 1988, PM's Address at Silver Jubilee function of "Patriot", *Indian Express*, March 30

Gandhi, Rajiv, 1988, PM's Address to Farmer's Rally, *Free Press Journal*, February 21; *National Herald*, February 21

Gandhi, Rajiv, 1988, PM's Address to CPP (I) *Hindu*, February 22; *Hindu*, December 8; *Hindustan Times*, February 21; *Hindustan Times*, July 28; *Hindustan Times*, August 31; *National Herald*, May 13; *Times of India*, May 13

Gandhi, Rajiv, 1988, PM's Address to the Chief Ministers, *Hindustan Times*, March 19

Gandhi, Rajiv, 1988, PM's Address to Farmer's Rally, *Free Press Journal*, Febrary 21; *National Herald*, February 21

Gandhi, Rajiv, 1988, PM's Independence Day speech, *Economic Times*, August 16, p 4, col 5-8

Gandhi, Rajiv, 1988, PM's statement on Gorbachev's visit, *Hindu*, November 22

Gandhi, Rajiv, 1988, Rajiv Gandhi's Address to Special Session on Disarmament, *Indian Express*, June 10

Gandhi, Rajiv, 1988, Speech at the AICC session in New Delhi, *Times of India*, November 22

Gandhi, Rajiv, 1988, Speeches
See Anon, 1988, Speeches

Gandhi, Rajiv, 1988, Speeches (Extract) Prime Minister Rajiv Gandhi, *Foreign Affairs Report* 37(9.10.11) September- November, p 101-124, figures

Gandhi, Rajiv, 1989, PM's Address to Bharat Krishak Samaj, *National Herald*,

February 7, news-item

Gandhi, Rajiv, 1989, PM's Address to Municipal Officers, *Hindustan Times*, June 6; *National Herald*, June 6

Gandhi, Rajiv, 1989, PM's Address to Nagarpalika Sammelan, *Hindustan Times*, June 15

Gandhi, Rajiv, 1989, PM's Address to Panchayati Raj Conference, *Free Press Journal*, May 5

Gandhi, Rajiv, 1989, PM Addresses Panchayati Raj Sammelan, *Hindu*, April 4; Thus, *Hindustan Times*, April 8; *Telegraph*, April 8

Gandhi, Rajiv, 1989, PM's statement regarding terrorism, *Hindu*, March 1

Gandhi, Rajiv, 1989, Population control and grass-roots development: Document, *Mainstream* 27(53) September 30, p 10-12+

Gandhi, Rajiv, 1989, Rajiv Gandhi addresses UPCC (I) Convention, *Times of India*, February 11, news-item

Gandhi, Rajiv, 1989, Rajiv Gandhi's Address to NSUI Convention, *Hindustan Times*, April 5

Gandhi, Rajiv, 1989, Rajiv Gandhi's Address to Seva Dal Convention, *Times of India*, May 13

Gandhi, Rajiv, 1990, Rajiv Gandhi's letter to PM on Punjab election, *Statesman*, September 22

Gandhi, Rajiv, 1991, Rajiv Gandhi's letter to PM, *Hindustan Times*, Febrauary 11, p 12, col 2

Gangadhar, V., 1991, Rajiv-baiters, *Sunday* June 9-June 15, p 94-95

Gangal, S.C., 1987, The India-Sri Lanka agreement, *Gandhi Marg* 9(5) August, p 259-263

Gangal, S.S., 1987, President and the Prime Minister, *Gandhi Marg* 9(2) May, p 67-72

Ganguli, Amulya, 1989, Rajiv Gandhi in history, *Statesman* (Misc), November 26, p 1, col 1-5

Gani, H.A., 1989, Prime Minister's Panchayati Raj, *Janata* 44(19) August 6, p 12+

Gargi, Balwant, 1982, Rajiv Gandhi: A politician without hang-ups, *Illustrated Weekly of India* 103(2) January 30, p 12-13

Ghose, Arabinda, 1991, Captain basking in Rajiv glory, *Hindustan Times*, November 10, p 16, col 5-8

Ghosh, Arun, 1989, The Economy and the Budget, *Economic and Political Weekly*, March 11

Ghosh, Soumya K. and Parsai, Gargi, 1991, Asthi special let off steam of emotions, *Hindustan Times*, May 28, p 1, col 4

Ghosh Chowdhury, Dilip 1984, Faction flight in Youth Congress come to fore in Bengal, *New Age*, 32(36) September 2, p 14

Ghosh Chowdhury, Dilip, 1985, Bengal Congress (I) new line up, *New Age* 33(48) December 1, p 7

Ghosh Chowdhury, Dilip, 1985, Bombs parts of agitation for Bengal Congress (I), *New Age* 33(42) October 20, p 7

Ghosh Chowdhury, Dilip, 1985, West Bengal Congress (I) beset by trouble, *New Age* 33(40) October 6, p 15

Ghosh Chowdhury, Dilip, 1986, Feud in Bengal Cong (I) stepped up after poll, *New Age* 34(26), p 16

Ghosh Chowdhury, Dilip, 1987, Academic platform used for Rajiv's political tirade, *New Age* 35(4) January 25, p 6

Ghosh, Chowdhury, Dilip 1990, Shekhar at mercy of Cong (I) and Rajiv, *New Age* 38(49), December 9, p 7+.

Giri, V.V., 1980, Poll for one party rule ... Prelude to Presidential form of Government, *Illustrated Weekly of India* 101(21) May 31, p 6-9

Gokhale, S.R., 1984, An adminocrat: New management concept, *Economic Times*, December 18, p 5, col 3-6

Gopa Kumar, 1984
See Anon, 1984, (Book Review)

Gopal
See full name, e.g., Raj Gopal, R.

Grant, Bruce, 1982, Of diplomats and politicians, *Indian Express*, April 25, p 1

Grover, Satish, 1982, Building for the Asiad, *Illustrated Weekly of India* 103 (34) September 12, p 44-45

Guha, R., 1991, Rajiv Gandhi: Can he provide a stable alternative? *Sunday* March 24-March 30, p 4, letter to editor

Guha Thakurta, Paranjoy and Taneja, Shiv, 1991, Hard times get harder, *India Today* June 15, p 80-82

Gupta, Indrajit, 1988, Untenability of Rajiv Gandhi's rule, *Mainstream* (Annual) October 8, p 29-30+

Gupta, L.N., 1982, Tripude antics fail to amuse Rajiv, *Blitz*, May 22 p 4

Gupta, M.G., 1987
See Anon, 1987, (Book Review)

Gupta, O., 1980, Power equation after Kamlapati, *Onlooker* December 15, p 10-17

Gupta, Pranay, 1985, Mr Gandhi goes to Washington, *Illustrated Weekly of India* 106(8) June 30, p 20-21

Gupta, Rajan, 1987, President-PM controvercy, *Mainstream* 25(28) March 28, p 6

Gupta, Ram Roop, 1985, Freedom fighters and Prime Minister: Interesting features of their horsocopes, *Organiser* 37(26) November 10, p 14-17+

Gupta, Ram Roop, 1987, Steep hildown trend in Rajiv Gandhi's life, *Organiser* 39(12) August 15, p 53-54

Gupta, Ranjan, 1986, Rajiv Gandhi's South East Asia Pacific tour, *Mainstream* 25(9) November 15, p 49-50

Gupta, Ranjan, 1987, President, PM controversy, *Mainstream* 25(28) March 28, p 6

Gupta, Shakhar, et al, 1991, Planned Precise, Pulverising, *India Today* June 15, p 27-29

Gupta, Shakhar, et al, 1991, An avoidable calamity, *India Today* June 15, p 38+

Gupta, Shakhar, et al, 1991, Assassination probe: Fitting the pieces, *India Today* June 30, p 42-44

Gupta, Shekhar, 1991, Friendly but lack lustre, *India Today* May 31, p 22-25

Gupta, Smita, 1992, Congress men no longer talk of chairsma, *Independent*, May 21, p 5, col 1-8

Habibullah, Wajahat, 1992, The Rajiv Gandhi Foundation, *National Herald* (Supplement), p 13, col 1-4

Hafiz M. A., 1991, Rajiv, V.P., Shekhar on firm ground, *Hindustan Times*, April 2, p 10, col 5-8

Hari, Jai Singh, 1990
See Anon, 1990, (Book Review)

Hanspal, H.S., 1992, An inspiring personality, *National Herald* (Supplement), p 11, col 4-6

Hari Kumar, K.N., 1988, Rajiv and the US: Trading Non-Alignment for Hi-Tech? *Mainstream* 26(29) April 30, p 17-26

Hari Kumar, K.N., 1988, Trading Non-Alignment for High Tech: Rajiv's record US visit, *Economic and Politied Weekly* 23(17) April 23, p 840-853

Hasan, Syed Majeedul, 1982, Why Rajiv Gandhi was displeased with Anjiah? *Sunday* 9(36) February 27, p 16-17

Hasan Suroor
See Suroor, Hasan

Hazarika, Sanjoy, 1991, For we shall never be young again, *Hindustan Times* (Sunday Magazine), June 2, p 4, col 1-8

Hemendra Narayan, 1982, No payment yet for Rajiv's air trip, *Indian Express*, April 10

Herle, Shashi, 1980, Trutu behind the demolition, *Onlooker* 42(19) October 31, p 9

Hindustan Times (Newspaper), 1991, A thorough probe, *Hindustan Times*, June 6, p 11, col 1, editorial

Inder Jit, 1984, Indira, Rajiv and succession, *Economic Times*, November 6, p 5, col 7-8

Inder Jit, 1984, Rajiv and the talks ahead, *Economic Times*, November 13, p 5, col 7-8

Inder Jit, 1985, More responsibility now on CPP (I), *Economic Times*, April 23, p 5, col 7-8

Inder Jit, 1985, Rajiv and his fourth mission, abroad, *Economic Times*, October 15, p 5, col 7-8

Inder Jit, 1986, PM concedes basic Gorkha demand, *Economic Times*, December 23, p 5, col 7-8+

Inder Jit, 1987, Controversy ends, issue remains, *Economic Times*, May 26, p 5, col 7-8+

Inder Jit, 1987, Let Rajiv follow Nehru's example, *Economic Times*, June 9, p 5, col 7-8+

Inder Jit, 1987, Parliament must debate gun issue, *Economic Times*, March 24, p 5, col 7-8+

Inder Jit, 1987, PM's Darjelling visit and Gorkhas, *Economic Times*, February 17, p 5, col 7-8+

Inder Jit, 1987, Prime Minister and the Constitution, *Economic Times*, June 16, p 5, col 7-8+

Inder Jit, 1987, Rajiv, Haryana Poll and new crises, *Economic Times*, June 23, p 5, col 7-8+

Inder Jit, 1987, Will Rajiv ride the rising crisis? *Economic Times*, July 28, p 5, col

7-8
Inder Jit, 1988, Rajiv's China visit and Nehru, *Economic Times*, December 20, p 5, col 7-8
Inder Jit, 1989, Singnificant gains of Rajiv's visit, *Economic Times*, July 25, p 5, col 7-8
Indian Express (Newspaper), 1992, Where is the evidence? *Indian Express*, April 2, p 8, col 1-2, editorial
Iyer
See also full name, e.g., Krishna Iyer, V.R.
Iyer, Mani Shankar, 1992, A loss of flair, *Independent*, May 21, p 5, col 1-4
Jaffer Shareef, C.K., 1992, Staunch votary of integration, *National Herald* (Supplement), p 9, col 3-6
Jain, Girilal, 1982, Political opponent or daughter-in-law, *Times of India*, April 11, p 2
Jain, Girilal, 1984, Grab for Rajiv Gandhi, *Times of India* (Sunday Review), December 2, p 1, col 1-8
Jain, Girilal, 1984, Nehru, Indira and Rajiv: Different styles, one objective, *Times of India*, November 14, p 8, col 3-5
Jain, Girilal, 1985, A brush with Indian reality: Not by pragmatism and high tech, *Times of India*, May 7, p 6, col 3-5
Jain, Girilal, 1985, Promise and fufilment: Problems Rajiv Gandhi may face, *Times of India*, February 6, p 8, col 3-5
Jain Girilal, 1985, Rajiv's India impatient to march ahead, *Times of India* (Sunday Review), January 27, p 1, col 1-8
Jain, Girilal, 1985, Rajiv's mission to Moscow: No need to shirk issues, *Times of India*, May 18, p 8, col 3-5
Jain, Girilal, 1985, The Rajiv phenomenon: India's search for a monarch, *Times of India*, March 19, p 8, col 3-5; *Times of India*, March 20, p 6, col 7-8; *Times of India*, Mach 22, p 6, col 7-8
Jain, Girilal, 1985, Rajiv Gandhi's visit to US: A possible turning point in policy, *Times of India*, June 4, p 8, col 3-5
Jain, Girilal, 1985, The year of Rajiv Gandhi : Pitfalls of accommodation, *Times of India*, December 31, p 8, col 3-5
Jain, Girilal, 1986, The challenge Rajiv faces: Continuing decay of Congress, *Times of India*, August 27, p 8, col 3-5
Jain, Girilal, 1986, Politics of Rajiv Gandhi, *Mainstream* 24(26) March 1, p 11-14
Jain, Girilal, 1986, Politics of Rajiv Gandhi: An outsider's view of India, *Times of India*, February 19, p 8, col 3-5, *Times of India*, February 20, p 8, col 3-5
Jain, Girilal, 1986, Rajiv Gandhi's personality: Impact on leadership style, *Times of India*, February 26, p 8, col 3-5; *Times of India*, Fecurary 27, p 8, col 3-5
Jain, Girilal, 1987, Challenge for Mr Gandhi: No room for compromise, *Times of India*, June 27, p 6, col 3-5
Jain, Girilal, 1987, Challenges to Rajiv Gandhi: President Zail Singh and V.P. Singh, *Times of India*, May 18, p 6, col 3-5
Jain, Girilal, 1987, A clash of interests: Rajiv Gandhi and V.P. Singh, *Times of India*, February 4, p 6, col 3-5

Jain, Girilal, 1987, Crisis of confidence: Challenge Rajiv Gandhi faces, *Times of India*, June 24, p 6, col 3-5

Jain, Girilal, 1987, Destabilisation in trouble: Rajiv Gandhi faces, *Times of India*, August 19, p 6, col 3-5

Jain, Girilal, 1987, Fight is for power: V.P. Singh's challenge to Rajiv Gandhi, *Times of India*, August 12, p 6, col 3-5

Jain, Girilal, 1987, Fight to the finish: Rajiv Gandhi versus V.P. Singh, *Times of India*, July 17, p 6, col 3-5

Jain, Girilal, 1987, Focus away from Rajiv: No natural allies for V.P. Singh, *Times of India*, September 9, p 6, col 3-5

Jain, Girilal, 1987, No anti-Rajiv conspiracy: Only convergence of interests, *Times of India*, December 16, p 6, col 3-5

Jain, Girilal, 1987, Political upheaval in India: Rajiv's blunder after blunder, *Times of India*, March 25, p 6, col 3-5

Jain, Girilal, 1987, President versus Prime Minister: New correlation of power, *Times of India*, July 29, p 6, col 3-5

Jain, Girilal, 1987, Prime Minister under siege: Compulsions of Indian democracy, *Times of India*, April 20, p 6, col 3-5

Jain, Girilal, 1987, Reagan has an agenda: Questions that Rajiv should raise, *Times of India*, October 14, p 6, col 3-5

Jain, Girilal, 1988, Chandraswami as linchpin: Attempt to blackmail Rajiv Gandhi, *Times of India*, April 5, p 4, col 3-5

Jain, Girilal, 1988, No anti-Rajiv conspiracy: Only convergence of interests, *Times of India*, December 16, p 6, col 3-5

Jain, Madhu, 1981, Nation remembers a leader but Subhash Saxena is forgotten, *Sunday* 9(3) July 5, p 32-33

Jain, Madhu, 1981, The family, *Sunday* 9(24) November 29, p 14

Jain, Meenakshi, 1985, In search of a strategy, *Times of India* (Sunday Review), October 6, p 1, col 1-8

Jain, Minu, 1991, What the stars don't fortell, *Sunday* June 9-June 15, p 60-61

Jaisingh, Hari
see Hari, Jai Singh; Anon, 1990, (Book Review)

Jakhar, Balram, 1992, The voice that stood for peace, *National Herald* (Supplement), p 9, col 1-2

Jalan, Bimal, 1991, Those were the days, *Sunday* June 23-June 29, p 54-56

Janak Singh, 1986, Failure to curb Bihar dissidence, *Times of India*, May 20, p 8, col 7-8

Janardhana Reddy, 1992, Nothing stood between him and poeple, *National Herald* (Supplement), p 8, col 1-4

Janata (Periodical), 1981, Distinction without a difference, *Janata* 36(39) November 29, p 1-2, editorial

Janata (Periodical), 1985, Congress (I), RSS and BJP, *Janata* (Annual Number) 40 (1), p 3-4, editorial

Jang, Bina, 1981, No babe in the woods, *Probe India* 3(5) July, p 20

Jaura, Ramesh, 1986, Politics of Rajiv Gandhi, *Mainstream* 24(34) April 26, p 26-27

Javeed Farid
See Farid, Javeed

Jayanth, V., et al, 1991, The gory end, *Frontline* 8(12) June 8-June 21, p 4-5 +

Jayaram, C.S., 1991, Blast device at forensic dept, *Hindustan Times*, May 30, p 1, col 5-7

Jayaram, C.S., 1991, A confusing scenario, *Hindustan Times* (Magazine), p 1, col 1-8+

Jayaram, C.S., 1991, Did killer's team visit Kanchi? *Hindustan Times*, June 6, p 18, col 3-6

Jayaram. C.S., 1991, Has the investigation been side tracked? *Hindustan Times* (Magazine), July 30, p 5, col 1-5.

Jerath, Arati R., 1982, Collecting crowds for Rajiv, *Indian Express*, May 16, p 5

Jeyaraj, D.B.S., 1991, Question of motive: Was it the LTTE? *Frontline* 8(12) June 8-June 21, p 25-26

Jeyaraj, D.B.S., 1991, The suicide killers, *Frontline* June 22-July 5, p 30-31

Jha, Ajay N., 1991, Post-Rajiv scene murky, *Hindustan Times*, May 31, p 7, col 1-3

Jha, Prem Shankar, 1985, New direction for politics: Rajiv Gaandhi's bold initiative, *Times of India*, January 8, p 8, col 3-5

Jha, Prem Shankar, 1986, Rajiv Gandhi's acid test: Revolt of the intermediate class, *Times of India*, February 24, p 8, col 3-4; *Times of India*, Feburary 25, p 8, col 7-8

Jhujhunwala, Bharat, 1986, Politics of Rajiv Gandhi, *Mainstream* 24(29) March 22, p 27-28

Joshi, Chand, 1980, Ashes imersed in many rivers, *Hindustan Times*, June 29, p 1+

Joshi, Chand 1982, Rajiv to wield the 'big broom', *Hindustan Times*, March 13, p 1

Joshi, Chand, 1991, Last tipoff was from terrorists? *Hindustan Times*, June 3, p 1, col 1+

Joshi, Chand. 1991, Lax security at forensic lab, *Hindustan Times*, May 30, p 16, col 1-3

Joshi, Chand, 1991, Rajiv assassination: More angles than facts, *Hindustan Times*, June 6, p 1, col 3-5

Joshi, Manoj, 1991, End of the road, *Frontline* 8(12) June 8-June 21, p 32-34+

Joshi, Manoj, 1991, The changing political scene, *Frontline* 8(12) June 8-June 21, p 18

Joshi, Manoj, 1991 A ruthless job: Who are the suspects? *Frontline* 8(12) June 8-June 21, p 21-22

Joshi, Manoj, 1991, Security puzzles, *Frontline* June 22-July 5, p 32-33

Joshi, Murali Manohar, 1987, A diversionary exercise to defocus the moral failure of Rajiv Gandhi, *Organiser* 39(24) November 22, p 5+

KGK, 1991, Selection of Sonia Gandhi: Inside story, *Onlooker* June 15, p 47-50

Kackar, Ranjana and Chaudhary, Shahid A., 1991, Will Rajiv be PM again? *Probe India* June 15, p 10-15

Kackar, Ranjana and Chaudhary, Shahid A., 1991, Will Rajiv be PM again? *Probe India* October 17, p 11, col 1-6

Kala, Arvind, 1989, Will a negative vote displace Mr Rajiv Gandhi? *Times of India*, October 17, p 11, col 1-6

Kalbag, Chaitanya, 1981, Spate of senseless tragedies, *India Today* 6(24) December 31, p 48-51

Kalbag, Chaitanya, 1982, The Opposition: The games old men play, *India Today* 7(4) February 28, p 14-15

Kalhan, Promila, 1980, A quite, young man in politics, *Hindustan Times*, October 27

Kalhan, Promila, 1982, PM visit to include Honolulu, *Hindustan Times*, July 11, p 8

Kalhan, Promila, 1991, A child who loved aeroplanes, *Hindustan Times* (Sunday Magazine), June 2, p 4, col 1-8

Kalkur, Ashok, 1991, The last post, *Frontline* 2(12) June 8-June 21, p 124-125

Kalra, Krishan, 1991, Fare well, my prince, *Hindustan Times*, June 4, p 11, col 2-5

Kamalanath, 1981, On Rajiv Gandhi: Nobody imposed him, *Probe India* 3(5) July, p 18-19

Kamalanath, 1981, Only the PM's son can fix the exploiters, *Onlooker* 43(12) July 15, p 38

Kamaruppe, 1991, Assassination and after in North-East, *Economic and Political Weekly* 26(22-23) June 1-June 8, p 1383, col 1-3

Kamath, M.V., 1981, Why Rajiv Gandhi? *Illustrated Weekly of India* 102(19) May 31, p 6-11

Kamath, M.V., 1982, After Indira Gandhi, Who? *Indian Express*, March 7, p 2-6

Kamath, M.V., 1982, Importance of being a sycophant, *Indian Express*, February 7, p 2

Kamath, M.V., 1984, Rajiv Gandhi's Prime Ministership, *Organiser* 36(28) November 25, p 4

Kamath, M.V., 1984, Will Rajiv make good? *Indian Express* (Magazine), November 11, p 2, col 1-5

Kamath, M.V., 1986, Absence of malice? *Illustrated Weekly of India* 107(17) August 20, p 20-23

Kamath, M.V., 1986, Bandying words with bandicoots, *Indian Express* (Magazine), June 22, p 2, col 6-8

Kamath, M.V., 1986, No bright ideas, *Indian Express* (Magazine), May 11, p 11, col 1-8

Kanju, N., 1982, 1981: A year of turbulence for India, *Caravan* 2(712) January, p 16-18

Kapoor, Coomi, 1990, A change of image: Rajiv tries to put his act together, *Illustrated Weekly of India* 111(27) July 8, p 10-19

Karanjia, R.K., 1976, The Nehru's: Father and daughter, *Illustrated Weakly of India* 97(46) November 14, p 6-19

Karanjia, R.K., 1981, Don't tampt fate, Mrs Gandhi, *Blitz*, May 30, p 1-2

Karanjia, R.K., 1982, Congress for dissidents, *Blitz*, May 15, p 1

Karanjia, R.K., 1982, Course of dynastic rule: Warning for Mrs. Gandhi, *Blitz*, April 10, p 1+

Karanjia, R.K., 1982, Dynastic crisis? *Blitz*, March 27, p 2

Karanjia, Russy, 1987, Case for the defence, *Illustrated Weekly of India* 108(28) July 19, p 32-35

Karat, Prakash, 1987, Separating religion and politics: Rajiv style, *People's Decmocracy* 11(11) March 15, p 3

Karlekar, Hiranmay, 1981, Rajiv: The politics of dynastic succession, *Indian Express* (Magazine), June 21, p 1, col 1-8, p 8

Karunakaran, K., 1982, Last laugh, *India Today* 7(2) January 31, p 51

Kashyap, Krishan, 1982, Men behind ASIAD, *National Herald*, May 2, p 1, col 1-8+

Katyal, K.K., 1991, An aggressive style, *Frontline* 8(12) June 8-June 21, p 122-123

Kaul, N.K., 1985, Congress(I) in an unenviable position in Jammu and Kashmir, *Economic Times*, July 18, p 5, col 7-8

Kaushik, Devendra, 1985, India, USSR and East Europe: Emerging trends under Rajiv Gandhi, *India Quarterly* 41(1) January-March, p 6-16

Kaushik, Poonam I., 1982, Rajiv goes through his paces, *Weekend Review* 3(10) May 29, p 7

Kelkar, B.K., 1986, Dissidence in Congress (I): A new chewing gum, *Organiser* 38(1) May 18, p 7

Keshava Rao, K., 1992, Rajiv Gandhi Technology Mission for rural poor, *National Herald* (Supplement), p 19

Khan, Masood Ali, 1985, Immensely successful Rajiv to USSR, *New Age* 33(22) June 2, p 8-9+

Khan, Masood Ali, 1985, Rajiv in Moscow, *New Age* 33(21) May 26, p 1+

Khandekar, Shreekant, 1982, Waves on the wane, *India Today* 7(12) January 31, p 48

Khanna, K.C., 1982: Year of Rajiv Gandhi, *Illustrated Weekly of India* 103(2) January 30, p 8-11

Khanna, K.C., 1985, A young man in a hurry: Hopeful signs of dynamic change, *Times of India*, January 9, p 8, col 3-5

Khanna, K.C., 1986, Protecting precious lives: A "soft" State cannot endure, *Times of India*, October 7, p 8, col 3-5

Khanna, K.C., 1986, Two-year of Rajiv Gandhi: A rudder jammed by drife wood, *Times of India*, October 21, p 8, col 3-5

Khanna, Rajesh, 1992, Rajesh, we will make it, *National Herald* (Supplement), p 12, col 1-4

Khanna, Vinod, 1986, Vichar Vibhag : Miles to go, *National Herald*, March 23, p 10, col 2-5

Khare, Harish, 1980, Anti-Congressism endures: Rajiv's failure to evolve, *Times of India*, October 10, p 8, col 3-5.

Khare, Harish, 1986, Challenge to Rajiv Gandhi: Issue he can no longer skirt, *Times of India*, May 5, p 8, col 3-5

Khare, Harish, 1986, Choice for Rajiv Gandhi: Away from charismatic leadership, *Times of India*, April 11, p 8, col 3-5

Khare, Harish, 1986, Congress and Rajiv Gandhi: Danger of Indian Marcoism, *Times of India*, September 6, p 8, col 3-5

Khare, Harish, 1986, Issues Tripathi has raised: Rajiv Gandhi should be grateful, *Times of India*, June 11, p 8, col 3-5

Khare, Harish, 1986, Organisational elections: Coping with political vulnerabilities, *Times of India*, October 6, p 8, col 3-5

Khare, Harish, 1986, Rajiv Gandhi's world view: Anti-Congressism to anti-politics, *Times of India*, April 25, p 1, col 4-6+

Khare, Harish, 1987, Dessidence in Congress: Rajiv Gandhi's strategy, *Times of India*, January 19, p 8, col 3-5

Khare, Harish, 1987, President, Prime Minister: No acquiescence, no confrontation, *Times of India*, March 2, p 6, col 3-5

Khare, Harish, 1987, Rajiv Gandhi on defensive: End of his brave new world, *Times of India*, March 24, p 6, col 3-5

Khare, Harish, 1987, Reviving the Congress: Main challenge for Mr. Gandhi, *Times of India*, May 17, p 6, col 3-5

Khare, Harish, 1988, The repackaging of Rajiv Gandhi, *Times of India*, March 29, p 6, col 7-8

Khare, Harish, 1989, Preparing for the pool: Rajiv's overtures to party, *Times of India*, May 17, p 6, col 3-5

Khare, Harish, 1990, Anti-Congressism endures: Rajiv's failure to evolve, *Times of India*, October 10, p 8, col 3-5.

Khare, Harish, 1990 Congress dilemma: Alternative to Rajiv Gandhi, *Times of India*, March 26, p 6, col 3-5

Khayal, Ghulam Nabi, 1981, All in the family, *India Today* 6(17) September 1, p 45-46

Kher, M.V., 1982, Infighting cost Congress (I) Jabalpur seat, *Sunday* 9(51) July 12, p 31

Kher, M.V., 1992, Naxal links with Rajiv assassins, *Times of India*, April 2, p 3, col 4-5

Khursid, Salman, 1982, Inclement climate for Congress, *Delhi Recorder* 3(4) June, p 36-37

Khushwant Singh, 1976, Man who gets the things done, *Illustrated Weekly of India* 97(33) August 15, p 6-15

Khushwant Singh, 1980, Destiny's cruelty, *Sunday* 8(1) June 29, p 8

Khushwant Singh, 1981, Rajiv: Reluctant bridegroom, *Hindustan Times*, May 13, p 9

Khushwant Singh, 1991, Rajiv and the stars, *Sunday* June 23-June 29, p 20-21

Kirpekar, Subash, 1985, Congress vote bank that failed, *Times of India*, October 23, p 8, col 7-8

Kirpekar, Subash, 1988, Rajiv Gandhi attaks Non-Congress Governments, *Times of India*, April 25, p 1, col 4-6+

Kirpekar, Subash, 1988, Rajiv warns Pak against medding in Punjab, *Times of India*, April 24, p 1, col 1-3+

Kohli, M.S., 1991, An adventurous spirit, *Hindustan Times* (Magazine), July 20, p 3, col 1-8

Kothari, Rajni, 1982, Stemming the rot, *Indian Express*, June 7, p 6

Kothari, Rajni, 1985, Rajiv Gandhi's election: End or beginning? *Economic*

Times, January 6, p 3, col 1-5+
Kothari, Rajni, 1987, Decline of institutions, *Hindustan Times*, August 10
Kothari, Rajni, 1989, Rajiv's Panchayat: A bonapartist vision, *Mainstream* 27(34) May 20, p 2-3
Kottary, Sailesh, 1985, Target: Rajiv Gandhi, *Illustrated Weekly of India*, 106(4) June 2, p 6-11
Koul
See Kaul
Kripa Shankar, 1988, Relevance of Gandhi to India's rejuvenation, *Mainstream* 26(29) April 30, p 11-12
Kripalani, J.B., 1980, Rajiv Gandhi: The succession qestion, *Hindustan Times*, October 15
Kripalani, J.B., 1981, Rajiv entitled to contest, *Hindustan Times*, June 2, p 13
Krishna Iyer, V.R., 1988, The Sri Lanka accord: An autopsy, *Illustrated Weekly of India* 109(14) April 3, p 32-35
Krishna Iyer, V.R., 1988, The Sri Lanka accord: A *post mortem*, *Illustrated Weekly of India* 109(15) April 10, p 38-41
Krishna Iyer, V.R., 1991, In search of truth, *Frontline* June 22-July 5, p 39-41
Krishnamurthy, R., 1991, Sleuths close in on Rajiv's killers, *Current*, July 6-July 12, p 9, col 1-5
Kumar, B. Tej
See Tej Kumar, B.
Kumar
See also full name/surname, e.g., Ajay Kumar; Prem Kumar; Prasanna Kumar, A.
Kumar, D.P., 1980, Rajiv Gandhi may join Party in October, *Statesman*, September 28
Kumar, D.P., 1991, Election scene: Congress prospects after Rajiv, *Mainstream* 29(32) June 1, p 4-5
Lakshman, Nikhil, 1985, The men who will now rule India, *Illustrated Weekly of India*, 105, (37) January 20, p 6-13
Lakshman, Nikhil, 1985, Where are his men today? *Illustrated Weekly of India*, 105(52) May 5, p 6-13
Lakshman, Nikhil, 1986, The Congress (I) cracking up, *Illustrated Weekly of India* 107(14) April 6, p 7-17
Lal
See full name e.g., Bhajan Lal
Lal, Thanhawala, 1992, Man love for the poor, *National Herald* (Supplement), p 18, col 1
Lamba, Asjeet, 1981, Rajiv campaign, *India Today* 6(24) December 31, p 4
Lamba, Asjeet, 1981, Rajiv Gandhi to fight Amethi seat, *Amrit Bazar Patrika* May 12, p 1
Louis, Arul B., 1981, India: The grandson also rises, *Far Eastern Economic Review* 112(27) June 26, p 22
Louis, Arul B., 1982, Arms for Pak will be discussed: PM, *Hindustan Times*, July 29, p 1, news-item

Louis, Arul B., 1982, PM denies Sikhs being wronged: Injustice to Sikh denied, *Hindustan Times*, August 2, p 16

Mahajan, Krishan, 1991, No SC judge to probe killing, *Hindustan Times*, May 26, p 1, col 1-4+

Mahavir Prasad, 1992, The end of an era, *National Herald* (Supplement), p 17, col 1-4

Mainstream (Periodical), 1983, Consensus and catcalls, *Mainstream* 22(9) October 29, p 1-2, editorial

Mainstream (Periodical), 1985, Much ado about nothing, *Mainstream* 23(46) July 13, p 1-2, editorial

Mainstream (Periodical), 1986, The missing factor, *Mainstream* 24(21) January, p 3-4, ediorial

Mainstream (Periodical) 1991, Rajiv's stability, *Mainstream* 29(28) May 4, p 1-2, editorial

Majeedul Hasan, Syed
See Hasan, Syed Majeedul

Malhotra, Inder, 1982, Warming up for 1985, *Times of India*, May 16, p 1

Malhotra, Inder, 1985, Cabinet making and after, *Times of India*, January 3

Malhotra, Inder, 1987, Political commentary: Britain's view of Rajiv, *Times of India*, July 2, p 6, col 3-5

Malhotra, Inder, 1987, Political commentary: Shades of the seventies, *Times of India*, March 20, p 6, col 3-5

Malhotra, Inder, 1991, Remembering Rajiv, *Sunday* June 9-June 15, p 83

Malhotra, Vijay Kumar, 1981, Official funds used to project Congress (I), *Indian Express*, November 25, p 3

Malik, Iqbal, 1981, Voices consonant and dissonant, *Indian Express*, November 23, p 6

Malik, Suyash, 1991, Murder most foul, *Radical Humanist*, 55(3) June, p 4-6

Man Singh, Surjit, 1985, Rajiv Gandhi and Indo-American relations, *Mainstream* 24(9-10) November 2, p 49-53

Maniam, V.S., 1987, A dazzling meeting of minds, *Indian and Foreign Review* 24(10) March 15, p 10-12+

Manmohan, 1986, Danger in the air, *Hindustan Times* (Magazine), December 14, p 1, col 1-6+

Marakkar, V.P., 1989, Rajiv Gandhi and the working class, *Indian Worker* 38(8) November 20, p 2-3

Masani, Minoo, 1987, Roots of President PM clash, *Times of India*, (Sunday Review), March 29, p 1, col 7-8

Masani, Zaheer, jt. author
See Tully, Mark and Masani, Zaheer

Mathews, K. M., 1984, Bogus Centnary of a bogus Congress, *Organiser* 35(34) January 8, p 7

Mathur, Girish, 1981, Rajiv's rivals fight to save their deposits: Congress (I) battle to win Muslim minds, *Blitz*, June 13, p 11

Mathur, Girish, 1984, Will Congress (I) continue Indira's policies? *Link* 27(18) December 0, p 7-9

Mathur, Girish, 1985, Rajiv's US visit may be as futile as Indira's was in 1982, *Link* 27(45) June 16, p 15-16

Mathur, Girish, 1986, How Prime Minister contains Congress unrest? *Link* 28(31) March 9, p 4-7

Mathur, Girish, 1986, Pranab: His business and Congress cultures, *Link* 28(44) June 8, p 14-16

Mathur, Girish, 1986, Whose Congress: Murli Deora's or Ram Kishan's? *Link* 28(40) May 11, p 4-7

Mathur, Girish, 1986, Why PM shouldn't let party drift to split? *Link* 28(37) April 20, p 10-12

Mathur, Girish, 1988, PM on peace mission, as Allahabad hots up, *Link* 30(45) June 12, p 10-12

Mazumdar, Sudip, jt. author
See Deming, Angus and Mazumdar, Sudip

Mehta, A.H., 1981, No complaint against Rajiv, *Hindustan Times*, January 21, p 8

Mehta, Dewang, 1981, Charan Singh: No visible sign of improvement, *Surya India* 5(4) January, p 24

Mehta, Vinod, 1991, Enter Priyanka? *Sunday* June 9-15, p 10-11

Merchant, Minhaz, 1991, Rajiv and after, *Illustrated Weekly of India* 112(23) June 8, p 14-15

Mirchandani, G.S. and Murthi, K.S.R., 1985
See Anon, 1985, (Book Review)

Mishra, Chaturanan, 1989, Rajiv Gandhi policies on Perestroika, *New Age* 37(2) January 8, p 8

Mishra, Chaturanan, 1989, Rajiv Gandhi policies on Perestroika, *New Age* 37(2) January 8, p 8

Mishra, Chaturanan, 1989, Rajiv's promises and performance, *New Age* 37(40) October 1, p 1+

Mishra, Sudhanshu, 1986, Mathur capable of stirring dissidence, *Link* 28(40) May 11, p 12

Misra, Gopal, 1986, Revamping the ruling party, *Commerce* 152(3898) February 1, p 196 +

Misra, Panchanan, 1985, Indian National Congress: Towards technological revolution, *National Herald*, November 17, p 1, col 1-6 +

Misra, Prafulla, 1986, Factional squabble in Assam Congress (I), *New Age* 34(34) August 24, p 6

Misra, Ravish, 1982, All set for 'mini' general poll, *National Herald* May 16, p 14

Mithani, D.M. jt. author
See Anon, 1988, (Book Review)

Mitra Chaudhury, Sreerupa, 1991, Rajiv Gandhi: Vikas ki aandhi, *Democratic World* May 19, p 6, col 2

Mitra Chaudhury, Sreerupa, 1991, Is terrorism, the way to all solutions? *Democratic World* 20(21) May 26, p 5, col 1-3

Mitra, Anirudhya, 1991, A formidable group, *India Today* June 30, p 46, col 1-2

Mitra, Anirudhya, 1991, Rajiv assassination: The inside story, *India Today* July 15, p 22-29

Mitra, Anirudhya, 1991, Startling break through, *India Today* June 30, p 45, col 1-2

Mitra, Ashok, 1989, Rajiv's reform agenda: Fulfilling the mother's dream, *Times of India*, July 3, p 6, col 3-5

Mitra, Chandam, 1989, A CAG-tag opposition: Neutralising Rajiv's populsim, *Times of India*, July 26, p 6, col 3-5

Mitra, Chandam, 1989, Rajiv Gandhi moves up: Congress takes the offensive, *Times of India*, May 29, p 6, col 3-4

Mitra, Chandam, 1989, The odds get longer: Rajiv Gandhi after black Sunday, *Times of India*, January 24, p 6, col 3-5

Mitra, Chandam, 1989, The Pensive party: Rajiv's non-discovery of India, *Times of India*, March 22, p 6, col 3-5

Mitra, S., jt. author
See Chawla, P. and Mitra S.

Mitra, S. and Chawla, P., 1982, Cabinet-carousel, *India Today* 7(18) September 30, p 56-64

Mitra, Sumit, 1981, Kisan Rally: Operation Ego message, *India Today* 6(5) March 15, p 16-21

Mitra, Sumit, 1981, Osibisa costly razze-dazze, *India Today* 6(21) November 15, p 129-131

Mitra, Sumit, 1982, Bhajan Lal: The artful manipulator, *India Today* 7(12) June 30, p 78-82

Mitra, Sumit, 1982, Doordarshan : A slow fade-out, *India Today* 7(9) May 15, p 53

MItra, Sumit, 1992, Rajiv Gandhi: A dream made and unmade, *India Express* (Magazine), p 1, col 1-7

Mitra, Sumit and Chawla, P., 1982, Government: Sprucing up the band, *India Today* 7(3) February 15, p 62 -71

Mittal, Rajiv
See Anon, 1982, (Book Review); Anon, 1985, (Book Review)

Mohammad Vazeeruddin
See Anon, 1962, (Book Review); Anon, 1985, (Book Review)

Mohan
See fullname e.g., Manmohan; Surendra Mohan

Mohan, Devendra
See Devendra Mohan

Mohan Ram, 1991, Who killed Rajiv? *Illustrated Weekly of India*, 112(23) June 8, p 6-11

Mohite, Gopal, 1981, Politics of loyalty, *Sunday* 9(33) January 31, p 18-20

Moopnar, G.K., 1981, No meeting with Rajiv Gandhi, *Statesman*, February 10

Moopnar, G.K., 1982, No IAF copter for Rajiv, *Hindustan Times*, May 15, p 5

Mukarji, Apartim, 1992, LTTE extends olive branch to New Delhi, *Hindustan Times*, March 29, p 15, col 5-7

Mukarji, Apartim, 1991, Lanka TV fails to show assassin's photo, *Hindsutan Times*, June 3, p 20, col 1-2

Mukarji, Apartim, 1992, Lanka assurance to India on Rajiv assassination, *Hindus-*

tan Times, May 8, p 12, col 2-4
Mukarji, Apartim, 1992, Sri Lankan dilemma over Prabhakaran, *Hindustan Times*, January 6, p 15, col 7-8.
Mukarji, Nirmal, 1989, Decentratization below State level: Need for new system of governance, *Economic and Political Weekly* March 4
Mukerji, Debashish, 1991, Power paralysis: Amethi yearns for the return of Rajiv as Prime Minister, *The Week*, April 28, p 38-39
Mukherjee, Pranab, 1982, New blood in politics, *Illustrated Weekly of India*, 103(3) January 31, p 30-33
Mukherjee, Pranab, 1984, The Leader of the House and the whips in United Kingdom and India, *Journal of Parliamentary Information* December, p 598-604
Mukherjee, Sadhan, 1986, Congress (I) drama only starting, *New Age* 34(18) May 4, p 1+
Mukherjee, Sadhan, 1986, Rajiv blues over Tripathi non-revolt, *New Age* 34(22) June 8, p 1
Mukhopadhyay Ashim, 1986, Rajiv's gift to West Bengal, *India Express* (Magazine), October 12, p 1, col 1-8+
Mumbal, Brihan, 1989, Maximum democracy and maximum devolution, *Mahanagarpalika Patrika* 36(6) August, p 2-6
Muni, S.D., 1986, Rajiv Gandhi's neighbourhood policy, *Mainstream* 24(25) February 22, p 4-6+
Murarka Dev, 1984, The assassination and after, *Mainstream* 23(15) December 8, p 5-6+
Murti, K.S.R., jt. author
See Anon, 1985, (Book Review)
Murti, V.K. and Sharma, Gautam, 1985
See Anon, 1985, (Book Review); Anon, 1986
Murthy, Sachidananda, 1991, Could SPG have saved Rajiv? *The Week* June 9, p 40-41
Murthy, Sachidananda, 1991, Power at hand, *The Week* Febuary, p 28-31
N.C., 1985 The chastening time, *Mainstream* 23(52) August 24, p 1-4
N.C., 1985, Chinks in the armour, *Mainstream* 23(49) August 3, p 1-2
N.C., 1986, Sunshine in Kashmir, *Mainstream* 25(9) November 15, p 6-7
N. Ram
See Ram, N.
Nagi, Saroj, 1991, A tragic end, *Illustrated Weekly of India* 112(22) June 1, p 6-11.
Naik, J.A., 1980, India that Rajiv may inherit, *Janata* 35(41) December, June 2, p 13
Naik, Subhakarrao, 1992, Rajiv: The innovator, *National Herald* (Supplement), p 20, col 1-3
Nalapai, M.D., 1992, The revolution unborn, *National Herald* (Supplement), p 14, col 1-6
Namboodripad, E.M.S., 1984, Will Rajiv Gandhi explain his stand: An open letter to Rajiv Gandhi, *People's Democracy* 8(52) December 23, p 7
Namboodripad, E.M.S., 1988, Rajiv Gandhi in his true colours, *People's Democracy* 12(15) August 10, p 1+

Nandy, Pritish, 1986, Defiant! P.C Sethi Ko Gussa Kyon Aata Hai? *Illustrated Weekly of India* 107(40) October 12, p 9-12

Nandy, Pritish, 1986, The man who knows too much, *Illustrated Weekly of India* 107(18) April 27, p 6-17

Nandy, Pritish, 1986, The men who tried to kill Rajiv Gandhi, *Illustrated Weekly of India* 107(27) July 6, p 8-17

Nandy, Pritish, 1986, Yesterday, tomorrow, *Illustrated Weekly of India* 107(2) January 12, p 8-17

Nandy, Pritish, 1989, The face-off at Amethi, *Illustrated Weekly of India*, 110(42) October 15, p 10-19

Nandy, Pritish, 1991, Stability and economic liberalism: Rajiv's new slogans, *Illustrated Weekly of India* (Supplement) 112(12) March 23, p 1

Narayan

See also full name, e.g., Hemendra Narayan

Narayanan, K.P., 1982, Sagar poll: Storm signal foı Congress (I), *Caravan* 1(713) February 1, p 35-36

Narsimha Rao, P.V., 1992, A crusader for change, *National Herald* (Supplement), p 3, col 1-6

Nayar, Kuldip, 1981, Is Rajiv Gandhi really native? *Sunday* 9(25) December 6, p 13

Nayar, Kuldip, 1981, No logic behind top bureaucrat's promotions, *Sunday* 9(8) August 9, p 37

Nayar, Kuldip, 1982, Mrs Gandhi likes sycophants, *Sunday* 9(37) March 6, p 9

Nayar, Kuldip, 1985, Rajiv Gandhi's 200 days, *Tribune*, July 25

Nehru, Arun, 1981, Charge baseless, *National Herald*, June 22

New Age (Periodical), 1980, Rajiv vs Maneka: Palace intrigues, *New Age* 28(32) August 10, p 1+

New Age (Periodical), 1984, Pious platitudes, *New Age* 32(47) November 18, p 2, editorial

New Age (Periodical), 1984, Rajiv refrain, *New Age* 32(52) December 23, p 2, editoral

New Age (Periodical), 1985, Disturbing pronoucements, *New Age* 33(28) July 14, p 1, editorial

New Age (Periodical), 1985, PM's US visit, *New Age* 33(25) June 23, p 2, editorial

New Age (Periodical), 1985, Struggle for national unity, *New Age* 33(2) January 13, p 2, editorial

New Age (Periodical), 1986, Grim warning, *New Age* 34(41) October 12, p 2, editorial

Niesewand, Peter, 1981, Indira without Sanjay: Rajiv no substitute, *Blitz*, September 20, p 20

Nigam, R.L., 1991, Rajiv Gandhi assassination and assassins, *Radical Humanist* 55(3) June, p 1-3+

Nihal Singh, S., 1981, Art of muddling through, *Indian Express*, October 27, p 6

Nihal Singh, S., 1981, Fall of the 'new' leader, *Indian Express*, September 9, p 6

Nihal Singh, S., 1981, Few signs of hope, *Indian Express*, December 30, p 6

Nihal Singh, S., 1982, All of India is a stage, *Indian Express*, April 21, p 6

Nihal Singh, S., 1982, Greatest show on earth, *Indian Express*, May 19, p 6

Nihal Singh, S., 1982, Making a leader to order, *Indian Express*, January 6, p 6

Nihal Singh, S., 1983, The heart of the matter, *Indian Express*, May 5, p 6

Nihal Singh, S., 1988, PM's propsoed China visit: Symbolism and substance, *Times of India*, May 28, p 6, col 3-5

Nihal Singh, S., 1988, Rajiv and Government battered: But Opposition fail to make gain, *Times of India*, May 10, p 6, col 3-5

Nihal Singh, S., 1989, Rajiv's China visit: Much work lies ahead, *Times of India*, January 3, p 6, col 3-5

Nikhil Lakshman
See Lakshman, Nikhil

Ninah, Sevanti, 1985, Rajiv's discovery of Bharat, *Indian Express* (Magazine), October 20, p 1, col 1-8

Nizamuddin, D.E., 1980, Changing guard, *Sunday* 8(18) December 7, p 66

Nizamuddin, D.E., 1980, Tears of many colours, *Sunday*, 8(2) July 20, p 58

Nizamuddin, D.E., 1981, Farooq Abdullah's growing maturity, *Sunday* 9(22) Novermber 15, p 66

Nizamuddin, D.E., 1981, Rajiv looking after Punjab, *Sunday* 9(22) Novmeber 15, p 66

Nizamuddin, D.E., 1981, Rajiv tastes infighting, *Sunday* 9(15) September 21, p 66

Nizamuddin, D.E., 1982, Anjiah's English was poor, *Sunday* 9(38) March 13, p 66

Nizamuddin, D.E., 1982, Congress (I) rally cancelled, *Sunday* 9(36) February 27, p 58

Nizamuddin, D.E., 1982, Even Amethi's animals are being nursed, *Sunday*, Febraury 27, p 38

Nizamuddin, D.E., 1982, Everybody is remembering Sanjay, *Sunday* 9(45) May 1, p 58

Nizamuddin, D.E., 1982, Missing the Rajya Sabha bus, *Sunday* 9(41) April 3, p 58

Nizamuddin, D.E., 1982, Rajiv: A quarter person, *Sunday* 9(5) June 12, p 58

Nizamuddin, D.E., 1982, Rajiv's friend Abbas, *Sunday* 8(9) September 7, p 66

Nizamuddin, D.E., 1982, Rajiv Gandhi's show: Who will pay this bill? *Sunday* 9(37) March 6, p 58

Nizamuddin, D.E., 1982, Rewarded for misconduct, *Sunday* 9(47) May 15, p 66

Nizamuddin, D.E., 1982, Who is Yashpal Kapoor fooling? *Sunday* 9(37) March 6, p 58

Noorani, A.G., 1988, Rajiv Gandhi: Immage and reality, *Indian Express* (Magazine), June 5, p 1, col 1-8

Noorani, A.G., 1988, Rajiv Gandhi's political invectives, *Indian Express* (Magazine), October 17

Noorani, A.G., 1991, A limited probe, *Frontline* June 22-July 5, p 42-44

Nungent, Nicholas, 1990, Rajiv Gandhi: Son of a dynasty, *Tribune* (Magazine), November 25, p 1, col 1-7+
See also Anon, 1990, (Book Review)

Oomen, T.K., 1987, Charisma and not king emperor, *Times of India*, January 22, p 8, col 7-8

Organiser (Periodical), 1985, PM's demagogy, *Organiser* 36(52) May 12, p 1+, editorial

Organiser (Periodical), 1985, Political pot-boiling, *Organiser* 36(43) March 10, p 3, editorial

Organiser (Periodical), 1986, Rajiv-Zia see-saw, *Organiser* 37(44) March 16, p 3, editorial

Organiser (Periodical), 1986, Ruling party crisis, *Organiser* 38(5) June 15, p 3, editorial

Organiser (Periodical), 1988, PM's progress, *Organiser* 39(46) May 8, p 3, editorial

Padgaonkar, Dileep, 1987, Soviet backing for Rajiv: Significance of visit to Moscow, *Times of India*, July 7, p 6, col 3-5

Padgaonkar, Dileep, 1990 The Congress will not deviate from secularism: An interview, *Times of India*, September 9, p 1, col 1-8.

Padmakumar, K., 1986, Politics of Rajiv Gandhi, *Mainstream* 24(33) April 19, p 31-33

Padmanabhan, Mukund, 1991, A question of identity, *Sunday* June 9-June 15, p 67-69

Padmanabhan, Mukund, 1991, The polls that weren't, *Sunday* June 2-8, p 18-19

Padmanabhan, Mukund, et al, 1991, The hit: Who did it? And why? *Sunday* June 2-June 8, p 14-17

Padmanabhan, Mukund, et al, 1991, How the arrests were made, *Sunday* June 23-June 29, p 62-63

Pal, R.N., 1984
See Anon, 1984

Pal, R.N. and Sudesh Rani, 1989
See Anon, 1989, (Book Review)

Pandit, C.S., 1981, Mrs Indira Gandhi very sure of her ground, *Amrit Bazar Patrika*, May 14, p 6

Pandit, Tooshar, 1982, Laughing stock of Andhra, *Sunday* 9(36) February 27, p 14+

Pandit, Tushar, 1991, A day with Rajiv, *Sunday* June 9-June 15, p 74

Pandya, Dinkar, 1986, No tears for the dissidents, *Link* 28(40) May 11, p 10

Panigrahi, Chintamani, 1992, Racing aganist time, *National Herald* (Supplement), p 8, col 4-6

Panja, Ajit Kumar, 1992, Facing challenges in Rajiv spirit, *National Herald* (Supplement), p 20, col 4-6

Parakal, Pauly V., 1983, Bombay AICC (I) Session: Confrontation while talking consensus, *New Age* 31(44) October 30, p 1 +

Parakal, Pauly V., 1984, Cong (I) manifesto full of tall claims, *New Age* 32(51) December 16, p 1

Parakal, Pauly V., 1986, Rajiv Gandhi should know some facts on linguistic States, *New Age* 34(42) December 28, p 3

Parakal, Pauly V., 1987, Destabilisation cannot be fought Rajiv style, *New Age* 35(17) April 26, p 1-2

Parakal, Pauly V., 1987, Stark reality refutes Rajiv Gandhi's claims, *New Age*

35(5) Feburary 1, p 1

Parakal, Pauly V., 1988, Rajiv Gandhi in same old style, *New Age* 37(50) December 17, p 1+

Parakal, Pauly V., 1988, Rajiv Gandhi's drive for one-party rule, *New Age* 36(7) February 14, p 1+

Parakal, Pauly V., 1990, Dublous role of Congress I, *New Age* 38(43), October 28, p 1.

Parakal, Pauly V., 1990, Rajiv trek back launch at Kanchi, *New Age* 88(24) June 17, p 1

Parakal, Pauly V., 1991, Rajiv Gandhi biggest destabiliser around, *New Age* 39(12), March 24, p 1, col 1-5

Paranjape, H.K., 1986, Mr Gandhi's economic policy, *Indian Economic Journal* 33(4) April-June, p 1-4

Parimoo, J.N., 1982, Warm welcome to PM in New York, *Times of India*, July 29, p 1+

Parimoo, J.N., 1985, Rajiv charms American: But US policy is another matter, *Times of India*, June 22, p 8, col 3-5

Parimoo, J.N., 1986, Virk's lawyers for dismissal of charge, *Times of India*, March 13, p 16, col 1-4

Parsai, Gargi, jt. author
See Ghosh,Soumya K. and Parsai, Gargi

Parsai, K.B., 1981, What does the future hold for Rajiv? *Weekend Review* 2(14) January, p 2+

Parthasarthy, G., 1982, Rajiv to go to USSR with PM, *Indian Express*, September 5, p 9

Patil, Vasantdada, 1981, AICC (I) post for Rajiv soon, *Times of India*, October 22, p 5

Pawar, Sharad, 1989, Closing rank, *Illustrated Weekly of India*, 110(50) December 10, p 6-9

People's Democracy (Periodical), 1985, Rajiv threat of emergency, *People's Democracy* 9(28) July 14, p 1+2, editorial

Pepole's Democracy (Periodical), 1989, The Congress (I) manifesto, *People's Democracy* 13(46) November 18, p 1, editorial

Phadnis, Umashankar, 1989, Indo-Sri Lanka accord: Need for reassesing realitics, *Mainstream* 27(40) July 1, p 5-6+

Ponkshe, Satyawrat
See Anon, 1987, (Book Review)

Pramar, Suresh K., 1991, Rajiv Gandhi's death orphans tribals, *Onlooker* June 15, p 46-47

Prasad
See also full name e.g., Mahavir Prasad

Prasad, Srinivasa, 1992, Rajiv's assassins were ready to strike in 1990, *Independent*, May 23, p 1, col 2-6

Prasad, Srinivasa, 1992, SIT files chargesheet in Rajiv case: Prabhakaran, 40 others accused, *Independent*, May 21, p 1, col 5-7

Prasad, Srinivasa, 1992, SIT files chargesheet in Rajiv case: Prabhakaran, 40 others accused, *Independent*, May 21, p 1, col 5-7

Prasad Rao, V.G., 1986, Congress cross voting in Andhra Poll, *TimesofIndia* April 1, p 8, col 7-8

Prasanna Kumar, A., 1985, Form Nehru to Rajiv: Forty years of India's foreign policy, *Triveni* 54(1) April-June, p 39-46

Prasannan, R., 1991, Bond of blood, *The Week* April 28, p 36, col 1-3

Prasannan, R., 1991, The driving force, *The Week* April 28, p 31

Prasannan, R., 1991, JD (S) will disappear: Rajiv Gandhi promises better contact with the masses, *The Week* April 28, p 32-33, news-item

Prasannan, R., 1991, Winning hand, *The Week* April 28, p 28-31+

Pratap
See full name, e.g., Anita Pratap

Prem Kumar, 1982, Congress (I) stakes in Haryana, *Statesman*, May 18, p 4

Puri, Anjali, 1986, What's nice kid like you doing in politics? *Indian Express* (Magazine), October 26, p 1, col 1-8+

Puri, Rajinder, 1981, Fighting Rajiv, *Hindustan Times*, June 3, p 9

Puri, Rajinder, 1981, Why Antulay will go? *Hindustan Times*, November 18, p 1

Quershy, Ahtesham, 1981, Rajiv's bid to stop infighting, *Indian Express*, November 24, p 20

Raghavan, A., 1982, Bells toll for Congress (I), *Blitz*, May 29, p 1+

Raghavan, A., 1982, Congress (I) in 82....at sixes and sevens, *Blitz*, January 16, p 9

Raghavan, A., 1982, Garhwal: Threat to Congress (I) dynasty, *Blitz*, May 8, p 9

Raghavan, Barun, 1982, Mrs Gandhi's troubles have only begun, *Sunday* 9(51) June 12, p 33

Raghavan, C., 1991, A challenging role, *Frontline* June 22-July 5, p 29

Raghu, V., 1991, Andhra Pradesh vandalism after Rajiv's assassination, *Mainstream* 29(35) June 22, p 29-30

Rahul Singh, 1985, Around the world with Rajiv Gandhi, *Indian Express*, June 30, p 6, col 1-8

Rahul Singh, 1986, Does Rajiv Gandhi still have anything to smile about? *Indian Express* (Magazine), November 2, p 1, col 1-8

Rai, Kalpnath, 1981, Rajiv carrying the Nehru flag, *Current*, July 11, p 5

Rai, Kalpnath, 1981, Rajiv has earned his place in politics, *Blitz*, June 13, p 4

Rai Singh, 1985
See Anon, 1985, (Book Review)

Raina, Ashok, 1991, Need he have died? *Hindustan Times* (Sunday Magazine), June 2, p 2, col 1-8

Raina, Jay, 1991, Rajiv allays minorities apprehension, *Hindustan Times*, May 14, p 1, col 4+

Raj Gopal, R., 1982, Karnataka: Little chance for Mid Term Poll, *Caravan* 2(714) February, 15-16

Rajan, K.R. Sundar
See Sundar Rajan, K.R.

Rajeswara Rao, C., 1984, Congress has piled up problems, *Economic Times*, December 12, p 5, col 7-8

Rajput, R.S., 1989

See Anon, 1989, (Book Review)
Ram, N., 1991, Rajiv had little time: Interview with Jyoti Basu, *Frontline* 8(12) June 8-June 21, p 113-115
Rama Rao, G.J., 1985, Capitalism paraded as socialism at AICC, *New Age* 83(19) May 12, p 1+
Rama Sarma, K.V.S., 1992, Man of destiny, *National Herald* (Supplement), p 5 vol 1-3
Ramalingam, N.K., 1980, Rajiv, Maneka must play active role, *Current*, July 12, p 10-11
Ramamurthy, Vazhapadi, K., 1992, An eminent Parliamentarian, *National Herald* (Supplement), p 18, col 1-4
Raman, R., 1986, Rajiv in blunderland, *Indian Express* (Magazine), March 16, col 1-8+
Raman Swamy
See Swamy, Raman
Ranadive, B. T., 1985, On the AICC (I) session, *People's Democracy* 9(19) May 12, p 1+
Ranadive, B. T., 1986, Inner conflict inside the Congress (I), *People's Democracy* 10(19) May 11, p 1+
Ranga, N. G., 1985, Congress since 1971, *Rural India* 48(4-5) April-May, p 57-63
Rangarajan, R., 1983, Beyond the Bombay session, *Link* 26(12) October 30, p 12-13
Rani
See also full name, e.g., Sudesh Rani
Ranvhi, Sharan, 1986, Dissidence on decline, *Link* 28(40) May 11, p 11
Rao, C. Chandra Shekhar
See Chandra Shekhar Rao, C.
Rao, P.V. Narsimha
See Narsimha Rao, P.V.
Rasgotra, Maharajakrishna, ed., 1990
See Anon, 1990, (Book Review)
Rath, Ramachandra, 1980, Let Indira choose the successor, *Current*, July 12, p 10-11
Rau, M. Chalapathi
See Chalapathi Rau, M.
Ravindra Nath, 1981, New Bhakti movement, *Indian Express*, September 8, p 6
Ray, Sunanda K. Datta
See Datta-Ray, Sunanda K.
Razdan, Deepak, 1991, Rajiv's opponent for Govt of poor, *Hindustan Times*, May 7, p 9, col 1-2
Razi, Syed Sibtey, 1992, Rajiv Bhaiya: A man of the people, *National Herald* (Supplement), p 6, col 1-5
Reddy
See also full name/surname, e.g., Janardhana Reddy
Reddy, G.K., 1982, India-Saudi Arabia joint Commission likley, *Hindu*, April 13, p 1

Reddy, G.K., 1987, PM retains image despite shortcomings, *Hindu*, January 1

Reddy, Pratap C., 1992, Rajiv's injection for high-tech medicare, *National Herald* (Supplement), p 12, col 5-6

Reddy, Sanjiva, 1981, Not enough done for children, *Indian Express*, November 15, p 4

Roy, Bhaskar, 1991, Ambiguous stand, *India Today* March 31, p 29-31

Roy, Bhaskar, 1991, An emotional farewell, *India Today* June 15, p 108, col 1-2

Roy, Bunker, 1985, For Prime Minister, a word of advice, *Mainstream* (Speical Number) 23(38) March 9, p 16-18

Roy, Subir, 1987, Economics of uncertainty: Policy options before Rajiv Gandhi, *Times of India*, April 10, p 6, col 3-5

Roy Chodhury, P., 1984, Soviet support for Rajiv Gandhi, *Link* 27(19) December 16, p 30-31

Roy Choudhury, P.C., 1985, The Indian National Congress: Sowing the seeds of political consciousness, *Indian Express*, November 24, p 8, col 1-5

Roychowdhury, Nanda Dulal, 1991, Rajiv Gandhi: Can he provide a stable alternative? *Sunday* March 24-March 30, p 4, letter to editor

Rudra Dutt

See Dutt, Rudra

Rustamji, K.F., 1988, Good Morning India, *Illustrated Weekly of India* 109(30) July 24, p 20-21

S.C., 1988, Focus: Rajiv's China visit: Balance sheet, *Mainstream* 27(14) December 31, p 3-4

S.M., Pseud, 1982, What does all this add up to? *Indian Express*, January 9, p 6

S.V., 1985, Well-don, *Mainstream* 23(43) June 22, p 1-3

Saari, Anil 1981, Can Rajiv save the Nirankaris? *Sunday* 9(25) December 6, p 43-45

Saari, Anil 1981, Sanjay's death was a personal loss, *Sunday* 9(31) January 17, p 22-27

Saari, Anil 1982, Yashpal Kapoor: The end is near, *Sunday* 9(33) January 31, p 42

Sachidananda Murthy

See Murthy, Sachidananda

Sadachari, 1981, Amethi wrong choice for Rajiv, *Blitz*, May 23, p 13

Sagar, Anand, 1982, In and out, *India Today* 7(5) March 16, p 35

Sahay, S., 1985, Mr Gandhi's Press Conference, *Statesman*, July 11

Sahay, Subodh Kant, 1991, Rajiv had been warned often, *India Today* June 15, p 46, col 1-2

Sahay, Vikant, 1986, Politics of Rajiv Gandhi: Measuring up to our expectations, *Mainstream* 24(29) March 22, p 28+

Sahni, Ajai, 1991, The dynasty ends, *Surya India* June, p 6-14

Sahni, Ajai and Dwivedi, S.K., 1991, The Bungler! *Surya India* April, p 22-23+

Sahni, Ajai, et al, 1991, The age of the pygmy, *Surya India* March, p 23-30

Saksena, Rashmi, 1991, The pug mask, *The Week* June 9, p 38-39

Salvi, P.G., 1987

See Anon, 1987, (Book Review)

Sanghvi, Vir, 1991, Encounters with Rajiv Gandhi, *Sunday* June 9-June 15, p 18-

28

Sanghvi, Vir, 1991, I cannot cling to office, *Sunday* March 17-March 23, p 66-69

Santosh Kumar, V.K., 1991, Last moment: A forensic view, *The Week* June 9, p 34-35

Sardesai, 1989, Gandhi, Gorbachev and India today, *Mainstream* 27(35) May 27, p 53-55

Sarin, Ritu, jt. author
See Shukla, Rajiv and Sarin, Ritu

Sarma
See full surname, e.g., Raman Sarma, K.V.S.

Saroj, Chiranjeev Joshi, 1982, Son will succeed Indira, *Current*, March 13, p 23

Sarojangi, 1991, Congress wants its way on Gulf policy, *Illustrated Weekly of India* January 26-January 27, p 1, col 1-5

Satinder Singh, 1980, Rajiv to enter politics, *Tribune*, August 3

Satyanarayan Reddy, B., 1992, A messiah of down trodden, *National Herald* (Supplement), p 18, col 6

Sayeed, Mohammad, 1986, State unit back High Command, *Link* 28(40) May 11, p 13

Scindia, Madhavrao, 1992, Progressive to the core, *National Herald* (Supplement), p 5, col 4-6+

Segon, Harish, 1987, Rajiv Gandhi's successfull visit, *Indian and Foreign Review* 24(21) August 31, p 6-9

Sehgal, Rashme, 1992, Trying to forget, *Independent*, May 21, p 5, col

Sen, Sumanta, 1985, PM's visit boisters Bhutan's confidence, *Times of India*, October 4, p 7, col 1-4

Sen, Sumanta, 1986, Factionalism in Bengal Congress, *Times of India*, April 21, p 8, col 7-8

Sengupta, Barun, 1980, And now, Rajiv, *Sunday* 8(3) July 27, p 35

Sen Gupta, Barun, 1980, Astrology and succession, *Sunday* 8(11) September 21, p 37

Sen Gupta, Barun, 1980, Men who matter with the PM, *Sunday* 8(18) December 7, p 23

Sengupta, Barun, 1980, Politics after Sanjay, *Sunday* 8(1) June 29, p 14-15

Sen Gupta, Barun, 1981, Cabinet shake up has merely been post- pond, *Sunday* 9(10) August 23, p 23

Sen Gupta, Barun, 1981, Could the next President be Mr Venkatraman? *Sunday* 9(25) December 6, p 30

Sen Gupta, Barun, 1982, Mrs Gandhi's troubles have only begun, *Sunday* 9(51) June 12, p 33

Sen Gupta, Barun, 1982, Mrs Gandhi will make big changes in mid year, *Sunday* 9(51) June 12, p 33

Sengupta, Bhabani, 1985, A tale of two visits, *Illustrated Weekly of India* 106(8) June 30, p 22-23

Sengupta, Bhabani, 1985, The year of living dangerously, *Indian Express* (Magaizne), November 3, p 1, col 1-8+

Sengupta, Bhabani, 1986, First year as Prime Minister, *Statesman* January 16

Sengupta, Bhabani, 1987, The fourth year, *Economic and Political Weekly* December 12

Sen Gupta, Bhabani, 1988, The green leaves of December, *Hindustan Times*, October 10

Sengupta, Bhabani, 1988, Poised for peace, *India Today* Janary 15

Sengupta, Bhabani, 1988, Rajiv Gandhi and his forty horses, *Economic and Political Weekly* May 7

Sengupta, Bhabani, 1989, The master and the novice, *Seminar* 363, November, p 31-34

See also Anon, 1989, (Book Review)

Seth, N.K., 1988, Commentary: PM's office, *Mainstream* 26(25) April 2, p 3

Sethi, J.D., 1985, A year of Rajiv Gandhi, *Indian Express*, October 25

Sethi, J.D., 1988, All the PM's men, *Illustrated Weekly of India* 109(4) January 24, p 32-35

Sethi, Patricia J., 1985, Rajiv impact lasts in United States, *Times of India*, July 3, p 8, col 7-8

Sham Lal, 1985, The national scene: Reading the fever chart, *Times of India*, January 12, p 8, col 3-5

Shankar

See full name, e.g., Kripa Shankar

Shankhdher, M.M., 1987, Rajiv-Reagan talks can open new chapter in Indo-US relations, *Organiser* 39(24) November 22, p 6

Sharan, R.H., 1986-1987, Prime Minister of India: The role of personality and social forces, *Calcutta Journal of Political Studies* 6(1-2), p 1-28, bibliography, footnotes

Sharan, Ranvhi, 1986, Dissidence on decline, *Link* 28(40) May 11, p 11

Sharma, A.P., 1982, No Rajiv hand in IA appointment, *Hindustan Times*, March 5, p 16

Sharma, B,N., 1981, Bansi vs Bhajan: A battle for survival, *Caravan* 2(708) November 16, p 19

Sharma, Gautam, jt. author

See Anon, 1985, (Book Review)

Sharma, Indira, jt. author

See Anon, 1983, (Book Review)

Sharma, Narendra, 1983, AICC: The consensus call, *Mainstream* 22(9) October 29, p 4-5+

Sharma, P., 1991, Arafat had warned Rajiv, *Hindustan Times*, June 3, p 12, col 1-3.

Sharma, Padam Singh, 1982, PM urged to punish Youth Congress rebels, *Times of India*, March 29, p 9

Sharma, Rajat, 1982, Opposition unity: Putting the piece together, *Onlooker* 44(2) January 31, p 17-19

Sharma, Rajat, 1982, Uttar Pradesh batting caste, dissent and crime, *Onlooker* 44(3) February 15, p 17-19

Sharma, Satinder and Sharma, Indira, 1983

See Anon, 1983, (Book Review)

Sharma, Udayan, 1981, World of Rajiv Gandhi, *Sunday* 9(24) November 29, p 12-13

Sharma, Vasudev, 1981, Five star future for Rajiv: Golden era for Rajiv, *Current*, June 13, p 1+

Sharma, Vichitra, 1982, Bhajan booed at Rajiv poll meeting, *Hindustan Times*, May 6, p 1+

Sharma, Vichitra, 1982, Campaigning Rajiv style, *Weekened Review* 3(10) May 29, p 7

Shastri, H.K., 1982, Defends Rajiv Gandhi, *Times of India*, September 29, p 13

Shekhar

See also under full name, e.g., Chandra Shekhar

Shenoy, T.V.R., 1982, What the Congress (I) lost besides the election, *Onlooker* 44 (10) May 31, p 14-15

Sheoery, W.G., 1985, Rajiv has wiped out the Congress (I) along with the opposition, *Organiser* 36(43) March 10, p 6

Shiraz, 1991, The Sonia enigma: The public loss of a private person, *Sunday* June 2-June 8, p 40

Shukla, Rajiv, 1990, Good bye? Can Rajiv Gandhi continue as Congress President? *Sunday* February 25-March 3, p 65-67+

Shukla, Rajiv, 1990, Security isn't cheap, *Sunday* February 25-March 3, p 7

Shukla, Rajiv, 1991, After Rajiv who? *Sunday* June 2-June 8, p 54-57

Shukla, Rajiv, 1991, Does Rajiv want out? *Sunday* January 13-January 19, p 30-35+

Shukla, Rajiv and Sarin, Ritu, 1991, After the dynasty, *Sunday* June 9-June 15, p 32-34

Shukla, Rajiv and Sarin, Ritu, 1991, A quiet sorrow, *Sunday* June 9-June 15, p 29

Shukla, Satyendra R., 1981, Congress (I) still a divided house, *Hindustan Times*, November 17, p 24

Shurygin, Veniamin, 1989, Rajiv Gandhi: A political profile, *Mainstream* 26(35) June 11, p 31-34

Sidhva, Shiraj, 1991, The letter bomb: Jagmohan accuses Rajiv Gandhi of misleading the nation over Kashmir, *Sunday* May 5-May 11, p 7

Sidhva, Shiraj, 1991, The Sonia enigma: The public loss of a private person, *Sunday* June 2-June 8, p 40

Silver, D.M., 1981, Indira's Rajiv gamble, *Onlooker* 43(10) June 15, p 20-22

Silver, D.M., 1981, Mind of Rajiv Gandhi: Think Indian, think big, *Onlooker* 43(10) June 15, p 23-25

Silvera, D.M., 1980, Meet the Government that works, *Onlooker* 42(19) October 31, p 10-13

Singh

See also under full name, e.g., Khushwant Singh; Vishwanath Pratap Singh

Singh, R. Bhagwan

See Bhagwan Singh, R.

Singh, V.P., 1981, Rajiv's victory is sure, *Hindustan Times*, June 2, p 13

See also Vishwanath Pratap Singh

Singhal, M.M., 1985, PM on test, *Mainstream* 23(38) May 18, p 11

Sinha, B.M., 1981, Bonanza for tax dodgers, *Probe India* 3(1) March, p 25-27

Sinha, Bharati, 1984, No protection for weak under Congress (I) regime, *New Age* 32(42) November 25, p 8-9

Sinha, S.K., 1984, A soldier looks at political scene, *Statesman*, July 8

Sinha Bhattcharya, Mira, 1988, Mission to Beijing, *Hindustn Times* (Magazine), December 18, p 1, col 1-8

Solanki, Madhavsinh, 1986, Congress decline in past year, *Times of India*, March 12, p 8, col 7-8

Sood, Upendra, 1992, Rajiv gave his today for our tomorrow, *National Herald* (Magazine) p 3, col 6

Southern Economist (Periodical), 1981, The Rajiv factor, *Southern Economist* 20(2) May 15, p 1-2, editiorial

Southern Economist (Periodical), 1984, The new dispensation, *Southern Economist* 23(14) November 15, p 1-2, editorial

Southern Economist (Periodical), 1985, Rajiv Gandhi at the helm, *Southern Economist* 23(19), Feburary 1, p 1-2, editorial

Sriman, R., 1992, Indian sports will always miss Rajiv, *National Herald* (Supplement), p 17, col 5-6

Srinivasa Prasad
See Prasad, Srinivasa

Srinivasan, S., 1984, Mr Prime Minister: Are you listening? *Indian Express* (Magazine), November 25, p 3, col 1-8

Srivastava, Manoj, 1985, Congress enters into a new dynamic phase, *National Herald*, July 7, p 1, col 1-6

Stewart, William, 1991, The next generation: Can India's republican dynasty produce more leaders? *Times International*, June 3, p 13

Subramaniam, Vidya, 1988, Will Rajiv Gandhi stand from Amethi? *Indian Express* (Magazine), November 6, p 1, col 1-8+

Subramanian Swamy
See Swamy, Subramanian

Subramanian, T.S., 1991, LTTE's overtures, *Frontline* 8(12) June 8-June 21, p 23

Subramanyam, K., 1987, Rajiv must resist US plea on NPT, *Times of India*, October 10, p 6, col 7-8

Sud, S.K., 1986, Haryana Congress on its wane? *Link* 28(25) January 26, p 49

Sud, S.K., 1986, No dissidents only opportunists in Haryana, *Link* 28(40) May 11, p 14

Sudesh Rani, jt author
See Anon, 1989, (Book Review)

Sulekh, 1982, Youth power no answer to gangster politics, *Blitz*, February 13, p 9

Sundar Rajan, K.R., 1982, Is Congress (I) cracking up? *Illustrated Weekly of India* 103(13) April 17, p 8-12

Sundar Rajan, K.R., 1982, Systematic strangling of democracy, *Caravan* August, p 15

Sunil, K.P., 1991, The plot thickens, *Illustrated Weekly of India* 112(30) July 27, p 20-12

Sunil, K.P., 1991, What is the LTTE up to? *Illustrated Weekly of India* 112(24)

June 15, p 6-11

Surendra Mohan, 1985, Rajiv Gandhi on stump, *Janata*, 40(95) March 10, p 7-8

Surendra Mohan, 1987, The Prime Ministers outbrust, *Janata* 44(10) May 7, p 9-10

Suresh Chandra, 1986, Rajiv Gandhi and the red-tape, *Economic Times*, March 11, p 5, col 7-8

Suri, Surinder, 1981, Mrs Gandhi's enigmatic charisma, *Illustrated Weekly of India* 102(33) November 15, p 30-31

Suri, Surinder, 1985, Presidential Prime Minister: New trends in Indian politics, *Times of India*, November 30, p 8, col 3-5

Surjeet, H.K., 1991, If Rajiv manages to maintain his present position, it will be a big achievement, *India Today* June 15, p 12, col 1-3

Suroor, Hasan, 1991, At close quarters: B.G. Deshmukh recalls Rajiv days, *Frontline* 8(12) June-June 21, p 117

Suroor, Hasan, 1991, The man and the leader, *Frontline* 8(12) June 8-June 21, p 116

Swamy, Raman, 1981, Sanjay Gandhi: A controversial tribute, *India Today* 6(1) January 15, p 15

Swamy, Subramaniam, 1982, Big game, *Current*, April 17, p1

Swarup, H., 1985, Rajiv Gandhi's triumphant visit to the dragon kingdom, *Indian and Foreign Review* 22(24) October 15, p 9-11+

Taban, Ghulam Rabbani, 1991, Post-Rajiv situation, *Mainstream* 29(34) June 15, p 19

Taksal, Vinod, 1985, Rajiv's timely initiatives, *Link* 17(36) April 21, p 28

Talib, Rasheed, 1982, Not to perverse, *India Today* 7(5) March 15, p 27

Talwar, Ashwini, 1991, Letter rogatory delivered to Lanka, *Times of India*, March 14, p 9, col 7-8

Talyarkhan, A.F.S., 1981, Linkage of Asian Games with Delhi's development, *Blitz*, August 1, p 19

Tej Kumar, B., 1982, Preparations for Ninth Asiad, *Indian and Foreign Review* 19(14) May 1, p 19-20

Tellis, Olga, 1981, Maharashtra flats and barl licences to MLA's for support, *Sunday* 9(26) December 13, p 39-40

Tellis, Olga, 1981, Why isn't Rajiv leaving Airlines? *Sunday* 8(24) January 18, p 36-37

Tellis, Olga, 1982, Antulay verdict has not quelled dissension, *Sunday* 10(2) July 3, p 39-41

Tellis, Olga, 1982, I was not surprised, *Sunday* 9(33) January 31, p 21-22

Thakur, Janardan, 1981, Mrs Gandhi's thoughtless thinking tank: Will it now be different? *Probe India* 3(5) July, p 23-24+

Thakur, Janardan, 1986, Does his answer lie in the stars? *Hindustan Times* (Magazine), November 30, p 6, col 1-4

Thakur, Janardan, 1986, It is easy to quote Nehru, *Times of India* (Sunday Review), May 25, p 1, col 1-5

Thakur, Janardan, 1986, No big toy for Rajiv, *Times of India* (Sunday Review), July 6, p 1, col 1-5

Thakur, Janardan, 1986, The intelligence network in a shambles, *Hindustan Times* (Magazine), October 12, p 1, col 1-6+

Thakur, Janardan, 1986, The stormy Arif, *Times of India* (Sunday Review), March 9, p 1, col 1-8

Thakur, Janardan, 1986, Who ever spoke ill of Rajiv Gandhi? *Times of India*, (Sunday Review), June 8, p 1, col 1-4

Thakur, Janardan, 1988, Rajiv Gandhi's discovery of rural India, *Hindustan Times* (Magazine), June 12, p 6, col 1-8+

Thakur, Rameshwar, 1992, Rajiv Gandhi: Visionary of New India, *National Herald* (Magazine), May 24, p 1, col 1-6

Thanhawala Lal
See Lal, Thanhawala

Thapar, Rajiv, 1985, Who is Rajiv protecting, *Economic and Political Weekly* 20(6) February 9, p 220-221

Thapar, Romesh, 1984, The Rajiv party and the Hindus, *Economic and Political Weekly* 19(50) December 15, p 2105

Thapar, Romesh, 1985, Rajiv's Bharat Mata, *Economic and Political Weekly* 20(41) October 12, p 1723

Thapar, Romesh, 1986, A Damaged image, *Economic and Political Weekly* 21(49) December 6, p 2113

Theodore, Stanley, 1991, Madcap's blue noon, *The Week* June 9, p 42, col 1-3

Thukral, G. jt. author
See Chawla, P. and Thukral, G.

Thukral, Gobind, 1982, Himachal Pradesh: Caste calculus, *India Today* 7(10) May 31, p 41-42

Times of India (Newspaper), 1980, Rajiv Gandhi, *Times of India*, August 16, col 1-2, editorial

Times of India (Newspaper), 1981, Misuse of office, *Times of India*, November 12, p 8, col 1-2, editorial

Times of India (Newspaper), 1982, Dangers of sycophancy, *Times of India*, February 5, p 8, col 1-2, editorial

Times of India (Newspaper), 1983, Rajiv's tasks, *Times of India*, May 20, p 8, col 1-2, editorial

Times of India (Newspaper), 1984, A clarion call, *Times of India* November 14, p 8, col 1-2, editiorial

Times of India (Newspaper), 1984, Not by mollycoddling, *Times of India* May 1, p 8, col 1-2, editorial

Times of India (Newspaper), 1984, Mr Rajiv Gandhi, *Times of India*, November 3, p 6, col 1-2, editorial

Times of India (Newspaper), 1984, To the hustings, *Times of India*, November 15, p 8, col 1-2, editorial

Times of India (Newspaper), 1984, Thugs at large, *Times of India*, September 15, p 6, col 1-2, editroial

Times of India (Neswpaper), 1985, After the mandate, *Times of India*, January 8, p 8, col 1-2, editorial

Times of India (Newspaper), 1985, Another shake up, *Times of India* October 18, p

8, col 1-2, editorial

Times of India (Newspaper), 1985, A blunt instrument, *Times of India*, February 23, p 8, col 1-2, editorial

Times of India (Newspaper), 1985, The right to know, *Times of India*, June 20, p 6, col 1-2, editorial

Times of India, (Newspaper), 1985, Mr Gandhi's odyssey, *Times of India*, October 30, p 8, col 1-2, editorial

Times of India (Newspaper), 1985, Moves in Maharashtra, *Times of India*, November 9, p 8, col 1-2, editorial

Times of India (Newspaper), 1985, A new work ethic, *Times of India*, January 12, p 8, col 1-2, editorial

Times of India (Newspaper), 1985, Not just a party, *Times of India*, May 7, p 6, col 1-2, editorial

Times of India (Newspaper), 1985, On the wrong track, *Times of India*, November 25, p 8, col 1-2, editorial

Times of India (Newspaper), 1985, PM darshan, *Times of India*, September 11, p 8, col 1-2, editorial

Times of India (Newspaper), 1985, Praise with purpose, *Times of India*, October 2, p 8, col 1-2, editorial

Times of India (Newspaper), 1985, Politics in war, *Times of India*, November 28, p 8, col 1-2, editorial

Times of India (Newspaper), 1985, A successful visit, *Times of India*, December 3, p 8, col 1-2, editorial

Times of India (Newspaper), 1985, Significant gesture, *Times of India*, May 29, p 8, col 1-2, editorial

Times of India (Newspaper), 1985, War on India, *Times of India*, May 15, p 8, col 1-2, editorial

Times of India (Newspaper), 1986, Breaking conventions, *Times of India*, September 16, p 8, col 1-2. editorial

Times of India (Newspaper), 1986, Courageous Mr Khan, *Times of India*, September 27, p 8. col 1-2, editorial

Times of India (Newspaper), 1986, Death of illusion, *Times of India*, May 23, p 8, col 1-2, editorial

Times of India (Newspaper), 1986, Disciplinary action, *Times of India*, April 30, p 8, col 1-2, editorial

Times of India (Newspaper), 1986, Indira loyalists, *Times of India*, May 14, p 6, col 1-2, editorial

Times of India (Newspaper), 1986, Issue is joined, *Times of India*, September 26, p 8, col 1-2, editorial

Times of India (Newspaper), 1986, Not to be written off, *Times of India*, November 14, p 8, col 1-2, editorial

Times of India (Newspaper), 1986, Refusal to oblige, *Times of India*, October 25, p 8, col 1-2, editorial

Times of India (Newspaper), 1986, The Sethi episode, *Times of India*, October 18, p 8, col 1-2, editorial

Times of India (Newspaper), 1986, The shots at Rajghat, *Times of India*, October

3, p 8, col 1-2, editorial

Times of India (Newspaper), 1986, Suppressing dissent, *Times of India*, March 14, p 8, col 1-2 editorial

Times of India (Newspaper), 1986, Test is not over, *Times of India*, June 4, p 8, col 1-2, editorial

Times of India (Newspaper), 1986, Tripathi speaks out, *Times of India*, April 26, p 8, col 1-2, editorial

Times of India (Newspaper), 1986, Tripathi strikes again, *Times of India*, July 10, p 8, col 1-2, editorial

Times of India (Newspaper), 1986, Unanswered questions, *Times of India*, March 6, p 8, col 1-2, editorial

Times of India (Newspaper), 1986, An unresolved crisis, *Times of India*, April 14, p 8, col 1-2, editorial

Times of India (Newspaper), 1987, Anti Rajiv campaigns, *Times of India*, September 25, p 6, col 1-2, editorial

Times of India (Newspaper), 1987, Appeal to the President, *Times of India*, April 24, p 6, col 1-2, editorial

Times of India (Newspaper), 1987, Confrontation is on, *Times of India*, May 14, p 6, col 1-2, edtiorial

Times of India (Newspaper), 1987, No comfort for Giani, *Times of India*, January 28, p 7, col 1-2, editorial

Times of India (Newspaper), 1987, PM on growth, *Times of India*, January 28, p 7, col 1-2, editorial

Times of India (Newspaper), 1987, Rajiv versus V.P. Singh, *Times of India*, March 27, p 6, col 1-2, editorial

Times of India (Newspaper), 1987, Seeds of trouble, *Times of India*, May 5, p 6, col 1-2, editorial

Times of India (Newspaper), 1988, In a combative mood, *Times of India*, May 5, p 6, col 1-2, editorial

Times of India (Newspaper), 1988, Leadership issue again, *Times of India*, July 27, p 4, col 1-2, editorial

Times of India (Newspaper), 1988, The PM's trip, *Times of India*, April 19, p 6, col 1-2, editorial

Times of India (Newspaper), 1988, Rajiv Gandhi to blame, *Times of India*, February 25, p 6, col 1-2, editorial

Times of India (Newspaper), 1988, A significant visit, *Times of India*, December 24, p 6, col 1-2, editorial

Times of India (Newspaper), 1988, State of the Nation, *Times of India*, August 16, p 4, col 1-2, editorial

Times of India (Newspaper), 1989, A good agreement, *Times of India*, September 19, p 8, col 1-2, editorial

Times of India (Newsparper), 1991, Best of both worlds, *Times of India*, Feburary 27, p 8, col 1-2, editorial

Tiwari, Narain Dutt, 1989, Waiting in the wings, *Illustrated Weekly of India* 110(51) December 17, p 6-7

Tripathi, Salil, 1986, Can the Prime Minister ever be safe? *Indian Express*

(Magazine), October 18, p 1, col 1-8+

Tripathi, Srinivas, 1988, Prime Minister fighting shy of visit to Amethi, *New Age* 36(40) October 2, p 1

Tulasi Daas, Majji, 1992, The pride of the Nation, *National Herald* (Supplement), p 7, col 2-3

Tully, Mark and Masani, Zaheer, 1988, The Rajiv years, *Illustrated Weekly of India* 109(20) May 15, p 32-33

Tyagi, Sadanand, 1981, Rajiv is man of destiny but he won't be PM, *Current*, June 20, p 3

Unnikrishan, K.P., 1991, I don't see Rajiv crossing 175-180 seats, *India Today* June 15, p 13, col 1-3

Varma, Umeshwar Prasad, 1989
See Anon, 1989, (Book Review)

Vazeeruddin, Mohammad, 1985, Piloting the country, *Tribune*, August 18, p 1, col 1-8

Venkatcharya, R., 1988, PM must prepare groundwork, *Economic Times*, December 18, p 3, col 1-8

Venkateswaran, R.J. and Mithani, D.M., 1988
See Anon, 1988, (Book Review)

Venkatraman, R., 1991, Rajiv excelled Nehru, *Hindustan Times*, July 3, p 1

Verghese, B.G., 1988, Getting more with less, *Indian Express*, March 10

Verma, Kapil, 1981, PM's plea to Amethi as a mother, *Hindustan Times*, June 12, p 1, 16

Verma, Kapil, 1981, Rajiv rekindles Amethi hopes, *Hindustan Times*, June 12, p 1, 16

Verma, Kewal, 1982, Where does Mrs Gandhi go from here? *Sunday* 9(51) June 12, p 25

Verma, Kewal, 1986, Rajiv Gandhi and secularism: Lessons from Muslim Woman Bill debate, *Mainstream* 24(38) May 24, p 51-53+

Verma, Shrikant, 1985, An insider's view, *Illustrated Weekly of India* 106(31) December 8, p 38-41

Vernekar, Raju, 1991, Rajiv death led to rout: Thackeray, *Hindustan Times*, June 22, p 7, col 1-4

Vidyadharan, Arvind, 1986, Rajiv's India, *Illustrated Weekly of India* 107(9) March 2, p 38-39

Vijay Dutt, 1981, Troubles of triunph: Can Indira-Rajiv work the Government that does not? *Probe India* 3(5) July, p 16-20

Vikramaditya, 1984, Will Mr Rajiv Gandhi be a better Prime Minister? *Commerce* 149(3834) November 24, p 814+

Viswam, S., 1984, Rajiv Gandhi faces history, *Mainstream* 23(14) December 1, p 7-10+

Viswanatha, 1991, Tamil Nadu under the Tiger's sway, *India Today* June 15, p 50+

Vishwanath Pratap Singh, 1982, My failure is total, *Onlooker* 44(3) February 15, p 20+
See also Singh, V.P.

Wajahat Habibullah
See Habibullah, Wajahat

Wariavwalla, Bharat, 1984, A dynastic democracy, *Illustrated Weekly of India* 105(33) December, p 34-35

Warier, K.U., 1989, Rajiv appeasing communalism: Daji, *New Age* 37(23) June 4, p 5, news-item

Wig , A.R., 1991, Delhi will miss Rajiv Gandhi, *Hindustan Times*, May 26, p 5, col 1-4

Willey, Fay, 1977, Indira's sure thing, *News Week* 89(5) January 31, p 21-22

Zakaria, Rafiq, 1986, How strong is Rajiv? *Illustrated Weekly of India* 107(45) November 16, p 10-15

Zehra, Nasim, 1991, Concern, disbelief in Pakistan, *Hindustan Times*, May 26, p 12, col 1-4

CICIL LIST

CONCEPTS IN COMMUNICATION, INFORMATICS & LIBRARIANSHIP

(CICIL)

General Editor: **S.P. AGRAWAL**

CICIL-1 Development of Library Services in India: Social Science Information
S.P. Agrawal Rs. 150

CICIL-2 Development of Documentation in India: Social Science Information
S.P. Agrawal Rs. 250

CICIL-3 UNESCO and Social Sciences: Retrospect and Prospect
S.P. Agrawal and **J.C. Aggarwal** Rs. 250

CICIL-4 INDIANA : A Bibliography of Bibliographical Sources
M.K. Jain Rs. 200

CICIL-5 Dimensions of Library and Information Science: Kaula Festschrift
V. Venkatappaiah (Eds.) Rs. 600

CICIL-6 Book Numbers: Some Indian Methods
M.P. Satija and **S.P. Agrawal** Rs. 100

CICIL-7 National Policy for University Libraries in India: Problems and Perspectives
N.B. Inamdar and **L.S. Ramaiah** (Ed.) Rs. 250

CICIL-8 Media Utilisation for the Development of Women and Children
B.S. Thakur and **Binod C. Agrawal** Rs. 150

CICIL-9 Terrorism: An Annotated Bibliography
Susheela Bhan (Ed.) Rs. 275

CICIL-10 Transnational Library Relations: The Indo-American Experience
M.B. Konnur Rs. 175

CICIL-11 Geography of Marketing and Commercial Activities in India (Documentation on Research Information)
R.S. Dixit Rs. 130

CICIL-12 Information India 1988: Global View
S.P. Agrawal and **J.C. Aggarwal** Rs. 200

CICIL-13 Women's Education in India: Historical Review, Present Status and Perspective Plan
S.P. Agrawal and **J.C. Aggarwal** Rs. 360

CICIL-14 Cultural Communication in India: Role and Impact of Phonograms
J.M. Ojha Rs. 220

CICIL-15 Second Historical Survey of Educational Development in India: Select Documents 1985-1989
S.P. Agrawal and **J.C. Aggarwal** Rs. 490

CICIL-16 Documentation Encyclopaedia of UNESCO and Education
J.C. Aggarwal and **S.P. Agrawal** Rs. 800 (set of 2 parts)

CICIL-17 Attitude Towards Information: A Study of Post-Graduate Teachers and Researchers in Social Sciences
N.G. Satish (in press)

CICIL-18 Librarianship and Bureaucratic Organisation: A Study in the Sociology of Library Profession in India
P.K. Jayaswal Rs. 175

CICIL-19 Literature Search
K.A. Isaac Rs. 150

CICIL-20 Child Education in India: Index to Scholarly Writings in Indian Educational Journals and Newspapers since independence
S.P. Agrawal and **Naresh Kanta** Rs. 100

CICIL-21 Lok Sabha and Vidhan Sabha Elections in India 1989 & 1990: Process and Results with Comparative Study of Manifestos
S.P. Agrawal and **J.C. Aggarwal** Rs. 250

CICIL-22 Islamic Studies in India: A Survey of Human, Institutional and Documentary Sources
Mohamed Taher Rs. 180

CICIL-23 Panchayati Raj: An Annotated Bibliography
N.B. Inamdar, N.G. Satish and **Anil Takalkar** 290

CICIL-24 Information India 1989-90: Global View
S.P. Agrawal and **J.C. Aggarwal** Rs. 500

CICIL-25 First Handbook of Psychological and Social Instruments
Udai Pareek and **T. Venkateswara Rao** Rs. 500

CICIL-26 Educational and Social Uplift of Backward Classes: At What Cost and How? Mandal Commission and After
S.P. Agrawal and **J.C. Aggarwal** Rs. 275

CICIL-27 Mass Media and New Horizons: Impact of TV & Video an Urban Milieu
H.R. Trivedi Rs. 180

CICIL-28 Indian Writings on Education : An Indicator to Indian Educational Journals Grouped by Subject Deseriptors 1979 to 1986 (in two parts)
S.P. Agarwal Rs. 900 (per set)

CICIL-29 Nation in Crisis
S.P. Agrawal and **J.C. Aggarwal** Rs. 200

CICIL-30 Information India 1990-91: Global View
S.P. Agrawal and **J.C. Aggarwal** Rs. 500

CICIL-31 Development of University Libraries in India After Independence
O.P. Gupta Rs. 270

CICIL-32 Handbook on Child : With Historical Background
Pramila Pandit Barooah Rs. 320

CICIL-33 Weaker Section in Indian Society : Undiscovered Past, Uncertain Present and Unpredictable Future Index to Writings in Indian Scholarly Journals and 10 National Newspapers Classified under 1500 Descriptors 1886-1990
S.P. Agrawal and **Rajeev Kumar Sharma** Rs. 600

CICIL-34 Communication Informatics and Librarianship in India : An Introductory Guide to Publications Based on a Survey of Libraries in Capital City of India
S.P. Agrawal and **Pushpa Rani Sharma** Rs. 720

CICIL-35 Problems of Collection Development in Special Libraries
M.S. Sridhar Rs. 225

CICIL-36 National Information Resources for Social Sciences in India : Mobilisation, Dispersal and International Enhancement
S.P. Agrawal Rs. 225

CICIL-37 Modern History of Punjab : A Look Back into Ancient Peaceful Punjab Focusing Confrontation and Failures Leading to Present Punjab Problem, and a Peep Ahead : Relevant Select Documents
J.C. Aggarwal and **S.P. Agrawal** Rs. 400

CICIL-38 India Information Sources : Economics and Business
Kyllikki Ruokonen and **Manohar Lal** Rs.

CICIL-39 Educational Planning in India : With a Slant to Educational Financing and Administration, Vol. 1, Reports of Committees and Commissions, Five Year Plans, Statistical Tables
J.C. Aggarwal and **S.P. Agrawal** Rs. 650

CICIL-40 Integrated Library System : Two Case Studies : Latin America and India
Maria Luiza Rigo Pasquarelli, Rosaly Favero Krzyanowski, Ines Maria M. Imperatriz and S.P. Agrawal Rs. 160

CICIL-41 Social Science Information in India: Effort towards Bibliographical Control
S.D. Vyas Rs. 300

CICIL-42 Higher Education in India Since Independence: U.G.C. and its Approach
O.P. Gupta Rs. 360

CICIL-43 Government and Politics in India: A Bibliographical Study of Contemporary Scenario Chronicling Rajiv Gandhi Era
S.P. Agrawal and **Rajeev Kumar Sharma** Rs. 500

CICIL-44 Second Handbook of Psychological and Social Instruments
D.M. Pestonjee Rs. 300